MW00653533

Interviews with American Composers

MUSIC IN AMERICAN LIFE

A list of books in the series appears
at the end of this book.

Interviews with American Composers

~~~

Barney Childs in Conversation

~~~

Edited by
Virginia Anderson

UNIVERSITY OF
ILLINOIS PRESS
Urbana, Chicago, and Springfield

Publication of this book was supported by a grant from
the Henry and Edna Binkele Classical Music Fund.

Library of Congress Cataloging-in-Publication Data
Names: Childs, Barney, interviewer. | Anderson, Virginia
    (Musicologist) editor.
Title: Interviews with American composers : Barney
    Childs in conversation / edited by Virginia Anderson.
Description: Urbana : University of Illinois Press, 2022. |
    Series: Music in American life | Includes bibliographical
    references and index. |
Identifiers: LCCN 2021024456 (print) | LCCN 2021024457
    (ebook) | ISBN 9780252043994 (cloth) | ISBN
    9780252052927 (ebook)
Subjects: LCSH: Composers—United States—Interviews. |
    Music—20th century—History and criticism.
Classification: LCC ML390 .I47 2022 (print) | LCC ML390
    (ebook) | DDC 780.92/2—dc23
LC record available at https://lccn.loc.gov/2021024456
LC ebook record available at https://lccn.loc.gov/2021024457

To all the composers in these
(and the missing) conversations.

Contents

Preface and Acknowledgments

The history of this book is both frustrating and promising. The composer Barney Childs recorded what he called "conversations (for they are hardly interviews in the precise sense)," with "younger" American composers beginning in the summer of 1972.[1] Childs obtained a faculty grant from the University of Redlands in California for travel, transcription equipment, and transcribers. Beginning in 1972, he sent out proposal letters to at least seven publishers. Every publisher turned him down.

At the time, publishers favored the previous generation of established composers.[2] Stravinsky died in 1971; books on John Cage and Elliott Carter were recently published.[3] The composers in Childs's interviews had not yet stood the test of time to be marketable. Deeply disheartened, Childs abandoned this project and in the 1990s finally gave a box of transcribed interviews to his former student Jim Fox in the hope that they might at last see publication. As Fox received them, almost all of the typed transcriptions lacked their original recordings; no dates, times, or locations were provided. What followed was a combination of a quest and a forensic investigation.

Publication History, and Its Absence

A motley crew of friends, students, and perhaps even hired hands—Cherrie Lynn Cox, Cynthia Jelliffe, Laura Sue Lloyd, Kathleen "Rustee" McCain, Angela Sanabia, and Ray Weisling—transcribed these interviews from tape. Childs noted in his draft acknowledgment that "each individual composer has been responsible for editing and polishing the transcription made of our discussion," though it is likely that not all had done so.

When Childs shelved the project, he stowed the interviews in a box in his spare bedroom and they lay there, untouched. I came to Redlands in the fall of 1972; after

1976 Childs and I became quite close. Occasionally Barney would tell stories about his summer of interviews (he was particularly nostalgic about his day spent with Christian Wolff on his farm), but he considered the interview project dead.

Composer Jim Fox, who received the interviews in Childs's final bid in the mid-1990s to publish them, was well-positioned to succeed, but the timing was off. Fox had worked with publisher Samuel French Inc., cofounded Silman-James Press, and founded the Cold Blue Music record label. His proposals to various publishers met with no success. Since then, however, interest in primary historical documents has grown and our music-historical perspective is different. We can readily agree with what Childs said in his draft acknowledgment: "the work of [these] 'younger' American composers . . . has done much to shape musical taste and direction."[4] For new generations, Ashley, Lucier, Johnston, Budd, and other interviewees have become our most important direct musical influences. In 2015 I was a guest speaker at a conference at the Orpheus Institute (Ghent, Belgium), which Christian Wolff also attended. I had chosen to talk about the Childs interview and Wolff's association with Cornelius Cardew in London and asked Fox for the manuscript. It became immediately clear that it was as fascinating as Childs had promised, so I asked for other interviews. At that point, the massive task ahead became clear.

The reconstruction process resembled documentary archaeology more than oral history. Childs's box held typescript transcripts of eighteen interviews and tapes of only one interview, that with Daniel Lentz. The typescripts appeared to be at different stages of the editorial process: some are either first transcription or a later draft. Some carry handwritten editorial marks, either by Childs or an unknown hand. In the interview with Daniel Lentz, a loud ground hum in the tape recording obliterated large sections of the interview. A page is missing in the interview with Joel Chadabe, but until recently the entire interview was missing. It was recovered in September 2018, when a transcriber donated interviews with Chadabe, Lucier, Mumma, Martirano, and Sahl to the University of Redlands.

Without the usual oral history data (tapes, dates, locations) for these interviews, I had to rely on the transcripts alone. We can say only that these interviews happened sometime in the summers of 1972 or 1973. At least one complete interview is still missing, most likely Pauline Oliveros's. Childs mentions hers among "24 out of a planned 31 or 32" interviews.[5] A thorough search of the holdings in both Childs's and Oliveros's collections (the latter at the University of California, San Diego) resulted in failure. The other seven or eight interviews proposed by Childs were never undertaken.

These conversations are, therefore, fragments. Aside from a draft preface, which consists mainly of acknowledgments, Childs left no other comments among his papers. Nevertheless, these fragments still provide a unique glimpse into American composition and its concerns at the time.

Acknowledgments

I owe endless thanks to the contextual essay authors for their cheerful acceptance of the task and their wisdom. I am also grateful for the goodwill and assistance from the surviving interviewees, and to the estates of the others. Many gave much needed clarification and corrections; Peter Westergaard and Sydney Hodkinson, in particular, closely edited their drafts. Jim Fox, the original keeper of the interview flame, was vital in bringing this project to realization. Thanks to the Barney Childs Collection, Armacost Library, University of Redlands. Laurie Matheson, Ellie Hinson, and Julia Laut at the University of Illinois Press gave invaluable advice. Thanks to Chris Brown for his honest and helpful reviews. Other sources of wisdom include William Brooks, Gordon Mumma, Charles Shere, James Pease, Jeff Gibbens, John Chowning, Peter Garland, Michael Byron, Mary Jane Leach, Beth Anderson-Harold, and more whom I may have inadvertently missed out. Finally, love and thanks to my husband, the composer Christopher Hobbs; and to my research assistants, Eri, Maia, Enchi, and Biqui. Barney, I miss you.

Notes

1. Barney Childs, unpublished interview book proposal, ca. 1974.
2. Among the publishers contacted were E. P. Dutton, W. W. Norton, the University of Alabama Press, William C. Brown, and Holt, Rinehart and Winston.
3. Richard Kostelanetz, ed., *John Cage* (Documentary Monographs in Modern Art; New York: Praeger, 1970). Contains a 1966 interview of Cage conducted by Kostelanetz and a collection of Cage's writings. Allen Edwards, *Flawed Words and Stubborn Sounds: A Conversation with Elliott Carter* (New York: W. W. Norton, 1971).
4. Barney Childs, unpublished acknowledgments in interview book proposal, ca. 1974.
5. Barney Childs to Holt, Rinehart, and Winston, December 15, 1972.

Interviews with American Composers

Introduction

VIRGINIA ANDERSON

The past is a foreign country. They do things differently there.
—L. P. Hartley, *The Go-Between* (1953)

L. P. Hartley's opening to *The Go-Between*, about an unpublished diary from fifty years before, serves as a caveat to the reader approaching Barney Childs's twenty-three "conversations." Almost fifty years after most of these interviews, they still seem, in historical terms, quite recent. Some of us were alive when they occurred; we know the music and its larger philosophical and technical problems. Yet the detail in these conversations—complaints about musical conservatism, minutiae about notation or electronic resources, the difference between East Coast and West Coast—may seem unusual to today's readers. Moreover, as published, it's an all-male party without the single woman composer who had been invited, Pauline Oliveros.

The German composer Walter Zimmermann's twenty-three interviews in *Desert Plants* (1976) cover a similar area as that of Childs, with overlapping subjects that include Christian Wolff, Robert Ashley, Alvin Lucier, Pauline Oliveros, Larry Austin, and Ben Johnston.[1] However, *Desert Plants* was published in a timely fashion; its readers would have understood the musical landscape much as Zimmermann did. Out of print for decades, *Desert Plants* reappeared as a valuable archival source in a second edition in 2020. But for all the similarities and overlaps in coverage between Zimmermann and Childs, the two projects are quite different. Zimmermann took his road trip through America as a young, twenty-seven-year-old outsider; Childs as an older, forty-six-year-old insider. The four-year gap between the projects is enormous: in 1976, the musical revolution from post-serialism, experimentalism, and minimalism to postminimalism was largely complete, whereas Childs took his conversations at the apex of that revolution four years earlier.[2] Thus Zimmermann's past is a slightly different foreign country to Childs's.

This introduction seeks to answer several questions: why were these particular interviewees chosen? What was crucially different in music about 1972–73? Why are there no women interviewees? Contextual essays that preface each interview show

how the interview fits into the life and work of each composer. These experts have
been crucial in bringing this book—one of Barney's last wishes as far as his work
was concerned—to fruition.

Barney Childs and the Interviews

Barney Childs (1926–2000) was a poet and composer who worked almost entirely
on the West Coast of the United States. Born in Spokane, Washington, Childs
was primarily self-taught as a composer and pianist. After service in World War II,
Childs won a Rhodes Scholarship to Oriel College, Oxford, gaining a master's in
English literature; he majored in English and minored in music at Stanford, where
he obtained a doctorate for a dissertation on the text setting of English madrigals.
Childs attended Tanglewood, where he studied with Aaron Copland and Carlos
Chávez, and where he also met several of the composers in these conversations. He
studied briefly with Elliott Carter in the late 1950s in New York City. Childs primarily lectured in English literature and poetry; he was the editor of *Genesis West*, a
journal of Beat and other poetry. However, music composition gradually took over
Childs's creative life. Still lecturing in English at the University of Arizona, Childs
founded a contemporary music ensemble and taught composition to Joseph Byrd,
later a prominent member of Fluxus. Childs increasingly identified himself solely as
a composer, though he taught poetry and literature for most of the 1960s. He was
dean of Deep Springs College, Nevada, an elite two-year men's college and working ranch, where Childs invited a number of American composers for residencies,
including Harold Budd and Morton Feldman. After his first official position as a
professor of music, at Milwaukee College Conservatory, Childs moved to the University of Redlands in 1971. He obtained a faculty research grant to conduct these
interviews in 1972 and 1973.

The Interview Project

Childs sent a letter to all prospective interviewees, much the same as this letter to
William Albright.

May 1, 1972
William Albright
School of Music
University of Michigan
Ann Arbor, MI 48105

Dear Bill:

I have just last week been fortunate enough to be awarded a University of Redlands
Faculty Research Grant which will help me get started on a project I have wanted

to tackle for some while now. This will involve interviews with "younger" American composers, these to be taped, transcribed, edited, checked out by you, and made into a book, maybe with some sort of short commentary preface. I plan to travel about this summer talking to people for this, and I think it important to include you. If you'd like to be in on it do let me know (using the enclosed mailback envelope) and say where you'll be in June and July—I'd give you some warning, of course, as to when I'd appear.

Further, I'd appreciate some suggestions from you as to other people you feel might be good to have in the book: could you list their names? I can't do everybody, but I'd like to have the selection process made in part by the composers included. Who do you think would have things to say you'd be interested in reading?

I'll hope to hear from you soon and, too, to have the pleasure of seeing you to connection with this project,

All best,
Barney Childs

The Choice of Subjects

Childs supplied a rationale for his choice of subjects in a draft preface:

> Any process of selection is sure to be satisfactory to hardly anyone but the selecter; the reader examining the list of composers represented in these interviews will probably complain of names omitted that should have been included and names included that should have been omitted. Nonetheless, I feel it to be important that some immediately accessible overview be available of the work of "younger" American composers, work often of major stature that has done much to shape musical taste and direction. . . . My direction in conducting these conversations (for they are hardly interviews in the precise sense) was to let each composer speak as he pleased on subjects of immediate concern to him; the results, as I view them, provide gratifying and challenging variety of opinion and conception as well as a candid and genuine personal glimpse of each composer as he appears in relaxed and immediate conversation.[3]

Childs focused on composers aged twenty-nine to forty-six who were influential in American music. His reference to "overview" and "variety of opinion and conception" indicates that Childs had intended to present a cross-section of new American music. Childs had a logistical limitation ("Some people I had hoped to include were not available when I was travelling about doing these interviews") and intended to feature composers who were important but not yet famous ("some others I felt to be sufficiently publicly available that they fell outside the line one has to draw somewhere.")[4]

Despite its limitations, Childs's selection is fairly broad. Many of the composers identified with the Cagean and Ivesian tradition. Most composers created electronic music, including computer music and live electronics. Several composers were exploring the nascent "new tonality" and crossover music, as well as microtonality. There are almost an equal number of composers from the East, Midwest, and West Coast. Since Childs had recently developed a Black music component in Black Studies at Johnston College (the "experimental" college at Redlands where Childs was professor of poetry), he was no doubt keen to interview Olly Wilson. He intended to include Oliveros. He also interviewed Donald Martino, Peter Westergaard, and Charles Wuorinen, three composers whose work was by no means "experimental."

Childs met most of these composers either at conferences or concerts. The University of Illinois, where Johnston and Salvatore Martirano taught, was an important experimental and avant-garde music center. The premiere performance of John Cage's *Musicircus* at Illinois in 1967 included Childs's *The Roachville Project*. Other musical activity in the Midwest in the 1960s included William Bolcom and William Albright at the University of Michigan and Phil Winsor in Chicago. The ONCE group (which performed music by Childs), followed by the beginnings of the Sonic Arts Union, thrived outside of the university in Ann Arbor. In the West, Childs knew composers at Mills College, the San Francisco Tape Music Center, and at the University of California, San Diego (UCSD). From the late 1960s, Roger Reynolds, Oliveros, and the contrabassist Bertram Turetzky taught at UCSD. Turetzky and Childs coedited the New Instrumentation series of orchestration books on extended techniques for instruments.[5] In New York in the 1960s, Childs knew Fluxus through his former student Joseph Byrd, Richard Maxfield, and Alison Knowles, who coedited *Notations* with John Cage, which included Childs's *Welcome to Whipperginny*.[6]

Childs knew many interviewees through the American Society of University Composers (now the Society for Composers Inc.), founded in 1965 by Benjamin Boretz and a committee including Martino, Westergaard, and Wuorinen. Childs was on the executive board and, with David Cohen, instituted regional conferences from 1971.[7] Childs founded the Advance Recordings label and released recordings of compositions by Wuorinen, Martino, Johnston, Bolcom, Winsor (*Melted Ears* [1967], performed by Albright), Robert Ashley and Gordon Mumma (in a recording from the ONCE festival, 1966), Martirano, Larry Austin, and Harold Budd.[8]

Many interviewed composers were former fellows in the Composers Forum at the Tanglewood Music Center. Childs was a fellow in 1953, when he studied with Chávez and 1954, when he studied with Copland. The latter year Richard Maxfield was also in Copland's class; Michael Sahl (who returned in 1955 and 1956) was in Lukas Foss's class.[9] Other alumni of Tanglewood include Martirano (a fellow in 1952 and 1955); Lucier (1959); Loren Rush, Charles Dodge, Martino, and Wuorinen (1964); and William Hellermann and Robert Morris (1967). Fellows in 1966—including Albright (who had also attended in 1963), Bolcom, Winsor, and Daniel Lentz, as well as Russell Peck (whom Childs had planned to interview, along with Ralph Shapey)—appear to have bonded in opposition to the Tanglewood course rather than with it.

Childs chose Martino, Westergaard, and Wuorinen for different reasons. Phillip Rehfeldt recorded Martino's *A Set for Clarinet* (1954) in 1964, and *B,a,b,b,it,t* (1968) in 1973 for Advance. Childs, then working on his notation paper, admired Martino's article on notation for extended woodwind.[10] As a poet and professor of English literature, Childs was drawn to Westergaard's 1967 work on a semiotic approach to the composition of sung texts.[11] Although this interview is striking for the clash between Childs and Westergaard on the "Princeton problem," they both clearly enjoyed discussing linguistics, text setting, and dramaturgy in Westergaard's opera based on Shakespeare's *The Tempest*. Childs may have intended his conversation with Wuorinen to follow his 1962 interview in *Genesis West*. This interview (updated and somewhat tamed in its reprint in *Contemporary Composers on Contemporary Music*, edited by Childs and Elliott Schwartz) shows no meeting of the minds between Childs and Wuorinen, who was then not "the least interested in the obscenities of Cage, Maxfield, and company."[12] The present interview is much more harmonious between the two composers. Having seen how Childs chose his subjects, we must then look at what they discussed, as the areas of thinking and practice in 1972 are different from our own.

Musical Concerns around 1972

New music was in a state of stylistic and ideological flux from the late 1960s. The postwar division between the post-Schoenbergian and Cagean traditions was still sharp.[13] These conversations show this division and also display concerns about history and education, notation, developments, and problems in electronic music, new demands on performers, and perhaps most crucially, the new "tonal" music.

The composers were concerned with history, the "new," and the next step. However, their compositional practice was far ahead of university practice, which was still based in the post-1800 classical music tradition. There is some exasperation in these conversations that students think of Cage as being "new," when many of the interviewees imply that he is an honored predecessor.[14] Just as intermedia, graphic, and text scores began to appear in university courses, the two most important intermedia movements had faded. George Maciunas wrote that 1968 was the end of the golden age of Fluxus, as members either left or were ejected.[15] In England, Cornelius Cardew and members of the Scratch Orchestra moved from text notation to minimalism or Marxist-Leninist realism around 1971.[16]

Innovations in notation increased sharply through the 1960s and early 1970s, both in indeterminate graphic and text scores, and also in symbols added to common-practice notation to convey extended techniques, such as Martino's articulation symbols.[17] Composers independently invented entirely different symbols for the same effect, leading to calls for an international standardization of notation. However, the problem of standardizing notation is almost unmentioned today. As new tonal

and minimalist works used common-practice notation, text and graphic notation
became less popular, with some exceptions. From 1973 William Hellermann moved
from abstract graphic scores such as *CIRCLE MUSIC*s to pictorial scores using
common-practice notation, and from 1974 Oliveros used text score notation for her
Sonic Meditations series, thus bringing "experimental" notation into minimalism and
postminimalism.

Electronic music brought new problems in notation, construction, and performance, as well as a legal problem. In the 1960s, copyright law considered the identity
of the musical "work" as intrinsic to the score itself, but most electronic compositions
were fixed as complete works in sound recordings.[18] Yet it was almost impossible to
notate the complex array of sounds in electronic music, some pop music, and free
improvisation. In February 1972, US copyright was extended to sound recordings,
thus changing the legal definition of the "work."[19]

The rate of developments in electronic technology was staggering. Studios needed
frequent and expensive upgrades to avoid redundancy. In the 1950s, electronic music
used banks of "black box" oscillators. In 1959, the first voltage-controlled synthesizer,
the RCA Mark II at the Columbia-Princeton Electronic Music Center (now Computer Music Center), was built. By 1963, the first Buchla synthesizer was launched at
the San Francisco Tape Center. Joel Chadabe employed banks of Moog single-step
analog sequencers to drive the Coordinated Electronic Music Studios (CEMS) at
SUNY Albany. In computer music, Charles Dodge had already created *The Earth's
Magnetic Field* (1970) and was working on *Speech Songs* (1973). Loren Rush had just
joined the Stanford Music Project (later the Center for Computer Research in Music
and Acoustics), one of the most important computer music studios in the country,
directed by John Chowning.[20] Ashley, Lucier, and Mumma had developed electronic
music in live performance in the ONCE group and Sonic Arts Union. Mumma
created electronic sound sources for the Merce Cunningham Dance Company that
could be activated by movement such as instrumental fingering or dance. Live electronics performance became easier to achieve in the 1980s when digital synthesizers
became portable and cost-effective.

Studio-based compositions committed to tape produced an aesthetic problem,
as a pair of speakers sitting static on stage lacked the action and danger of live performance. Martirano proposed to create aural movement and surprise by placing
banks of speakers around the performance venue, powered by his Sal-Mar synthesizer.
Compositions for performer and tape supplied the live element. Stuart Dempster
and Charlotte Moorman were among those specializing in these works. "Super
virtuosos," as Childs called them, specialized in normal virtuoso technical prowess,
plus extended techniques such as preparations, multiphonics, and special embou-
chures, sometimes with electronic amplification or processing. Stuart Dempster and
John Schneider, who have contributed essays in this book on Loren Rush and Ben
Johnston, are two such specialist performers. Performers were also increasingly asked

to play extremely quiet pieces in which little happened. The challenges—to repeat figures accurately (for wind players without rest or breath), to project a good tone at *pianissimo possibile* in registers that were easier to play loudly, and for an entire ensemble to count tempos accurately through long periods of silence at extremely slow speeds—created a kind of virtuosity in miniature.

One of the major talking points in these conversations is the new diatonicism, part of a general tendency to step away from experimental and avant-garde process toward harmonic concord, often with a clear narrative content. Other names for these new realist styles at the time include new tonality, pretty music, or simply minimalism. These new approaches to composition elicited questions that would only settle with postminimalism a few years later.

Composers gradually became less focused on generative systems and more on narrative and harmony. In 1971, William Bolcom was the guest composer for a Contemporary Directions Ensemble concert at the University of Michigan, titled *The New Diatonicism*. In an article about the new romanticism in electronic music for the *New York Times*, Larry Austin wrote that synthesizers had promoted "the new romantic movement in electronic music." Yet they wanted to avoid nostalgic pastiche. In his interview, Austin defended his statement: "What I mean by New Romanticism . . . is that NEW Romanticism is a new love of sound, without any other preconceived notions at all; you simply love sound."[21] The remainder of the 1970s marked closer ties between the new experimental scene and popular music, including Budd's association with Brian Eno and Obscure Recordings in London, and the establishment of Lovely Music. American music moved into a more central, and more respected position in Western music by the end of the 1970s.

Being American

In 1972, however, American music was marginalized, with African American music further marginalized. The first issues of the *Black Perspective in Music*, a landmark journal devoted primarily to African and African American concert music, appeared in 1973, claiming that not only music by Black composers, but also all modern American music was disenfranchised by the dominant culture.

Then, American music was in what Leonard Meyer called "fluctuating stasis": a stylistic plurality of movements with distinctive and sometimes conflicting theories and aesthetics.[22] However, no matter what style, American music was perceived to be less valuable than European contemporary or historical music by concert music institutions. Their situation parallels the late 1960s counterculture as Raymond Williams described it: a variety of separate subcultures (antiwar, revolutionary, Black rights, communes, alternative spirituality, and so forth) having individual group concerns as well as sharing either an opposition toward the dominant culture (the Establishment) from within or proposing an alternative to it and remaining outside it.[23] Martino complained of the funding of concerts of music by "Beethoven and Company," leaving little support for advanced new music. Emergent hegemony appears in the tendency for value to be accorded from the dominant culture. T. J. Anderson noted that "the sources, the idols continue to be what's going on in Paris, never what's going on in America," explaining that American colleges ignored Cage and that Karlheinz Stockhausen held more influence than John Coltrane or other Black composers.[24]

The clearest need for an opposition to the dominant musical culture appears in "(M1) American Music," by Wadada Leo Smith in 1974. He explained that Scott Joplin and Charles Ives were marginalized by a "politically and racially motivated" worship of the European tradition.

> Because of this point of view, nowhere in America will you find the music of Ives (even though he was white) and certainly not the music of Joplin (a new serious art music presented by a man who was black) being considered for performance to the same extent as you would any of the European composers who were contemporaries of these men. In fact America has been so content with its European-culture adaptation that it has put statues and other pictorial representations of the great composers of Europe in all of its halls and auditoriums. It is impossible to find an American black or white man represented in this way.[25]

The interviewed composers viewed American music as distinct from the dominant European tradition. Sahl felt that being American involved responding to one's heritage, including Jewish songwriting, and that "American" composition was a matter of finding one's roots. Some, including Bolcom and Lentz, came to the realization of their American identity while residing in Europe. Bolcom, studying at the Paris Conservatory, was condemned for "une rupture de style" for including a spiritual in his primarily Boulezian quartet. The revival of Joplin's piano music only occurred in the 1960s; his opera *Treemonisha* was heard first in excerpts by Bolcom, Joshua Rifkin, and Mary Lou Williams in 1971 and then reconstructed in its entirety by Anderson in 1972. Recordings of Ives began as a niche market in the 1950s, after his death; this interest would increase in time for his centenary in 1974 and the US Bicentennial in 1976.

The 1972 interviews (especially those with Albright, Bolcom, and Sahl) show that the lines between "art music" and other modern music had become blurred, and they would eventually become meaningless in all but the most academic music. Moreover, the "counterculture" in concert music was occurring throughout Europe as well: the first Festival Nuits de la Fondation Maeght in Saint-Paul-de-Vence, France, in 1970 (concerts by Albert Ayler, Sun Ra, Terry Riley, and La Monte Young); the International Carnival of Experimental Sound (ICES) at the Roundhouse in London in 1972 (dubbed "the Woodstock of the Avant-Garde"); alternative venues such as the Kitchen in Greenwich Village (1971), the Logos Foundation in Ghent, Belgium (1968), and the London Musicians Collective (1975). With guidance from Gavin Bryars, Brian Eno launched Obscure Recordings in 1976, which featured music by John Adams and Harold Budd (with Marion Brown). Other European supporters include Walter Zimmermann, the author of *Desert Plants*, and Wim Mertens, who wrote *American Minimal Music*.[26] By 1980, the new American music "counterculture" was much more central to international arts than in 1972.

The regionality of American music was also a common topic. Childs told Bolcom that "There is no musical environment in New York." Bolcom answered, "There is no scene in New York!" But he admitted, "It's the only place in America where you can get some kind of general exposure to and in the arts." At Tanglewood, the Californian Rush said, "I was really disappointed that I didn't come well-prepared with Stetson hat and cowboy boots and six-guns, because that's what they expected." Some regional disputes occupied a very small geographical space (in New York City, Uptown versus Downtown); others spanned the continent (East versus West). Music scenes flourished in Ann Arbor, Chicago, Berkeley, and Los Angeles in spite of, of more likely because of, the distance from and isolation of their location from New York. Some of the musicians in these regional scenes were tied to regional universities, like the University of Illinois. Some, like the ONCE group or Childs's Tucson New Art Ensemble, programmed music independently of the local university.

Childs, just beginning what would be almost twenty-five years working at the University of Redlands, was deeply linked with the West. As a poet, Childs celebrated the landscape, including evocations of his frequent mountain and desert hikes and of incidents in which he had explored California history. As a composer, Childs similarly explored location: his two pieces at the time of these interviews, *Of Place, as Altered* (1972, for five clarinets) and *Of Place, in Particular* (1973, for soprano voice, tape and chimes) are musical, and most likely dream, landscapes.[27]

The spirit of place thus lies at the heart of Childs's thinking, and in the thinking of many composers in these conversations. Childs and the composers assumed these distinctions, but due to the time in which he lived, he missed others.

What Childs Missed

Childs focused on a wider and newer area of American music than academic publishers would accept; what he left out lay even further from most academic study in 1972. Creative music (and free improvisation in general), intermedia, and women composers were ex-nominated (excluded by definition) from this discourse through 1972 and beyond. Childs clearly planned to include Pauline Oliveros. Why not others? That there are no women in this book is particularly shocking today, as is some of the language and the near-universal exclusion of feminine pronouns throughout.

To find out how many women Childs could have interviewed, I informally polled musicologist and composer friends and colleagues; I searched online lists and in the Childs materials themselves.[28] I found that if we accept the landscape of modern concert music in 1972, he missed very few. When Childs asked his interviewees for candidates, Oliveros was suggested second only to David Behrman, who also does not appear in these interviews. Harold Budd recommended Thea Musgrave, who had then recently moved to the United States from Scotland. My informal poll and the online lists suggest that some women composers were excluded according to Childs's limitations; those who were older (Lucia Dlugoszewski and Musgrave), younger (Joan La Barbara), or who lived outside the United States (Gloria Coates and Annea Lockwood). The remaining list comprises twenty women composers in three areas of activity: those in jazz, popular, and commercial music; the academic experimental and avant-garde movement; and the Downtown minimalist and intermedia scene, including the remnants of Fluxus.

Composers working in popular music and new jazz include Carla Bley, Wendy Carlos (then working as Walter Carlos), Carole King, Joni Mitchell, Annette Peacock, Grace Slick, Dorothy S. Moskowitz, and Jeanne Lee. Pop, rock, and musical theater of this time was not within Childs's area of interest, and stylistic segregation was still very strong at the institutional level in 1972: few if any books mixed modern popular and classical music. Although Black music improvisation was clearly avant-garde in the 1960s, it was seen as having a separate tradition. When Austin, Rush, and Oliveros explored music improvisation, they did so as American experimentalists, but as Anthony Braxton, whose explorations were similar, said two decades later, "even though I have been saying I'm not a jazz musician for the last 25 years; in the final analysis, an African-American with a saxophone? Ahh, he's jazz!"[29] From the mid-1960s, the Association for the Advancement of Creative Music distinguished score-based "classical music" and improvisational "creative music," which became increasingly linked with the American avant-garde throughout the 1970s.[30] In 1972 Braxton released a full album of his titular graphic compositions.[31] Childs and Elliott Schwartz included Braxton, T. J. Anderson, and Pauline Oliveros in the second edition of *Contemporary Composers on Contemporary Music*.[32] By 1998, omitting them would have been unthinkable.

Women composers of experimental and avant-garde music include Pauline Oliveros, Joan Tower, Nancy Van de Vate, Ann Silsbee, Maryanne Amacher, and Sorrel (Doris) Hayes. Of that group, Oliveros was the most established composer at the time. Others may not appear because they were at an early stage of their compositional lives. Joan Tower was then a serial composer within the "school" of Vladimir Ussachevsky and other composers. Gordon Mumma noted: "Barney's focus was on the renegade and exploring composers. If he had been assembling these articles a decade or more later, I'm sure he would have had [Meredith Monk, Laurie Anderson, and Joan La Barbara], and such as Annea Lockwood."[33]

Monk, Anderson, La Barbara, and Lockwood were involved in Fluxus and other early Downtown movements. Childs knew Fluxus through Joseph Byrd and Alison Knowles. Byrd dedicated his *Four Sound*Poems* (1962) to Lucia Dlugoszewski, Judy Winkler (now Judy Eda), Diane Wakoski, and Charlotte Moorman—all New York artist-composers—when he was corresponding with Childs.[34] Childs dedicated one of his first indeterminate works, "Interbalances III "(1962), to Charlotte Moorman and wrote about sound art as music in 1969, but scholarly discourse considered these movements to be performance art, not music.[35] Mumma proposes that Childs may have seen these artists (and Monk, Ono, and Knowles) as performers, not composers. Mumma comments: "One factor for Barney's lack of connection with women composers was that he was not himself broadly active as a performer. His primary cultural milieu was in the college-university realm, of mostly 'backward-looking' into history. In that realm he was something of a renegade with his interest in the arts of the present. Through the 1950s and 1960s women composers were flourishing, but often not recognized (or known) unless they were also active performers; e.g., Pauline Oliveros and (then just beginning) Meredith Monk, Laurie Anderson, Joan La Barbara."[36] This theory would explain the omission of other possible interviewees, including composer-performers like Glass (recommended by two composers), Riley, and Young. Most of the interviews here are with composers in university work. Had Childs interviewed more Downtown composers than Hellermann and Mumma, the gender balance in this book would have been different, but it would have had an even smaller chance of publication. Finally, the definitive answer to his choices died with Childs.

Thus the issue is trickier than it first appears. Following Hartley, we must accept that they did things differently in 1972. William Brooks writes, "Although we may not celebrate Childs' decisions, to condemn him for them is to declare that yesterday is sufficiently like today that our values can be transferred whole-hog from now back to then. That runs counter to Hartley's dictum that the past is 'foreign' to us; we inevitably enter it as an unsolicited cultural interloper, and measuring it against our standards is a kind of historical colonialism."[37] Music in 1972—its landscape, thinking, theory, and practice—is thus simultaneously familiar and foreign.

The early 1970s was a time period defined by continued anti–Vietnam War and civil rights protests, and while second-wave feminism was in full swing, it didn't have nearly the stature of other contemporaneous, social-political movements. While some of the composers in these interviews are participating in countercultural protest, most are benefitting from the elite, conservative, and largely segregated American university system as a patron of the arts.

While speaking from the "foreign soil" of the early 1970s, many of the composers Childs interviewed made predictions about the future. I hope that readers are struck by the prescience of some of these prognostications and, at the same time, are able to forgive the others that in hindsight are risible.

The Essays

These interviews are arranged alphabetically by surname for convenience; but, as we do not know Childs's intentions, they can be read in any order. The writers of the essays that precede and contextualize the interviews include critics and journalists, music theorists, historical and critical musicologists, performers, colleagues, and former students. They mediate between then and now and contextualize these conversations within the work life of each composer. The final word must lie with Barney Childs, in answer to a question from Sal Martirano: "It's a very selfish thing for me, because it's such fun to hear and be challenged and discuss with people whose work I know. It's a tremendous banquet for me, just partaking of everybody. As with you and the 'when the ink is dry, you are through,' this same thing is true here: that my own personal reaction is simply that when the thing is finished, that'll be it. I have no personal stake in it or anything like that; I'm an agency who's getting things that aren't available for people who will also find it exciting and challenging." This is such a "Barney" statement: enthusiastic, selfless. I hope that the reader will enjoy this long-delayed project.

Notes

1. Walter Zimmermann, *Desert Plants: Conversations with 23 American Musicians*, 2d ed. (Berlin: Beginner Press, 2020).

2. Keith Potter, "1976 and All That: Minimalism and Post-Minimalism, Analysis and Listening Strategies," paper, First International Conference on Minimalist Music, Bangor, Wales, September 2007, http://minimalismsociety.org/wp-content/uploads/2016/01/Keith -Potter.pdf.

3. Barney Childs, unpublished interview book proposal.

4. Ibid.

5. Barney Childs and Bertram J. Turetzky, series eds., The New Instrumentation, 7+ vols. (Berkeley: University of California Press, 1974 ff.). This work includes volumes by Turetzky (contrabass), Thomas Howell (flute), Stuart Dempster (trombone), Phillip Rehfeldt (clarinet), John Schneider (guitar), and Lou Ann Neil (pedal harp).

6. John Cage and Alison Knowles, eds., *Notations* (New York: Something Else Press, 1969).

7. Marshall Bialosky, "A Brief History of Composers' Groups in the United States," *College Music Symposium* 20/2 (1980): 37–38.

8. Jerry L. McBride, "Advance Recordings: Innovative Label for American Twentieth-Century Avant-Garde Music," *ARSC Journal* 50/1 (2019): 1–43.

9. Childs later released Richard Maxfield, *Electronic Music* (Advance Recordings FGR-8, 1969), on the Advance label; Sahl and Childs conducted a decades-long correspondence.

10. Donald Martino, "Notation in General—Articulation in Particular," *Perspectives of New Music* 4/2 (1966): 47–58.

11. Peter Westergaard, "Sung Language," *American Society of University Composers, Proceedings of the Second Annual Conference*, April 1967, 9–36.

12. Barney Childs, "What Concerns Me Is Music [interview with Charles Wuorinen]," *Genesis West* 1/1 (1962): 16.

13. Leo Treitler, in "The Present as History," *Perspectives of New Music* 7/2 (1969): 1–58, presents the factions as opposing historicist constructs (4).

14. Not just students: Stephen Davies, "John Cage *4'33''*: Is it Music?" in *Themes in the Philosophy of Music* (London: Oxford University Press, 2003): 11–29, presents a recent example.

15. Clive Phillpott, "Fluxus: Magazines, Manifestos, *Multum in Parvo*," in Clive Phillpott and Jon Hendricks, *Fluxus: Selections from the Gilbert and Lila Silverman Collection* (New York: Museum of Modern Art, 1988), 15.

16. Virginia Anderson, "1968 and the Experimental Revolution in Britain," in *Music and Protest, 1968*, ed. Beate Kutschke and Barley Norton (Cambridge: Cambridge University Press, 2013), 184–87.

17. Martino, "Notation in General."

18. A musical composition could not be registered with ASCAP without a score, thus prohibiting future revenues for broadcast and performance.

19. "Copyright Registration for Sound Recordings," U.S. Government Circular, 56, https://www.copyright.gov/circs/circ56.pdf (accessed May 3, 2020).

20. Jon Appleton at Dartmouth, mentioned by Christian Wolff in his interview, would develop the Dartmouth Digital Synthesizer (later the Synclavier), the prototype for all digital music processing today, in 1976.

21. Larry Austin, "Music; Can Electronic Music be Romantic? Composer and Electronic Music Practitioner," *New York Times*, September 19, 1971.

22. Leonard B. Meyer, *Music, the Arts and Ideas: Patterns and Predictions in Twentieth-Century Culture* (Chicago: University of Chicago Press, 1967), 102.

23. Raymond Williams, "Base and Superstructure in Marxist Cultural Theory," in *Culture and Materialism* (London: Verso, 2005 (original article in *New Left Review* 82 [1973]), 41.

24. Joseph Hunt and Thomas J. Anderson, "The Black Classics," *Black Perspective in Music* 1/2 (1973): 159.

25. Leo Smith, "(M1) American Music," *Black Perspective in Music* 2/2 (1974): 112.

26. Wim Mertens, *American Minimal Music* (London: Kahn and Averill, 1983; orig. Belgium, 1980).

27. Childs sporadically kept a dream journal that often focused on location.

28. I searched letters from the interviewed composers in answer to Childs's call for suggestions for possible interviewees, the records of ASUC, sites recommended by the International Alliance of Women in Music, and other sources, including a call to colleagues on Facebook for women born between 1930 and 1943 who were known composers in 1972.

29. Anthony Braxton, in *Soundpieces 2: Interviews with American Composers*, ed. Cole Gagne (Metuchen, NJ: Scarecrow, 1993), 36.

30. Smith, "(M1) American Music."

31. Braxton, in *Soundpieces 2*. Though Braxton's graphic scores appear earlier, *Saxophone Improvisations Series F* (America Records 30AM 011–012, 1972, LP) is the first substantial recording in this style.

32. Elliott Schwartz and Barney Childs, with Jim Fox, eds., *Contemporary Composers on Contemporary Music*, expanded ed. (New York: Da Capo Press, 1998).

33. Gordon Mumma to author, e-mail January 25, 2020.

34. Eric Smeigel, "The Singularity of Sound in a Plurality of Vision: The Early Works of Joseph Byrd" (liner notes), in American Contemporary Music Ensemble, *Joseph Byrd: NYC, 1960–1963*, New World Records 80738, 2013.

35. Joseph Byrd to Barney Childs, unpublished letters 1960–67. Barney Childs, "Indeterminacy and Theory: Some Notes," *Composer* 1/1 (1969): 15–23.

36. Mumma e-mail.

37. William Brooks to author, e-mail September 8, 2020.

1 William Albright (1944–1998)

ROBERT FINK

The career of William Albright epitomizes both the joys and the sorrows of what would come to be known during his lifetime as "postmodernism" in contemporary music. Albright was an unruly talent, a prodigious performer on both piano and organ who used his virtuosity to champion other composers (both living and dead) while his own musical ideas often flowed from improvisation and the wide stylistic range of his concert repertoire. He had practical success as a composer, especially in the specialized genres where he uniquely excelled (organ and piano, liturgical music) and whenever his strong identification with the expressive power of ragtime, blues, jazz, and popular song allowed him to flout the compositional orthodoxies of his time. As he half-seriously informed the audience at the 1993 premiere of his jazz-tinged *Fantasy Etudes* for saxophone quartet, his music tended toward "messy diversity, as opposed to boring unity"—they audibly tittered at the implied transgression.[1]

To Erik Santos, a former composition student, Albright's signal virtue was *empathy*, his superpower the ability to assimilate almost instantly the signature moves of any other composer: "It seemed that there was no stylistic wall that he could not and would not pass through. His oeuvre is truly a garden of exotic concoctions—ragtime, classical, klezmer, renaissance, aleatoric, acid rock." Santos eulogized Albright as the enthusiast and "optimist" who was "reverent in his irreverence," but modernist-identified critics ended up dismissing such polystylism with faint praise, as when Paul Griffiths led his *New York Times* obit with the oddity that Albright had composed ragtime pieces for the organ, "which had probably never had rags written for it before."[2]

Albright, of all people, would have known just how irrelevantly wrong this was. As a performer, he had premiered William Bolcom's shattering *Black Host* for organist, percussionist, and electronic tape in 1968, and was thus a bystander to the annihilation, during the work's climactic "detonation" of noise, of a gentle little ragtime episode Bolcom had written for, yes, the mighty pipe organ. It was the sixties; there were a lot of pieces skittering along the edge of societal and musical collapse in those years, and you could tell whether a composer was hip or square by what was allowed to survive the composed-out riots sweeping the concert halls of America. Bolcom's *Black Host* ended with the organist thundering in B minor, closing the door on hope and change—but Albright's own entry in the end-of-the-world theater sweepstakes, "The BEULAHLAND Rag" (1967–69), was more sly, more prophetic of what would actually come after the general collapse that musicologist Leonard Meyer, surveying the aesthetic wreckage of 1967, predicted for Art as a goal-directed humanist endeavor. Ushering in a post-canonic musical world, the work's narrator, who has been barking Hitlerite speeches and other gibberish into gathering clouds of free jazz, atonal improvisation, and taped noise, turns to call, at the peak of chaos, on the impersonal power of the Afro-diasporic musical spirit: "We will now shake the earth's foundation with the 'BEULAHLAND RAG'!" What he actually sets loose is the irresistible syncopated second strain of Scott Joplin's "The Maple Leaf Rag," eight bars of which bring down the house (and the curtain as well).[3]

It seems inconceivable today, but many classical patrons might not have recognized the quote from Joplin's most famous work; in 1969, ragtime piano was a dead style, suitable only for pianolas in ice cream parlors. But at the same concerts, Albright, who had already composed several note-perfect exercises in classic ragtime, would play his own foundation-shaking Grand Sonata in Rag, with its first movement subtitled "Scott Joplin's Victory." At the time of his interview with Childs in 1972 or 1973, Albright was seen as a standard-bearer, along with Bolcom and Gunther Schuller, for the (quite literal) reintegration of ragtime and other African American "learned" piano styles into contemporary art music, an antiacademic crossing of the musical color line typical of the funky late 1960s and coeval with the jug band revival that swept across the corresponding precincts of the pop-folk world. Albright's ragtime compositions from the 1970s might once have seemed like willful exercises in blank pastiche for the "historically deaf" (Frederic Jameson), but in fact they present an alternate history of American music in which Scott Joplin *did* triumph, and in which a useful Black compositional lineage was thereby preserved. It is difficult to imagine the contemporary success of African American pre-jazz revivalists like Jason Moran, Reginald R. Robinson, and Dom Flemons without these postmodern ragtime fantasies.

In his maturity, Albright's signature achievement as composer and teacher was to harness the explosive power of vernacular music to the systematic musical craftsmanship inculcated by academic modernism. In his most successful works—like the *Organbooks* he wrote in the tradition of his mentor Olivier Messiaen, or the expansive *Five Chromatic Dances* for piano (1976), perhaps his masterwork—the restless play of generic signifiers is grounded by surprisingly rigorous control of pitch and a fastidious ear for timbre. Late in life, he began sorting his compositional output into four basic expressive modes, only three of which (aggression, sensuality, humor) accord with stereotyped images of pop-influenced American postmodernism, in the vein of John Adams or Michael Daugherty. Albright's fourth expressive interest, spirituality, might surprise those familiar with his mercurial rags, but as the longtime music director of Ann Arbor's First Unitarian-Universalist Church, he produced a series of practical religious works that generally avoid polystylism and disclose a strong transcendentalist impulse.[4] Some bear the imprint of 1960s minimalist repetition (*An Alleluia Super-Round*, 8vv, 1973), while later unaccompanied choral works show an exquisite sense of text painting and harmonic color.

William Albright: Interview

BARNEY CHILDS: So many younger composers who had similar ideas in music were all at Tanglewood the same summer.

WILLIAM ALBRIGHT: That was a crazy summer. One of the most inspiring (and challenging) events of my life was the coming together of several very acutely aware people, common souls, who could converse on many different levels. Their music, of course, is worlds apart.

BC: Even now?

WA: Each has individual things to say—they may converge at certain points. Bolcom may write rags; I might write rags as a kind of a half-joke. Maybe things are common between Phil Winsor and myself or Dan Lentz, or Russell Peck, in terms of being good guys, having something on the ball in music. Why this should happen is anybody's guess; maybe there was a slipup in the administration. That sounds libelous! But it was a good summer. We had things to contribute, we gave to each other; more important, we all kept in contact. Some friendships are quite binding from that time. Certainly Phil Winsor; Peck I've known for a long time; others.

BC: You can't say that there's any similarity between your work.

WA: Only as it reflects itself in the overall spirit of younger composers now. Doesn't that sound rather presumptuous? There's a certain spirit of freedom. It sounds like old Charles Ives talking about freedom, individual spirit. You march in there, do your thing and ram it into the future. It's also the freedom to do whatever you want; freedom of tradition, in a sense, although not totally.

BC: Freedom *from* tradition?

WA: I think so: the traditional establishments as they might be portrayed. At the risk of oversimplification, there have always been East Coast establishments, certainly in literature. Mark Twain faced this in relation to the Eastern Establishment. The post-Emerson school, for example; pretty stodgy and conservative, as is not entirely equivalent in music. But establishments grow up in various places. One says this with a grain of salt because East Coast people speak of the Midwest as being a certain kind of establishment and vice versa; and Midwest people speak about West Coast people as being an establishment. It always seems like that from the outside. All of us at Tanglewood were from quite widely separate parts of the country.

BC: That's curious.

WA: Phil Winsor from Chicago and part of the West Coast; Bolcom from the West Coast and a little bit of East Coast; myself basically from New Jersey; Peck from Michigan; and so forth. We could have each re-created the image of one establishment or another but refused to do so—and found that we were in common agreement about a lot of things.

BC: One of which is this ability to do what you want.

WA: Consciously so, at least when you *talk* about music. When you do it you're not consistently aware of these things. Of course, that would be folly to think that you're always thinking about outside events. Music is just music; it's just the sound of it and that's all; you don't think about who you're going to please or what you're doing at any particular time, finding what's inside your head and putting it down on paper or creating it in sound. For a number of composers—and a lot of them feel this way—there is a degree of freedom, getting away from feeling that you're at the end of something or that you're carrying on any sort of tradition. This is difficult to do, because you'll always be holding to tradition in one way or another, even if you write down a C natural. How many people have written down C natural before? But one *can* get away from a lot of the establishments. Goodness knows that contemporary music in this country (or the arts in general, if you want to expand that way) have not had an easy go of it. They don't have the general respect of middle America, or lower-class America, as opposed to Europe, for example, in which the arts at least have lip service of respect, if nothing else. Most people will grant you the *right* to be a creative artist and feel that you are a useful part of their society. They have the tradition of this; they're *told* this. If the occasion arises, you say in a village in France or Germany, "I am a composer," you receive a modicum of respect. It's somewhat head-swelling too, that you do have respect. In America you don't have much respect. You either have to burrow yourself into a university somewhere where you can be included in a larger intellectual community, or you can go out and *try* to establish yourself as a composer in a society that is unlikely to agree that you are indeed a composer.

BC: Do you feel that there's something wrong about "burrowing into the university"?

WA: That's a good question. I don't think so. I've often had the feeling, as many others have, that one should try to make a go of it as a real person, in the sense that American society implies that you're a real person. I have relatives from San

Francisco: "Why don't you get a job?"; "When are you going to earn money?"; "When are you going to be a worker?" The work ethic equates a certain kind of professionalism with that. Being an artist can be portrayed or seen as a scab in society, a "parasite," as the communists would say.

BC: But at a place like Michigan, where there is a very strong contemporary music climate, where younger composers can really feel at ease and flourish, this is a pretty good thing.

WA: Definitely the university is a worthwhile aim and it certainly is as good a profession as one can find. I myself am enough of a middle-class American to believe in raising a family and having enough money to shelter myself and my wife and my child, so one comes to the conclusion that you have to get some kind of employment. Why not use at least some of the skills that you have? Not all situations are interesting. Some are completely stifling. But if it's as good a situation as one can find anywhere, why go off and be a waiter in a restaurant? You don't need that experience just because you're a writer, for example; that romantic notion of being a hand laborer just doesn't make any sense. Take advantage of what the situation has to offer. This way you can get some sense of having the respect of being a creative artist. This doesn't excuse not trying to communicate with a larger audience, or trying to change the situation so that you could integrate yourself within workaday society, so you can gain that kind of respect.

BC: Are you thinking of music as a tool for polemic purposes?

WA: I'm thinking more in terms of its commercial aspect. Commercial music has a very simple formula. It's good if it sells, whereas in "concert" or "classical" music, that certainly doesn't hold true. In fact, the least salable item is often the one that gets the most talk in university communities. Commercial music has very much a fascination for me, as it has among several of the people we were talking about previously. The idea that someone can establish themselves with an enormous audience—Burt Bacharach, Joni Mitchell, James Brown, or the Motown industry—these are incredible musical experiences on many different levels. They are of course aware of the commercial aspects. On the other hand, they have individuality and creative abilities. They believe in themselves just like "real composers" do; there's no question that they are that. Therefore it has a definite fascination for me—the wide communication of it. The justification of being a composer is there in commercial music, whether on the artistic fringes, writing jingles or whatever.

BC: How successful has the rag record been in getting at that commercial communication?

WA: There was talk about putting a couple selections on a 45, including "Brass Knuckles" [1969], which was a collaboration with Bolcom and myself. It was "discovered." I have heard that "Brass Knuckles" has caught on in kind of a commercial way. People will use it consistently in classrooms. I don't know why; because of its zaniness, perhaps. It's too sophisticated for general listening audiences. Yet it has a kind of earthiness: a kind of thumb-the-nose, punch-in-the-stomach feeling maybe that people respond to—just like they like *The Godfather*. Of course it never got anywhere, because it doesn't have any of the ultimate commercial appeal—it's not a song, it doesn't sell—but it has done reasonably well for a classical record. What can you expect? The music is fairly sophisticated. It takes a musically trained listener to fully appreciate it.

BC: What about rags in your own work? This is something else that present in the younger composers, much more openness of available languages. We did Peck's *Automobile* (1966) at Milwaukee. The second movement very clearly draws upon commercial music. And Phil's *Melted Ears* (1967). Do you think that this does obtain with your generation?

WA: Yes, except I think it's getting to be passé now, if you can sense anything in the wind. I hate to try to pin things down. That's a problem with critics. They're always trying to codify. They try to digest what might be going on in the avant-garde world or a mass readership. It wasn't so many years ago that all the New York papers were filled with items like "The composer world is divided into two camps: those following Milton Babbitt and those following John Cage." One doesn't think in these terms at all, at least I don't. Where I came from, you follow your own course and do what you like to do. Certainly a balloon has been punctured. There's no consideration that there's a purity of style any more. If it ever held any water, it is dead now. Of course, Charles Ives burst this bubble a long time ago. So what are we doing except following in the footsteps of Charles Ives? Establishing a tradition in his name.

BC: Does it make any sense to talk about style?

WA: Style doesn't imply anything to me. If someone wanted to codify me as an artist, they would have great difficulty. Journalists throw up their hands and say, "Well, he's doing a lot of things." The articles usually come out as a hopeless jumble of items that don't have anything to do with me. I suppose the diversity that's present could contain the recent interest in amalgamating styles, where the freedom of manipulating musical ideas has become the freedom of diversity. "Diversity" is a favorite word to try to incorporate all that might be going on.

BC: OK, what about *Organbook* [I, 1967; II, 1969]? This is a very diverse collection of . . . not "styles," but drawing on the resources of an instrument and its entire literature.

WA: I was drawn to the diversity of elements, trying to assuage a number of styles, not feeling that these are in conflict. You're not treading on anybody's toes. A number of pieces are like that; certainly your music incorporates many styles. All my friends are interested in that. If you want to tie any direction to that, it's the amount of diversity, both among the people and in their own music.

They're not afraid to do anything that they want to do. On the other hand, there tends to be a certain consolidation of that feeling. There's not quite the "going out in all directions" that there was few years ago, maybe it's because it's become less hip to do it. I'm cynical about trying to pin things down in that way because things change so rapidly. I'm virtually out of the ragtime thing. It was beautiful for a particular period, but it was also sort of precious. It's gone now, and now every other composer is writing it, and . . .

BC: . . . just in time!

WA: Right, I'll escape while I have the time! Of course the original turn-of-the-century music is justifiably here and is good.

BC: What about your role as a performer?

WA: I certainly spend more time performing than composing, because I like it better. I like working with composers, working with audiences, getting that visceral response from them. I try to get that in a sophisticated way. I'm not shooting daggers into the audience to get an emotional response, or throwing spoons. But I do try to get an emotional response, whether it's in an informal quasi-classroom kind of situation where I'm talking and demonstrating, or whether it's in a very formal proscenium. The challenge to get across that barrier is enormous: trying to get some kind of response from an audience that is that cynical about what you can do.

BC: You're working with an instrument which perhaps has more built-in prejudice about it than any other—except, maybe, the harp.

WA: The organ is a curious instrument—a very complicated one, with a rich history and a complex society surrounding it. A lot of it is church-oriented and still is, but it's a secular church. It's not connected with God necessarily. Everybody has a different association. You mention "organ" and you can see their mind running back to childhood events. The society of organists is a curious one that I don't enter into very flexibly; I tend to be on the outside and to be regarded with some suspicion. I'm often accused of destroying the instrument for the simplest things (it might be just a hand cluster of some kind). This is "violating" the instrument and its nature—not in reality, it's just the sensibilities of the particular person who is saying that. Whenever anybody says, "Well, how can you play with your arms?" I say, "It's kind of curious to play with your feet, too."

BC: Are contemporary composers really beginning to think of the organ in different terms?

WA: There's been initiative among organists to encourage new music, thank God! It certainly needs to be revitalized after a couple hundred years of virtual stagnation (with a couple of exceptions). Many traditional Western nineteenth-century instruments have gotten good service by twentieth-century composers: piano, flute, violin to a certain extent, the viola recently, cello certainly. Because of its curious encloistered nature, the organ has always been off in left field. It's a wacky instrument; because of its very diversity (every instrument is different), it can't be controlled. You can't know all the possibilities. It's an open-ended situation for any organist. You play a recital and it's like re-creating a piece on a totally different instrument. Often you have to rethink the substance of the piece to make it come off. The goal is to communicate with an audience, and this would be different for each instrument. I wish I could televise the appearance of my playing a neo-Baroque German organ in Montreal to the audience, which unfortunately was not able to see what I was doing because I was in a balcony. I had two assistants standing on either side of me in order to accomplish the elaborate color changes in much of the music I was playing, and they were working like incredible dogs. They were pulling, and reading. It was like a ballet performance (not one I'd like to go through too often!) because it was incredibly difficult. The appearance of the organ and the organist has even been exploited in some pieces that I know about. It is such a visual thing—equivalent to an orchestral conductor. Just as certain pieces of music use the conductor as kind of a visual element—the [Toshiro] Mayazumi *Metamusic* (1964), for example—the organ itself is a visual delight. It's a de Sade–like contraption.

As a performer, I use this as an advantage to get my message across, or get the message of the composers that I'm playing across. It's always fun. I value the effort that I put into it so highly. Each concert will be different. One occasion a piece I play will be a flop, the next will be an enormous success. There are so many intangibles involved. Whereas you know more about what's going to happen if you're playing the piano. That Steinway's going to be wheeled out, it's going to be so many feet long, the keyboard's going to be so wide, and it's going to have so many notes on it. There'll be large differences among pianos, but nothing that you can't manage with a few minutes' practice and overcome if you're confident. But with the organ, it's a real trip every time you do it.

I enjoy giving the concerts, even with the amount of preparation it has to take in advance of an organ recital. I think the initiative of the organists has helped encourage organists to write for it. Certain specialists in contemporary music, like Sacher in Germany, some French organists, and perhaps myself and a few other Americans, have encouraged them. What I often tell the American Guild of Organists groups that I speak to occasionally, it has to be go to your neighborhood composer and say, "I've got a recital. Will you write me a piece?" This way the repertoire gets expanded.

BC: Or write your own.

WA: It's not the most fun to keep pumping your own piece. This year I'm going to do a whole program of literature—a whole bunch of stuff stacked up in my room that I haven't gotten around to. Bolcom wrote a couple of pieces. One's called *Hydraulis* (1971)—a long piece which is non-Christian; it's Jewish. I want to do Phil [Winsor's] piece again. Your piece is up. I hope I don't have to do anything of mine to fill the gap! I'm not considered generally an organist, per se. I'm outside of the general mill of organists. I don't feel comfortable with them, and they don't feel comfortable with me.

BC: You feel much more comfortable with composers?

WA: I have more to communicate with them. I do a lot of piano playing now, a lot of ragtime and contemporary music concerts, and as an instrument, the piano is probably more rewarding. It's a more complete instrument. I don't struggle as much with the piano as I do with the organ, and it's a lot more fun to play. I think that it's one of the marvelous inventions of man. A very complex one, too, when you think about it. It took a long time, a lot of years of development to come out with something that is really as flexible as the piano is. It can play so many roles.

BC: My objection to much contemporary piano literature is that there's so many "total piano" pieces. It's like the total bass piece, the total trombone piece. You get a tape of the available sounds and then you write a work which includes everything you've been told about on the tape, plus, hopefully, some things which you've thought of, too. This establishes an end point at a gamut of clichés. One end point is the traditional literature—piano players learn to play a repertoire, they don't learn to play an instrument. At the other end, it's the super piano piece for tape, amplification, sticks, mallets—the whole bag.

WA: Rubber chickens!

BC: Right! Somewhere in between there's something viable. But the instrument bores me sometimes.

WA: Yes, the extraordinary manipulation, what I call "marginal" sound possibilities of an instrument, can be OK. It can result in aesthetically satisfying events from time to time. But the pendulum is swinging and there's more interest in the real original musical qualities. There's some richness to be found there. This is not to say that I don't "approve" of anything. Anything goes, obviously. This is the whole basis of the ethic today: you really *can* do anything. You do what you do to make an intelligent musical statement. You're more likely to be on the track if you stay sober and investigate what the piano sound really is. Cage's *Cheap Imitation* (1969) is a good example of a current piece that does just this: it exploits almost primarily that mezzo-forte piano sound, the best qualities of the piano sound. Played on a good piano it's just gorgeous.

BC: You're mentioning communication, audiences. If everybody can do what he wants to, is there any reason any longer to think about compositional process as a musical force?

WA: Sounds like a dull word.

BC: It's what students in analysis learn to look for, what critics and record-jacket guys try to tell you about.

WA: I always feel a negative reaction to a word like that, because not that often do you think about the process that's going on. Composition is not a process; it's the end result. It's the existence of sound in space. This is what you are trying to make audible, what you hear in your head. This is how I feel, not to imply that this is the way to compose, because everyone's different. "Processes": serial composition has implied some of the most artificial constructions that man has ever devised in any of his arts. Intellectual processes that only have vague references to appreciable sound, of communicable sound waves.

BC: What makes a piece of music communicate?

WA: That's completely undefinable. If something comes from within you as a necessity, or something makes sense to you, it will communicate. I feel strongly about the word "communicate," although that sounds like a romantic notion of some kind. It is a reaction to the noncommunication that is encouraged in the university ivory towers: the half or quasi-rejection of commercial values to promote "inner" research of some kind. Even though it's not a conscious effort, it's more important to communicate. In the initial stages of composition I speak with people by composing. I can't just talk to myself. There's no need to write things down if you're talking to yourself or keep a diary. One wants to talk just like you and I are talking now, over a cup of coffee and a couple of good cigars. It's one of the most interesting experiences a man can have. A piece of music is not that much different. If it's a difficult piece, it might be rough going in communication. If I started a discourse on the fourth dimension to you, but I wanted to make you understand it, I would try to give it some foundation that would interest you. It's somewhat similar in music. You want to give your composition a foundation or "halo" of communicability, to draw people into your private world. If it's *all* privacy, then people won't give a damn. Who cares about it any more? The university will encourage this, because you are playing to smaller, select audiences. You don't even have to combat the local music critic very often. That doesn't even concern you; you don't even know what a review is! Which is all educational experience, even for the composer.

BC: Should the university be training how people should listen? Is it our job to do all of the work? Shouldn't the audience make some kind of gesture of its own to get where it wants to go?

WA: You're asking whether they should be entirely complacent with a "show me" attitude?

BC: Do you expect anything from an audience?

WA: I expect an audience to be open-minded, as Ives says, have their ears clean and not be burdened with prior expectations of trying to be comfortable. Ives was fighting against the same kind of attitude in a much more difficult situation than we have now. By comparison, young composers are comfortable, with nice situations. Charles Ives's situation was quite different. He fought the whole time against the "comfortable" nature of music. This is important. The audience should be willing to have a new experience. If they are, how can you lose?

BC: Does the inclusion of other media help them? Tapes, lights, dancers, balloons . . .

WA: No doubt, probably because it looks like TV. You can communicate with the lowest common denominator if it comes on like TV, especially if it's simpleminded and more pretentious, as most media pieces tend to be. You tread on dangerous ground with the media thing. While it has a great many virtues— certainly I've used them like anybody else—I tend to be increasingly reluctant to employ other devices. I do have something I can do with pitches—even C-E-G—that could be interesting. I like to work with those elements, rather than trying to cloud the issue with so many extraneous elements. There's too many interesting paths to pursue in music. Go to an instrument, play a few notes, and you realize there's a whole world out there that you don't even know about yet. People talk about "Everything's been done before, everything's been used." That is not true. What is true is that everything's conceivably available now, but not everything has been discovered.

BC: Charles Wuorinen asked once what the next revolution was going to do if this one said anything goes.

WA: They might say, "nothing goes." If it's a pendulum situation, it might be a consolidation. This may indeed be taking place now, although I'd be the last one to say what it is. I leave that for the pop journalists. In fifty years they'll say, "Maybe something's happening now." Musical diversity is important now, and the willingness to communicate with an audience on basic levels without sacrificing quality of music. These things are not necessarily mutually exclusive.

BC: When you were studying with Messiaen, did you tune into things that were going on in Europe?

WA: A number of things. I'm not a total jingoist as an American composer. A lot can be learned in a world community of composers. American music is as strong as anywhere in the world, if not stronger, but for very objective reasons. The composers seem to be more willing to try out anything; they tend to be less circumscribed by tradition. They tend to be a little bit freer in their attitudes, less constrained than many of their European contemporaries. Perhaps more knowledgeable, too.

BC: Could this be the nature of their musical experience? The American composer often is an instrumentalist, has often played for a living. Winsor was a trumpet player, Rush is a piano player, and so on. They played sometimes to keep themselves going. There is still a European conservatory tradition, that perhaps the knock-about-ness is not available to them yet.

WA: One can be a twenty-four-year-old composer in Europe. There is a small amount of money available from state funds for composers' commissions for young people, if they have the right connections. But that is combined with a less opulent life style. They pursue the goals of being a serious composer. There's a lot of things to be learned. One can't ignore what's going on in Europe or tromp on anything that's imported. It is better to be objective: that it's all worthwhile. I can be interested in it all; it can be accepted on its own merits. To lump all European music into the wastebasket, just because it's neocolonial, doesn't make any sense. We've passed beyond that particular stage. We still have to establish the reputation of American music in Europe. But on these shores it's worth considering, without falling into the old trap of thinking that everything imported has more substance to it, than anything we can come up with. This, in traditional concert life, is the Sol Hurok syndrome, which touches us in various ways. If we go into institutions, we feel this pressure.

BC: About your eclectic tastes; you said you like to watch everything. You like to listen to everything too?

WA: George Cacioppo once accused me of having the most eclectic taste of anyone he had known. To a certain extent he's right, because when I get together with him I'll put on a piece of Balinese music, Dionne Warwick, German organ music, or [Carlo] Gesualdo.

BC: Do you ever feel you want to use this in your own music?

WA: No. You don't feel when you're doing it as if it's going to be fodder for the mill; only the spirit that excites you in a particular instance.

BC: You're not an eclectic listener; you're hearing similar things, but the shapes are different.

WA: I always come back to Charles Ives. He's been an animating force for me, even though my music is not that similar. It's not as rugged, individualistic as Ives, because of all that he was, and it's much more conditioned by the last fifty years and the twelve-tone experience. I can't escape that . . . yet. I'm still hearing a lot of those sounds (many composers do), but I often come back to him as an animating spirit. Somehow the fantastic freedom with which he dealt is just inspiring. I think, if he can do it why can't I, whenever I feel myself being constrained by some school or tradition.

Pop music has been an interesting force in my life. I enjoy all kinds of pop. There's a lot of hackwork, of course, especially in the lyrics. I've written a few pop songs.

BC: Both lyrics and music?

WA: Lyrics and music. It's great fun to do. The music is easy; you know how to make the harmonic rhythm right; the stanzas and so forth. But to get the right turn of words, the right inference of using the English language is very difficult, but very exciting.

BC: You're backwards in this case. Mostly a mindless evocation goes on in the lyrics, there's no real attention to . . .

WA: To detail? Sometimes there is, sometimes there isn't. Some of the great stars of the '60s had marvelous musical ears. Their music was created either by them or by extremely competent professional producers. They were often breaking ground within their individual fields. Very few mistakes were made. The chord changes were good, with some exceptions. It takes knowledge to play I-IV-V properly. There's a skill to doing them well and doing them imaginatively. And certainly the blues: when I, IV, and V are done well is something else again. Some of the blues numbers which I've been learning; some of Meade Lux Lewis's stuff which I just enjoy so much.

BC: I used to play that in high school.

WA: I've learned some of that now. You don't pretend to be anywhere in the same class, but it's great party style, and you get a great response from it. The lyrics are sometimes casually treated; even if the thoughts are OK, there's not the care that Cole Porter would have taken, or the old masters.

BC: The lyrics that infuriate me are pretentious, quasi-symbolic (Donovan, for example), where a lot of phrases essentially mean nothing at all, but there's this feeling that they ought to mean something to you.

WA: That's easy to pull out of your hat. To try to integrate the continuity and interesting word structure and sound structure takes real skill to do. I've enjoyed that—when you get just the right turn of phrase, something falls into place in a structured sense. Maybe you're just writing the old limerick form, with the rhymes in the right place.

BC: Have you ever written any so-called serious music with that vocal content?

WA: No, I've never written much vocal music.

BC: What about the second movement of your *Automobile* (1966)? This is a marvelous integration of the pop tradition. There's enough blur from its randomizing that you get this nightmare collage quality.

WA: There's a very carefully constructed and conceived example. It's all integrated; it's fairly loose integration, which makes it different from much of my music. I often struggle to get very close integrations. For example, if I juxtaposed jazz or ragtime against more chromatic dissonant sounds, I would try to find points of tangency among them all and work them out, if not in a logical fashion, at least in an intuitive fashion—to find all the inner workings of these various sounds. I call them "sound worlds," as pretentious as that might sound. You have different spheres, and then bring them together. They create the same inner tension that the tonal system might do among chords, like dominant, tonic, or other hierarchies of sound. This animated music for a couple of centuries. You can do the same thing, utilizing different available sounds. The more care you take with it, the more successful it's going to be. Although I can appreciate how the composers work, I don't care too much for a kind of "casual" juxtaposition, just as you might walk down the street and be bombarded with sensations of Colonel Sanders and used cars and things.

BC: Well, in a sense you are. You play Dionne Warwick, you play Balinese music, you play Gesualdo—in a sense you're getting at this kind of variety, but you're not using it in direct, immediate collage.

WA: Collage may be old hat now. I don't know whether you feel that way or not. Some of my young students frighten me; they tend to be much more conservative in their attitudes than I am. Five or six years ago an undergraduate composer would be excited by the whole "avant-garde" thing. At least I felt myself involved in that swirl.

BC: You try to be hip.

WA: You tried to know what was going on constantly beyond the fringe, or the cutting head of the avant-garde. Now I find that the cutting head of the avant-garde is writing string quartets in 4/4. The pendulum has swung back to a gross conservatism among many students. This may be a lack of curiosity about what's going on, and this is where I part company with many of them. On the other hand, look at the university establishment of twenty years ago, and what were they encouraging? It was twelve-tone. They were encouraging Bartók, Stravinsky, and looking at the brazen, post-Webern school with some shock and dismay and complete incomprehension. Now that situation has changed; a different generation of kids come along and now they're preaching a different Bible.

BC: If you think of the "group" phenomenon—ONCE, the San Francisco Tape Center, New York in the 1960s—all are very young guys who are rebelling. The ONCE guys were all people who couldn't stand [Ross Lee] F-I-N-N-E-Y. The same with the Tape Center, and with Joe Byrd and Terry Riley and so on in New York. But these are all guys in their early twenties, who *forget* that.

WA: They're looking for a different set of values now, and the situation changes very quickly. What those groups were doing is now considered somewhat old-hat among the younger generation. Certainly as they become more "establishment," it's inevitable that they should become less avant-garde and more part of a tradition.

BC: So the *real* "new diatonicism" is NOT *In C*, is not *Cheap Imitation*, but is string quartets in C Major. That's scary.

WA: Several of us staged a "Contemporary Directions" concert in Ann Arbor called "New Diatonicism." Of course it's not convenient to stick everybody who's writing something that's quasi-diatonic in a category like this. I can see grimaces on people's faces, knowing that the label has been stuck on. Who wants it; who needs it? But it was a very successful concert, a very beautiful presentation of sound. It included *In C*; works of Winsor, Bolcom, Lloyd

Rogers, and Douglas Leedy—people who are more interested in a diatonic approach to music than a chromatic approach.

BC: The term "new diatonicism" has a great "mosquito" value that comes back to plague its inventors.

WA: It just implies that it's already an establishment; it's no longer the new play-thing. It was an important trend of 1965, and therefore has a place in the university conscience. Now it's on to bigger and better things.

BC: I'm charmed that the concert was had, that the title was invented, and that those works were played.

WA: It scandalized the older establishment too, as it might well. They saw no logic in this kind of turn-around, or turn-forward. They couldn't accept this logically, especially where they were steeped so much in European chromatic tradition. This is hard for them to see. My first piece was twelve-tone. If you had your idea of a concert of "Opus 1" . . .

BC: That's startling to me because of our age difference that this would be what you did.

WA: In 1961, this was *the* thing to do. I virtually reject the sound in that piece as part of my language, whatever that might be. That doesn't appeal to me any more. It had negative aspects. The world of sound is big and has enormous possibilities of beauty. Although this had a certain grotesque beauty, it is not getting to the heart of the matter: investigating the nature of sound. So after working with serial processes and going through the book A to Z, I decided that it was not for me. On the other hand, that experience has influenced me; the chromatic sound still exists in my music and I do use it frequently. I think it's a viable sound, and it can be used intelligently with very great effect.

BC: How do you feel about electronics?

WA: I've used tape a great deal. Tape is an adjunct; sounds that egg on performers into worlds they'd never imagined. *Tic* [a spectacle for two groups of performers, soloist, films, and tape, 1967] is a strange piece. The psychology of the play-ers is hard to handle. Finally you turn out the lights and turn on this massive tape, and people lose their sense of cool and go crazy. I think that reaction is probably more interesting to me than the experience of the piece, which being a mixed-media piece is dated already and doesn't excite me much. The reaction of the players is very intriguing. It's almost always the same, this going ape: it's as if you'd opened a jack-in-the-box with inhibitions.

BC: Like one of those monsters on the late show—you open the chest and out it comes. You were talking about, in connection with the pop world, the impre-sario, the importation of culture.

WA: I tried to hedge various sides of the argument. The situation's so complicated, it's hard to see things in terms of black and white.

BC: That we have to see things in black and white is, in turn, a European intellectual construct. The best thing that's happened in this country is that we don't.

WA: There's a lot of excitement in our field, which intrigues me. It keeps me coming back, as jaundiced as I might get about the composer's situation. You read something, hear a new piece that's exciting, or talk to a friend who has exciting things to say, and it keeps you going. I'm totally committed to the world that exists, and the older I get the more committed I am to it. I do feel that the battles are worth fighting just for the worthwhileness of hearing good sounds.

BC: We talked about you people at Tanglewood. Now you can be aware of what they are doing even if one person is in Michigan, one person is in Virginia, one person is in Utah. People are more mobile, with the result that when you play the Contemporary Directions Concert, you're *not* playing just Michigan composers, you're playing Bolcom, Peck, Austin, whoever.

WA: A lot of people would want to be much more parochial and create little enclaves, medieval fortresses, but our numbers aren't so many that we can't keep supporting each other. As I get more experience, I tend to accept and enjoy experiences that I might have rejected offhand at first. Communication is better now than in the past. You hear, for example, what goes on on the West Coast, with the establishment of journals. Not all of them are totally successful this way; some tend to beat their own drum a little bit too much. It was interesting that a journal promoting West Coast music and all of the activities there all of a sudden devoted six pages to European activities.

BC: On the other hand, Peter Garland's magazine, *Soundings*, is really the closest thing to the *New Music Quarterly*. It's a "handmade" periodical—it's not a slick thing at all, no big university behind it.

WA: This is healthy. They may or may not last very long; that's not the point. There are things going on all across the country, too. Also it's not a matter of just New York, or of just Los Angeles, of just this or that place. It's spread clear across the country and exciting things are happening.

BC: This again is an American thing: grass-roots-ism. Back fifty-sixty-seventy years—Ives, [Lou] Harrison, [John J.] Becker, [Carl] Ruggles are all in their own areas, doing their own things, nobody's paying attention to what's happening. They're not part of the aristocratic establishment in New York.

WA: There's not much frontier left to conquer in this country, geographically. The West Coast was the last frontier. Maybe there are frontiers in Utah or something of which I am not aware. But you can think of our forefathers being a strange mixture: misfits in Europe, adventurers, ne'er-do-wells of various kinds, various stripes. Often a very conservative kind, of course, but at least with enough invention to pick up their roots and skedaddle to an adventure which they didn't know anything about. That spirit is still alive in this country, and may indicate the kind of adventure that goes on in music. We don't have to create a masterpiece each time we write a piece. What kind of trends do *you* see happening in this country?

BC: Much the same as everyone. The trends are getting more intense and lasting less time, and they're much more sweeping. Like collage, which is the most recent thing to rise into meteoric blaze for a while and fade away. It used to be that when university students started doing it the pros were pretty well tired of it. Pauline Oliveros says Fred Rzewski wrote that live electronics are big in Europe, and she wrote, "So it's time to start doing something else." But you can't find out what's going on until you talk to people. Larry Austin had a recent article in the *New York Times* where he discusses the new romanticism, but this is a very loaded term.[5]

I certainly agree with everything you've said about the individual independence of composers. It's the American thing: push out, do your own work, and not care. The best composers are those who've done this and not teamed up with any club. I don't want to talk about people who, with a perfectly viable "Americanische" style, suddenly discovered that they had to be serial to be hip and became serial, and then they had to be indeterminate to be hip and became indeterminate. They were writing the same bad music. X [name redacted] is a very good example. Here's someone who's always been two hundred yards behind the bandwagon. Five years from now you can be sure that there will be an X piece reflecting what happened in 1972.

WA: I'm sure he's probably honest about it. It's as if he does this consciously and has a real dedication, and sees no artistic fallibility in doing it. A kind of extreme case; but there are lesser cases, unfortunately, that don't even handle it as well, musically, as X does.

BC: I think the '60s were peculiar because younger guys felt "I've got to be on that bandwagon." Not your generation but the next, the guys who are now in their late thirties. There's a lot of sort of rushing to get on that side of the post.

WA: I sense a lack of curiosity among some younger generation composers. Maybe this is a dangerous aspect of the independence: you can go to Fertilmenken, Minnesota, and write your Great American Symphony without being in communication with your colleagues. This not being aware of what's going on is a bit dangerous. I value the knowledge of my peers and my colleagues and the whole world of music. It's not because I will use those things in a piece, or be so flirtatious with whatever comes my way, but just because it makes me happy to be a composer knowing that there are people struggling with the sound world just as I am.

BC: And coming out with intriguing solutions.

WA: It tends to have something that's more rooted in music rather than in fads. Does sound itself go in and out of fashion now, I wonder?

BC: That's a very good question! I think it does.

WA: Does the approach to the beauties of the sound go in and out of fashion? It might, as different attitudes come to the fore. I like to think that I can imagine a good sound, that I can hear one and re-create it in a piece. For that reason I do a lot of experimenting at the piano. Stravinsky often experimented with sounds on a piano. People who aren't pianists tend to do things more in their head. But I like the idea of my fingers slipping, you know, and getting something entirely new.

BC: More so than with the organ?

WA: You don't really experiment with the organ. It's not a flexible instrument; it's a heavy monster that you grapple with. My doing this fairly novel work made me a certain reputation as an organist, but I really don't appreciate the organ as much as I do the piano. I'm working on several projects now. When I get around to it—and I don't have the initiative all the time—I have some demand to do church and organ music. I might see that through, although I don't know whether I'll have the energy to do it. I'm intrigued by writing some children's piano pieces. My wife, being a piano teacher, is constantly inundated with loads of crap published for children. There's very little that's of meaningful quality or is inspiring to a child.

What I've done so far is widely eclectic; it's a grab bag of all the things I'm interested in at that moment. I won't be writing organ music for a while; I'm sick of that. I'm pretty much finished with writing ragtime; that was a thing of the moment. There's all kinds of exciting ideas I can pursue. It's merely finding the right one at the right time. I find deadlines help very much in this.

BC: I suppose a lot of it is the fact that you play yourself. When you get a tape back from a performance from Hog Jowl A & I, and it's just an appalling mishmash of what you had intended, it's discouraging.

WA: Some of the best performances I get, I do myself. Maybe this is partly imaginary, but I enjoy performing much more than composing. It's more rewarding for me in many ways.

Notes

1. "William Albright Introducing World Premiere Performance of *Fantasy Etudes*," YouTube, https://www.youtube.com/watch?v=qjkOVhjn_oI (accessed July 20, 2019).

2. Erik Santos, "Requiem for Bill Albright," *Perspectives of New Music* 37/1 (Winter 1999): 36; Paul Griffiths, "William Albright, 53, Composer of Ragtime for the Organ," *New York Times*, September 23, 1998.

3. Leonard Meyer, "The End of the Renaissance?" in *Music, the Arts, and Ideas: Patterns and Predictions in Twentieth-Century Culture* (Chicago: University of Chicago Press, 1967), 68–86. Excerpts of Albright's "The BEULAHLAND Rag!"—most notably its Joplinesque ending, can be seen in the 1969 short film *Caprice Will Become the Rule*, made at Portland State

University and now available online at its fiftieth anniversary, https://www.youtube.com/watch?v=uz4Qm4VAYFo (accessed July 28, 2019).

4. Albright's list of "expressive modes" follows the biographical sketch provided by the online finding aid to the William Albright Papers at the Bentley Historical Library, University of Michigan, https://quod.lib.umich.edu/b/bhlead/umich-bhl-00135?byte=182038 869;focusrgn=bioghist;subview=standard;view=reslist (accessed August 2, 2019).

5. Larry Austin, "Can Electronic Music Be Romantic?" *New York Times*, September 19, 1971, sect. D, 15.

2 Robert Ashley (1930–2014)

KEVIN HOLM-HUDSON

When Barney Childs interviewed Robert Ashley in 1972, Ashley had been at Mills College for only a year, in the midst of a creatively barren period.[1] This may account for Ashley's somewhat pessimistic tone in assessing the contemporary music scene—the "professional orchestra domain, which I consider to be obscenely against American music; they're against music as any sort of magic thing. . . . I decided that that was unhealthy, that I wanted no part of that." The ONCE festivals were conceived by Ashley and Gordon Mumma, self-described "university rejects," who were met with indifference in their efforts to promote electronic music; "we couldn't get anybody at the university to believe that you could be interested in those things, so we just had to do it ourselves." This is, of course, a profoundly American idea—the icon of the do-it-yourself "maverick American composer" goes back to William Billings.

Ashley advocates for local, grassroots music making, informed by place: "I want to play music that comes from me living right here." The work of ONCE led to similar localized activity in other communities: "In every university in the United States right now that I've been in for the last five years . . . there are the young guys who just want to change it . . . for local reasons. Very seldom do you find a person who has grandiose ideas about conquering. He just wants to make the local scene richer for him. It makes it wonderful."

In 1966 Ashley formed the Sonic Arts Union with Gordon Mumma, Alvin Lucier, and David Behrman; still active in 1972, this ensemble also comes into the discussion indirectly. When asked, "What things have you heard recently that you feel to be interesting?" Ashley shares brief descriptions of recent work by Mumma, Lucier, and Behrman.

Ashley also reveals several ideas and preoccupations that would significantly shape his later work, thereby documenting some of his career-defining insights in their nascent state. For example, discussing the declining role of the concert virtuoso, Ashley speculates about "a very natural running out of repertory and a very natural shift into another type of playing." Here Ashley may have been thinking of his long-time collaborator "Blue" Gene Tyranny (formerly Robert Sheff), who performed in the ONCE festivals and is best known for creating the role of Buddy (the World's Greatest Piano Player) in *Perfect Lives* (1978–80), in which he demonstrates his prowess as a new kind of virtuoso improviser.

Ashley also discusses the different temporal experience in works of long dura-tion: "I'm trying so hard now to work at pieces that you listen to in a different time duration. It isn't a matter of they're being longer than ordinary pieces or longer than traditional pieces, but they pass at a different rate." This interest led Ashley into documentary video (his "television opera," *Music with Roots in the Aether*, lasting fourteen hours) and to *Perfect Lives*, an "opera for television" in seven thirty-minute episodes. As Ashley later told another interviewer, "It's okay to sit in your room and listen to a record over and over again when you're fifteen, but if you do that when you are forty, people think you are crazy. But the funny thing is that we've actually allowed ourselves that free time in television."[2]

Ashley also shares several ideas that ultimately point to his piece *Automatic Writ-ing* (1979). Ashley evidently began work on this piece in 1974, with some recording taking place at the Mills College Center for Contemporary Music.[3] One interesting idea he shares here concerns music meant to be experienced at home, conceived for the phonograph record. Other composers had done this (Morton Subotnick's *Silver Apples of the Moon* was commissioned by Nonesuch Records in 1967) but Ashley made *Automatic Writing* as much *about* the home-listening experience itself as it was a work to be listened to at home. "I'm getting very interested in music that you don't pay attention to, sort of music for hi-fi. I'm interested in the listen-ing process. For instance, most of my musical experience in the past twenty years . . . has been through records. And you can't help noticing that it's a very peculiar experience because the time zone is different from the way your attention spans are different—the different perception faculties are working at different rates. So I'm trying to make music that is good for listening in your home over loudspeakers." Ashley also seems to allude to *Automatic Writing* in his discussion of his fascina-tion with speech: "I've always been very interested in verbal texts, in the meaning of things that people say. . . . I like the idea of talk. I can't explain this very clearly, but I like the idea of talk as being a scheduling process for our listening. . . . I like the idea of listening to English as if it were a foreign language. . . . When people talk, I try to listen to them as if I didn't understand anything about language, as though they were just moving their mouths. I like that. I like the pauses . . ." This interview fortuitously captures Ashley at a nexus point in his career. The ONCE festivals had come and gone, having made their point for the creation of new music outside the cloistered walls of academia. The Sonic Arts Union was still active, an early composers-as-performers collective that was a model for later ensembles such as the Bang on a Can All-Stars. Ashley's administrative duties at Mills left him little time for his own creative work—but that does not mean that his mind had lost any of its fecundity. Indeed, the works that emerged in the late Mills period and erupted soon thereafter—*Music with Roots in the Aether, Automatic Writing, Perfect Lives*—all had roots in the early 1970s. This interview affords us some tantalizing glimpses of what would become some of Ashley's most pioneering and best-known work.

Robert Ashley: Interview

BARNEY CHILDS: What's your retrospective view of the ONCE festivals?

ROBERT ASHLEY: I'm vain as to think we were one of the first, yet I'm not so vain as to think we invented the idea. It was just current. We got in circumstances that were very good for us: four or five guys in Ann Arbor who were compatible. Ann Arbor was not so big that we couldn't negotiate and not so small that it didn't mean anything. It was just an ideal circumstance: a university community. University communities are where music is interesting these days, and will be.

BC: But you were all university rejects.

RA: We were. I didn't mean that the university as such played such a big part. I've always been scornful of people who come out for Real Music, Real Art. They're into a professional orchestra domain, which I consider to be obscenely against American music. They're against music as any sort of magic thing, or any cultural thing. They're in it for the bucks. Then there are European counterparts—like [Pierre] Boulez, who has been attacking the university composer the last couple of years. Of course he works in a situation that is much more closed than any university system. Having taken a good look at the so-called professional real world, I decided that that was unhealthy, that I wanted no part of that.

BC: But it is curious that so many of you guys with talent decided it at once. It fell into itself, apparently, and there it was.

RA: Don Scavarda and George Cacioppo had both graduated from the University of Michigan and didn't find any place for themselves in the so-called professional world. Roger [Reynolds] was there as a graduate student. Gordon [Mumma] was about Roger's age, about five years younger than I am. He tried to be a university student and just failed completely. I was there through peculiar circumstances. I already had a master's degree in piano and had not done any composing at all, so I was looking for a place to compose in, and I was very interested in electronic music. Columbia was absolutely outrageous, totally beyond my financial resources. I had just gotten out of the army, I had a GI Bill, and since I had lived in Michigan I could go to school there. I went back there for practical reasons and it didn't work out. I was a disinvested student. So, aside from Roger, who was still in the department, the four of us were either out of it and having nothing to do, or else not in it.

BC: About electronic music: it seems, listening over the years, that there was a distinct new ground being broken. We've played *Fourth of July* for electronic music classes. People were turned on by the work, wanted copies of it. There was an openness sound in those days with electronic means, which just wasn't happening anywhere else.

RA: It was just because Gordon and I hit it off so well. We were such close friends; it's a small place, so we saw each other daily for hours. We were both rabidly interested in electronic music without having had the opportunity to meet anybody else who was. We had great admiration for [Karlheinz] Stockhausen. The two *Studies* were two things that we had, and [Vladimir] Ussachevsky, and whatever was around in 1957. We couldn't get anybody at the university to believe that you could be interested in those things, so we just had to do it ourselves; reading all the books, building the equipment, etc.

BC: There's a sophistication in technique in those early works which just isn't present anywhere else that I've been able to find in those years. There's an inventiveness that is very exciting.

RA: This is a very particular point. The aesthetic of world music is overall, in humanistic terms, a good idea. I'm interested in African music and Indian music, and pieces from Europe. I don't mean to sound like a right-winger who says, "Well, America first, blah blah blah." We recognize some very mystical, mysterious connection between the area that a music originates in and the honesty of that music.

BC: How about the philosophy of that music and the honesty of that music?

RA: The goal of trying to influence the world with your music comes out of nineteenth-century politics rather than out of any musical idea. That could happen in Europe because Europe *was* the whole world for a while. You had the idea that you could be *the* most important composer in the world, if your world was only Europe. We outgrew that. We began to realize that there should be a lot of different kinds of music.

BC: This goes along with what we were saying about music for the area in which you are. You are not trying to impress guys in New York, in London, or Darmstadt.

RA: I really don't want to impress those guys over there. I like the idea of the musician or the composer being a sort of freak—an oddball in his environment. If you take him out of the environment, people can observe him the way Barnum used to exhibit midgets. You take an African or an Indian around, it doesn't seem like he gets hurt by that traveling, because his music, his roots stay back where he came from; he only suffers when he gets cut off from them. But that is totally different from trying to make a music that encompasses the whole world. The idea that we could all be sharing the same music seems so dull, so flat. I don't want to play Indian music. I don't want to play African music. I hate that idea. I want to play music that comes from me living right here.

BC: Africans, I'm sure, don't want to play our music.

RA: I think you can count on that. Ha! This idea came to me because I had to unlearn the European idea of conquering the world. It's such a bullshit idea. . . . I still like to have guys come in. I like the idea of the traveling oddball.

BC: America is a traveling oddball culture to begin with. America made Barnum, after all; Johnny Appleseed, Ives and Ruggles, and all.

RA: Ives's music was peculiarly regional. Coming out of the time that he came out of, it's amazing. It's even more amazing than his technical [innovations]. Everybody in his time was absolutely imitative of European music—to the letter! The prizes went to the guy who could sound most like he studied in Berlin.

BC: But how much has this changed?

RA: It's changed considerably in the last fifteen years. That idea is more and more acceptable in the United States, along with the idea that conquering the world is less and less acceptable. It seems so hard for us to outgrow that idea, but we have outgrown it.

BC: In any art it probably seems so . . . although many of the arts have been ahead. Graphic arts, film are beyond music. Maybe music has caught up, but ten years ago it hasn't.

RA: You're right. They were ahead; I don't know why. I guess it's because that, along with the idea that music was an international skill, was the idea that you brought a lot of skills to music. That also seems sort of peculiar to me. The idea that you would make a skillful music, so that only a few people could do it, seems to me to be outrageous.

BC: How much are you into computers now?

RA: I've had almost no experience, but I'm very interested in computers. I just haven't had time since I came to Mills.

BC: Do you have the wherewithal if you do?

RA: Not really, but it's becoming more practical. There is not the wherewithal anywhere, the way I think of computers. So many composers are getting on to what the computer can do. Not that they weren't always on to it, but they're getting on to the idea that computers should be decentralized. That had something to do with our electronic music at Ann Arbor, too. At that time the idea was that you had to build a large studio, and only a few people use the thing. And everybody worshipped the European successes and put them on. And everybody worshiped Columbia-Princeton. The idea that you could just make your own equipment and make music was going to set us free. And the people are beginning to get that idea now about computers. It's a recent concept that you could have a small, relatively inexpensive, computer. You want the music computer [to be] no more expensive than very classy studio equipment that only does music. If you get that kind of installation, then you can start dealing with computers as though they were musical instruments, not as bookkeeping slaves, as in *2001*. You want the computer to produce your musical ideas. You don't want to manage something that someone else has already laid out. It's like being a virtuoso.

BC: What's happening to the virtuoso? You have more super-instrumentalists in the last fifteen years than ever before: out-of-sight guys who play wild things that people twenty years ago would never have dreamed of. Is there still a place for writing the super flute piece, the super viola piece?

RA: I don't notice those pieces being written. Most of the super virtuoso players, inasmuch as I read the papers, are playing real, that is, nineteenth-century virtuoso music. Once in a while you will see some commission, but it's usually not a very good piece for the instrument, because we've gone away from that. The only person who comes anywhere near it is Xenakis writing for Takahashi. I like Takahashi's playing, and I like Xenakis' musical ideas, but I don't think that's where Xenakis is strongest. And I certainly don't think that's where Takahashi is strongest. Maybe that's where his *career* is strongest, but those pieces don't show him off as a pianist as well as a lot of other pieces.

BC: So you think that gradually the instrumental virtuoso is shipping out?

RA: My feeling is that there'll be a very natural running out of repertory and a very natural shift into another type of playing. The virtuoso player is not unequipped to do other things; he's just programmed to do that particular kind of weird thing he does. He's obviously capable of being part of a very powerful musical activity.

BC: The virtuoso is a nineteenth-century concept, and it too is fading out. But getting into your point of approaching instrumental music, I think there's still a place for the virtuoso. Not in the nineteenth-century sense, but in the sense of a composer laying on him certain new ways of looking at real-time sound, instrumental sound, acoustic sound. That still makes the super players a part of new music.

RA: I always think of the virtuoso ideal as having more to do with entertainment.

BC: Well, that's the concert format that comes with it.

RA: In other words, the virtuoso player is a guy who has trained himself to do a particular virtuoso thing. Some guys can play the Brahms Violin Concerto very well and other guys can whistle with bottles. If you really get into the world of sound, then you find yourself in a situation where you value the guy who can whistle with the bottles to exactly the same degree as the Brahms performer.

BC: I wouldn't like a world in which the virtuoso instrumentalist wasn't there serving the composer who is coming at him from directions where he was learning fingerings he didn't dream was there.

RA: I would like to dream of a world, at least a temporary one, where we could get rid of the virtuosos.

BC: You're surely not going so far as saying to ship out instrumentalists?

RA: Well, I just wish they would all stop being virtuoso!

BC: What you're objecting to is the virtuoso mentality. But you will still welcome guys who could blow like hell on flutes and horns.

RA: Yeah, definitely.

BC: If you want to make a career playing nineteenth-century pieces, that's one bag; but if you want to get into new music you have to forget all that. You have to know about the fingers still, because that's going to be demanded of you. At the same time, the whole nineteenth-century virtuoso music has to ship out and you have to get into a new way of thinking about sound.

RA: There are so many virtuosos—almost everybody, if you give them the chance, can do something unique with an instrument. But if that's all there is, I'm not interested in it at all.

BC: Do you have student composers who are strong instrumentalists who carry this thinking over into their work?

RA: At Mills, right now, I have one composer who is a spectacular flutist. But her master's degree project was a film of oscilloscope patterns that she generated by very, very unusual ring modulation techniques. The film was a very high-tech solution to the problem of how to film oscilloscope patterns, so it had nothing to do with flute playing. I have another student who spent his whole undergraduate career playing the Moog. He considers the Moog his instrument.

BC: That's the nineteenth-century virtuosity, isn't it?

RA: Well, he doesn't consider it as an instrument that he plays: the Moog is his orchestra. Among the other people, there is a very good pianist who the farthest-out guy we've got. Right now he's into contact microphones. There are a couple of people who don't play instruments at all.

BC: I'm not trying to say the composer has to be the virtuoso.

RA: I know. I'm just trying to give you examples. I don't have any examples of people who exploit any of their instrumental training. In fact, those two have completely rejected their instrumental training as being a handicap.

BC: This bodes ill for the conservatory-trained player.

RA: I can't imagine what's going to happen to those players. In their conservatory training they are getting neither practical experience in the areas in which music is growing—one doesn't have to be a composer in the old way—but they are not getting experience with ensemble ideas that have been developing since the last fifteen or twenty years. Nor are they getting any sort of practical exposure to the areas in which virtuoso playing is still pretty relevant, which is popular music or jazz. They are neither getting that nor are they getting the very rich ideas of recent concert music. So they are just being trained in obsolete skills.

BC: Trained to make buggy whips.

RA: I can't imagine what their future is going to be.

BC: What about people who don't know much about computers, tape, who do write for the virtuoso concert ensemble? Is this a viable compositional stance, in terms of what is going to happen and what is happening?

RA: I can't imagine how. Assuming that my predictions that music is going to become more decentralized are coming true (and I can't see any reason why not), any time you start a small group in some city, as soon as the thing gets any strength, as it overcomes all those outside influences, as it becomes associated with its own local strengths, then it's going to start developing local compos- ers. I can't imagine how those local concerts are not going to do radical things, because they're going to be cut off from those traditions. There's always going to be that conflict between the economic society that establishes the ensemble and the real musical inputs. Those conflicts will be overcome in every situation because the musician is just there, doing it.

BC: This extrapolates what you're saying about the regionality of American music. The composer or the young super-instrumentalist who comes to Omaha or wherever is no longer going to have roots connected. He's going to be in the sphere of the action there, which is going to break him off from these roots and plug him in to what's happening immediately. It's going to make him go this way, and if he can't handle that, then he's in serious trouble.

RA: At the same time people who will be furnishing his musical ideas and who will be working with him are going to be more cut off than he is because they haven't had that skill training.

BC: But here he is coming green and MA'd from Eastman, and he's encountering a curious local focus which is independent and developing and real, and he's going to be cruelly snapped from those roots that he had.

RA: You see it happening all of the time. I don't have to predict what's happening. It's happening in very profound ways. In every university in the United States right now that I've been in for the last five years, there is tradition based on some concept of what music should be like (usually the older people), and then there are the young guys who just want to change it. They want to change it for local reasons. Very seldom do you find a person who has grandiose ideas about conquering. He just wants to make the local scene richer for him. It makes it wonderful. It means that every community you go into has composers and players, and they're getting along wonderfully. They feel perfectly confident that what they're doing is valid.

BC: In ONCE, was this already showing? You had plenty of bright young players. One of the exciting things about ONCE was the incredible number of play- ers that could do these things, and they were being wooed away, broken away from whatever conservatory or university plug-in they had. You've given me an answer to something I've been wondering about: the importance of things like ONCE. It affirmed the local focus and the local power to work toward a new music in a real original sense.

RA: Well, in retrospect I'm proud that we never tried to transplant them. We got really wonderful letters from some guys that I won't even name that said, "we'll do the exact same thing here." We always used to think that was just terrific. There was very little of, "Well, we'd like to come study with you." In fact, if a guy said he'd like to come to Ann Arbor and be part of it, we discouraged them. We'd say, why don't you do it where you are and then we'll communicate? We just did that instinctively because it was in the wind.

BC: How do you think those composers for ONCE feel now? Do you think there's a distinct mark left on them from this kind of stance?

RA: We've all had strange fortunes. Gordon is very happy with [the Merce] Cunningham [Dance Company]. In a peculiar way Cunningham is very provincial. The Cage idea has always been uppermost. The Cunningham music has always been this one idea. In spite of the fact that they traveled, they're not achieving fame in the same way that other dance companies are. Roger left early; he's had a very strange career and spent a lot of isolated years. I stayed in Ann Arbor and went on with the ONCE group, which was more theatrical. I was still not making a living in music. George has worked at the radio station for fifteen years. And Don Scavarda has pretty much given up the active social life. I guess everyone was getting tired. I don't think that that is necessarily sad, though I regret sometimes that Don Scavarda has not become a world-famous composer.

BC: The idea of fame and the picture on the cover of *Time* magazine: do you think composers in this country now are less concerned with this? That the whole nineteenth-century-hero thing has shipped out? That none of us now are really concerned about "making it"?

RA: It's such an impossible dream—unless you're just completely batty, you don't think of it. I can't imagine where having your picture on the cover of *Time* magazine would mean anything for more than a week and a half. Like Andy Warhol said, "Everybody's famous for fifteen minutes." In a practical sense, if you do something and you get recognition for it, it makes it easier to do the next thing. But you can accomplish that locally, too. Some very spectacular things can be done without anybody knowing about it except your immediate friends.

BC: This is now important. In an older aesthetic, you didn't do the spectacular thing unless it would pay off in the big cultural center. Now, if you can make the piece go in your own scene, that's what counts.

RA: It comes out of real musical experience. First, we didn't get into the virtuoso concert-stage thing about music because we anticipated that that could be very shallow. If you have a musical scene going that is local and very strong, it's as rich for you as eating good food. You don't need anything else. You listen to

African music on the records. Music is magic for them. You just do not need the European idea that you can conquer the world. Second, the bigger, more influential, more broad you try to make your music, the thinner it gets. You don't want that as an experience, to be on a concert stage. It's very unpleasant to be on a concert stage giving a piece the audience hates. We get the idea from history—Stravinsky and those guys—that that experience is supposed to help your career. But we all know that's bullshit. It leads you to a situation in which people don't like your music; finally you die, then people like your music. Everybody realized that was a horrible idea. The idea is to have fun in music while you are alive.

BC: I'm glad you said that. If there isn't an immediate enjoyment then it isn't worth doing. You're thinking posthumously, saying, "OK, they don't like it now, but by God, this performance is going to be historical." In the Cage retrospective album there's the awful, awful performance of the *Concert for Piano and Orchestra* with half the players purposely fouling up and playing *Rite of Spring* and things. I have a horrible suspicion that Cage put up with this, despite his terrible misgivings, because he has an old-world sense of posthumous winner-ness.

RA: Well, you can't win 'em all. Cage has been so farsighted in so many ways, if he seems to be slightly fame-oriented, he can be forgiven.

BC: You brought this point out in the Feldman interview, where you said that we could give a festival of personalities.[4] Just list the names. You don't have to play any music, you just have the people. It's a very profound judgment.

RA: We had so much fun getting those concerts ready. It was so rich for us. I don't know if you saw it, but Gordon and I were doing twice-a-week performances with Milton Cohen . . .

BC: Yeah, in the Space Theater.

RA: Every Tuesday and every Saturday for four years we played for forty or fifty people. It was very popular, a wonderful experience to make that kind of music for those people. That was the richest experience in my life. I just can't stand the thought of giving a concert and laying it on people for historical reasons. Sometimes people don't like my music. I can't change that. But I like it when people like my music.

BC: I think we all do.

RA: Obviously we're in a very transitional, difficult period. Cage's performances are largely given for people who don't like his music, and that's very unpleasant. But there are people who do like the music and who get it on with the music in that situation.

BC: Especially with Cage, so many of them nowadays are young cats who think, wow! John Cage, big daddy, we've got to go hear that. It's a sort of historical halation that obtains around these people. They'll go to hear this guy because he is a name. They won't listen to the music, but they'll say, Wow! It's like the Satie-ism, with the buttons and the whole thing. They're not hearing the goddamn music.

RA: This year, I was teaching some pieces by Cage and Cage's students because I wanted to deal with certain ideas. There were three or four Cage performances that were very big performances, good performances. And these students said, "Well, that was very easy to take. That's nice music. There's nothing far-out about that." It was just so easy for them to be in the presence of the Cage thing, and I think that they understood what was happening. They didn't see it as being historical.

BC: That's encouraging, because there's a kind of cold-blooded "graduate-student-ness" that says, "Yes, we're listening to this because it's historically important," and they don't enjoy it.

RA: Another thing: audiences in the US have always been taught to like the musician. They've been taught if you didn't hear it in New York it was some-how unreal. We got across the idea that we believed in it, then the audience started feeling that this was our music, too. There was no big deal. It was no weirder than anything else they did on a day-to-day basis. A large number of close friends of the music went to all the concerts, and they knew the music of John Cage and the music of Barney Childs as well as they knew my music.

BC: You told me earlier you haven't had much time recently; you've been setting up the studio. What are you going to do next?

RA: Let me see how to say this. I'm getting very interested in music that you don't pay attention to, sort of music for hi-fi. I'm interested in the listening process in an intellectual way. Since I stopped playing the piano most of my musical experience in the past twenty years has been through records. It's a very peculiar experience because the time zone is different from the way your attention spans are different—the different perception faculties are working at different rates. So I'm trying to make music that is good for listening in your home over loudspeakers. It's a very distinct change for me, because at Ann Arbor, which was played weekly for live audiences, my music became progres-sively more theatrical. I became much more involved in the time situations that happen when a lot of people are there, and that developed into a bunch of purely performance pieces. I hadn't even figured out a way to write [them] down; they are not easily notated. They *are* real pieces. They have all of the problems of dance notation or theater notation.

There are two directions that I'm interested in. One is a very peculiar per-formance situation. You go because you know that something very odd is going to happen. Or else you listen through the loudspeaker. When you go to the place, what's odd, obviously, goes beyond just sound. You're expect-ing not just sound-producing behavior but gestural. I went through that so intensely for about six years that I came to a point where I wanted to leave

Ann Arbor because I was so wrapped up in it, and I was starting to think of this as background music. Coming to Mills was good because it cut me off from my other musical culture. I'm trying so hard now to work at pieces that you listen to in a different time dimension. It isn't a matter of they're being longer than ordinary pieces or longer than traditional pieces, but they pass at a different rate.

BC: An interesting thing is connected with this: the idea of the long piece like *In C*, where audience attention is recast over time in a way which is completely un-nineteenth-century. On the one hand you have the nineteenth-century event-flow. You've got the big theme, you've got the big development. On the other hand you've got the short Darmstadt microphenomenal post-Webern event-flow. What's happening now in the pieces that I'm really turned on by there is a spaciousness of operation that can get away from the microphenomenal Darmstadt thing and away from the nineteenth-century, theme-heroic business, and at the same time take a lot of time and still be a reshaping of what's happening over time with sound.

RA: It's obviously just habit that somebody would want a piece to last a certain amount of time. The idea that an hour is a long time spent listening to music seems so bizarre to me.

BC: Well, that's a preconception, a built-in thing.

RA: The tendency all through the late '60s, from the whole '60s—not so much Gordon, but Don Scavarda's and my tendencies from 1960 on—were toward very long, demanding time things.

BC: Will these pieces be essentially electronic or instrumental?

RA: Oh, they will all be electronic, because the speakers are electronic. The impulse source could be the voice, or anything that you could manage, but the sound should be made for the loudspeakers. The attention, the way the music goes by, should be made the way you listen to records. I haven't yet made a successful version . . .

BC: No, you haven't had the time.

RA: I've been trying. I've done a couple of pieces that approach that, but it's just a whole new thing.

BC: If somebody commissioned you for a bassoon concerto, you wouldn't write it?

RA: Yes. There's no danger of that. I've cut myself off from those things, too.

BC: In other words, you're availing yourself of a medium that wasn't there ten years ago. Well, it was available in vision ten years ago, but now you have the tools to do it.

RA: The other reason I wanted to leave Ann Arbor is I started thinking about these long background music pieces, and I wanted very much to use recent electronics—multitrack and all the stuff that's in a real classy studio. I didn't want to get involved with that in Ann Arbor, so when the chance came to

come to Mills, which didn't have those facilities but which I foresaw might
have them, I took it. I was perfectly happy to work at Mills building those
things because I wanted to use them. It was the same old problem: you don't
have the money. You can't go into Sierra Sound or Wally Hyder and say here's
my $4,000. You still can't conceive of things that way. So I had to find some
situation where I could make up the kind of studio that would allow me to
work on those things.

BC: This is essentially the kind of thing whereby liveness would not exist, essentially. [The thing] somebody is going to get is a tape . . .

RA: No, I'm not interested in liveness at all. In fact, I'm very interested in the idea
of there not being any personal aim attached to it.

BC: Is this an aesthetic, or an immediate composition?

RA: I'm just interested in those things. We could play examples right now. When
you came into the room, African music was playing. We weren't listening to
that music as though we were at a concert. We were talking, but we both were
listening. That's the way I listen to all records. I never buy a record, put it on,
sit down, and memorize it. I don't like to do that. I can't deal with music in that
way. I buy a record, Sam buys a record, Mary buys a record. The old experience: you put it on and you'll hear a cut you've never heard before, on a record
you've been listening to for four years. That's what I'm trying to work with.

BC: That's getting into a curious range of aesthetic perception. People are thinking
in these terms in a way they haven't done before: the way people handle things
with their ears, what you pay attention to . . .

RA: Right. Listening to music in your home, to say nothing of earphones, is going
to become more and more productive. There are people now who consider
themselves to be totally immersed in music who almost never go to a live
concert. Now *that* strikes me as being the way to go.

BC: That's a new audience, a new way of hearing too.

RA: It seems that that aesthetic is going to become very rich. When I listen to
popular music, jazz, I see that evidence very strongly. Popular music has changed
so concretely from 1965. There are records now by groups that hardly make . . .

BC: . . . and if they do make personal appearances, what you hear is not really
what you hear on the record. If this is what's happening, what will happen to
liveness? Is it going to ship out eventually? We've talked about the Julliard-
trained player who learns to play the clarinet piece . . .

RA: The situation's going to become more generalized, less and less concerned
with music as we know it now. People invent interesting reasons for going
somewhere, reasons may involve sound and they may not. Conventional theater
is a bummer, we all know that. It's almost as bad as conventional concerts. But
there are still things that you go to that are very hot.

BC: Some composers are getting back into the conventional concert situation and are saying let's regard this as a ritual as such, and work musically out of that. Keeping all the disadvantages and all the errors in mind, they regard these folk up here in a sonic and visual focus, as a kind of ritual, starting with that as a given.

RA: Then the sounds have to be more interesting. Once you've experienced what electronic music does to you, then the sound of the clarinet is pretty dull, like a bad electronic instrument. And the sound of the solo violin: if you mistakenly go to a string quartet concert, you're disappointed in the sound. The theater is more or less amusing, depending on how stoned you are, but it's very canned. The sounds are just absolutely stupid.

BC: In your Feldman interview, he said he couldn't stand the sound of the violin E string, because it brought back that whole virtuoso violin school. It was there, inherent in that instrumental sound.

RA: It's so dumb; you go to an orchestra concert and there are sixty-five guys playing as loud as they can play. It's just absolutely boring by anybody's definitions.

BC: Do you think that technical advances are going to permit this? There has been tremendous advance in four or five years in synthesizing equipment and technology. We're about five stages away from the days when you guys had three Viking decks on top of one another in Ann Arbor. Do you think the tools are there? Are you satisfied with the resources?

RA: The only resources that you can foresee the consequences of are the cheapness of the materials. Electronic music instruments now are still too much nineteenth-century style performance-wise. What we haven't dealt with is to build your own instruments, now that the circuitry for peculiar sounds is getting cheaper. The tendency is not going to be toward centralizing those things on the synthesizer but toward decentralizing.

BC: In other words, you are disposing handily and profitably of the cheap nickel-dime synthesizer. Instead of leveling and universalizing, this is opening up.

RA: Let's say you could build the circuitry that makes a very interesting piece. The circuitry cost you $50. There's no reason why you shouldn't build that piece, play it, and then dump it. There's no reason why it has to fit into any larger pattern. That's a piece, and then there's another piece and another piece. And your closets are no more filled with boxes than they are filled with parts. Except the sounds have changed: you're dealing with new, more interesting sounds.

BC: A lot of tape composition today is terrible cliché sounds. Composers are limiting themselves just as the nineteenth-century violinist was limited by tradition. A lot of tape pieces are just as instrumentally constricted by what's there.

RA: That's to be expected. On a particular level, the fact that a lot of pieces sound alike is a good sign. People have recognized that particular cliché as being something very ordinary. It couldn't be any more cliché than the E string. Or the piano. If I hear one more piano sonata! Not because of anything done with the notes, but the sound of the piano is so boring. It's just the same old thing.

BC: One thing on the list that people for years have gotten into is new ways of handling time—maybe not in a conscious sense. I don't mean *In C* or Steve Reich pieces, but regarding a long duration in quite a different way than anybody has ever regarded before. This is an American thing—you don't have it in Europe. I saw [Aloys] Kontarsky play all the Stockhausen pieces. He did an optimal arrangement in *Klavierstück XI*: the big page was cut up and arranged in pieces, in order. Apparently he was scared of the temporal responsibilities of not having this order. You talk about a work that lasts an hour. I know an instrumentalist who says it's impossible to write a piece that lasts an hour. I disagree. In a nineteenth-century sense yes, it is impossible to write a piece that lasts an hour. But in the 1970s or late-1960s sense, it's probable. You can redefine the temporal arrangement of sounds that they can last an hour and be very moving. This depends on a new thinking about expressivity. If you are listening for two or three hours, like we were listening to the African music, it's possible for things to happen and be very valid and meaningful, if these terms carry any weight any more.

RA: Obviously, in your own home you listen for two or three hours. So you just have to break the habit in the audience of feeling that when they go to a concert, a different place, things have to happen on schedule. Once you get the idea across that a piece is valid for an hour and a half, then it is the audience's problem to handle it.

BC: What you're dealing with is canned expectation patterns, where you get restless after the official concert length. At CalArts [California Institute of the Arts], on a concert with Hal Budd and Dan Lentz—the pieces were clearly too long for the audience. They weren't prepared to deal with a piece with five sounds which lasted half an hour. Yet at the same time, in a funny way of listening, it was too short.

RA: There *are* some pieces that are too long; there are pieces that *are* too short. If you get the idea that all concerts are going to last five hours, then people just have to learn to deal with that in a physical way. They have to learn to be more comfortable. The seating for concerts is all based on the idea that you can stand that physical strain for an hour and a half. If you want to listen to something for four hours, you have to have a different physical situation. Those things the audience just has to handle on their own; in other words, the audience always listens to what is happening. If the musicians are making four-hour pieces, the audience will say, well, the piece was long, but these guys were making it and we have to listen to it. If theater turns into a seven-hour event, then you have to learn to take a lunch.

BC: But I don't think people are trained to listen. Your concept of home listening is a different audience than the canned concert audience. They expect six or seven works and after an hour and twenty-four minutes they are going to applaud for two curtain calls and take off. But that's not the audience you're interested in.

RA: No! I wish that audience would disappear. I don't see that happening anywhere else. That seems to be a skeleton or fossil; it seems to be left over. The pieces or the events that you see that are interesting are just not like that.

BC: What have you heard recently that you feel to be interesting?

RA: The music I hear the most is by Gordon. Gordon's on a performance kick. He's getting very much now into a theatrical sense that I enjoy, into certain personal projections and building instruments that just do one piece. He's done a new piece called *Anagramatics*, which is based on a circuit that he built that he wears on his body on a sort of extension cord. He plays the trumpet in the piece, and the circuit is responsive to the velocity of what he wears on his hands. It's a very theatrical transposition of the sounds that he can produce with the trumpet. Alvin Lucier is very interested in exploiting that notion of the concert situation being heard in a larger environment; he's always trying to bring the outside into the concert. David Behrman is doing very simple circuitry that makes good sounds. I like those pieces very much. A guy that I work with at Mills just did a piece that uses complex drone effects that are made on the synthesizer, inserted in which are cues for performance of comparable drone effects. Any particular instrument in this ensemble arrives at his drone pitch through a sound gesture that can only be done on instruments. So he's got a juxtaposition of something that can only be done on electronics, which is very unchanging, juxtaposed to a thing that can only be done on an instrument—you can't do it on a synthesizer. It's a very human gesture. And they're interrelated on cues, so it makes for a big droning sound which has these two elements in them.

BC: You're talking in terms of sound, which is very good. When I asked you what you were doing, you talked of raw things coming into the ear. How do you feel about just sounds for the ear, given works that you are going to do for the listener's home set, say? What sort of sound *Klangideal* have you? Are we beyond the Cage thing where any sound the process produces is a good sound?

RA: Well, I liked Cage's idea very much, but I've been very interested in the notion that instruments produce sounds that you couldn't imagine. Since we have a whole bunch of new instruments, we must expect a whole family of sounds that don't exist right now. So I'm interested in thrilling aspects. The thrill doesn't lead you to another situation; it's a momentary thrill. Maybe a way of letting you off the hook is built into that structure so your attention span can relax; then you're prepared physically, rested, for the next sound.

BC: This has always been part of your aesthetic, hasn't it? This is also true in your earlier works. There's a sense of coming into new, startling sounds and contexts.

I'm thinking about *[The] Fourth of July*—one of the big tape pieces. There is always a surprise around the corner. You're waiting, and there it is, and you didn't really expect it. Then you get into it, you are aware of it, you've stepped up into the next plateau and all of a sudden, there's something else. This is something that you've always done.

RA: I can't pretend I'm controlling that. That idea of the attention of the listener waxing and waning on some interior schedule is like you are cooperating with him in some way. I don't like the idea that you control his attention rates, but there is something very fundamental to him and you try to get in on it. It's like a treasure hunt where you put things in the right places and people will find them. I'm interested in sound, but I can't describe exactly how I arrive at those points where you hear the sound. What I hear from your music is the same thing. It's just a different principle of trying to arrive there. People are interested in new sounds. That comes right out of Cage. He says that if you listen to the real environment, you hear new sounds continually. That environment can also include new instruments which make new sounds. Whatever you do makes a new sound as long as you're using new instruments.

I've always been interested in verbal texts, in the meaning of things that people say. This was true of *The Fourth of July*, and it's true of my most recent pieces. I like the idea of talk as being a scheduling process for our listening. I'm trying to reevaluate what it means to talk to someone, to figure out what other level exists in the actual sound production of the words we use. I like the idea of listening to English as if it were a foreign language and the idea of listening to words that you know very well in a detached sense—as though you're listening to them without even having the power to speak; as though you were a person from Mars and you've come down to hear people making strange sounds with their voices. The notion that we would think that the Martians would arrive at an understanding of our language on the level that we understand it seems very vain to me. They're liable to name a whole new pattern that has nothing to do with the words and that we don't even understand. When people talk, I try to listen to them as if I didn't understand anything about language, as though they were just moving their mouths. I like the pauses . . .

BC: The shapes, the gestures . . .

RA: . . . I like the way they articulate what we consider words with other sounds. So I don't think I've written three pieces in my whole life that didn't have words in them.

BC: David Antin mentions a version of a Cage piece in which there is somebody speaking Swedish, and he doesn't know Swedish, but there is this sense of gesture and shape and sound which is going on. And he knows it's language-based, but he doesn't know the rules. And yet it's very meaningful.

RA: You can understand. If you really *listen* to somebody *talking*, you get ideas that are not even in the language. Obviously, if we had to deal with all those meanings we couldn't get anywhere. I am interested in the fact that we use the whole speech apparatus to make these strange sounds. The idea that I'm talking to you and making sounds and that you are talking back to me is so weird.

BC: Some of the language-synthesizing people have done that. They've tried to get into those sounds in a raw material sense. And what about theater? Very few works you have written don't have speech in them. In a sense, speech is theater. If you watch a guy in a phone booth talking, you watch the gestures—he's trying to orchestrate. Suppose you have a work which someone's listening to, but he is denied these gestures that you're making on the phone when you're talking to someone. You're in the booth and you're making these gestures—he can't see them, but you're making them anyway.

RA: Well, that's what I'm trying to sort out in getting away from Ann Arbor. From '63 until '64 my pieces got to be increasingly theatrical. They didn't involve sound any less, but there is just no equivalent in notation for these pieces. You can't do a videotape; that's almost as bad as trying to write them out. They got away from me; they got so impractical. The sound pieces and the loudspeaker pieces were such an abrupt change from the theater to no theater. Suddenly you want no theater at all. I'm probably more involved with theater than any composer, and that's why I'm so out of it now.

BC: In a different way, in the opera, the theater and the sound are indistinguishable. You can't take one off and say here's the piece.

RA: I got into a type of theater like public address, but really complicated. The idea of the concert as theater is so campy that I just reject it outright. It's absurd to say that a bunch of people sitting on stage playing clarinets is theater. Because it's just too dull—it's not theater at all. I'm hoping to get a sound thing that has no theater at all.

BC: That's going to be very difficult, because you've been thinking in these terms.

RA: It's really the opposite, where there's absolutely no movement, just sound. But for other composers that's still very rich. Just because I've stopped being interested in that sort of theater, it doesn't mean other people should. The kind of theater that has sound embedded in it is still very rich, and the relationship between the sound and what you're seeing is so subtle. It produces entirely artificial sounds that don't exist anywhere else. They are as artificial to your experience as the sound of a concert, but they are not cliché. They are very unusual sounds that you never find them anyplace but there. More composers have been working on that, too. Gordon is definitely working on that, and I think Alvin is, too. People who have come out of the theater production are doing interesting things. The Living Theatre people, Julian Beck, come in through the theater. They came too much out of the theater tradition; they were more interested in what the voice was doing than in the sounds themselves.

Notes

1. Kyle Gann, *Robert Ashley* (Champaign: University of Illinois Press, 2012), 48.

2. Melody Sumner, Kathleen Burch, and Michael Sumner, eds., *The Guests Go In to Supper* (Oakland, CA: Burning Books, 1986), 101.

3. Robert Ashley, *Automatic Writing*, Lovely Music LCD 1002, 1996, LP, liner notes.

4. Morton Feldman, "An Interview with Robert Ashley, August 1964," in *Contemporary Composers on Contemporary Music*, ed. Elliott Schwartz and Barney Childs, with Jim Fox (New York: Da Capo, 1998), 363–66.

3 Larry Austin (1930–2018)

THOMAS S. CLARK

Barney Childs's interview with Larry Austin begins with a conversation about improvisation, a mode of music making very much of interest in the late 1960s in America. It is fitting that the conversation itself unfolded as a sort of duo improvisation. Barney was a composer buddy and friend of the Austin family in California. Larry's wife, Edna, remembered his visits and late-night conversations between these two kindred thinkers.

By the time of these interviews in 1972 or 1973, Austin was well-known as a champion of new music improvisation, as he had also emerged as a leading radical voice of the avant-garde. In the improvisational realm, two accomplishments stand out. Austin's founding work with the University of California at Davis New Music Ensemble became a pioneering example followed by other composers-performers (including my own New Music Performance Lab, established at North Texas State in 1976). Some phrases spoken in the interview were slogans of this exploratory world: "free group improvisation" and "open style."

Austin's breakthrough composition, establishing both his credibility and notoriety, was *Improvisations for Orchestra and Jazz Soloists.* Premiered in 1964 by the New York Philharmonic, conducted and championed by Leonard Bernstein, and reviewed in the *New York Times*, the piece merged prescriptive writing for orchestra with the freewheeling improvisation of a jazz combo in a neo-Baroque *concerto/ripieno* sinfonia form. Described as "third stream," *Improvisations for Orchestra and Jazz Soloists* was an intentional collision of styles, like physicists smashing atoms together in particle accelerators to see what flew out.

Austin became the voice and face of turbulent times in new music with his establishment in 1967 as editor and publisher of *Source: Music of the Avant-Garde.* These magazines—if you can call these rich compendiums of cutting-edge musical experiment that—vividly expressed the "anything goes" and "death to tradition" spirit of the movement. In this interview, Austin articulates that mindset: "I'd like to dissociate myself from . . . all the other musics that are being composed and played and espoused and enjoyed today in the world."

Austin raised "the eternal problem of dissociating yourself from your own past" as the main problem of composing. Removing composer intent and choice from the musical experience was a John Cage concept embraced by Austin at the time. Having hosted Cage as a guest composer at UC Davis in 1969, Austin became a close and lifelong associate and friend. His best tribute to Cage was a beautiful 1982 piece, . . . *art is self-alteration is cage is . . .,* in honor of Cage's seventieth birthday.

Years after this interview, however, while remaining an admirer of and collaborator with Cage, Austin had mellowed considerably on this question of personal experience and intent. His composition professor role necessarily involved helping students achieve perspective on their musical experience while expanding it to better inform their compositional choices. Our coauthored book, *Learning to Compose,* is all about the compositional process, using personal experience and taste as well as deep knowledge of craft to design elegant musical forms and structures.[1]

Another important aspect of Austin's avant-garde is what he calls "the beautiful ritual of performance," conjuring the whole trend toward performance art. Austin's radical piece *Accidents* (1967) is all about the performance. As described in the interview, it featured theatrical elements as well as a game scenario for the performer who was to try to play through a rapid, complex piano texture without ever letting the keystrokes produce any sound.

Discussing neoromanticism, Austin proposes the term "new romanticism," the subject of his recent article in the *New York Times,* and defines it in this interview simply as "a new love of sound without any other preconceived notions at all"—not retro but again striving toward "open style."[2] This return to personal expression was new enough that its terms were unfixed. Childs mentions having attended a concert of this kind of music titled "New Diatonicism," as the two debate the stylistic and aesthetic parameters of each term. (A personal note: I played in the New Diatonicism concert while a member of Contemporary Directions at the University of Michigan, an ensemble supported by the Rockefeller Foundation. Another piece on the program was a poly-tempo experiment, *Alma Redemptoris Mater* by another California composer, Douglas Leedy. Although I doubt Austin was at the Ann Arbor concert, Leedy's piece strongly resembled Austin's later lyrical poly-tempo 1981 work, *Canadian Coastlines: Canonic Fractals for Musicians and Computer Band.*)

The love of sound explains the fascination at the time with the emerging medium of electronic music, "in love with continuous electricity, electrical sounds." Austin was an avid practitioner of electronic music as the technology was born and progressed. It is ironic that his comment in this interview is somewhat casual: once he had "explored the resources" and celebrated the sounds, he claimed, "then you think about doing something else." In fact, however, his electronic explorations persisted and pervaded his later music, evolving into computer music and constituting the vast majority of his overall compositional output over a long, prolific career.

Austin became a leading practitioner and researcher in computer music, hosting in 1981 the major International Computer Music Conference, founding in 1986 of the Consortium to Distribute Computer Music, and serving as president of the International Computer Music Association (1990–94). *Larry Austin: Life and Works of an Experimental Composer* documents the many creative streams pursued by Austin throughout his wide-ranging career.[3]

Larry Austin's work as a respected professor and leader of professional organizations seems a sharp contrast to his iconoclastic image as the radical of *Source* magazine at the time of this interview. That's not what Austin meant, though, when he invoked the term "schizophrenic." He was talking about the dual identities as a jazz improviser and "official" composer of fixed pieces. But he was both a radical iconoclast blowing up traditional expectations and also a patient researcher and builder, whose later music is complex, precisely crafted, and sometimes quite beautiful.

Larry Austin: Interview

Also present was Stuart Petock.[4]

BARNEY CHILDS: Looking back at the Davis New Music Ensemble, historically or in any other way, how does it feel? You're connected with the festival of new music groups, which is going to happen in England this summer.

LARRY AUSTIN: I'm not a part of groups now.

BC: But you were, very thoroughly, in those days.

LA: I probably should have gotten out a lot sooner than I did; on the other hand, that would decry the marvelous associations that I had. All these people (at least most of them) are still my very good friends and musical buddies. What did it do? It had to happen to me at that particular time, now that I look back on it. Why we did it in the first place? Personally, it grew out of work I was doing in composition. Free group improvisation seemed to be very important to me. That came out of the piece *Improvisation for Orchestra and Jazz Soloists*, in which there are two sections that simply said, "Do it." In 1961, "doing it" was still a fairly new concept.

BC: Indeed it was. It wasn't as new in the western part of America as it was elsewhere.

LA: In '61 we were all into that—Robert Erickson and so forth. We were probably one of the first to formalize free group improvisation without schemes. But they grew out of this experience that I had in that piece, working with jazz solos. We had a fluent improvisatory language.

I was a jazz musician and improviser from way back, and never associated that with my "official" composing. I realized that I was indeed kind of schizophrenic as a composer, so I tried to solve this personality problem that I had through my music. It wasn't as silly as that, but that had something to do with it. Out of that, the confluence of events, and the lucky accident that Stan Lunetta and I, Art Woodbury, Wayne Johnson, and Richard Swift were all in the same place at that time, made it logical that we should get together for experimental work in group improvisation. We did it one summer in 1963. The group came out of a compositional need; the compositional need was satisfied after the first year. I'd done it; we'd found pieces that we played. Then it was a matter of composing again. As a matter of fact *Continuum* (1964) was the first post–New Music Ensemble piece; it is a direct result of the experience I'd gained.

BC: You said earlier that the improvisations reached for audience involvement.

LA: In the first place, we didn't do it for that reason. Yet we found that that was one of the phenomena, because the audience realized and believed that we were making music on the spot, right in front of your eyes! They became involved in the excitement of the act, and you can interpret "act" in any way you want to. Because it was theatrical when we performed in front of an audience.

BC: There's a dramatism, a tension.

LA: Sure, a marvelous drama about whether or not the next gesture is going to work!

BC: Do you think that dramatism has left music now?

LA: Oh, no. I'm much more dramatic in my works now than I was then.

BC: That sense of excitement: you never stopped working for that.

LA: Yeah, that's always been part of my work.

BC: You're concerned with the audience in a special kind of way—a reaching out, a personal warmth in so many of your pieces. But this *does* still animate you? Like the '60s; nothing is more distant to us than the last ten years, you know. It's easy to look back at the '30s or the '40s and feel kitschy, but we look back at the '60s and we feel "Gosh, how alien it must have been!"

LA: Alien, but I have a morbid interest in revisiting some of those experiences. In fact, improvisation is interesting to me again. I've been away from it, per se, since late '65. Beyond that time we did improvise as a group, but it was a single piece and we really didn't create anything valuable. We were a commercial commodity by that time. Usually when that happens I lose interest right away.

BC: Do you think that it's important for music in the last twenty years that so many young composers originally started with some jazz background? You talked about the "schizophrenia" that you inherited as a jazz thing. But there are so many guys who are really into jazz, too. Do you think it shaped what was happening out here in a special way that was denied people before?

LA: I've never compared experiences with anyone who has had as specific a background as I have had, except my good friend Art Woodbury. Art is a great jazz improviser. I'm the first one to say he's really a composer and he's the last one to claim that. I shouldn't say something if he thinks he isn't, but he's the only person I've ever really compared notes with whom I think is a really great jazz improviser. I don't know whether I am or not—I always had a lot of fun, and still do. In fact, during the last two years I revisited that experience, which is out of the '40s for me, playing in a student jazz band here. No one could play jazz: I was the only one who could play jazz, who could improvise on the spot. I *think* they all thought it was marvelous; maybe they thought it was awful I had good times revisiting, and got bored after about six months.

BC: Do you think boredom is a part of composing?

LA: Oh no. I'm terribly thrilled, excited about it all the time.

BC: That's good. This morning you were saying you don't consider yourself a musician any more, you consider yourself a sonic artist.

LA: With the recent pieces I'm doing . . .

BC: That is what your stance is now.

LA: Stance? You could call it a stance. It's a stance, because I don't *really* believe it myself.

BC: What does it involve as far as you *do* believe?

LA: I'm discovering at age forty-one that the main problem of composing is the eternal problem of dissociating yourself from your own past. Some composers could learn that rather good lesson, and where they fail is that they *don't* dissociate themselves from their own past accomplishments and failures. For instance, one of the pieces that I cherish most is one of my greatest failures. I won't say which piece, but I associate with that piece because it's a failure. I definitely want to dissociate myself from the successes.

Then there are all other musics that are being composed and played and espoused and enjoyed today in the world—gee, that's a big scene—and I'd like somehow to dissociate myself from that. Or find a couple of genuine musics and make a situation where there might be the possibility of a hybrid idiom coming out of it.

BC: You've done this with media.

LA: I'm interested in new idioms and mixing idioms now, but I've always been doing that anyway. First, jazz and so-called classical art music: they were brought together because Darius Milhaud said, "Why the hell don't you bring your jazz background out in your work?" I resented that, because it pointed up a weakness in my personality. And because I resented it I then began to consider it as a serious thing to do. It took three years, but I finally came around, and mixing idioms was pretty natural. Now I think that that is a recognized compositional resource, not just by me, but by practically every composer who's thinking today. Richard Teitelbaum, for instance, has been experimenting with mixing Indonesian music with Indian music with jazz with electronic music, and so forth. What *usually* happens is something very vulgar and awful. But sometimes something comes out of that is really very unique.

BC: But this seems to me a contrary movement, because in works like *Brass* (1967) and *Bass (A Theater Piece in Open Style for String Bass, Player, Tape, and Film* [1966]), there's an intensely limited use of the media without branching out into other genres musically. But there's an attempt to integrate the media into a non-self-conscious totality.

LA: Some people call my stuff very self-conscious and very self-indulgent.

BC: Why—do you *feel* self-conscious?

LA: Not at all. But these people probably have some point to make.

BC: Do you listen to them?

LA: I'm affected by them. I wonder if they're right, but those weren't my motives. *Brass* and *Bass*—I've just gone beyond that scene now. They go together with a piece called *Accidents* (1967). *Bass* was portrait of Bertram Turetzky, the first one that I called a theater piece. *Accidents* was another portrait, of two people, David Tudor and Frederick Rzewski, but they were really the same kind of person. *Brass* was for the American Brass Quintet. Then there were other subsidiary theater-piece portraits. There was even a portrait called *Magicians* (1968), of my own family. And then the last theater-piece portrait is *Walter* (1970), the most recent one. Those earlier pieces were concerned with the *situation* of music, the beautiful ritual of performance, more than anything else. I framed what I thought Bert did, stylized it, but I also made it somewhat surreal. In that first piece, *Bass*, the player (Bert) wears or has a mime face (whiteface, and tails, and white hands) and he does stylized gestures with his hands in front of a screen, *lanterna magica* fashion. That was my vision of him on stage, and it was the only way I could write a piece for him. I guess he wanted everybody to do a piece for the bass, which maybe accounts for the title, *Bass*. It's sort of a grotesque situation that you're given as a composer. It's not romantic at all to think about a guy in tails walking out on the concert stage with this big huge pregnant fiddle (his bass is pregnant-looking), and he looks like a bass. It is B-A-S-E—it's "base." It has none of the refinement of a string quartet . . .

BC: You're projecting the personality of the player. *Walter*, as I understand it, is an extrapolation of the player's self, and the player's instrument.

LA: When I got to *Walter* I had understood the process pretty well, and that's why I've exhausted that whole thing. I don't have any desire to do that again, because I can still draw things from *Walter*. With *Bass* there were still unsolved problems. It was somewhat of an unsuccessful piece; it was a study piece.

BC: I was very impressed when you told me that *Uncommon Canon* (1963) and *Squares* and so on were study pieces. I had never heard of a composer nowadays who really put serious time in on study pieces, études, for his own compositions.

LA: You don't know that you're doing them at the time, but you can look back on them and see. I don't think you can put that much serious effort into a piece such as *Bass*, which involved a film, an elaborate electronic music tape, and a very complex score. In fact, I have an experimental prototype of that piece. I actually played that piece on the bass and recorded my performance with the tape, then transcribed what I had performed. No one will ever hear that sketch.

BC: In a sense you're going back to the improvisation as a fountainhead from which these things grow.

LA: Improvisation is a funny term. It's one we understand, but having gone through that scene with a couple of improvisation ensembles—one within the New Music Ensemble, and then one in Italy that I worked with—I don't think there's any such thing as improvisation beyond the first session. The first session is indeed exploratory, and that's what I think describes improvisation. Because then you have to *make do* with the materials and resources you have: we'll make music no matter what—here it is and this is what we got. Beyond that you should try to make music, rather than improvise sonic relationships. You should try to make music. So improvisation is an experimental period.

BC: How do you account for the fact that there are so very many groups today?

LA: That's because the Europeans are very much behind the times. They discovered "the group" ten years after the fact. I hate to say that so arrogantly, but it is true. The group phenomenon, which we've all gone through in the United States—with encounters and sensitivity things and all—we did musically, before they ever discovered it psychologically. But the Europeans, particularly the English, are discovering this, and just are ecstatic about it. They're also into the antihero thing which we were into in '65, '66. The primacy of idea doesn't mean that everybody else that comes afterwards is bad; it does mean that these people have deprived themselves of information and experiences that were available to them. Of course there's an ocean, and that has a lot to do with it. ICES (and all the groups there) is a long-overdue festival. Maybe that festival should have happened five years ago. Maybe it really did someplace; I don't know. But it's happening, and these young groups and young fellas will discover things faster than we discovered them. They probably have already discovered the problem of how you don't really solve any problems in a group—at least musically. What you do, fortunately, is to create new problems. A composer who doesn't cause himself to be influenced by other people or put himself into other various situations where he can be influenced is not causing new problems for himself, and hence his music becomes eclectic.

BC: You think the thing about "problems" is important. Somebody must have problems; it's not just "do the same piece over again." You feel you have to have some kind of a challenge—an immediacy of problems, of wrestling with something—like you were talking about the theater pieces.

LA: I always do. I don't know whether I *have* to do that, and maybe the day will arrive that it all becomes terribly facile and easy. But I'm getting on—I'm forty-one years old.

BC: Don't knock it!

LA: There are two pieces I'm working on now, and both present big problems for me. One's for tape and violin; the other's for organ and tape. And they both use the same tape, and this is part of a series called *Quadrants* Event/ Complexes No. 1, 2, 3, and 4 (1972). I've done two of them. They present big problems because everything is too pat. In other words, I have solved so many pre-compositional problems now, that I'm a little suspicious of the facility I'll have in realizing the piece. So I'm rethinking the whole thing. I may just throw it all out and say, "To hell with it; I thought I was going to do four pieces, I'll do two." They're already done and I'll rethink, and we'll go into a new piece. On the other hand, I may then go ahead and do the original conception. So I'm scared of the term "problems," because that conjures up all sorts of internal turmoil. These are just workaday conflicts for the composer. They're exciting conflicts, very necessary to get the juices running inside. One thing in composing I have learned is that you have to wait. You have to wait and let it "cook." I used to get scared of that. I thought that maybe I'd dried up.

BC: Panic sets in!

LA: Right! And so you simply wait.

STUART PETOCK: What about "inspiration" instead of "problem"?

LA: "Inspiration"—we've all been afraid of that word for a long time. It was used poetically so much. In our denial of the hero image for so long, even though we really did secretly know that we were heroes, we want to get away from that. Also, that used to conjure up the idea of some magical thing happening. There is such a thing as inspiration—yes, indeed. And that it goes along with "perspiration" and all those other words . . .

BC: And "constipation" . . .

LA: And constipation: getting it out.

BC: This fits in with your article in the *New York Times*, "Can Electronic Music Be Romantic?" The idea of inspiration is essentially a romantic concept.

LA: Yes. I believe in it too.

BC: But what is the new romanticism, as such? The *Times* article is essentially about electronic music, but is it also in instrumental music? Or are instruments passé? Clearly, they are not.

LA: I may write passé things, but if I do, it's my fault, not anybody else's. As much as other people might think that I'm "stylish" and "on top of it"—in fact I'm almost paranoid about this—I just don't think about those things. I'm a very practical man and, at least in the last five or six years, usually the impetus for a piece stems from a commission. Simply that. I will accept a commission when the person knows my music (not everything, but a good portion of it) and has accepted *me*, and wants something from *me*. Then once we've agreed on the medium, then I'll set to work. The relationship with Walter Trampler [violinist who commissioned *Walter*] was that way; it's been that way with everyone. But I've not gone to your original question about new romanticism.

BC: This is a very challenging term. I saw a program from a concert at Michigan where they had titled it "The New Diatonicism." They played [Terry Riley's] *In C* and a couple of Cage things, and they seemed to suggest that it was a swing back toward the diatonic.

LA: I think that's a very naive approach. First let me say something about calling anything anything, because I don't want to fall into the past traps of third stream, structuralism, etc. Nor am I pretentious enough to think that I have my finger on it. However, it just seems so obvious that we have come into a phase over the last two or three years (and maybe it'll last two or three more years) of a genuine love of sound. I'm not talking about color, I'm talking about the phenomenon of sound. And this is the very same kind of talk that was going on in the mid-nineteenth century; Liszt talked about "the sound." What I mean by "*new* romanticism" (and I don't mean neoromanticism! That would be the phoniest of all! As a matter of fact I think new diatonicism is neoromanticism) is that *new* romanticism is a new love of sound, without any other preconceived notions at all; you simply love sound.

BC: But hasn't that been around for twenty years?

LA: Not in the same way. The point I make in the article is that not before '66 that solid-state synthesizers got out and began to become generally available to individual composers was it possible for us to have access to these instruments, so that we could invent sounds and enjoy the world of sound as long as we wanted to and indulge ourselves in it. Before that time, we'd all visited the studios, or tried to get into one, and it took ten years, and it was really awful. I guess for some people it's still that way, but it's their fault—it's not the fault of technology. I compare it to the invention of the piano by Cristofori in 1709. What first happened was, "Gee—gosh, crazy instrument!" How did they play the piano and how did they write for it? Just like the fucking harpsichord! Mozart wrote all these sonatas: they could have been just as easily, in fact more appropriately, for the harpsichord. In fact, those early pianos probably weren't as *dramatic* an instrument as the pianos of Beethoven's day. Instrument systems have *everything* to do with what a composer writes. Comes Beethoven. Obviously, pianos have improved by that time, but it took a hundred years (not nearly as fast as everything's improved today) and instruments were getting better, well-tempered, and all. Beethoven began to realize the possibilities. But it took him half his sonatas to finally get around to writing a dramatic piece of music: by God, listen to that sound! Then Liszt, Schumann, and Chopin celebrated the sound.

BC: It's that celebration that we're getting back to now.

LA: Exactly that: the celebration of the sound of the synthesizer. Over the last five or six years these guys have gained a fluency on these instruments. We've now discovered the sound of electronic music rather than all of the gestures and mannerisms that were so much a part of the early "classical" period of electronic music. It just has to do with the history of the technology and how things have developed. Gordon Mumma, Robert Ashley, Pauline Oliveros, David Behrman, I humbly suggest myself, David Tudor, Frederick Rzewski, and La Monte Young: these people are all in love with the sound that electronic music systems make; in love with continuous electricity, electrical sounds. That means that we finally have discovered what the nature of the medium is. All this banging on the piano is in a sense comparable to that, in the *Hammerklavier*, every Liszt piece. In fact the pieces that go with orchestra, you might as well not have the orchestra there. That was some kind of an accoutrement, extra baggage. These were perfectly fine musicians, composers, but they didn't need to write for the orchestra! They had the piano—what else did they need? That's exactly the same with electronic music composers—what else do they need? We don't need the orchestra or anything. Except that now I seem to be coming back to that, because I've gotten a modicum of technique there, and I've explored the resources of the equipment I have. You study it and celebrate and enjoy a lot, then you sit back and say, "Well, what do you know about that?" And then you think about doing something else.

SP: Do you find the problems relating the electronic media to an orchestra the same as relating a piano to an orchestra?

LA: There you have a mixing of media. I think that that's really a hybrid mixture of media; and it's a tough one.

BC: Would you write such a piece?

LA: I've done *Catharsis* (1965), which mixed media. It's an anarchic situation where it destroys the orchestra, meaning that they do everything as counter to their training and to the roles that they play as oboists, flutists and violinists. I didn't mean it as destructive. It happens that way, though; it upsets everyone. In that context, electronic music seems to fit in, because electronic music in the mid-'60s, when I did *Catharsis*, still seemed destructive to most audiences: here's the "mechanical monster" coming in. I put two things together. One was the technique of freeing a group from its usual criteria of performance, and the other was the medium of electronic music, which was "destructive," and which the orchestra members thought was some kind of threat to them economically. It was a fierce thing to do. It was in the style of the '60s polemic. We all did that polemical thing, and I don't think it was wrong to do it. We did it last fall in Oberlin, and it was a lot of fun. It's almost a "camp" piece to me now; I feel funny about it. Anybody who takes it seriously today, I say, "Come on!"

BC: You were saying that there's an American school of "how to write music."

LA: Well, it's an American school of how to write music European style.

BC: And you think that this is still widespread, even in 1972?

LA: It still rears its ugly head in young people, and this is an awful thing that we get stereotyped young composers from that school. Of course, the academic composers may accuse me of the same thing; that they get stereotyped "free-form," "far-out" composers. What is wrong is that they are lost souls and have really become systematic musicologists. Somebody in Nashville last fall asked . . .

BC: What were you doing in *Nashville*?

LA: I was the majordomo for the first mixed media festival that Gilbert Trythall put on at the George Peabody College for Teachers.[5] It's a good little school in Nashville. And Gil is a nice guy and really did yeoman service. Four concerts; it was mostly southeastern United States composers. There were some northerners from Southern Illinois, and there was one person from Syracuse. I gave a lecture—you know, the "master composer" bit—and I was terribly embarrassed, but also gratified that these things were happening. And there were some really good pieces, by the way. One of the questions they asked after my talk, mainly about the new romanticism, was: "What do you think about Milton Babbitt?" I said he's a good buddy and we have drinks together. I think that this polemical thing, this kind of confrontation of philosophies is past. I'm sure that Milton would feel the same way. It's the young people who have the wrong idea about the importance of that empirical approach. I would consider what Milton's followers do is a hyper-technical thing. I consider what we did in the '60s as an anti-technical thing. And right now I think both approaches are wrong. Young people should take up a more dialectical approach, saying, "I don't espouse hyper- or anti- things." It doesn't mean they espouse some kind of innocuous middle ground. It only means that they want to get at music, that's all! I don't want to start talking twelve-tone, or serial, or jazz or whatever, I just want to make my music. The people at CalArts [California Institute of the Arts] have that attitude. I'm really impressed with the kids who come out of there who've been sending me pieces lately. They've got a very—excuse the expression—catholic, tolerant attitude.

BC: Talking earlier about un-music or non-music, you weren't sure that what you were doing was really music, in the sense of the word. In other words you were postulating some sort of redefinition.

LA: You accused me, Barney, one time—and I've thought about it ever since, it's probably right—of intellectualizing everything I do. I took that as a caution, and said maybe I'd better back off and not say much about anything. On the other hand—and I look back maybe ten, twelve years? then I can talk about my own music—I *think* what I did in the early '60s was an *anti*-musical thing. I needed to clear my head, get rid of the schizophrenia, and have a whole catharsis of musics: get it all out. I don't care whether jazz, post-Webern, *any*thing, get it out there. *Continuum* has that sort of cathartic flavor, but it's controlled. Open style was that, too: getting it all out there, letting it hang out, and going straight ahead. John Mizelle even named a piece *Straight Ahead* because he felt that was the kind of attitude people had.[6] I got more pro-music after that; I just simply swung over, and no more improvising. I began to be very much in love with the rituals of musics, what we see, and what the whole thing is, really. Once I'd purged my ears with anti-music, I began to start doing films and things like that. So I guess there was a sort of pro-music period, which culminated, I think, with *Walter*. I really feel that's a pro-music piece, even to the point of digging up museum musics to put overlays on. I wrote duets with Telemann, Vivaldi, and all, and I felt like I was hand in hand with those guys.

Now I'm not so terribly interested in both approaches. I see them as techniques, and not as art ends. My recent music has to do with getting rid of the phenomenon of choosing and of making choices, getting rid of taste; trying to extract my personality, but getting outside it by making it non-music—unmusical. This series of pieces called *Quadrants* has that as its goal. I *think* I'm unsuccessful, and that doesn't mean that the piece doesn't work—it means I'm unsuccessful in dissociating myself from past experience. However, in trying to do that, maybe the piece comes off. What it's involved me in is actually a renewal of interest in serial procedures, and extracting my personality from my work. But I find it impossible.

sp: Why do you want to do that?

la: I don't know. And I didn't know why I was doing these other things when I was doing them either. I can't answer that question.

sp: Do you know Krenek's position on that? Krenek complained that inspiration was conditioned by factors over which the composer had no control, such things as whether the asparagus he had for lunch was fresh, or whether his mother beat him when he was a child. And so Krenek said, in order to obtain complete autonomy [over] what the composer wanted to do, was to remove his personality, since his personality was really not his own making. But now, I gather, this is not the way *you* feel?

la: Maybe I still have that old schizophrenia. Because I use this as a technique, making an *un*-music. Whenever there's anything I've put down on paper, or make on a tape, that associates with anything I've done before, or anything anyone else has done before, then I exclude it—as a limitation, as a rule. However, I don't exclude something I consider original happening, such as enveloping the audience in sound and having swirling sounds. That, at least as far as I'm concerned, is fairly original. It's been done many times before in other ways, but the way I approached it was original. In that sense, it hasn't qualified as "music" yet, by its originality.

BC: So that's the *un*-music.

LA: Yes. It may be the old business of trying to renew yourself. I hope that's the business of all composers. Some people would accuse me of newness for newness's sake. And I always say "Yes, that's true," because that's extremely important for a composer. I can't imagine that he would want to recompose something.

SP: Aren't you afraid of kitsch?

LA: Well, that *is* recomposing something, only in a banal way. What you're talking about is novelty for its own sake. That's what some people equate newness with. I think it is rethinking everything you had thought worked before. You continue to do that—you don't accept premises: you continue to reexamine them. That is renewing and making things fresh.

BC: I'd like to get back to the idea of open style, which has always seemed to me a very challenging idea. Have you abandoned this concept? Maybe personally you have, but is it still something that counts with you?

LA: I can't get rid of my past entirely, so I guess maybe something could be related to previous works. Maybe people will always say "Yeah, he did have it nailed then when he said 'open.'" I'm a very western kind of guy, and so I'm open, and so my music still is an expression of that trait, where your biggest defense is telling everything you know, expressing every thought, and not saying anything when you don't know anything. That's also one of my greatest weaknesses. But Texans are like that a lot.

BC: Pauline, too?

LA: Yes, I think so, but also very sensitive. She's one of the most sensitive women around—and the most female—really, a very female person.

"Open style": I was using that term in reaction to a situation when I was there in Italy in the summer of 1964. We had just moved there, we were in Rome in an apartment, and I felt imprisoned in a closed society. That was the basis for the term. I was doing a string quartet at the time, and then I did a clarinet-and-piano piece for Bill Smith. The term just struck me; I was inspired to say this was going to be in open style. I didn't say it was going to be in "open form" because all the pieces were in very closed form; that is, they had spans of time, they weren't processes. But the reason I said "open style" was to make things seem as open as musics that I had heard or could imagine, but didn't yet know what processes or ways to do it that were available to me. So I said that those pieces were "study pieces." But they went toward the piece which I considered open form, which is *Accidents*, my first open-form piece.

BC: You've said that you thought this was a very American kind of piece. Why?

LA: It's defiant, for one thing. Americans are a defiant bunch. We keep on doing it! I wish we'd stop some time, or get off. But we are defiant. The piece was a challenge to begin with, because John Gillespie, who was then writing a book called *The Musical Experience*, called me up one day in 1967 and said, "Larry

Austin, I'm doing this book; and the last thing I want to have in this book (one of those eternal music appreciation books) is to have an actual piece by a composer. I want it to be 'aleatoric,' and since you're an 'aleatoric' composer . . ."

BC: Did you hang up?

LA: No, I didn't hang up. You see he's a musicologist, and I can understand his ignorance and his non-understanding of the situation. So I listened. And he said, "I'd like to commission you to do a piano piece, be 'aleatoric'! You know, you do chance pieces." I said, "I've never composed a chance piece in my life." And he said, "Oh?" Never mind, I'll do it, because the idea was the next logical step. If I'd been pretending that I was doing open pieces by saying "open style," then the natural thing was to try to do it. And that piece is a very defiant piece. That year Karlheinz [Stockhausen] had been here with his closed structures and David Tudor had been here with his very openness. And David said, "Larry, I'd like to have a piece for me, by you," which I felt to be high compliment. I said, "But you don't play piano any more." And he said, "You'll figure out something." Therein lies the challenge. I put the two things together, plus I was going to have a tour to Europe and Rzewski's group Musica Elettronica Viva was going to have me in Rome, and I wanted him to do a piece. So on the way over I got the ideas for this piece, which is *not* playing the piano. What you do is to try not to let the hammers strike the strings.

BC: But sometimes . . .

LA: . . . they do indeed. Those are the accidents, and then those sounds are transformed by the practitioner, who's sitting there in control. I think that next time we do the piece, I'll probably have a different attitude about it, but at that time, it's a battle between the practitioner and the non-pianist, or the nonplaying pianist.

BC: The non-piano.

LA: The non-piano. Of course, as I've always enjoyed saying, the perfect performance is silence. Then I always say, "I'm happy to report that I've had twelve unsuccessful performances of this work."

BC: But they were close. What about the black light?

LA: That's hard to trace. I was beginning then to get interested in magical things, theater, and things like that. I couldn't conceive of a piece by that time that would not have its own preordained context in which to exist. Right now I don't feel this way, but at that time I felt that I had to control all those things, and so I had to set up the context. And so I wanted David to be a fantastic figure; I wanted him to appear as a ghost. It's a very corny idea, but it came from the music. I don't keep all of my notes, but I'd like to go back and research the real reasons behind that. The black light made it possible for me to suspend the score, which is on layers of acetate; it meant that the notes would seem as if they were suspended in air. I couldn't figure out any technical means of doing that; in fact, it turns out there's a very practical way of doing it. The mirrors are much more significant than the black light. They reflect the visage of the performer so that the audience can see the hands and the features and the innards of the piano. I'd always been amused by the fact that at piano recitals everyone sat on the left-hand side, and so I thought I'd accommodate them and have his back to the audience and mirrors all around so that they could see everything he was doing. Again, it gets back to this defiance of conventions.

BC: Again, you're thinking about the audience here. If the piece is going to be heard by you only, it's one thing; and if it's going to be heard by them, that's another thing.

LA: That means that I'm a terribly self-conscious person.

BC: No, no. I was saying that it seems to me humanistic, where there's a warmth that's going on, that you want to "embrace" these people.

LA: That's not for me to say.

BC: Yes, it *is* for you to say, because that essentially you're building in the audience, and I think that *Accidents* is an immediate demonstration of this. You're putting up these mirrors, but you're not part of the performance except as the audience is concerned.

LA: Except also—and this is a key to understanding *Walter* in a way—it also is narcissistic to have mirrors all around you as a performer. You rather admire that.

SP: Why call that narcissistic?

BC: That's the whole virtuoso bag—there isn't a virtuoso yet who hasn't been narcissistic.

LA: He loves it.

SP: But to say that it's extreme? Maybe it's the sort of thing that could be done in moderation.

LA: A recitalist just can't be moderate about his ego. He just has to believe that he's the end of time.

SP: Let's all run out after the performance and get the papers and see the reviews! Narcissus wouldn't have done that.

BC: If the papers had been around, he would have!

LA: At any rate, performers would really like to have a bunch of mirrors in front of them to see how great they look. In fact I'm sure they *do* practice in front of mirrors, and tell their students to.

BC: That's the "bigger-than-life" thing, the virtuoso thing.

LA: David, of course, caught all the innuendos, and Frederick Rzewski and, in fact, most of the pianists and non-pianists who've played the piece have caught that, and delight in the irony of the piece.

BC: Do you feel that the composer has a responsibility to the audience? Or do you feel that he just lays it on them and says "All right, fellas, take it or leave it, there it is."

LA: A lot of people would say that I just say, "Fuck you, here it is."

BC: I don't think you do.

LA: I certainly hope that everybody will enjoy himself; I guess I could say that.

SP: Would you be crushed if the people didn't?

LA: Well, if I were crushed I would have probably stopped composing and killed myself a long time ago.

BC: Or you'd be selling insurance or pumping gas.

LA: I've had reviews right along, and I'm only puzzled when those kinds of reactions come. I can't understand, because I was so loving. I thought that what I did was going to be such an enjoyable experience intellectually, gut, and everything else for them. I don't mean "enjoyable" in a superficial sense, I mean enjoyable for the total experience—realizing that, gee, I make contact with that experience. I really do relate to the audience very much. I couldn't possibly do my things in a vacuum. However, the size of the audience doesn't matter to me. It can be two people, three, or anything—not the kind of commercial success that perhaps some people associate with relating to the audience.

BC: Does that bother you that there isn't a commercial success?

LA: No, it couldn't, because I've never been commercially successful. If that had bothered me, I would have stopped composing a long time ago. No, I'm a virtual commercial failure.

With all humility, I would say that I owe a lot to Music with a capital *M*, and it's given me a lot: all that kind of garbage, sentimental stuff. You just have to stop sometime and pay some dues, so I'm going to try to do the best job I can. I think I did it partially with *Source*, but on the other hand, I got so many benefits from that personally. I got more from that than I gave to the music world, so I still feel a little guilty because of it, and I have some catching up to do.

Notes

1. Larry Austin and Thomas Clark, *Learning to Compose: Modes, Materials and Models of Musical Invention* (Dubuque, IA: Wm. C. Brown, 1989).

2. Larry Austin, "Music; Can Electronic Music Be Romantic? Composer and Electronic Music Practitioner," *New York Times*, September 19, 1971.

3. Thomas Clark, *Larry Austin: Life and Works of an Experimental Composer* (Raleigh, NC: Borik Press, 2012).

4. Stuart Jay Petock, professor of philosophy at the University of Nevada, Reno.

5. Now part of Vanderbilt University.

6. Dary John Mizelle (b. 1940), composer and trombonist.

4 William Bolcom (b. 1938)

GAYLE SHERWOOD MAGEE

In 1972, William Bolcom stood on the cusp of an exceptional career as a world-renowned, remarkably prolific composer. This interview captures Bolcom just as his works were beginning to circulate through publications, performances, and recordings. Two early-1970s LP collections showcased Bolcom's pianistic and compositional talents: *Heliotrope Bouquet: Piano Rags 1900–1970*, with original and historic rags for piano; and *Bolcom Plays His Own Rags*, which included the solo piano version of the *Garden of Eden* suite.[1] Additionally, Nonesuch issued a collection of contemporary organ music by fellow composer William Albright that included Bolcom's *Black Host* in 1971, the same year that Bolcom's *Hydraulis for Organ* was published in an edition by Albright.

Despite this recognition, Bolcom was in a professional transition, as evidenced in his frustration over the New York scene—or lack thereof—and his disillusionment with academia. Four years earlier, he had left an unsatisfying yet secure position at Queens College, CUNY, followed by temporary stints as composer-in-residence at Yale University (1968–70) and New York University (1969). His divorce from the university system would be short-lived, as Bolcom accepted a position at the University of Michigan the following year: he remained on faculty there until his retirement in 2008.

In Ann Arbor, Bolcom completed most of his major works (to date) including his magnum opus, *Songs of Innocence and Songs of Experience*, which he had started in 1956 as an undergraduate at the University of Washington. His plan to set William Blake's two volumes of illustrated poetry still occupied his thoughts in this interview, some sixteen years later, and the massive composition gestated for nearly another decade before Bolcom completed it in 1981. The work premiered in 1984, first in January in Stuttgart, Germany, followed by an American premiere in April at Hill Auditorium on the University of Michigan campus, while a 2005 Naxos recording featuring the university's ensembles conducted by Leonard Slatkin received multiple Grammys. Not only did a university position supply Bolcom with much-needed security and support for composition, but it provided him with the opportunity to reconsider how composers were trained, especially regarding the place of popular music within academia, thus addressing many of the concerns about isolation and dogma voiced in the interview below.

Bolcom's temporary rejection of academia is only one salient aspect of this reveal-ing interview. The concept of synthesis is a recurring theme in the discussion of his and others' music, along with "stylistic rupture," the seeming opposite of synthesis. The interchange of synthesis and rupture is perhaps the most recognizable component of Bolcom's compositional voice, one that owes much to Blake's conception of the marriage of opposites and the integration of vernacular and elite voices. Bolcom's contemporary and later works continuously experiment by synthesizing the full range of modernist techniques with the inherently tonal world of popular music, often rupturing the former through the presence of the latter. In this light, it is fascinating to hear Bolcom's views on everything from the Beatles and Pink Floyd to vaudeville and ragtime.

Indeed, this interview took place in the midst of the ragtime revival, with which Bolcom remains closely associated. Two years prior to the interview, he wrote perhaps his most performed and recorded composition, "Graceful Ghost Rag." Ragtime served as a connection to an authentic American musical past for Bolcom and other contemporary composers, including Albright, his close friend and future colleague at Michigan. As Bolcom describes it, rediscovering classic ragtime and writing new rags felt like "picking up a dropped thread of our emerging American tradition" that provided a counterbalance to the mid-century focus on European methods and models.[2] The mid-1970s would see ragtime circulate in mass media on an unprec-edented scale, spurred by the ragtime-based soundtrack of the film *The Sting* (1973) and including national performances of Scott Joplin's opera *Treemonisha*, featuring Bolcom's orchestration. Bolcom's work in ragtime went beyond the dozens of original rags that he would eventually write to include scholarship, editions, and recordings.[3]

Although Bolcom describes himself quite modestly in the interview as a "pretty good" pianist, his recordings suggest otherwise. While his considerable pianistic skills were already well-developed in 1972, Bolcom expanded his activities as a per-former as accompanist and musical partner to mezzo-soprano Joan Morris, his most important collaborator and future wife, whom he met in 1972. The following year, the duo started performing together.[4] Their numerous recordings and national tours showcased Bolcom's growing catalog of cabaret songs, many of which would become repertoire standards: "Lime Jello, Marshmallow, Cottage Cheese Surprise," "George," and "Song of Black Max," to name only a few. In addition to original works, Bolcom and Morris contributed to the rediscovery and popularization of popular songs from earlier eras, particularly from the first half of the twentieth century, as part of a nationwide movement toward recognizing and celebrating American music on its own terms.

Bolcom's other collaborator on the cabaret songs was lyricist and poet Arnold Weinstein, with whom Bolcom had worked on early, experimental theater pieces. Of these, the best known is the war satire *Dynamite Tonite* (1963), which was supported by the Actors Studio through funding from the Rockefeller Foundation and lead to an off-Broadway premiere in 1964.[5] Bolcom and Weinstein would produce more cabaret-theater pieces (*Casino Paradise* in 1990), along with three full-scale operas for Chicago's Lyric Opera: *A View from the Bridge* (1999), based on Arthur Miller's celebrated play; and two cocreations with film director Robert Altman, *McTeague* (1992), and *A Wedding* (2004, based on Altman's 1978 film).

All of these projects lay ahead of Bolcom, on the midwestern horizon far from the disappointments of New York. Looking back on his earlier self, Bolcom reflected: "I have changed a lot since, but I feel I followed that path pretty closely in my subsequent career or careers."[6] And our musical world is all the richer for it.

William Bolcom: Interview

Also present was Tracey Sterne.[7]

WILLIAM BOLCOM: Even though I am no longer, at this particular moment anyway, affiliated with any kind of university or college or music school, I have remained a composer.[8] That usually is the end of most composers' careers. When they have no longer a job in the university they stop writing. What they stop writing is usually "*Disquisitions 27* for Heckelphone and Prepared Tape." But I'm not writing any more like that, and I don't think I ever did.

BARNEY CHILDS: How long have you been in New York?

WB: Off and on since 1961; I really settled here permanently in 1966. My basic interest in New York had to do with the theater world, because in my time in Paris when I was a student there from '59 to '61 I wrote an opera called *Dynamite Tonite*, which at that particular time explored my interest in popular music, a tendency of which I was a little afraid and ashamed. People who had the musical training I had were not supposed to be interested in popular music. I always was interested in popular music, but I suppressed it, like a good boy, and wrote wrong notes instead.

BC: Did you play jazz or pop music?

WB: I used to love doing that, but I did it for money to put myself through school. At the University of Washington, I worked all kinds of funny little jobs. Not infrequently, I would do a dance or stag-party job on Saturday and play church on Sunday morning, which of course has set my whole philosophy of life to now.

BC: Did you play organ, like Bill [Albright]?

WB: I played organ in church, but I've never played organ seriously like Bill.

BC: You don't think of yourself as a performer?

WB: I think of myself as a pianist. I play piano pretty good, but I'm not an organist. I played organ because there was an organ job in Everett, Washington. I'd finish my stag-party job at two o'clock in the morning and then take a Greyhound up to Everett from Seattle, and I'd play organ in the morning. I would nap; then I would go off and work nights at an elevator job in a hotel in Seattle called, at that time, the Edmond Meany. That's how I put myself through college. I had a little scholarship from General Motors, who in those days didn't give you full scholarships. They gave you $200, paid your tuition, and I did the rest myself. I also played a lot of dance-band jobs. In those days I don't think that I could call what I did "jazz." We would try things that might be interesting, but after all, we were up there in the boondocks, in Seattle. Any time you started trying thirteenth chords they would throw you out and throw in somebody who could play a schottische. That's how it was. Actually, I got to the point where I liked the schottisches better than all those things the progressive jazz-ers were trying to do in those days. I never did like the Modern Jazz Quartet. They were very popular when I was in college, but I couldn't stand all those pseudo-fugues. I really like the real ones by Bach better. But this was all part of the basic training in the business of being a musician in America, whatever that particular strange imponderable is—something that I don't think many of us serious musicians have ever really gotten into in a real sense. We all think of ourselves as we would really like to be: in some marvelous never-never land of our image of what Europe . . .

BC: We want to be heroes.

WB: We want to be heroes of some kind. We all read biographies by Robert Haven Schauffler of Beethoven and Schumann and the rest, and I read Romain Rolland's *Jean-Christophe* and I wanted to be that. Gosh, I educated myself musically when I was a kid by going to the library and starting from the As and working through the Zs. I played through everything from Arensky to Zimbalist. I didn't know better. I liked what I liked. When I was eight years old, we went down to Sherman and Clay in Seattle. I picked out a record of *The Rite of Spring* and made my parents' life a hell for several weeks. I played it over and over and over again because it drove me absolutely into ecstasies. They finally didn't give me any trouble after a while. (I think I cowed them at an early age.) But that was really very nice of them. It probably shortened my poor father's life, but it did have a strong effect on my musical education.

But in the meantime, my background consisted of doing things involved with popular music. So I never really was raised (as I think often happens with people in a more conservative conservatory training) with a strong backing in "the classics," period. We had really nothing very much of our own, but we had the offshoots of everything. The last vaudeville in the United States was probably played out in Seattle at the Paramount and Palomar, and theaters like that. We had an Orpheum theater; that's been torn down, the Palomar is gone, the Paramount. But I remember when I was a kid there were vaudeville acts: trained dogs and acrobats. But that was the last of it, and it was pretty terrible. I talk about these things and everybody says, "My God, when did you grow up?" And I say, "Well, I was born in 1938," and they say, "How do you know about all that stuff?" and I say, "Because we had it out there ten years after it was dead everywhere else." That's the way it was. Some of the old vaudevillians ended up in the National School Assemblies. When I was in junior high school, an old guy, Clement May, came and did recitations from Shakespeare. All the kids hooted and hollered at him, but I loved it. I went back to see him afterwards and saw him in his little makeshift dressing room, drinking straight from the bottle, and I told him I thought he was good. I was eleven and I was shocked at how drunk he was. He was old, and decrepit, and disappointed. He probably was very corny on stage. But I've always had this strong interest in popular theater.

At the same time, I went through all the changes that happen to composers in the '60s. You know, when we were all writing with what is well-known as the international fellowship style: minor ninths instead of nice triads and the rest. Luckily I chose to study with Darius Milhaud.

BC: In France?

WB: At first in Mills College. I'd spent a summer in Aspen in 1957 and we got along very well. He thought that maybe I'd like to come and study with him, and I thought so, too. Milhaud's chief strength as a teacher lay in the fact that he was terribly interested in exposing his students to everything that was going on without making any kind of judgment. He is not, and never was, a parochial kind of person. He likes what he likes, and he doesn't like what he doesn't like. He never liked Brahms. I loved Brahms when I was about eleven or twelve, but I think I've outgrown Brahms. Milhaud was aware of everything around and had a certain kind of fearlessness that I always like about him. Also, he was interested in popular music. One of the things that struck me was that he didn't have this snobbish attitude about it.

When I went to Mills (1958) I was aware of what was happening at Berkeley; there was this intense, miserable, Schoenbergian, serious, everything-must-hurt quality about most everything they wrote. Always "we must be serious, by God." I never quite bought that. I mean there are very profound and important things to be said with music, but music is like life, and there are so many things that happen in it. The terrible thing that has happened with music in the last few decades is that it has almost, by some sort of force of will, limited its spectrum of expressivity into a very small area. We have so much, and so many things to be said, that *can* be said, that have been dealt with in many other arts. One of the nice things about pop art was that it opened up certain areas of thinking.

BC: But this seriousness has been fading out in the last ten years.

WB: Of course it has; I never bought it. But I *tried* to buy it. I went through the whole darn thing. When I was a student in Paris, I was a big Boulezian. I even tried to write like that a little bit. This was of course student stuff, but at the same time a wild streak also would come out in me. I only won second prize in the Paris Conservatory *concours* because in the middle of my serious quartet [No. 8, 1965], I started doing a fantasia on a tune similar to "Rock-a My Soul in the Bosom of Abraham." Henri Dutilleux came up to me with the other judges, and said, "C'est une rupture de style." That was the end of me. I got second prize; I would have got first prize if I hadn't "ruptured the style." Then it got worse.

Probably the big thing for me was the Beatles. They had enough nerve to go ahead and do what I wanted to do before, which is to put things together. And even though their means were probably more limited than a lot of so-to-speak classically trained composers, they began to synthesize things. I knew that was always where I'd wanted to be. That was, I guess, where I really began to part company with the whole academic thing in a serious way. I was not terribly interested in doing what the Beatles did, but I felt that what was most wrong with the large part of what has come to be called "serious composition" today is that it is hermetically sealed into a small area of human experience. And that is the natural consequence of the fact that the people who *write* it are locked into that small area of experience. After a while you begin to have a feeling that the only way you can really exist as an artist is *at large*, and I realized that I had to somehow or another exist "at large."

The problem has been ever since, how do you do it? I must say every once in a while going back into academia attracts me, because, my Lord, your bills are paid, you don't have to worry about what's going to happen next week. I'm sitting here every day; you never know what's going to come in next month. It's been like that for three years: I truly love the freedom, I have nobody to answer to. There's not a person to whom I have to say I will agree with you in order to keep my job. That's what I like. What I don't like about the situation is that it would be a little easier for me to be able to sustain a long piece, a long thought, if I had a little more tranquility. So I hope that maybe with a few of my recent projects I'll be able to buy some time. I might be able to go back into academia if I was able to call the shots. It would have to be a situation where I could do that.

But I don't want to have a situation like I had at Queens College in 1966 to '68. It was straight out of Kafka. We had twenty electric pianos and I had forty little girls, two at a piano. Each one had false eyelashes that came out a foot and a half from their head, they wore cheap perfumes, and they had little long fingernails that clacked on the Wurlitzer piano keys—those little electric Wurlitzer pianos, those horrible sounds? You can imagine twenty of them, in the same room, hacked away at by forty pairs of hands all playing "Mary Had a Little Lamb" at the same time. I had to do this four times a week. That's how I made my living at Queens College. Queens needed the money from their tuition to support the department. Practically everybody taught the music-for-education-majors course, even the senior professors. You never got out of it. I also taught music depreciation. Gang-bang piano, as I called it, and music depreciation. Out in Foundation U. or Cow College Extraordinary you probably are several removes from this kind of confrontation with the reality of the education game. It probably is better, but I suspect that it may be simply the other side of the same coin. That's what scares me about going back into education. I have this terrible suspicion that we are teaching people to go out into a world where they will not have jobs. And that is unforgivable. I don't feel honest about spending somebody's four years' tuition to keep me and my fifteen kids just so that person can find out that there is no need for another heckelphonist in the Royal Philharmonic or the New York whatever. That's where I feel bad about the teaching situation.

At Queens I'm working along with composers who sit there, intensely suffering over their three notes a week. I suddenly wondered: what world are they living in? What is going to happen with *them*? Because even the most serious efforts in the whole history of Western music have always, to an extent, depended on a very strong basic connection with the real world. I've always felt that, in the end, the esoteric depended on the exoteric in order to live. And this is the basic fact that's been lost in the basic *Weltanschauung* of a lot of our contemporary music.

I want to be able to have the range of the esoteric and the exoteric all together in some way; I really want to make a synthesis in the largest possible way. Maybe I felt that in order to do this I had to get out there and get a few knocks: well, I've been doing that. And it was not completely by will, but because I simply could no longer stay at places like Queens College, that I resigned. When I resigned, Charles Burkhart came up to me and said, "I can't understand: why have you resigned? Look at the security you are giving up!" And I remember looking at him, and I didn't have to say anything. I suddenly realized what those guys, those people teaching gang-bang piano, are: they consider themselves artists and they haven't ever faced anything, and their music has never faced anything. They are living in a world that I can't believe can continue to exist. I keep thinking, my Lord, it's going to all crash around them someday and they have no protection, they don't know anything. I suppose in a funny way that this is what's been wrong with their music, too. In the end we have to survive somehow in the real world. At the same time, *in* this real world, make a statement that will be as complete as we can make it.

BC: Do you think other composers are seeing this and moving out?

WB: Yes, I see it more and more. A lot of them have felt the same claustrophobia I felt. I don't think that many of them have made the jump I've made. I made the jump partly out of will, partly out of circumstance. I don't necessarily think it's one or the other, but I feel that whatever I come out with is going to be from a different point of view from those who are still safely ensconced in the "Company of the Blessed." I do feel one thing: that something that was very strong and prevalent and cramping in the '60s is very definitely over. I see the fear syndrome disappearing; people are no longer as scared as they were either of making a statement or not. All those noisy tempests-in-teapots perpetrated in music festivals in the middle '60s, which never really got anywhere, only had their force because they happened within a very circumscribed and tight little environment.

BC: Many people say that New York is still the tightest little musical environment of all. There is no musical environment in New York.

WB: There is no scene in New York! There *is* a group who are involved with Columbia-Princeton. They are hanging on, on a little raft, and I feel sorry for them. There are also people who do three-hour improvisations in lofts. People do this, people do that, but there is *no scene in music in New York*. I came here originally because of my interest in theater. I had no illusions about the New York musical scene. I also felt that the need for me, personally, was to understand New York. This is where you were really going to have to "deal with the Man," as Black people say. It's the only place in America where you can get general exposure to and in the arts. That's why I came here. It wasn't because I was interested terribly in what was happening with Charles Wuorinen, Hugo Weisgall, and Elliott Carter, because these people didn't really interest me that much. I wasn't here for the musical scene any more than I was interested with the musical scene in Paris. I went to Paris because I was fascinated by the idea of going to Paris, and I went to New York because I was fascinated by the idea of going to New York. I'm a kid from the sticks. I don't know anything about big cities. I'm fascinated by big cities. What is this peculiar phenomenon that draws everybody together to suffer in harmony, or disharmony, whatever it is that everybody is here for? Anyway, I was here for that.

New York has taught me some idea of the possible and the impossible, where it is necessary to work with the system and where it is necessary to work outside the system. I'm simply gearing up for whatever battles are necessary, and the best place to do that is where the real mess is. At least one value of New York to me has been in the shedding of a lot of illusions, including the one about "great art." Because although I believe in great art, I believe in the deepest best human statement that can be made, I know that it's not going to happen in Lincoln Center. Everybody knows that by now. But would you believe that if you were out in Two Silos, Wisconsin, and didn't know better? No—you have to get here to find out it isn't true. And you have to experience it firsthand to understand it really truly. People from out of the city have this kind of whole fantastic syndrome about New York. I get letters and they just have no idea.

TRACEY STERNE: We got a letter from Pittsburgh. They said, "We humbly ask you to listen to this tape, please don't be prejudiced against us because we come from Pittsburgh." I cried.

WB: They don't see, they just don't see. The only thing different about New York is that the people who are attached to the culture business have got the least illusions about what it's all about, in most cases. Maybe they need a few.

I always had the strong feeling that there was a very important contact had to be made somehow between me and somebody out there. It's like this: Baudelaire was not considered very good by the Parnassian poets; he wished to break their rules all the time and at the same time be honored by those guys. Some of the Parnassians were good poets, but Baudelaire is the only one now who hits you in the gut. We are almost in the same bind today. The Parnassians were artificial, the group around the Russian Five were artificial; in that whole need to impose artificial restraints, we have had very much the same thing in America. Whoever thought the criterion in music was what system you went by? Systems are for somebody who is really not sure of where he is. I remember Donald Martino (God, what a talent!) saying, "If you are not sure of your own talent, at least you can fall back on the system." I remember he said that in Tanglewood in '66.

BC: That must have been quite a summer, by the way.

WB: It was a funny time. That's where I met Bill [Albright]. I wrote *Black Host* because of Bill. He's such a fantastic organist, such a hell of a guy, such a musician. And I thought, wow! Here's a chance to do this big crazy bla-a-a-ck ugly piece, so I just let all the stops out. Before that, there was still a certain timidity in my music.

BC: So that was a big piece for you.

WB: It was probably my emancipation declaration, in a way, I wrote it in La Jolla, California, in my first and most important sense on a trip: I took an LSD trip. I took a few since, but I won't any more. LSD, as with many others, are all pop drugs, and they turn you into pop syndromes, because they tend to brutalize. But they also tend to make things terribly direct and almost impossible to miss. That was the excitement for me; suddenly being able to see things in that clear way, making a statement that could be clearly understood. I played the tape of *Black Host* when I first got it back from Bill, for rock people, the Pink Floyd, everybody else. It was the first piece of mine that I can remember playing for people that hit everybody in some way, and it did a thing for me. I suddenly said: my golly, I have gotten hold of something. I'm no longer dealing with just those little guys, the brethren, my little fraternity. I'm all of a sudden writing pieces that I don't give a goddamn what they think of, if I ever did think in that way. A certain syndrome is still true among a lot of composers. I think of them as junior executives in an insurance company: they want to see where their little pin is on the board.

TS: They want to be loved!

WB: They want to be loved, accepted, or something. They are going around "getting performances." I remember Bill Sydeman always used to talk about "getting performances." The way he said it, it always seemed to me like raping an audience. Getting performances, like getting a girl; grabbing her, opening her up and *getting* her, rather than making love with her. And that's the way so many people think about it. They don't even listen to anybody else's piece on a concert; they just sit there and *get* their performance. The real meaning of writing a piece and having it played (which is really a social act) was completely lost, and denigrated and vitiated by composers having gotten into some sort of crazy, self-destructive ego-thing, which had nothing to do with real ego-gratification, just a kind of dry-humping with music. It was dead; it was nowhere. I never could do it. It was so nice suddenly to write a piece and people would say "WOW!" Russell Peck would talk about what great things you got back from audiences: that could seduce you. All the same I did want to stay with something that everybody could understand. The only people who didn't understand it, by the way, were people who'd say, "Hmm, you're using all those triads, you're using all those minor and major chords, don't you realize that's not twentieth-century language?" I'm so glad they didn't understand, because I thought: if they did, I'd be in trouble.

BC: What are you writing now?

WB: I'm now starting—as a matter of fact I just finished it in my head—a big quartet for the Concord Quartet. I started it in '67, and now it's pretty well all finished except for the last part. I have to think about it. The Concord Quartet—Mark Sokol's little group—asked me, so I'm going to do that for a concert next year. The big thing which I've been wanting to do for fifteen years and I'm just starting—I've already got sketches for it—is a big full evening on the "Songs of Innocence and Experience." I have several songs already written for it, but it's going to be a continuous thing, which will include an extremely simple, and also a very complex, music: all the things that need to be said. Often the simplest thoughts can be handled with the "complexest" music and the most complex thoughts can be handled with the simplest music. You understand what I mean. I've thought about Blake since I was seventeen, and I've been a

Blake nut ever since. When I'm drunk enough I can quote large passages of Blake from memory, even parts of the prophetic books. Now I feel almost to the point where if I can get a good piece of time, I can sit down and write the damn thing. In the meantime, I'm finishing up this quartet.

BC: Do people ask you if you've cast away style, that you have no "personal" style?

WB: I hope to hell I *have* cast away style.

BC: In *Dream Music #2* [1966], for example; people say, "What's all that jazz doing in there?"

WB: I never have even heard that piece—the one with the vibraphone? I wrote that piece for Frank O'Hara's death. Frank was a beautiful man. When I first got here in '61, there was a whole group of people I got to know through Arnold Weinstein, who I wrote *Dynamite Tonite* with. And I got to know a lot of painters; Larry Rivers, [Willem] de Kooning, and Franz Kline, who was one of the loveliest and best of them all. A great artist, the only man who was able really to make statements with simple black and white that are still as telling as they ever were; they really, really hold up. De Kooning gets tiresome. But Franz Kline: I remember when he died it just broke my heart, because he was truly, truly a good man. Larry Rivers: an opportunist, but I love that thing he did with the Prudential Plaza.

Do you know that story? He was given $87,000 by Prudential Company to paint the biggest mural in the world on canvas. He said fine, give me the money first and I'll do it for you. So they gave him 87,000 bucks and he went out and bought another El Dorado Cadillac. You know, he has a new one every year. He scuffs up the seats and bangs it up—he doesn't care. It's a terrible mess by the end of the year; he has to give it back and they only give him fifteen cents for it, but he gets another one. That's the way he is. And he painted this great big painting for the Prudential Plaza in Pittsburgh or Philadelphia or wherever the heck it is, depicting American Revolutionary soldiers in blue costumes trampling on the faces and hands of the Black and red and yellow people of the world. Prudential have it down in some huge basement someplace and they won't show it. What a great thing to do! In a way it was a great coup. Hurra=y for Larry . . .

I wasn't really close with most of that bunch, Jane Freilicher, Rivers, all of them: I knew them mostly through Arnold, but it was the sense of community that was there, that I felt part of. That's gone; I saw several of them at a party recently at Lukas Foss's, and we had very little to say to each other. It's been more than ten years, after all.

Well, the importance of Frank O'Hara. Besides being a hell of a poet (a very inconsistent one, but he wrote some really great poetry), Frank was the one who brought everybody together. There *was* a community in those years. When I was first here in the early '60s, I spent six, seven, or eight months at a stretch doing a show or something, I was in and out a lot, and I was going to school. Frank was a kind of Jewish mother for the whole bunch. We all had a sense of being in the thing together because of him. It was terribly important to Frank that everybody kept together, so he just simply made it happen in the ways he could. He was a person who lived kind of a soft, strange life. He was a curator at the Museum of Modern Art and he was living from hand-to-mouth all his life. He was a homosexual, and it was even rougher to be a homosexual in those days. But I don't think there ever was a gentler man, a beautiful man. When I came back to live here solidly in '66, one of the people I wanted to look up and say hello again to was Frank, because I really thought the most of him, even though I hardly knew him really. Then I found out that he'd been hit by that damn beach buggy out on Fire Island. So I wrote that piece; what I tried to express in that piece was the softness of the man. When Frank died, that community I spoke of went with him. I still would like to hear it some day.

BC: This is the piece about which people say, "Why have you got all that jazz in here"—rupturing the style . . .

WB: I love rupturing style. The only way to find a style is to destroy style. Frank was a jazz nut, by the way. Do you know his poem on Billie Holiday?

BC: How much does writing and playing rags influence what you write?

WB: *Dream Music #2* was 1966, before I discovered Joplin. I didn't discover Joplin until that following fall. I got that through Norman Lloyd, whom I went to see in the fall that year, and I said "hi, how are you doing?" He said, "did you know there's a ragtime opera by Scott Joplin?" Ragtime I knew of, like "Alexander's Ragtime Band," and if I'd heard of him at all, and I'm not sure I had, I'd heard of Scott Joplin because of the "Maple Leaf Rag." Everybody knows that, of course, through fifteen thousand bastardized variations. Then I ran into Rudi Blesh, who was also teaching at Queens College. I asked him, "do you know anything about this opera by Scott Joplin?" He said, "do I *know* it? I happen to have a copy, do you want to see it?" I looked at it, and I fell in love with *Treemonisha*. It did what I had wanted to do all that time; it brought it all together, and that was what's exciting to me about Scott Joplin. Ragtime as such doesn't interest me two hoots. But I'm interested in people who put it together, successfully or not.

People who have interested me a great deal in the last few years are people like him and like Eubie Blake who put it all together, who made a synthesis, who did what I thought was absolutely necessary and had to be done. They haven't been given the due they deserve. Because they *did* do it and they didn't do it artificially, like people like Aaron Copland and I don't know who the hell else tried. Eubie Blake likes to write English waltzes, and writes very nice English waltzes. But he's a Black man, and we're not supposed to listen to Black men doing English waltzes. He's not supposed to be able to do them, but that's what he *loves* doing. "I'm Just Wild about Harry" was an English waltz that was made into a one-step because the star of his show, *Shuffle Along*, said you can't have a waltz in a Black show.

But Joplin and Blake and a few others, those guys put it together. They were so important to me, because they did what I had been trying to do all that time. My interest in ragtime is minimal. I love to play ragtime because it makes me feel good. I remember coming back after teaching gang-bang piano at Queens and playing ragtime and feeling better. What opened things up for me was that those guys were able to make a synthesis without doing it in some intellectual kind of way; they did it on the simplest level, which is the hardest.

BC: What about people who tried to synthesize media? It was very popular five years ago, say.

WB: It depends on who they were and how they did it. Scriabin tried to synthesize light and sound, right? Did he do it? And if he didn't do it, why didn't he do it? *Because he was operating from the effects rather than the causes.* The usual excitement about mixed media—let's put all this stuff together and blow everybody's mind—is working again from effects rather than from causes. However, somehow this can be done. You can synthesize practically anything with anything, but you have to work from causes, to work from *why* the sound is interesting, from *why* the lights are interesting, *why* the dance is interesting. Otherwise you end up with a three-ring circus. I prefer a three-ring circus because it doesn't pretend to be anything but a three-ring circus. In order to collide, two elements have to have something in common. And to find that common element, *which is there*, requires discovery from the inside out, rather than the other way around. Mixed media was a desperate maneuver in a lot of ways, but it did some things. I did a few mixed-media pieces myself for the heck of it; they gave me commissions. I don't think that they were of any importance in my particular history and I don't think that they will be remembered, because they weren't really what I wanted them to be. They were not a synthesis, and to me, that's the most important thing to make.

BC: You say in the notes for the *12 Etudes*: "Why write etudes?" There's a kind of historical specter that you are banishing: don't write (or write) what our time says you must write.

WB: I wrote the *Etudes* because I was interested in the technical problems involved; also because they were a collection of pieces that turned out to be études, as I'm sure you can guess. As I said in these notes, there was a time when a number of pianists were running around trying to learn the "modern music," because they felt that was the only way toward survival. There was a little while when you had to put in some abortion by XYZ in order to finish out your program and not let everybody think that all you could play was Bach and Mozart.

BC: A "Modrun" number.

WB: Yeah! "modrun" music. There were all these people who were trying to equip themselves technically to do this. I went into these problems with enough concentration to want to figure out which things were interesting to me that had and had not been explored by the piano literature before. By the time I wrote the notes for those études (several years after having written the pieces and having gone through several stylistic changes, the most important of which was writing *Black Host*), I could look at them another way. I thought they were all right as music, and I still think they are really all right, but all of a sudden I found myself having to ask all over again the question of why did I write them. And I don't know; I guess they were a technical kind of problem that had to be solved somehow. There's more to it than that, because they also were meant to have a certain kind of unity—the Chopin études, the Schumann study pieces, the Paganini Caprices all have that. In a certain sense I cut my teeth on them; certain molars, certain bicuspids of the mouth formation of the composer had to be cut that way. I did them in that kind of spirit, but at the same time I was dealing with a lot of stylistic problems, and I felt that perhaps I solved, or at least opened up, some of them.

What's happened with me in the last few years is a change: I don't look at the *Etudes* as something I would write today. I find them just too dense and too complicated; I wouldn't write that many notes per square inch now. I might again sometime, but at the moment I don't want to. At the moment I want to be very clear; like Nixon, "I want to make it perfectly clear." It's not because I want to make it clear for *them*, I want to make it clear for *me*. I really don't care what *they* understand so much as I care that *I* understand what I'm doing; if *I* really honestly understand what I'm doing, then *they* will. At least I've got to know what I'm doing, I've got to be sure that everything that's gone into the moments that I have constructed is absolutely boiled down, and now I want to do it with the least shrubbery possible. At that particular time I was still quite interested in the shrubbery. I think that's the difference between me in 1965–66 when those were written, and me now.

BC: The quartet, for example, is going to be shrubless?

WB: It depends on what you mean by shrubbery. There were certain people who felt that [Anton] Webern had no shrubbery. Only with him, you're seeing the notes through the shrubbery. I love Webern; I think that the best of him, which is the earliest stuff (like those early Five Pieces for Quartet—that's marvelous), was simple, straight, terse statements. With Webern, the shrubbery is still there, only it's implied rather than expressed, it's encapsulated. The first movement of Opus 21 is Mahler's 9th in miniature. He could use so few notes *because* all that shrubbery was still around; the post-Webern guys misunderstood what a *super-romantic* he was. He summed up with two notes what everybody before took two hundred to say.

Now that shrubbery is gone, through no fault of our own. Webern could *afford* to be indirect. But what I need to do now is to make the straightest possible kind of statement I can make, and I can't afford not to be direct any more. I have no place to hide. I can't make a statement behind the safety of any kind of artistic format, I have no -ism that I can say I'm behind any more. So I've got to do it as straight and quick as I can. That's what I mean about shrubbery. I mean, there's shrubbery around Mondrian. It isn't the question of whether the statement itself *looks* very simple—it's more of a question of what is required *around* the statement to make it intelligible. I want to make it so that you don't *need* all that to see. Yet I think this can be done in such a way that you can say everything you need to. It's not just simplifying or bastardizing or Bowdlerizing, it's making your music intelligible. Yeah, it's as simple as that.

Notes

1. William Bolcom, piano, *Heliotrope Bouquet: Piano Rags 1900–1970*, Nonesuch H 71257, 1971; and William Bolcom, piano, *Bolcom Plays His Own Rags*, Jazzology JCE-72, 1972.

2. William Bolcom, liner notes, *William Bolcom: Complete Rags*, John Murphy, piano, Albany Records TR 325, 1999, CD: online at http://www.dramonline.org/albums/william -bolcom-complete-rags/notes (accessed July 12, 2019).

3. See, for example, Robert Kimball and William Bolcom, *Reminiscing with Sissle and Blake* (New York: Viking, 1973); and Bolcom, piano, *Pastimes and Piano Rags*, Nonesuch H-71299, 1974, LP.

4. The duo continues to perform on a limited schedule as of this writing. See also Joan Morris, *Let Me Sing and I'm Happy: The Memoir and Handbook of a Singing Actress* (Hillsdale, NY: Pendragon, 2018).

5. David Garfield, *A Players' Place: The Story of the Actors Studio* (New York: Macmillan, 1980), 196, 228.

6. William Bolcom to Gayle Sherwood Magee, e-mail July 31, 2019.

7. Teresa (aka Tracey) Sterne (1927–2000). Concert pianist and director, Nonesuch Records, 1965–79.

8. *Transcript note, 1974:* Mr. Bolcom has since taken a job with the University of Michigan.

5 Harold Budd (1936–2020)

VIRGINIA ANDERSON

Harold Budd is arguably the most Southern Californian composer. With Daniel Lentz, Budd inspired a community of composition (much more diffuse than a "school"), beginning with "pretty music": an expansive style of intimate, close-miked instruments, sung and spoken text with sensual or meditative topics, reflecting what the British composer Gavin Bryars called "non-doctrinal spirituality."[1] In his "soft-pedal" piano style, Budd subsequently moved from notated scores to produced recorded works.

Originally a jazz drummer, Budd studied composition at Cal State University Northridge and the University of Southern California, where he was taught in the post-Schoenbergian tradition. Interested in the visual arts, Budd sent Mark Rothko his work, *Analogies from Rothko* (1965). Through Rothko, Budd met Morton Feldman and Budd's musical aesthetic changed. His first work in that alternative scene was minimalist. Will Johnson called *VII* (1967), "the most conservative piece" at the First Festival of Live-Electronic Music.[2] Other works included *Candy Apple Revision* (1970), a red piece of paper reading "Candy Apple Revision, D-flat Major, Harold Budd May 1970." Budd explains to Childs that the score is both decorative art and music to be performed. "It's not a notation, obviously. I mean it to be a pretty little thing, and it does exist as a piece of red paper. . . . At the same time, I *mean* that chord sound."

Childs released Budd's first album on Advance Recordings with two works, *Couer d'Orr* (1969), for saxophone and organ drone, and *Oak of the Golden Dreams* (1970), for Buchla Box.[3] Budd began teaching at the California Institute of the Arts (CalArts), where his students included Michael Byron and Peter Garland. While still a student, Garland cofounded the journal *Soundings*. *Soundings #1* includes three text pieces by Budd.[4] All were earlier works, as Budd was in a two-year creative hiatus: he had out-minimalized himself with *Candy Apple Revision*.

Budd returned with *Madrigals of the Rose Angel* (1972), the first and, for Bryars, strongest of Budd's works from the 1970s.[5] It was a deliberate step: "I purposely tried to create music that was so sweet and pretty and decorative that it would positively upset and revolt the avant-garde. . . . Hard as is it is to imagine now, the prettiness of my music was very much a political statement at the time."[6] Budd denied any direct associations in the title. "It's not really a madrigal, of course, and there probably is not a rose angel. They're words that I put together because of their attractiveness to me."[7]

In Delius's Sleep (1974), a commission by Childs for his duo with Phillip Rehfeldt, has typical "pretty music" traits: smooth piano arpeggios, soft clarinet, sleigh bells, and an unhurried pace. Budd's harmony avoids traditional direction and drama. He credited Childs: "There's another kind of harmony you've talked about for years I didn't catch onto for a long time: when you have a chord and it goes to another chord, you have produced a harmony." Budd decorated his manuscripts with ladybirds and butterflies, stylized leaves, and other "pretty" drawings.

Bryars visited California in 1974 and suggested *Madrigals of the Rose Angel* to Brian Eno for his experimental record label, Obscure. Eno brought Budd and the saxophonist Marion Brown to London to record *The Pavilion of Dreams* (1978), an album suite that includes *Madrigals of the Rose Angel* and *Bismillahi 'Rrahman 'Rrahim* (1974, with Brown).[8] Budd and Eno collaborated on *Ambient 2: Plateaux of Mirrors* (1980), where Eno processed Budd's solo piano, and *The Pearl* (1984).

Unlike Eno, Budd abhorred the term "ambient": "I'm slammed into that category. . . . I feel like I've been . . . kidnapped into something I know nothing about and have no interest in at all."[9] Rather than being "a note composer," Budd now worked directly to recording, often as an improviser, and his "soft-pedal style" of piano performance was his preferred category term.[10] Budd formed his own Cantil label, and released albums with the Cocteau Twins, David Sylvian, John Foxx, and others. His work includes paintings, installations, and poetry (*By the Dawn's Early Light* [1991]). Budd publicly quit composition with *Avalon Sutra* (produced by David Sylvian, 2004), but subsequently recommenced with collaborations like *Jane 1–11* (2013), with cover art and videos by Jane Maru.[11]

One gets a sense in this interview of what Budd no longer is—the earnest educator—and a little of Budd's humor. Some of my fondest memories include afternoons drinking and listening to Hal and Barney exchanging quips and anecdotes. But the interview depicts Budd's enduring aesthetic in which the listener inhabits an expansive time space, the instruments are beautiful, and harmony is merely one good sound that moves into another good sound, often "because the goddamned thing is pretty." These "pretty" traits influenced the sound world of other composers, including Jim Fox, Rick Cox, Michael Jon Fink, Michael Byron, John Luther Adams, and Budd's contemporary Lentz. As a legacy, they still do.

Harold Budd: Interview

BARNEY CHILDS: In the notes for the record jacket for *New Work #1*, you say that about 1970 your whole musical thinking changed with *Candy Apple Revision*. Why was that?

HAROLD BUDD: Barney, I think it was just latent. When Dan Lentz and I used to get together, I started discovering what I wanted to do (and he also). We provided a catalyst. In talking things out, it suddenly occurred to me to do what we goddamned well wished to do. It was that simple. One thing was "sounds." Most composers are interested about making interesting sounds. Interesting sounds, somehow or other, remain interesting sounds. Except for performances, it's the only place you experience the "art stuff" about music. I got infected with the notion of not being able to do anything other than experiencing the "art stuff" about music. Some pieces became, therefore, examples of my day-to-day thinking. It became increasingly difficult, if I ever wanted, to divorce my musical language from the things I looked at. To get much less metaphysical, I also like this idea of making music that is decorative, in the same way that a vase is decorative. It has a function to it. You put flowers in it, you put it in the home, but you put it there for a reason. It's because the goddamned thing is pretty. Aesthetically, it's about as deep as interior decorating, but that's good enough unless I change my mind. *Candy Apple Revision* [1970] was not a piece as such, because it's almost too radical, but it's just terribly pretty.

BC: So how did your interest in art alter these stances? I know it has, because the Rothko piece [*Analogies from Rothko*, 1965] is earlier.

HB: Those art works made an absolutely direct statement. It required no special knowledge other than the eyes to see color. I would have liked to make a music that I would respond to exactly the same way. It's pretty, it does the right things, and you put it away until you see it again.

BC: Which would leave you open, as I'm sure you've found out, to assault from people who say, "You've ignored all the 'musical' premises as such."

HB: Of course they're all wrong [*laughter*]! I've zeroed in on the musical stuff. They've done all the other stuff: that whole business where the music justifies itself because the system it employs is a product of its system. I don't care if it's Cage. Cage is responsible for more than his share of quite lovely, exquisite pieces; he's also responsible for the kind of piece that stands as the proof of a system. These are the pieces that I don't care for, but most people who like Cage's music do care for. That second generation of Cage people got interested in something that I have never been interested in. It is not John Cage; it is thinking about the making of the thing that Cage did better than almost any others. He also made some awfully nice poetry, awfully lovely pieces, and that has been passed [over]. The same with Lou Harrison. Harrison made a career off of the stuff that Cage abandoned, and that was not the hip road. Cage doesn't need any apology. The Cageans who came later made awfully good systems—maybe they were improving, or even *proving*, Cage's system—but not pulling it off nearly as well. The proof is a plethora of string quartets with "aleatoric" (so-called) stuff in it that people are getting PhDs for. That doesn't take much balls to do that. What takes a lot of balls is to just forget the whole thing: to simply go on and do what's necessary.

BC: How many people are doing *that*?

HB: Not really very many.

BC: With the students you work with, how do you get this vision over to them? How do you keep them from simply imitating the surface? Or do you care?

HB: I care to the extent that it is very trying to put up with bad music. But I'm not very pushy in that regard. Any reasonable person can slip. Someone's doing something but something's not right about it, and so they ask someone else. Through some kind of long, simple process—having enough beer together, having enough coffee together—a certain point is made. It's accepted or rejected, or it goes through that synthesis process. That's certainly the way I've dealt with the students that I think are writing awfully good music. I didn't have anything to tell them, really. Maybe I made it cool for them to do what they wanted to do anyway. But they were writing the kind of piece for me that they *assumed* that an avant-garde composer wants to see. And I did not want to see it.

BC: Salzman and others point out this work and that of yours as sort of the "typical West Coast work." Larry Austin has talked about "western" music—is there a "western" style? If so how do you feel connected with it?

HB: I think there's a West Coast style. But it's impossible to say exactly what it is or who is doing it. In the mid-'60s the art that was made here on the West Coast was remarkably different than it was elsewhere. You in particular are not just a little bit responsible for that. It also has roots in a lot of people that you don't really like—Harry Partch, for example. It's possible for a gunfighter never to have met Bat Masterson, but he still was pretty good. I've never lived on the East Coast or anywhere other than the West Coast, but I feel that to be the case. When I've talked this over with Richard Teitelbaum, who's an East Coast man, he comes up with the same conclusions. He'll point out painters from the '30s, like Mark Tobey and Morris Graves, who are peculiar to living on the Pacific instead of the Atlantic. There is something about it, but I don't think there's any kind of self-conscious "coast-ism."

BC: Teitelbaum participated in this sort of immediate post-Cagean thing in New York—La Monte Young, Terry Riley, Joe Byrd—all West Coast people in this sort of export-come-back again, like Poe exported and came back again. But do you think that now in 1973 we could say, "Yes, there is still a sort of identity"?

HB: No, I don't think so, and that's pretty good, too. It was important for a while; when Larry [Austin] was at [UC] Davis, he brought a certain regional pride to it. Because there's no question: most of the guys out here were writing thoroughly better music than the guys back east. At the heyday of *Perspectives [of New Music]* there was no publicized alternative. Everyone knew that was a lot of shit, that it was "bad art." Everyone was independent, and there was an underground nexus, almost, of people who knew it also. The state that we live in—the distance of our border exceeds that from Manhattan to Savannah, Georgia, for Christ's sake. But somehow we still have kept in touch. Larry was good at making all the noises necessary to create an identity; regional pride, perhaps. This is what he did in me. Those pieces written around 1965 and thereabouts were infinitely better than theirs. [Robert] Ashley had something to do with that, too. He never was out here, but he wasn't a New Yorker. Those were awfully good, very important pieces.

BC: It's curious to look back on it and say, yes, we can now deal with this as historical force and historical fact. It's *you*, it's the way it was. At the same time, you say now we'll start writing an article about it; we can immobilize it in plastic or amber.

HB: Yeah, that's going to happen now. You're right; someone's going to make a lot of money on it.

BC: Do you think there's a danger of "establishmentism" settling itself in the west?

HB: Ah, yes I sure do. You bet I do. I think that with *Source* magazine . . .

BC: I thought you might have mentioned certain universities.

HB: But universities have never participated in West Coast art. They have always divorced themselves from that. They have always been sick sisters from their East Coast counterparts. They have never been interesting. They have never contributed anything to all that necessary art stuff. It's just as well, because they're strong enough as it is. They turn out composers by the fistful. Every one of them has a DMA [doctor of musical arts] to prove it. They come out of these universities all the time. Absolutely worthless.

BC: So you think this new *Source* is the . . .

HB: I think *Source*'s contribution is going to be chronicling the thing that made them necessary at one time. They really are not necessary any more. They're awfully good, I admit. Their heart's in the right place. Dreadfully dull stuff. Maybe it's the nature of making a magazine.

BC: Well, there's *Soundings* and *Numus West*. That's this part of the world.

HB: No, it's quite easy to do exactly what you feel is necessary these days.

BC: Why aren't more people doing it, then? Or maybe they are, but they feel what's necessary is not right.

HB: They're still playing to a kind of audience. They may even be their peers, but they're not very free people. [Karlheinz] Stockhausen said something years ago that always grated on the academicians: he only cared for a piece of music if it shocked him. There's a great deal of truth in that. You certainly can't be shocked by aggressive avant-gardism any more. It's boring, dreadful stuff. Its necessity has slipped by years ago. I'll tell you something. There's very little music that I actually . . .

BC: I agree. I'm finding less that I like to listen to, so I listen less and less.

HB: There's about a fistful of composers that I can consistently count on to lay out right. Not like I'm a judge, but it's simply inescapable fact. The others are doing all that stuff. I think that's wonderful, but they're really performed far too often.

BC: Isn't this a melancholy prospect when you have to teach? When your fireball young composer has to come up against this—what does that have to do with us? Are we Judas goats, leading him into an arena where he's going to get his neck carved?

HB: If the guy finally ends up doing what he wishes, he's solved all his problems, except the personal poetic ones, in terms of style and other professional music stuff. That goes by the wayside; he's already solved his problem. He's really smelling out something that he or she can't escape; it's something that keeps pulling him. It's a neurosis, but a good one, the kind that you want to have. You've got to nurture it. Don't go to someone to expunge yourself of this dreadful desire to write gorgeous music!

BC: Do you think it is a desire nowadays? Don't you think they want to be hip? I think this is deadly.

HB: Terrible. I don't understand that, but they must think there's something there. I don't see it myself, but that's OK. Maybe that's a phase they have to go through?

BC: Twenty years ago the hip thing to do was to have every measure in a different time signature. The piece could've been re-barred in 4/4 with a couple 3/8 bars, but that didn't make any difference. Nobody was going to play it if it looked that way. So, is it really possible to teach them anything? Either they come to you already doing it, or . . .

HB: From my own experience (not very extensive), the ones that already have their bag of tricks down are going through the motions of getting their degree. They're buying their degree.

BC: In the last couple of years, has your interest in performance of your music faded? If you're concerned with the immediacy of an art, does this include performance? Talking about *Candy Apple Revision*; essentially it exists as itself. All you have to do is look at it, and partake of it, and it doesn't have to be performed. But on the other hand, it does indeed have to be performed.

HB: It does have to be performed. I wanted that portion of it that is my handwriting to be a tip-off about exactly what I meant. It's not a notation, obviously. I mean it to be a pretty little thing, and it does exist as a piece of red paper. I didn't do that blindly. At the same time, I *mean* that chord sound.

BC: *Madrigals of the Rose Angel* [1972] is *clearly* performance oriented.

HB: Absolutely.

BC: In a sense you're getting back to performance, but you're coming back to a different level. You're coming back to do a different thing with the sound than you would have before. You're coming back to performance as a different function in regard to the notation than before, and a different function in the ear of the listener than before, simply by the nature of approach to what's happening, by the opulence of implication in the score, and of the sound. So performance is just as important, but in quite a different way. I mean, it's not like you write a Fugue in C major . . .

HB: . . . and then someone reads it out for you. That's correct. The emphasis is shifting, that's for sure. Maybe even to the point I would prefer to be the performer.

BC: A lot of people are doing it.

HB: Sure. I'm not unique in that respect. But the music that I'm doing is much different. For example, a composer whose piece does not exist without his performance of it, is not translatable to someone else: that is one thing. Mine is that, *plus* something still different. For God's sake, it's written out so that some second party could do it. But that isn't the point of it. If I believed in an aural tradition more, there would be no need to notate them, because my feeling about those pieces is not simply one of high regard for them as a piece of music, but I feel the emotional side of that kind of piece so strongly, maybe even dangerously. I'm not kidding; I don't want it fucked around with by people I don't know very well. It's really tough, man; I can't get to the nib of it, mostly because it shouldn't be talked about anyway.

BC: I've heard so many people say at concerts when they're asked to talk about the music, "Well, words are nothing; you should listen to the music; if you hear what's there you don't need to talk about it." I won't buy that, but I certainly won't *discount* it as a view. On the other hand, where you have the ten-minute explanation complete with diagrams and set theory, that's equally repellent.

HB: The difference is that they *can* talk about it if they want. But they choose not to because they're lazy, or they simply don't want to. They feel a regard for the people performing, they don't want to talk about it. But I'm talking about something that I can't say. It can be talked about, but I can't do it.

BC: Essentially this has become much more individual, both from the inside—that is, how it's written—and from the outside—that is, how it's done, how it's performed. In a sense, it's anti-virtuoso.

HB: In the tactile sense, it's anti-virtuoso. Mostly because I'm not a tactile virtuoso; I can't do all that stuff.

BC: But that doesn't enter into the problem; it would be foolish to say it did.

HB: All those elements that Lentz hears in Beethoven that I don't—all the black side of human nature which is becoming increasingly attractive in art, a neurotic, erotic thrust—is enormously attractive.

BC: Well, it's *re*-becoming attractive, in a sense. You can't think of anybody in 1942 doing anything except sturdy, healthy, Boy-Scouty; in your phrase, the "American populist symphony." It's an honest, naive, good thing: painters who used to go paint grain elevators—WPA writers' projects. There's music paper still left at the College Conservatory in Milwaukee that says "WPA Music Project" on it. I should have brought some back with me, because it gives me a great feeling to write on that paper! But this [emotional content] couldn't have [existed] in 1940. It certainly was present in about 1890, and it certainly is present now. One can see it coming in the use of other people's music, quotations; this coming to terms on the immediate surface ear level with a sort of sumptuousness, sensuousness of sound, and on the non-ear level with these concerns that you're mentioning. But it's not nearly as hip as it may be (and hopefully never will be).

But how much has this to do with the Romantic personality? I've always thought that the real breakthrough was with the empiricist philosophers, when somebody was sitting up there telling you that you were just a sum total of your experiences and your associations, and that what you thought of next was what your mind produced next, not what a logical rhetorical rule fabricated for you. But then the Romantics could say what counts is how I *feel*. We've shipped out all the world-machine classical rules. Clearly my sensibility is that sensibility, since I feel it more clearly than you clowns down here in the valley. My sensibility is what counts, my sensibility is artistically expressible in these terms. So you get Shelley: "I fall upon the thorns of life! I bleed!" That's where the thing starts. It submerges for a while, and then it comes back again in a very curious way. And this is a *RE-coming* back, in a doubly removed sense. You were saying you should write down what you want to hear, young composers should just put it down. It sounds like I'm building some sort of a category now, which I didn't intend to do, because I don't like isms. The [move toward] quotation is a harbinger of something that hadn't happened before and it was malhandled and shat upon.

HB: But it was done by guys who had no business doing it, because it wasn't very honest. It was well-thought-out. These guys are crafty: they know how to write music, they put those notes down one right after the other. But it's not honest. It's done for all kinds of very curious purposes: commissions and . . .

BC: But if you take the Mozart song in Loren Rush's [*Danse le Sable*], this is quite another matter. We don't stop and say, "Mozart!" when we hear that. We don't even *think* that if it's working right, something strange, a creepy something, is evoked. It's the same thing that you and Dan are doing in pieces which have echoes of an earlier time, and yet they really aren't. When you were replaying *LOVERISE*, I was struck by how much the opening six bars sound like a Chopin prelude, until you get to a particular chord change; then you know it can *never* be a Chopin prelude.

HB: If Loren Rush showed [*Dans le Sable*] to someone who didn't give a shit, they'd say, "Well, this is a very clever music hall theme." They're right at one level, but they've missed the point completely! He might as well have never shown it to him.

BC: I really sort of derailed you, because you were just getting at something. You were getting at the idea of the black side of things.

HB: This can get so confused and mixed up, but it seems that some composers write inscapes that are designed to exorcise themselves of their devils. Actually some of it's pretty good art. But I'm not trying to escape from those devils. I'm delighted to rediscover that they were there. I knew they were there when I was a kid, and I had a wonderful life with them, until then it became necessary to become a reasonable person. And I'm delighted to rediscover them.

BC: Some people would say that's *naïf*, with an *f*, and a dieresis over the *i*. I'm very personally part of that, too.

HB: You mentioned the quote from Shelley, that initial development of extreme romanticism in the nineteenth century. Those guys that came afterwards who had the gift, had time to look back and make judgments about what romanticism had been, never pointed out the fact that yes, it was unreason*ing*, but that's not the same thing as saying it was unreason*able*. The way you feel about a thing is not the same thing as saying the way you *feel* about something. It's different somehow. You can have a reaction to a work of art. You can confront almost anything—a very lovely piece of music, for example—and have a certain feeling about it. Which is not the same thing as zeroing in on *a* feeling that's either triggered by an action of yours or by someone else. It's simply taking it, grabbing it unreservedly, going right up to the hilt with it; and my own thought is that it's impossible to exhaust it. But it has nothing at all beneficial; it's only *it*—it's part of being human.

BC: This gets down to the relationship that what one is making in a work of art with the whole past experience. You have pieces that are resonances from past experiences: *Healdsburg Plum* and some others. What do we plug into when we're writing a piece of music? Is it simply a kind of orderly survey? Or is it a poet with his "eye in a fine frenzy rolling," waiting for Inspiration with her finger of fire to come down and ignite his pen and drive it across the page? Clearly you are getting back into a kind of immediacy of contact with yourself that you couldn't do without the device, but on the other hand, the device has been absorbed and built in. You no longer have to accede to the "when in doubt, write a fugue" thing that bothers so many composers.

HB: I don't know. At the moment, the process is not really a process. There was never an honest-to-God waking moment in the past two years that the damn thing simply isn't with me. It doesn't mean that I sit down and "choringly" whip out another Hal Budd piece! It simply means that it's wholly unnecessary to divorce that activity from drinking a cup of coffee or a can of beer. My drinking a can of beer is not at all parochial. The drinking of it is, but my imagination at every moment is right there all the time. So I don't need the devices, if that's what you're asking, even if it means memory . . .

BC: If there *were* any devices implied in my question, that would have been the one.

HB: It's omnipresent. I have to make the same kind of decisions, but that's the craft part. I have the ability to write a note down and know what it sounds like.

BC: I was discussing this morning about what a teacher ought to do. I said that essentially the teacher teaches you the craft and he takes you up to the edge of the roof and then he throws you off and sees if you can fly. If you can, great, and if you can't, well, there's a lot of money in double-entry bookkeeping as a career.

Is there any valid external judge on music that one does? Clearly, we're past the stage where the critic says something in the *Nowhere City Bugle* after the concert and we are stricken to the vitals by what he says. Are we like early romantic artists who are also arbiters of our own selves? Are we self-sufficient by this time that we can proceed without needing it? When you get a bad review, what do you think, other than "what a clown this guy is; what an imperceptive bastard this guy is"?

HB: To be honest, I just don't know what their function is. It's strange, because I rely on critics for all kinds of things—whether or not to see a movie, for example. For example, Orson Welles's *Touch of Evil* is an absolutely sensational film, but I've never read a critic who didn't say otherwise. So I rely on them for something that I think they probably know a bit more about: the history of *la cinema* and all. But when it comes to music, I swear to Christ I don't know what to say. I don't think they're helpful or harmful. Mostly I think they're making a better living off the stuff they're talking about than the person who's responsible for it.

BC: Who watches the watchman in our/this case, who are our monitors? Do we *need* them? Did past artists need monitors?

HB: This business about being a critic is a very formal situation. These people get paid by journals to say something intelligent. Whereas criticisms that you or I might make, for example, about someone or something, are really the right ones as far as I'm concerned. They're not published, but that doesn't mean that that information isn't available. It's available, clearly; it's just that you don't have to pay a dime for it—it comes for free. Now that's a better form of criticism, in that these guys are a result of *that* kind of talking about the artist. I don't think that what they have to say here actually has to do with newspaper reviews. For example, Ruskin was right when he trumped Turner and *some* of the Pre-Raphaelites. He was clearly wrong with William Holman Hunt. But what these guys have to say is not based on what Ruskin had to say in the journal anyway. As a matter of fact the *only* reason they're saying anything about them is because Ruskin said *something* about them. It's publicity. And I don't know what the function is beyond that.

BC: But do you suppose these *artists* are concerned, on the other hand, with what the prints or the dailies say?

HB: Apparently so, but I don't think it was in terms of whether or not they thought they were doing the right thing. It has to do in terms of just being plain stupid, like Ruskin slandering Whistler and Whistler taking him to court. That was clearly libelous; there was no question of it. Critics have no reason to do that. They have a right to do it, but that doesn't *give* them the right.

BC: Most of the people who really made the impression are, one way or another, keeping themselves before the public through some extraordinary means of style. Yet nowadays in music, the people who are working hardest to keep themselves before the public eye are the people, mostly Europeans, who are the infinitely *dullest* people. PR is tracking well for them. And it's been one of my theories about American music is that the guys really don't much give a damn about critics or audiences or anything else. They're interested in making the piece work. I like to think that's still around.

HB: I think it is. I can't imagine any person about whose art I think a great deal changing [their work] for something as crass as the critics. I was once asked, do I think composers—I guess they were talking about *avant-garde* composers—write for an audience. I said no, no, absolutely never. It's not the *same* thing as saying that they don't *have* an audience. Of course they do. Some of them have enormously big audiences. Some of them have a small extremely devoted audience. At that kind of level that's OK. If it's a small audience, that's fine, because it's another way of being very friendly to people you like a lot. But having a big audience without compromising about it, like [Morton] Subotnick and Cage, for example, that's gravy, because it's a noncommercial art to begin with. And guys that *depend* for the amount of money they're used to making in a year on an audience very clearly must have that. Movie composers, for example, can't afford to make a mistake. Even when they do it right, obviously it's a mistake anyway.

BC: How important do you think is teaching the craft?

HB: I don't think it's critical. There's certain kinds of stuff you can't escape. If you're going to write a harp piece, then there's no reason in the world why you, along with anyone else, can't learn you've got to change the pedals occasionally, or you don't get sounds. If you refuse to do it, then you're *saying* it's not important, but you can't possibly mean that. If your intention is to write a harp piece, then you're going to get a harpist to play it. If you learn what that harpist's language is, what they know best—you can expand on it. So that craft part is one thing. The study of harmony is interesting. First of all, harmony that you learn in colleges can be taught in one semester. A lot of guys would lose jobs if anybody found that out! But there's another kind of harmony you've talked about for years I didn't catch onto for a long time: when you have a chord and it goes to another chord, you have produced a harmony. Then you say to yourself, oh yes, is it good or does it suck? You start discovering for yourself—is this good, is this bad, is this melodic line making it? Even if it's improvised over a drone, does it make any difference? You have learned certain "craft"; it becomes something else, actually: technique. You do whatever's necessary to do the right thing. Yes, there is a formula—man, just being sensitive to what the hell it is that's going on in your own art. In particular, just opening your heart to the thing and trusting your judgment, that's craft.

BC: It's hard to abandon the landmarks of models. I think that as long as you stay with the landmarks, you're never going to write a piece that lasts longer than a minute and a half. "Panic City" is too intense after that. You're panicky about pitches, and you're panicky about resolutions. If you can just say screw the parameters, just put it down.

HB: There might be some reason to have a violinist, for example, learn as much about the craft as the people whose music they play.

BC: Oh dear, now you're into this thing about what else ought you to know. If you're a super-skilled virtuoso trombonist, should you be forced to pass a piano proficiency requirement that says play "The Star-Spangled Banner" in five keys? If you could play it in five keys *at once*, that would be another matter!

HB: No. That has come about to keep complete incompetents from losing their jobs at major universities. Of course that's not important, unless you're will-ing to do something with it if that's pertinent to the art, you're going to either make yourself or re-create for someone else. I don't see the point. Good ears, big hearts, open minds: there's no substitute.

BC: I surely hope not. Stravinsky's idea about music being incapable of expressing anything.[12] Are there certain gestures in music that automatically stir certain responses in human listeners? Is music supposed to "communicate" something?

HB: It's not supposed to, but I think it does. I don't think that's its function, be-cause language does it better. If you want a cup of coffee, language is the way to get it. Art is capable of changing your life, and good art most certainly cannot help but do that. Now, if that's communication, OK, but that's not usually what those guys mean. That's the old Western world tradition of seeing that diagram of the composer, the listener, the performer, and drawing the triangle. Well, the triangle is a neat blackboard adventure, and it's very convenient to show people who may not have thought about it, but it has absolutely nothing to do with the topic at hand.

BC: Can it communicate what *you* want it to?

HB: Yes. I believe that very strongly.

BC: So therefore it'll work. I think people approach it a different level, the "five pounds of potatoes on the grocery list" level. Why does music have to be "ennobling"? Why does it have to be thought of like a carillon ad I saw in a magazine some time ago, about music that "lifts your soul to other spheres"? One of your relatives dies, so you endow a carillon and put it in your university's tower.

HB: That's not the same thing.

BC: But the public thinks it is. Students sometimes think it is.

HB: People who want it to be true have felt so, or *they've* been told by someone who had it told to them, somewhere along the line. But I really don't have any quarrel with that. I do see what Lentz means when he talks about those last quartets of Beethoven. Choose a piece—it depends on each person. I don't think every piece communicates at the same sort of level. Sounds like a sociological talk on NET [predecessor of PBS], doesn't it? "Communication and relevance"? Nonetheless, I really believe in that *stuff*, that *something* that's there that is capable of so many extraordinary things. They're unspoken and they're so perfectly obvious, that if you have to pinpoint it to someone, they've just missed the point. You can't assume all that for everybody—maybe because I'm not interested in everybody—but friendship, love, and other things are formed, if it had to be analyzed, from a very complex bunch of stuff. There's a lot of reasons for that; among them is what makes one have a high regard for a good friend's work. That says an enormous amount about what's there. I like certain persons' pieces, for example, for the same reasons that he or she is very close to me.

BC: Suppose you like somebody's music and you can't stand him?

HB: I don't know anyone like that.

BC: Or, better, liking somebody very, very much and yet his pieces are appalling.

HB: I don't know anyone like that. There are people that I like, certainly, but like "very, very much" is a much different thing.

Notes

1. Gavin Bryars, "Harold Budd," *Contemporary Composers* (London: St James, 1992).

2. Will Johnson, "First Festival of Live-Electronic Music, 1967," in *Source: Music of the Avant-Garde, 1966–73*, ed. Larry Austin and Douglas Kahn (Berkeley: University of California Press, 2011), 116.

3. Harold Budd, Richard Maxfield, *The Oak of the Golden Dreams*, Advance Recordings FGR-16, LP, 1970.

4. Harold Budd, *Pauline Spring Piece* (1970), *Sun Pieces* (1968) and *Vittorio* (1969), *Soundings* 1 (1972): 12, 13, 14–16.

5. Bryars, "Harold Budd." Budd's return included *New Work #1*, mentioned in the interview.

6. Harold Budd quoted in Paul Tingen, "Harold Budd, American Vision," *Sound on Sound*, January 1997.

7. Harold Budd interview with Vincent Plush, Yale University Oral History of American Music, Los Angeles, May 3, 1983.

8. Harold Budd, *The Pavilion of Dreams*, Obscure Recordings 8, LP, 1978.

9. Budd, "Drinking Scotch."

10. Ibid. Budd has intermittently composed "notes"; for example, *Them Old-Fashioned Love Songs* (1992, clarinet and piano), a gift for Christopher Hobbs and Virginia Anderson.

11. Harold Budd and Jane Maru, *Jane 1–11*, Darla Records DRL 287, CD/DVD, 2013.

12. "Expression has never been an inherent property of music. That is by no means the purpose of its existence." Igor Stravinsky, *An Autobiography* (1935; reprinted London: Calder and Boyars, 1975), 163.

6 Joel Chadabe (1938–2021)

SARA HAEFELI

Joel Chadabe was just entering the most productive years of his career as a composer and pedagogue when he sat down with Barney Childs for this interview. Chadabe was teaching at the then SUNY Albany (now the University at Albany) and had just written some of his first pieces for live instrumentalist or instrumentalists and electronics, including *Echoes* and *Shadows and Lines,* both composed in 1972. Chadabe was emerging in the new music scene as a significant innovator in electronic music and is recognized today as a pioneer in the development of what he calls interactive music systems and interactive composition. He is the founder of the Electronic Music Foundation (EMF) and is the recipient of numerous awards, including the Society for Electro-Acoustic Music in the United States (SEAMUS) Lifetime Achievement Award.

In 1966, Chadabe purchased his first modular synthesizers and the next year he commissioned Robert Moog to design and build the Coordinated Electronic Music Studio (CEMS) at SUNY Albany, the design of which he discussed in a 1967 *Perspectives of New Music* article.[1] The CEMS system included "an extended array of sound-generating and processing modules, an automated matrix mixer, and a digital clock," as well as "a bank of eight analog sequencers with customized logic hardware for running them synchronously, asynchronously, in succession, or in any combination."[2] At the time it was the largest collection of Moog sequencers, and it enabled Chadabe to process sounds created in performance and route them to a sound reinforcement system.

Chadabe created his 1972 piece *Echoes* so that the percussionist Jan Williams could interact with his own sounds as they were transformed and broadcasted throughout the performance space. Chadabe describes the interaction of the performer with their own sounds as a conversation: "If we think of the first percussion sound as something that is 'said' by the percussionist to begin the conversation, the sound as it emerges from the loudspeakers is a 'reply' to which the percussionist, in turn, replies, and so it goes throughout a conversational performance."[3] Writing for *Grove Music Online*, Burt Levy and Gregory Reish describe Chadabe's music as sometimes "rhythmically complex timbral kaleidoscopes" and sometimes as "catchy melodies in jaunty rhythms."[4]

Given Chadabe's musical and technological interests, one might be surprised to learn that he studied at Yale with Elliott Carter. But early innovators in tape music had a significant influence on him, especially John Cage, Earle Brown, Morton Feldman, and Christian Wolff, all of whom participated in the Project for Music for Magnetic Tape in New York in 1951. In 1971, Chadabe organized a performance of Cage's multimedia, computer-assisted composition *HPSCHD* (1969) at SUNY Albany and has continued to be devoted to the piece, either organizing or taking a significant role in almost a dozen performances. In a letter to Harold Hersch regarding a performance of *HPSCHD* that Hersch was planning for San Francisco in 1972, Cage wrote that Chadabe "was the last person to solve the technical problems" for the piece, of which there are many, and that he "might save you some time and worries."[5]

Cage's identification of Chadabe as a "problem solver" seems apt given that he approaches composition like many experimentalists, namely, as creative inquiry, or, simply, as research. Chadabe has consistently promoted the exploration of the creative and social potential of technology (in the creation of new instruments or new approaches to performance) and new applications of technology, including the documentation of environmental sounds.

Echoes of Chadabe's engagement with Cage—and particularly with *HPSCHD*—are found throughout the interview as Chadabe and Childs discuss issues central to Cage's philosophy, including subjects such as *process, material, form, theater, notation, participation*, and *technology*. But Chadabe is not a blind devotee; some of his musical thinking deviates significantly from that of Cage. For example, Chadabe's description of process is different from Cage's (Cage would never speak of "rules"), and although Chadabe is devoted to discovering new sounds he is not interested in indeterminacy as an essential condition.

Many of the issues discussed in the interview have remained central to Chadabe's life and work. For example, his discussion of the end of modernity, and of compositions as bounded, framed "masterpieces," is a subject he returns to in a 2004 article for the journal *Organised Sound*.[6] And the idea that contemporary musical languages are often in conversation with innovations in science—specifically innovations in quantum physics—is a subject he often returns to, most recently in a May 2019 talk given at the Centre for Interdisciplinary Research in Music Media and Technology at McGill University.[7]

It is clear from the interview that Chadabe is a dedicated and thoughtful teacher. Many of the issues raised in the interview about professionalism and the role of the university in the arts seem as fresh and pressing today as they were in the 1970s. Chadabe notes that one of the benefits of teaching electronic music is that there is "no pedantic academic tradition. . . . No textbooks, no pedagogical methods." This is no longer the case, and ironically Chadabe's own 1996 monograph *Electric Sound: the Past and Promise of Electronic Music* is today one of the most widely read texts and his music is part of the pedagogical canon of electronic music.

Joel Chadabe: Interview

BARNEY CHILDS: Not many people into electronics to the degree you are also write pieces for performers. You're not sold one way or another; you do both.

JOEL CHADABE: I'm sold both ways. The concerns of technology do not need to be related to mediums; they're more related to structures. It's very difficult to find a solution to instrumental writing that isn't part of the language of the past. In a funny way, almost everything I hear for instruments seems very tired—with exceptions, of course. The twelve-tone school, the European instrumental style, seems to have completed and turned back upon itself, which is why I mostly write for instruments in connection with electronics.

BC: So it's simultaneous.

JC: When you work with instruments and electronics, you're making a drama of mediums; you're putting a human player into a technical situation. Pieces written for instruments and tape in the classic studio sense are very often juxtapositions of media. For example, Jacob Druckman's piece for trombone is man-against-machine. [Mario] Davidovsky's pieces are the tape elaborating on what man does to greater extents of opposition or cooperation. But it's always a definite relationship between the human player and the technological means. It still is: I'm able to work now on pieces for instruments and electronics because I've found a way of handling that particular problem that interests me.

BC: How much has the recent rise of very strong virtuoso instrumentalists had to do with this?

JC: Most of my instrumental writing lately has not been very difficult technically, partly because the virtuoso school seems to be so tired. The dazzling things that many instruments do seem to come out of orchestration books.

BC: You were talking about the dramatism of the player against technology. Do you conceive your scores in a sense of dramatism like Carter?

JC: My music now is very different from Elliott's. In his pieces, Carter determines each event, works out the details very carefully. When he's finished, he's presenting an entire proposition that is worked out in every aspect. I usually think of a piece in terms of a process. "Process" is a word that's used in different ways and by different people to mean different things. I mean the rules of a game: once they're established, then I set up the details in a composition. For example, when I'm writing for an instrument in electronics, I think what kind of process is the electronics doing? What kind of process is the instrument doing? Then how do they combine?

BC: In a tape piece, where you control the rules of the game and move within these rules, are you taking over the instrumentalist's function?

JC: That's just an electronic process.

BC: How much are you in control of the process?

JC: Completely.

BC: At what levels? How much pre-compositionally are you in control, and how much immediately are you in control?

JC: Let's talk about automation, because that's the name of the game. By analogy, if the first level of automation is building a car, what does that mean? The first level of automation is no automation. You build a car with tools with your own two hands; you go out there and hammer away, shaping metals. You decide every detail about the car, put it in place, and decide the color it's going to be painted, etc. In the second stage of automation, you build the machine that builds the car. The machine does exactly what you would do, except that the machine has thirty hands where you have two hands. This is automation for efficiency. You could put it another way: memory automation. It's like player-piano rolls: computer memories that tick things off more quickly than a secretary could do. I am doing none of this, because memory automation is the use of technology as a tool for efficiency.

The next step of automation is process automation. In this, whatever machine you're using calculates. You present the problem, stated in terms of the rules of the process. The machine then gives you the specifics. For example, in a computer graphic, different lengths of lines were fed into the computer—widths of lines, angles of departure—and the computer was told to scramble them randomly. When I'm working, I decide the materials that are going to be used and how the control systems will operate, and that defines the rules of the game, and then they just go by themselves.

BC: What struck me about your article in the ASUC [American Society of University Composers] *Proceedings* was the concept of levels of process.[8] There were two or three levels of process working themselves through the apparatus, each one of which was independently operative.

JC: Absolutely. I would call it "scale": the same process should be manifested in different scales.

BC: How many of these scales are going to be audible in the sense of listener-extractable, or does that matter?

JC: They're all audible, all sensed. It has a lot to do with perception. When we look at something, it's important to notice the texture and say, "How was that done?" If it looks like it must have been constructed, contrived, put together by an artist, then it's memory automation or it's not automated at all. If you conclude that no artist really could have done it that way, then it's process automation. That computer graphic has to be process automation. The idea of a process for me has a great deal to do with grace. I think of it as being very effortless, easy, elegant, and very lyric.

BC: The device for doing dominates setting up the material. You *hear* ahead of time, rather than generating solely a paper process.

JC: Yes. In the work I do, you're always working in the presence of the sound.

BC: Paper process—does this bother you? Too often pieces today are judged on somebody being able to articulate how he did it. When you read an analysis, you say, "Wow! he's done this, he's done that," and the actual sound follows as a kind of trailer.

JC: It's terribly boring, because of all the program notes we used to read, five, six years ago dealing with a certain placement of a hexachord, very rarely describing what the piece was about. Program notes that truly elucidate the piece are one thing; program notes that don't are quite another. It's a whole different aesthetic—twelve-tone music, serialism. It had a lot to do with electronic music, but now it's very much different.

BC: Was thinking about electronic music a step back [from serialism]?

JC: Not at all. It ran a parallel course with electronic music; it very often cross-fertilized, but it's not that one thing actively helped the other. It's no coincidence that the serialists thought of separate notes being defined by rows that gave qualities of pitches, dynamics, attacks, or loudness. That means really that a sound is defined in terms of amplifiers, filters, oscillators: all of these separate components working together to form a system. It's a concept of systems that doesn't hold true today.

BC: Why not? We have many more systems available to us now than we ever did. It's easier to lean on them as a kind of aesthetic. Some electronic composers do. Instead of a realization of a serial apparatus, people say here's the electronic realization of these various levels of process I'm concerned with. These tend to stand for something musical. In having various levels of operation, is there not an attempt to make this replace another kind of musical thinking? To say the electronic processing on these various levels is what's happening, what counts, that's my rationale for making a piece. Instead of just saying certain serial apparatuses are those things which, when set in operation, make a piece.

JC: Yes, there's a similarity. There's a great deal of process automation in serialism. The idea of setting up different rows, right? The first step is the selection of the materials, then the arrangement of materials, and then it's automated.

BC: You get to the end, plug it in and Lo! There's the notation and the realized piece of music.

JC: There are several real differences. The first is, what is the musical material? Serialists think of it as notes, and I think of it as sound. That, you might say, is a difference of scale. I don't mean musical scale on certain steps, I mean the level at which you approach a sound. Instead of taking a sound as a fixed entity, I'm concerned about something lower than that: how sounds change. In other words, waveform changes; everything comes from that.

BC: What happens to pitch?

JC: Most electronic sounds don't have clearly defined pitches, so it's something that can be worked with.

BC: But many electronic composers stand by the pitch class system.

JC: That's just imposing an old aesthetic on a new medium.

BC: Pitch has become subordinate through the use of these means?

JC: Yes, but it is not an arbitrary judgment, it comes from the material itself, one of the things that electronics has opened up at the end of different kinds of developments. Cage, for example, created so many new sounds simply by noticing sounds that were around and admitting them into the world of music. If then you try to categorize sounds, what a violin plays seems very limited in terms of all possible sounds. How *do* you categorize sounds? You can categorize them in terms of spectrum types, for example. Then that harmonic spectrum that we associate with pitch music is one out of four or five different sounds, and by no means accounts for the sounds that are around us. With electronic music, curiously, the most interesting sounds are not [part of the] harmonic spectrum, are not completely periodic waveforms. For this reason, to limit oneself as an electronic composer to periodic waveforms is a very arbitrary limitation and has nothing to do with the potential of the medium.

BC: But working with instruments at the same time you are stuck with the pitch continuum.

JC: It's a big problem. My interest isn't in the relationship of pitches to non-pitches (sounds); my interest is in the drama between the two mediums. If anything, I wish instrumentalists could play instruments that don't play pitches.

BC: Do you write for the instruments as though they couldn't play pitches?

JC: It varies.

BC: Getting back to dramatism, what should a piece mean in dramatic terms?

JC: It's not a question of what a piece should mean, it's what a piece *is*. In other words, if anyone does anything in the arts, they are a model of a kind of activity. Mind you, that's not always true. In many compositions, for example, the idea is not to pay any attention to the performers.

BC: In existing compositions?

JC: Most of the compositions from the '50s.

BC: Has this changed?

JC: Very much so. John Cage and many other composers are very concerned with the activities that the performer does.

BC: That gets you to theater, doesn't it? How much are you concerned with that?

JC: As theater, not at all. I'm not at all concerned with making a stage spectacle, but I'm very aware of what a player is doing on stage in relation to other things happening in a musical situation.

BC: With a performer you are stuck with a set of theatricalities, willy-nilly. With a cellist or an oboe player, certain things must be done.

JC: Taking a very conventionally notated score by an older composer, for example, a performer just reads the music. To interpret that from the point of view of the performer's activity, you would say that he's being told in every conceivable rotational way what to do, and he's doing his best to do them and to add whatever he can. You might picture that as a kind of totalitarianism. Obviously that's not the case and it's funny to think of it in that way. Clearly, in most of that music, we're not meant to watch the performer; we're meant to listen to the music—the performer is only a vehicle. But recently it's become much more a focus of attention, to be concerned about the very activity that the performer is bound to on stage, and to think in terms of that kind of activity.

Again, we come back to a type of automation, because the whole idea of a process automation is that there are guidelines within which freedom occurs, whether it's automated by the machine or the performer does it. In other words, the rules are set up and then the rest of it just spins out, creating all the detailed events. Many pieces by John Cage, Lukas Foss, and various other composers do just that.

BC: How much does that freedom, or the need for it, operate in the things you do?

JC: I don't know.

BC: What is the role of the performer, then? In terms of scales, is he going to have to rethink himself, musically, before he can play?

JC: The performance of new music is in a very problematic stage. Not from any professional point of view—there's a great deal going on, which is very good—but from the point of view of the role of the performer. It seems that most things that performers do are no longer fresh, that the whole gambit has been run. This does not mean that every possibility has been covered; it means that there's a significant change occurring now. The old issues have in a certain sense been discarded and that the new issues are not yet clear. So a new language or a fresh kind of attitude has not yet come about. There are many remarkable examples, though, that might point the way. Wanting to search for new sounds further complicates the whole thing.

I first collaborated with Lukas Foss on a piece called *MAP* [(*Musicians at Play*), *a Musical Game*, 1970], where the players reacted in certain different ways to several tapes and played a variety of instruments in very unconventional ways. That was a very refreshing, very unusual performance situation. It's not been notated yet; that is, there is no particular type of notation to denote those kinds of fluid relationships. Perhaps there's a great deal yet to do with working with performers in creating a piece without a notation.

BC: Is this because of irremediable basic inadequacies in notation? Or are composers going to demand that notation keep up?

JC: For one thing, notations tend to fix things; for another, the conventional notations we know have to do with older kinds of music.

BC: So notation must be reviewed?

JC: The notation will follow the music. I don't think the problem is with the notation; the problem is a lot more conceptual.

BC: Here [at SUNY Albany] you work largely with undergraduates. What can an undergraduate gain from this thinking? Is it natural for young people today to agree with composers, or is it something they have to live with for a while?

JC: I haven't verbalized these things before. The trick to working with undergraduates is that I don't push any ideas; I create the opportunity within which we can all work together. I often regret that because I'm there on the scene working so hard, I very often provide a model that is imitated. [But] none of my students write music that sounds anything like mine. It is very important that an undergraduate learn enough different things so that they can choose their own way, so I can't teach them any one particular theory. I can only make them aware of everything that is going on and let them find their own solutions to their own problems. I underteach as a teacher.

BC: Are you happy with the results?

JC: Absolutely. I go increasingly more in this direction because my experience shows me that it produces more professionalism. Many of the undergraduates here are equal to the professionals that I've seen elsewhere in composition.

BC: Why is that?

JC: Because they care so much about the results of what they are doing, because they are not stupid.

BC: There are professionals by implication who really don't care . . . does this bother you?

JC: No, I think it's terrific!

BC: You've spent a lot of time in Europe. Do we still have a dichotomy of attitude between what's happening there and what's happening here?

JC: Much of the music in Europe that I hear comes in one way or another from the '50s.

[*Missing page.*]

JC [ON CAGE]: I know of no students here who have purposely tried to imitate him, but at the same time like his music very much.

BC: What do they learn from it?

JC: That music can be free and doesn't need to pay attention to the neuroses they bring in. Much of what Cage stands for is that it's enjoyable. It's the lightness, the grace, the excellent quality, the flair for sound, the fun, and the humor.

BC: How about Cage's concern for process?

JC: It foreshadows what I'm talking about: Cage automates in exactly that same way. Lately he has been doing it with the *I Ching*. He determines specific events with the *I Ching*, the exact materials he's going to work with and to what he's going to apply the *I Ching*.

BC: To these younger people, he is still somebody to whom serious attention is paid. There's no regarding him as they might regard [Anton] Webern—as historical.

JC: No, they regard him as very present on the musical scene.

BC: How about your colleagues, not necessarily at Albany: do you think this regard is shared?

JC: No. To many traditionally trained musicians and "professional" musicians, Cage's ideas are too divorced from the rules of nineteenth-century music. What he stands for is too opposite to the mainstream of traditional music to be easily accepted by musicians. Furthermore, musicians usually think in terms of the musical world, and that's a mistake in dealing with Cage's music.

BC: And they see it as unjustifiable?

JC: Ideas that don't fit into previously thought-up categories.

BC: You're getting into the whole realm of ideas. Are the sounds the result of ideas, or do the ideas dominate the sounds? That's important.

JC: The more I work in music, the less musical I become, in a way. As a general trend in all fields, it's the interrelationship between many different things. It's very difficult for me to think of "a" professional musical world. More and more I see the word "professional," not meaning high standards of excellence, but rather activity that had nothing to do with the general problems involved. Maybe it's because composers read more magazines. It has nothing to do with musicality; it has a lot to do with types of activity that aren't exclusively music. I find it very hard to think of music as a thing apart from kinetic sculpture or other processes. For example, some traffic lights on a boulevard in Brooklyn sense traffic and record accordingly, so that when traffic is light, the lights are more likely to be red, and when traffic is heavy they are more likely to be green. Processes like these become models in art and music. It has much to do with my general feelings about technology: one of the crucial problems that bring about changes in thought that are becoming of extreme importance.

BC: Is the increased technology reflected through computer composition?

JC: Much computer composition that I've heard seems to be very naive musically, but it's very natural to use a new medium to say older things at the beginning.

The way technology will change our basic perceptions is not yet completely clear. *That's* where the real problem is, and *that's* where the real change is going to take place. It's not a question of tools; it's the way these things will change our basic perceptions of the world. Hopefully technology will someday make politics obsolete soon.

BC: What do you do with a bright young student who feels this compulsion, but doesn't know how to do it? It's common to wish to participate, to be aware. How can they get into it?

JC: It's important for teachers not to conceptualize their students as receptacles to be filled with knowledge, but rather to create a situation in which learning can take place. There are two ingredients: the ability to participate and do whatever professional activity is involved, and constant models. It's very important to have people coming up to the university to lecture and do concerts—a constant parade of personalities, different kinds of activity—and to have a place to talk to the students. Ideally, a university should be a gigantic entertainment center where concerts, plays, and exhibitions are going on. Classrooms ideally should be places to discuss this and its historical implications, to learn the skill to do things in the same field of action, and hopefully be left enough alone to develop a sense of the professional; that is, what it means to do a good job.

BC: That's the hardest thing of all to get across, to have pride in what one is doing.

JC: It's more than that. When a student doesn't feel that it's his job, he feels that he's the teacher's agent: he has no responsibility for the act and the teacher does. The student has to do it himself. One learns by doing things and one finds the answers to questions once the questions arise. It's very important to make those questions arise through activity. If you throw a student into a TV studio and say, "Now put on a program," he's going to ask a lot of questions.

BC: Here they have a chance to do this in a way they may not in other places—putting on concerts, preparing your own or somebody else's work.

JC: It could happen anywhere. Albany is hardly a hotbed of experimental education.

BC: What about the student who is not going to be a professional composer?

JC: He should be treated exactly the same way.

BC: What about other things he'll learn in a standard academic musical education? A lot of people put down the academic disciplines—analysis, theory, counterpoint—as stricture, "detractments." What can the student gain from this orientation?

JC: It's not that a student shouldn't learn about counterpoint, harmony, and tonality; they should know that. The question is the way it's put in teaching. A student is likely to spend three years studying harmony, a year studying counterpoint, several years in analysis of tonal music and the performance of tonal music, and then perhaps one semester in contemporary music. That student will come out of that school having overlearned tonality, and feel ill at ease with twentieth-century music. It's doing a great disservice to the student in practical terms, as well as, in my feeling, to education. That part of the profession is finishing; it is no longer possible for a concert pianist to play nineteenth-century literature exclusively and make a living off it. One must understand the problems of the contemporary and its time.

BC: Why write music? One doesn't make a living at it, it's not the kind of thing that the society wants: why continue?

JC: I write music mostly for curiosity: to discover new kinds of sounds, new concepts of structure. Much of my music long ago shows a certain naïveté; in many cases I simply wasn't aware that other people had done it.

BC: You had to reinvent the wheel.

JC: That's why it's so important to have an extremely good knowledge of contemporary literature, so that you don't solve other people's problems. Wallace Stevens said that his idea of paradise was starting where the other people left off. I'm mostly concerned about exploration.

BC: It's more than simply a solving process for you, isn't it? There's more in the immediacy of sound as you make it. Any well-trained graduate student, like the monkeys and the typewriters, can write music. He can solve set problems, but he's not going to be musical.

JC: It always comes back to talent, and to what Louis Armstrong said, "It don't mean a thing if it ain't got that swing." That's part of the problem: not to approach the thing from an academic point of view. It's an exploration of the way things tend to work. Many people view music as a very isolated and specialized language; they think in exclusively musical terms, solving exclusively musical problems. I'm not so concerned about that. The arts have developed in two different ways. One is a kind of historical development of a grammar in the arts that's handed down from teacher to pupil, and it goes on for generations. It's true in all the arts. Cubism would have been unimaginable without Cézanne, for example. Babbitt's style would have been unimaginable without Schoenberg's, [Pierre] Boulez without Webern. We take these things so much for granted as one thing developing from the other, yet it had to happen that way. More than artists or other art fields, musicians are historically oriented, always studying their own language. Much of musical education has to do with this idea of a specialized language.

BC: Do you think they've become historical determinists?

JC: At least they're so imbued with this historical concept that they lose all perspective of their present art. Another way that the arts develop is a certain kind of contemporaneity. A composer decides to do something that has little to do with the historical language as it comes to him. Feldman talked about that when he used the phrase "stepping out of history" to describe his own music. That kind of reaction to history was neither a rebellion, nor was it an acceptance; he just had nothing to do with history. I suppose, in a sense of continuity, that Feldman more or less achieved that. Except Feldman is also a very specialized musical thinker; when he talked about "stepping out of history," he talked about it only in musical terms. I'm not so concerned with purely musical terms. I try to be a general artist who works in music as a medium.

BC: And in what terms? Carter was often using nonmusical models (I don't want to say programs) for musical structures from cinema, painting, literature, from immediacy of living everyday situations. These are reflected or refracted into the music. I take it you are thinking in the same terms.

JC: Yes, except that the specifics are somewhat different. They weren't when I was studying with Carter. Carter is one of the most interesting people I've ever met, and one of the most knowledgeable. What's interesting about Elliott and his music is that he really has not been in the professional world in the sense that some composers have. He has purposely remained aloof from the "specialized language" concept of music; he worked out his own absolutely unique style.

BC: What is style? Can we legitimately talk about it?

JC: I suppose that style is the unique idea of a particular composer's personality, expressed in his music.

BC: You are not concerned solely with music or writing just for sounds; there's more to it.

JC: Yes. Also, if Elliott Carter were solely concerned with the specialized language of music, his recent pieces would not have developed as they have. His concepts of form, of motion, of time, of the way things work in relationship to one another, parallel many concepts in science. If one knew on what level to make them, one could find comparisons between the relationships that quantum mechanics tries to fix between different kinds of changing quantities, and Carter's music. One of the marvelous things about a piece of music is that it presents, simultaneously, all of these details and relationships and at the same time a total universe. It defines its whole world in which it exists. I find that remarkable about music in general. Carter's *Concerto for Orchestra*, for example, is not only extremely complex in the relationships between the instruments, but it also has an overall comprehensive simplicity of one simple sound.

BC: Are you suggesting that the closer we stay to a kind of Schenkerianism, the better off we are in writing and analyzing?

JC: If you mean by [Heinrich] Schenker the idea of a hierarchical form, no. I'm interpolating from my own point of view, but as I think of that hierarchical form, I don't see recent concepts of form in the same category. To speak of a form existing on different scales is not to speak of a hierarchical system. Schenker's concept of form was very industrial; it's like a mass-production line, like a factory. The nature of that form is that separate subsystems—each of which has its own, different components, all of which cooperatively together form a subsystem—cooperate together to form an overall system, and all these systems combine to form a supersystem. I wouldn't say this concept of form applies today. Today, if anything, it's not thinking in terms of specific entities that relate together as subsystems, but rather of different activities, all of which are different aspects of the same process.

BC: You're making it a dynamism, rather than a fixed set of relationships.

JC: It's change oriented rather than material oriented. The question isn't what material is being used, the question is how does it change. And the question isn't how does this material and that material fit together into *one* self-contained system, the question is what are the rules by which they operate, that make them form as part of the same process. Schenker's system is extremely centralized. It's a concept of a large corporation or a government. The type of structure that I'm observing is completely *de*centralized, where the most general rules of process apply to all the different multitudinous aspects.

BC: Given this process of change, alteration, or organic development, doesn't this admit something that is fundamentally alien to the whole functional nineteenth-century bag? This questions the idea of permanence. We can now admit that impermanence is acceptable, that we are not trying to make an eternal masterpiece.

JC: "Masterpiece" is a very complicated word. For one thing, it's the very end of a period of science and of art that we're seeing now; it's the very end of the development of a whole language.

BC: Are you thinking of it in terms of cycles?

JC: Yes, or large-scale historical periods. The science that started in the period of the Renaissance is ending today.

BC: You started it that early? You're not starting with Newton?

JC: The whole idea is the causality of this approach that science presents. For example, in the "if, then" proposition, the point is if that everything comes to a conclusion, and the music also comes to a conclusion, it's what I would call a directional reasoning.

BC: Do you agree with [Leonard] Meyer when he calls these things teleological, the goal-directedness of music?[9]

JC: Absolutely. We've reached the ultimate degeneration of that way of thinking, by accepting all of history in that same way. It's no accident that we've become so historically minded now, because naturally in terms of the "if, then" proposition, we are at the "then" part and that's the "if," so we arrive at the present. This makes us look backwards into history and create "masterpieces" that are historically oriented. Not only is the reverence of Beethoven and Mozart as great composers absolutely Philistinism, not only is it the greatest disservice to these composers to call them "great," but it's extremely important to understand that it's these last few generations that have created this mass of masterworks. There's no God-given truth about their compositions being masterworks.

BC: If Beethoven did not exist, we would have had to invent him.

JC: That's another way of putting it. So now you ask about masterworks today. There are, in a much simpler sense. A masterwork is any piece of music that so elegantly, simply, and graciously sums up a certain idea—the piece that states it most clearly is a masterpiece. Now whether that piece endures throughout history is another problem, and it's linked a lot with the notation, symbolically.

BC: Roy Harris is quoted as saying that Webern's work is no good because the pieces are too short.

JC: That's absurd, because every piece of music creates its own idea. It's absurd for another reason. One of the peculiar aspects of tonal music is that it has a beginning and an end; that's an extremely important point. It's like pictures with frames. I don't know if you've observed by chance that, in museums, masterworks of the eighteenth and seventeenth centuries usually have very large, ornate frames. This somehow seems very suited to these paintings as part of the whole presentation.

BC: The boundary is part of the whole painting.

JC: These paintings are absolutely separate from life; they have beginnings and endings. So does Beethoven, so does Webern, because after all what Webern did is to miniaturize Beethoven's forms. Today, pieces don't have beginnings and ends, paintings don't have heavy frames—they seem to spill off their canvas into the rest of the room.

BC: How about the symbolic, linguistic, aspect of notation?

JC: It's a practical problem today in terms of preserving a great deal of electronic music for the future; tape can't be expected to stay in very good shape for much longer than ten to twenty years.

BC: That's the impermanence thing.

JC: Yes, but it's not aesthetic, it's in terms of practicalities.

BC: I was thinking more in terms of symbology, in the sense that structures grow out of styles, and styles grow out of symbols. In the eighteenth century, the whole world appeared in a set of rational symbols, hence musical shapes, hence musical expression, hence painting with a frame.

JC: When a student studies traditional notation, they're bound by that language. A problem now is that there is no language to study for electronic music—no theory, no notation.

BC: A lot of it is a-notational. Trying to write for performers as though they were non-pitch-limited is part of it. You're trying to move them off the game board into a new area where they can feel at ease, just as you can with electronic sound.

What is the role of Cage and others in thinking about musical structure? How badly does this damage eighteenth-, nineteenth-century concepts of the fancy frame and the picture?

JC: No one person can damage anything. Cage is Cage as a person. Cage could only have come up with his views because he lived at a time in history. Cage tuned himself in to some other aspect of the world than the traditional musical language he studied with Schoenberg, consequently making everyone aware of the use of the rest of the world as a musical resource. He was the first in a long train, but there are many different ways of going about it.

BC: What is the implication of admitting that there is impermanence, formally or structurally, that there is alterability, in terms of a whole artistic system?

JC: It has to do with the accessibility of art and the way people understand it. To the extent that people understand the art, they do not believe in masterpieces. It's very hard to find a contemporary artist who treats Rembrandt as a contemporary musician treats Beethoven; there's simply no emotional involvement. Clearly, Rembrandt was a terrific artist; clearly, the way he worked has very little to do with the issues of our time, and it's simply not an emotional problem. To the extent that people understand music, they'll enjoy it, they'll keep on creating it. The idea of composers being great is clearly an unfortunate attitude that rests upon ignorance. If there's any kind of a trend, I think it's toward participation. It would be very nice if a group of people in a neighborhood got together and decided they wanted to have a concert series.

BC: Henry Brant was trying to do that in Bennington.

JC: That large-scale participation in planning concerts and putting them on would be marvelous.

BC: People at a concert are really watching themselves hearing the music. They know that it's a masterpiece; there's a big printed multipage program that refers to it in that way. They don't hear any sounds.

JC: I'm sure of that. They're so self-conscious of being in the presence of dead masters that they are completely unaware of the music. I've witnessed this at the Metropolitan Opera, where people sit with serious expressions through the funniest scenes of *The Marriage of Figaro*. The Metropolitan Opera production reinforces that view because they're staged so badly, the theater doesn't get across anything.

BC: Even now—and it's very late in this century to still be clinging to this soggy log—so many of us, even of our generation, are still accultured to this way of listening. It's very difficult for many to get out of.

JC: It comes down to structure, Barney. This idea of directional form in composition began to go out of fashion around 1914. Around 1920, things changed very dramatically; that's when most people lost touch with art. Still, the arts had a great deal to do with that direction. Many artists used the same objects in their work, just out of perspective, placed in different juxtapositions. Only very recently, different alternatives—especially in technological art—are happening, where people can relate to [art] differently and tune in in a different way.

BC: A new ground of perception is being provided for them, handily enough to replace one that they were not used to.

JC: I've noticed the same thing happening in music. People whose tastes in instrumental music are very conservative might well like the most advanced electronic music.

BC: Someone into electronics said it was scary to get twenty- and twenty-one-year-old kids who are aesthetically at the stage he is now, but just have skipped all the previous steps and have just plugged in. They haven't paid any dues in the sense of having to restructure their whole set of beliefs in terms of the new. They accepted it easily; they just go "Pow," and there it is.

JC: It's happening. One of the nice things about electronic music right now, and technological arts in general, is that it requires no previous artistic experience. This is marvelous for education.

BC: Equally marvelous is that it demands a very immediate and precipitous development of a personal aesthetic in its own terms. Since electronic music as it now stands in a popularizing sense is way ahead of what it was five years ago, is this a good sign? Should we have nickel-dime synthesizers in every high school?

JC: Absolutely. Many people think electronic music is elitist, and quite the contrary is true. It's the most nonelitist, because it requires no previous musical education. If a kid wants to play in an orchestra, he has to have studied the instrument before; with electronics, he can be making sounds right away and begin with musical problems on whatever level.

BC: The musical problems that he is forced into would be the screen, then. In other words, there isn't fifteen years at the conservatory as a barrier.

JC: And there's no pedantic academic tradition. One exciting thing about any new field is that there are no textbooks, no pedagogical methods. That is a terrific advantage.

BC: Technologically, what happens next? I'm not asking you to make any crystal-ball statements. One thing about electronic music has been that, no matter where you plug in, you still have to run like hell to stay in the same place, because there are so many radical changes, things metamorphosing like crazy.

JC: Another way of putting that is that there's so much work to be done with technical understanding. In a way, our problems with technological arts are the same as human problems of understanding relationships in a technological society—that's why they're so valuable. Going into any problem in depth is difficult for any one person. Right now there's a lot of simultaneous activity going on in different places; everyone's trying to work out his own problem. Hopefully a good electronic music teacher makes people aware that the machine problems are not exclusively musical problems. If someone can operate a computer to make music, then he knows how the FBI uses that computer to store information.

BC: Or Kresge's [now Kmart] uses it to bill customers.

JC: In short, using these technological tools in an art form is a great deal.

BC: Are you standing behind this as an extra benefit? That music is a handmaiden of technology? This familiarity with the way the world goes is a bonus? We're treading very perilously closely to a doctrine of music as political or technological polemicism.

JC: I don't really think that. I do think that music is bound up with other things in the world, that it is not a specialized language. The study of applications of technology in music is no different than the study of applications of technology in other things. It's just that *this* is its particular outlet. Furthermore, a composer should remain solidly in touch with the rest of the world as he writes. And scholarships, taken into seclusion, isolation, and so on, are detrimental.

BC: I still think I have the tattered remains of a point, because in all the arts in this country there has been a small maverick tradition of isolates: painters, poets, composers.

JC: But these people weren't isolated from life—they were isolated from the profession.

BC: Very good. You've answered my question.

JC: Ives saw the profession as being isolated; it was and still is, which is my point. The musical profession views music as a specialized esoteric kind of language.

BC: That's the old high-priest thing, where you study twenty years and you can then step up to where the masters are.

JC: Part and parcel of calling Beethoven great. One should be very profane when dealing with great composers—never vulgar, never discourteous, but always profane.

BC: That fits perfectly. In a sense even the most eccentric is still immediately in touch with living in a way that a lot of professional hacks are not.

JC: That's why they were so eccentric; they left the professional world to embrace life.

BC: What are we to do as composers with the professional world now? Someone invented the university music department, from which most of us take our lifeblood. Many people think it's the worst thing in the world that we have to be chained to this.

JC: It's how you conceptualize the university. If one views the university as an ivory tower in which scholars can refine their sensibilities and develop specialized languages, not only Latin and Greek but also music, that's true. It's very detrimental to any kind of vitality in the arts. I don't view the university that way at all, although too often they are that way. Universities in this country are extremely important social institutions, partly because of their educational value. But a great deal of their educational value stems from the real importance of the university, which is that it's the only place where a noncommercial activity can take place. In that way universities are terrifically important to the profession at large. It's extremely important that real research, real exploration that has no commercial rewards, be done at a university, because it's the only place that that can happen. It's not a preparation for anything; it *is* an important social function in itself. Since I myself am very noncommercially oriented, a university is very strongly my field of action. At the same time, I don't have the slightest feeling that I'm in an ivory tower, that it's tame, reclusive, or oppressive.

BC: Many feel it's oppressive. They say my business is writing music, and I don't want to go to committee meetings, I don't want to teach theory. I want to do my thing.

JC: Many people outside are doing things that they don't want to do. I guess there's a certain amount of everyone's life that is spent in doing unpleasant things, but if those things make one's life, it's unfortunate. I find that an extremely selfish point of view, though, and perhaps these people shouldn't be at universities.

BC: But they can't be elsewhere, because they're ill-equipped: they cannot go out and starve.

JC: I understand, but even so perhaps they shouldn't be at the university. I don't have a whole hell of a lot of sympathy for them. I do consider it very selfish, because these people don't contribute anything to the university scene.

BC: Given the university system as it stands, it seems that there is still a lack of communication among composers, which is largely geographical: there is a West Coast thing and an East Coast thing. But in the west, we don't really know what you are doing, and you don't really know what I am doing. This is bad. There should be some way that all of us can take from one another in a dialogue.

JC: I agree. A lot of traveling, exchanging visits, is very important.

BC: Exchanging scores and tapes has helped, lots of mail action. And travel. The university helps, because it does allow people to go. You get people here. What was the reason you used? It was important, because the students ought to "bull" with these guys, not just hear them standing on the podium. Here's a person from X State, miles away, that the students may have read about and have never seen live. Even hearing him live on the podium is something else, but if they can drink with him . . .

JC: The whole point is to foster informal contact. We do it personally; we have parties when people come to town.

BC: This is a benefit. Our whole orientation has got to be different than, let's say, a European country where since 1250 there has always been one center of culture to which everyone goes. When I was at Oxford, all the talented young people went to London. That was where it was, that was where you got into a kind of aristocracy. There were half a dozen cities that did it. Here we don't have that.

JC: Here the trend is very much towards decentralization away from the big cities, and it's very healthy.

BC: We have to face a whole new approach to thinking about music. It's no longer what a New York, a Chicago, or a New Orleans critic writes.

JC: Critics in general are very poor and are extremely detrimental to the understanding of music. They foster the old attitude of mentioning what's good and not good. They don't explain the musician to the public—they evaluate the music.

BC: I've always felt it would be lovely to have a concert with no composers listed on the program. The critics would be stone dead as to what to say. All the punch cards would not come down; they would have to talk about it musically, they couldn't plug in the clichés.

JC: Critics are terrible and doing a great disservice to music. The quality of musical criticism is extremely low in comparison to the quality of film, drama, literary, and art criticism.

BC: Especially in art criticism. This has its own dangers: in some art magazines you have a whole critical establishment which feeds upon itself. And in some learned disciplines, in anthropology, the reviews in journals are part of the literature to a degree that they are not in other disciplines.

JC: Much of the burden falls upon the composer to write critical articles about music. It's an interesting kind of situation to be in; I don't think it's paralleled to such an extent in the other arts. I don't know of any artist who's written books about his art in the way that many composers have. And composers do it largely by the default of critics understanding music. Also, the critics that I know of don't have composers as friends; in short, they're not working in the composer's musical world. This also tends to support the idea that critics judge music. I often find [Harold] Schonberg's statements in the *Times* irresponsible. Sometimes I agree with him, but often for different reasons. His dislike of serialism . . .

BC: Don't composers perpetuate this to some degree? Because of this decentralization, one tends to team up with the home club. There are still patches in the west in which the mention of the names Columbia and Princeton are anathema. And I'm sure it works backwards. I don't know the east well enough, but I'm sure there are people in New York who feel that anything west of Philadelphia is a raging wilderness.

JC: In a certain way New York is a very provincial city; much of the activity that occurs in New York occurs nowhere else in the world. In many ways the New York profession is very ingrown, and that's extremely unhealthy. To most Manhattan-dwellers, everything outside of Manhattan is Texas.

Notes

1. Joel Chadabe, "New Approaches to Analog-Studio Design," *Perspectives of New Music* 6/1 (1967): 107–13.

2. Joel Chadabe, *Electric Sound: The Past and Promise of Electronic Music* (Upper Saddle River, NJ: Pearson, 1996), 286–87.

3. Joel Chadabe, "Echoes," Joel Chadabe, https://joelchadabe.net/echoes/ (accessed July 30, 2019).

4. Burt Levy and Gregory Reish, "Chadabe, Joel," *Grove Music Online*, January 31, 2014, https://doi.org/10.1093/gmo/9781561592630.article.A2256311.

5. John Cage to Harold Hersch, September 13, 1971, John Cage Collection, Northwestern University Library, Northwestern University, Evanston, IL.

6. Joel Chadabe, "Electronic Music and Life," *Organised Sound* 9/1 (April 2004): 3–6.

7. "Joel Chadabe—Music as Emergence," YouTube, posted July 22, 2019, 1:03:23, https://www.youtube.com/watch?v=zATg_yFCNpQ (accessed July 30, 2019).

8. Joel Chadabe, "Technical Report: The CEMS System," in *Proceedings of the Fifth Annual Conference, 1970* (New York: American Society of University Composers, 1972), 69–73.

9. Leonard B. Meyer, "The End of the Renaissance?" in *Music, the Arts and Ideas: Patterns and Predictions in Twentieth-Century Culture* (Chicago: University of Chicago Press, 1967, 1994), 68–84.

7 Charles Dodge (b. 1942)

FRANCES WHITE AND JAMES PRITCHETT

When Barney Childs interviewed him, Charles Dodge was known as one of the young composers inventing the field of computer music. In 1972, making music with computers was still a difficult task requiring what was, at the time, rare and highly specialized machinery. Even the most fundamental equipment was a cause for excitement. Dodge is thrilled to have a digital-to-analog converter—the device that turns digital data into audible sound. "It really is great," he says, clearly delighted to have the rare chance to work with such a system. At about the same time in Princeton, for example, composers had to take an hour's drive to Bell Labs in Murray Hill, New Jersey, to convert their digital samples into sound they could hear. It is easy to forget how difficult it was to get such basic equipment that, today, is mass-produced, cheap, and ubiquitous (you probably have at least one digital-to-analog converter within arm's reach right now).

Computer music had its own culture in the 1960s and '70s that arose naturally from the requirements for making it. It was by necessity largely an academic endeavor: there was no such thing as a personal computer. Computers were largely the domain of engineering faculty working on government contracts, but interest in their applications to sound was widespread, and composers were able to get access to make music with them. In the private sector, Bell Labs was the leader in the field, with researchers such as Max Mathews, Joan Miller, and John Pierce creating the first general-purpose computer programs for composition: the MUSIC series of programs (MUSIC IV, MUSIC 360, etc.). Like the research environments they were attached to, composers using computers began working more collaboratively. Some of the early adopters, like Godfrey Winham at Princeton, had a natural talent for computers and helped newcomers get started.

In the very early days of computer music, composers had to have certain personalities and characters to put up with the conditions in the field. They were opportunistic;

they would work with whatever equipment or sound-creating means came their way. Like all truly creative people, they were willing to drop their preconceived ideas about what they were doing and instead let their work reveal its own path, often shaped by the limitations of the technology available. They were supremely patient, willing to deal with the unreliability of hardware and software, often producing rather meager sonic results. But they were curious about sound itself and about how digital technology could create and manipulate it. They believed in a limitless universe of sound to be opened up by the computer. It was a future that was just around the corner, waiting in the next stack of punch cards.

Charles Dodge fit this profile of a computer music pioneer, but, as revealed in this interview, he is not someone who is primarily interested in technology. The overriding concern for Dodge is that his music always be about humanity, never machines. At the time of this interview, he was fully realizing this and was just encountering the technology that united the human and the digital, the technology that would lead him to create the music that defines his career: speech synthesis.

In the interview, Dodge describes a trajectory familiar to many composers who work with computers: frustration with analog equipment, discovery of computers, initial experimentation without much in the way of exciting results, and finally, a first musical work. Dodge's first computer composition was *Changes* (1970). Here he used the computer to create synthetic percussive sounds in a rhythmically and texturally complex context. For a young composer working at Columbia and Princeton, the influence of Milton Babbitt's music was very much in the air, and the aesthetic of *Changes* reflects this. The original plan was to include a live percussion part, but the work needed sounds that could not be created by physical percussion instruments. In particular, the computer was required for some of the pitched and timbral components—including, interestingly, some that deliberately attempted to create vocal effects. In this piece, like those of many of Dodge's peers, the technology was used as a way to transcend the limitations of live instruments.

It was the introduction of a natural element into the realm of computer synthesis that began to spark Dodge's imagination. In *Earth's Magnetic Field* (1970), he mapped data about the interaction of solar radiation and the magnetic field onto musical parameters (pitch, register, dynamics, etc.). This resulted in his first computer work that displays his mature musical voice. Though fully synthetic, it is often unabashedly beautiful, with gestures that are unpredictable and deeply natural and musical. At times the choice of timbre in the work intuitively evokes a sense of brilliance, which is fitting for the content of the piece.

The discovery of speech synthesis fully opened the door to Dodge's mature style. In this interview, he discusses very early work on "a videotape opera"—what ultimately became *Speech Songs* (1973) and *The Story of Our Lives* (1974) (the video accompanied the latter work, and used actors lip-syncing to the tape part). The final compositions that resulted are remarkable; the surreal and yet undeniably human nature of the synthetic speech perfectly mirroring the surreality of the poems by Mark Strand. It was also an original musical use of the voice—speech itself as music, rather than a "singing voice" as music.

Dodge developed an uncanny ability to orchestrate with synthetic speech, and *Speech Songs* foreshadowed his masterpieces *Cascando* (1978) and *Any Resemblance Is Purely Coincidental* (1976–78). In *Cascando*, a setting of the play by Samuel Beckett, the imperfections inevitably present in synthetic speech perfectly portray the character of Voice, hopelessly flawed himself but trying—desperately trying—to tell the right story. The somewhat inhuman quality of the synthesized speech becomes deeply human and oddly moving in the persona of Voice. In *Any Resemblance* (for piano and computer-generated sound), Dodge analyzed Enrico Caruso's iconic performance of "Vesti la giubba" from Ruggero Leoncavallo's *I Pagliacci* and then resynthesized the voice to suit his own musical ends. Initially, Dodge highlights the comical qualities of the synthesized voice, and so at first it seems a joke. But as it draws to a close, searing reverberant pitched auras transform the voice into an agonized shriek, and the work coalesces as a wrenching evocation of the tragic clown Pagliaccio. All of this music is in the future at the time of this interview, but in Dodge's conversation with Childs we hear a composer who senses the possibilities for a deeply human music made using computers, someone reaching out and just beginning to trace the contours of his own musical world.

Charles Dodge: Interview

BARNEY CHILDS: Your work with speech synthesis: why are you interested in it, your whole interest in computers?

CHARLES DODGE: Business is booming! I'm working on two pieces at the moment. One of them is virtually done and one is virtually started, and that is pretty good for me. But I ought to go back and talk about how I got into the whole thing. I was commissioned to write a work for Tanglewood in the summer of 1965, called *Folia*, and it is finally coming out this year. While I was there, I met J. K. Randall, who was also commissioned. His work entailed tape. I was not too impressed at the time with the sound. I thought it was rather Hammond organ-like and was disappointed (it is, by the way, now a piece that I like very much). That was after my first year in graduate school. In my second year in graduate school, I took an electronic music course at Columbia with [Vladimir] Ussachevsky, and I just couldn't work in the studio. The equipment was always breaking down; it was never the same way twice. It was almost inherent in the equipment that there was no reproducibility. What you got out one day was unique. I found it very difficult to experiment with finding different sounds because I couldn't really test anything. It was a disaster; I didn't do anything for about a year except complain about the equipment and produce a few sounds.

The next year, I took the computer music course at Princeton. Godfrey Winham taught the course that year, and he and I really hit it off very well. I found him to be an articulate person. I learned a tremendous amount from him, not only about computer science but just general intellectual subjects. I really got the beginnings of a good education out of that course. Everybody in Columbia and Princeton had free computer services and use of equipment. The [US] Defense Department was getting bugged that guys at these universities on Defense Department contracts were paying for this computer time and that it was free for everybody else. So they finally lowered the boom and said, "Shit, man, we're not going to pay for that computer time if nobody else is!" So there was a period there in the summer of 1967 where nobody used the computer at Princeton or Columbia much. The days of indirect charging for computer time was finished. The next year I worked at the IBM Thomas J. Watson Research Center at Yorktown Heights, New York, on a small computer with a cathode ray tube.

BC: Were you employed by IBM?

CD: I was what was called a contractor without pay: contracted to make sounds with the voltage on the cathode ray tube. I messed around for most of the year and didn't produce anything very interesting, but I learned a lot about computers.

The next year I started doing computer sound synthesis at Columbia on the IBM 360 model 91. I finished *Changes* that year and spent most of the summer at Columbia Computer Center. The next year I taught at Princeton; that year I finished my dissertation, and there were a lot of other things going on in my life. I was in a bad state. I went back to New York (I had moved to Princeton and lived on a farm for a whole year) in the summer of 1970 to this apartment, and in August did a work called *Earth's Magnetic Field*. I began teaching at Columbia again in 1971. Through the joint effort of the Columbia Computer Center and the Columbia Physics Department, I was able to get a digital-to-analog conversion system. It's a four-channel stereo sound computer system. It really is great, so that's what I've been working on.

Also that year, when I was waiting for the conversion system to arrive, I got interested in speech synthesis. The previous summer, 1970, just before I moved to New York, Godfrey Winham taught a course at Princeton in the mathematics of sound processing. Winham's course was good background for doing speech synthesis. It told the mathematical expressions for a lot of acoustical stuff, and that's pretty important for synthesizing speech. In the middle of that year, 1970–71, I started working at the Bell Telephone Laboratories on the system that Joseph Olive had set up, and produced the examples you heard at Houston. Then Columbia got its D-to-A [digital-to-analog] conversion system, and I got a commission from Ronnie Anderson to write a little piece for trumpet and tape, called "Extensions for Trumpet and Tape." The relation between trumpet and the tape is this: I wrote a piece for solo trumpet, then recorded Anderson playing the trumpet part on tape, and then converted that tape from regular tape-recorder tape to digital tape for computer. I wrote computer programs which add reverberation and modify the sound, then I fed those tapes back out for the tape recorder. The performance consists of Anderson playing the piece live with this tape of a modified version of his playing it previously. It should sound as if he's playing the same composition in a room as it is coming off the tape, but where the two are interacting makes it sound like the size of the enclosure that he's playing in is changing size. At least I hope that will be the effect—that's what I'm aiming for.

The other piece that I'm working on is, for lack of a better term, a videotape opera. It uses computer music and then synthetic speech on poems of a friend of mine. Then all of that goes together with the computer film I'm making. The poems are both by Mark Strand, a better-known obscure poet: "When I am with you I am in two places at once, when you are with me you have just arrived with a suitcase which you pack with one hand and unpack with the other." That's the first poem. The film starts out with a picture, probably a still picture of two people looking at each other, and on the soundtrack two voices are modified, repeating words and phrases from the poem and creating a kind of otherworldly effect on these words. The advantage in using synthetic speech over just recorded voice is that you can control the inflection very carefully, and you can repeat things exactly. You can create a wide variety of emotions and expressions. You can represent emotions, turn people's heads with the sound of a voice. This part is really what interests me about computer music these days, is that it is a way of getting with film. That's very important; with film you can get at a lot of situations that are very closely related to the way we live.

I've come through academic music education, which I don't regret in any way. I learned a tremendous amount; I think it is very good for me to have done all the usual bullshit that one does in getting his academic education. Now I feel that those were my student days, and now I'm a man. What interests me most about the way I'm living these days? The way I'm thinking these days? The people I'm seeing? What interests me is thoughts, of course, but also feelings: the wide range of human experience instead of just abstract patterns that you think of as the classic academic piece. Not just only patterns, but also the way that people react to those patterns. They don't always have the same effect.

BC: If someone came up and commissioned you to write a solely instrumental piece, would you still do it?

CD: I've enjoyed writing this trumpet-and-tape piece. Having gone so deep into the computer thing (I really did, and now I'm almost out of touch!), I'm enjoying coming back out of it now. Tape music is almost a practical thing; by doing tape music I can get a professional-quality recording of this composition. This spring, rehearsing *Folia* with Jacques Monod conducting, was quite an experience. It's a student piece really, but the instruments sound so good! So I'd be pretty easily persuaded to write an instrumental work. Maybe I don't have too clear of an image of what I'm doing, except that these videotape operas really have the greatest possibilities.

BC: Has the work with computer sound led you to continue thinking about musical organization? In what ways has it opened up your thinking in terms of structure?

CD: Yes, it has. The videotape opera really consists of two types of sound. There's synthetic speech, which is modified in different ways, and the background to that is a whole mess of tones that are glissandos up and down. It's hard to explain, but at one point the thirty-two tones equally spaced in intervals from 30 cycles to 12,000; and they all start glissandoing. In the course of a minute they all come together to a single tone in the middle, and then move back apart. It's a fabulous sound; one you couldn't begin to get any other way. You couldn't get it with instruments, you couldn't get it in the classical studio, you can only compute it. It's beautiful; it just sounds fantastically clean. When the thing is almost together there's a tremendous amount of beating, and they all come together for a second and then there's no beating at all, and then it begins beating again. The rate at which these things go up and down, and the distance that the tones travel, are the basics in this musical structure.

BC: You're getting into different parameters.

CD: You sure are, and it's only possible with computers. That's a special case. There are billions of things that you do with computers that you could never do any other way, but most of those billions of things just aren't very interesting. It's possible to write music with 93½ tones to the octave, but who perceives music that way? I think that foremost in my mind, at all times when I'm composing and listening, is what is that music getting across to somebody who has my musical experience? With synthetic speech and the visual stuff, you've got to ask some different questions; not just what is that getting across to people with my musical experience, but what is it also getting across to people with my psychological experience, my emotional experience, my maturational experience; a whole lot of different parameters. It's the difference between writing opera and writing symphonies.

BC: But there really isn't anybody else with all your experiences.

CD: No, there certainly isn't, and there never is. But that's the kind of question, nonetheless, you have to assume. I always assume that the ideal listener is sort of my alter ego.

BC: Eventually we all, whether we like it or not, are writing for the audience of one. This is the audience that we say, "It approves," before we let the piece out, or "Can I fix it so that it approves better?" I have a lot of trouble, as anyone who has taught music has had, with people saying, "It doesn't communicate; you're not thinking of the audience in these terms." One wonders if the whole audience bag doesn't need to be redefined.

CD: I'm having different experiences these days. The first side of *Earth's Magnetic Field*, for example, is diatonic, in the key of C.

BC: It's an astonishing sound.

CD: You don't have to be musically literate to hear it. So there you're communicating with practically anybody that has a foundation of Western music on a pretty simple level.

BC: I think it's possible for somebody who knows very little about the very sophisticated levels of *Changes* still to enjoy the music. The thing that always comes up is how much should the listener really have to hear before he possesses the music in some kind of way that the composer wants him to?

CD: I'm not very absolutist about it, but the person who goes to a performance of *Don Giovanni* and follows the libretto, doesn't listen to the music very carefully, and is moved by the situations in the plot of the drama, may well leave the opera feeling satisfied. But that might not even be [a] sufficiently deep experience to pass an opera course in the liberal arts college. There you have two possible levels of the same experience. Everybody approaches music with their previous experience, and obviously some people don't have the previous experience necessary to appreciate the music of Schoenberg or Stravinsky, much less the music of Barney Childs and Charles Dodge.

BC: How much should the composer ask? Can we ask more than just people who are turning the "on" switch and letting the sounds just flood into their heads? It's always a revelation to students to discover that after half an hour of study of a Webern piece they can hear what's happening. But there is certainly a lot of post-Webern work in which this can never happen, as far as I can tell.

CD: I really don't feel capable of discussing this aspect of music; you probably end up making some very compromising statements. You can find a person who may well appreciate some piece of recent contemporary music who doesn't understand the first thing about Schoenberg's *Variations for Orchestra*. What does that mean to have a person who can understand some recent piece and not understand this classic? I think it's too bad. Like you find people who can't appreciate Mozart but who can really get into Beethoven. That just means their musical experience is a little narrow. I suppose it's desirable to have one's musical experience as broad as possible. It's similar with composers. I don't think you can tell him he should write for as broad an audience as possible; the key there is "should." *Should* what? Maybe I don't want to. One of the nice things about musical life in America is that you can do pretty damn much what you please. There are limits, but for a very good reason; our musical life is college and university centered, and there is no national board or national radio network.

BC: How did you feel when *Folia* was being recorded and rehearsed and all of a sudden here is something that was past which is brought to life again?

CD: I felt funny about it, actually; the last time I was really into it I had conducted it. I had a fascinating experience. My performance in concert took nine-and-a-half minutes or so; this recording is twelve minutes. OK, I forced the metronome markings slightly when I conducted it. Jacques Monod interpreted it rather more slowly, and the effect is fascinating. This performance was very good; there are maybe twelve things in the whole goddamn recording that are wrong. This includes a wrong note in the viola, the percussionist meant to hit one cymbal and hit a different one, and things like that. What interested me about comparing this experience and my doing it myself with Monod's doing it was that Monod was completely, internally consistent. He did this slower, but by his doing it slower the phrasing comes out unbelievably beautiful. By doing it fast the way I did it, you get the overall form coming across very easily, but the way the phrases contribute to that form is rushed, helter-skelter. I actually prefer his conducting to my own. And as to the piece, it was interesting to come back and learn the notes again. Basically I thought, "My God, the piece isn't really as bad as I thought it was!"

BC: You're not ready to disavow your early works?

CD: Not that one. There are a lot of early works that I disavow. From '65 there's that piece, from '66 there's an orchestra piece [*Rota*]which I don't know if you've ever heard.

BC: No, I haven't.

CD: I wish we had a tape of that. It was played first by the Iowa symphony and then by the Milwaukee Symphony.[1] Art Weisberg went out to Milwaukee one spring, in '68. Not a good performance, but not Weisberg's fault, certainly. I've just been listening recently to the Iowa recording of that work; it's a piece that is almost completely satisfying to me. I had gone to see *Parsifal* shortly before this, and the sections will go on for twenty-five minutes, the piece just building up to a climax. What I tried to do in this piece is something like that; you have one big gesture, the piece is about sixteen minutes long, and it almost worked. It's a devilishly difficult piece to play. It starts out just completely chaotic with the winds, the brass, and the percussion just sort of all playing millions of notes, and doing things in and out of each other, and just almost making no sense. It goes on like that, and it does it some more; for five or six minutes before the strings play, there's just this incredible chaos going on. In the middle of these big splashes, the strings come in and start playing a unison, then they branch out into two parts and then three parts. Finally, the strings are spread out in a great big register playing four or five different parts, and this other chaotic activity has just gone like that to nothing. The mechanic activity's extremely fast; like fifteen things happen in seconds, so it's just tremendously fast.

The string part is just very relaxed, and it winds down to the first violins playing a single line, with the other strings playing a pizzicato accompaniment, and then they stop; and then the winds, and then. . . . What you've had is a mixture of everything, then the strings are isolated, then there's isolation of the wind timbre, of the brass timbre, with the percussion timbres and then, after a short pause, the last section of the piece reinterprets the first section of the piece. Now, instead of being chaotic, the elements that were simultaneous are now successive, so that it kind of picks the previously chaotic part apart, and plays the thing successively. And it almost works!

BC: The interesting thing about this is that there's a kind of dramatism inherent in the concept. What is so pervasive today is a sense of organic growing in a piece, that there is a constant—often dramatism but not necessarily—in a piece. There's no longer pouring it into the cake tin and coming out with a cake of a fixed shape.

CD: That's right. Godfrey Winham once made a statement which had an effect on me; he thought that pieces of music that he liked were ones in which the background activity was also apparent in the foreground.

BC: A challenging statement.

CD: Yes; we could probably argue about every word in his statement, but I have some kind of intuitive grasp of what he's talking about. It's what you find in Mozart's symphonies. The classical composers will have, say, in a five-chord succession, not just chords but also key areas of the piece which are treated in large sections. He's talking about having the four or five chords right in the foreground. An indication toward the larger scope of the piece, and that's tremendously challenging. In this aspect of twentieth century that you mentioned, pieces which grow, how to have that growth kind of shown not just only in the large but also in the small, that's really where a composition is born. We can all sit down and dream up a dozen large forms in which we would like to hear our music, OK? But it's in the composing out between this concept and the actual sound of the piece that our real skill and effort lies.

BC: At the same time, we can neither be satisfied with nor totally reject, let's say, the Darmstadt microphenomena, instantaneous events. If there is a large sense of gesture, it is apparent only standing very, very far back.

CD: I don't like pieces like that. It's just that you have to stand so far back in order to see the thing. I like something that I can sort of get into, feel a part of.

BC: In some work I just finished, I've been concerned with foregrounds which become backgrounds, and backgrounds which become foregrounds. You perceive them as the same activity that was going on before, but there will be something else which is more out in front.

CD: One of the questions you always get asked in these interviews, and I'll answer it, is where are things going?

BC: I try not to ask that!

CD: How do you like the scene, are you pessimistic or optimistic? I'm really very optimistic at the level of talent that we see in our colleagues, the level of competence throughout the country in all of the technological stuff, which you would expect. But I'm also rather encouraged by not just the ability to work with technology, but also of the real concern for what it all means, the real concern for human expression. Where does the human being fit into all of this, this tremendous philosophy of technology?

BC: How do you approach it?

CD: Well, I guess in the videotape operas, you have the human problems dealt with very directly.

BC: But you can do that with tape.

CD: But you can do that with words.

BC: But with sound, nonverbal.

CD: I guess with nonverbal sounds, what I'm interested in is kind of communicating to larger groups of people than I have been. In the last, say, four, five years, I've lived in situations in New York and Princeton where people are writing pretty esoteric music. My music has not been very esoteric; I've never been very comfortable writing that. And in *Changes*, which is a work that has a lot of verbalization, is a piece for which people who can still listen to jazz from the late '50s and like it to get a kick out of, because it plays on those kinds of similarities. Even that piece, which is probably as esoteric as I'll ever write, has its easy-to-read side.

BC: But it isn't sufficient in your search for good communication just to drop down a couple of notches and write instantly accessible . . .

CD: No, I can't do that shit. I could do it, maybe, but I don't want to do it. The only reason would be if I wanted to make a living by my composition, and I don't that much. One of the marvelous things about late twentieth-century America is that it's possible almost to be a country-gentleman composer. You have this job at the university that pays the rent, and then you really can spend your composing time investigating interesting problems instead of making a living.

BC: [Charles] Ives goes so far as to suggest that it's better if what you make your living at and music are not the same.

CD: That's certainly the case with us; I mean I don't see my teaching career as being my composition career at all. I do my teaching career, because I enjoy studying old music. And I enjoy studying contemporary music too; it's a kick. And I haven't found anything that I get that big a kick out of.

BC: Would you go back to Iowa if they offered you a fat job?

CD: I might. I went back to Iowa and took my kids to visit their grandparents this summer. It's beautiful country, and the people there are warm and their style of life is somewhat more measurably paced. I might not, too, though, because I really like New York. Only in the last few months have I begun to like New York. I went to Europe; I gave nine lectures about computer music. I started in London, Paris, Brussels, Utrecht, Munich, Berlin, Stockholm, and Oslo, and all over the goddamn Western Europe. I was so impressed to find these cities that I've heard about all my life are very beautiful, but how different New York is from a European city. And I knew from my own experience how different New York was from anywhere in America. The place is just fantastic. When it's clear, which is about one out of every ten days, those buildings in Lower Manhattan, if you come across one of the bridges, are just gorgeous. It's really quite a unique place.

BC: "Earth has not anything to show more fair . . ." [William Wordsworth, "Composed upon Westminster Bridge, September 3, 1802"]

CD: That's how I feel about New York. But it has its drawbacks, of course. I'm very lucky to have a job now at Columbia, and if for any reason that relationship terminates I'll probably have to look for a job outside New York. In that case I'd certainly consider Iowa, as a place that I really like, a place that I have a tremendous admiration for.

BC: Suppose you were offered a job at *non*-Iowa.

CD: Same thing. Having grown up in the country, I just feel that I have more options. I like the country.

BC: Some people outside of New York still have the myth that New York is a giant closed shop. This isn't nearly as pervasive as it was.

CD: That's how people used to feel. But I haven't found it that way.

BC: There are still some pockets of resistance.

CD: People who really think that New York is . . . ?

BC: Anti-Christ.

CD: Anti-Christ? Well, sure, it's a very complicated place, and there are those awful elements, hell yes! Very important decisions that affect the musical world get made in back rooms by two or three people, and they happen to be in New York. What does that have to do with me? For sure, there's a lot of stuff going on. What I appreciate about New York is its diversity, its tremendous diversity. It's a lot going on good, and there's a lot going on bad.

BC: I'd like to talk about one of those things which you're connected with, which is ACA [American Composers Alliance] and CRI [Composers Recordings Inc.], in what directions you think this can move. CRI is a unique project, because it is for the composer in a funny way.

CD: Oh, yeah. In the last four years, I've been involved with different organizations. Among them, and most important to me, has been ACA and CRI. It's always been my principle that things affecting composers' lives should be run by composers, because although there's a considerable amount of inefficiency and often difficulty surrounding that approach, in the long run it seems to me

to be the best kind of combination. With things which were run by foundations, other interests get served there first. Composers in particular tend to get
lost. Maybe it's a way of protecting myself from too much frustration, by being
involved with ACA and CRI. Although they're quite small by the standards
of the elite professional organizations, they're vey important to me since I'm a
composer and their activities affect me.

Now, what ACA has done in the past is to duplicate some of the functions of
ASCAP and BMI. Not that we'll do that in the future. What we're becoming is a
composer-owned and -operated publishing house, which will print catalogs and
distribute all the music of its members. It will make it possible for performers
throughout the country to really know what's being written and not just coming out of the big publishing houses, that it's also coming off our pens which
is still manuscript. I think that's an important part. Also, ACA is trying to get
personal appearance gigs for its members and, by George, we got two! This is
possibly prophetic: we got two lectures for composers in a mental hospital.

BC: So this will hopefully expand?

CD: I sure hope so. Although ACA founded CRI, and CRI is one of these ACA
projects that succeeded, it wasn't known really whether it would or not. We're
going to put out this year our two-hundredth record. There's a lot of nonsense
on CRI, but there are also some very important recordings. And I think that's
worth it. Now that's just a matter of attitude; a lot of people take a look at the
stuff that isn't so good, and say it's not worth it. I'm not that kind of person. I
tend to look at the valuable things and say well, maybe it is. Otherwise many
of those things might not have gotten done. Like the early recordings of Ives;
that was just astonishing. ACA should have been the instrument by which Ives
became known to the American public.

BC: All these American pieces that nobody ever knew, nobody would have ever
heard for another couple of decades.

CD: So I'm pretty optimistic about that scene. It's got some problems, but I think
it can just be an important resource to composers.

BC: I think that the composers realize that it is really for them.

CD: Well, it surely isn't for the benefit of the fat cats in the house. Some of us
work pretty hard to keep the organization going as a matter of pride. It would
be a real shame if we let it slip through our fingers. There was a point where
ACA just couldn't hold. I must say, I just got a kick out of making things work.
Who doesn't, really?

BC: Clearly working with computers has infinite ranges of potential. But aren't
these largely denied most of us because we don't have special know-how or the
apparatus? It seems to be that there are maybe ten guys in the country who are
really well enough grounded in working with computers that they can make
music other than just thirty-second noodles. And this seems to me a pity.

CD: I agree, but working with computers to make music is not easy. You've got to invest a lot of time. I've got some graduate students now that are doing pieces that are several minutes long, and this is in their first year. God knows these graduate students are busy in different things; they haven't been working in this full-time. I wish there were some kind of central clearinghouse; there ought to be a national center for computer electronic music. Say, around Washington, DC, where composers can go and learn it for a year or two, and know enough to take it back to their universities.

BC: How much actual work would be involved, given somebody who has all good intentions and knows nothing about it? What would it take?

CD: Let's say you went to Columbia for a year, to Princeton or Illinois, no problem. Shit, if you came to Columbia for the fall semester and took this computer music course, inside of a few months you would be capable of realizing a piece.

BC: But then the second problem, as you were suggesting, is putting it in backwards.

CD: That's a different problem. Basically you don't need to know much about computers in order to make the music. The first computer piece I did, I knew almost nothing about computers. I knew how to punch cards; I knew if I put the deck of cards on this counter, a day later I would find the output to that job, resulting from this, so that's about all I knew. So you really have to attack in many different ways. J. K. Randall was never really into implementing programs; he's always finding someone who can do it well. I'm getting that way; I have a programmer now who does a lot of the shitwork. I don't enjoy that. Tuck Howe would be happy to spend the rest of his life just doing little programming problems, and he probably will.

BC: You actually teach computer programming.

CD: I'm lucky to have a course right in my specialty, and my teaching is really a different career. Here's one case where it's almost very close. I don't really talk about music that much; I just help them learn how to use the computer. I keep trying to improve the way I teach it. This next year I'm going to do it rather different.

BC: There's so much in there that many composers would like to experiment with, to expand their own musical grasp. Yet it isn't as though you can just go over to another building on your campus and say I want to learn.

CD: No, and that is a drag too. I've talked to John Clough and Tuck [Howe], who are working on a book. You see the big trouble that my students have, that everybody's students have, and the big trouble when I was a student, is that you'll hear somebody's computer piece, and it has these sounds in it, how do you get your hands on the specifications for these sounds? Impossible; there's very little communication. On my doctoral dissertation was a catalog of the computer centers, a catalog of the computer sounds and changes. So if anybody wants one of those sounds he can belt them out if he knows the language in which they were written, which is another problem.

BC: And the language seems to change remarkably fast.

CD: It does, but it seems to be settling down now for the next few three or four years with IBM Music 360. What I'm going to do for my students is get a lot of test tapes, with the computer programs that produce the tones on the test.

Note

1. It is unclear which ensemble Dodge means by "Iowa symphony." It may be the University of Iowa orchestra, as he had graduated from the school in 1964.

8 William Hellermann (1939–2017)

JAY M. ARMS

Like many of composers of his generation, William Hellermann's work is difficult to categorize. His creative output encompasses musical composition, sculpture, photography, graphic design, theater, dance, and narration. He often fuses these different media into a single artwork that is not wholly of one discipline or another, such as a sculpture that also functions as a musical score or gestural approach to playing an instrument akin to choreography. Blending different media, however, is not the ultimate aim of his creative practice. Hellermann intended his music to function primarily as social endeavor; its purpose is to bring people together.

Hellermann's musical career began as a jazz trumpeter and guitarist in Milwaukee, Wisconsin, but he soon developed an interest in classical and flamenco guitar. In 1961 he traveled to Spain to study guitar with Rafael Nogales, and adopted as his performing persona Guillermo Brilliante, a translation of his name into Spanish. While living in New York and performing regularly, he developed extended approaches to guitar performance that informed his compositions for other instruments, including new methods of preparing the instrument, exploring timbre as a structural device and sound as a by-product of gesture, and engaging new perspectives on virtuosity and the limits of physical performance. Hellermann wanted these aspects of his work to function as more than mere "sound effects" and "extended techniques," but for them to have meaningful and perceptible consequence on the music at a deeper level. One telling piece from this era is his *Passages 13—The Fire* (1971) for solo trumpet and magnetic tape. In this piece, the trumpet performs highly soloistic passage work with a tape accompaniment he composed in the Columbia-Princeton Electronic Music Center. The trumpet part derives from the Marian hymn, "Alma Redemptoris Mater" by Hermannus Contractus. Each phrase of the hymn is presented in what Hellermann calls a "troped" form with interpolations he composed in a free-chromatic approach to pitch and a "free-flowing, dramatic sense of pacing."[1]

The drama culminates at the end of the piece, when the trumpet plays the unaltered hymn in its entirety with a haunting background provided by the tape.

Hellermann began developing his own approaches to musical notation in the early 1970s, often claiming that "hearing is only another way of seeing."[2] He ultimately came to consider the look and content of the score itself to be as important as the sounding music, and these works generally invoked a sense of theater and multi-sensory experience. He first developed his graphic notations in his piece *Columbus Circle* (1970) and the subsequent series *Circle Music 1, 2, and 3* (1971). For these pieces Hellermann used a set of drafting tools to devise a notation scheme that indicates relationships between performance events (not necessarily sounds) and patterns of recurrence among those events. Whereas the materials of a given performance are left open to the performers, the process of enacting those events is fixed within the piece's cyclic structure and expressed through geometric figures based on circles.[3] The second *Circle Music* piece was premiered by the free improvisation group Il Gruppo di Improvvisazione Nuova Consonanza while Hellermann was living in Italy after receiving the Rome Prize in 1972.

Building on these works, Hellermann began a new series using unconventional notation called *Visible Music*. Unlike the previous *Circle Music* series, *Visible Music* sought to integrate the visual score with the sounding music, uniting form and content as well as the senses. These works use the conventional five-line staff notation presented in unusual contexts or on unusual materials. *In the Mind's Ear* (1973), for example, depicts the score as a flat landscape, with the staves running from the bottom of the page and flowing back toward the horizon. Partially framed by an open door, the striking image focuses the eye on the distant vanishing point where the parallel lines of music—like the actual musical processes notated on the staves themselves—seem to converge. Other pieces from this series would place music notation on everyday objects, leading to Morton Feldman's observation that for Hellermann, "everything is music paper."[4] *Experimental Music II* (1975), for example, uses three-dimensional note heads floating in test tubes with staves drawn on the outside. *Wind Music I* (1977) has note heads affixed to the frame of a fan, with the staves drawn on the blades. Hellermann referred to such works as "conceptual per-formance sculptures," which may be realized in sound or simply appreciated visually.[5]

Later in his career, Hellermann sought to support the experimental music and arts communities of New York beyond his role as a composer and performer. With the aim of bringing together his work and communities from both aural and visual arts, he founded the SoundArt Foundation in 1982.[6] Throughout the rest of his life, Hellermann used the SoundArt Foundation to help finance and advocate for artists and composers by hosting exhibitions, concerts, and other events. One of the major contributions of the SoundArt Foundation was the *Calendar of New Music* that Hell-ermann compiled and published regularly. This print publication provided announce-ments for upcoming new music concerts throughout New York City, and for many years it served as a primary means by which composers and enthusiasts would learn about what was going on in the scene. Accompanying these initiatives, Hellermann cofounded the DownTown Ensemble with composer and clarinetist Daniel Goode in 1983. They founded the group with the intent of forming a repertory ensemble, in contrast to contemporaneous ensembles dedicated to performing the works of a single composer. Since the group's founding, the DownTown Ensemble has performed, commissioned, and premiered works by many composers within and outside of New York, fostering and expanding a supportive community of like-minded artists.

While his music displays much in the way of technical rigor and formal clarity, Hellermann always considered the people who would play and listen to his music, composing in a manner designed to foster meaningful musical and social relationships. This concern can be found in various configurations in his fully notated scores, musical structures designed for improvisation, graphic scores, and interactive sculptures, among other media. This concern perhaps is most evident in his efforts to bring together communities of experimental artists through organizations like the SoundArt Foundation and the DownTown Ensemble that aimed to do just that. In this interview—conducted just prior to Hellermann departing the United States for his residency for the Rome Prize, beginning his *Visible Music* series, and forming his vision for the SoundArt Foundation and DownTown Ensemble—he elaborates on his creative and social concerns at that moment, foreshadowing major developments in his work in the coming years.

William Hellermann: Interview

BARNEY CHILDS: In the pieces of yours I know, whether they're graphic notations or not, there's a real interest in a sumptuousness of sound, a real physical presence of a perceptible sound. Is this typical of what you do?

WILLIAM HELLERMANN: In a sense. I'm very concerned with sound quality, particularly with the motion of sound apart from sound effects, unusual tone-color combinations, or *klangfarben* melodies. Central to all of my work is how to use sounds that were traditionally excluded from musical structures so that they function. It's important that these new sounds function as *the* musical ideas, not just as sound effects.

BC: Not only are they pulling their weight in the immediate structure, timbral structuring is going on, too.

WH: Right, although I've found it impossible to get that intellectual about it. However, the timbral aspect should be pointed out because most people only know my earlier works.

BC: Do you disown these earlier works?

WH: No, I don't. I like them. But they were still Webernesque in some respects.

BC: What was your Opus 1?

WH: My Opus 1? That was when I was eleven or twelve. I did some piano pieces—
short pieces in classical style, a little Beethovenian, which is strange since I had
had very little exposure to classical music. Most of my listening was to jazz. I
started in a school program where they give you a band instrument. No one in
the family was much of a musician, and the lessons were free. I began on the
trumpet; by the time I was sixteen (I was tall and looked older than my age),
I began playing around a sort of jazz, nothing very heavy. I was never truly a
jazz musician. You remember the Dixieland-cum-swing arrangements that one
would play in various social centers? That's what we were doing. I also studied
the piano. Then I had one of my front teeth knocked out.

BC: How?

WH: Playing basketball. I was mostly into sports and hot rods. Anyway, my front
tooth got knocked out so I had to stop playing the trumpet. Somewhere around
that time (I was eighteen or nineteen) I heard Segovia play the classical guitar.
Until this point, classical music to me was really only Tchaikovsky and light
popular-classical music. I hadn't heard much else. I took jazz very seriously,
despite the things I was playing. I would drop into the one record store in
Milwaukee that carried jazz and ask: "Did you get anything in that's good?"
because you almost never heard anything on the radio. Later I was getting
Coltrane, Miles Davis, Duke Ellington of course, and Charlie Christian. For
the guitar, he was very important for me. That first influence was jazz, but only
recently I bring this up. Before, I didn't think it was relevant. But people say
continually they hear a jazz side to my music, which I don't entirely agree with.

BC: This is true of almost everybody in your generation.

WH: I guess you could say almost everybody.

BC: There's so many guys. Terry Riley plays saxophone.

WH: Unless one was brought up in a certain milieu, jazz was the only serious music
around. Serious classical music was almost never broadcast. Many composers
did a lot more playing than I did. Bill [Bolcom] still does. I agree there's an
influence. Still, I don't want to give the impression I was a real jazz musician.

BC: It's a subliminal influence.

WH: Perhaps. All my serious early listening, and to an extent playing, was in
that area. Guitar was the strange next step, and that put me in contact with a
different kind of music. I loved to play. It wasn't so much the style of music
itself; it was the joy of playing. There is something very physical about playing
an instrument.

BC: The kinesthetics.

WH: I like that word, kinesthetics. It refers to something that is very important
to my music, more so now that I'm actively performing again.

BC: It seems your work isn't theater; it's an amplification of the natural choreography that an instrumentalist would have.

WH: I feel a greater identification with dance than with theater. Not that I've composed music for dance. I've played some for dance concerts only in the last month or two But I've found that I connect with dancers or theater people that work with [Jerzy] Grotowski's ideas, which are more movement-oriented than traditional theater. Also, modern dance in New York right now is some of the strongest work in the arts. It's the physical thing that got to me with the guitar. There was no one to study with in Milwaukee, so I began working by myself and listening to recordings. I studied a little bit with someone when I was in Madison, at the university, but the method was outdated. I also worked a lot with flamenco guitar.

BC: Manitas de Plata?

WH: I was most excited by Sabicas. He made a great impression on me. The first person I really studied with was in Spain. I flew to Europe for three hundred bucks—the very beginnings of these student flight plans. I worked with the guitarist Rafael Nogales in Madrid for the summer. That was '61. After Spain, I came back and finished up my degree. Then—this is classic, even corny—I landed on the Lower East Side of New York, guitar in one hand, my cat in the other, and a fifty-dollar check that I couldn't cash.

BC: What inspired you to come to New York?

WH: I no longer wanted to do anything but music. I wanted to study guitar, and I didn't know of any well-known guitar teachers anywhere else except in New York City. I came with a painter friend and moved into a basement on Seventh Street with no heat. We sat in the St. Mark's Theater every night watching a triple feature with the bums. Finally, the painter threw in the towel. He had a girlfriend back home and was missing her very much, so he left. When all my money had run out, I got a job sorting stock certificates for the Chemical Bank and I found a nice one-room place on the Lower East Side for twenty-five bucks a month or something. So finally I had a room, a guitar teacher, and a job. That's about all I did for the next six to eight months. I knew no one; it was a beautiful period.

BC: Were you writing?

WH: I was doing some writing, but I was really into the guitar. I wrote some guitar pieces, all of which I've thrown away. Then Jackie came over from France. We got married and moved into a bigger place also on the Lower East Side. I began studying piano again, not to be a pianist but to be able to read through scores. I also began formal studies in composition with Hannah Hall. She worked out marvelously for me. She had been a student of Stefan Wolpe; after a year, she sent me to work with Stefan. I studied with him for three years off and on.

BC: Your work doesn't show it.

WH: Other people have said the same thing. I could play some pieces that do to some extent . . . at least, you can draw a connection. I was very close to him and I can't put him up too high. It was a marvelous experience. I worked with him after he had developed Parkinson's disease. I've been told that he wasn't as adamant about his own way of working then as he had been before. There was always a special intensity in working with Stefan. He would always give of himself 100 percent, but he needed disciples. This eventually caused problems. As a consequence, though there was never any personal friction, I saw less of him. I wanted to continue, since his insights and spiritual view of music were an inspiration to me. However, it was difficult, particularly as his health weakened.

The lessons were marvelous. He never said a word about how to write music. We analyzed other people's music, mostly: Debussy, Beethoven, and occasionally modern pieces, often his own. I would show him anything that I was writing. Talking to people who knew him, this was quite different from the way he had worked up until a year or two before. In the past, he had been wrapped up in questions of method and system and what one should or should not do if they were going to write a piece of music. In contrast, I remember one of his remarks that was characteristic of our work together. We'd been three or four hours working on the "Hammerklavier" Sonata—Stefan was a very heavy analyst, systematic and very poetic at the same time—when he just looked up and said whimsically, "You know, it's all just witchcraft."

Our work together was always very careful—intellectual, never sloppy—but in no way academic. He was not interested in the new numerical systems. He often said, "I don't understand how people can write music with so much bookkeeping." He has been very influential in my life in the sense of combining discipline and rigor, and the freedom of spontaneous insight. Putting your finger on the poetry of what's going on, and then, once you have that, not being afraid to be as rigorous and as complete with the implications of that as possible.

I've noticed how this works in myself. I get excited by performance techniques that lead off into things that don't fit into the structure of a composition. I then find that by analyzing them along lines I got from Stefan, I can pin them down to their essentials, and by creating symbols and graphic arrangements work them into a definite structure.

BC: But you didn't get graphics from him.

WH: Not at all. The graphic thing was very simple evolution. I'm clumsy as a writer. My handwriting is impossible. So, I got a drawing board, triangles, templates, and technical pens just to make my scores legible. Later, when I was really involved in timbral, performance-oriented pieces using unusual sounds, I found I could use these templates to develop sign systems that did more than merely translate a performance action into a written symbol; they had a family relationship with one another. That led to ideas and structures I'm sure I wouldn't have discovered elsewhere. In my case, the transition was from just trying to make neat scores to doing pieces that look much like graphic designs.

I must say I've never yet been able to do a graphic piece that didn't have a sound [idea] first. Even my *Circle Musics* [1, 2, and 3; 1971], which look completely graphic, and are open to many different realizations, grew out of fairly specific musical ideas. They actually get most of their graphic character from the simple fact that the score is drawn as a big circle. This came from my desire to give a form that isn't based on linearity. The idea of a beginning and an end began to feel false to me, especially in dealing with emotions and feelings, which seem to be *matrixed*, rather than formal events.

BC: You're animating this into audible terms.

WH: I really see the *Circle Musics* more as resources for making music than as scores in the conventional sense. Lately I've been performing a lot of graphic music with pictographic symbols—lines move up and down to give pitch; register shapes; loudness and softness given by line thickness—the things that are often done in notating tape pieces or instrument and tape pieces. As a performer I can love to do these, but as a composer I have difficulty feeling excited by it.

With the *Circle Musics*, I got into a side of musical graphics that is non-pictographic, dealing with abstract symbols. For example, in *Circle Music 3*, a square, circle, diamond stand for 3 different events. They can be any events the performer chooses. It is necessary that there be a relation between the choices made for any given symbol. That is, all the players should realize a square in a similar way and it should be different from the realizations chosen for the circle and the diamond. Transformations of these basic events are indicated graphically by having the symbols either filled in or not filled in, and by superimposing symbols (a square inside a circle, or a diamond inside a square, etc.).

BC: But this is not merely notational, this is organic to the concept of how the performers can react.

WH: Not really. I don't think it is purely notational, but the square symbol doesn't imply what anything should be. It doesn't look like any one sound, such as a knock or a glissando.

BC: You aren't imposing that sort of limitation.

WH: The question isn't of imposing limits, more that these pieces are concerned with composing on the basis of pure relation without referring to any specific material. They are pure syntax without a semantic element being necessary.

BC: That's the whole notational hang-up: the idea of the sound image, as Ezra Pound develops "image," and the syntax of these things.

WH: The distinction between syntax and semantic as developed by Chomsky played an important role in shaping my attitudes towards musical notation, even though I don't completely agree with him. Conventionalized music notation was concerned with indicating what happened, not with the relationships between what happened. Yet it seemed that if music is about anything, it's about relationships . . . if you want, grammar. The *Circle Musics* result from taking these notions of a pure syntax and trying to work them out in musical terms. On the other hand, my other recent pieces like *Ek-Stasis II* [1970] and *Passages 13—The Fire* [1971] go in the other direction and notate unusual sounds in as precise a fashion as possible.

BC: Despite this, there is still an immediate and very attractive sound world happening. I don't believe it is because of the performance; it may happen whether you coach the performance or not. What interests me is this immediacy of sound is still there despite the very pristine order in the world that the notations themselves set up.

WH: Thank you—you've put your finger on what I'm after. There was a break that took place in my work. It wasn't earth shattering—going out at midnight, screaming to the gods and then burning all my early music or anything remotely like that—but rather a coming-to-terms with sound first before thinking of music. I first became involved in writing pieces in close personal contact with performers; for example, *Ek-Stasis II*. I got a commission to write a piece for timpani and piano from the timpanist Jesse Kregal. Since Jesse lived in Portland, a friend of mine, Howard Van Hyning, set me up with all of his timpani. I must have spent about twenty hours banging away on his timpani and the other percussion he had lying around. I'm really grateful to him for this as well as the personal assistance he gave me.

Finally, I worked out a special, unique performance setup based on the idea of having the sound from one instrument being directed into another so that the resulting sounds were produced by the intersection of two or more instruments. There were the timpani, of course, and placed just above the heads, bongos, temple blocks, and a cymbal on one timpani. Since the timpani had the pedal tuning arrangement they could do glissandi and at the same time give a glissando to any sounds reflected into them. I began to work at first rather freely, improvising, fooling around with all those potentials. What happened with various sticks? What happened with various rates of speed? When I felt I really had control of the different performance techniques, I made up symbols for them.

With symbols, any set of them naturally generates their own context that is a kind of language with special possibilities for growth. This is very important to me as a composer. Once I've made up the symbols, I can think with them, arrange and pattern them. These symbols lead to combinations and events that I don't think would have occurred to me elsewise. They are a way of seeing the sound; they lead to not only a sharper understanding of individual sounds, but also create a whole different context in which to hear the sound. This has been particularly relevant to the *Circle Musics*.

BC: When you are composing a score with the metasymbolic thing you've gotten into, how much of it is the eye?

WH: Out of the symbols grow relationships that are investigated in making the piece. It's like language. You have a certain scramble of words there; suddenly, a new arrangement occurs to you—you've got a new insight. The eye plays an important role here, but it's not for the eye. The eye is simply a tool. What I'm getting at is that composition is only a means to produce music; it's not music. Composition uses written symbols as its means. It uses them actively to generate ideas, not only passively to notate preexistent ideas. The point is that I've found this to be true for not only my graphic pieces, but in my more-or-less traditionally notated works as well. Take my trumpet and tape piece, *Passages 13—The Fire.* For the plunger mute, I use six different settings, from completely closed to completely open, indicated with special symbols. I needed to do this because on the tape part I had sounds that were similar enough to this mute effect, that by controlling them I could get the trumpet to weave in and out of the tape part.

Incidentally, I'd like to say this because it's not a common approach to tape and instrument music. It is something I've done instinctively from the beginning, and now that I am aware of it, I feel strongly about it. That is, working to get a whole resonant body of sounds so that the instrument is not set off apart from the tape. There's none of the man-versus-machine scenario implied: to have the instrument and the electronic sounds appear to emanate from one source, without violating the true nature of the instrument. I want the instrument to be there, and I want the player there as a person, and I don't want the tape to be removed from that. I want the two of them to "fit" together. What used to be done by having things come together on a triad, I want to accomplish by coming together timbrally or with similar motions. I stress "motions" because by "timbre" I'm usually referring to sounds that are full of inner activity, that come about by a complex of performance actions.

BC: This is choreography.

WH: I think it is. Sound, for me, is movement. When we talk of timbre, we're really talking of different movements and not static color states. The difficulty is, these things are usually confused by the ear and in notation. There's always the overall sound, the total color or texture, but this is made up of many small complex inner movements, all variable, which give the life to the sound.

BC: So there it's together and yet there is an independence. There is more than the setting of mass against mass.

WH: One thing Wolpe gave me is a strong interest in polyphony. All of my timbral pieces are really polyphonic, not in the sense of many pitched lines, but as the precise joining of different independent actions. Also, something related to this I probably got from Stefan is the interest in doing virtuosic music. Pieces where the fitting together is very complex. The excitement of players being at the edge of disaster: the player completely up front, as the master of his fate at least for the moment. I get excited by a performer who is totally into his instrument, where his mastery, his life, is completely bound up in playing.

BC: You're not dramatizing him in the nineteenth-century sense.

WH: No. I don't see virtuosity as a hero thing. I see it as a greater revealing of the person, in a very special way, through his instrument. What happens when someone is doing the thing he really cares about and spent his life learning how to do, and doing it well is, in some way, a life-or-death matter. And then to give him pieces based on unusual ways of playing that we work together and by the nature of their difficulties, make him confront his instrument as well as himself, differently.

BC: Is this going to work for performers who are someone else [other than a specific virtuoso]?

WH: It has to, in order to be a piece. In composing you have to start somewhere. I start from people—their individual ways of moving and playing. The trick is to work up the piece in a way that is faithful to the original inspiration and yet not limited to it. This is my concern with notation: to get a structure fixed as a performance event, open enough that any performer can get into the piece in a personal way and closed enough that he must deal with something more than his own habits. I'm very excited by the act of performance: the performer coming on stage and not just doing his own thing but coming to grips with a text, a defined thing, that demands all the skill and understanding he has.

BC: A lot of fuddle is being written now about people turning off from the concert format. From your comments about interaction and performer participation, you still are not really worried about it. The idea of what people could call the "concert ritual" is important to you.

WH: Actually, it is. I've given the question a lot of thought. The first thing is that the concert hall is not a home base, a natural medium. It is only a mode of presentation. In the twentieth century one of the worst things that has happened to our so-called classical, or serious music, is that our home base is rooted in the concert hall: an unnatural, plastic affair.

Beethoven's music didn't start in a concert hall. Liszt and Chopin played in salons. Lead Belly [Huddie William Ledbetter] played on back porches and the fields. Jazz grew up in the nightclub. There's no music that we know of—marching music, band music, dance music, so-called serious music—that didn't grow out of a time and place associated with a people and a culture. And then, after this, the concert hall comes along as a means of distribution. It serves it up to more people.

They bring in a group from Cambodia. We go down and pay our two bucks and listen. We wouldn't hear them otherwise. But that music didn't start on the stage; it grew out of a whole way of life and is intended to be performed in a different place. And it still communicates this. So, to that extent, there's nothing wrong with the concert hall in the same way there's nothing wrong with a phonograph record. They are a means of bringing an experience to more people. But, when they become the home base, which everything is supposed to grow out of—when music is written solely for the concert hall—then, something is wrong. It's a real problem we all face. We can't get away from it. Twentieth-century music has not been written for or done much in another kind of environment.

Today we are beginning to get away from this with the loft scene in New York. Out in the Middle West [is] a gymnasium-type space that's beginning to come into play—some place of presentation where you know your audience. I don't mean the colleagues or fellow professionals, but an audience whose values you know and you identify with and address your insights to. Then things live: they have an identity, they have a time and a place. And the concert hall system can't really get very much in the way of this. It's when somebody sits down to write a string quartet to be done in Carnegie Hall that there's something wrong—something no longer authentic or real. It becomes, somehow, a package operation, like writing music only for the money.

This is, for me, the concert hall problem. Not the falseness of an outmoded ritual, but of looking on the concert hall as an institution with roots when it just doesn't by definition have any. Too many composers have been writing their music for a mode of presentation instead of for real people and a place. That's a major problem of contemporary music. Art needs identities with people out of which what it says acquires specialness above and beyond being an aesthetic object.

BC: Yet so many people nowadays are writing, saying that the whole concert hall thing is wrong, it's crippling, it's a binding ritual.

WH: Well, you can talk to a writer or a poet, and he'll tell you the same thing about the publishers. It's not so much the basic idea that's got us messed up as the people that are running it and how it's tied up in the total economic system.

BC: You're about to go over to Europe; what are you going to do? What about that bag over there? I know you're not *worried* about that.

WH: I am, to be frank about it. I decided I had to get away from it all last fall. In America, this means asking a foundation to send you to Europe. Lately, I've had to spend too much time on the phone arranging rehearsals, teaching, judging scores, appearing at meetings to explain and/or justify new music. I filled out an application, and now I'm going to Rome for a year or two. Europe isn't a strange place for me. I've been over a number of times to visit and for performances and I've always enjoyed it. But the thought of a year? I was really upset about that and I wasn't sure I wanted to go. I really like New York. It's been such a real stimulus, and I feel that I am going to miss it. I really have mixed emotions about this. I may be the only person who is going to Europe who really doesn't want to.

BC: But that's why it would be valuable.

WH: Maybe, but I have high hopes certainly that, if everything else goes wrong, I will have the time to get into certain things that I want to work on.

BC: Which are what?

WH: I've a number of pieces to write. Some four or five ideas I've sketched out over the last two years and haven't had the time to work on. In addition to that, I want to come to terms with the implications of my past work: where it's going and how it fits into the larger scheme of things. Until now, each piece I've written starts from its own premise; I've worked hard to compose those pieces in a way that is faithful to their initial idea. This has meant, however, that I've written radically different kinds of music, in terms of the materials and techniques involved. I think this has been a good way to work. But I'd like to see if there aren't some connections or correspondences that I've overlooked and try to develop those.

In many ways, music is really about process, or what I referred to before as "syntax." The *Circle Music* series, *Round and About* [1970] and *Columbus Circle* [1971] deal with this using graphics and leaving the decisions concerning materials up to the performer. Also recently I performed a new piece, *Part Sequences for an Open Space 2 (Table)* [1972], that incorporates theatrical means and which deals with this question on a much larger scale.[7] It's two-and-a-half hours long and involves four musicians, four dancers, four actors, and five sets constructed around the performing space. It's certainly the most ambitious work I've done and, in many ways, is a turning point for me.

In all these works, I've been concerned with carefully fixing a system of relations, which then stimulate a performer to discover his own means of expressing these relations. On the other hand, my other recent pieces like *Time and Again* [1969], *Ek-Stasis II* and *Passages 13—The Fire* work in a different direction in which all the details are fixed. The performer is given specific material as stimulation to his imagination; from this he must discover the syntactical relation that will make the whole thing hang together. To the extent that both these approaches work, there's no problem. However, an open process too often leads performers to find only trivial ideas. Too many players need specific sound events, motives, something concrete in order to be stimulated. But, with totally notated music, somehow—no matter how original the materials are—one is back to the old business of reciting lines.

The question comes up because of my strong belief in the role of the performer in music. As a composer, I see my role as being a stimulator or initiator of performances, not as a creator of cultural objects, and I want to rethink the

ways of doing this. There's also the business of roots, or more exactly, reestablish-
ing a social basis for contemporary music. This is a big question facing music
right now; I feel that, for the first time in our [twentieth] century, composers
are beginning to accept that the ability to draw people together is the only
thing that makes music interesting. Because of this, music is really going to
get it together within the next five or ten years.

BC: I think it's doing it now.

WH: It's starting now; I feel a new spirit animating things. It's one of the main
reasons I feel bad about leaving at this time. Composers and performers are
beginning to do music for an audience and on a basis that puts music up front
as music instead of hiding behind the sanctity of cultural institutions, universities, of being serious and above it all. Also, there's a new spirit of cooperation. I
sense less of a spirit of competitiveness. I even would say that music is entering
a period that could be what the early '50s were for American painting. For the
last seventy years, modern music has been pretty much of a disaster. Excluding
those really great accomplishments by a few individuals, which will always be
the case, the general level has been so low and of so little impact, that music is
rarely even considered as part of the cultural scene. Possibly, music is just now
entering the twentieth century.

Music had the toughest time, in a way. In the nineteenth century, music was
king; theater was melodrama or opera without music. Dance and painting had
qualities that quickly seemed out of place in their past form for the new age.
Whereas music *was* Mozart, Beethoven, Wagner, Brahms. Even today, most
movie music, background music, and popular ballads could have been written
in the nineteenth century. It's only literature that seems to have succeeded at
being a major cultural force through both centuries, especially in America.
Poetry, novels, essays . . .

BC: Novels, yes, but not poetry.

WH: Well, Ezra Pound . . .

BC: Yes, but you're talking about nineteenth-century . . .

WH: That's another thing. Still, twentieth-century literature has been the major
traditional art form, whereas for music, it's really only jazz. Jazz is perhaps
the twentieth-century music. At any rate, right now things are going to catch
hold for music. What's going to help is that we have begun to get away from
this idea of working on the basis of "the next step." Schoenberg has serialized
pitches, now let's serialize rhythms, then dynamics. It's like [Pierre] Boulez
saying, "Schönberg est mort": let's do what he did, only more so. We must live
up to the imperative of the historical moment. This has infected America very
much, particularly New York. "What is the next step in history? One must
march with time. If you don't, you're simply out of it." This just doesn't make
any sense in the American context.

BC: This is our ritual, this does turn out to be an inherited European thing.

WH: Yes, history is a very strange source of inspiration. One always goes on from what came before, but when you're dealing with borrowed history, something is false. In America, we've always had this problem. Take the "Americana" styles of Roy Harris, Aaron Copland, and William Schumann, for example; somehow they are all so French. They're also very self-conscious, but that's understandable. In a way, I can understand the attraction for Schoenberg and the twelve-tone technique that came after the war more easily. It was so radical and, being technical, it seemed outside of history, but of course it wasn't. As long as one is just dealing with musical techniques, any of them can work to produce a great piece.

BC: The potential is never exhausted. It's just awful hard sometimes.

WH: Wolpe used to talk about how ideas become exhausted. No matter how strong their intrinsic value was, they finally lose the possibilities of renewal through no fault of their own. He felt this way about the tonal system. I wonder if this is still true. Perhaps it is possible for ideas to regain their future, also, through no fault of their own.

At any rate, I would say that at this time everything has again become an open question. I don't see any one way of working as having a favored place in the future. It seems that the whole idea or newness, of being original, has lost its appeal. To have an original personality is one thing. But this business of working to make a "contribution" by doing something that hasn't been done yet—serializing another parameter, smashing a cymbal instead of a violin, or developing some new piece of technical apparatus—doesn't lead us very far. This thinking is very bad for the imagination. It begs the questions of "what does it all mean? who is it for?" Who wants to listen to music that's written for history? There's got to be some other animating purpose behind it.

At last these things are changing, I think. Even in New York, which has always been America's bastion of cliques and movements, artists are much more open to what other people are doing, without feeling threatened by the differences with their own work.

BC: That's where we split with Europe.

WH: Yes, in Europe everything has to be categorized. One has to be part of a movement; one works to have an oeuvre. Before one's work can have meaning, it has to fit into history. A Swiss music dictionary or encyclopedia wrote to me, asking to have a form filled out on myself, giving information for their next edition. One of the questions blandly asked, "who are you the artistic disciple of?" That question is impossible to imagine in the American context. One thing, though; the European composer always has the sense that when he writes a piece he is addressing the nation.

BC: It may have been the conscience of the nation.

WH: That can be a very good thing. It leads to pretension and an inflated sense of importance, which has always bothered me in Europe. On the other hand, when the works are good, they have a quality of being really major, a quality that says "Listen, this isn't just a piece of music." Our freedom to do pretty much what we want in the arts in America leads to a situation where what one does doesn't matter. This bothers me; it's the explanation for why so much American music doesn't seem to really dig in beyond its initial good ideas and personal dualities. I would like to see more coming to terms with things beyond oneself. For example, take twelve-tone music. In America, most of these works were conceived as modest essays into perfect musical form. In Europe, with [Karlheinz] Stockhausen and Boulez, working out of a similar concern with techniques and formal procedures, there is the overriding desire to reorder the universe. Now that's nonsense, but it gives the music a whole different quality. I'm still talking about the need for communication with an audience here. History is the way it works in Europe. America has yet to find its own way, at least as far as "serious" music is concerned.

It's very interesting; there isn't a name for the music we do. Contemporary music, modern music, new music: all words that the public associates with pop music as much or more so than with, well, "classical" music. This doesn't seem to bother other composers very much. "A rose is a rose by any other name . . ." So why get hung up on words? Still, people give names to things they recognize. Those that scoff at getting hung up on words still refer to country rock, folk rock, city blues, country blues, hard rock, acid rock—an endless list of hairline distinctions. At the same time, music critics assert that they can't tell the difference between John Cage and Milton Babbitt. This means our music doesn't exist for America. It seems very likely that popular music will be the music taken seriously in the next century, the same as nineteenth-century music, classical music, was taken seriously by this century. Pop music has acquired an identity, a body of associations that people can relate to. The traditional distinction between the popular arts and the classical arts is that the popular arts are rooted in the moment, the passing fad, and, hence, temporary, while the classical arts are rooted in a place, the nation, the total culture of a civilization and, hence, are timeless. For twentieth-century America, this has changed. It's classical music of the past which seems dated, not popular music. Perhaps it is pop music which constitutes our shared experience, whereas no matter how finely made classical music is, it can't make up for never having been part of our life.

One thing that bothers me so much is that the problem seems to hold only for music. American painting, dance, theater, movies, literature, all have an identity, not only in America, but in the world. Poetry, for example; I'm especially bowled over at the incredible way our poets express themselves with a natural, purely American voice, and at the same time have an age-old quality. Not the history we were talking about before, but a spirit of history.

BC: And that is very real in this country, because it is so immediate.

WH: A special sense of history, not as concerned with systems to fit into. Berio said in a talk how, when he walks down a street, he sees history all around him and how he would like to get that into his music. Having been in Europe, I understand what he means, but when I walk down a street, it's not the same thing. Take [Charles] Olson and [Robert] Duncan, the Black Mountain School, and West Coast poets, they have this way of bringing in the Middle Ages and Renaissance and making it all part of the American experience. And the way Gary Snyder brings in the East.

BC: What's important about Snyder is not the East, but the poems about discovery and awareness in the mountain west. It's not Olson's *Maximus* poems, because there's still so much Europeanism in Worcester [Massachusetts]. But being a forest lookout, a logging crew member, Snyder is really finding the new world fashion in the way that nobody in Europe could ever understand.

WH: Without any apparent effort. That's what's so beautiful about it.

BC: Do you know any of the new Canadian poets? There's about five of them you should read. They're so much more recent than we are, and still have so much sense of this historical growing.

WH: No, I'm afraid I don't know them. But I would like to say that Robert Duncan made clear to me how quotes could work as something more than a literary device, or as a camp thing. I mean, the way he uses quotes to enlarge the field or, as he says, to make things belong not only by fitting in, but also by the resonances of the whole or the inclusion of forms within forms. There's a way of getting outside, beyond a specific time, without losing a sense of place.

BC: Getting time to work for you so that you can see place in a different way.

WH: Also, their work gives the impression of going out on a limb, risking new forms, without seeming experimental.

BC: Of course not; the only experiment was if you viewed it as a European. Then you'd said, "These guys are out of their gourd."

WH: Here there is a ring of history, authenticity, of a people, the whole roots thing.

BC: The whole sense of awareness about what's there.

WH: These are all qualities I'd like to see more of in music. Not the involvement with history we talked of before. Music has been so much more wrapped up with Europe than other American arts. This seems absurd. I don't think that the European experience is that relevant any more.

BC: You've come to terms with it, you've turned your back on it, but it's still with you.

WH: I don't know if I've come to terms with it, but I've turned my back on it.

Notes

1. William Hellermann, "The Composition and Structure of *But . . . the Moon . . .*" (DMA diss., Columbia University, 1978), 6.

2. William Hellermann, "Letter to Philip Corner, April 15, 1976," in Theresa Sauer, ed., *Notations 21* (New York: Mark Batty, 2008), 96.

3. Hellermann, "Composition and Structure," 6.

4. Morton Feldman, quoted in William Hellermann, "Visible Music (The Score as a Sore to Be Rubbed)," *PAJ: A Journal of Performance and Art* 33/1 (January 2011): 87.

5. Hellermann, "Visible Music," 90–92.

6. See William Hellermann, ed., *Sound/Art* (New York: SoundArt Foundation, 1983), for documentation of the SoundArt Foundation's early showings.

7. *Part Sequences for an Open Space II*, premiered Loeb Student Center, New York, 1972, http://www.soundart.org/whlngrsm.html (accessed August 17, 2019).

9 Sydney Hodkinson (b. 1934)

DAVE HEADLAM

Winnipeg, Manitoba, is one of the coldest cities on Earth, but this forbidding locale nonetheless produced composer, conductor, and all-round warm personality Sydney Hodkinson. I knew Syd at the Eastman School of Music until he retired from teaching composition and conducting in 1999. Syd was a gregarious fellow, full of sarcastic humor, and his expressive voice resounded through the halls of Eastman. He enjoyed teaching and renewed his own faith through his students, all the while offering streetwise cautions about how the world would, of course, crush their artistic spirits, but with a twinkle in his eye that said everything would turn out. On doctoral exams, Syd brought his infamous test score for a chamber combination of incongruous instruments; each part was full of unplayable notes and unmusical gestures, with unlikely tempos and articulations, and woe to the student lacking the wit and wisdom to see through the joke! Syd's sense of humor was his calling card.

Syd came of age in the shadow of Milton Babbitt's "Who Cares if You Listen?" proclamation that came to symbolize the compositional world of the late 1950s.[1] Rather than being an "academic composer," however, Syd was more of a "Beat composer," describing others in the "groovy" terms of his time as "cat" and "man"; but, even as the hippest cat in the composition department, Syd was nonetheless extremely learned. As part of both the old guard and the avant-garde, he rejected nothing of value from music history. Confronted with the competition of all of recorded music, Syd responded with a polystylistic language: tonality and popular music styles commingle wittily in his music. This approach functioned as a refuge; in response to Childs's question about the general "rediscovery of tonality" in the air at the time, Syd responds with his rationale: "perhaps a certain natural just fedupness with ugly sounds. Too much note-spinning."

For composers of Syd's generation, the university ivory tower was both their salvation and their prison. The academy confronts creators with, as Syd notes, that "old bugaboo of communication." Here they could write pieces for the "cat in the next office," for a "tremendous intellectual stimulus," but the victory was a hollow one: "pieces that end up that way, you ought to write 'em and chuck 'em." From their academic offices, these composers were separated from the people they longed to engage with their music. Syd above all didn't want to "shut the door off to that humanity out there," but he feared that "what I write ain't gonna communicate to even a small part of the world."

Nonetheless, this interview comes from a time (1970–72) when Syd was working on a Ford Foundation Contemporary Music Project Grant as artist-in-residence in Minneapolis. The grant was part of a series designed to introduce young audiences to new music and to place composers into society. In referencing this opportunity Syd used words like "duty" ("But I felt a duty, if that's not too maudlin a word to use") and "creativity" to reflect the mission of bringing music to real people. He found that "there's no difference in doing a piece for grade four kids and writing the Great American Symphony." At the end of his time on this project, Syd pursued this direction in *A Contemporary Primer for Band, for Wind Brass and Percussion Instruments* (1972) in three volumes, for easy, intermediate, and advanced.[2] These pieces are *aesthetically* above the high school level but offered a training ground in new sounds and compositional methods, as part of a general trend toward an outreach of modern music in education, such as Brian Dennis's *Experimental Music in Schools*.[3]

While eloquent on the role of the arts in general, Syd did not want to analyze or even discuss his own music. "I will not discuss a work that I am working on with anyone, not even with my *frau*. Now, you will say, 'Shit, what a romantic idea!' I really do that. When a good colleague intellectually wishes to discuss some technical facet of composition, or someone says at a cocktail party, 'Well, what are you writing now?'—in both cases I will remove myself one step and talk about the work that has just been copied or is at least all completed. I will stay one behind."

Syd's website lists some 250 works in nine categories with multiple commissions and awards that range from a jazz-inflected liveliness with flashes of humor—in titles such as *Another Man's Poison* for brass quintet (1970), *Hit and Run Praeambula* for harp and percussion (1997), and *Interplay: A Histrionic Controversy for Four Musicians* (1966)—to a more restrained "New Music" fare such as *Potpourri: 11 Very Short Pieces* (2009), *Epitaphion: Lament* (1990) and the Piano Concerto no. 1 (1997–2004). A humorous example is a piece for clarinet/saxophone, piano, and tape called *Dissolution of the Serial* (1967). This nine-minute exploration begins with a Pierre Boulez–inspired "post-serial" piano texture of aggressive single notes combined with a clarinet part starting from the third movement of Olivier Messiaen's *Quartet for the End of Time*. The counterpoint grows more manic, with the clarinetist gasping for breath, until the piano seems to tire of the tedious texture to dissolve the serialism into more consonant, thicker textures, and popular rhythms, including (at 4:30) a quote from the Serial Anti-Christ Richard Wagner's opening to *Tristan*. A minute later we are in a cool jazz saxophone solo that leads to a boogie-woogie piano (5:50).[4] Players' shouts and other vocalisms accompany a transformation into "American Songbook" territory, and the piece ends with a return to the opening manic energy, with ever-increasing back-and-forth riffs and quotes, both verbal and musical. The final passage features piano ragtime at a breakneck tempo under a cacophony of verbal jousts. The piece is virtuosic and hilarious, much like watching Syd holding court at a faculty meeting.

Syd's artistic credo is perhaps most clearly expressed in his answer to Childs's query about support for composers in society. Here is the composer I remember well: he is sincere and takes his craft seriously, and he seeks to build bridges between musicians. This is his contribution. And of course, as always with Syd, a spoonful of humor helps move the process along.

Sydney Hodkinson: Interview

BARNEY CHILDS: What [are the] entertainments and problems that you found as a town composer?[5]

SYDNEY HODKINSON: There are two unusual aspects with these CMP [Contemporary Music Project] grants: (1) one gets away from the university environment, and (2) the two-year continual contact with the professional world and the time in this grant to get through some educational things. Those are the two main virtues.

I've tried to write some "school music" within my normal university schedule, but it's difficult because of the pressures of the university life. When you write a piece, it's usually one that you really want to write; you aren't going to take time to write that junior high string orchestra work or talk to some junior high band director. Even the good ones are "suspect" to the composer. It works both ways: they also may distrust the composer.

Since the position was touted as a resident composer, I could be used in any manner by theater companies, dance companies, professional orchestras. When I came, I got a few phone calls from local educators. Many of these—and this area is very typical—were elementary and high school orchestra directors who said everything I knew already about the state of education. Most of the published stuff was a crock; wouldn't I like to try and do something with the kids? One band director said at night he'd turn on his FM radio, hear some Ligeti and say, "Gee, that's going on in the real world, but I don't have anything like that to expose to my students." Right away that puts him in a new level far above most educators. He wants to do some of these things, and wouldn't I be interested in writing some?

And I did write a couple of pieces. I found a poet who teaches philosophy at the University of Minnesota who had great short children's poetry—little animal stuff—so I wrote a dozen of those for elementary and high school choirs.

I used techniques that are au courant in composition in the last fifty years. I wrote D major elementary school first-position works for strings. And in doing both of those elementary school pieces for strings and choir and I had the time on the grant, this fostered the idea for my band primer.[6] I decided to write for band because there are a lot of them, and because I approached three or four local band directors, "What do you think of this idea to try and get the kids to loosen up their ear balls," and they agreed with me. But I think it will be a long time before people will purchase or use this.

BC: I disagree. I was happy to hear that it tentatively had a publisher.

SH: Contracts haven't been signed yet, but I hope they will. I shouldn't talk about the publishing world yet, but it depends a lot on what that publisher does with it. Publishers push Harold Robbins, who doesn't need it, but will not push someone else like an Al Greenberg or some novelist who needs a push.[7] It's a bad business proposition. The reaction in the Twin Cities to the initial copies that I've sent out is very positive. I want to get feedback from the educators because these people were not only interested, they were intelligent folks who spent five days a week in the classroom with children.

In fact, the nicest things that have happened to me from an educational perspective have been invitations to go into their classrooms, to do the CMP bit as they write it up in their blurbs. It was a very nice experience to hear these grade four and five kids six months ago do my choral pieces, some of which were very difficult. But they did not know how difficult they were. And if the teacher is willing to spend a little time, they can get great things out of those kids, as I knew would happen (I'm not sure the teacher did). The kids surprise you; they are often ten light years ahead of where the teacher is. They would suggest ways to perform the pieces, and they came up with better ideas than I had.

But that aspect of the CMP grant—in other words, here is a live composer who doesn't wear frilled cuffs and a wig and he's not dead—has always been useful in any program. You can't tell what good you would ever do, but if you only reach one or two out of a class of seventy, probably those one or two otherwise would not have been reached. I don't mean the budding young musicians; I mean the guy who will be a junior executive for the 3M Company in twenty years and will complain when he's on the symphony board that they aren't playing contemporary work.

What is most upsetting is to see the current state of art education. But all composers, all my friends, all my colleagues feel the same. I did a camp up in northern Minnesota last summer and a sophomore majoring in music at a college exclaimed, in all seriousness, when I played the third movement of the Schoenberg, Op. 16, "Surely this is not music?" That attitude's still there. I always knew it was there, as does any composer. I found presenting new music very difficult to do, even with the time this grant enabled me. There's no difference in doing a piece for grade four kids and writing the Great American Symphony. It takes just as much energy. It's just that the piece is thirty-eight seconds long instead of thirty-eight minutes. But I felt a duty, if that's not too maudlin a word to use, because I can do that for some people. That was the main reason for the primer. Why not put it all together in a collection and come up with simple ways of trying to get the kids to appreciate a cluster chord as being a reasonable musical solution? They might even like it.

BC: It is progressive. You introduce new notations, a couple each time, as well as traditional musical notation, and it does move through a whole gamut.

SH: Once, while rehearsing these pieces I did for *elementary* school string orchestra, one of the attending high school directors said, "My God, you wrote this like it was all first position in half notes, but aesthetically it's still way above my high school kids. Can I play them with my high school orchestra?" There are kids in the high school who didn't know what the word "simile" meant, for example; they had never been confronted with it. So when I wrote my primer, I introduced free rhythmic notation along with *ritardandi* and the standard terms, which the director is free to ignore or to accept. In that sense, it's very much a textbook, as any primer would be.

BC: You are especially qualified to get into notation because of your work with the Contemporary Directions Ensemble. You are so familiar with what works and what does not, things that are simply notational gingerbread and others that are valid and usable. You didn't have to do a lot of ground clearing before you sat down to do it.

SH: In that sense, the primer is a little suspect from a purely personal compositional, creative point of view. I did not hesitate to write a piece or two that would employ a notation that is in wide use, although I don't do it in my so-called serious music. Whenever the music looks different, performers often think that it's a product from some lunatic fringe. Of course it isn't at all, it's going on all over the globe. This is hard to sell, especially for those who would never buy a collection like this and think that income is my peculiar penchant for doing it. But it is not that at all. As one guy put it, "the big crusher's going to come, when now that you've got the kids ready to play this stuff, where's the stuff for them to play?" One guy last week offered this comment: "Well, now I have 'primed' my kids. I'll buy your primer now that my kids are primed." Give me a piece that is not "dissonant" because it has a minor second in it, or it's ersatz Debussy, or in modal harmony, all passing under the guise of "new music" for educational works.

Things are changing, although not as fast as one would like. In the next year or two, since I will go back to my conducting position, I will try and encourage some of my colleagues to investigate it. There is a lot educators can do about encouraging composers in their locale to create works. There again, they say it's already been done, but it really hasn't; not written by what we know are the good guys. I would like to entice a [Paul] Chihara or a [Peter] Westergaard to write music for kids, you see.[8] I hope I can do this.

BC: One problem is that some of us have suitable pieces, but nobody knows about them. How do we get it out? You have a springboard now from which you can operate.

SH: Perhaps not. Publishers could do a lot to bring these works to the attention of school musicians. First of all, a publisher has taken works of this sort on as a so-called prestige item. He knows it ain't gonna sell like the *Overture in B Flat* by a "school" composer or an arranger. At the same time, he will take out a half-page ad in *Music Educators' Journal* to push *Overture in B Flat* so that everyone knows about it. Hey man, let's pick up on this arrangement, and not push the good new American composer who has taken time to produce an unusual work that is "contemporary" in the best sense of the word. I feel the publisher needs to do a little more soul-searching along those lines.

That gets into another area. I don't have a major work published in this country. They are all published in Canada or Europe. The only way they would ever get knowledge of them would be through knowing me personally or they would come on them by accident. *Armistice* is an example. Alexandria, Minnesota, did a performance of *Armistice*. They sent up to Canada and got the score, but it was only because the director heard of this. He didn't know the piece existed until a fellow Twin Cities orchestra director told him about it.

BC: The grapevine is about all we have going for us. Let's say you do a piece for trumpets and a trumpet player will tell another trumpet player.

SH: It's unfortunate that the publisher won't appreciate. . . . Sure, it's unusual. It's not that marketable. But it seems to me he could expend a very little cash and a little bit of effort to promulgate works that would fall into that line, because it would expose the educator to more of it, and then he'd give it a try. But at least push it a little bit. There's no push.

BC: Did you also have time here to do your own work? Or were you caught up with educational works?

SH: I was brought here on a grant. A local committee of artists, businessmen, managers, theater directors, [and] a dance company was formed to bring me. I'm now in a community outside a metropolitan area that has close to a couple of million people and it's often hard for them to come into town. They have their own artists here, thoroughly competent, professional men and women. Since I'm grafted on top of the ongoing cultural activity, it's difficult to get a foot in the door, which is why the grant was for two years instead of one; because after the first year, you get to know people and then it starts to happen. I did a lot more conducting than I thought I was going to do. I conducted the Minnesota Orchestra. I got a commission from the local civic orchestra (which is very good—a typical community orchestra, but of really quite decent quality). So I didn't cop out on my own work. I wrote a piece for the St. Paul Chamber Orchestra; they recorded it a year ago. It was professional work. I've worked a lot harder than I thought. I came with the idea, not that it was going to be a vacation but that it was going to be so great to do nothing but to get up in the morning and not worry about teaching a class or grading papers, and that I didn't have to worry about support for myself and my family—I could just write. But I kept extremely busy. This included things outside of the composition; for example, lecturing, conducting, talking to the League of National Jewish Women, play a little [Pierre] Boulez. Again, immeasurable results: you don't know what good you are going to do, but you produce works. I've written an awful lot of music here.

There's an insidious thing; one of the reasons I was happy to take the grant is that the university environment is not that great for the composers. Now there are many who do not feel this way. I am not sold on the "artist in the university" as being a viable answer to the question: how to live in a society that really doesn't care about what work you do. The main reason is because there is an especially good music school here. I happen to work at one of the main music schools in the country, and you get to rub heads all the time with good minds. This is all great, but there is a certain self-consciousness, a certain intimidation, that can result if you don't watch out. The professional contact and the educational "insertion" are not there because of that. I was especially grateful to get the grant for those two reasons. In addition, to get out of the cloistered hall of the university in order to meet the truck drivers and the professional musicians was very nice.

BC: Why did they stop the project? It would have been a bonanza for everybody.

SH: They just ran out of bread. I would hope executives are trying to think of ways to extend this. The project itself is now becoming more and more interested in the things they can do in teacher-training institutions to help the people who are being unleashed on our kids to get a little smart about contemporary music. It's touchy because whether we like it or not, the composer is feared. I think if there is any one little thing I may or may not have been able to do with the teachers, the professional musicians or the kids themselves, was to show them that I am sincere in my work. I like what I do, I do it fairly competently, I work hard at it, I'm serious about it. There is always this problem to break down the distrust that seems to extend between an artist and any type of purveyor of the art or even an interested teacher. And a basic good comes from just building social bridges.

BC: Yeah. Enjoy a good cigar. Been known to drink in public once in a while.

SH: I umpire Little League baseball games. I enjoy my kids. I'm a member of their community, and just because I write this funny-sounding music doesn't make me all that suspect as an individual. From that point of view, the project itself is very valid. I have no idea how they intend to extend it, although I know they are trying to get funds to find ways to do this, specifically those that involve the community. It's a tough row to hoe in this country because new art is just not that important. I sat on the arts council here, for example, and tried to broach the problem, but the reaction of the newspaper and the sports director on the TV station was "We can't do this with the arts because no one's interested." Well, how interested is the public in the sports syndrome? Possibly it's because they are continually confronted with it. How many pages in the local paper are about high school basketball? They'll report that down to the nth score at night on TV, yet some sixteen-year-old piano player who made an audition comes on the evening news only by accident. The "arts" are all sub rosa and suspect. It's not an important part of American life. The kid that plays the oboe in the orchestra is almost always looked at askance.

BC: Don't you think that there is a slight relaxing of this now? When you and I were in high school, if we were interested in music we were real freakos. Now the musician in high school, thanks to rock groups, is much more a culture hero than he used to be.

SH: I would agree with you, yes, that certainly it has changed somewhat. But then, when I was in high school and we were blowing [Count Basie's] *Jumping at the Woodside.*

BC: [Duke Ellington's] *C Jam Blues.*

SH: We had our share of acceptance in the school: I could play baritone saxophone.

BC: Let's take the people who not only like the university atmosphere, and find it ideal, but are not interested in getting out of it. They couldn't care less whether a high school down the street needs a work for orchestra. They are involved in writing masterpieces.

SH: As many years ago when Milton Babbitt wrote that article for *High Fidelity,* "Who Cares if You Listen?," there's much truth in that. I don't really see any serious young artist reading that article and not agreeing with it, because it's the way things are. The artist's main responsibility is working, producing things, and all the trite sayings are true: "To thy own self be true." I certainly understand and respect that attitude. I think it's a matter of degree where my difference comes with colleagues who feel as you've described. I don't mean to suggest that I'm debasing anyone's art, but I'm talking about the old bugaboo of communication. It's a matter of degree. I know men who, it would be fair to say, do write pieces for their colleagues. There is a tremendous intellectual stimulus one gets from this. Personally, the pieces that end up that way, you ought to write 'em and chuck 'em, or temper them later with other considerations. Again, it's been foisted on an audience by the gap.

People could say of me that I really want to bridge the gap. I don't wish to do it if I have to get out on the road with them sitting eighty miles away, without them getting on the road too. I would be willing to walk perhaps fifty or sixty of those miles, but they would have to walk their share, too. I would even say that I would go more than halfway on the double-edged sword just to try and get them to appreciate serious artists. I care whether my music doesn't communicate to *some*body. But who? I would like my music to communicate more to performers than the cat in the next office, without question. Yet I know full well what I write ain't gonna communicate to even a small part of the world.

There is a certain debasement that one can foist onto one's art to write "the successful piece." Honestly, I don't believe that I do that. But then, any composer can say that, depending on how she views her own integrity. "I still write in the Dorian mode because I believe that the Dorian mode is the music of the future; that's the way I hear it." And he still firmly believes that. But I'm aware of these feelings that I react to in the university. I don't like 'em. The awareness of it is enough for me to take care that I don't shut the door off to that humanity out there, by worrying about some highly intellectualized problem.

BC: In your role with the Contemporary Directions Ensemble, you are the way many potentially gifted or giving musicians would like to be. The only channel they have to see what is happening now is through what they hear played by any new music group at any university. And yours happens to be a peculiarly good one, one which reaches out.

SH: I have mixed emotions (which I am happy to confess to you!). I go back to my school next year pretty much as a conductor. I have the Contemporary Directions group, a wind ensemble, a concert band—and I'm a little scared. I like the music making. I played clarinet on a tour last year. Bill Albright and I went on a tour of the boonies in Minnesota and played. The composer-performer is certainly necessary—there are a lot of good ones around, as you know. They do a lot of good for relationships with the general audience. However, there might be better ways. Where I work in Ann Arbor, the situation is unusual; composers one or two decades before I got anywhere near the University of Michigan had built up an intelligent, educated audience for new music. We can give concerts for five or six hundred people sometimes, and that's very rewarding. Since we have a good student body there, I honestly try to divorce myself enough to separate the conducting, the objective music-making part of it, from the compositional. I have music I dislike, but as a conductor, my attitude is entirely different in presenting a work to a public. I have been put down for this; the group could be better, some people argue, if they have a specific point of view to present. To do music of only a certain class of East Coast or a certain class of mid-West, or western, scores; to only do the European mucky-mucks. I do not feel this way at all. Furthermore, not only should you do a wide range of repertoire, you should buck them up one against the other. I would go out of my way to put Harold Budd right up against Elaine Barkin on a program. I also can see the value of having a piece of Corelli on the program, although I won't be doing that with my group. But, again, that's a very unusual situation. But I'm not so sure in an outside community that concerts of contemporary music as such are all that valid. The people that do come presumably are interested, of course.

BC: But they are the same people. You're not getting the girl who said that the Schoenberg wasn't really music.

SH: By and large you're not getting a lot of those music students, man. You're getting the interested BA kid and the art student, but I hope this will change.

BC: This leads to the level of performance. Michigan has for the last five or six years turned out a remarkable assortment of very gifted new music players, and I assume that right off they can play dead guys' music just as well or better because of what they've been doing. This is not only an advantage for you as a conductor: you know that these people know what the horns are for, but also you have to keep them on their toes in works which will challenge them, which will make them realize it's not just the old conservatory routine that they have to do.

SH: Maybe this is the primary reason why I'm going back to my school: the quality of the students, the faculty interest is above average. I'm not calling it "good." The studio teacher who would allow his student to perform this work of John Cage and not be afraid that it's going to hurt the way he plays the "Waldstein" is not rare. This is not to say that even in a school like ours I am not confronted by teachers who still feel there's been no good music written since Bartók.

I feel even stronger than ever as a member of a faculty at a university, this crap about the cello teacher complaining because the kid couldn't hear a minor third and then yelling at the theory teacher because he's not preparing his kids adequately in the dictation exercises is bad news. Or the music education teacher who puts down the caliber of some trumpet player. The compartmentalizing goes on, especially in larger schools. We are all responsible for the education interdependently of all those kids. In the work I do, I rehearse carefully a new piece of Davidovsky, and when they leave that room I hope they can play a better Bach sonata. Particularly in Ann Arbor, because of the work done by [Ross Lee] Finney, [Leslie] Bassett, and [George B.] Wilson, building up these concerts and audiences for a long span of time, you get large general audiences, you not only get the faculty but more students who come. They say, "My God, you're drawing twenty people to the recital of the Three B's and you're getting five hundred to concerts where you're doing the newest music." The earliest piece in the last concert I did in Ann Arbor was circa 1969. Here's an audience.

They are performers; they want to get out there and play when people will hear them. And therefore a fermentation goes on, and even a couple members of the faculty would knock at my door and say, "We want in on this and we see this is happening." And the waiting list of kids wanting to partake of the ensemble—playing student-composers' works as well—grows continually. Hell, it's just good education. Many young students now don't feel it's got to be the capital "M" Masterpiece to warrant their attention. They can spend time on the works of a student composer without feeling bad about it. They will even learn something. They'll come to grips with contemporary techniques, and when they get out, hopefully, they'll be able to pass it on to their own charges.

BC: You must have a pretty thorough look at new music through the scores you get for Contemporary Directions.

SH: It's not unusual for the old composition "pile"—in one of the composition department offices—to have a good two-to-three-foot stack of scores. I'll have a dozen arrive every couple of weeks.

BC: This puts you in a very special position to see what's happening. I don't think that anybody is loony enough to say that where it's at is any one place. There has been a change in what people are writing in the last four or five years.

SH: This thing snowballs. I'm a practicing conductor. I get scores—any conductor does. I don't get as many as Bernstein did. The word gets around. A year ago here, in Minneapolis, I got a fairly extravagant package of scores and records from Romania. I heard works last week of very young Czech composers. Of course, perhaps it's not so unremarkable, due to communication these days—speaking very generally—-they're all into the same thing. Writers are rediscovering tonality; you can't tell the difference from something that's coming out of Savannah, Georgia, or Prague. There are always surface dissimilarities, but basically there was a certain universality.

BC: Where is this rediscovery of tonality coming from? Why did it happen?

SH: Perhaps a certain natural just fed-upness with ugly sounds. Too much note spinning. I don't know how other composer-conductors react to this. I am aware of it, so I think I handle it okay. I don't want to be all that aware of the world and all the activity. I look, but when I get down to the drawing board myself, I do not feel consciously influenced. I'm still there doing my own thing whether I spent the night before studying a work of Marek Kopelent, say, that the ensemble is going to do. But I can see such a thing becoming insidious. You could spend so much time just trying to keep up, seeing what's going on, that you don't have any time to do your own work.

With communications today, and with all this stuff arriving, it's not all that difficult for me to locate new works. I expend effort to get scores from all over the world and I get a lot of assistance from other colleagues who do the same thing at other schools. But with communications being what they are, it becomes very facile to join the bandwagons. We can Boulezify, Pendereckify. Any amount of this with young students is probably a good thing, and one of the advantages of the school where I am (they have a very large and certainly excellent quality class there) is that they get to hear all these concerts.

However, I find myself, certainly in the most recent decade of my own life, caring less and less about what's going on "out there," even though when I'm back at school I'm studying scores for performance on pretty much a day-to-day basis. I don't ride the tide of those things, to be washed along with them. That's the main reason I enjoyed teaching sixteenth-century counterpoint for many years. I looked forward to conducting arrangements of Bach toccatas with my wind ensemble. I am an advocate of the old Bartók syndrome: I don't think I would be a good teacher of composition. I don't relish the thought of spilling my blood over a piano keyboard, telling some kid how I *really* feel about some aesthetic matter of pitch control or what have you—highly, highly personal matters, because that would take a lot of creative energy from me. There would be no energy left when I sat down at my own drawing board. That's what we're told was the reason Bartók taught piano, not composition. That works for me. I enjoyed my sixteenth-century counterpoint courses because, man, I could switch gears into another world I loved. I enjoyed studying Monteverdi, Gesualdo scores, but it was a different kind of energy expended. It didn't use up any so-called creative juices; they were still there when I felt the need or had the time to start pourin' 'em out.

BC: What about that doctrinaire defense of style, or the need to justify what one is doing? In the past decade or so, the validity of the composer's stance has been increasingly dependent on how he can articulate what he did.

SH: That is precisely what I meant about the insidiousness of the university setting. One must remember that a learning institution often demands analytical/theoretical "positions" to validify some more or less dogmatic position. If a composer does it and still produces good works, that's cool. I don't do it. I have certain personal fetishes about this kind of crap. I will not discuss a work that I am working on with anyone, not even with my *frau*. Now, you will say, "Shit, what a romantic idea!" I really do that. When a good colleague intellectually wishes to discuss some technical facet of composition, or someone says at a cocktail party, "Well, what are you writing now?"—in both cases I will talk about the work that has just been copied or is at least all completed. I will stay one behind. I remember in my late twenties not doing that, and I talked myself out of some good pieces! All that energy talking about something that was not yet completed, and I was all talked out. Again, it is a personal thing, but I like to save that energy up for me. It becomes the loneliness that's a part of any artist's existence, not just in composition. And in composition seminar, I don't want to be asked "Why?" by some really smart brainy kid. I know why. It's very personal. It's my gut he's talking about—good, bad or indifferent. The piece may be a crock, ultimately. It doesn't matter. It's mine and I don't want his wit, his sharpness incising into my spleen, man. That's a very common attitude, I think, among composers. Even when you talk specifically about technical matters it has a "general" aura about it: if you are talking about the bar you just wrote, or the bar you're going to write tomorrow, in my experience, then that bar has become changed. Composing is *lonely* work, Barney; that piece is my child.

BC: Would you teach a contemporary analysis course if you had your choice?

SH: Well, next year I'll be teaching a course, "Conducting New Music," which is, in effect, how I view the conducting process. In order to understand, say, [Boulez's *Le*] *Marteau* [*sans Maître*]—to prepare it for a public performance— you analyze it. I do nothing different in preparing Loren Rush's *Dans le sable* or the Mozart G Minor, both of which I conducted here last year. You study the work in order to make performance decisions, and analyze that score—you tear it apart. I will be doing that in this conducting class. The kids do not have to be taught how to beat a 7/8. I have taught analysis courses of twentieth-century works—Schoenberg, Stravinsky, etc.—but the conducting class will be involved with later things that the Contemporary Directions Ensemble is doing. We'll approach them from an analytical point of view. Of course, it's difficult. In some pieces you can still smell the ammonia—if you're going to do a new work of Seymour Schifrin and it's just arrived in the mail, you dig into it. It ain't like looking at the Mozart G Minor, but the processes are the same. You try to get into the work and base your decisions on what you see. Your decision and your analytical technique is based on what you know in the past about the style of a certain work, how it fills or carries on its own "history." That's how I would approach the conducting class because one should adopt different attitudes towards different styles. All of them certainly are rampant today in musical composition, as I'm sure that the composers in the book you are writing now will indicate. Because there's a lot of musics, man.

I find a lot of men and women—really good composers in America alone, to say nothing of Europe—that are really interesting. I find it exciting as a conductor because it's like dropping the pebble in the creek. The ripples go out—and it's so active and so fruitful. I'll counter that by saying that five years ago, when I started conducting a lot of contemporary music, I thought there were hundreds and hundreds of composers all writing great stuff. I found out rather to my dismay that once I got past all my favorite classical twentieth-century works—the Varèse and Webern that hadn't been done at certain places, the Ives—I came down to a list that indeed was not as large as I thought, although it was still plenty large.

I don't mean it pompously, but I maintain a very catholic taste. I feel I *have* to as a conductor. I would never throw out a work of a thoroughly competent professional composer because of some stylistic view judgment I would make based on my own creative work. Never! I'm afraid there are a lot of composers who do. I don't agree with that because there is too much going on—the musics abound. Colleagues at my school have felt free to tell me they were totally offended by some of the music I've conducted, to say: "I really dug, you know, that one piece, but like, that other bag . . ." That's natural, because they're responding as an audience to a style. I take each work for what it is, to do it as well as I possibly can. I think that's why so many composers are performing.

If the public can be made aware that there are good works out there and if it's well conceived, well directed, well rehearsed, good players, and a good piece, how can you lose? There are such pieces, and there are conditions for allowing that to happen. That must be nurtured outside of the CD Ensembles and groups like that. I'm looking forward to the wind ensemble. I think I can do the same thing with the damn wind ensemble that I can with the CD group. As a conductor and a performer, it's my duty not to cloister off any particular style further, not to further horse-blind my audience. Any "blinders" have got to be torn off. And, as a performer, one has a duty to do that.

BC: However, in writing your own works . . .

SH: That's a whole other ball game, Barney. I would behave in the depths of my sanctum sanctorum, the way you or any artist would behave. That's personal. There, my likes and dislikes abound. You know, I've changed in my own work.

BC: You sure have.

SH: No more or no less than anyone, by growing up. When I was young, I was very conscious of style. When I was thirty years of age or so, I forgot about it. Which, looking back on it now is a sign of growing up a little. Years after that, I've discovered that, by forgetting about it, I've gotten somewhere.

BC: You weren't interested in writing anything because it was hip to do?

SH: No. I think the main reason is my upbringing. As a youth, I got into Eastman on dance band charts. I was a straight—and mediocre—dance band player. I was nineteen before I entered school in Rochester. I had been highly influenced by current theoretical matters, abstractions. I happen to think that many of my pieces are what I would today call very intellectual pieces. But some friends wouldn't agree. That's all totally immaterial. I know what is in there and I think ultimately if there's a reason, that's the end of it. At the end of the piece for Bert Turetzky last year [*One Man's Meat*, 1970], it degenerates into blues. I have a great fondness for blues, remembering one's roots. It's the natural thing; you've got fond memories of the old days, and blues in F for me was a beautiful and complete musical memory, so it's there in my music.

One of the high school kids up here in Minnesota heard my *Interplay* [subtitled "*A Histrionic Controversy for Four Musicians*," 1966]. We got to talking about "what was the composition like to you?" I discussed certain parts of the *Interplay* to try and clear up for this fifteen-year-old boy about what a composer does, how I conceive. We talked about different ways it can be done, and we played a little bit of the piece. He remarked how similar he thought it was to Frank Zappa. It's a simple point to make, I need not prove this one.

Looking back on it, the time when I forgot any self-conscious sort of the style attitudes, at that point my music acquired profundity. Each piece demands its own solution. Another bad thing at the university: often one will, after completing a work, try to stride out all the time. There is so much effort put into that search for "originality." Especially in the last two years, I've felt absolutely no compunction about writing two works that could be construed as "the same." But just because of the largesse of time that I had and the *joie* (I called it, being given two years to write), I had no qualms at all about just writing. The actual composing becomes harder for me every year. This is another stock thing to say, but I do feel that. You become more self-critical. We get fussier, but at the same time along with that fussiness, for me, is getting it right. That fussiness is counteracted by the necessity to put out.

Benjamin Britten, in "On Receiving the First Aspen Award," said something very profound.[9] He was discussing the university life, where a student would spend all that time writing "the dissertation." I'm paraphrasing highly, but the young composer would work on some austere, big, or great orchestra piece, when his proclivity was for writing good children's piano pieces instead. University studies can do damage to that. It won't give that student the free mind to write his children's pieces without feeling badly about it, as if he's letting somebody down—worst of all, her/himself. It's a crock. At the same time, the opposite is true also. In my own music I've gone back, for example, recently, and looked at Stravinsky's '30s and '40s pieces that I did not know. As far as compositional matters go, I subscribe to the various trade magazines and journals. A composer that does not read does so at his own peril, because who's to say what will bear fruit for him later?

It comes back perhaps to how I feel as a conductor, so maybe there is some tie-in that even I don't realize. There's a lot of grist out there for the compositional mill. I don't think anyone can ignore blatantly any whole "style" of an art being obliterated because of some indoctrinated attitude inherited from the teachers one had—or for him to say, "Oh, that's crap, I won't have anything to do with it." Life's too big, art's too big.

BC: Where does that stand in approaching a piece that you're going to write? Of course we're all making things for the ear, but does it have to do more than that for you? Is there more of you in it than merely the gut and the ear?

SH: There's a great deal more for me. Now you're getting a little closer to where I live. I have felt in the past that an erroneous manner in my compositional idea was the way I work. It's got to sit around a while; I won't start a piece until the whole thing is there. I have tried, in some works, not to do this. I failed miserably. I know many writers who wouldn't dream of working this way, but I have to hear it, understand, formulate it all, by and large, before I even get into the first sketches. I can appreciate why that might be a bad thing to do, but I can't apologize for it because it works for me. It naturally works better with some pieces than with others. But I seem to require, because of my conservatism, my own nature, the rather careful blocking out of a span of time, knowing and controlling what goes on. I still may be too much of the western man nowadays. I can appreciate and understand the composer's attitude that would be diametrically opposed to mine on that point of view. I am in essence saying that in the macrocosm—a structure of some kind—I am ruling out the surprise, the accident. I hasten to add that in the detail, in the microcosm, all kinds of things could happen. I don't know why I sound apologetic for it! Maybe that's again my own self-consciousness. Though I don't get in there and work into it until I can block out—I know that the piece is going to do this. There might be a choice, but in the end the choices might be somewhat similar, and I know what the overall shape is going to be. Depending on what sort of piece it is, this may happen in a month or it may take a couple of years; it's happened both ways. I appreciate how much pure surprise I have not allowed for, but evidently it doesn't seem to bother me because that's the way I've been working. Just because I've tried to put a feeling to talk to you with words about how I would respond in a compositional situation gives a kind of aura to you that I, indeed, might not mean at all. (I adore surprises!)

So that's the frightening part. But that's how the compositional idea is to me. It's something you hear, you manipulate and then you compose. Let me put it in reverse: let me make it clear that I do not sit down blindly, put that pencil on the sketch paper and see what happens. I don't function that way. It might be tied to my total lack of ability at the piano. I play the world's *worst* piano. I struggled through that obligatory secondary piano course and tried to play the D minor Invention at the end of two years of study at half-tempo. Although I work at the piano from time to time just to check things out—it's nice to hear—I can't go at it blindly. I can't sit down and see where I'm going to be led. At the same time, I wonder, am I not doing so when I think about a piece? I don't know. It's not uncommon for me to spend six months thinking about a composition. You think and you think, and then, as it takes its shape, you start to write it down. I am very conservative in that respect. I tend to mold; I tend to start with X, and then comes X^3 or X^1, and then maybe the Y.

I do tend to structure—one thing does tend to lead to another, and in that sense my works would be constructed or developed.

Each guy and gal finds their own solution in some way of working, and then proceeds. After that he's just complementing that with ways of allowing that initial feeling to bear fruit as the situation demands. Putting out a piece, we all have our own little methods of trying to get at it as painlessly as possible. I certainly would admit, though, to a fear of "what would have happened if . . ." I'll have to admit there's that fear—but at this stage, I can say that although these thoughts troubled me a little, it certainly is not bothering me enough to change the manner in which I am going about it right now. Each work varies.

BC: How about live electronics?

SH: An FM radio station at the University of Virginia let me in from midnight until 4 a.m. when it was free. I passed through what everybody did—the stages where you splice all that tape together and come up with a decent two minutes and it's cost you six months of your life. Live electronic usage right now is for me very interesting because there are many interesting sounds you can get down in real time, compared to the way things were five years ago, to say nothing of two years ago: it changes overnight. It comes back to what you said before about the old grist for the mill. If they are usable, OK. The advantage I have—it gets back to the old jazz thing for me—I enjoy spontaneous improvisation. The typical concert situation of course has obvious advantages. Many people particularly aren't familiar; even in large towns when they haven't heard a lot of electronic music, people still applaud a speaker only with great reluctance. That really isn't a factor—it wouldn't make the music any better.

But I find the spontaneous improvisation of live electronic music very interesting. Every day they're coming out with things on the market. By and large, a lot of rock musicians I have met use the equipment for exactly what it was put out for. They never really give it much thought—which is just their point of view, which is to reproduce their favorite tunes. Miniaturizing the electronic equipment just makes it so portable they can cart it around. A couple of scores have come in for the Contemporary Directions Ensemble using octave dividers and timbral-modifying devices for large-ensemble works, but I don't think they are common enough—they're prohibitively expensive in many cases. Any conductor will see that he needs an X machine attached to his bass clarinet and will say, "Well, I won't do that." We used to do that twenty years ago if the work called for three bassoons and you were in a school that had only two bassoon players. But guys are using them. The whole computer thing—it's very exciting, if you can get good folks to make good music out of it. It's the same as anything else; if good guys spend some time on it, hopefully they will be able to do good things. The mediocre guy will just do mediocre things.

Notes

1. Milton Babbitt, "Who Cares if You Listen?" *High Fidelity*, February 1958: 38–40, 126–27.

2. Sydney Hodkinson, *A Contemporary Primer for Band*, 3 vols. (Theodore Presser, 415-41113, 415-41114, 415-41115, 1972).

3. Brian Dennis, *Experimental Music in Schools* (London: Oxford University Pres, 1970).

4. Timings refer to Sydney Hodkinson, *The Dissolution of the Serial* (F. Gerrard Errante, clarinet-saxophone, William Albright, piano), in Leo Kraft/Sydney Hodkinson, *Kraft/Hodkinson*, New World Records/Composers Recordings, NWCRI 292, 2010 (1971).

5. Hodkinson had received a Ford Foundation Contemporary Music Project grant as artist-in-residence in Minneapolis. http://www.sydhodkinson.com/Biography.html (accessed August 1, 2019).

6. *A Contemporary Primer for Band: A Collection Of Musical Studies for Any Number Of Wind and Percussion Players* (Theodore Presser, 1972).

7. Alvin "Al" Greenberg (1932–2015), American poet.

8. Paul Chihara (b. 1938); Peter Westergaard (1931–2019).

9. Benjamin Britten, *On Receiving the First Aspen Award: A Speech* (London: Faber and Faber, 1964).

10 Ben Johnston (1926–2019)

JOHN SCHNEIDER

At first glance, Johnston seems an improbable candidate for title of Subversive Radical American Composer. The 2016 New World Records release of all ten of his string quartets made headlines in the *New York Times*, and at the age of ninety-two Johnston was elected to the American Academy of Arts and Letters. Yet in 2012, *LA Times* critic Mark Swed wrote, "More than 20 years ago, the music critic John Rockwell described Ben Johnston in the *New York Times* as 'one of the best nonfamous composers this country has to offer.' What has changed is that Johnston is now, I'd suggest, our *best* nonfamous composer."[1] Earlier, Swed called Johnston "probably our most subversive composer, a composer able to make both radical thinking and avant-garde techniques sound invariably gracious."[2] His sly revisionism has given birth to a most extraordinary catalog of diverse works, embracing a bevy of mid-century compositional techniques. These techniques can be traced in his work leading up to the following interview with Childs.

Johnston had an early interest in intonation. He studied with Darius Milhaud, John Cage, and Harry Partch, though Johnston recalls Partch telling him that, "If I or anyone else ever claimed to have been a student of his, he'd cheerfully strangle us."[3] The master's degree and studies at Mills College with Milhaud that followed his apprenticeship with Partch led to a job at the University of Illinois in 1951 that would last another three decades. There he met John Cage and, during his first summer break, he traveled to New York to help cut tape with Earle Brown for Cage's *Williams Mix*. By the mid-1950s, Johnston was eager to scratch the itch of just intonation, those pure tunings he had so enjoyed with Partch. Within a week of taking a Guggenheim Fellowship at the Columbia-Princeton Electronic Music Center in 1959 to work with Milton Babbitt, Johnston realized that the new, much-ballyhooed RCA Mark II sound synthesizer was incapable of producing the subtlety of pitch variation needed for his microtonal projects. Babbitt chided him: "You know, nobody can hear those intervals," to which Johnston replied, "I can, Milton. Can't you?" He chose to study composition with John Cage instead, under whose tutelage he produced his first *String Quartet*. The ever-acute Cage gently confronted Johnston with a simple question, "You're not really doing your own thing yet, are you? Why aren't you?"[4]

Johnston's first completed work upon returning to Illinois was his *Five Fragments* (1960), his first using the ratio-based intervals of just intonation. "I remember asking myself, 'What ever happened to harmony?' Harmony was valued very highly in my thinking and it was a tangible loss to feel when it was under-emphasized. Working with harmony for me at that time was like opening a door in a building where most of the doors were shut."[5] By 1964, Johnston's researches resulted in the *Sonata for Microtonal Piano* and *String Quartet #2*, and his first theoretical article, dealing with tuned complexity in the pitch domain. "The 'emancipation of dissonance' did not solve the problem of harmonic freedom. While rendering permanently obsolete the old black-and-white division into consonant and dissonant, it in no sense abolished the tonal hierarchy."[6] He later explained: "I wanted to enlarge the tuning horizon in my music at least somewhat beyond the limits Harry Partch had opened up in his music. Also, I was determined to generalize the tuning concepts that Partch had introduced so that no composer would be bound either by the limits the design of ordinary musical instruments imposes, or by the new, but also restricting limits imposed by Partch's own instruments."[7]

To organize these new materials, Johnston discovered the concept of the tuning lattice, which graphically represents the pitch relationships of just intonation scales. It is an array of points in a multidimensional pattern, with each point corresponding to a ratio (or pitch). "The lattice demonstrates harmonic neighbors (that is, ratios in near proximity are consonant, those farther away being more dissonant). . . . To 'explain' a dissonance in this manner *justifies* it to the ear; it is heard as a natural and inevitable result of a constellation of less complex ratios."[8] It turned out that pure ratio tunings make available an entirely new melodic and harmonic vocabulary. "Just Intonation requires a pitch usage that might well be described as *the emancipation of consonance*, and the use of hexachordal combinatoriality (to trot out one of the special gems in the terminology) to achieve control of microtonal harmonic modulation could only be described as leaving twelve-tone organization thoroughly behind. Subversive."[9] Subversive indeed! Johnston sought to disrupt the established notion of an inviolate twelve-tone equal-tempered octave and to extend the parameter of pitch to embrace a complexity at least as diverse as those being explored in the realms of rhythm and timbre. At the same time, ironically, he made his music more accessible. Johnston's genius lay in his ability to achieve both goals with wit, grace, and formidable intellectual rigor while simultaneously navigating the avenues of the institutional establishment with considerable political acumen.

Which brings us to this 1972 or 1973 interview with Barney Childs, as the two discuss tuning, lattices, aesthetics, experimental work with computers, dance, virtuosity, indeterminacy, Johnston's influences (Debussy, Partch, Milhaud, Cage), other working composers, performances of his music, and more. The infectious camaraderie between the two is palpable.[10] At the end we are suddenly aware that this is a forty-six-year-old composer who, exactly in the middle of his career, is just on the verge of a major breakthrough with the *String Quartet #4*, "Amazing Grace" (1973), with much more to come.

Ben Johnston: Interview

BARNEY CHILDS: Your interest in tunings: how do you feel now, as opposed to ten years ago?

BEN JOHNSTON: I started very gradually. Temperament first interested me about the problem: when I began to learn what the physical acoustical picture was like it didn't seem very satisfactory at all. It amounted to Helmholtz. I remember one lecture that is not quite as unusual as it seemed to me at that time. I was twelve years old and attended a lecture by a physicist at the conservatory in Macon, Georgia. He talked about acoustical relations, phenomena, and Debussy. He tried to show with recordings the use that Debussy made of these sonorities. He first pointed out that harmonic progression in Debussy isn't functional— that any sound, any conglomerate, would work as well as any other because of that. The tonality is contained in the melody, so there is no reason for the harmony to have to bear that burden. Debussy was fascinated with sonorities related to the higher octaves of the overtone series. The lecturer felt that even the whole tone scale was an attempt to reproduce those sounds to some extent.

I got interested, but it led nowhere because I wasn't in school. Ramon Douse, my first-year college music teacher, was interested and reinforced it later. It's very curious how the whole thing filtered down. He had picked it up from Roy Harris, who obviously never did anything with it himself, nor was he even seriously interested to my knowledge. But it sounded as if Harris knew about Harry Partch. He had apparently made a fuss about that somewhere in Minnesota or Wisconsin: one of those schools at which he taught at some time. I didn't do any more than write a couple of papers for English class, because the music classes at William and Mary weren't much. It was only later that a musicologist who was teaching at Cincinnati Conservatory of Music treated me to a real discovery of Partch, when I was getting a master's degree. That was before the conservatory joined the university [University of Cincinnati]. Gunther Schuller went there about the same time, but Schuller did not attend this school, and I did not know Schuller then.

I became so interested in Harry Partch that when I got that degree, I had just gotten married and my wife and I decided to take off to the West Coast so that I could become apprenticed to Partch. So we—my wife, Betty, as well, because she was actually used on some of the recordings—went as apprentices, which is the right word. He didn't do any teaching; he actually sniffed at it disdainfully. He didn't believe in any sort of teaching except self-teaching. I did what he wanted me to: work with his instruments so as to learn by ear. I collaborated with Harry on *The Wooden Bird* [1951] and did the intoning on *Dark Brother* [1942–43], which was a relatively hard piece to learn. I got a kind of perfect pitch by then so that I could home in on a note and be sure that it was right. But that's never been very secure for me, especially where voice is concerned, because I have very poor vocal coordination.

That was the beginning of it all, and I did nothing with it. When I left Partch, I went to study with Darius Milhaud, got a degree from Mills College, and then I got a job at the University of Illinois. Later I arranged through John Garvey, who was at that time chairman of the music festival, to get Partch to Illinois. He stayed for several years, then left and then came back. He was affiliated with Illinois in one way or another for a substantial amount of time during the '50s, and several of his new works were done here. The most important one probably was *The Bewitched* [1955]. I don't like *Revelation in the Courthouse Park* [1960] as well—and he did these two and another, *Water! Water!* [1961].

I finally decided a few years later to quit just thinking about these things, and I bent my own compositional efforts to that direction. I had gone through a number of changes, writing neoclassic stuff to begin with, and then I got interested in serialism. It was what most people did, even Stravinsky. I underwent that change; it was largely a passive response to the winds of fashion as one gets them in compositional circles. But that came to a screeching halt. First, I retuned the piano in a very, very elaborate way and wrote a piece, the *Sonata for Microtonal Piano* [1964], which took me five years, because it was extremely hard to learn by ear, which ultimately I had to do. That just *didn't* come easily. I've always been interested in just intonation, and very little in tempered systems, partly because temperament produces finite and closed systems, while just intonation produces open and infinite systems. In practice we can only deal with finite portions of such systems; we need systematic reasons for limiting the infinite possibilities if we do not wish our design decisions to be arbitrary. My study of scale order has given me a theoretical framework within which I can cope intellectually with a variety of kinds of order, ranging from highly indeterminate schemes to extremely precise determinate ones. I am especially interested in ratio-scale order in the case of pitch and rhythm. I tried to cope with both these parameters in this way in the piano sonata (in the case of pitch, also in a serial way); but the ratio-scale ordering of pitches is really interesting, again because of tuning innovations. That's where I come back to just intonation. That makes a bigger difference than anything else.

BC: As you developed compositionally, you also had to develop theoretically. You had to go through a whole musical self-discipline above and beyond that which somebody who was not trying to develop his own technique went through.

BJ: That's true. It was really frustrating to spend five years on a piece, especially on no more than a ten-minute piano piece. If you'd ended up with an hour-and-a-half of super-*Hammerklavier*, well, it might palliate you a little, but it didn't, and doesn't. The whole thing was really an effort, but in spite of that I wrote the Second Quartet [1964], one of my most successful pieces. I almost tossed it off in the middle of that. So the effort trained me. I knew what I was doing, though I wouldn't have been confident to answer a question about it at that time. I felt buffaloed by the whole thing.

One thing that was hard was that I was trying to exert so many controls over the music that it actually went against many personal idiosyncrasies of mine. Consequently I'm not doing elaborate pre-composition any more; it doesn't really turn me on while it doesn't actually turn me off. It was the thing I had to go through. That's largely the background. I feel right now that through a project that I've been working on with Ed Kobrin, I have understood deeply (in phase 1 of that) what the possibilities are. And because of this attempt to put it in the form of a computer program, it has had to become just crystal clear to me what's going on.

BC: Along with your compositional demands and your investigation of the theory, have you had to investigate an aesthetic? I don't know too many composers who are so concerned about the immediacy of aesthetic implications of a system as you are. This is something I'm interested in—it's not simply given you process and shape to work with, it has also forced you to rethink a whole kind of very personal and different musical aesthetic.

BJ: I'm not satisfied with a lot that goes on at present. I don't like to go to concerts. I overcome that because, professionally speaking, I just plain have to. Now, what do I want to do? I'd rather experience the music in the direct way that you can when you sit down with your hi-fi and simply drink it in, but I haven't been able to do that either, for various reasons. I've been buried in this very intellectual discovery. But the aims aren't intellectual.

BC: The aims seem humanistic.

BJ: Yes, the aims are different from that. Sometime in the mid-'50s I had a conversation with Bessie Schoenberg, who's a dance teacher at Sarah Lawrence. Or was—I guess she's retired now. It was on an occasion that I'd done some incidental music for a play of Wilfred Leach, who teaches there now and she asked me about my musical points of view. I quoted Suzanne Langer to her in support of one point. She said she didn't like Langer; she felt that the idea of trying to get all that stuff intellectually straight was destructive, and that it shouldn't be intellectually straight because that wasn't the basis for the decisions and actions that you had to make anyway. I told her that my interest was in using intellect to destroy that effect. In another context, I feel too that it's not serialism, but that cast of mind that leads to the search for total serialism that is stifling. In my opinion, that constitutes a misuse of the intellect for organizing music or organizing any kind of art. Just as [Karlheinz] Stockhausen probably had to write "How Time Passes," but not for that purpose: rather for the purpose of bringing things into line with things that are empirically observable, as constants in people's perception of music.[11]

It gratifies me a great deal lately how I'm now using seventh partial relationships in music. I wasn't doing that before, which means I've notched up on the overtone series. Partch has been using not only seven but eleven for a long time, so this is no great daring thing that I've done. But it amounts to a wish to cover the whole ground thoroughly, which Partch never has been concerned with. He just went in there and took what he wanted and made what he wanted to make out of it. I really find that my interest is as much of a theorist as it is a composer. While that's true of him too—he's written a hell of a good book on theory, *Genesis of a Music* [1949], and I hear he's releasing an updated version of it [1974]—still, his behavior as an artist is very much towards the improvisatory, the free, and the self-taught, among others. He's not an intellectual composer, although there's plenty of intellect there. I have been intellectual in the way I function, but it's been using intellect to destroy the stranglehold of the intellect. Now I'm dissatisfied because I really don't know quite what I want to do with rhythm when I'm starting to write a piece. I guess I'll have to find out what I want to do with that. It's certainly not a new field. Some of the things that I've done with rhythm are better known than other things.

BC: I was thinking back one step yet from that. You're on published record in getting at how the composer thinks about what he's doing. Is there an immediate integration of means, whatever they may be, with a kind of stance the composer has to have? It seems that you are seeking to articulate this.

BJ: It's because I have to. I feel so unsatisfied by what is going on that I have to do something about it. John Cage pushed me into doing something with the computer. As usual with him, his reasons were in large part very pragmatic. He felt that the computer would supply me with the right intellectual tools to get the results that I was looking for and that I should learn about it. Of course, I haven't tried to become a computer expert, I have collaborated, and this is where Ed Kobrin comes in. I should say right now that I don't like to work with other people on anything but an equal basis. I treated Jaap Spek equally when we did tape pieces together. It made it possible to work with him. He's a very demanding man to work with, but because I treated him equally, it was as much his piece as it was mine, because he took part in the creative decisions. Similarly, it is as little that I make all the musical decisions and Ed does all the work with the computer as I can make it. It's too much that way, but that's mainly because they were my root ideas from the beginning. Now that we get into phase 3, where it begins to be a matter of what we do with these machines, it's very much more his baby than mine. A lot of the stuff he's been working with I never will understand, at least anything like he does. So collaboration is another thing I've been interested in, because I've been doing it for more than twenty years.

BC: Certain pieces, like the *Do-It-Yourself Pieces* [1969], are essentially collaborative with performers.

BJ: That's why I like them; that's why I did it. That aspect of indeterminate music seemed right to me. We should bring the performer right into it. Also in phase 3, when Ed and I get this thing on wheels, we will be handing a lot of the composition to the performer right there in situ, on stage, so that the performer too will be making compositional decisions. He will be making them out of a context that we provide.

BC: In other words, you don't trust the performer carte blanche.

BJ: I've tried that, and it doesn't work too well.

BC: So you're providing limits within which he's going to work.

BJ: Yes, and we're writing for a different kind of performer. Rather than David Tudor, who's only too able and willing to do this kind of thing, we're doing a commission for Paul Zukofsky. Paul Zukofsky is a remarkable musician, but you wouldn't expect him to just improvise a piece. David Tudor has in fact done that; the Busotti pieces are nothing but a clear instigation.

BC: Do you think that having performers of this caliber has made much difference to our generation of composers?

BJ: It couldn't help it. Good lord, so many people have written difficult things even if they themselves in some cases weren't expert performers. I'm thinking of Harvey Sollberger, in particular, and also Charles Wuorinen, in that twelve-tone post-Webern, post-Wolpe technique. It's so technical, so damn virtuosic and hard to play, that unless they were virtuosic themselves, I don't really think they could have written successfully the pieces that they have. Insofar as I find the music interesting, it's largely because of that virtuosity. That's the human part.

BC: Speaking of virtuosos, the very first time I met you, you said that you'd always been interested in writing a dance piece in which none of the gestures were completed, in which the gestures became altered or stopped or diverged somewhere. This seems a reflection of the interest in the performer as contributor.

BJ: If you were going to make a dance like that, you'd really have to be a dancer. Of course, this is the thing about modern dance (and I mean modern ballet, as well): the choreographer has to operate as a performer. We don't do that in music, at least not as much. Many students I encounter now aren't so much like this as the people who have gotten jobs, having finished their training. These are very much performance-oriented, and very often good performers.

BC: A lot of them are jazz musicians, too.

BJ: A good many. That whole tradition has been a part of what has been going on. Not that very many are writing jazz. Some do so, but that's not most of what's happening. It's not that use of it like Copland; it's not even the kind of music that Schuller has made.

BC: It's part of a way of looking at things that grew out of playing.

BJ: So many of these people have been performing in ensembles. The era of the Rockefeller-supported performing group has drawn a lot of composers in, and even when it wasn't Rockefeller (we had very little support from Rockefeller here), we worked it out that way. So many of these composers were very much performers. Letting the performer into the act that way, they understand better how to do that than I did, because I never have tried to be a performer. Although I have used the piano as a tool, I certainly never was a real performer, not even a second-rate one.

BC: But given virtuoso performers, it's possible for a composer who doesn't play to still participate in a partnership.

BJ: Well, my experience doing music for dance people for so long gave me that, in that it was impossible for me to think of functioning as a choreographer. But I got a real feeling for how to let them do what they wanted to do and then work with them in such a way as to complement it. There were cases when the people I had to collaborate with were less experienced than me, when it was necessary to bolster their confidence and give them the feeling, "Why sure, this is your baby, it isn't mine, it isn't a piece of music which we're going to put on a dance concert, but it's a dance. And that part is up to you." Of course that's a more blatant collaboration. The most recent thing I've done in that way is a rock opera, *Carmilla* [1970].

That is a foreign idiom for me, as foreign as making up ragas for Indian musicians would be. I understand that too, but from my point of view, which is different from theirs. And I'm not a rock musician, certainly. But it does work as a piece and it's partly because I made no arrangement of that piece, nor did any one person. The ensembles themselves, with prodding from [the saxophonist and composer] Jim Cuomo, made the arrangements.

BC: Do you find that with the demands you are making, that performers have a difficult time doing pieces that you write?

BJ: Yes. I write hard music, and it's always a mess. They never can play it at first, and things sit around for a long time with nobody playing them. But I've actually been lucky that way, because a few times the right performers have made all the difference. Two people performed that piano sonata. Claire Richards did it first. She worked her fingers to the bone over that because it was entirely alien to her as a performer, almost as much as it was to me as a piece. She did a good job with it. Then Neely Bruce took it over. He also did a good job with it—an entirely different job, which was revealing, because it's a terribly tight piece where everything is specified. Yet the feel of those two performances was fundamentally different. They also used a different order for the movements, which is permitted in that piece.

BC: I'm not thinking so much about precision groups or individuals, but the orchestra.

BJ: You know the only orchestra piece I got off the ground, except for early works. I have two earlier orchestra pieces that I should not show anybody. This one was due to the fact that Eleazar de Carvalho felt that the festival [Festival of Contemporary Arts at the University of Illinois] here had given him a real boost at a time that he needed it. He wanted to show his gratitude to the people who had made it possible. The two principal people were myself and Jerry [Lejaren] Hiller. He offered to do Hiller's *Hieronymus* [1966], but Jerry didn't finish it in time. It's a big project, and Carvalho was more interested in that than he was in mine. But I did mine, and Jerry didn't do his. So he put mine on and it was good, especially considering that he gave a generous amount of rehearsal compared to what you usually get. We used a number of hours of work during the week. An all-out effort had been made with the parts to ease all the bumps out of the way, and technically we didn't have so awfully many hang-ups. The percussion players did not rehearse in advance as I had advised. That's just uneconomic, I guess.

BC: That's just one of those things that works in a school but doesn't work in a professional situation. But usually the percussionist is going to be the guy you can count on to do the job. You cannot count on the strings.

BJ: No, but what about when the string players are the percussionists? Because we had that there. Two of the percussionists were real percussionists. One of them was a nut, but he could play. The string players—back line of the violas—and the orchestra piano player were so tired that they couldn't make it. So one whole section of the piece was a mess because those people couldn't really cope with their parts. The piano interior and the piano percussion simply weren't up to it.

BC: How about the new piece for winds and voice? And the tuning problems that led you into it?

BJ: This is really the newest piece, and it isn't even finished, inasmuch as I project seven movements and there are now only three. It's a song cycle, and therefore the main thing about it is the voice. But it's voice with two instruments. They have to be treble instruments; for at least one of them, flute won't work, because it doesn't go low enough. So in effect it's a reed piece. I would also say any low instruments would be nice if you use male voice, because that would put the whole thing down. But I wouldn't want the accompaniment way up and the male voice down below, because in this case it wouldn't work. The organization of counterpoint is Renaissance or medieval. And it *is* counterpoint, so we have a set of vertical relationships which are reached by melodic performance. It's even harmonic counterpoint.

That's to exploit one feature of the theory that I have been working with so much; the theoretical arrangement of the pitches is a lattice, providing a complete picture of the just intonational manifold of relationship. You have a set of repetitive relationships which you could call a cycle of fifths in one direction, and then you need another direction in order to have a cycle of thirds. In diagonal movement through this we get typical triadic material. If you introduce still another variable—yet another pitch organizer, basic interval type (I've used seven)—you need another dimension. So one has a system, a three-dimensional lattice which is like a three-dimensional graph. It's hard to visualize.

The pitch aspect of the piece was put together by designing an *Urlinie* that passed scale-wise through a large number of notes, all of which are available at one place or another in the matrix but which lie adjacent to each other in the scale if you project all these notes down onto one linear continuum. The way to get from one note in the *Urlinie* to the next note is to follow a path on the matrix, then all the pitch relations that you have one by one are consonant, and therefore tunable by ear. Everyone has to listen very carefully and tune by ear to everyone else. It's very like Renaissance music in that way. It's like trying to perform [Carlo] Gesualdo; in fact I believe Gesualdo did write in that way. I wonder whether it was something of that kind in what Stravinsky was so interested in Gesualdo. At least it's a good reason for being interested in Gesualdo!

BC: How about the percussion?

BJ: I first did the instrumental parts, which provided the harmonic basis. The voice lies on top of these, having adjacent intervals that are free in the otherwise strict structure. I didn't tie down the voice; I wanted to have more freedom to make it expressive. And so each note of the accompaniment—we are using the oboe and clarinet—represents a tempo, it has a speed. A is 440; OK, that's a speed. Now I took an "octave" of 440—shades of Stockhausen! In actuality, I do owe this idea to Stockhausen. But he doesn't do it, really; it doesn't fit his theories actually because "How Time Passes" presents a proportional theory that has been imported into a serial context, and in serial music, it undoes the serialism. Such proportions, applied to pitch, certainly don't yield twelve-tone music any more. In this case, I took an exact octave of it. If A is being played in a tempo which happens to be an octave of A, it's being played by one of those people. If the other note is F, why then a tempo of 4:5 of the other tempo is being played. This gives you *Knocking Piece* [1962] rhythm.

In this case, I had seven entering as a feature, so we have 7 against 4, 7 against 6, 7 against 8, and so forth. *Knocking Piece* doesn't have any of those relationships. I decided to express 5 by 1, 3, 5, for example, leaving out 2 and 4, similarly to express other rhythms by leaving out notes, which I didn't do in *Knocking Piece*. Actually, it says in *Knocking Piece* that you *can* do that. It's permitted, but nobody ever does, because they're already scared to death of getting all those tempos to work correctly by cross-rhythms. And when you're in cross-rhythms, it's much harder to learn if you leave out notes. What it amounts to is a very irregular-sounding rhythm.

BC: You left notes out?

BJ: Yes, the people who were going to play it found it just out of reach; particularly the younger of them just simply threw his hands up and said, "I can't play this." So we aren't making them play it. They're going to Hawaii shortly, and they wanted to program this piece. They may not even manage to program but one out of the three songs—two out of the three, to be optimistic. But they are performing it without percussion. With Peter Rumbold, who's taking Ed's place in collaborating as assistant on this project, I thought we would use the MUSIC 5 program, which is operative now with the computer on campus here, to generate the percussion parts synthetically through the computer and then let the performers play with these. But it isn't going to work; it takes too long. There's too much work, so the deadline can't be met. So we're having the piece minus its percussion. It really sounds very Renaissance. The deceptive thing about that piece is that it sounds so ordinary. You hear these triads and yet you really don't know where they are, tonally, and they're not any place you can tell if you try to pin down where they are in terms of any familiar tonal system. Here is a three-dimensional system; you can be awfully close to something familiar, but you're *not* actually on it. The fascination of the piece actually exists in the nearness of these relationships. In this case, there are very small intervals—more than 143 per octave. It's really a dense system, but they're not used as successive or simultaneous notes, so that there's no attempt to exploit that side. In this piece, you get really unusual progressions which are effected by it.

BC: The modulations.

BJ: It governs the modulations—exactly the same as rhythmic modulation, metric modulation.

BC: With percussion it will be a special version.

BJ: Yes, exactly. It is almost an ultimate use of metrical modulation. That's why it's so hard, because that isn't an easy technique.

BC: I was interested that you'd had the idea of some of the proportions from Stockhausen. Since you do not work on many pieces and you follow your own line of development, if you got the question "Who has influenced you?," you would have to answer, "Hardly anybody."

BJ: That isn't true, because this isn't the only kind of music that I do. I do some things that can be performed. If I only did this kind of music it would be prohibitive; also, I don't think I would be very happy to do only this. There has been a lot more influence from various people. But actually, it's probably true; it doesn't sound very much like anybody, just as in a way *Knocking Piece* doesn't. It was just an idea that I developed to its logical conclusion.

Of course, there's metric modulation itself. I became acquainted with that idea, as I guess most American composers did, from Elliott Carter. I admired both those first two string quartets very much, more than any of his later pieces. He really was doing something interesting there, far more than the way he uses pitches, which I don't find of any particular interest. (I tried to talk with him about this—he was here teaching on a short stint one year—but he just didn't understand what I was asking him, and he's not willing to talk about his own music very much. So it wasn't very fortunate.) But I had really become interested, more from Elliott Carter than from Stockhausen. Of course "How Time Passes" crystallized that idea in a way that it probably wouldn't have if I hadn't read it. I was trying to face the *Die Reihe* challenge, in 1959, when I read that. I was impressed by it as something I should take into consideration—a sort of equivocal way of saying "impressed."

I haven't been obviously influenced too much by Partch because he scorned that so much, so verbally, and so explicitly, that I would scarcely have dared. There's a little bit of influence, of course. Generally speaking a lot of influence there has been theoretical, because I've studied *Genesis of a Music* very closely. There's not much faking in that book. It's really all there.

I found a big influence from John Cage, but not the one that so many people get. He interested me very much in indeterminacy, in the idea of leaving large amounts of the piece for the performer to do and collaborating in that way. It reawakened my awareness of that. His whole life has been collaboration, because he has been, since a relatively young age, the musical director of the Cunningham Dance Company. But he has posed a set of terms in which both collaborators would have a maximum amount of freedom. This is a very interesting thing to have done, just as many other practical things that he did. Like facing the problem of the vagaries of the piano interior with its preparation; you could never get the same preparation twice because there are no standardizations in the screws. They don't build those screws in order to weigh the same amount: the alloy would have to be exactly right. You are so far away from anything fixed that I'm sure it suggested to him that there was no reason for things to be fixed. Why shouldn't they be completely unfixed? It's a logical step from those prepared piano pieces to indeterminacy.

I wouldn't have been tremendously influenced by Cage if it weren't for knowing him personally. Certainly he's had a great effect on me. He's one of the most interesting people I've had the privilege to know. That of course makes a big difference, with the result that I did a lot of the things I might never have become interested in just out of respect for him. He drew my attention to things which probably I would have passed by.

BC: Or come to later.

BJ: Maybe, in another way. At least I owe him a great deal. At one time I was much influenced by Milhaud. I profited from studying with him. When I was writing neoclassic music, Stravinsky fascinated me for a long time. He still does in a way, and it's the same pieces that did then, not the late ones . . . the middle more than the early. I was once influenced by [Paul] Hindemith but never had any contact with the man. I liked that fourth-y sound. I also read his book, and it was enough of a challenge for me to try to organize phrases in that way at one time.

BC: Do you make any effort to have any of these earlier things performed?

BJ: Now and then—until recently I wasn't doing it. I haven't been producing much in the last year or two. Yet people have wanted to play things, so I've gone back to a few pieces and taken them out of the mothballs. I've been rather pleased. I wasn't upset at them at all. I didn't feel embarrassed—they were better than I thought they were.

BC: There is a certain difference about the generation of American composers of which you are a part, that what they are doing is new in a real sense.

BJ: I'm not sure what you mean. I've felt being part of something in that I recognized that I was following a line of action that so many people followed: person after person writing diatonic modal pieces in dissonant counterpoint with lots of rhythmic activity. There was a big Stravinsky influence, and also a big Bartók influence on me. Particularly I liked Bartók's string quartets so much—and some of the late pieces as well. The ones in which he became conservative again fascinated me because, having gone as far as he did—let's say with the piano sonata . . .

BC: . . . the second fiddle sonata.

BJ: Yes, those pieces—and then to write the violin concerto. This is really very interesting. That's neoclassic again—in that case neoromantic. There was a big interest in Bartók, especially rhythmically. I got more out of Bartók's rhythms than I did out of Stravinsky's, although they're really very similar. Bartók could have written the rhythms in *Les Noces* just as well. It's that Middle Eastern European folk thing that both of them at one time were interested in. Jazz played a large part in some of my development. Not that I was any great jazz musician, but I made my living playing piano for a while and doing some arranging, and that's been an influence, and a continuing interest of mine. I like to listen to good jazz. I'm not so much of a buff that I collect records and know it all, but it's a pleasure to me.

BC: I was thinking of the point beyond which everybody went. Think of any ten people, and they each went into a different thing which was not predictable; from the middle-Stravinsky sound, then the serial, then all of a sudden something happens. You see people going in funny, unpredictable directions. And they're not even consistent one to another. This produces a number of extremely individual composers, which did not happen in the previous generation.

BJ: No, it didn't. When we look at those people in the previous generation who have accommodated themselves to this, it's interesting. It's been mostly they've gotten involved with the electronic music. Merrill Ellis certainly went all out to embrace the new thing. Then there are people who turned to one type of synthetic music or another, like Morton Subotnick. Morton's younger, and really is of a different generation in spite of the fact that he's the same age as a lot of people we're talking about. I think of him along with Gordon Mumma and the ONCE people, although I like what they do much better than what he does.

BC: But if you go back to [Arthur] Berger and [David] Diamond and [Vincent] Persichetti . . .

BJ: An interesting person to look at in that light is Mel Powell—an interesting set of transitions. He really was one of the best jazz pianists going, and then Hindemith, and then after that serial, and finally electronics. I guess what he mostly does now is electronics. The whole thing has been toppled and turned: things that took twenty or thirty years—a real generation—to mature passed by within a decade, or even less. You're forced to reset everything. When you get to a certain age, you eventually ask yourself, "Well, this is all well and good, but what am I really interested in? What had I really better start doing?" And that isn't the same for everybody. The only people who have moved in a similar direction to me I don't know personally. I'm thinking of Lou Harrison.

BC: It's an American stance from that whole generation. Ives is the prototype, but younger men, too. People who just did their own damn thing: [Carlos] Chávez's early works, John J. Becker, [Dane] Rudhyar, from whom Jim Tenney is resurrecting a lot of scores. Very exciting stuff.

BJ: I'll bet it is; that kind of neo-Scriabin . . .

BC: These are people that you wouldn't have had in Europe.

BJ: What about those people in Europe that never made it because of that conservatism? The traditions and all didn't make a niche for them. They weren't strong enough to force through. Most of the European microtonalists, with the possible exception of Alois Hába, but all the rest of them, [Ivan] Vychnegradsky and people like that. There they were doing those things, and yet really ended up leading nowhere.

BC: But in this country you had people who are doing the work and could continue doing it.

BJ: The thing is, in this country *nothing* leads anywhere.

BC: Exactly, because you can have someone like Conlon Nancarrow who goes off to Mexico and builds player pianos and writes these pieces for years and years and nobody knows anything about it. Maybe occasionally they get commissions, but how many of us get commissions to speak of?

BJ: Actually, I haven't had very many commissions lately that have affected me very much. I feel guilty about some of them. The harpsichordist Antoinette Vischer, who was the occasion of John Cage's *HPSCHD* [1969], commissioned me to do a short piece. All right, it doesn't amount to much in money; it's just something I should do. But how am I going to write something? I would want to really represent the experimental side of what I do. And yet I can't figure a way to tune the keyboard that satisfies me. I don't think I'll ever try to write another piece in the same way that I did that piano piece. It was too hard to do, and a second time would be, I think, not much easier.

BC: There are all sorts of ornate compromises you have to use in the orchestra piece, with doublings and triplings to get the tunings you want.

BJ: It had to be tricky. It's very interesting what that did to the color of it, though, because it had all kinds of surprising changes of color. I had thought it would probably have a bolder sound than it did. Betty [Johnston] said it sounded impressionistic to her. She's not a musician, though, and I don't think that's to be construed to mean it sounded like Debussy or Ravel, but rather the sort of thing you mean if you are a painter and say "impressionistic." That's how all that started as a term in the first place.

BC: Still, the university does undertake the care and feeding of composers.

BJ: That's what's happening, still is, mostly. Some few have managed to band together in concert situations.

BC: This is our group syndrome.

BJ: The day for that seems to be almost past. It's a '60s phenomenon, really. Now the number of places where they perform is almost, I think, curious. I figure it may be the case—this gets back to what we were talking about right at the beginning—that it's necessary for some trends of development that really became blocked by the twentieth century to continue to develop. Therefore a new formulation of it all needs to be made, and I think that's what I have. Perhaps we may find quite a resurgence of things that will depend partly on how successful I am in making it really workable in concerts.

BC: How workable do you want to make it?

BJ: I don't know. It would be nice if the concept were possible for other people and didn't involve such a wrench of coming out of the whole way of thinking into something else. Yet in a way the development has all been very logical and very solid. So I would not want to change it in that way. I think what I've been doing makes sense. It may be hard to play, but it makes sense.

BC: Have other quartets looked into the second quartet?

BJ: It was performed in Tokyo on the Crosstalk series. Darryl Dayton, who is in USIA [US Information Agency] and has been a great support, was giving it to a Romanian quartet. I don't know whether they've done it or not, but this would make then three groups who have actually done it. Reports were that the Tokyo group performance was pretty good.

BC: Did they have the recording?

BJ: Of course. Now that it's been done, it's much easier. One might even get performances from groups who aren't into that kind of thing. It was really hard for the Composers Quartet. They spent an awful lot of time on it, and it was *work*! I was at the last sequence of rehearsals, and there was not much that needed change. They had worked on it to the point where even where they were doing things that sounded different from what I had thought, I preferred to let them alone, because they made sense out of it. I found that I wasn't too wedded to an imagination of the piece, so I didn't mind. They play it rather more romantically than it would have to be played. That's what they got out of it, so it's perfectly legitimate. It would be possible to play the whole thing a little more coolly, and it might have more bite. That's the way I would expect the La Salle Quartet to play it. They haven't. They actually originally suggested that I write it. When I finished writing it, they were occupied with other things, specifically the Lutosławski quartet, and they didn't want it. So I got very little encouragement about the piece from them. Sal Martirano was responsible for getting the Composers Quartet interested in it. I had met some of them, but he knew them well.

BC: What about other works: do you find that there is interest in them?

BJ: There's been some nibbling about the orchestra piece—Lukas Foss, for example—but they don't return the score, damn it, and I haven't got the money to get it reproduced.

BC: But things like *Knocking Piece* get played.

BJ: Yes, although every time I've heard it outside of this context, I've been disappointed. It isn't that I tell people how to do it; it's that the Illinois conception of the piece is lyric, and nobody's else's is. They really use a lot of imagination in the timbres of the piece, where the Buffalo performance was merely very accurate. Emmanuel Ghent became quite interested in the piece, went to the performance, and really checked them up on the score. He's into rhythmic complexity much more deeply than I am, and he said it was awfully accurate. Well, I've got the tape, and it is. But it's as hard as nails: a mean-sounding performance, which is OK—that's one thing the piece can be. There was a performance in England that was just awful. A performance in North Carolina didn't even get through the whole piece. So I don't really know what all these performances amount to. I wrote a basic étude, and a lot of percussion players regard it that way. So it's very useful for that. Then the inevitable: one of the people who played the piece decides to do it as a solo. Bill Parsons did it with drums because he couldn't single-handedly cope with the inside of a piano. I think he stopped short of that.

BC: How did it go?

BJ: Not bad. It bothered me a lot more that it was drums, because there's really little interest in that by comparison. It shaves a whole side of the piece off. Much more is lost there than in an oratorio performance of an opera.

There have been performances of that. And a lot of people have played the *Duo [for Flute and String Bass*, 1963]. That seems to be the going thing. Unfortunately, there are two just out-and-out mistakes in the piccolo part, notes that simply can't be played, so I get frantic telephone calls every now and then. That's purely because I didn't know certain limitations of the piccolo. I regarded it too much as a transposed flute. But it's too expensive; Joe Marx had that engraved in Japan, so he'll probably never put out another edition of it. So corrections are just out of the question.

BC: You should probably have him add an errata sheet.

BJ: I should talk to him about that.

BC: Should we really talk about music rather than write it?

BJ: I don't know. The next thing I want to write about is tonality, because it really begins to interest me quite a lot. I already tried to make the point with that talk I gave at the ASUC [American Society of University Composers] on the microtonal panel. There was far more to tonality than history had allowed, the big problem being that most of the people who insisted on it were being merely conservative. They were simply looking back nostalgically, and they reflected that in what they write. That's not the point at all. The real point is that new systems can be worked out, and that the whole idea of systems of harmony is not dead.

The conception of consonance and dissonance is more useful than to throw it all away, which is exactly what's happened. And I don't think Hindemith's approach to the problem was nearly fruitful enough. It was obvious it worked in a way, but most people that learned it as a system eventually just discarded it because it was too much trouble. I find that actually this system of harmonies that make up a key isn't a tightly knit system of related chords. I've found a way to generalize that principle, and it is quite interesting. It does affect intonation very directly, as I would have expected it to. So one has the possibility of a very new way of making music. And so many other aspects of music making right now are in flux that it's hard to figure what to do. I can show the computer how to design an *Urlinie*, how to design a harmonic progression and so forth, but I have not yet been able to get it to make interesting rhythmic decisions. If I were to make a rule that all pieces had to be like the song cycle I was speaking of, well, that would be easy enough, although still hard to perform.

But, dammit, it wouldn't be broad enough for all pieces; you can't tie them down to something like that. The analog, the direct parallelism of pitch and rhythm, is an oddity. One might handle them analogously, and that's interesting. But it would be like using a metrical modulation system—though much freer and more full of possibilities than that. It's interesting that proportional design lies on the level of chord-to-chord and note-to-note progressions, whereas with rhythms, it tends to lie in most people's work on a phrase level. That's what was radical about *Knocking Piece*, that there it lies on a note-to-note level—bar to bar—so quickly that you have no chance to really adjust. But whereas that's an interesting rhythmic idea, it's simply not sufficient. Kobrin and I are really trying to make a system where very different pieces could be made by the computer plus performers. Therefore, we have interesting varied possibilities. I wish I could show you the efforts we've made along this line of getting this *Urlinie* thing, because that is really going to work nicely. We have practically taken care of the pitch problem for the composition. Something will happen, and you'll have the feeling of progression. That's what, it seems to me, gets lost in most twelve-tone works. People just don't know how to make it go anywhere from a pitch point of view. The hexachord system and all other forms of combinatoriality are simply the boy trying to do the man's job. They won't.

Notes

1. Mark Swed, "Ben Johnston Shines in MicroFest Spotlight," review, *Los Angeles Times*, April 26, 2012.

2. Mark Swed, "Ben Johnston," *Chamber Music*, March–April 1995, quoted in Bob Gilmore, introduction to Ben Johnston, *"Maximum Clarity" and Other Writings on Music*, ed. Bob Gilmore (Urbana: University of Illinois Press, 2010), xi.

3. Ben Johnston, "The Corporealism of Harry Partch," in *Maximum Clarity*, 227.

4. Frank J. Oteri, "A Conversation with Ben Johnston," *New Music Box*, January 24, 2007, https://nmbx.newmusicusa.org/a-conversation-with-ben-johnston/.

5. William Dougherty, "An Interview with Ben Johnston," *Van Magazine* 101 (April 19, 2018), https://van-us.atavist.com/i-did-that.

6. Ben Johnston, "Scalar Order as a Compositional Resource" (1963), in *Maximum Clarity*, 28–29.

7. Ben Johnston, "MicroFest 2006 Keynote Speech, April 15, 2006," *1/1: Journal of the Just Intonation Network* 12/3 (Fall 2007): 7.

8. Ben Johnston, "Rational Structure in Music (1976)," in *Maximum Clarity*, 68.

9. Johnston, "MicroFest 2006 Keynote Speech," 8.

10. Childs had previously analyzed Johnston's work in "Ben Johnston: Quintet for Groups," *Perspectives of New Music* 7/1 (Autumn–Winter 1968): 110–21.

11. Karlheinz Stockhausen, "How Time Passes," transl. Cornelius Cardew, *Die Reihe* 3 (1959): 10–40.

11 Daniel Lentz (b. 1942)

VIRGINIA ANDERSON

Alongside Harold Budd, Daniel Lentz originated "pretty music," a style and philosophy that launched "the post-avant-garde 'California Sound'" from 1970.[1] Lentz's interests include political protest, conceptualism, eroticism, early music, religious ritual, wine, theater, and visual art. This interview was largely obliterated by a tape hum, but the fragments are compelling.

Lentz and Childs begin with "biographical shit." Lentz's education includes study with Alvin Lucier at Brandeis, a Tanglewood Summer Fellowship, European festivals, a Fulbright grant to Stockholm, and a lectureship at the University of California, Santa Barbara. His early work, *Fünke* (1965), written at Brandeis, is a spiky post-serial avant-garde piece with a lead flute, jazz drummer, and occasional shouts.[2] *Hydro-Geneva: Emergency Piece #3* (1968) features a list of fifty thousand people killed in the Vietnam War.[3] Lentz founded the California Time Machine (CTM) in 1968, a group best known for its conceptual pieces, including *Air Meal Spatial Delivery* (1969), in which the group radio-telephoned their San Francisco performance to the venue while flying to their next concert in Vancouver.[4]

Lentz lasted only two years at Santa Barbara. In 1969, the department chair walked out on a performance of Lentz's *Gospel Meeting* (1965),[5] an electronic theater piece in which "a man, holding a Bible, paces the stage . . ., while his assistants pass a collection plate among the audience."[6] If religious blasphemy hurt Lentz's teaching career, sex killed it. At that year's faculty recital, Lentz offered *Love and Conception* (1968, for piano, page turner, two to three radio stations, and tape), based around a pastiche Schumann piano sonata first movement. The grand piano sounding board, fixed with transducers, acted as a loudspeaker through which local radio stations broadcast one of Lentz's tape pieces, a review of that piece, and the piano piece. During this last broadcast, the pianist and page turner danced, stripped, and then began love making as the curtain closed.[7] Lentz's contract was not renewed. He adopted his young daughter Medeighnia's term for UC Santa Barbara, UniNursery, to describe conventional higher education.[8]

Two pieces mark Lentz's move to "my version of 'tonal music.'"[9] The score to *LOVERISE* (1970, for singing pianist and optional film) includes chord symbols with the direction, "Piano licks are meant only as suggestions (possible interpretations) of the chords." Visually, *LOVERISE* includes marginal jottings, and drawings, including a penis growing increasingly erect on each page.[10] A wealthy ninety-year-old patron commissioned *Canon and Fugle* (1970–71). As his patron's tastes ran to Stephen Foster and Lentz had given up modernism, "it was a natural step (or jump) to compose a work that was 'pretty,' but also incorporated my interest in keeping my music in that 'state of becoming.'"[11] At the premiere, attended by many faculty members from CalArts (California Institute of the Arts), "Only Hal [Budd] stuck around later, and 'got it.' Like me, he was stuck in that world of 'babbittry' (both of us added a touch of jazz to our then 'modernist' language)."[12]

Song(s) of the Sirens (1973, for clarinet, cello, and piano) was startling in its recorded release in 1975.[13] This piece includes bell-like reverbed piano arpeggios and cello melody, a close-miked, sibilant, seductive voice speaking broken phonemes, then detached words, then full phrases. At the last minute, the clarinet emerges to support the speaker. The piece ends in a final tremolo crescendo. *Song(s) of the Sirens* and Budd's *Madrigals of the Rose Angel* (1972) firmly established the California sound and are clearly post-minimalist years before the commonly accepted 1976 watershed.

Wine is central to Lentz's music and life, both as religious ritual and in gastronomy. *You Can't See the Forest . . . Music* (1972, for three speakers, wine glasses, and delay system) was written for his post-CTM group Budd, Lentz & Stoerchle. *Missa Umbrarum* (1973), first performed by Lentz's next group, San Andreas Fault, includes rubbed and struck wine glasses, broken and extended speech patterns, a whispered "sexy Sanctus," and a harmonic structure underpinned by 118 "sonic shadows."[14] Lentz references non-Christian sources, including his distant Seneca ancestry. *O-Ke-Wa* (1974, for voices, drums, bone rasps, and bells) is based on the Seneca Dance of the Dead. *Apologetica* (1996) uses the Chilam Balam sacred books of the Maya of Yucatán, plus Hopi and Navajo words and colonial texts.

Some references are patently "American." "eagleCREDO" from *wolfMASS* (1988), written for the Lentz Group, his ensemble through most of the 1980s, suddenly moves from Renaissance counterpoint to Ivesian quotation via "The Battle Hymn of the Republic," "Battle Cry of Freedom," and "When Johnny Comes Marching Home." *Continental Divide* (2003, for string orchestra) has "American" open chords, melodies, and dancelike tunes while retaining Lentz's musical language.[15] Lentz is often ethical, moving, and contemplative. *Ending(s)* (2018, for string ensemble and tenor) sets two haiku; the first by a survivor from Hiroshima, the second by a sixteenth-century warrior poet who subsequently died in battle; "In Paradisum" from the Latin Requiem; and the formula for an atom bomb.[16]

Recently Lentz has created an Illuminated Manuscripts series: three-dimensional sculptures made from acrylic, on which graphic symbols are painted, and including a digital recording of the piece. "All of the Illuminated Manuscripts appear as abstractions, as a musical score itself appears . . . symbols floating in space, but carrying a sonic message that, when performed, becomes Music."[17]

Lentz and Childs banter playfully throughout this interview. As the conversation flags, Childs suggests that they turn off the tape, and Lentz agrees: perhaps the perfect ending to an interview.

Daniel Lentz: Interview

This interview is fragmentary due to tape failure.

Biography and Groups

BARNEY CHILDS: Can you tell me biographical shit, so I can tie this down?

DANIEL LENTZ: I have three birth dates published, from '41 to '43. I want eventually to spread that out so thinly, that after I die it would have to be a "circa," such as in [Jacob] Obrecht. It's very elegant. You have actually a question mark with him: "?–circa."

BC: It would be a giant musicological problem for some clown to have to solve for a master's thesis. The locale is fixed?

DL: Actually it is. Pennsylvania, Latrobe.[18]

BC: That's a famous town.

DL: Yeah. Arnie Palmer.

BC: You studied at Brandeis?

DL: I studied at Ohio University in Athens. And St. Vincent College in Latrobe, Pennsylvania—it's a monastery-seminary. I got my bachelor's degree there and then two master's degrees, theoretically, at Ohio. I have a sixty-hour master's degree. Then I did PhD work at Brandeis. I did the course work and a couple of the languages, but I never wrote the thesis.

BC: Driving up we talked about the California Time Machine. You told me about all the pieces people wrote for it. Since '60–61 there has been a great rise of new music groups, like the ONCE group and the Davis people [Larry Austin and others at UC Davis]. Why is this?

DL: Probably for the same reason as in industry. There's been a great rise in consulting firms, external groups determining what was happening in a particular business. I can't get my finger on exactly why the group thing, but I see signs that it's fading right now.

Europe

DL: It's a nice place for music to visit, but it shouldn't want to live there! I have lots of pieces done there, like performance pieces, which are very difficult to do here.

BC: There's a better audience?

DL: There's more of one.

BC: Do they regard what you are doing as different than you do?

DL: Yeah. The first time I had a piece performed in Europe was about five years ago. I had written a piece in '64 and it was performed in '67, at one of these festivals where there was a seminar the next morning and everybody talks about his piece. [Roman] Haubenstock-Ramati was the moderator. His criticism was adamantly against the structure of this particular piece; that it was a lot of things mixed and going very fast—the way I wanted to write the piece. An event lasts for a second; then another event lasts for two seconds, then one second, then two seconds, and absolutely no relationship between the events. I really didn't think of this until afterwards, riding a train back to Sweden, that Haubenstock-Ramati listening to that would be like him watching American TV. You have the breakups, the commercials and whatnot. The piece was very well performed, but . . .

BC: . . . misread.

DL: Shit, that was a long time ago. I'm not very fond of the piece, but I was defensive about it. Going back on the train, I was reading [Marshall] McLuhan; finding out about linear and horizontal thinking. The difficulties that African natives have when they see a TV and they can't quite make it out because it takes more of you than the screen gives.[19] I made this analogy in the piece; there was no way you could hear it going that way. You just can't make those links that we can make.

BC: You've never trained in it.

DL: I've had quite a few things similarly received since then for different reasons. You get a completely unexpected reception to a piece over there. I had a piece done by Dutch television. My idea in this piece was to have them perform it and pass it through and have the sounds come out of either full or empty Rice Krispies. They took this as a big pop-art event, because it was Rice Krispies. All I thought was of "Snap, Crackle, and Pop"—I thought of sounds either snapping, crackling, or popping, or doing none of these. Different sounds went through an empty box, or a full box, or through no box at all.

Electronic and Tape Music

BC: One thing that interests me about your new scores is the way that electronics are used much differently than I've seen. There's a very tight integration with sound as the endpoint. It's not just somebody turns on a tape and there's a tape playing. There's the whole sound process . . . It's different than what Larry [Austin] and those guys were doing: everything is amplified and altered, but you don't like that?

DL: No, the last piece I wrote was called *Sermon: Saying Something with Music* in 1966, which for me was a long time ago. But I'm not that old.

BC: Musically it was a long time ago, too.

DL: It was a string quartet for people who gave sermons and played at the same time. And they went through seven modulators. [*Bad tape; unintelligible.*] But that was the last one, because I got to hear that piece right after I wrote it. It wasn't exactly my thing—those electronic alterations become just other instruments that are used to defend musical thinking.

BC: But you don't do that?

DL: I'm getting away from that.

BC: How confident are you? Can you read circuit diagrams and do wiring and that sort of thing?

DL: I've done that.

BC: You think that's important? Pauline [Oliveras] is also qualified to do that.

DL: Pauline is probably a good example. I don't want to get negative, [but] the whole electronic thing has seen its day. It's like the SST [supersonic transport].[20] People just got fed up getting the pollution. Which we've gotten in the music, too; there's an awful lot of it.

BC: Yet colleges are expanding tremendously: buy a studio, have courses, everybody's got to have an ARP [synthesizer], have seminars.

DL: Well, when it hits the "UniNursery," you know it's dead.

Style and Strength

DL: A guy can tell if they hear a piece of yours or mine or Russell Peck's. You can tell when there's strength or power. It could be a very bad piece, but you can tell when the strength is there. And that's what people resent first. They know they are in no position to say right away if it's a good or bad piece, but they're in a position to recognize its strength. And when they recognize that strength, they've got to be threatened. Only because that's one more of the "biggies," which everybody thinks they themselves are in and don't want to be crowded.

BC: Yeah, that's it.

DL: They can have good weak pieces.

History and New Music

BC: We're still in the shadow of somebody like Stravinsky. This is still the masterpiece thing.

DL: Yeah. We're all looking for the right . . . which ain't gonna happen. There are too many rights to make a wrong. To coin a phrase.

BC: I think it's a good point. Did you look at the *Perspectives* [*of New Music*] issue with all the tributes to Stravinsky?

DL: I haven't seen a *Perspectives* in six years.

BC: Everybody that they could get wrote a tribute or comment. Most of them are maudlin. It really is very discouraging. There are one or two irreverent and genuine things.

DL: I'm more encouraged by the bad ones. I get discouraged when I see a fantastic idea, which I've never seen in *Perspectives*. And I wouldn't expect to see them.

American Music and History

BC: Something happens to me more nowadays, and I wanted to see if it happens to you, too. I hear fewer pieces by contemporary composers that I like. The pieces that I hear are tedious. Contrarywise, the pieces that I do hear that I like, I like very much.

DL: I'm a bit different because I hear fewer and fewer pieces these days. I'm a little more isolated.

BC: Do you think it's important to hear new pieces? Does it matter to you to hear what other guys are doing?

DL: Oh, it interests me to hear other pieces. I know that my circumstance doesn't always permit that. I've got to travel great distances to hear pieces. I get a better chance of hearing what's happening in Europe.

BC: But you don't get a better chance of hearing what's happening here.

DL: No. I think the American pieces played there aren't really representative of what the Americans are doing. As I'm sure the European pieces we hear over here . . .

BC: Those things are selected, although we tend to know better what's going on in Europe now than they know what's going on over here. Because there's so much PR—so many over here are teaching, and so much lionizing.

DL: Up to a point, because they know more about our young guys. [Terry Riley's] *In C* must be played every day over there. You get very little of [Urs] Peter Schneider or the equivalent—a very young European with a lot of go.

BC: There are young guys who are doing exciting things.

DL: It's so damn hard to compare continents, because ultimately you get down to the fact that you know very little. They were omitting us when Ives was here, and they had made a very big mistake. We probably would be making the same mistake by not acknowledging the fact that things are happening there, just because we don't hear them. Maybe Russia's where it's at. But who heard American pieces in 1910? What would you have thought if you lived in Vienna and you were hearing what was played in America? You wouldn't have heard Ives, McDowell or any of the really interesting people. You would have heard the academicians. There's probably still something to be learned by that.

BC: How about performers? I guess it's a cliché that performers today are much more able to handle the demands put upon them by composers.

DL: In their fingers they are. I'm sure this has always been true that in 90 percent of performers, their nerves end at the knuckles; at least their sensibilities end there. I can't see where that's changed at all. It doesn't interest me because I'm learning to build in safeguards.

BC: It's an idea that . . .

DL: . . . took me a long time to learn. I prefer to perform them myself.

BC: That was the point that was made at the concert at CalArts the other night—Hal [Budd] saying that this was a piece for him to do and that nobody else could do it. I'm sure somebody could after hearing him do it, but you want to dummy-proof the thing.

Juvenilia and Legacy

BC: What have you done with all those old works?

DL: I have tapes. I have, surprisingly, almost everything I've ever written or performed.

BC: How many pieces?

DL: Counting electronics? Probably fifty pieces.

BC: That's a lot of pieces. You started late?

DL: I started writing music when I was a little kid. As does everybody when there's a piano in the house—and paper. My daughter is doing the same thing. I have never even said a word to her, but she has already invented her own notation. I wasn't quite that sophisticated, but somehow there used to be paper around and I would write little things. Nothing came out of it. I got into jazz and I played all the Louis Armstrong charts and went into Dixie. In high school I arranged for the jazz band, and that was the beginning of my writing. Then I went to college. I wrote a piece for brass septet, which in retrospect was very Bartókian. But in 1959 in Pennsylvania, that was plenty modern. Everybody read it in a rehearsal, but they wouldn't play it. They went through it once and decided it wasn't worthy. I didn't have the confidence at that time to know that I had something that they didn't have, so I quit [composing] until I graduated from college. That summer I was already just twenty-one, and that's when I started again, writing pieces.

BC: Do you think it's possible for any promising young composer to get anything out of an academic [education in] four or five years?

DL: Yeah, you get angry. I'm for the old-style education in that sense. I had the advantage of a bad education, and I think everybody should have the same advantage.

BC: I agree completely. John Gates and I were talking about a composer (who shall remain nameless) who doesn't really enjoy listening to music.[21] I was saying that I found his pieces dull, and John said, but he doesn't like music, as such. He can't put a record on at three in the morning and get tearful about it.

DL: No emotional aspects.

BC: I'm not sure this is guaranteed. Part of it is what you said about a bad education, but part of it is a kind of cantankerousness you've got to have. Essentially you get tired of guys saying "You can't do this, you've done this badly." And you have to say, "Screw you, Jack, I can and indeed am going to do it."

DL: That's like a little anecdote. In my study with Roger Sessions at "Wangletood" [Tanglewood] . . .

BC: What year were you there? Were you there the same year that [Phil] Winsor and Peck and all those guys were there?

DL: Yes.

BC: That must have been a ball.

DL: It was a good year. Winsor was just going through a divorce; an exciting character to be around. And Bill Albright, Dave Borden, Paul Chihara, Peck. Thumbs-up for some; thumbs-down for some. I went to Roger Sessions. You've got to pick a teacher, and I had a choice of Gunther Schuller, George Rochberg, Donald Martino, and Roger Sessions. And anybody in their right mind would go for the old man. I took a piece that I had done a long time ago, but at the time I found that they like to have a piece played there. They preferred that you wrote it there.

BC: This has always been true.

DL: I pretended to be writing this old piece. I would take a little bit in at a time. And the first time I took something, he said I *hadn't* been giving myself enough problems. Because he had come especially from Princeton and that was the mathematic ethic: problem solving. That's what music was to these guys. And old Roger had just been getting into it himself, just enough to be able to articulate these things. Babbitt would have been incapable of saying something like that because it never would have occurred to him. I gave this answer off the cuff (which is not true at all) that the reason he can't see the problem is because of the perfection of the solutions! Because everything was so smooth in the piece, he didn't see the problems. And I hadn't really been writing music like that anyway.

BC: Did you try writing such a piece? Counting up to twelve and or anything of this sort?

DL: In school I did, but not very much after that. I started getting into octaves which I thought was really early.

BC: Do you enjoy listening to [jazz]?

DL: No.

BC: You don't feel as some people do about popular music today?

DL: No, I've gone through it. You hear a rock band of ten people and you think, what are we doing wrong? Everybody's sitting around getting smashed and having a good time. This is interesting because Alvin Lucier was here a couple of years ago. I got this position of Regents Lecture, which became one of the reasons I was hired. It was right in the middle of the big rock surge: after *Sergeant Pepper*, well after the Beatles, right at the end when they were really fine. It always has concerned me that academic modern music completely removes itself from any popular reality. It's discouraging when you thought of Woodstock and all, but I've never gotten that concerned to do something about it. But I talked to Alvin once. I'm sure it's not even his idea, but it impressed me at the time because it was so obvious. The difference between that music and one of Cage's pieces was that you went to a rock concert, you did your thing, danced, and you went out, and when you left you left the music. Whereas you were not supposed to do this with so-called serious pieces. What it's supposed to do is that when you leave, it goes with you. Permanently: that it actually changes you and that the other doesn't.

BC: You think music ought to do that?

DL: When I was a kid I thought it should. I'm not so sure.

BC: When you hear pieces that impress you, do they stay with you? Do you think, "Wow, what a good thing"?

DL: Actually they do, unfortunately.

BC: Why "unfortunately"? They do with me a great deal.

DL: Because the bad pieces do the same thing. That's the whole point of this story. Certain pieces stay a very long time, really.

BC: Then my question about my decreasing satisfaction with what I hear is essentially not true.

DL: Well, you're getting less satisfied because you're probably hearing more things; because more things are getting written. You know, there aren't any more good ones being written.

BC: It's the same percentage.

DL: Two years ago I would have been disappointed even raising the issue of good and bad—a little less socialistic now. You see, there's still good pieces and bad pieces.

BC: We're stuck with the good and bad things. It's been ingrained into us, our generation. Our children may not have that, and maybe this would be of value. I would have agreed with you two years ago.

DL: We're getting there. Guys in positions such as yourself should start writing bad pieces. Try to be as bad as you can. Pretty soon, if you're really successful at your badness, you'll notice it starting to turn where there will be no distinction between really good and really bad. By then you've eliminated the whole issue.

BC: I don't like the "good" and "bad" idea because it seems so terribly dependent on my own set of responses. But there are pieces that I just enjoy a hell of a lot. I can't say this is good or this is bad; I just can say goddamn, this is great sounds doing good things. And they stay with me.

DL: Well, normally that would be a good piece.

BC: I had a big hassle with some guys at ASUC [American Society of University Composers] after a paper I had read, where I put down the idea that the more compositional decisions you make, the better the piece is apt to be. This leads up to total organization being total salvation. I said no, this isn't so. I got a lot of flack from people from the other coast—particularly a guy from Princeton who had just published an article saying that this was indeed true, that it's the number of pains you take in solving compositional problems. That's why what Sessions said is interesting. It seems that we inherit, whether we like it or not, the view that you're not setting yourself the problems. It becomes an exercise rather than something much more near or immediate.

DL: It's going to take an awfully long time. Who knows? It could just disappear. My only problem is getting started: stop drinking enough to get down and do some work.

BC: We all have that problem! A poet friend of mine said that so many friends of his had died recently because of violence and hang-ups: sex, liquor, dope, and so on. At the time, it didn't seem to me to be quite true about composers. Composers seem to be more resilient. The worst thing that happened to them is they stopped composing. They didn't kill themselves.

DL: Let me think about that. Probably the reason—see if you like this or not—is that it's easier to be a poet because all you have to do is say you're a poet and produce some poems. But music is much more in its own little world; to get there far enough to call yourself a composer and then go one other step where you are recognized as one. [*Tape cut out.*]

BC: You don't think a great many more people are calling themselves composers?

DL: Probably not any more than ever, which is neither here nor there. It's probably just as high of a proportion.

BC: It seems to me there are more people calling themselves composers. Maybe in Europe there are more people. I had a talk with Peter Schat under very interesting circumstances, because his parents run the Schat Bakery in Bishop [California], and he came up to Deep Springs.[22] There are hundreds of composers. Their work is printed and things are performed.

DL: That's in Holland. It's not that easy here. There, first, you call yourself a composer and then everything's pretty much done for you, if you lay the work in their hands. Here you've got to do that for an awful, awful long time before anybody, if ever, takes it seriously.

BC: It seems that you do a lot of work, that you work steadily and perhaps more than a lot of people I know. The orchestra piece is a long hard job. In other words, what you have been doing is extensive. It's not that you just sit down one afternoon and you have a piece.

DL: I do that kind too, you know. When I said fifty pieces, I don't really count those.

Wine

DL: I like what I've been working on these last six months.[23] I call it *Fermentations* because the word "fermentation" implies . . .

BC: . . . growth . . .

DL: . . . or an aging, because most of them use wine to some degree. I use that because I've been drinking wine. Well, you saw the wineglass. That would be a predecessor to this whole thing I'm working on.

Composition, Performance, and Life

BC: You're getting back writing pieces for you to perform.

DL: Half of what I do is that and half is like writing the orchestra piece. It's really a big move for me. But I'll end up performing it in some way or conducting it.

BC: Will you go back to conduct that Utrecht performance?

DL: I'm trying to swing that now. A union problem—the Dutch have a strong union. Last time there, I had a couple of pieces done and I participated from a distance.

BC: Would you say you are better known in Europe than in this country? For this reason, that you've been there a number of times?

DL: I don't know. I think I'm unknown anyway; I'm destined, so I don't really worry about it. I really like going to New York. I get disgusted with staying here. We've moved, since we were married, twelve different places. Which tells you something about me, not her. But I'm almost going out of my head, this long in a town. Going to New York just doesn't quite do it for me. But for some reason, when I'm nine or ten thousand miles away, I really dig on it for a month or two, but that gets . . . All the cobblestones become part of your brain! But I'm anxious to get back. I'm fed up with California.

BC: The students I have have this need to go, to constantly change. They'll come to [Ben?] Johnston for a year and then they'll drop out and go somewhere else.

DL: I always stayed with school. I went to the monastery college because I had no other choice. I couldn't get into any other. My father made me go to college; otherwise I wouldn't have gone. It became a choice of working or going to school. These are all little justifications of why I'm different than your students.

BC: You're older, for one thing. Better at it, for another. What would you have been if you hadn't gone to college, do you suppose? Well, actually, that's an unfair question. Nobody can tell.

DL: Jesus, probably been in lumber, like my father is. I would probably have been a jazz musician, actually. A combination of college and the cold sore on my chops got me out of jazz; got me out of playing with my lips and more into the fingers.

BC: So many people in their thirties now are also jazz musicians or have been.

DL: In the nineteenth century, most of the composers were something else. Most of them were probably . . .

BC: . . . improvisers on the keyboard.

DL: Jazz is very mechanical; it has to do with mechanical ability. It's natural that jazz gets created like Beethoven's improvisations got created, and it's natural to start going into the other bag. It's still probably not very interesting.

BC: I don't know, there's a hell of a lot of people that have been in jazz at one time or another: La Monte Young, for example, or Terry Riley.

DL: I could name almost everybody I know. Hal [Budd] . . .

BC: . . . Bill [Bolcom] and Peck and all. And Austin and Phil Winsor were trumpet players.

DL: Alvin Lucier was a drummer.

BC: Mostly trumpet people and keyboard people.

DL: That's why I like trumpet people.

BC: It seems to me that the generation that grew up after the war is the first generation in American music which is genuinely its own. If you look back at David Diamond and all those guys, they're still under the shadow. They're not their own.

DL: Some of them, amazingly, have made the change, although they're part of the other generation. Even in some cases they have actually led it, like with one hand tied behind their back. What's going to be funny is the young guys aren't going to go back and untie their hand. More likely they're going to tie the other one.

BC: They're going to try.

DL: It just seems very natural. But we've been successful, and this is almost autobiographical: we went through the war too. A different war, and in many senses more prone to be set to music: the Vietnam War. We've been pretty successful in eliminating it, musically. I see like the magic year of '69, which besides being a good year for Burgundy was also a good year to get rid of politics. Last night

I heard the first political piece I've heard in two or three years, at the height of the Vietnam War. I guess it had something to do with the reescalation. It was a Richard Teitelbaum Maoist piece, and it's embarrassing to see that again, because it doesn't make one ripple of what it's intended to do.

BC: Once Stu Dempster played a piece which is a trombone in a giant refrigerator carton with holes cut in it. Dempster kept popping out of it; parts of him kept showing up here and there. At one part a hand came out with a flag, and it looked to me like the Beaver Patrol or something. I thought what a great thing! It turned out to be the Cambodian flag. I was really very angry to find this out. It was such an obvious, gross kind of button pushing.

DL: Well, your book's about a specific generation, from thirty to fifty?

BC: From twenty-five to fifty.

DL: Well, the people I respect are in most cases around my own age or into their mid-forties. From twenty-five to fifty, I guess. I still like some thirty-five-year-olds better. But I think we're getting a little more open-minded. We differ from guys ten years older than us. I don't know a lot of guys—[Robert] Ashley, Lucier—but they seem a little more bitter, a little more closed-minded. If anything, we've opened that up and it's freeing us too. Ultimately, I think we will do much more of the same thing, too.

BC: Well, don't forget that a lot of people as they get older start to panic slightly. Where are all the goodies? I'm old enough now that I ought to be getting them and I'm not.

DL: "Goodies" being what?

BC: Fame, fortune, reputation, recordings, performances.

DL: Once that comes along, you've got to start getting worried. You should be happy, but you've got to be worried, too, because it usually comes side by side with vestigiality in most cases. But you aren't asking very many really musical questions, which is nice.

BC: What would be a musical question?

DL: If the interviewer was Milton Babbitt, the question would come from his consciousness and would be fairly easy for me to answer. Some of the vocabulary would be missing or out of joint. But it's a hell of a lot easier to do. I didn't mean to say that's what you should be asking. It's probably what you *shouldn't*. It should take care of itself.

BC: I just want people to be themselves and say what they want to. Especially when one listens to other people, one is interested in what other people are doing, one knows them, one is concerned with them. I mean, it's foolish asking somebody, "In your opinion, sir, is tonality dead?" or something.

DL: Very much so. The concern with it is dead. I have answers for questions like that because as a teacher you get asked those questions. I have such a fantastic set of answers—a lot of very automatic ones, but which in some cases I took a week to work out an answer. I had like stock, off-balance kind of answers. You can reverse a question very easily by giving an off-balance answer. Like one of Cage's beauties: the afternote to the *Lecture on Nothing*. If you've ever tried that in real life, it's fantastic what it does to the person who just asked the question. Or the David Tudor answer to the student's question, "If you don't know, why do you ask?"

BC: It's pretty scary. I don't like games.

DL: I bet if you went to England, you'd run into a lot of that. They have a history of that—the wit thing.

BC: That's quite another matter.

DL: But wit can get so devastating. Once I took a charter flight from Los Angeles to London, which was three days late. By the time I got to London I hadn't slept for three nights and all I was doing was drinking. Flying at the time frightened me. I got stopped in customs, and I had two numbers in my sock. It was supergrass in those days. What they really wanted to know was how much money I had. I had just gotten a grant from UC and I had about $1,500 in cash, which got me through the line pretty quickly and they never got to my socks. I ended up in this house in Cambridge, of all places, though I had landed in Heathrow. The house was built in the sixteenth century. But I only knew the American I'd gone there with. And everybody was British, but only one Englishman, who was a journalist. There was an Australian, South African, Rhodesian—their girlfriends and wives. There was an English girl, too—a cockney. This was in the middle of Vietnam, and the American had a whole different connotation than when you were there in the '50s, when you were still a hero. They found that we were very fragile when it got down to it. But the big thing was these games the Australian, especially, and the British journalist played with me. That constant wit, man. I was quite proud of myself when I got right down to it. There was pressure on and I usually could deliver in that circumstance, but, at that time, I got thoroughly nonsensical but it completely disarmed them. There was absolutely no logic to anything I said, but it was delivered with a lot of speed. They thought there were things they didn't understand from California.

I said that only because of that game thing, which there was so much bigger with the English. I wonder if English music uses this thing that is so natural to the English. I haven't been to England very much but there's the Scratch Orchestra; Cornelius Cardew's *Schooltime Compositions*, which are little games. That's very charming. But that's probably a natural outgrowth of that kind of wit. A guy like Cardew can't get it out in real life and he gets it out in music in some weird, obscure way, if you know those pieces.

BC: I know some of his earlier ones. Well, what else do you want to say?

DL: I don't know. I don't exactly feel as if I've said anything.

BC: Let's turn it off for a while.

DL: Absolutely.

Notes

1. "Support Your Local Independents," *LA Weekly*, July 31, 2002, https://www.laweekly
.com/support-your-local-independents/ (accessed August 25, 2019).

2. Daniel Lentz to the author, e-mail April 29, 2013.

3. "Daniel Lentz: Music for Rental or Purchase," http://www.daniellentzmusic.com/
daniel-lentz-music-rental.html (accessed August 23, 2019); Bob Dickinson, "Interview: Daniel Lentz," *Mouth Magazine*, June 26, 2014, https://themouthmagazine.com/2014/06/26/
daniel-lentz/ (accessed August 25, 2019).

4. Daniel Lentz, interview with Vincent Plush, Yale University Oral History of American
Music, Los Angeles, May 4, 1983.

5. Dickinson, "Interview."

6. "The Electronic Theater Music of Daniel Lentz," *RadiOm*, 1967, 30:08 min., available
at Internet Archive, https://archive.org/details/C_1967_08_XX_01 (accessed August 23,
2019). The score is part of "Three Pieces (Lentz)," *Source* 3 (1968): 43–49.

7. Dickinson, "Interview."

8. Medeighnia Lentz Westwick was one of the cover art designers for Daniel Lentz,
wolfMASS (1986–88), Aoede Records AR103, CD, 2000.

9. Daniel Lentz to the author, e-mail March 9, 2016.

10. *Soundings* 1 (1972): 17–21.

11. Dickinson, "Interview."

12. Daniel Lentz to the author, e-mail April 25, 2013.

13. Montagnana Trio (John Gates, clarinet; Caroline Worthington, cello; Dolores Stevens, piano), *Spell*, ABC Command COMS 9005, LP, quadrophonic, 1975. Pieces include
Per Nørgård, *Spell*, Barney Childs, Trio for Clarinet, Cello and Piano, and Lentz. Also
see *Song(s) of the Sirens* on *Dancing on Water: Marty Walker, Clarinets*, Cold Blue Music
CB0005, CD, 2001.

14. Dickinson, "Interview."

15. Daniel Lentz, *Continental Divide/Ending(s)*, New World Recordings 80815-2, CD,
2019.

16. Ibid.

17. "Art," Daniel Lentz, http://www.daniellentzmusic.com/daniel-lentz-art.html (accessed
August 24, 2019).

18. "Daniel Lentz," in Joseph A. Comm, ed., *Legendary Locals of Latrobe, Pennsylvania*
(Charleston, SC: Arcadia, 2015), 70.

19. While singling out Africans as uniquely unable to understand television is highly
problematic, the ability to decode visual images requires a kind of literacy. Similar to how
we learn languages, we acquire visual literacy through persistent and extensive exposure and
acculturation. See for example, Neil Cohn, "Visual Narrative Comprehension: Universal

or Not?," *Psychonomic Bulletin and Review* 27 (2020): 266–85, https://doi.org/10.3758/s13423-019-01670-1.

20. The United States canceled a four-year project to research and develop supersonic air transport in 1971 because of the expense and environmental concerns.

21. John Gates, clarinetist and member of the Montagnana Trio.

22. Peter Ane Schat (1935–2003), Dutch composer.

23. *Fermentation Notebooks* (1972), for mixed choir.

12 Alvin Lucier (b. 1931)

RONALD KUIVILA

At the time of this 1972 interview, Alvin Lucier was composing live electronic music focused on the creation of alternative material relations to sound. These pieces involve the complex interplay of a physical process with images that serve as a shaping influence. For example, in *Music for Solo Performer* (1965), a performer's brainwaves are amplified and diffused to loudspeakers that in turn activate percussion. This suggests an image of total control in which the composer's mind has a direct, unimpeded path to the sounding music. But the application of electrodes to the performer's scalp suggests the vulnerability inherent in any medical procedure. And, since the physical generation of detectable brainwaves resists intentional shaping, the piece actually unfolds according to the involuntary waxing and waning of attention, which shapes the unmetered somatic rhythms of neural activity.

Throughout the interview, Lucier mentions various generative images that have served or might serve as organizing principles for pieces of this kind. These images tend to be quite specific while retaining a level of abstract generality. The epigraph to *Vespers* (1968) provides a useful example: "for any number of players who would like to pay their respects to all living creatures who inhabit dark places and who, over the years, have developed acuity in the art of echolocation, i.e., sounds used as messengers which, when sent out into the environment, return as echoes carrying information as to the shape, size, and substance of that environment and the objects in it."[1] Realizations of this piece do not attempt to represent bats or their sounds so much as create an aural experience sympathetic to their way of being in the audible world. The original realization involves four performers who are instructed to move from one specified point in a darkened space to another, guided only by the echoes of impulses produced by handheld directional speakers called Sondols. The performers are able to start and stop those impulses and change their rate. But such changes are made in support of the process of echolocation by differentiating the pulse streams of different performers. In order to enforce their dependence on echolocation, the performers wear sunglasses or blindfolds.

While the title is derived from the Latin name of the family of bats (*Vespertilionidae*), it also invokes evening prayers in the Catholic liturgy. This mirrors the animism of the epigraph and ritual overtone of the performers' task. The result is a performance where simple pedestrian actions and the incidental humor of the sunglasses acquire greater and greater poetic force as they somehow result in music of subtlety and charm.

In this way, *Vespers* illustrates how a generative image can establish a material relation to sound and shape and how that relation is enacted. In this approach, the intrinsic theatricality of an unconventional performance action (walking around a concert hall while pulse streams are beamed) acquires greater focus through the simplicity and specificity of the task those actions enact (echolocating oneself through the hall) and the poetry of the generative image that informs those tasks.

In the interview, Childs asks about the role of "fancy" and "imagination" in Lucier's work in order to better understand how these pieces extend beyond "a kind of reality and helping man orient himself in an immediate way." He proposes a triptych of three scenes from a saint's life as presenting an imaginative approach to the "real world." Lucier pushes back somewhat by observing that the religious would believe that a saint *could* appear in three places simultaneously, and then he describes how engineering concepts define his *Room Simulation No. 1* (1972). The implication is that faith and science both describe "real worlds" of different belief systems, and an artist might engage with either or both. He then invokes another belief system in the form of a Javanese saying, "We have no art; we do the best we can," to illustrate that invention in these pieces is directed at how best to enact a specific physical encounter with sound using readily available materials. The choices made are *pragmatic* rather than fanciful.

However, that invention finds its shape within the generative image he identified in the piece. For example, when Lucier describes *Queen of the South*, he comments that "the imagery comes from alchemy" in relation to the physics of the Chladni plate. But the realization of the piece is purely physical with "no other idea" than the physicality of the sand figures that can form out of vibration patterns on a plate activated with sound. Thus while "fancy" and "imagination" certainly enter into the recognition of the potential of juxtaposing the imagery of alchemy and the Chladni plate, the actual realization of the piece remains resolutely focused on the physical phenomenon as physics, while the pragmatic approach to realization resists an explicit representation of the underlying generative image.

Interestingly, Marshall McLuhan emerges as a possible influence lurking behind this discussion. For example, his *Understanding Media* contains the line "'We have no art,' say the Balinese; 'we do everything as well as possible.'" A few paragraphs earlier, McLuhan suggests that human survival may depend on the recognition of the truth of Wyndham Lewis's observation that "The artist is always engaged in writing a detailed history of the future because he is the only person aware of the nature of the present."[2]

However, where McLuhan deploys a kaleidoscopic range of images and examples to articulate large-scale claims about media and human experience, Lucier places intense focus on physical sonic experiences on the margins of conventional musical attention. Hopefully, the reader will find a useful counter-history of our obsessively designed present in the way Lucier's carefully chosen pairings of image and physical phenomenon succeed in musicking what just happens to be.

Alvin Lucier: Interview

BARNEY CHILDS: You said that although you wrote electronic music, you didn't use synthesizers.

ALVIN LUCIER: Well, all you need to change your mind is an idea. The minute you zero in on something, positively or otherwise, then you immediately see the opposite. I never liked synthesizers because they're somebody else's packaged idea, a low common denominator. The guy that designs them has to think of academic institutions and so forth. Then it struck me that I was being superior. If I had been an Italian in the eighteenth century, I'd certainly be interested in the new instruments that they were building; I'd go to Verona or Parma, wherever they were being made—the rash of string compositions that came out because of the technology of the time. So then I thought, hell, these are my instruments! There's a move now back to simpler things. Because it's part of American technology, and technology is responsible for pollution (the ecological thing), people that haven't been successful in electronics are putting it down. It struck me that if you take that attitude, the musical instruments that you're going to use are simply those instruments that come out of somebody else's technology. A piano is a very expensive instrument, but it's somebody else's technology.

Several things happened at the same time. I didn't really study an instrument very well; I played percussion, but I refused to study. I studied piano off and on, but it was such a psychological burden that I didn't really study an instrument and [that's] why I didn't go into music until a late age. But instead of my thinking it's my fault that I didn't study a musical instrument like everybody else did, then why couldn't I think that's because they're not my instruments? As a young person, there was a lot of pressure on me to play the violin because my father was a violinist, or to play the piano. I thought something's wrong with that. I'm American, and this is pointing towards the music of another time, another culture. I figured that out very early in my life, which is the reason I didn't go into music soon enough: the pressure was "you can't go into music if you don't go through these particular channels." So making electronic music is natural for me. It dawned on me that if I believed in electronic technology, and if I believed that we must go on with it and find new instruments, then I'm morally obligated to make pieces for synthesizers, because guys are making them. I go up to ARP [Instruments] and I speak to the guy who designed the 1047 filter. He's just as much an artist as any artisan ever was. I can talk to him about his filter; he's delighted. I'm doing things with it that he never dreamed would be done with it. He feeds back on my ideas; and it's just a perfect symbiotic.

BC: Perhaps like violin makers . . .

AL: Why should I be alienated from the people that are producing the instruments, even though I don't like the package? So I am obligated, if I regard myself as an interesting composer, to use these instruments so that I can in turn change what the manufacturers actually think about them. I go up to ARP just thinking about tunes and timbres; I can say I'm going to take the IBM 1130 computer and use your synthesizer as a package of components that are conveniently put in one box. I'm going to have the computers—four channels of voltage output, which was made available here—and use those four voltage channels to control four components on your synthesizer to simulate an environment change. That should be interesting to you, because it's like the automobile. The first cars were made in the image of the previous technology: the horseless carriage. Now you build a synthesizer in the image of a piano, and you've got a keyboard, and you tune it . . .

For instance, for the set of compositions I'm doing now—one that I did at the Bremen festival [Pro Musica Nova, 1972]—I used two voltage-controlled amplifiers, the filter, [and] the reverberation device, to simulate changes in room space. Changing the values of where the filter is gives a crude simulation of going into a big room or a smaller room, when you hear the room tone change. And if it is computer-controlled, then you can do it at a very fast speed. Their oscillators can respond to that. I use the ARP synthesizer for that piece, but not in a way that that synthesizer has hitherto been employed.

So instead of staying away from it, I can look at it as a package of components and I can turn that little 2600 synthesizer into the means of simulating environments. My visions would be that someday we'd set up permanent installations. We'd have special synthesizers, so that we'd have a space that could continually change. I could do that now with a conventional B-flat synthesizer. Instead of staying away from it, you can go and change your ideas about it. I think that that's a very important thing to do. Because we're so alien—we hate ourselves in a way (don't we?) in the United States.

BC: It's fashionable.

AL: It's fashionable. When you go away to another country, you go to Europe. Art is always from somewhere else. All right, they make synthesizers—they're just guys who are trying to look at a market, at what composers are doing. If I isolate myself, then I'm thinking I'm superior, and that's very elitist. And I'm dead set against that.

BC: You've been to Europe a lot with the Sonic Arts Union and on your own, and clearly they like what you do or they would not have you back. What have you that they like? Or what did they have that you like?

AL: We're doing something that they don't do. I think it's very clearly a situation of supply and demand. The German, Italian, and French electronic studios produced those classic tape music pieces. But in America (I'm using the people I associate with here) we've been committed to the live performance of electronic music for a long time. The Sonic Arts Union has been doing this as a group since 1966, but Gordon Mumma and Bob Ashley started it very much earlier. I didn't get into it. When I was in Italy as a student, I did an electronic piece, *Elegy for Albert Anastasia*, in Milan in 1962, but I didn't really finish it until 1965. But that was a tape piece; I didn't get started with live music until my solo performer piece using the brain waves. That was in 1965. And I thought a lot about that when I was doing that piece. Everyone I talked to had the idea to tape record the brain waves and then speed them up and slow them down as a raw material. You can see using brain waves at different octaves, different transpositions. Of course, the idea of the EEG is the theatrical element of a guy sitting there producing beautiful sounds by just turning on and off his alpha. But the situation's even more beautiful, because it has to do with plugging in, being plugged in.

BC: So many of your pieces involve human beings in a way that nobody else's work does. There's a very immediate feeling. *I Am Sitting in a Room* [1969] and *Vespers* [1968], where you're going about in a dark room, there's always this sense of relating to a human person in a funny kind of intimate sense.

AL: That's what we're all doing. We all want to relate to each other in an intimate sense. I don't regard the fact that we're in an electronic environment as technology. You pull the switch on a light, you hardly think of it as technology. It's the environment—like sunlight, like air. We're in that environment; there's no getting around it. Therefore, we're having whatever intimacies we have with other people in this environment. You put the lights out to be more intimate, right? But you put sounds in the background. Yet I'm trying to relate to the word "intimate." The EEG is one of the most intimate things, tapping somebody's brain waves. For instance, a person in my family who had some psychological problems was treated in that way, until they decided to take an EEG. And when they did, they found out there was a trace of mild epilepsy. So finding that out—and that's a very intimate thing to find out about somebody—changed their whole idea about what to do with this person. That happens again and again in the world—that's very poetic; that's the situation we're in. Astronauts have electrodes all over them to monitor their heart, and that's a very human situation now.

I would rather use electrodes and a differential amplifier than a violin because I believe that art can help you survive in your environment. And if your environment changes, your art has to change so that you can keep helping people understand what their environment is. I would hope that a piece like that shows people what an intimate situation those things are. Art that repeats; for example, Andy Warhol's piece that has many Green Stamps in a row.[3] You could say, "What the hell is that? It's just a bunch of Green Stamps." Green Stamps are mass-produced by the millions, but when you take a look at them you find that no two Green Stamps are alike. In an age where everything's repetitious, we're all afraid that because we can produce things en masse, everything, and consequently everybody, will be alike. That piece of art that Andy made teaches me that even if you do mass-produce things no one thing is alike. That changes my mind about the fact of mass production. I'll buy a car like everybody else's. Why should we have a plethora of different kinds of cars, when in fact you can get cars that are exactly alike and you find out that they're not? That's an important thing to know to help people survive.

BC: If somebody commissioned you to write a wind quartet, you simply would say "Pass"?

AL: No, but I would reinterpret what a wind quartet could be. In the first piece I talked about, the computer-generated simulation of spaces, *Room Simulation No. 1* (I call it the Bremen piece), I used four channels of computer-generated voltage control. Right away, four channels gives the idea of four performers. When I was in Bremen, the wonderful string quartet the Societa Communistica Italiana performed. I never heard the program because we were preparing ours, but I was able, outside the door, to [hear them]. They played with great skill and were very committed. I thought, what if they asked me to write them a piece? If I made the Bremen piece using components of a synthesizer, which had been an instrument that I didn't have any ideas for, then if I don't have any ideas for a string quartet, I could reinterpret my idea of string playing and have them do the four channels of voltage. I could tax their ability to change amplitude. If they're an excellent quartet, they must deal with slight changes in amplitude all the time. I could make them be the four changes. The first violinist could be responsible for changing the reverberation time of these imaginary rooms, and so on. So that you could interface—I hate to use these terms . . .

BC: Good. I'm glad you're twitchy about "interface."

AL: Interface, but I was going to use the word "couple." I would then couple the string quartet with my idea of spaces. It would be a beautiful idea that the quartet, which always plays in a space—chamber music in a "chamber," and I underline the word "chamber." In this instance the quartet could change the size of its chamber, simultaneously. You could even have the real-time situation develop that they change it, and as it changes, they change their idea of what the next move would be. So I could write a piece for string quartet.

BC: One might assume from hearing you and your work that you were solely interested in a reality and helping man orient himself in an immediate way. Yet what about that part of art which is fancy? Imagination? Obviously, in changing room shapes you are moving into this in a way. You're not eliminating the whole concept of art as something you *can't* do. I'm thinking of a painting of three scenes from a saint's life. In one part of the painting he is coming down a hill, in another part he is standing. He's in the same picture three times. This is an imaginative approach to the "real world" as they thought of it.

AL: Of course, that came out of the way they saw the real world. If you were religious, you would believe that that saint could appear three places simultaneously. The idea we're talking about: changing the sizes of rooms is really an engineer's idea. I'd really love to be asked by a city or school or government to design rooms with an architect where we could change the sound situation in the room for particular purposes: in order to teach at one hour, in order to be a dry space or a reverberant space. So that's one idea. The other idea I'm still doing, but I'm doing it on my own. I almost don't think of it as art, I think of it as doing. The Indonesians have a great saying in Java: "We don't have any art; we just do the best we can." In my idea of changing spaces, it is personal and intimate and I would use the string quartet. I'm doing the best I can. It interests me more than to make it an engineering problem. So I don't quite know how to react to your word "fancy." When I hear that word "fancy," it means "extra," putting something in the piece that doesn't have to be there.

BC: I don't mean that. It's the dream part, the imagination part.

AL: That's getting to be my biggest problem. If the world is going badly, what good are my dreams? Do they help? In the past, our ideal artist does what he does, and they spin off, and it's beauty and that's enough. Because it will help people. Then you think, "Help who?" Who does my work help? Your work? People; who are *the* people? When you talk about imagination, I don't know why, but I make the connection with mysticism. At the time that Chinese communism is coming to the fore, things like astrology, the occult, are coming to the fore, maybe for two or three particular reasons. One reason probably is that society in America is so horrendous for a lot of people that they retreat into the mystical. It's a retreat; it's an escape. If that's the case, then it's bad. If you read Mao, there's no place for that in the Chinese society, because it doesn't help. If there are problems to be solved, the most important thing is to solve those that one can see and do something about. I've done recently two pieces in which the ideas came from alchemy. I'm concerned about them, because if I believe what I just said, then I shouldn't be doing that, because alchemy's not going to help anybody. On the other hand, *The Queen of the South* [1972] is a very physical, material piece, which involves performers making operations, a responsive surface upon which is sprinkled sand or stream material. The performers make sounds into the plate; whatever the material of the plate is, that excites the plate, and there's a well-known physical phenomenon that the sand will disperse . . .

BC: . . . in high school physics where you saw the plate bowed . . .

AL: The piece is a very simple application of that principle. It has much to do with alchemy, where you repeat the same operation on physical phenomena. You don't change what you do, you repeat it exactly and hope that other things come into play so that the transformation is made. Even though the imagery comes from alchemy, the piece itself is very materialistic, physical. It has no idea beyond that. The players can physically react and respond and push around the sand on that plate. The idea is that if they do it together they discover their own collective imagery. A guy wanted me to install this in an outdoor civic community situation, which I'd be delighted to do! Just let people come in and play onto the plate, see what images they have. I got to this idea through an occult, esoteric way, but when I really think about it, it's as physical as any piece I do. And in that way it's important.

BC: At the same time, all the pieces are revealing. In other words, the players are going to always discover something in your works. Which answers my question. Although the input may come from alchemy, this isn't reflective in a programmatic sense, it is merely a transmission that helped you help the player to find out things.

AL: The title came to me through Pauline [Oliveros]. Pauline and I are old pals, and she came east last year in October, and I drove her up to Vermont. That was a very good trip. I drove her up to Dick Higgins's in Vermont, a twelve-hour ride—just gorgeous autumn. We drove up through the Connecticut River Valley, which is very beautiful. When I first came here, I had a very strong idea that the Connecticut River was the source of energy for me in some way. It's an old tidal river; it's four hundred miles long. I took some students up to try to find the source. And I always wanted to make a piece about this river, but it never came to me.

But I drove Pauline and Lin [Barron] up the Connecticut River to visit Dick, and it turned out that we both had commissions from Gerald Shapiro's new music ensemble in Providence. And Pauline was searching for a piece, and Mary, my wife, was along. Pauline's very interested in promoting any female artists, which is a wonderful thing, and Mary was feeding Pauline images, because Mary's a visual artist. I thought [that since] we were both commissioned, chances are both of the pieces will be played on the same program.

Next few weeks I read Carl Jung's book on psychology and alchemy; it's filled with excerpts from alchemical texts. I came across this alchemical text about the Queen of the South, which can be an image for *sapientia*, the wisdom of God. It's curious because the wisdom is female, which is a wonderful, important idea, particularly now when the women's liberation . . . The idea that in another time wisdom could be thought of as feminine, whereas for most of our lives wisdom is always associated with the male, interested me. And I got it through my great respect for Pauline.

So even though alchemy's esoteric, it's pertinent now, particularly when women's liberation is such an important social matter. I guess it's OK to go back in time and go out to imageries that come without, in order to help something that's happening within. Mao would say whatever imagery China has that serves the purpose of helping people—even if it is from a time in China when there was feudalism—I think it's within; it's a good idea to use that.

BC: You said you didn't have an instrument. Don't you think that the chorus is your instrument?

AL: I got into choral directing obliquely. I went to Brandeis; they had a choral director who was very excellent, but he had other jobs, and Brandeis wasn't his first job. I was a composer, and Irving Fine—a wonderful man who did a lot for so many people—always wanted a committee of composers. While I'd been at Brandeis I was active with student brass groups—I think I had the worst brass group that ever existed! I think I probably gave the worst concert of brass music that ever was heard, but that's all right. I was "peppy"—I had that American pep, organizing—and Irving, being a choral composer and a former choral director, thought that he would take a chance on me. There were no other instrumental conductors, but his predictions turned out right, because my ego wasn't concerned with doing the B Minor Mass. I was more oriented towards doing contemporary music for composers.

I got very tired of it, because you push people around. Choral directing on that kind of level, you have to discipline, you stand up and talk and scream at people. I hated it. I remember doing a piece of Seymour Shifrin, who joined the faculty. It was a very difficult piece: you had to play tablas and sing at the same time. I had to really browbeat some advanced students. One pianist wasn't good enough. I had to tell him he couldn't play it. It was a terrible experience to say to someone, "You're not good enough." So then I thought, why the hell do this kind of music? Seymour Shifrin's got those high standards of performance, but it's terrible to keep somebody out, and you might think of making art where anybody can come in. We have to do that. For those people that want to learn an instrument and be proficient, that's also a wonderful idea; but you have to make an art where everybody can come in.

BC: How much has your experience with music of different cultures here in the [Wesleyan University] ethnomusicology program shaped your future compositional thinking?

AL: Well, I'm very respectful of other cultures, and I think about it all the time; I think about the word "intrusion" into other cultures.

BC: That's a great geological word, by the way.

AL: I also love the word "insertion," which they use in the moon shots. The insertion into the field of another planet is just a marvelous idea. As my thinking has turned to politics, I think intrusion and insertion is unavoidable. It's where violence and aggression and pain come from. And the places where the intrusion occurs, the in-between places, are the places where I think change and ideas come from. It's unavoidable. For instance, in Java, the gamelan now is being tape-recorded and is being taken to social functions. You frown, and I frown; but somehow that's unavoidable. I have a very good friend here, Sita, who plays a rebab, a Javanese instrument. I was thinking how could I compose a piece for her. I learn that the rebab is an Arab instrument that gets to Java because of a religious invasion by the Arabs. It goes historically through the race, so that when Islam got to Java it intruded on what was Javanese, and now that is Javanese. One's intrusion, changing other cultures, is inevitable, as communication does that. If you call somebody on the phone, you intrude on his room, his space. You can have no phone, but it's unavoidable. So the main problem that we face is the question is how to do it in a very beautiful way.

One of the first ideas you have in a community like this is to mix the musics. That's beginning to happen. North Indians and the South Indians are beginning to play together, which is of historical interest. It's a new event that the North Indian tabla player will play with the South Indian player. The Javanese gamelan man very much liked my piece *I Am Sitting in a Room*. I think it's got to do with the fact that where he sets his gongs up, the placement of instruments is very [important]. In Java the idea is that the music already exists and you've got to pluck it out of the sky. The idea of *I Am Sitting in a Room* is that these particular resonant frequencies already exist in the room. My simple-minded tape recording into the space plucks out resonances that are already implied by the natural structure of the room. If [the gamelan man] can understand that, then we're not very far apart.

I've stopped myself from making a piece using a blending of the cultures. But what I'm working on now is a big, long, chant-like song which will be computer-composed. I'm asking all these people here to donate me a song from their particular cultures. They "donate" the song, like you donate blood. I would have all the songs going, unheard, simultaneously, in a computer program. The computer, with some formal structure that I make up, will then choose songs in real time—not so much snatch bits, but lock on to one, and then statistically move to another. So you'll be at points where you're 27 percent in Java and 33 percent in Arizona, the Navaho land, and so many percent on Amsterdam Avenue. At certain points you'll know where you are, and at other points you won't. The result will be a song that somebody sings; the computer won't make the sounds. It will be a song that somebody sings, which will have all of these elements in it. But I hope by doing that I don't hurt anyone's particular music.

Collecting the musics of other cultures is only historical collecting; it's what a musicologist does all his life. We studied the Baroque and then we exhausted that. Now instead of going back in time, we're going horizontally out in time, and it's a legitimate thing to do. But it's only a transition stage. What has to happen is, and what I'm going to work on very hard now, is creating a new kind of music for me; not blending, but seeing deep connections which a future music could have.

BC: Will the song be accompanied?

AL: I don't think so. I'm friendly with an American Indian. On occasion, if we're doing something specific, he'll sing some chants that are appropriate for what we're doing. I drove him to the airport once early in the morning, and he chanted on the way. He wasn't being artsy-craftsy, you know, it's just what he does. He believes it, and this was a chant when you go on a trip, and it's about a particular road. And when we take a steam bath together, he'll sing the sweat bath songs. I'm just becoming very interested in that chant-like idea; there's one horizontal line which does so much.

BC: Other members of the Sonic Arts Union that I've talked to, and you too, suggest that it's really a rather independent coalition of people, that often you don't know what one another's doing until you get together.

AL: Yeah, we're a very bizarre group, and we don't really succeed in a funny way, but that's why we stay together.

BC: Why do you suppose that there is this group-ness, like the ICES [International Carnival of Experimental Sound] festival? I looked at the list and there's groups from God knows where; you know, it's just one after the other. Clearly, the San Francisco Tape Center and a couple of other outfits in the very early '60s are vital in this country to the whole musical development, and are unrecognized as such.

AL: I think it comes from the times. People talking about extended families where more than one couple lives together. I think that we have learned that it's possible to be intimate with more than one human being. And groups like the ONCE group—well, they had to form, they were in an alien artistic environment, they were connected with a university [University of Michigan] that was antagonistic towards their new ideas. And what they did, which was very beautiful, was that instead of going to the Big Apple, they made Ann

Arbor just a wonderful place to go—Ann Arbor, a little university town in
the Midwest. I would drive twelve hours and go to hear their concerts in the
Veterans of Foreign Wars ballroom. And they did it out of a need to survive in
an antagonistic environment. Now, the Sonic Arts Union . . . I don't feel that
need, that survival thing. I don't think any of us want to promote ourselves
the way that other composers go around and promote themselves. There's a
certain amount of shyness, so that when you form a union, it's for pieces.
Bad things go along with that, too: sometimes the concerts are very hard to
mount, sometimes someone has a longer piece which detracts from someone
else's, sometimes we don't place the pieces right because we don't know what
they are yet. Well, I said before that we're not successful—I meant that we're
not slick in that way. Some of our concerts are a little awkward, but we enjoy
that awkwardness. And we say in our publicity that we pool our electronic
equipment; that's true, but the real particular reason we're together is more of
a social one. We happen to like each other and it seems to work. You've always
had orchestras; you've always had chamber music. So why can't four guys who
like to do electronic improvisation get together because you like to play with
other people? The idea of playing alone is not as interesting as playing with
somebody. So these particular groups are just what we've always had.

BC: What's happening in the way people handle what's called (I think erroneously)
"form," and what a lot of people like to call "structure," and the relationship
of a composer to his sounds?

AL: You mentioned transformation. First, we're very aware that society is being
transformed. Isn't everyone aware that they, plus the social groups that they're
in, are undergoing transformations? The transformations are processes that
originate and move in their own particular ways by laws which come out of
them. If you believe in God, God is "the mover" of society. But if you don't
believe in God, which most people don't, then of the social forces moving
(even Mao, the idea of contradictions), the two forces are always in action;
they're never static. Things are always moving within themselves and that idea
that things can be transformed by laws which come from themselves instead
of externally, from God, is a fundamental idea. John Cage understood that
idea when he says he doesn't want his pieces to imitate the natural world, but
wants them to copy nature's way of operation.

BC: This too is a very old idea. "Nature methodized," as Pope said.

AL: *I Am Sitting in a Room* does that. In that piece, two very ordinary things are
going on. One is speech, which is very ordinary; the other is tape-recorded repetition, which too is a very simple idea. Plus, you find out that nobody's speech
is ordinary. In that piece, no matter how many times you repeat the process,
you can still hear the rhythmic structure of speech. Everything gets destroyed
but that, which is a very wonderful thing to find out. Now, by doing two very

simple, ordinary, banal operations, you get a beautiful result. That's my idea of art; a very *accessible* idea, that means that people can do very simple things and get beautiful results. Anybody with two tape recorders, a microphone, an amplifier, and a speaker can do that piece.

BC: So you're not concerned with exostructure in a piece; the pieces, in a sense, generate their own nature.

AL: When you used the word "fancy," and I thought you meant "extra," I wouldn't do anything else in that piece. That doesn't serve its purpose. I got the idea from Bob Ashley that speech is song on a beautiful, very simple level, and that I stutter makes me aware of those things. You discover in that piece that everyone's speech is interesting. I'm content, I trust that fact; I believe that fact. A European composer (I use the word "European" in all that we know it means: meaning, structure, and so forth) wouldn't be content with a simple spoken paragraph. He or she would program it, put vowels and syllables into certain categories, and so on. Whereas discovering the rhythm of unaltered speech is very beautiful. I would rather hear the changes that the repetitions bring about than to impose some extra idea about speech that I have. That would only serve to fuck that piece up. And particularly Americans: I think we've learned. My God, isn't that an old American idea? You read Thomas Wolfe, who's content with pages of names of American cities. We have those beautiful names; we're content to just read them off.[4]

BC: In both there is this submergence into the experience in a very immediate way: long descriptions of train rides, long recitations about banquets and so on. A very sensory kind of immediacy.

AL: In England, [Cornelius] Cardew just attacked John Cage in a very vitriolic, stupid attack. One thing he says was that he tried doing one of the *Variations* unamplified, with just horn and guitar, and he found that it was a desert. That was the word he used, meaning "no substance." Now in a week I'm going to drive out to a desert where a people live: the Navaho. If you're an American, you don't think a desert is boring. Cage proved that to us, and I thought that was one thing that we Americans had discovered. Isn't that one of the most beautiful things to find out—that your speech is beautiful? I quoted the Javanese: "We have no art; we do the best we can." If you regarded your speech in that light, then you'd try to talk beautifully. I can do that, and that is a very important social function; it makes us trust and believe in those things.

BC: Is Cardew putting that down, too?

AL: No, he's talking politically, and he's on the right track, you see. The English are in an intolerable situation: composers are poor; English musical society is just awful. As a Maoist, Cardew attacked Cage and then [Karlheinz] Stockhausen. I agree wholeheartedly in the attack on Stockhausen. He was saying that Stockhausen was using vulgar displays of mysticism.

BC: If an American [instead of Stockhausen] had written *Hymnen*, he would have used high school bands playing high school fight songs instead of national anthems.

AL: It's not that piece; it's more like *Stimmung* and other pieces that are direct thievery from say, La Monte Young or John Cage. Mao says in his talks to artists, "Art for whom?" For the people? Well, the Chinese people are more homogeneous, since they have not been a technological society. The Peking Ballet that we all saw on American television can be understood by any Chinese person in the remotest reach of China, whereas the Merce Cunningham Dance Company—I shouldn't say "understood"—doesn't interest everybody. We deplore the fact, perhaps, but because we are a technological society we could, theoretically speaking, stop it and go back to agriculture. If we did that, then everyone would be doing the same thing. Therefore, we could have a dance company devoted to one form of dance that would interest everybody. But since we are in a technological society, there can be many things happening at the same time, and you can choose. We're affluent in that way. I always wanted my pieces to be loved and understood.

BC: Yes, the important thing is that you are reaching out, but you're doing it without any kind of political hokum, invoking past muses or anything. You're working simply with human beings.

AL: Yes, for *The Queen of the South* I had wonderful experiences going into factories—United States Steel, for example, junkyards, a welding shop—to discover about pieces of metal. I talked to a young executive guy at United States Steel. Now, he didn't know anything about steel and he wasn't sympathetic to me. He didn't want me to go into the warehouse because he knew I wasn't going to buy two tons of hot rolled steel. I finally talked him into it. He didn't know what he was talking about. I went to another steel place, and I got to talk to Billy. Billy is the guy who knows what's in the warehouse, and he said, "Well, what do you want it for?" I explained to him, I want a piece that is responsive to sound, that would have a particular ring to it. Now I told lies; I said, "I want to make a reverberation plate," because I thought that these people would understand that more. But I got much better response from the people who work with the metal, who touch it. The Maoist view is that particular wisdom comes by operations, constant working on materials. You extract the wisdom out of the material; thus, the materialistic ideal. *The Queen of the South* is exactly like that. The players have to play it a lot until their relationship to that plate is just like my relationship to air. I breathe it and I don't think about it. And like John Cage—I owe him the contact mike on the chair—if it were the best contact mike in the world, you'd get the essence of the fiber and quality of the wood.

BC: This is very scholastic, isn't it? What you're doing is getting at informing essence through this. "Chairness" is what you're trying to . . .

AL: Right. Cage has been doing that. For Cardew to misunderstand that and say that Cage is using electronics as some kind of alien gimmickry (he uses the word "gadgetry"), what does that show? I mean, what is a flute? It's a gadget to me, it's alien to me. We all want social equality and the end of oppression. But Mao could do it in China because it was agrarian. That's where he split with the Soviets, in doing it with the peasants instead of the industrialists. That's just unthinkable in America—we're just not that kind of society. Instead of my wanting to write heroic songs, many people would play with that plate and strew material on that plate. I'm looking at that plate now. I step on that plate every day and I feel it. By doing that piece, you'd get at the essence of *your* sound production into the qualities of the plate and of the strewing material . . . And you can change it. I've used salt and silica sand. In making the piece I've had to find out about sand. I haven't constructed a serial, abstract piece built on some idealistic philosophical system. I've gone down to hardware stores, and I've talked with guys who touch materials, and I say, "Well, do you think this'll be good for my piece?" And usually the guy who touches those plates can give me the right piece. I'm trying to connect on that kind of a level; and I don't think that because I use amplifiers to help boost my signal into the plate that it is in anyway alien and unsocial. I think that anyone who attacks Cage, or myself, just doesn't understand; it's a stupid short-sighted view.

To get back to transformation, as I said before, every day I feel myself change. Probably in the old days you didn't get that air of change, because of God, and God didn't change. The church changed, I suppose, but there was this static quality of life.

BC: We've just now had to challenge the idea that one of *the* features of art is permanence, static.

AL: It's very complicated; many Eastern people don't believe in changing the environment despite the ideas of intrusion, transformation. These ideas are important because they mean different things. We dominate the financial world, and we do it badly. We're polluting our atmosphere. On the other hand, we shouldn't stop changing things, because you could change things for the better. If you're making your music for God, then you make a music that doesn't [change]. Now, when we are transforming ourselves in just colossal ways, then of course our art, the pieces we do, will transform. That's why alchemy is so important, because you do the same operation over and over again until it begins to change, and then you go from one stage to another.

BC: Well, *I'm Sitting in a Room* is an alchemical piece.

AL: Yeah. I did another piece with an alchemical title, *Gentle Fire*, the fire that you [use to] heat the retorts, and you can make the material by fire. I feel rather guilty about this piece, because I was talking about idealism and how, if you use mysticism, you can't say there's a better world somewhere else when this world has got so many bad things. But [Merleau-Ponty?], the French phenomenologist, talks about being able to dream and being able to change things in your dreams. For example, he describes being in a room in Paris and hearing the street sounds, which can be oppressive. But if you could, in dreamlike fashion, transfigure them—think of your room as a boat rocking on the ocean and the sound of the street sounds being the sounds of the ocean—then you can transform that oppressive situation and dream it to be something nostalgic, being in a boat in the sea. I once again used synthesizers, because the British group Gentle Fire use live electronics. I wrote down about 125 everyday images that implied unpleasant sound like car accidents, warlike sounds, anything tearing, burning, destroying. Then I made another set of images, another 120-some-odd images which were ambient sound effects that had more pleasant implications. Sometimes you'd get the images in both columns, so that you could see that one image was pleasant and one wasn't. The idea was to use electronic devices, synthesizers, to transform the images in one column to the images in the other column. And if you pair them up in a random way, you get an unexpected connection. A computer programmer made me a program so that the computer printed out the twelve thousand combinations: crackling fire becomes crunching snow; so-and-so becomes something else.

There were three versions of the piece: first, to tape record these and transform them by synthesizer; second, to do it in real time, to deploy a microphone outside and have a programmed situation where to transform them. The third idea was that if you did this enough it would teach you. You could design an imaginary synthesizer with a low-pass filter, a band pass filter, or an envelope generator, so that you could make these transformations in real time—you could tolerate daily life by carrying around this perfect model. I thought that electronics could help you learn that. Then I started thinking: that's escapism. Instead of changing the amount of cars that go by that make the noise, instead of passing a law saying you can't do that, you escape into like a dreamlike world. I don't enjoy that idea. I'm worried about whether the piece is just an escape valve. But I didn't want to stop doing the piece because I had that idea, and if it isn't a good idea, then the piece won't be good. But if it does help people hear, that's what we're doing: help[ing] people hear differently. And that piece could be the basis of a whole school year of hearing envelopes of one sound, just by transforming them. You could also find out what it is in a sound that you're able to recognize if you play with transients and envelopes and filters. The idea of transformation is in that, plus the fact that it's very down-to-earth. It's not abstract; there it is, the steel plate, a visible sound. You know, it's not technology, it's an environment.

BC: Similarly, you don't agree with people who say electronics, as every other musical medium, has to have some sort of structure, carefully worked-out process imposed upon it before it can be justifiable in musical terms.

AL: I don't believe that. It's a hard question, because the idea of imposition—if you don't impose, if you don't like the idea of imposition, then you'd never make political change. It's the same thing as changing the culture, say, like the rebab in Java. If you felt that, there would be no change. Mao, for example, makes no bones about imposition of ideas on the whole, including people. So, in these ideas that we're talking about is a whole problem: the world.

Notes

1. Alvin Lucier and Douglas Simon, *Chambers* (Middletown, CT: Wesleyan University Press, 1980), 16.

2. Marshall McLuhan, *Understanding Media: The Extensions of Man* (New York: McGraw-Hill, 1964), 66, 65.

3. The work is Warhol's *S&H Green Stamps* (1962). S&H is a retail store, and green stamps were an early loyalty-incentive program. Customers received stamps with purchases and could redeem them for merchandise.

4. See "The Promise of America," in *The Complete Short Stories of Thomas Wolfe*, ed. Francis E. Skipp (New York: Charles Scribner's Sons, 1987), 482ff.

13 Donald Martino (1931–2005)

BRUCE QUAGLIA

Although many of the milestone achievements of his career still lay ahead
of him in 1972—including winning the Pulitzer Prize in 1974 for his chamber work
Notturno (1973)—Donald Martino had already arrived at a mature aesthetic and
compositional technique that was grounded in the twelve-tone system. Martino's
approach to music making, though always rigorously founded, was preeminently
imaginative and sonorous. The twelve-tone system, which he observes to Childs in
this interview, "has been terribly misunderstood by people who have never worked
with it . . . [who have] never 'played the game'," provided for him a basic resistance
to work against for dramatic and expressive purposes. For Martino, a lifelong lover
of games, especially tennis, it was unthinkable that a game or musical work would
not have structure or rules, even though these may creatively evolve once a new piece
was under way. These constraints provided the basic challenges that were essential
to the fun and satisfaction of composing new works.

Likewise, the physical challenges of performing Martino's music were always a
primary component of their drama. Conceived for professional performers, Martino's
music was unapologetically difficult, advancing extended instrumental techniques
and their precise notation, while pushing the very limits of what was then considered
"playable." This produced another kind of dramatic tension. The struggle to execute
a passage accurately and expressively was a part of the work itself. Martino thought
the work eventually suffered when younger players began to perform these difficult
passages with the appearance of relative ease: "For example, when *Parisonatina* was
first performed, you could hear the difficulty in getting from one note to another,
in the skips and shifts that were necessary. But over time, and here is a real trap,
players have resolved many of those difficulties, so that the piece in some 'electronic-
sounding' performances I have heard has lost its tension, its drama."[1]

At the time of the Childs interview, Martino had established a successful academic career, having taught for a decade at Yale (1959–69) before moving on to the New England Conservatory, where he chaired the composition department from 1969 to 1981. He would remain based in the Boston area, holding endowed chairs at both Brandeis (1980–83) and then Harvard (1983–92) before retiring. Martino had already given up on writing academic articles by the time of this interview, noting to Childs that "to write an article takes time that I can't afford," but he had already published two very important ones during his Yale years. His "Notation in General—Articulation in Particular," which so interested Childs, addresses the problems produced by variable interpretations of the same musical symbol and emphasizes the responsibility of both the performer and composer to resolve these issues into a more standardized practice.[2] Martino was always concerned that the notation and appearance of his music convey not only precision, but also the emotional expressivity of the music itself. In order to gain greater control over the publication of his own music, and to retain the revenue generated from it, he founded Dantalian Publishing in 1978. This allowed him, for example, to reissue the score for his solo cello work *Parisonatina al'Dodecafonia* (1964) with the distinctive multicolored notation he had used when composing it for his colleague, Aldo Parisot. The original publisher had rejected this notation to produce a less expensive black-and-white score. These colors denote the manner of sound production used on the cello, which change quickly between *arco*, *pizzicato*, *col legno battuto*, and non-pitched sounds produced by striking different parts of the instrument. Martino's handwritten scores were always ornate and beautiful, and these details remain preserved in all of the works published by Dantalian.

Martino's second article from the 1960s, "The Source Set and Its Aggregate Formations," has been cited by virtually every subsequent author who has written about twelve-tone music.[3] Proceeding from earlier work by Milton Babbitt, Martino offers his own detailed catalog of the even partitions of the aggregate, providing a map of how twelve-tone combinatorial sets may be generated from these.[4] This article also provides insight into Martino's conception of the twelve-tone universe, which is not based on ordered row classes, but is primarily conceived as a succession of partially ordered aggregates related through their subsets. Lines articulate aggregates by using musical parameters such as register in works like *Pianississimo* (1970), or by their manner of sound production, as in *Parisonatina al'Dodecafonia*.[5] The aggregates are determined by a consistent yet fluid use of hexachord types that are reinforced by their shared trichord partitions. This results in a characteristically episodic musical surface because the musical character follows these harmonic shifts, often producing rondo-like chain forms. Such "chain-rondos" begin as early as the *Trio* (1959), and then appear throughout the 1960s in works like the Concerto for Wind Quintet (1964), *Mosaic for Orchestra* (1967), and the Concerto for Cello (1972). The expressive impetus of these techniques was to create a mercurial musical experience, to "move abruptly and dramatically, suddenly dropping us from one kind of sound world to another . . . to transport the listener from one kind of musical moment to another."[6] The work as a whole emanates from the pitch structures that Martino tells Childs are "perceivable only in the very background of the music," but the evocative musical surface that the listener comes into expressive contact with always roils up from those same deeper compositional processes, emerging as improvised play.

Throughout this interview, Martino delivers a forceful defense of complex music that may at times be misunderstood as mere complaint. It is not; it is an echo of that tone established earlier by Schoenberg himself, a composer who has been misunderstood. Martino argues for an expressivity that is grounded in advanced techniques and based on a drama of struggle that originates with the works of Beethoven. Nevertheless, he finds the shallow worship of "Beethoven and Company" by contemporary audiences to be an obstacle to the vital evolution of modern music. Martino's stated view "that the only thing that we're really into is writing music that we believe in," expands on Babbitt's argument for advanced music in his 1958 article "Who Cares if You Listen?" and enriches it with a social and humane context.[7]

Donald Martino: Interview

BARNEY CHILDS: Some years ago you published an article in *Perspectives* about notations for articulation.[8] Have you gone on thinking about this?

DONALD MARTINO: I am always concerned with the problems of notation, but I have not extended my ideas about the notation of articulation. First, the article presented conclusions based on years of practical application; it was the last step in a process. Second, after the article was published I composed a number of pieces for orchestra. The concept of articulation in the article derived from my earlier preoccupation with small chamber ensembles. My conception of the orchestra as an extended chamber ensemble led me to construct massive counterpoints of as many as sixty real voices; thus, elaborate articulative differentiation seemed unnecessary.

But symbols of articulation (like all music symbols) must reflect an emotive as well as a technical intention. No other composer today devotes more time and effort to emotive notation than I do, or is more concerned with expressive content than I am, and no composer is more severely criticized—by the press, at least—for the lack of such concerns. In any case, I hope that my orchestral scores of recent years reveal a symbology sufficient to project the dramatic as well as the technical aims of the music.

BC: How about the solo pieces?

DM: I guess I forgot about *B,a,b,b,it,t* and *Strata* [both 1966], two solo works each for clarinet, each adhering more rigorously than ever before to the precepts expressed in my article—but these were written in one and five days, respectively. So, in my mind at least, the orchestra has dominated me for the past six years.

Most of these notations for articulation evolved from my understanding as a player of how to produce certain sounds. I'm always surprised by the reaction from performers. A clarinet player came to interview me about my article; his annoyance with it was alarmingly overt, as though I were attempting to limit expressivity rather than to increase it. I thought I had been clear enough in the article on this issue. I have always suggested that the composer notate what *he* hears as accurately as is possible. As a composer, *I* hear musical events complete with their performance—perhaps because I have never stopped thinking of myself as a performer. Since that ideal imaginary performance of my music includes a diversity of timbral, rhythmic, dynamic, and articulative nuance, my notation has developed over the years into a kind of performance editing.

BC: It is more a codification and clarification.

DM: I would like to see these procedures clarified for the composer who's concerned with their structural use as pitch adjuncts.

BC: You have thought of them in those terms?

DM: Yes, in those terms, among others.

BC: Would you regard yourself as a classicist in terms of using the set?

DM: No. Certain people who write twelve-tone music would claim that I don't write twelve-tone music at all. These are the classicists. But the twelve-tone system is a set of guiding principles to build upon and develop. It would have ceased to guide me long ago if the system were confined to a few basic unextendable laws, or to extensions with no option. I've come to look at the system more as I have worked with it almost the way the tonal system can be looked at; that the basic principles often are perceivable only in the very background of the music itself.

BC: Each work then, is like a new bottle for old wine?

DM: Not at all true. Each work has a different bottle; it always contains wine, but the wine is never exactly the same. I'm fed up with this cult of newness for its own sake. What seems to be new often later proves to be superficial. And too frequently the *new* is a cover-up for lack of substance, or simply ignorance of the *old*. It is not newness, it is novelty.

Although I've hardly been repeating myself, I have been less concerned over the years with fetishistically producing *new* pieces than with producing *pieces*. To try to be completely new in each piece is to ignore evolving a personal language and to risk exhausting one's talent prematurely. It is often true that the piece which presents a new idea presents it less well than a later piece, when the idea has become completely assimilated into the composer's vocabulary. He can transform novelty into substance. Of course an idea can become stale with overuse. So the sensitive composer whose concern is newness, not novelty, will search out new and exciting ideas. If his ideas do not seem so new to other people, perhaps they are listening for novelty.

In one piece I'll find certain fulfillments and also unanswered questions. The next piece will answer them and pose new questions. The Concerto for Wind Quintet [1964] was a piece in which I investigated a number of things that I had been thinking about. I'm not sure it is a good piece; in certain ways I think of it as a bad piece because it's stricter than many of my other works. But I was able to learn about certain processes so that later I could work with them freely. The Piano Concerto [1965], one of the few pieces of mine that I am *really* fond of, is an outgrowth of all those ideas. It came naturally. I didn't have to do all that work; the work had been done in other pieces.

BC: Does it bother you that the solo pieces and the small ensemble pieces don't get played very much because of the demands on the performers?

DM: Aldo Parisot played the cello piece as much as thirty or thirty-five times a year for many years. Other people have tackled it. Fred Sherry plays it extremely well, and Joel Krosnick has played it a couple of times. Each of my solo pieces (for example, *A Set for Clarinet* [1954]) was written for a specific, first-rate player. Interestingly everybody who studies the clarinet buys the *Set*; every teacher teaches it. Yet to my knowledge, only three or four people play it in public each year. I don't really care about that. Sure, I love to have pieces played in public, but it serves a function and I am confident that one day it *will* be played in public more. The *Set* does not now represent the same level of technical difficulty that it did in 1954. The *Trio* was regarded as an impossible piece in 1959, and excellent players premiered it. They put on a performance that was really terrible, and for many years there were only terrible performances. I participated in a number of terrible performances as the clarinetist. But this year a group in New York played it and it was incredible; and recently I coached a group of students at the New England Conservatory who put on a performance that was as good as any performance of Beethoven they played.

I write difficult music, but I have never written anything that is unplayable; by my standards as a performer it is not nearly as difficult as it is judged to be. It may be at the margin of playability for most professionals, but ultimately it becomes more playable, even relatively easy. As a matter of fact, *Parisonatina* has disturbed me because in 1965, when Parisot premiered it, you could feel the strain. The stress was part of the expressive content of the piece. I don't write a skip or a change of timbre unless I know what goes into it. I don't want the performer to spend the next five years learning the piece so well that it sounds as though it were played by two hands at the piano.

BC: That's the price for multi-performance.

DM: I don't know what the answer to that is. A certain amount of feigned difficulty is required even in the *Set for Clarinet*, which I wrote as a clarinetist with the instrument pretty much in my hands. In one place it's two notes separated by three octaves. Today's virtuoso clarinetist can play it with relative ease, but it should not be played that way. If it is played glibly, some of the natural energy of the piece is lost. There is psychic energy in physical motion. *It has to come across.*

BC: So the pieces are more dramatically involved in performance.

DM: They are *very* dramatically involved in performance! In later pieces like *Parisonatina*, a complex set technique delineates pitch-timbral events. Each event evokes its own unique expressive character, and the aggregate of these events unfolds the drama. The dramatic and expressive results are equally important as the technique and logic. As an undergraduate at Syracuse, I learned this old-fashioned notion that music should present some dependent combination of the mind and the soul. When you set constraints such as the twelve-tone system, it's not always easy to produce that kind of marriage, but that's what I'm after. The main difference between *A Set for Clarinet* and the *Parisonatina* of ten years later is that *Parisonatina* reveals a more perfect marriage.

BC: Your piece in which the dramatism is most intense is *B,a,b,b,it,t.* Every time I see Phil [Rehfeldt] do it, there's the feeling that one small move and he's crashed and burned.

DM: Well, I went to college with the idea of becoming a great clarinet player, and I write a piece with the performer in mind. Performers seldom feel that at first, but usually they come around.

BC: How do you like teaching undergraduates?

DM: I have mixed feelings. When I have a good student, I feel good; when I have a bad student, I feel bad. I take my responsibility as a teacher very seriously, but I think that students have changed. At graduate school at Princeton, I studied with Milton Babbitt the first year I was there, in 1952. Few people had heard of him; he wasn't that much older than I was—about thirty-six—but it never occurred to me that I could not learn from Milton Babbitt. He was a professor of music, a composer. I assumed that he had something to teach me, so I listened to him. The next year I studied with Roger Sessions; the age difference was much greater, but still I thought I must learn from him. I didn't unquestioningly accept everything these men said or did; I came to them with respect, an open mind, and some sense of the difference between their achievements and mine. Now kids come to me, Roger, Milton, or anybody, and say, "Who the hell are you? What the fuck have you ever done?" It makes it very difficult to communicate. It's frustrating because although I frequently wish I never had to teach again, I've learned a great deal and I've developed things in strange ways which I would not have developed if I hadn't taught.

Because of it, some important things have happened to me. *B,a,b,b,it,t* itself developed out of a class. One day I felt like talking about my instrument, and I showed the kids how you can roll up a piece of paper, shove it in the bell and get a half step lower. Of course I didn't get a half step lower, but a whole step lower. I immediately thought, if a whole step, why not six octaves! I spent three months rolling up pieces of paper, and finally came up with a whole chest of crooks. I had extended the range of the clarinet by two octaves and a tritone. That was important, not because of the piece, but because it was an exciting adventure for me, and my students too, because they participated in the discovery. When I communicate what I discovered long ago, I am less effective as a teacher than when I reveal before the students the very process of discovery. I share with my students what I am doing, they share with me what they are doing, and I hope we learn from each other. The kid who comes in and says, "I've done these three notes, now where do I go from there?" is the student I cannot teach. But if he's the kind of student who thinks, feels, and has natural intuitions about music, I get something out of that. I hope we both do.

For as long as I can remember, I've worked an eighteen-hour day, seven days a week, because my enthusiasm was equally great for each task I undertook, whether it was teaching, writing, or cabinet building. As the years go by, the desire to just sit and write music all day long becomes greater and greater; the inability to do that becomes more oppressive.

BC: And as one progresses academically, the opportunities become less.

DM: I've given up writing articles. I don't deal with words easily. The smallest article is a monumental effort, much greater than writing a piece of music. To write an article takes time that I can't afford. I've given up program notes. Every time I've written a program note, I've unwittingly induced people to say things about my pieces that they might not have said if they had just listened to them. I've withdrawn from lots of things, simply because I'm not fast. I'm not like Milton, who can do a thousand things at once. I can do one thing; however well I do it, that's all I can do.

We talked about performers who can perform things that were non-performable earlier. There *are* real performers today who know *exactly* what you want them to do, and have the dedication, the technique, and the inspiration to go beyond what you've indicated, too. These are the people that we're writing for. Speculum Musicae, Collage, the Group for Contemporary Music, the Boston Musica Viva. But these groups are struggling along financially. If we had only accurate and expressive performances of our pieces, then a few more people would like them. If you go to a concert and listen to those "professional" performances of past pieces that you know and love, or present pieces that you might come to know and love, they're pretty dismal. Once in a while somebody comes along and plays it the way it should be played, or chooses the piece that ought to be played. I just don't believe that all of those pieces by Beethoven and Company are that good! And if all of those company pieces aren't that good, then *all* those pieces by me can't be that good, either! A lot of them have to be routine, and if you're lucky, you've got a couple of really good pieces in your whole life. You sit down in the Tanglewood Shed, and listen to some routine company piece, routinely played, and you wonder why anyone bothers. Then the crowd stands and cheers, and you become aware that this crowd would cheer for anything—so you wonder why they're not playing *your* pieces.

BC: The orchestra pieces obviously take a great deal of time and a great deal of care. Do you get one performance? Two?

DM: I have reservations about almost everything, but the piano concerto (my favorite piece, the one piece that I really love) has had one performance in its life. *Mosaic [for Grand Orchestra*, 1967] was premiered in Chicago, not terribly well, but then they only had three hours of rehearsal. It was played beautifully in Munich, Gunther Schuller conducting, with fourteen hours of rehearsal, and finally at the New England Conservatory, with Schuller again conducting. The rehearsals almost provoked a riot; students resisted.

BC: Did that surprise you?

DM: Not that much—mainly the string players. Music teaching is too conservative, and string teachers are the worst offenders. Woodwind players could do virtually anything; they looked to the challenge with excitement. But string players authoritatively proclaimed that you didn't know what you were doing. If you wrote a harmonic for the string bass, the player would say that there was no such harmonic. You would have to go and put his finger down and show him that it did in fact exist. That was the last performance of *Mosaic*. Ultimately, with a few extra rehearsals and a little prodding from Gunther, they demonstrated that a student orchestra with a sensitive, dedicated conductor and about twelve hours of rehearsal *can* do that piece. It's as much a conductor's piece as it is a player's piece. It is one of the simplest works rhythmically that I've written recently, so it requires that conductor who will take the license that will make it supple. There are tremendous balance problems; it has an enormous collection of instruments, sometimes each playing different things at once. So I don't feel as badly about it as I feel about the piano concerto or my cello concerto, just finished, which may not get played at all. It was written for Aldo Parisot, and now it's not for him. This may be my last concerto.

For concerti you need not only the soloist, but a conductor. Why should a conductor conduct a new concerto? What does he get out of it? He has to learn a new score; he must share with the soloist most of his god-ness and at the same time risk almost certain disapproval from all quarters. The soloist might get something out of it, but certainly not as much as from the Dvořák Concerto, which is a guaranteed hit. The soloist has to have immense dedication and audience appeal as well as the muscle, politically, to convince the conductor to do it. The conductor then has to convince the orchestra board, and if successful, with virtually no rehearsal time, face the skepticism of orchestral players, the audience, and critics alike. Even if the premiere performance is a success, the chances for additional performances are slight. Three years on a concerto—it's not worth it. But most of my pieces are commissioned, and [so] at least one performance is guaranteed.

BC: What was the last piece you wrote simply on your own hook, with no request or commission?

DM: *Seven Pious Pieces.* They were written in the winter of 1971 on seven successive Sundays, and they're settings of Robert Herrick, for a capella chorus. They are little tonal-type pieces cryptically derived from the twelve-tone system. But since 1959 I haven't written anything else just because I wanted to write it. There has always been someone asking.

BC: Have these choral pieces been done?

DM: The Harvard Memorial Chapel chorus will do it in the fall.

BC: What do your students want to write?

DM: Usually more than I can handle. I don't believe in telling them what they should write. I believe that from their earnest desires will come the mistakes by which they will learn. As a rule, I don't think they should be set tasks, nor should they have formalized instruction in compositional techniques. Most of the kids are a little worried about whether they are any good. I worry about damaging whatever spark is there. They should learn how to criticize themselves, but not at the expense of their desires to do what they want to do. So it's a balance between reinforcing their egos and gently leading them to positive and productive self-criticism. Sometimes you'll see ten or twenty different things that should be corrected, but you will criticize only one. There will be other sessions. To criticize too many things at one time could confuse and disillusion them.

Most of the kids come to me thinking they know who I am, what I stand for, and hence, what I want of them. Often they are misguided, especially when they expect me to talk about the twelve-tone system. I don't want to talk about that to them when half of them don't even know what a phrase is. Besides, I'm not propagandizing any system, but I am deeply committed to what I do—all I expect of my students is commitment to an idea. I'm also afraid that if they embrace a systematic rigor too soon it will cause a crisis which they are not yet mature enough to cope with productively as musicians. As a student, I saw this happen to many of my colleagues; they either quit composing or quit thinking.

I'm disturbed that music teaching is in a way pseudo-intellectualized. Students come to me with graphs, charts, tables: stuff which they think will guarantee something. But first they must have an ear, musical intelligence, and a submerged reservoir of musical experience to guide them. True, they must continually use rational processes in the composition of their music, but premature intellectualization is often a cover-up for severe aural inadequacy. Moreover, the student's inability to cope with his own charts and graphs frequently stems from his failure to realize that such pre-compositional plans are only as valid as the aural phenomena they represent. The plans and the sounds must be conceived simultaneously; the pre-compositional moment cannot exclude sound images. So too often musical intelligence is cast out in favor of the seemingly seductive rational. The result of that is frustration, disillusionment, the destruction of self-reliance, and the wasting of those early years which are so vital to the development of the ear.

BC: This intellectualization is not limited . . .

DM: It's rampant! And we are responsible for it in certain ways. Our immediate predecessors got where they got because of the way they talked about method. We learned that we should talk about it, and *we* got sat on for talking about it. You have to be mature enough to understand what it's all about. You can tell a bright college freshman who has an IQ and SATs somewhere beyond count about this or that, and without having an ear and without having listened to any music, he can produce the most incredible monstrosity, logical though it may be. He can justify everything. He can tell you *why* the E goes to F and *why* it doesn't go to E flat, but it's wrong. I hear a lot of composers laughing at me now, saying, "But if zero goes to one it's right, that's all there is to it." I don't feel that. You *make* zero go to one in such a way that it is right.

I'd like to get back to a one-to-one relationship student to teacher. But it's pretty late for that; besides, no one could afford it today. There are all sorts of baby things that ought to be learned about music, and those baby things can best be learned when you are a baby. By the time you get to college, [age] eighteen, you are ready to start doing something, and graduate school is obviously too late. *It should all happen much earlier.* It's a pity that what we call music education in this country is certainly not dedicated to teaching people to use the ear.

They also must be taught a healthy respect for the professional. One thing really annoys me in this country is not the amateur involvement in music but the *way* amateurs are involved! In the past, the amateur had a healthy respect for the professional. He *knew* that he was an amateur, he knew what a professional was. He knew what music was about, and he honored it as part of his society. Here it's worthless. We've created a monster with our Music 1 courses. We cultivate the amateur by conning him into believing he's a professional. He then goes on and becomes *the* professional, the man who calls the shots. We're in trouble because we're playing for the approval of the amateur professional.

If you have a revolution, the people who take over seem always to take their predecessors as a model. But when have you ever had a really cultured society as a model in this country? You're not a country like Germany, which as a nation started out with a sense of its own inferiority and felt that it had to import art and did so. (There are more translations of Shakespeare into German, probably, than into any other language.) When the aristocracy gave way to the bourgeoisie, the model was art, culture. Whether they *really* understand what they listen to is not important. It *is* important that the vehicle is there. I don't think that we will have it unless Madison Avenue gets into the act.

A composer like Milton Babbitt waits until he's fifty to be published, and any young punk in Europe will be published by the time he's twenty-three if he's just got three notes on a page. I wonder how long the human spirit can take that kind of disillusionment? Teaching at a school, I was told, "Why, we can't play that guy's piece—it's not even been published!" I say, "But it is published by so-and-so," but they say, "That's not a publication, it's not even engraved." When I hear that kind of absurd snobbery I get sick. Then our concert audiences listen to new music and old music with the same ear, but they've been told that *the company* is good, so they applaud with vigor. They've been sold a bill of goods.

BC: Somebody at the University of X told me that when the electrician walks on stage he gets two curtain calls.

DM: Because he makes more money than anybody there. It doesn't pay to be a composer or a teacher. You can make more money as a truck driver: you can have a decent car, a decent home, and you are a person of respect in the community. But if you write music, you do something that no one wants. Therefore we have no respect. I just can't believe how Roger Sessions can go decade after decade with the kind of neglect he's had in this country. The Boston Symphony hasn't played his music for ten years. Yet he's come through it in such a way that he writes better music than he's ever written. So there *are* such spirits. But it's easier for those guys in Europe; all they have to do is announce that they've done something different, and everybody says, "Well, he's the authority, he ought to know," and a star is born.

BC: And maintained . . .

DM: . . . because their society demands it. When *Mosaic* was performed in Munich, I went out into the main foyer—I had just taken my bows, so some people knew who I was—and people pointed to me in such an awestruck manner that I was embarrassed. Not "Yucch! there's that awful person!" You can stand up straight with that response. Basically it isn't important to most of us whether we make a lot of money or have fine clothes and houses. One wants a little respect; without it, one must develop a strange plastic ego. The number of talented composers we have in this country is astounding, but they don't have the credentials of success—no place to go, dead end.

BC: What about foundations?

DM: I benefit from them, but in a certain way damage has been done because of them. They've taken responsibility away from established performing organizations such as the Boston Symphony. "Let the foundations do it," is their attitude. You end up with one of the foundations who support music on once-only, matching grants; or a Little Society for Contemporary Music concert at Carnegie Recital Hall with twenty-six people there, all thirteen of the composers who are being played and their wives. Ultimately, the life of a composer is at its best when he's working alone and making the discoveries he enjoys. If he has done it long enough, he doesn't expect the performance to be very good, he doesn't expect the critics or the audience to love him. I guess he expects, deep down, that sooner or later *somebody* will!

BC: Can composers help each other?

DM: I'm so pessimistic about it all. I shouldn't say this; composers have helped me a tremendous amount. Yet I've been on juries, so I know about how prizes can be given. I *never* think of it as something that supports my ego. I always think, well, the guys on that committee were in my camp, not because I wrote a piece that somebody genuinely liked, or because anybody had any respect for my work. Composers can help in that way at least, but they're all competing, after all, for something that doesn't exist. I wonder why we don't help each other more, because we need reinforcement from each other. We have so pitifully little else to look forward to; we have such small salaries. There are no big rewards at the end of the rainbow. For Leonard Bernstein or some people, there are big rewards: lots of dough, penthouse apartments, and vacations on the Riviera. But the rewards for most of us are so slight that I can't figure out why we cut each other's throats so much. Let's start a new camp whose only criterion for membership is professionalism, where styles and systems are no longer proper biases, and let's all belong to it together.

BC: Is this a leftover of careerism?

DM: It's not even a leftover. I'm not sticking up for the original founders of ASUC, but however presumptuous and arrogant some of those who founded it might have seemed (and I was one of them) the motivations were good.[9] The founding fathers (or the founding punks, because we were all so very young) had assumed that there was no such thing as career. Nevertheless, I haven't seen Charles Wuorinen turn away commercial career opportunities; I would never turn any of them away. We all hope that someday the New York Philharmonic will play one of our pieces, that everybody stands up and cheers for hours, the critics all rave, and we all exit in gondolas. Of course, we all expect that to happen someday or other. It's misguided.

BC: If you wanted to be cold-blooded and crafty, you could make a work in which you really didn't believe which was sure to get kudos. The models are everywhere.

DM: It is a knack, a gift, a talent to be able to do that. Some people have it; other people don't. There are things that you learn in your life which, try as you may, you cannot eliminate. When I was little, I learned that when I went in front of the altar, I genuflected and made the sign of the cross. Today, even though I'm not a churchgoer, if I walk into a Catholic church, I genuflect instinctively. I'll even nod my head when profanely I say "Christ." These things become a part of you. So the college years were vital. They taught me lessons about integrity, about what I was supposed to be. I'm not sure that I want to, but I just can't give them up. I have a star, I follow it, and ultimately I write pieces that I think I like at a given moment. After all, I'm just a listener like everybody else. Cage once wrote that composers are one thing, performers are another, and audiences are another: what could they possibly have in common? I'm a listener and a performer as well as a composer; I can't separate myself. I write for myself, of course, as a listener, as a performer, and as a composer. I expect other listeners, performers and composers to like it. I am always shocked when people don't like a piece of mine.

Recently I listened to a piece that I had written fourteen years earlier and was genuinely moved by it. I didn't want to go to that concert because I thought, "My God, how could I possibly have written such a horror?" But at the concert I listened with new ears and I really liked it. When it was over I said to myself, "For the first time in my life there's going to be an ovation. People are going to like this!" People went *plunk . . . plunk . . .*, and I thought, that's just the way it always is. Maybe they're right, but I'm not going to believe it; as long as I don't believe it, I'll keep being happy when I do it. That's what it's all about. These are the moments when I'm in my study—doing this, discovering that, finding something I like. If I don't think that what I liked then was so good two years later, that's not so important because I'm onto another thing.

BC: That's the making of the music.

DM: Seldom do I experience that it's being played to my liking. But there are three or four performances of *Parisonatina* with Aldo playing in which he really did something; it moved me. I recall one performance in 1960 or '61, Billy Masselos playing my *Piano Fantasy*, in which I really thought he made some music, made good decisions. I still listen to the tape of that performance with pleasure.

BC: But that's a pretty good percentage.

DM: What, four times in twenty-five years?

BC: The way things are, you're damn lucky you got that.

DM: If you get less, *how* can anyone know whether the piece is good or bad?

BC: I'm not trying to say this is good; it's the way things are. One is thankful that there are moments, few though they may be, when it *can* happen. It reaffirms that it may yet happen again, and yes, I was right. So your story about being moved by the work is very meaningful, because you reaffirmed yourself; you were able to take something from it: that it's not all a fake.

DM: The piece is loaded with defects.

BC: That doesn't matter. That it got to you in that funny way all of a sudden is what counts. And yes, by God, it *is* there, even though the evidence from the other 364 days of the year overwhelmingly suggests that it may not be.

DM: Thank you.

BC: As composers we have to condition ourselves, as a kind of hair shirt, to live with mediocrity.

DM: That's why I want my commune. I was born into a second-generation Italian family—to be accurate, half Italian and half German Swiss. My father came from a family of nine, my mother a family of eleven or twelve. They went to work as children; they didn't have a high-school education, and they put their lives into me. They married before the Depression; they suffered it. They taught me the value of the dollar—all things that aren't essential to the spirit of the artist. At the same time, something made me move in another direction. The two things are still there within me: the one hand that says, "Why the fuck should that truck driver make more than I?," and the other that says, "Who cares about the nickel?" They're there in most of us because we were brought up here. That isn't to say that we should scorn the dollar. But the European reveres money in a different way. He is capable of distinguishing the value of the individual from the value of his estate. But there still is the career market issue, an incentive that causes us to cut each other's throats rather than help each other.

I've gotten much more career-wise at my age than certain people, many of whom deserve it more than I, and it's probably getting better for me. But I'd like to shear away all of this. I'd like to find twenty composer-performers who don't give a damn about their careers, who are willing to go off with me and learn what we have to learn: how to write music, write and play for each other, criticize each other, and educate our children. I don't really mean a commune (I don't want to share my wife with anybody), but a community. It is the only alternative to isolation I can see. Colleges are not going to do what we were told they were going to do; and they, too, think they can't do it. We have to do it for ourselves, but we can't do it individually. I'm not about to spend the next thirty years of my life writing only solo clarinet pieces.

It's the old story. There's no audience for what I do. I know from practical experience that there isn't, but I continually delude myself into believing that there is. Every new piece is for an audience; I think it's a fine, great piece.

BC: Perhaps when you're eighty-five there will be a giant Martino retrospective in New York and everybody will love you as they did [Edgard] Varèse and [Stefan] Wolpe?

DM: That would be nice if I'm still around, although our oppressive copyright law might still be around. Everything that is played on that retrospective has to have been composed after I turned thirty-three, otherwise I will derive no financial gain from it. My family won't benefit from my death; my present royalties make it unlikely that I will leave them even a modest sum. People don't realize that it costs lots of money to write music. The only tangible assets I could leave would be royalties from my music, which in fact won't give them a nickel, no matter how popular I become in death, because they won't own them. Our copyright law assumes that the author will receive a reasonable initial return on his work; this assumption does not hold for serious music in America. By the time a reasonable return might be realized, the works are likely to be in the public domain. That's why there is no gain. This fact would be easier if I could convince other people that there isn't any gain, that the only thing that we're really into is writing music that we believe in, and to found a community of people who believe in the idea that I'm doing music. That would be a community I could live in, and I think I'd be happy. But I'm just tired; I no longer want to have to be afraid—as was the case when I was trying to get from an instructor to an assistant professor to an associate professor to a full professor—that what some idiot said in the *New York Times* would probably be accepted as truth by some guy who had nothing to do with composing but sat on some committee at some college and had the power to knife me.

BC: What's the role of analysis? Can analysis be of any use at all, outside your own knowledge of what you are doing?

DM: This is very complicated; the kind of issue on which if I say anything I will immediately know I'm wrong. I have to talk out of both sides of my mouth. On one hand, you acquire a certain level of personal growth to use analysis properly. And it seems that analysis, at too early a stage in one's development, can lead to very dangerous results.

I believe that the student should keep writing lots of music. He should use analysis only as a tool, not as an end result. Historically analysis, as a discipline, came after the fact. As a creative tool it must come during, and sometimes even before the fact. But recently the false impression has been given, often unwittingly, that the analysis is equal in value to the composition and that one must begin each composition by constructing a plan that is so complete that it is synonymous with the work. This procedure can take place; the creative process occurs in many ways. But it is unlikely to occur in this fashion or, if it occurs, it is more likely to be successful in the hands of the more mature composer who has come to be able to predict in the pre-compositional stage more of the events which must occur in the composition.

I have written a few pieces in which the preplan approached an analysis. But I more generally begin with a vague ground plan: timing, structure, large gestural shape, and some equally vague notions about the detail. From this I may proceed to a more rigorous set of definitions or I might plunge directly into the work, allowing the rigor to unfold. For there *is* an unconscious level, as there *is* a conscious level. The unconscious changes the conscious; the conscious changes the unconscious. More precisely, one has to have a body of acquired knowledge that is stored and can be summoned up reflexively. It's really not intuitive, but this faculty must be allowed to assert itself.

The ideal is to have a student who at some level of his training has two separate parts of his being: the composer and the student. As a student, he learns about analysis. He doesn't learn that a piece is A flat to G to E flat to C, and say to himself, "My God! *The company* was thinking of *that*! I must think of something like *that*!" No. He learns what happens. He writes his pieces, gradually develops his critical and analytic faculties, and he doesn't develop an inferiority complex about it. Later on he learns to use analysis of his own ideas as a tool to develop his own spirit. Of course the student must learn by making mistakes, but not at the expense of the ego.

I am disturbed not by analysis, but by the lessons which our students seem to learn from it. The young composer, intimidated by the literature of contemporary analysis, unable to perceive its fallacies and seduced by its obvious beauty, will all too often force on himself a rigorous model which he is incapable of realizing. It is no better for having been constructed pre-compositionally than any other model he might have constructed post-pre-compositionally. Often his stubborn commitment does not permit him to perceive that the model has failed or that he has failed the model. Whereas if he could have been receptive to that inner self during the process, another model might have evolved which he could more effectively have realized. Why is model X better than model Y? It's just different. There is no model that is bad or archaic; there is no model that cannot be made to work.

Analysis is useful, even necessary, at all stages of composing. I can't imagine composing without continual critical inspection, especially of those passages that I have written with a minimum of calculation. It is amazing how often such passages further incite the creative process. I began writing my piano concerto in 1958 as a series of sketches for a piano piece, which I finished. One of the sketches, only about five or six complete bars, remained. The sound of these bars pleased me but they were based on a very unrewarding set, seemingly non-extendable by any process I was then aware of. I put the sketch aside, but in 1964 I saw that it wasn't one set, it was the union of two sets. There was an upper melody, a bass line, and an internal area which was a sort of accompaniment. The accompaniment made up one hexachordal set and the outer voices made another. I began to think of the outer voices as the piano set and the other as the orchestra set. As soon as I allowed myself to think of this tripartite union of two different set types, I immediately wrote the piece. And without that analytical moment I don't think I would have gotten beyond five bars.

BC: What about people who dismiss serial composers as simply mathematics-mongers?

DM: The twelve-tone system has been terribly misunderstood by people who have never worked with it; it's very easy to misunderstand when you've never "played the game." And we have said things that have done us a disservice; we've been tremendously misunderstood. I have said to classes, "I'm not going to talk about the emotional content of music; I don't ever want to hear you in my analysis course talk about 'a bombastic cadence'; I don't want anybody to have an orgasm in front of me over this piece, simply because that's not something I can discourse upon. Not because that level of music is not there. I have no language to describe it, but it's there." I can say these things, and I'm openly criticized for talking technical horseshit. We've never said that nothing else exists; we've only said that's what we know how to talk about, or more properly that's what we *think* we know how to talk about.

I'm sort of a mystic; either one is a composer or he is not. Anybody who produces some music that makes some sense, that has shape and design, that moves from here to there coherently, is thinking big things. You may not be able to test him on an SAT score, but he's thinking those things, and it may be on a nonconscious level. I suspect that anyone who has studied composition has experienced that moment of revelation when his teacher has uncovered the unconscious in him. As you write more music and become your own teacher as well, you become aware of that happening all the time. You perceive it almost as the astral body, standing away, perceives the physical body. You don't have to think about thinking to come out with coherent music. If you don't think, danger! If you think too much, danger! I believe that the ultimate moment in getting it together is the moment at which you learn to juggle when it is appropriate to calculate, when it is appropriate not to.

So analysis, formal training, is extraordinarily important as a vehicle, not as an end. Currently we tend to teach it as an end but use it as an insidious kind of vehicle. After all, the classroom teacher is probably a composer, probably disillusioned by his proper audience, using that class as his audience. I used to do it myself: that was my ego trip. Bullshit! That's really dangerous, because you're falsifying the case. Therefore a lot of the classroom experience is falsified experience, a lot of it is showbiz, and a lot of it is destructive. The analytical experience is not being used the way it should be used.

I see this and lament it, and yet I see another side of it. I see this poor bastard who considers himself a composer forced year after year to teach theory, which is not his forte. That's got to be destructive. In the concert hall he's derided; in the academic world he's not permitted to do what he believes he can do; when he would talk most excitingly about the things he believes in, he's made into a kind of a hack. He often uses that teaching experience as the one great moment of glory in his life. That's why I don't like the distinction between the composition and theory faculties; the theory faculty is usually composers who are never allowed to teach anything related to their personal investigations in music. I went through it, where I was not allowed to teach as a composer for the entire ten years of my tenure. The system did damage to me, it did damage to very gifted people who were there with me. I would like to change the system but can't.

Notes

1. James Boros, "A Conversation with Donald Martino," *Perspectives of New Music* 29/2 (Summer 1991): 225.

2. Donald Martino, "Notation in General—Articulation in Particular," *Perspectives of New Music* 4/2 (Spring–Summer 1966): 47–58.

3. Donald Martino, "The Source Set and Its Aggregate Formations," *Journal of Music Theory* 5/2 (Winter 1961): 224–73.

4. See Milton Babbitt, "Some Aspects of Twelve-Tone Composition," *The Score and IMA Magazine* 12 (1955): 53–61; "Twelve-Tone Invariants as Compositional Determinants," *Musical Quarterly* 46/2 (1960): 246–59.

5. For more detailed analyses of both works, see William Rothstein, "Linear Structure in the Twelve-Tone System: An Analysis of Donald Martino's *Pianississimo*," *Journal of Music Theory* 24/2 (Autumn 1980): 129–65.

6. Boros, "Conversation with Donald Martino," 222.

7. Milton Babbitt, "Who Cares if You Listen?" *High Fidelity*, February 1958: 38–40; 126–27. The title is not Babbitt's but an editor's.

8. Childs is referring to Martino, "Notation in General."

9. The ASUC is the American Society of University Composers (now Society of Composers Inc.).

14   Salvatore Martirano (1927–1995)

KEVIN HOLM-HUDSON

When Barney Childs interviewed composer Salvatore Martirano in May 1972, Martirano was on the cusp of finishing his Sal-Mar Construction invention—one of the first real-time interactive electronic musical instruments.

Martirano's most famous electronic composition is the multimedia piece *L's G.A.* (1968) for "gas-masked politico, helium bomb, and two-channel tape," created with filmmaker Ronald Nemeth and poet-performer Michael Holloway. The live-performance component of this piece involved Holloway delivering a dramatized rendition of Lincoln's Gettysburg Address, with increasingly incongruous accents (a southern gentleman, a Nazi military officer), his voice eventually distorted to a cartoonish squeal by the introduction of a mixture of nitrous oxide and helium gas. The political commentary of this piece, with its uncomfortable allusions to the riot-gear-clad Chicago police at the protests outside the Democratic National Convention in 1968, fit the late-1960s Zeitgeist perfectly.

Martirano next turned to work on the Sal-Mar Construction, a large electronic-music instrument built using parts from the inactive ILLIAC II computer, in 1969. The Sal-Mar Construction was Martirano's response to several compositional problems. First was the composition as a fixed entity, as he described to Childs: "music . . . is analogous to going to see a movie. Once you've seen the movie, you possibly might want to see it again, twice, but most people don't go to see a movie three times. I certainly don't go to hear a composition three times."

A second frustration had to do with the time-consuming nature of tape composition—creating the twelve-minute tape part for his composition *Underworld* "took over 3000 hours to produce because each note had to be separately shaped, spliced in a chain, and finally mixed with 8 other channels to form a 9-channel whole."[1]

Finally, Martirano was aware of the limitations of collective improvisation: "any tailoring that I could do to the abilities of the particular people that I was working with could never be really as interesting as the things that they would just do normally."

"I'm less interested in 'music' per se," Martirano told Childs. "I'm really interested in the activity that *I'm* involved in less than what it's going to sound like. I've really grown away from the whole idea of what things sound like." In other words, the *process*, not the *product*, interested Martirano: "I'm constantly a beginner. At the point where I've got experience and can handle something, I'm already tired of it."

The Sal-Mar Construction was a hybrid digital-analog instrument, using transistor-to-transistor logic circuits to drive analog modules such as oscillators and filters. The performer can provide input from any of 291 touch-sensitive switches, and can also input sequences of numbers that would be converted to musical data. Circuits allowed for selecting either manual or automatic control of input functions, and the instrument also allowed for independent control of pitch and register (octave).[2]

One innovative feature allowed the performer to switch from macro to micro parameters of a sound. A report Martirano prepared for the University of Illinois in April 1971 provides details of his work in progress: "varying quantities of information are controlled in a scale of perceivable steps that range from a pseudo-random set, through permutations that are predictable to a significant degree, to a totally predictable set." Furthermore, "an analogy to traditional composition exists, considering that particular patching patterns are developed over a period of time. In performance a composer can improvise, better said, *compose* in real time, within a large set of musical possibilities." The Sal-Mar Construction even allowed for pseudo-random sets to "program the dimples and pimples in a shape that custom has conditioned our ears to expect in a musical sound."[3]

Although at the time of this 1972 interview Martirano claimed the Sal-Mar Construction was still unfinished—telling Childs "the idea's almost finished"—he had in fact already given public demonstrations and performances of his instrument. A July 1970 performance was reviewed by Bernard Jacobson for *Stereo Review*: "Martirano was working with his new electric console, in company with a bunch of extemporizing instrumentalists, a couple of dancers, and any amount of pulsating visual and aural imagery projected on screens and fed into little speakers that dangled all over the room."[4] With Martirano's typically wry humor, these public performances were often given titles like "Look at the Back of My Head for a While."

Childs's interview documents the instrument in its "research and development" stage. Martirano explains the instrument's design and the issues of choice versus chance and degrees of control afforded by the instrument, even allowing for the machine to acquire a "personality" through responding to a performer's inputs over a history of performances. Interaction (or "interference") with the more automatic functions of the program was accounted for in three ways: a REST control that "overrides the program," a HOLD control that "enables the user to inhibit evolution of the program," and modulation with other programs (amplitude modulation or frequency modulation, for example).[5] Martirano asks: "how much of the role should be taken over by automatic predetermined control, and how many overriding capabilities do I want to have available?"

Martirano even speculates about using the Sal-Mar Construction's circuits to control other media: "the important thing is the control system. . . . It's not completely out of the question that in attempting to get into new fields and new technologies . . . that I would try to develop an interface with, perhaps, television. The most important thing . . . is the control system, not what it's controlling." This intermedia application is evocative of some of Robert Ashley's contemporary work, especially his "Illusion Models" ("hypothetical computer tasks," composed in 1970).

The Sal-Mar Construction is now housed in the Sousa Archives and Center for American Music (SACAM) at the University of Illinois at Urbana-Champaign, where it is maintained and occasionally still played. Ken Beck has shared his experiences in learning the instrument in a series of blog posts.[6] One gets the impression that the Sal-Mar Construction is an instrument with vast potential, as unique as each individual who takes the time to learn and play it.

Salvatore Martirano: Interview

BARNEY CHILDS: I'd like to talk about what you're doing.

SALVATORE MARTIRANO: It's the *next* thing I'm deeply in, which developed as a result of trying to get into something less abstract. Now after about two and a half years I'm ready to get back into something that's more abstract. And writing.

BC: Now that the machine is finished?

SM: No, it's not finished. The idea's almost finished.

BC: What is the idea? How does it work?

SM: There's a history to that, too, to do with the impossibility of getting together with a group of musicians to produce music and a desire to get into a less dependent activity. When I first started, I wrote music; when the piece was on the page, it was finished. The performance was just so much sugar frosting. I was happy to hear it, take the bows, and have people say "That's fine!" Then I came to Illinois, which proved to be an enormous turning point in my attitudes. For the first time I was no longer isolated from the performing community. It was actually possible to get together with marvelous players, so a period of tailoring pieces to the particular abilities of these players followed. I then realized that any tailoring that I could do to the abilities of the people that I was working with could never be really as interesting as what they would just do normally. The motivation of using my musical ideas as an orientation for another group became less important. The idea of tailoring the piece for, let's say, seven people would mean that I would look at their abilities and that would be its focal point. At the same time, I'd be taking advantage of all the things that they were best able to do. So I then had an improvisation group, with everybody listening to each other and playing. It was a leaderless group.

BC: This was back in '68, '67?

SM: Yeah, '67, '68. That group of incredible musicians worked for one summer: four to five hours a day, six hours a day, playing together.

BC: Did you make any tapes?

SM: I've got about thirty hours of tape of this improvisation. Usually we'd just turn the machine on. Listening back, those improvisations sound really great—they were excellent. There could never have been any agreement within the group as to what was happening—as to the quality of it, the value. Everyone within the group seemed to evaluate the result on the basis of his own performance. At some point there were so many psychological problems within this group that it stopped being fun. It turned tense.

BC: Wasn't this a natural thing to happen with any group of highly talented personalities together for that length of time?

SM: [Ronald] Dewar said: "I just don't want to hear another note of new music!" And I understood what he meant! There was no convention, no place to lean on; there were no rules—or so it seemed. Although listening to the tapes, there were obviously rules: the style is consistent from tape to tape. I began to get more involved in performance. I did a lot of conducting, but that seemed not very satisfactory. The percentage of musical density as opposed to the organizational density just proved to be too far out of whack; that is, 90 percent of the time was spent getting people together and 10 percent spent doing something. Although we put in many hours of rehearsal on pieces in ad hoc groups, it could never really get heavily into anything musically.

I started thinking, "What can I get into by myself where I can control the pace?" that can only be dependent on interaction, but still is oriented towards performance. I decided to make an instrument which would be generally divided into two functions. One would be the manual control that I would exercise over it; the other would be automatic, predetermined circuits which I could route. In a sense it activated large collections of things as opposed to what we think is a single collection, like any one note is composed of so many different things. Taking the one-note idea at a time over the piano—ten, fifteen, twenty, thirty, or forty notes if you use elbows, and controlling larger quantities of information—I found out that quantities actually make a lot of difference.

BC: Did you have to learn electronics to do this?

SM: Yeah. Before that it was black box, turn knobs, and listen—the real innocence. But this required a great deal of study about a new field. It is quite interesting to get into something you know nothing about as a result of a decision, as opposed to getting into something as a result of some natural law which pulls you there.

BC: Much of your time had to be spent in very intensive personal learning?

SM: Right. What would be the electrical devices and mechanisms? It's a new technological study.

BC: That also had to include a lot of computer study, too.

SM: The study of logic circuits turned out to be much less complicated and a much more explicit way of expressing structure than set theory in the tradition of serial technique. The background is still musical, but as soon as things are translated into ones and zeroes, the output of your ideas becomes very explicit, simple and checkable. The modifications of an idea are traceable and notatable. The reasoning processes that govern role manipulation writing for instrumentalists and instruments are just not that explicit. A very small detail on the machine that I'm studying now has to do with a shaft of filters—the study of the proper logic to judge the rotating rods or wheels. I've got an idea for the audio spectrum as being a varied-sized-circumference wheel. The values that apply to a larger rotation or circle can be scaled down to smaller sizes, and once the window within the wheels is set, it would be possible to shift this window up or down. A number of these wheels operating simultaneously, or coming in or coming out, changing the density, would be one way in which one person could control a large quantity. This idea, in conjunction with the study of a programmable shift register-programmable input, breaks the set of permutations into varied sized groups. The idea now is to steer: a performer or composer will steer between different-sized groups, selecting certain permutations. The thing is kind of a silly idea when you realize it, and that's within a random set. If it's long enough, any piece of information that can possibly exist has to form some segment of a random set. I'm much more conscious in looking at available off-the-shelf logic circuits and making use of them.

BC: You're the only one that will really be able to do anything with this instrument. There won't be any others made?

SM: My God, I hope not!

BC: How long has it taken you from the first actually getting your feet wet and actually putting things together?

SM: It's almost three years ago when I first started getting involved.

BC: And for three years steadily, you've been totally given to this.

SM: Right. The last time I can remember a single effort continuing so long was the Mass, written in '52 to '55. A forty-seven-minute a capella Mass.

BC: You wouldn't do that again, either?

SM: No!

BC: As you said in the beginning you're thinking now of reapproaching the problem of written music, performing music, with a different kind of feeling. It's obvious that it would have to be different than before.

sm: I'm less interested in "music" per se. I'm really interested in the activity that *I'm* involved in less than what it's going to sound like. I've really grown away from the whole idea of what things sound like.

bc: But you're still concerned with sound? When this is through, you will use it?

sm: Yeah, there'll be a concert.

bc: It's going to *make* sounds.

sm: I'd like to see if it can pay for itself. It's expensive, and it doesn't fit in with any of the guidelines of any of the supportive institutions. There's a credibility gap when I go to the scientists, and the humanities and the musicians think it's equipment, as if a transistor collected a salary! "We don't want to put any money into your equipment!"

bc: Do you have no objection to your early instrumental music? You still wish it to be heard?

sm: That's correct. Whenever anyone comes over, I'm willing to play for them.

bc: Something interesting about your output as a totality is a series of major single gestures, each one of which encompasses a particular kind of musical exploration. It ties it up in a package and says, "There! That's that!" There's *Underworld* [1965], which combines live electronics, performer sound. You repeat yourself less than practically anybody I know.

sm: Everyone's going to find himself operating in certain worlds. The two extremes of the possible worlds have to do with the abstract hypothetical person who's constantly looking for something new to expand his information in a horizontal way, as opposed to the funk pianist who spends seventy-five years getting into something in a vertical way. Now the greats of the musical tradition tend to be of the funk pianist class. I've given up any illusions about becoming one of the greats of music, because my orientation, my personality, is of the horizontal class. So I'm constantly a beginner. At the point where I've got experience and can handle something, I'm already tired of it. Being in the university has contributed to this in allowing me the freedom where it was possible.

bc: This is not just any old university; this is a special one. I know many universities where you wouldn't be allowed to develop on those levels that you're working on. As you said earlier, you couldn't have done the "virtuoso" performing pieces without the virtuosi here. Although these works were written for specific . . .

sm: *Underworld, Ballad* [1966], and *L's G.A.* [1968].

bc: Do you find that other people are interested in performing these?

sm: Not *Underworld.*

bc: Why not?

sm: It's just very hard. You need four percussionists, two string basses, tenor sax, and four actors. But *Ballad* gets quite a few performances.

BC: *Cocktail Music* [1962] has become a standard repertoire item.

SM: Even though now it's no longer available—there are a few published copies extant! I get letters all the time from people who want *Cocktail Music*.

BC: Are you going to reprint it?

SM: No—it's too much trouble! Can you really enjoy performances when you're not there? I like the idea of people performing my music, but I don't know how much trouble I want to go to. It takes away from what I'm doing now.

BC: But after you come out the other side with this, perhaps there'll be a time when you'll have wound up what you're doing now, tied the ribbon, set it aside, and you'll move out again.

SM: I have some plans for a period of kooky pieces. I've been able, from time to time, to spend long periods on one thing.

BC: This is the way you work, isn't it?

SM: *Ballad* was written in three days, but of course it's one of those strong controlled, structured pieces in a lot of ways.

BC: Do you feel you're on the side of the controlling structure people today rather than the non-control, non-structure people?

SM: The non-control is something that no one can avoid. What's inside of you is the irrational element. The control only represents a connection with others. Systems represent bridges to what other people are doing. You try to include enough of the things that they're doing with the hope that you'll build in some connection between the things that you're doing and what other people are doing. Now everybody's got the other part (I never thought of them as being opposite parts): you just can't avoid being yourself.

BC: So each piece is a new stance but with the same one's self and one's connections; a reappraisal of these relationships perhaps, a restatement in a different way.

SM: What changes as time goes on? I think the quantities rather than the qualities. When having the note last for ten seconds was not long enough, this was tripled. In order to attract attention to itself, it had to last for thirty seconds, or go faster than ten notes a second. So in order for sound to have any extraordinary characteristics so that it will be noticed at all, it's got to do something that pulls out of the ordinary. Therefore any set of time-volume-pitch considerations has to constantly be readjusted as time goes on, so that it will not be thrown into the great mass of unnoticed sound which we're surrounded by. So it is very simply changing quantities.

BC: The common practice is always with us, whether we like it or not.

SM: [David] Gilbert and I were talking about what relates to what other people hear. I never thought it was necessary to talk about not-verbalizable subjects: feelings and emotions. It's interesting to talk about things that have some meaning. If one's real-time conversations are translated to the written page, they gain a new life; the sum total is not completely comprehensible. But I'm always reluctant to edit anything that is real-time tape-recorded. I'm getting further and further away from the idea of editing. *L's G.A.* was my last editing job.

BC: It was also your last piece before you started on this, wasn't it?

SM: Yeah. Notes with this machine that I'm working on have really become very cheap. Let 'em disappear. They can be repeated, by the way. It would require remembering what I've done, and then that would have to be coupled with the desire to repeat it.

BC: *L's G.A.* is a visual as well as an audible piece, and to some degree *Underworld* is too. What about this machine you're working on now? Is there going to be any visible counterpart, or is it simply going to be sound?

SM: Well, consider that a particular *piece* of music as we know it is analogous to going to see a movie. Once you've seen the movie, you possibly might want to see it again, twice, but most people don't go to see a movie three times. I certainly don't go to hear a composition three times. Usually when I've heard it once, I've heard it; if it's an event, that event can only take place that first time. If I know enough music of a particular composer, I sometimes don't even have to hear the newest piece the first time. I assume that I've already heard it. There's so much information available, why make any hard-and-fast rules about what you're doing? Are you going to go hear every first performance? No. This machine is oriented toward popular tradition. It'll never be successful; this is what it would *like* to be, as a group has a following. It might be as oriented toward drug-culture listeners: people who get stoned, lay on the floor, and listen with their own dreams about themselves. So it probably will be received in the other way. People will come to hear it and they'll say, "Oh, that's what it is." That's what I'm saying: notes have gotten cheap in the sense that I don't have to hear the same ones. I'm more interested in just listening to variations of the same thing. And something like what you would imagine jazz to be like.

BC: In a sense that's what classical serial music is, isn't it? Variations on twelve pitches; "arrangement" of twelve pitches? I noticed in the literature you refer to serial procedures in earlier works, which suggests that you're still thinking in that direction.

SM: This also is an attempt to get support. It's necessary to connect with things that are known by the reader. Actually, the things that I talk about are the least important; the first thing that you talk about just happens to be some random place in the list. I don't even know if there's anything important any more to talk about. Just go along step-by-step, hammering one nail in at a time.

BC: We're stuck with that, though, because we can't do it any other way. Nobody's invented a way to "interact." There's not going to be a visual analog; there won't be any multimedia. This is solely a sound-producing machine. When one comes to partake of it, one will "hear."

SM: That's not really correct. The important thing is the control system. It seemed easier for me to try to construct an interface with sound. It's not completely out of the question that in attempting to get into new fields and new technologies and information that I don't have at this point, that I would try to develop an interface with, perhaps, television. The most important thing, the closest thing to me, is the control system, not what it's controlling.

BC: OK, I see. The *product* is going to be immaterial.

SM: I think so, in a way. That's a hard one to face.

BC: Once you have the system, that's all you need to be concerned about. You know it will do what you want it to do in the ways you've made it do it: you can trust it.

SM: I like that idea.

BC: After that, what happens is simply resultant.

SM: I thought about these twenty-four speakers hanging around. It might be possible to extend pipes out from the top of the machine and suspend the speakers from these pipes. Another idea might be to put this whole apparatus on a rotating wheel and make a merry-go-round. That part of the idea is the frosting; the sound output is also.

BC: That's getting into a visual extra-bonus situation. What about acoustics? When you're giving a concert on it, will it matter where this is done? Will each hall be different?

SM: My guess is somewhere between 3,000 and 8,000 square feet of floor space surrounded with a mattress that's 25 feet, 50 feet in diameter, and then outside the circle of 50 feet to have chairs. So it'll be an arena idea, the public being invited to lie down on the mattress and have the rotating merry-go-round.

BC: When you take it on tour next spring, you're going to be put in whatever they've got, be it an old barn or a fancy new music hall. May it not make major problems?

SM: I don't see why it should, because it's now in a small room about 12 feet by 20. The idea of the source of sound moving at the same time the sound is moving is an interesting sidelight. I wouldn't say that was the most important part of it.

BC: *Underworld* gets into this too, because there's a spatial division of players.

SM: All music is into that. I'm talking about the source of sound moving at the same time the sound itself is moving through the space. You're talking now about the *same* sound set up with instrumentalists placed around the room. They're not producing the same sound—they're different sounds. The fact that the sound is in phase with itself as it moves around the room and bumps into that self produces some complicated Leslie effects![7]

BC: That's why I was curious about the hall if you have this sound going around bumping into itself in strange places, even though it's coming from a central locale. Audiences in different parts of the hall are going to be hearing different things regardless of what's coming out of the middle.

SM: It's set up now so that four music programs can be circulated in different patterns, or each of the programs can be trapped in a certain part of the hall, while another program might only pass through it occasionally. So if I spot a group of troublemakers in the corner, I can put one program of unpleasant sounds and then race through with something very rasping, which, when it gets back to the good side of the people, can become quite pleasant.

BC: How busy will you be performing this? It sounds like you are going to be extremely, virtuosically busy.

SM: I consider the most interesting and deepest problem about what I'm working with to be the calculation of what my human time is, and trying to make some kind of comparison with what machine time is. How much of the role should be taken over by automatic predetermined control, and how many overriding capabilities do I want to have available? What do I want to be bothered with? In its simplest sense, a random collection is entirely controllable just through manipulation of the range that it's allowed to work in. Therefore, a random collection that's operating in a very narrow window might be really quite adequate for putting dimples and pimples in the envelope of the sound. I could make it therefore relate to traditional instrumental music of the past. That's to say, you don't always want to have dimples and pimples in the envelope of a sound. But this would seem to be one of the first options that anyone working with electronics would want to develop, the ability to have more flexibility.

BC: It will be possible to make no decisions, to start the thing going and say, "OK, for a while I'm going to make no personal control at all."

SM: Right. It'd be possible to go out for a smoke.

BC: And come back a little later and say, "Here, I'm stepping in, taking over." In other words, you can pace your own tempo of controlling against what's happening.

SM: Right. Control will be exercised when a compelling opinion appears.

BC: As with any other instrument, the more you get into it, the more will be gotten into it.

SM: There's no lack of possibility for turning on a sequence of events which are unexpected to a listener. I don't know to what degree it'll be possible to turn on a sequence of events that would be unexpected to myself, because I've already expanded the horizon of what I consider to be something expected.

BC: So just as any virtuoso instrumentalist knows his instrument immediately and totally, then you too will have this capacity. It will be composing and improvising combined in a very real sense.

SM: I think it'll be impossible for me to devise something that would be unexplained. I would *like* to be able to try that . . .

BC: To have it surprise you.

SM: . . . but I don't think it would be possible. Has anybody ever worked with that idea—trying to set up a situation where the results would be completely unexpected?

BC: Some people have talked about trying with various indeterminate things. But I don't think it works. Do you see any chance at the other extreme that you'd tend to fall into clichés?

SM: Big chance.

BC: The question is of course, "When is it a cliché and when is it a favorite lick?"

SM: My favorite twisted fifth finger! The broken wrist brush stroke on a canvas. That mannerism!

BC: But it has so many possibilities that I think you'll have a lot of room to move in. You can simply say, I don't *choose* to work this way. Or you see something coming and say, "No, thanks, I'll choose this." The control is constant and immediate, as I understand it; your potential is never any the less.

SM: I'm thinking very carefully about overriding options, inhibiting evolution: one button that kills all sound according to whatever happens to be programmed at that moment. We're thinking about seventy-three different sound sources, which are divided into four groups. Each of the four groups will have a soloist, and an accompaniment that varies in size, from a quintet to a thirty-five piece orchestra. The information that's fed to the soloist will be also fed to the accompaniment and changed by some function. So the accompaniment will actually always be a function of what the solo instrument is doing. What this would translate into, specifically, is adding a particular collection, which would then itself be translated into a collection of voltages, to the information, or subtracting a particular collection of voltages, or *both* adding and subtracting. So the information controlling the soloist, the accompaniment then becomes totally dependent on the soloist. Except the soloist can be shut off.

BC: What happens to the accompaniment?

SM: It can continue to accompany.

BC: It's accompanying itself, or accompanying a nonexistent solo. But it is controlled by the soloist, and if there isn't any soloist, what controls the accompaniment?

SM: The control system controls the soloist; it also controls the accompaniment. It's a parallel system, four wide. And each of the four systems Y's into a soloist and into the accompaniment. Before going into the accompaniment it goes through a device which generates a function of the information that's available, and that then goes through D-to-A converters, and the analog voltages then control the analog part of the circuits. And the sounds that will exist are synthetic voice sounds, synthetic percussion sounds, synthetic . . .

BC: Synthetic *any* kind of sounds. But would you think it possible to tape a performance and say, "OK, here is a piece"?

SM: I'm thinking of commercial output at this point; maybe a four-channel tape.

BC: Each one of these recordings then would be different, unique. It would be whatever piece you wanted to call it.

SM: I don't know. Maybe it would develop a personality like Pergolesi, so that they were just different pieces by Pergolesi.

BC: But for those people who don't have a chance to hear the apparatus live, to hear you do it, there would be an interest in some sort of commercially available performances. Of course, then you wouldn't have to worry about when you send a score out and you get a tape back and the tape is terrible, the performance is mangled beyond redemption. We're all aware of that bad moment.

SM: Yeah. I think that anyone writing today must definitely have to stop when the ink dries.

BC: I agree. The rest of it is not your concern.

SM: Right.

BC: You said you're allowing *Cocktail Music* to sort of fade off into a limbo, perhaps. Are you going to retire other pieces?

SM: Yeah, I'm starting to charge very high rentals.

BC: That's the best way in the world not to get performances.

SM: It's a way that saves me the trouble of packing it, of getting it back. I had a performance of *Ballad* in Philadelphia on April 31st; here we are into June, and I still haven't gotten the music back. There are notations in the parts, which are in colored pencil, which means that they're not reproduced. I just really can't imagine a performance that's going to add very much to what we did here, with Don Smith singing and John Garvey. They're the people that it was written for.

BC: It's difficult after hearing Don Smith to imagine anyone else singing it, as a matter of fact.

SM: He's far out; fantastic. But what he does in that piece is *nothing* compared to what he's doing when he's just sitting there just playing and singing by himself. As much as that piece allows him to stretch out, it still inhibits him. I think it's one of the most successful pieces for allowing somebody to express themselves at the same time that they're orienting toward a reference. It's very successful that way—and it *still* doesn't make it.

BC: This is what you've been thinking about all along, in the machine and in the earlier works too, that there be a set of controls. You're limiting the random set so that he's moving inside a certain structure, but still . . .

SM: This summer you're traveling around the country, speaking with different people. You must be getting into some really . . .

BC: It's a very selfish thing for me, because it's such fun to hear and be challenged and discuss with people whose work I know. It's a tremendous banquet for me, just partaking of everybody. As with you and the "when the ink is dry, you are through," this same thing is true here: that my own personal reaction is simply that when the book is finished, that'll be it. I have no personal stake in it; I'm an agency who's getting things that aren't available for people who will also find it exciting and challenging. Also, there simply isn't any literature on our particular generation of American composers. I consider there to have been some exciting things that have happened since about 1950 in this country; music is never going to be the same because of a bunch of people. And I'm not trying to sound jingoistic or anything . . .

SM: Well, there's a tradition of that in America. We've never been able to really develop that cooperative thing. It's been talked about a million times . . .

BC: We're a lot closer to it than we were.

SM: I find that the reception for music in recent times is really declining: audiences are falling off, no one goes to concerts any more. It's just not an interesting activity, socially. There used to be some social activity involved in going to concerts.

BC: Is this because the music is repellent to them?

SM: Listening to music doesn't seem to be a very interesting activity any longer.

BC: How about records? Everybody buys records. *Everything* is now available. If you want to hear it, you just put it on; you don't have to find a performance of it. With some pieces, that's the only way you can hear them. How many times am I going to get a chance to hear *Underworld* live? If I'm lucky, once, maybe. But if I have the record, I can put it on. Why go to a concert? And yet you're going in the face of this yourself, in producing something that's so essentially concert-oriented.

SM: True. I don't know how to explain it, except that what I'm doing now is what's interesting, rather than what I *will* be doing on the West Coast in some hall.

BC: You may find it just as interesting in its own way, because after all you will be realizing the whole three or four years of thinking, which is very personal and very real and very demanding. The actual process of doing will be as demanding as designing and making the instrument. And you haven't made it easy for yourself. You've made it as difficult for yourself as you can. And it's a good thing; you're setting up a wall and saying, "Can I bust this with my head?"

SM: I think you've got it right there. That's really what it's been like, to make it as hard as possible.

BC: Your instrumental pieces do this, too. Each one of them is a big reach. I don't know any of your works that are less than a complete commitment on your part, and demanding a complete commitment on the part of the players. So you're constantly reaching through your pieces for something. There are no easy pieces.

SM: Yeah, it seems it has to do with trying to make something extraordinary that is physically taxing. Probably the physical labor is one of the more important parameters in what I'm trying to do. It's not like trying to express myself or express music, or that I had a melody in my mind. It's not that at all. It has to do with climbing the highest mountain and all that: what's impossible? I'd like to have been presented a long list of impossible things and then one by one . . .

BC: . . . Bust 'em!

SM: Right!

BC: It seems then that you are into music as an act of making, of doing. The making of the music, the making of the instrument, the achievement of the goal in terms of activities is what counts. There's no rope which is attached to your inner emotionality. The other day Ed London and I were mentioning, as Yeats said in "Sailing to Byzantium," the idea of artifice, in the best sense of the word, "the artifice of eternity." In a sense, one is *making* something; the process of making involves him in a situation, which has to be exhausting to finish. But once it's done, then that's it. That's as far as one goes, because one has then either broken down the wall or not. It's time to go on to something else. I think this fits in quite well when you say some people extend themselves horizontally, who write the same piece eighty-three times.

SM: That's the tradition of great music, writing the same piece eighty-three times, and finally, the depths at which the pieces can speak to someone. In the first place, writing a piece eighty-three times you finally get the message across!

BC: Yes! We are told nothing succeeds like repetition, but the problem is that essentially you're writing the same piece. I've never found that you ever write the same piece twice.

SM: Well, I did, in a certain sense, in *Octet* [1963].

BC: But that's also a virtuoso performance, the making of that, taking something which is a complete solution to one set of problems, and trying to make it a complete solution to some degree a contradictory set of problems.

SM: That's legitimate—picking those particular instruments to express the piano lines.

BC: Piano lines, piano concepts, piano sound. Does the *Octet* get performed much?

SM: No.

BC: I wonder why? Too hard?

SM: No. It belongs to a period of sound that is associated with our fathers.

BC: Properly so?

SM: Not so much "properly" except that it's natural for it to be neglected. Then again, composers who work with ad hoc ensembles and haven't built up a repertoire for a particular ensemble themselves can't really complain if something doesn't get performed. If you write a large number of pieces using that instrumentation, then you get into the bag of the small instrumental ensemble. Then you do get a lot of performances simply because you've got a lot of work available. The reason a piece doesn't get performed is usually because people don't happen to think of it. When I was conducting and choosing pieces, it was a matter of available information much more than careful discrimination of what to play and what not to play. We consumed music. In those summer workshops we just chewed it up.

BC: So it would help the composer who was concerned about performance to have some kind of PR system?

SM: I think the first thing you should do would be to produce many works that have certain physical dimensions that are in common with each other.

BC: Right. You can make a channel anywhere—it just has to be a big enough channel for it to have a chance to spread out. Certainly, this is a time when performing groups don't want to go to much trouble, so pieces that have large effect (I'm talking about quantity) with a small demand in terms of service are the most successful. Much rather rehearse two hours and play thirty pieces.

SM: And I can see both sides of the story.

BC: Have you thought of writing "easy" pieces, so to speak? The task you'd set yourself would be "Can I produce a work of such a nature that it would be playable within two hours?" I would feel when I had finished it that I had done the job, something that instantly would become part of the repertoire.

SM: It's not as if I lacked ideas in this direction. It's mainly desire. What changes an idea from something hypothetical in the head and puts it on the page? Something happens. That's never been an automatic thing with me, of immediately transcribing ideas to some kind of record. Most of the ideas I've had, I've said it's not worth bothering with. The few times I have done things in this manner they have actually been quite successful, so it's hard for me to make to evaluate, positively, the result of an enormous effort when compared to a smaller effort. Because it seems as if you're always able to do something that's pretty much along the same lines as far as quality, whatever that quality is. Almost anything you do will have it whether you spend a lot of time at it or not. So I choose the harder problem not really from the desire to produce something that's going to be really high quality. It's just that seems like a more interesting kind of activity; I prefer doing something that is not easy.

BC: I didn't mean to imply that we couldn't do this sort of thing, but that sometimes it's just not interesting.

SM: It's just not an interesting thing to do. The *result* might be quite interesting.

BC: The result might be great, but there's a certain challenge and demand in it too. So we say, "Fine, I can write a sonata for baritone horn and piano because there isn't one everybody'd love to play."

SM: *L's G.A.*, for example; the effort is in the editing. The rest of it's quite easy. The concept's the simplest Fibonacci set of proportions, scraps from ten years of fooling around with tape, and just hustled together as far as discriminating between what goes where. Most of the time there was spent with very carefully adjusting volumes, balances, splicings, and cutting out clicks. There's where the big effort is. It's not in the structural concept.

BC: Or even in the musical concept, if we can talk about that. You already had that. You knew what you wanted it to do.

SM: It's quite a simple musical idea: go on for a long time with a sound. I made some experiments with a class, putting a sixteen-inch Electrovoice through a long thirty-two-foot carpet tube [that's used to roll carpet in] and pushing that in Smith Hall with sixty watts, then fanning something between forty and fifty cycles through that tube—and through two A-7's that are up about twelve feet high into the hall, forming a triangle with the tube on the floor and the two A-7's at either side. We were able to produce standing waves in the hall so that as you walked and talked your voice would modulate acoustically, you'd get sums and differences, right in the space. So the idea of *L's G.A.* was to create a low canvas which in any hall would creak (though less noticeable since they're not focused), create standing waves, and allow people to have the physical feeling that comes from this sound in a room. That's a simple idea; you really don't have to spend more than thirty seconds thinking about it. Once you've had it, you've had it.

Notes

1. Salvatore Martirano, "Progress Report #1: An Electronic Music Instrument Which Combines the Composing Process with Performance in Real Time [April 1971], http://www.jaimeoliver.pe/courses/ci/pdf/martirano-1971.pdf (accessed June 26, 2018), 24.

2. Ibid., 13.

3. Ibid., 8, 12, 24.

4. Bernard Jacobson, "'Travelog' in Illinois," *Stereo Review* 25/1 (July 1970): 50.

5. Martirano, "Progress Report #1," 25.

6. Ken Beck, "Learning the SalMar," *Beck's Good Word* (blog), http://www.ken-beck.com/words/2011/09/ (accessed June 26, 2018).

7. Designed by Don Leslie, the Leslie cabinet was originally intended for Hammond organs. It consists of two speakers—a woofer and a high-frequency horn—that spin in opposite directions. The spinning, along with tube amplification, creates a liquid, shimmering effect. Joe Albano, "Understanding the Leslie Effect," Ask Audio, February 21, 2019, https://ask.audio/articles/understanding-the-leslie-effect (accessed April 8, 2021).

15 Robert Morris (b. 1943)

ROB HASKINS

This interview dates from Morris's tenure at Yale University (1969–77), a pivotal time in his career that precedes an extensive period of scholarship as a music theorist. Although he had explored post-tonal theory in school and hardly entertained any thoughts of scholarly activity, the interview reveals evidence of this emerging interest—for instance, his adaptation of transformational grammar for one composition (*Entelechy* [1969]), brief remarks on projecting atonal pitch relationships on a formal level, and a general conviction, expressed throughout, that composers—especially himself—should learn as much as possible. Morris taught Forte's theory on the side to graduate students during his first years at Yale, and also interacted with a number of Yale theory students who became important scholars in their own right—for instance, Bo Alphonce, whose work with invariance matrices was crucial to the development of Morris's own thinking.[1]

Nevertheless, when he gave the interview, Morris's contribution to Yale's intellectual climate was primarily through composition, and even his extensive work in theory clearly seems intended as a broad and exhaustive guide to composers—something to stimulate their imagination rather than prescribe technical recipes.[2] With Childs, he alludes to this interest as an antidote to a certain complacency he observed in new-music composition and a call to identify and write a new music that can realize its full potential.

Morris's solutions at the time drew from his work with electronic music and his knowledge of world music traditions gained in part from his doctoral studies at the University of Michigan. An early example of both can be found in the electronic work *Rapport* (1971, rev. 1973 and revised for new technologies in 2010); here, a synthesizer player responds to two prerecorded stereo tapes of nearly eighty excerpts from many musical traditions, using the instrument to modulate the four channels of tape sound to create an environment in which the excerpts interact with each other.[3]

Rapport indirectly comments on the work of Cage, who (along with Milton Babbitt) notably shaped Morris's thinking as a composer—specifically Cage's *Variations IV* (1963) and *Rozart Mix* (1965), both of which offer a rich collage of other music. Cage's works differ in that Morris is more committed to transforming the music in significant new ways. While Cage projects the Buddhist principle of interpenetration by simply presenting the excerpts unaltered, *Rapport* demands the performer know the stereo tapes very well; he or she becomes an informed and active agent in the process of transformation.

Another electronic interest, perhaps of greater import, is tape delay in *Rapport*, which Morris describes as a means of fixing material, especially lengthy material, in the memory. Such delay systems essentially create canons, and various kinds of canons abound in Morris's work. At the same time, Morris connects this lengthier sense of time to other traditions like Japanese Noh music, where an extremely slow temporal unfolding is heightened by anticipation for the next pattern.

Around the same time of this interview, Morris would soon pursue this goal more comprehensively with a series of works that intertwine the concerns of various world music traditions with his own. For example, *Varnam* (1973) uses canons with close time intervals to evoke tape delay and to facilitate a deeper listening engagement with long strings of melodic material. The melodies themselves—played by Western instruments (piano, clarinet, violin)—draw from the seventy-two South Indian Melakarta scales of Carnatic music practice, each occurring within a ten-beat rhythmic cycle articulated by finger cymbals. The dense textures produce a rich, constantly shifting projection of the melodic intervals; though superficially similar to minimalism, the changing content and density of the music create a sense of change and progression little explored by the minimalists.[4] The percussion part, furthermore, lends another layer of structure and indeed of expressive excitement, the counterpoint frequently complementing and animating the pulse stream of the canons in surprising and dynamic ways.

As mentioned above, Morris's interest in serial music led him inevitably toward serial procedures using twelve-tone materials, resulting in a large body of research and music created while a professor at the University of Pittsburgh (1977–80) and at the Eastman School of Music (1980–present), including for many years a dual appointment in composition and music theory. For this music, Morris makes use of arrays, in which multiple melodic lines unfold twelve-tone rows whose rich interrelationships offer seemingly limitless possibilities for listening.[5] These techniques have also been linked, in new and thought-provoking ways, to Morris's ongoing concerns with aesthetic principles from other musical traditions. The 1992 work *MA*, while considerably beyond the period Morris discusses with Childs, nonetheless demonstrates how the concerns there continued to have far-reaching implications for his later work. The work's array structure deeply manifests Buddhism in that the various transformations of the *MA* row create a vast network of relationships inviting multiple strategies of attention. Morris aptly compares this network to Indra's Net, a celestial assemblage of jewels through which one can observe not only a single jewel's perfection, but also the totality available by considering all or some of the jewels in various relationships.

I have spent some time discussing techniques and formal principles of Morris's work, but these are largely incidental to the expressive experience, which suggests a complex interplay of emotions that changes the more one listens to it. In this sense I believe Morris's work fulfills the promise he expressed most forcefully in the interview—the necessity for a composer to recognize where new music could travel so as to produce a body of work and experience worthy of its promise and apposite to the emotional lives of performers, listeners, and composers in the complex but ravishing world of intersecting cultures in the current historical moment.

Robert Morris: Interview

BARNEY CHILDS: Would you elaborate on your interest in transformation as a compositional resource?

ROBERT MORRIS: I don't know if it's really a resource, any more than C-sharp is a resource. If we are speaking of what we hear, transformation is a kind of pun: trance and form. In traditional music the fugue, sonata, and especially the variation are good examples. Generally, when anything occurs with anything else—one transforms the other, modulates it in a sense. So transformation is one of the basic musical givens and is, in this sense, trivial. Its use in new music is more global than ever; transformation becomes the primary gesture in the composition. The idea is to lead the listener from a zone that he's more or less familiar with into places he would normally not go if he were merely told about them. I think of pieces like *Rapport*, which I played for you, as hikes where you start out and explore the countryside. The composer's responsibility to the listener is to provide a very interesting hike. But the direction of travel, what you see on the hike, what order events occur in, etc., are relatively unimportant matters. You keep returning to things you know; then, at another turn, you're someplace you've never been before. Often when you transpose something complex into something simple and recognizable, the familiar feels very strange; this emotional result is what a lot of new music's about. We're reexamining the whole of Western and non-Western musical traditions, because in a way new music has progressed to the point where it has come to a dead end. Classical electronic music is a good example, because it not only negates the visual aspect of seeing music performed, it also negates the notational aspect of music. That represents, in a sense, a dead end: the sensory cues are diminished to sound itself.

I was brought up on radio rather than television. When television came along it was very astounding; you could actually see *and* hear things. But my daughter finds the radio "experience" very strange, because it isolates the aural from all the other sensory modes. So nowadays, in electronic music and in new music in general, we keep looking back toward all the traditions we have, trying to reassess them and bring them all in to the present. In that respect, a composer has very much the same goals as a musicologist, because he's trying to make music that's supposed to be "dead"—music that's strange or hardly played, for instance Persian or Japanese classical music—alive again. We try to reinvest pieces of music with a new kind of liveliness. We do this by changing the orientation of the listener, so we hear these pieces of music in a new way.

BC: That's what you're doing in *Rapport*.[6]

RM: Right, but it's also more. It's an attempt to discover those musical impulses that inform all kinds of music, beyond merely trying to hear various musics in a different way. It represents an attempt at discovery of the beautiful things that can happen in all kinds of music, to put them all together and to have them interact—in fragmentary and, of course, more natural gestures.

BC: You've done that in the tape part of the piece. There are seventy-eight excerpts from a cross-section of musical experiences. Did your provision of a live alter-ator (whatever you conceive your performing role with the synthesizer to be) arise from a wish to replace the visual?

RM: That's part of it, but it's primarily to make this music alive. Listening to the tapes alone—which is a lot of fun, actually—most people play a game of musical recognition. Each time the performance goes on, the performer of *Rapport* attempts to reevaluate the formal moment, the sound he's working with, based on how well he knows the tape of seventy-eight excerpts. A performer shouldn't play this piece if he doesn't know the tapes very well. Such a performance would be terrible; very arbitrary at least. A lot of the rehearsals should be devoted to listening to the tapes and getting to know them very well.

BC: There's been interest in the last five or six or seven years in what's variously called collage, magic theater, or quotation. How do you fit this particular piece into this?

RM: I've had a few interesting experiences with "quotations." A few years ago, another composer, Wayne Slawson, and I put together a piece called *Much*, which is also a tape piece. We took a poorly recorded orchestration Wayne made of a Prokofiev march and used it as source material, modified it one way or another. This was the first piece in which I had to deal with a so-called quote, but we decided in a particular performance of this work to add live music in traditional styles. I wrote a "Haydn" trio and a "Bach" fugue to go with it. I had a helluva lot of fun writing these two pieces, and I think I produced pretty good replicas of the styles. As a composer, I sensed a great rapport with the tradition of Western music. Here I was writing old music, and there was a weird satisfaction, but I didn't want to explore it too much. I didn't want to get in that bag because the primary role for me as a composer was to expand and to transcend tradition rather than to emulate it. Unless these quotations are used to some effect other than just saying "Here's something beautiful that's in the style of Beethoven, etc.," I'm not that interested in it. (Even though I may feel it really is beautiful.)

Somehow—and this is probably a moral issue rather than a musical one—I feel that a composer's responsibility today is to broaden himself, to transcend rather than to emulate a tradition. It may be that some composers who are working with quotations are trying to reexamine this older music, but if they do quote, they must transform the material in some way—at least make a frame around it. If the frame is merely three more successive pieces in other styles, this may be not sufficient. The role of the performer in *Rapport* is to make sure that the spirit of the musical excerpts can permeate the experience of the entire piece in as many ways as possible given prevailing conditions. Thus the vectors leading to *Rapport* are different from those that other composers have followed.

I don't know if it was conscious or unconscious, but there is a real attempt to put Western music in its rightful place in *Rapport*. After all, classical Western music is a thousand years of music written for the aristocracy or clergy. Only in the nineteenth century do you begin to get any mass public appeal. But other kinds of music are just as beautiful and complicated and have just as many traditions associated with them. Of course, due to ethnomusicology, more people are becoming aware of these traditions. The composer in me wishes to communicate this interest, but I can't just do it by emulating—composing in the style.

BC: There were very few jazz excerpts, if any.

RM: There are seven, but they were rather submerged in that performance. They probably would have been more apparent if you'd heard another performance. I like jazz very much; a lot of friends have been involved in it, although it's the only type of music that I can't really improvise on the piano.

BC: You're not writing instrumental music then?

RM: I'm writing instrumental music, but the last few pieces have been with electronic modification. In fact, in '69 I wrote *Entelechy*, with ring modulator, which involved a form in which there were sections whose orders were determined by certain rules. These rules come from the theory of transformational grammar, so that a certain structure was always possible if you obeyed the rules. Then I wrote recently for tape-delay system and string trio, which is a fairly accurately notated piece.[7]

I should say something about my interest in the tape-delay system. Terry Riley and Pauline Oliveros have used it, and other composers before. When I was a teenager I got two tape recorders together and tried it. The interesting thing about it is that it's an instant memory. It "auralizes" things that normally you don't remember.[8] It makes it impossible, in a sense, to forget, which makes the temporal sequence of events in a composition much longer than they can be under normal conditions. You can develop long segments of time. In some music—for instance, Japanese Noh music—there are places where the music gets very slow. But if you know that music, you know the drum patterns that are occurring; there's tremendous anticipation for the next pattern. But this dilation has really not been the case in Western music. So the tape-delay mechanism stretches out time, gives you a larger, wider range of expression. Also, it's necessary in new music, when we use sounds that are extremely complicated, to give the listener time to really get to know them.

BC: What things did the string trio play?

RM: There were often canonic events, so that there were multiple delays in the ensemble as well as on tape. The piece is arranged so that the tape could capture things and not be immediately played back. Later on you could play them back and return to something that had occurred much earlier in the composition. The string trio played gestural things exploiting many of the almost clichéd effects that you find in modern music since 1950. There are so many techniques and clichéd things that a composer uses now. God, 90 percent of the pieces you hear are very boring. *Pithoprakta* was an interesting piece in 1955 when it was composed, but now I wouldn't want to hear it. It's been ruined by pieces that have imitated it—just like [Anton] Webern has been ruined by people who have imitated him. And, by the way, attempting to come to grips with Beethoven by writing Beethoven may ruin Beethoven.

I was talking about string writing. There is a desire to go back to very simple writing, tunes for instruments, to use the instrument the way it was more or less designed to be used. I haven't found yet that I want to take advantage of this use in my own music. So I've been trying to use electronic modification to expand further the realms of instrumental sound. Some composers have gotten around this problem simply by incorporating theatrical events. Some of those pieces are very effective for that reason. I remember, of all pieces, a very interesting realization of *4'33"*. There was a presence about those instruments on the stage that was astounding. Whoever choreographed that four minutes and thirty-three seconds must really have had that in mind; you had a feeling of each instrument's tradition. Had they played something, the effect would have been lessened. Incidentally, the concept of an instrument as totem occurs quite frequently in primitive musical cultures.

BC: In George Brecht's piece *Saxophone Solo*, the score is simply the word "trumpet." When we did it in Tucson, we brought out somebody who was a known trumpet player with a trumpet in a case; he took the instrument out, held it up, showed it to people, put it away, and turned around and left. The "instrumentness" is sufficient to produce, to imply the music. But again this goes way back—this was 1961.

RM: I would like to do a piece where people could actually touch the instrument, which is something that nonmusicians don't get a chance to do very often.

BC: Is it conceivable that you would write a piece just for the instruments—if somebody commissioned you to write a wind quintet, for example?

RM: I'm writing a flute concerto right now.[9] I haven't given up. I didn't mean to give that impression.

BC: I didn't mean to imply "given up," but have you moved completely away from that?

RM: For a while. Part of the reason is that it is so difficult, performance-wise, these days, to write anything that demands any precision in time, pitch, or any parameter. Yet I've found that, after so many pieces which allow things to "occur," sometimes you get some better results by *writing* it down, rather than waiting for somebody to come up with it. A lot of composers have come to that conclusion. For instance, [Karlheinz] Stockhausen's new piece, *Mantra* [written 1969–70], is a piece that you could almost conceive of him writing in 1951. It's very strange. Although there's a ring modulation of the pianos, the piece is very rhythmic and is very consciously serial again. It presents a sequence of motives from the immediate level all the way up to the highest structural level of composition.

Thus, some composers seem to be returning to earlier conceptions of musical form and instrumental use. Daniel Lentz said to me a few years ago that he thought that the "Oriental" experience was over. He meant by that the long-line kind of piece—just one thing that repeats again and again, and you get sort of high on it. He wanted to get back into writing for instruments in a very specific way. I feel that way sometimes, but I see blocking this all the paraphernalia of the last ten years in instrumental writing, which hasn't really led anywhere. It's made musicians unhappy, and these resources are more or less used up very quickly.

BC: You mentioned "to avoid arbitrariness."[10] Are you against arbitrariness?

RM: Not exactly. I feel that, when you write for an instrument, there should be something that the player really can feel, that his experience on his instrument is relevant to what he's playing.

BC: But isn't that being changed?

RM: That's true. Schoenberg is no longer a problem. There *are* new people, but a good many of them do not like playing pieces that involve them doing anything but playing notes. Although they find that playing a very complicated series of pitches and rhythms, etc., can be very satisfying per se. But I see the same kind of balking that you see in more traditional lines of musicians. So in order to use instruments well, we have to take advantage of their history. Again, this goes back to styles and quotations, but somehow that doesn't seem the right solution to me.

BC: That, again, may be why you found electronic music more suitable.

RM: I'm also interested in expanding electronic music into a larger field than just the auditory.

BC: Your piece that has the oscilloscope part, as well.[11]

RM: *Lissajous* is an attempt in that direction. It will be a film, and it will primarily remain an abstract situation. I was thinking of using film as a kind of a score: projecting a film on a performer who is playing, and he has certain relationships with that film. Rather than being presented to the audience, the soundtrack of the film could be a series of instructions (a kind of score) that would go to the performer via an earphone; and he would do things in synchrony with the film. The idea is to use a different kind of score, to get away from the score on paper. This is the main reason I like electronics and the things it offers a composer: it really frees you from the printed page and instructions, verbiage, and its iconic representation. My best music is often composed in such a frame of mind. Very often I can't write it down because I would have to make too many compromises from the original idea. Many composers have felt this; all the experiments in notation that have occurred in the last twenty years are attempts to find ways of hearing sounds again in a new way, or at least trying to present them the way the composer wishes them to be heard.

BC: You're interested clearly in the eye here, as well as the rest of the "media," whatever it's called now.

RM: Right. The composition becomes then a sensory show where you dominate one sense and let the other ones be freer, and you keep moving between the various sensory modes.

BC: The sound part of the oscilloscope piece is really secondary?

RM: In a sense.

BC: You composed it to produce pictures?

RM: There's some give and take. Some very beautiful sounds made very dull images, or were so sonically complex that they really didn't amount to anything visually. Then there were some very beautiful, extremely tactile oscilloscope patterns that sounded plain ugly. So I kept on mediating between the eye and the ear. The idea of the piece is that one can "see" the sound as well as hear it, so I had to limit myself to this problem.

BC: The viewer is simply going to hear the sound as accompaniment to the pictures.

RM: That's possible, especially when *Lissajous* becomes a film; after all, you go to the movies to see things. But I'm not particularly upset about that.

Throughout this interview I've been saying that we've reached a kind of end point, and that now we have to assess everything and move on from there. I don't know how many other people whom you've interviewed have had this feeling, but I certainly do these days. For instance, the words "contemporary music" and "new music" no longer apply to serious music. In fact, I had to ask somebody else the other day what kind of music I was writing because I didn't have a word for it. He provided me with a great term: "hard music." Now we're trying to find a new conception, a new direction. I wonder if all of the so-called revolutions that have happened since 1945 have been evading this problem. We have to decide in a very conscious way about where we're going to go and what we're going to do, and then stick to it. We may make several decisions of this kind. I remember being in this frame of mind when I was about nineteen. I was beginning to know what was going on musically in the world, rather than just what music I was able to hear on records, or see scores of. Then the world seemed very open. But now I have all my own music behind me, and it's more difficult to say, "Well, now I will just move in a new direction." It's that tape-delay playing back, you know!

BC: Thinking about one's own past work in that sense is a curious idea. It might entirely be possible for you to collage a piece out of your own past work as a kind of "revisitation."

RM: It's been done. I feel that that's very narcissistic. How many people would actually understand such a piece?

BC: Wouldn't it be just for you? Homage to yourself?

RM: Yes, but I can do that without really writing a piece. When you actually do get down to writing, you're doing it for someone else. How many pieces do we all have that we just don't write down?

BC: True. But how many pieces do we write down that nobody will ever hear anyway?

RM: That's another problem, a very pressing problem.

BC: This is another obvious answer for the electronic solution in that you don't need to rely on performers. Performance opportunities can be snapped up whenever they arise, rather than waiting for five super wind players, for example.

RM: That's the way it goes nowadays. If you have two or three tape pieces that people know about, they'll keep on writing you for tape pieces, but try and get a second or third performance of a piece that has fairly large instrumentation. In fact, if you want to write a piece that'll get played a lot, you have to write it for two or three instruments and tape possibly, drafted from the modern music quintet or octet, which always includes a flute, double bass, a soprano, a percussion player, etc. I'd rather write a piece for three oboes.

BC: I've had that trouble, writing for freak combinations and instruments. I have a piece for E-flat contrabass sarrusophone and solo percussion, for example, which has never been played because there simply are no E-flat contrabass sarrusophones in working order. Well, it has once, very much to my surprise— there turns out to be one in Oklahoma.

RM: The situation in performance is really horrible today.

BC: Back in the West, we provincials tend to regard New York and New England as full of performance opportunities. It ain't so?

RM: I don't know. Certain composers get performed often enough. The performers that play this kind of music are associated with certain composers. That's the way it works; if you're outside that circle, if you're writing a different kind of music, it's difficult to get performances. Recently I got interested in trying to do a piece which used groups of four instruments: four cellos, four flutes, four sopranos, four basses, and piano four hands. I've had a difficult time trying to get a performance of this work because of the problems with instrumentation. Not only that; certain people on certain committees tend to disparage a piece that is not written in traditional or currently fashionable notation or does not seem to be the result of some set manipulation.

BC: What do you feel about sets?

RM: My feeling about all of the technical stuff is that a composer really has to know all of it and then choose what he wants to use. I have not too much sympathy for people who complain about this or that technique without really examining it totally.

BC: In educating the young you would expose them to as many . . .

RM: I wouldn't just say, all right, now we're going to learn twelve-tone technique in depth, because there's so many other things to learn, too. But one should know enough to get into the literature. Sets have a certain heuristic value, and when you read what Schoenberg said about the use of sets in his lecture on twelve-tone music in 1931, you find that his main concern is primarily chromatic completion and motivic integrity.[12] Many composers use rows in this way, a grab-bag technique. But as for the structural implications of the row, from the microcosm to the largest level, the ironic thing Schoenberg's music shows us is that there isn't any connection between these two domains. Here is a composer who uses very intricate atonal pitch connections on the surface of the piece, but yet uses traditional form at the larger levels. If there's any lesson to be learned from Schoenberg, it's that there isn't any necessary connection between pitch events on the foreground going into the background. There are such connections on the gestural level, but I don't think there are in terms of atonal pitch relations.

In tonal music, there is a much more intimate connection between large- and small-scale events, but in spite of all the Schenkerian research that has been going on in the last twenty years, this is being contested by a lot of people, implying that we really don't perceive the foreground as being the embedding of relationships that occur on the largest level of composition. That's the strange message of Schoenberg.

BC: This idea about foreground and background brings us back in a new way to the transformation idea. In *Rapport*, for example, I was struck by its very richness, the "tapestrial" quality, which catches you up. It's what you mentioned about Oriental music, where you're listening in a different kind of attention. This is essentially what happens with this work.

RM: There's a tremendous richness on the foreground, which I was trying to do very consciously in many of my pieces recently. I don't want to give up that hypnotic effect. On the other hand, I hate pieces that have no surface detail. A lot of pieces have gotten into this problem recently. We specify only the very large aspects of the composition; we leave foreground either up to chance or fate. This experience becomes dull very quickly. We have the same experience again and again.

BC: So if there is a low density of surface detail, it should certainly be organic.

RM: It should be very new, very astounding. *In C* is very astounding the first time you hear it. But *In C* actually has a beautiful wavelike motion on the foreground. I like *In C* very much, but there are a lot of imitations of that piece now on the scene. A whole brand of composers (I've heard a lot about them, never met any of them), very young, not even twenty some of them, are very much into drones and things like that.

BC: The curious thing about this of course is that *In C*, although it was written in 1965, is really a 1960 piece. All that stuff had been done, tied up in a package in New York in 1960 and '61. It infuriates me that CBS sees fit to publicize it on the record jacket as a "trip." They're trying to plug it into the whole later market. The piece isn't that at all.

RM: That's one of the things that new music can say. One of its virtues is that it preceded this extension of consciousness by twenty years at least. You can even go back as far as *The Rite of Spring*. We felt in 1968 that younger audiences were really going to flip out on new music, but they didn't flip out so much. They asked us embarrassing questions about acid and speed—if we used them when we composed—but they really didn't hear the music. We weren't able to figure out why. Perhaps it was because really pure (ideal) musical responses are rare, all the more so when the style is unfamiliar. In any case, we were unaware how dependent new music is on tradition.

Regarding musical responses: certainly responses to theatrical events, performers doing other things besides playing on their instruments, are universal.

BC: Like the marching band.

RM: Yes, parades.

BC: You don't much care for pieces that are minimal in that sense. *In C* isn't very minimal, really, because there's so much immediate foreground. But I can think of certain other works.

RM: Well, it's where you say, "Yes, that piece had to be done." But I feel that about other pieces as well. There are many one-time pieces; the majority of composers don't realize this. They keep on writing the same one-time piece over and over again. There's a history of this in Western music. When you go back to the thirteenth-century motet, so many guys were writing thousands of these motets that could only be performed one day during the year because of the liturgy. Then we have the chanson, the sixteenth century; literally volumes and volumes of those pieces were composed, much more than could ever be performed. We're seeing this again, as reams of cluster pieces, texture pieces, drone pieces, clone pieces, etc., are written over and over again.

BC: You're a putter-together.

RM: I feel that I am.

BC: I don't like to use the word "synthesizer." It's like saying, "Are you an electronic composer?"

RM: Right. But my main impulse is to avoid ideas which are one-time events and to capitalize on things in traditions of music that really can be expanded, transcended. I mean by this "one-time thing" that the music can't be transcended; in other words, it's there. If you go one step beyond it, you are at a dead end.

BC: That takes you into aesthetics, of course. It's very difficult. Who is going to be the transcending person?

RM: I wouldn't want to put it that way. That's a thing that really distinguishes this time from others. I don't believe there is any composer today that should be singled out as being greater than any of his many colleagues, including Stravinsky and Varèse, who some people have singled out for this honor. Music nowadays is a very open and complex field of activity, and no one person could be said to represent it.

BC: Are there people who believe that to try to be Mr. Music is a worthwhile goal?

RM: I'm sure there are people who believe that it's possible. I don't think it's possible; if you're trying to do this, you're banging your head against a wall. Given the state of performance now, given the real problem of finding any kind of patronage for music—I don't only mean monetary patronage, given the social priorities in the USA—the "towering genius" of music has no place to go. At Yale this year a lecturer from Holland made a big case for Franco-Flemish music being vital in the history of Western music. We still find this kind of cultural attitude in Europe. In the USA we don't have the same kind of history, and it leads to having all composers be more or less equal. We know what X does and what Y does and what Z does, and we may admire them for doing that, but I feel that composers, or at least a lot of younger composers, have a lot of mutual respect for each other.

BC: Competition . . .

RM: There's still a lot of competition for performance, but when you get composers to the rail and really talk about music, you find that they're much more liberal in their approach toward what's going on. People will be doing a certain kind of music but really admire what's going on in another camp. Partly the reason for this is because each center—the New England states versus the Midwest, or the Southwest, or Canada, and other areas around the country—has its own time and place of music. In the '60s, Urbana and Michigan were very important places, although this was not recognized at that time. And nowadays, a lot of activity is going on the West Coast. Sometimes I feel a little isolated out here.

BC: It looks as though Yale is readying itself by getting young new people.

RM: Right. Three or four young composers around here now are somewhat attuned to the way I feel about music. Understand that Yale is a very academic institution. Many people who get hired here are hired primarily on their academic attainments, which are not always the best criteria for making interesting music. But some of the people that have been hired recently are interesting. I hope that it's going to continue, but as far as the scene today, tenure remains very difficult to attain if you're a composer, unless you're interested in writing theory.

BC: This is true in other universities too, unless the composer is hired as a special big name.

RM: And those guys either have tenure someplace else or they don't need it. But European influence is waning. The country is standing on its own two feet. When most of the major European composers are associated with American universities, it implies that they know where music's happening. They might also feel like it's virgin ground, that they can kind of come in and inseminate the population. But they're finding out that it isn't so easy right now. Many of the composers, young people, who are around are not that impressed with European traditions. Maybe this is partly the reason why you have these very young composers interested in a music that is totally non-European.

BC: Do you think a composer should know "world music"? Is this part of what his training should be?

RM: I feel that one should learn everything. The minute I hear about something, I want to explore it fully. Other people may say, "I'll just trust my intuition and go in the direction I want to, and if something is in sync with the way I'm going then I'll study it." That works very well for some people. I need to know a tremendous amount of things. Some of them never influence my work at all, but others are very important.

BC: There's the perpetual argument: can you really teach composition, or are you just teaching people to polish up skills that they may use?

RM: I don't know the answer to that, except you can't teach composition by teaching skill, technique, etc. You have to make people aware of techniques, but what you try to get a young composer to do is really trust his intuition, and follow it.

BC: Can the university do this?

RM: It has to. Whether or not it can or can't is really quite irrelevant, because so many teachers of composition have this approach.

BC: Does the academic clutter get in the way?

RM: Sometimes. It depends on the kind of head a person has. Some people really enjoy learning theory, have a secondary interest in it. If you were interested in English literature, it wouldn't be "clutter" in terms of composition. Composition is a very personal thing, ultimately, and studying with someone is relevant inasmuch as you believe in that person and inasmuch as they're responsive to your own needs. This becomes difficult when you're dealing with people who have very little experience in composition. Then you try and get them to form simple pieces of music, or to actually take out a score and talk about it, because that will encourage them to find out what their responses are.

BC: With the new studio are you going to be giving direct instruction in electronic music?

RM: We have a course in electronic music. You have to teach a little acoustics. You have to make people feel comfortable with electronic means. Some people are intimidated by them, believe it or not. You have to give them exercises so they refine their techniques to the point of competency. It's very much like teaching somebody how to make a score, in a way. But you must also encourage them to expand their techniques beyond a certain level. When a lot of composers get to electronic music, they learn one particular technique and then use it in about ten pieces. This has led to certain composers who have a very limited approach to electronic music composition. They don't trust synthesizers, nor computers; they've found that splicing tape, etc., works fine, that additive synthesis versus subtractive synthesis is the way to make music. Their music suffers from the limitations of such techniques. On the other hand, cutting, handling, measuring tape is very tactile, and the synthesizer and computer entail a less kinesthetic experience. Perhaps these composers just have been unable to become comfortable with newer means of making electronic music. I might add that the composer who refuses to splice or make precompositional decisions will also be limited in his means of expression.

BC: Does thinking structurally about a piece of electronic music pose different problems than thinking structurally about a piece of instrumental music?

RM: Of course. Although after you go back to instrumental music after you've done some electronic music, they begin to influence one another. Sometimes the result is music for both media together.

BC: How much of the literature of electronic music should a student know?

RM: You're getting back to "knowing" again. You should know as much as possible.

BC: So he should soak up the existing literature as well?

RM: It's a good thing, but you always have to make the distinction between those things that are worthwhile hearing and those that are not. For instance, the early

Cologne pieces: one or two of them are probably interesting to listen to now. Others are instructive as typical kinds of sequences or sound events. However, it would probably be a waste of time to listen to all of them. It is great value to have the budding student of electronic music hear a good variety of electronic music so that he senses the extremely wide spectrum of aesthetic and technical trends in the field. It is important that the student see that electronic music is not merely a style, especially when many students come to the studio knowing very little about the history or literature of the field. Believe it or not, courses in electronic music often do not spend much time listening and talking about existing compositions. This is like studying sixteenth-century counterpoint without looking at, much less singing, one piece by Palestrina, Lasso, Josquin, etc. (Of course I don't think there is much necessity for a composer to study early music in order to help him compose the music of today.)

BC: In the electronic music class at a large state university, you get people who are going to be music educators, you get clarinet players, people in the studio band who want to find out how to make those sounds for their rock group. What about these people—should they be separate?

RM: No. They should be very much part of a course for everyone. They'll meet people who are very seriously involved in electronic music, which is very good, because by meeting these people they'll learn a lot more how to use the equipment than they would if they were in their own class. If people want to use electronic music for film scores or just sound effects, why not? I have no objection to it.

BC: Do you need a studio like this to teach the course properly?

RM: A very fine studio is necessary. I began studying electronic music at the University of Michigan, which has a good studio, and I was spoiled. I had machines that always worked. So when I went out into the field, I knew nothing about electronics (aside from patching components together) and I felt greatly at a loss. That's part of learning about electronic music. Perhaps you'll learn more about the technical aspects of electronic music in a studio that has certain malfunctions or limitations. On the other hand, it's very important to have the best possible equipment, otherwise your imagination is too limited—you have to keep on watching out for flutter, noisy amplifiers, etc. Your flexibility's gone. However, a limited field to work in is easier to start in electronic music. Sometimes people feel that there are so many different things to make they don't know where to limit themselves at the beginning. After a while in the studio, professional or not, you think that you've exploited everything, then an idea hits you and it opens up the whole studio again. By the way, that's a problem that keeps coming up. You have to move beyond the existing conceptions of music; you have to wait for the right idea. You can't compose music every day and have it amount to anything. Very often I'm upset by the problem that everything's been done, there's nothing new. I don't know how many other people feel that way.

BC: How about style in electronic music?

RM: That's very often dependent on the studio.

BC: There's a danger that certain apparatus tends to impose its "personality" upon the composer. Can you recognize all the pieces done in a certain studio?

RM: That's true. That's not any more of a limitation than, say, being able to identify an oboe piece. There need not be this kind of limitation, but it almost always exists, because people have just so much imagination. When you're around other composers in a given studio, you learn from each other, and you begin to develop certain ways of going about things. Some "electronic" composers will actually teach these techniques and say, "Well, *this* is electronic music, and anything else . . ." This results in a particular studio's music sounding alike. Perhaps this tendency is the result of composers stressing the technical aspects of electronic music and not spending enough time on the essence of what each composer needs the medium for. A confusion of ends with means. This is another reason why a mixed group of students in classes in electronic music and lots of listening is a good thing. Finally, a lot of the music you hear coming out of a studio are first pieces by a composer in the medium: thus they're bound to reflect their origins.

BC: Do you hear quite a lot of new music performed?

RM: Not too much. I'm not the kind of guy who says, "There's a concert out there, let's go." I have a lot of recordings and hear lots of tapes. There are a few pieces that I thought were really beautiful. One of them was *Hymnen*.[13] But nowadays it's not so attractive to me. We had a very interesting performance of *Hymnen* here recently. The Yale symphony was the prime mover. They sent for the tape of the work, and eight loudspeakers were set up around the quad. The third part of the piece, the third region, was performed with orchestra. About 200 people got together, practically all the groups that were involved in music throughout the whole university, and a fantastic happening situation resulted which often obscured the music almost totally. There were wonderful events: squadrons of airplanes flew over the performance space, hundreds of people milling around doing various pageants, a dictator roving through in his convertible, all kinds of nationalistic parades, etc. I like that one can take a piece of music, and then jump off with it into something beyond it. In a sense, they really wouldn't need to have played the piece. The piece is just the initial idea that led to this fantastic event. That's beautiful, because that's the way I feel about pieces that I really like. They're not their own end; we can move from them, they open up something.

BC: Can a Westerner really get into something like South Indian music?

RM: My first response to non-Western music was due to the wife of my piano

teacher; she loaned me some seventy-eight recordings of the music of Uday
Shankar, the North Indian dancer. I was immediately struck by the beauty and
strangeness of the music. Then the next year I heard Ravi Shankar in one of
his very first trips to this country. Again I was extremely impressed; I bought
the two commercially available recordings of Hindustani music. From then
on I studied and listened to a great variety of Eastern music on my own. In
1966, while studying toward my doctorate at the University of Michigan, it
seemed natural that I should minor in ethnomusicology. Under the tutelage
of William Malm and other professors I became very familiar with the musical
and anthropological aspects of music throughout the world. I decided to study
the sitar, and after two months it became painfully clear that I had to make a
choice—study Indian music on a full-time basis and give up my pretensions
of being a composer or continue as I had been going and keep my interests in
Indian music a hobby. I chose the latter because I had started too late; after
all, an Indian musician starts studying music at age five. It was not as if I could
never feel at home with a particular type of non-Western music, but I wanted
to be good at it. Other people who have managed to be successful in both
worlds at once merely differ temperamentally from me. Perhaps my Western
training has inhibited me from taking a chance. I had too much to give up, at
least in my own mind.

First it was mainly North Indian music; now I'm more interested in South
Indian music, perhaps because there are real composers there. I can really feel
their personality in their pieces, which is not so easy in North Indian music.
There's a composer named Tjagaraga, who lived around the time of Schubert
and who is considered *one* of their greatest composers. His music is very beautiful. But the relationship of the composer to the performer is very different in
South Indian music. The composer provides a nuclear composition which is
embellished differently in each performance. Since there are at least five major
schools or dynasties of Karnatic music, there are at least five different versions
of Tjagaraga's music. Imagine five or a thousand radically different versions of
Beethoven!

BC: Say you are writing a flute concerto, are you going to use non-Western material instrumentally?

RM: The glissando, if that's a non-Western material, in the flute part. I don't want
to make a literal translation of some structural feature of non-Western music,
like a scale or a rhythm. I feel that that simply takes the technical resource
out of this environment and makes it manneristic, ultimately. But one gets a
feeling from a certain music that you can try and express in another. There's
a certain joy in South Indian music that's just unlike anything in any other
kind of music in the world. I can't get at it and that's very frustrating, in one
sense. On the other hand, that makes this music very special. There are a lot

of such things in these other kinds of music, all kinds of experiences that are not like anything else.

BC: Perhaps "acultural" in our terms: one can't know this music, really, without having grown up with it.

RM: Perhaps. Yet listening to it, trying to understand it, prompting other people to play it, reading as much as you can about it, and trying to write it down can get you near enough to feel its spirit. A lot of times I've learned most about this music by transcribing it as accurately as I could. Sometimes that's the best way anyone can learn about music—whether it's in their tradition or not. There are certain aspects of this music of which I will never be able to be part. I remember meeting some Indian students in a laundromat near Tanglewood. We struck up a conversation, and it turned out they were very homesick. I mentioned I had some recordings of North Indian singers and they practically begged me to invite them up to our apartment. When they arrived and I began to play the records, all of them broke into tears. It was very moving, but I'll never feel that way about Hindustani classical music.

There are some composers around today who are trying to capitalize on that nostalgic experience, not to mention the programming of 1950s rock 'n' roll tunes on certain radio stations. This aspect of nostalgia bothers me a bit, although some of our basic preferences in music may be deeply rooted in nostalgia. For instance, the Seventh Symphony of Beethoven was one of the very first pieces I knew. But I'm not clear whether I like it because of this or whether I like it because it's really a fine piece of music. The whole world of music is just out there. You can go into any record store or turn on the radio, and you can get practically anything. This availability has led to an impasse. If things are equally probable, and their number increases rapidly, the probability that any one of them occurs becomes increasingly less. I was writing a lot more music and being much more polemic about my views when I knew much less about music and much less about what was going on. Nowadays everything seems to be so much more complicated and diverse. I feel somewhat alone, in the sense that there seems to be no "One True Church of Music," as a friend of mine put it. On another level my responses to music are very rich. There are many composers that I've met that have practically no response to music. In other words, they don't listen to it. And that's more important, ultimately, than writing it.

BC: What they produce is therefore . . .

RM: You can't be sure. Sometimes one of these guys that seems to be totally uninterested in music will write a piece that will strike you. That's one of the very strangest things: that you may have heard pieces by people you don't know, and think, "Well, I'd really like to get to know that person," or "I *wouldn't* want to know that person at all." You find out, ultimately, that it really doesn't matter; you can't infer from a piece of music a particular personality trait very often. The worst situation is when you like a piece of music by someone and then you meet him, and it's just horrible. That's the most trying situation of all, since it's very difficult to keep enjoying the music after such an encounter.

Notes

1. Robert Morris, "Some Things I Learned (Didn't Learn) from Milton Babbitt, or Why I Am (Am Not) a Serial Composer," in *The Whistling Blackbird: Essays and Talks on New Music* (Rochester, NY: University of Rochester Press, 2010), 31.

2. See, for instance, Robert Morris, *Composition with Pitch Classes: A Theory of Compositional Design* (New Haven, CT: Yale University Press, 1987).

3. The four original performances of the work are available through the DRAM database, https://www.dramonline.org/albums/robert-morris-rapport (accessed August 23, 2018).

4. I am aware of only one example: Steve Reich's *Piano Phase* (1967), where changing pitch content over the three sections of the work creates a comparable effect.

5. Each row is related to all the others by the classic transformations of twelve-tone practice (typically transposition and inversion with transposition), with small parcels of each combining vertically with others to form twelve-tone aggregates without pitch duplication.

6. *Rapport* for prerecorded tapes, electronic music synthesizer, with tape-delay-system (1971, rev. 1973 and [new version, with DSP software played in real time] 2010), https://www.dramonline.org/albums/robert-morris-rapport/notes and http://ecmc.rochester.edu/rdm/morris.works.html (accessed August 31, 2019). The old score appears in Robert Morris, "Remembering Rapport," *Open Space Magazine* 12/13 (2011), http://the-open-space.org/issue-12-13/.

7. . . . *Delay* . . . for string trio and tape-delay-system (1971; revised 1973).

8. "Auralize" is used here in the informal sense of sound communication and memory rather than the more modern, formal sense of the process of rendering a soundfield audible, using anechoic recording and computer data.

9. *Streams and Willows: A Concerto for Flute and Orchestra* (1972).

10. It's difficult to know what Childs is referring to in this question. Morris does say earlier in the interview that a performance of *Rapport* would be arbitrary if the performer didn't know the tapes well, but it is more likely that Childs is referring to Morris's earlier complaints about the overuse of "clichéd effects" in modern string writing—the idea that to simply trot out the same effects again and again is somehow arbitrary.

11. *Lissajous* for prerecorded tape and oscilloscope (1971; film version, 1973). Notes: http://ecmc.rochester.edu/rdm/notes/lissa.html (accessed August 31, 2019).

12. Arnold Schoenberg, Radio Lecture on the Variations for Orchestra, op. 31, Radio Frankfurt, March 22, 1931.

13. Karlheinz Stockhausen, *Hymnen* (1966–67).

16   Gordon Mumma (b. 1935)

MICHELLE FILLION

In the first week of July 1972, Barney Childs interviewed Gordon Mumma in New York during a brief hiatus in the latter's busy schedule. Childs had prepared assiduously. He gently guided their conversation through the primary channels of Mumma's activity in recent years—as composer, performer, instrument-builder, and wizard of sound technology with the Merce Cunningham Dance Company (with John Cage and David Tudor) and the Sonic Arts Union (with Robert Ashley, David Behrman, and Alvin Lucier), preceded by his pivotal role in the ONCE festival in Ann Arbor (1961–65).[1] Fundamental to Mumma's work has been the value of collaboration in the creative process, whether with people, instruments, or electronic resources. Moreover, by 1972 Mumma was heavily involved in FM telemetry, a collaborative live-performance process by which the sound materials are generated electronically by the physical motions of the performers, as most recently explored in Cunningham's *TV Rerun* (1972) and his own futuristic *Ambivex* (1972) for cornet with what he calls in the score a "phantom myoelectrical telemetering system."

Childs's interview occurred at a pivotal moment in Mumma's career. It neatly intersects an intense roster of activities over the entire year that provided the content and context of their lively interchange. At the outset of this period came Mumma's collaboration at New York's Museum of Modern Art (MoMA) in December 1971, which featured Cunningham's solo dance event *Loops* paired with the first of Mumma's live telemetric works, *Biophysical and Ambient Signals from FM Telemetry*. February 1972 saw the two-week Cunningham Dance Company repertory season at the Brooklyn Academy of Music, which included the premieres of *TV Rerun*, for which Mumma's *Telepos* (1972) was swiftly adapted, and *Landrover*, with his live-electronic collaboration with Cage and Tudor. The third premiere, *Borst Park*, was danced with Christian Wolff's *Burdocks*, with Mumma on horn in the onstage ensemble.[2] This repertoire was also featured in the Cunningham Dance Company's spring 1972 tour in North America. Sandwiched among Mumma's Cunningham commitments was a series of Sonic Arts Union events, kicked off in New York at MoMA (February 19), and including a short European tour capped by their quartet of premieres at Pro Musica Nova, Bremen, Germany, in May 1972.

When Childs sat down with Mumma, the latter was fresh from the sixtieth birthday celebration for Cage at the New School in New York (June 30, 1972), as featured in this interview. Mumma was about to leave for a short teaching stint at Dartmouth College in later July, followed by his participation in the International Carnival of Experimental Sound in London (the so-called ICES festival, August 13–26, 1972), for which he wrote a review.[3] From there it was off on the whirlwind two-month European tour with the Cunningham Dance Company that brought the ensemble to the Festival of Arts in Iran, the Venice Biennale and St. Mark's Square, Belgrade, the Warsaw Autumn Festival, Sadler's Wells in London, and cities in Germany and France.[4]

The close of the Cunningham tour in Paris initiated a turning point both for the company and for Mumma. February 1973 would see the final major American tour of the Sonic Arts Union in Upstate New York. Its members were increasingly engaging with the academy. Mumma quickly followed suit, beginning a full-time position at the University of California, Santa Cruz, in September 1973. It would convert to a professorship in 1975. Although Mumma's new entente with academia required that he curtail his touring activities and loosen his connection with the Cunningham company, it also encouraged his planned reengagement with composition for traditional instruments to which the interview alludes. Accordingly, Mumma's self-distancing from the lure of "the academic thing" throughout this interview, capped by his insistence that "freedom is more important to me than the sense of security" afforded by a university appointment, must be taken with a grain of salt.

Among the topics touched on in the interview, the ONCE festival in Ann Arbor assumes pride of place. The handful of years since the last festival had seen its importance swell to a degree "even greater than I would ever have imagined." Here Mumma signals ONCE as an "amazing proving ground" for a young bunch of "pretty obscure kooks," many of whom had "gone on raising hell in various successful ways." Among these was Childs, whose *Interbalances VI* (1964), with Mumma on horn, had been featured at the fourth festival (February 26, 1964).

The interview identifies the early 1970s as a turning point in electronic music, as the availability of increasingly inexpensive and portable commercial equipment facilitated live-electronic music by soloists or small ensembles. Yet Mumma's vigorous engagement in do-it-yourself electronic instrument building—most recently the telemetric belts for *Telepos* and the telemetric glove for *Ambivex*—also promotes a healthy skepticism of large, bolt-down, one-size-fits-all institutional studios as fitting none.

The swirls of controversy surrounding the programs of ONCE and the Sonic Arts Union had provided a tough school in how to deal with backlash from audiences, critics, and concert organizers, particularly in the high-powered hub of New York City. It is no wonder that the topic returns repeatedly. Mumma has always been concerned with the ambiguous role of the critical press and of audience response in shaping what a composer does. He echoed the sentiments probed here in a communication with John Zorn first published in 2009: "Audience reaction has no bearing on what I compose. . . . My work may have some influence on the thinking of others, but that is not my compositional intention. With few exceptions, the audience is an unreliable mirror with which to evaluate one's own creativity."[5] At the base of these words is Mumma's unshaken confidence in "what I had done and what I was doing," a sureness of voice that permeates his creative work and how he speaks of it.

Gordon Mumma: Interview

BARNEY CHILDS: What has your work been like with the Cunningham dance group?

GORDON MUMMA: Fundamentally, it was David Tudor's idea that I should work with them. They needed some technical assistance. Electronic technology was getting out of hand—between John [Cage] and David, they had every new toy going. When I joined them for a summer European tour in 1966, they had what at that time must have been the world's largest malfunctioning toy box. Since then, we've worked on a collaborative basis, the three of us, technically as well as compositionally. Probably half of the new pieces is done by John Cage, David Tudor, or myself, recently more in combination. The other half is outside composers' commissions. We must have an average of two new works a year; this year it's been three, so that's ten or twelve works since I've been with the group.

The collaborations started with a movie score that we did for a film [*Assemblage*] of the company in San Francisco (KQED) in 1968. Since then we've done a couple of pieces: one in which we worked at the same time, and another we divided up into sections.[6] I do one, David does one, and John does one. Which one comes where is decided immediately before each performance. We've established a way of working [in] which we all have to be responsible about what we're doing, but which leaves us a great deal of freedom. To call it collaboration may be stretching it, when each of us has a third of a piece completely independent of the other. Yet we think individually about what will be good for the others, either because it's in opposition or complementary.

BC: How much of these pieces are composed in real time? How much are pre-composed?

GM: It depends on the circumstances of each piece. With the dances, I'm personally becoming more interested in things that are not so much musical pieces as
such, but rather things that happen because of the circumstances. For example,
I did my own new piece for the company for a dance work called *TV Rerun*,
called *Telepos*—the word I invented. I designed some belts which contain accelerometers for the dancers to wear. The accelerometers are attached to oscillator
circuitry on the belts and are transmitted by FM wireless to the orchestra pit.
It's a telemetry operation; the nature of their movements and their positions in
space when they're not moving make up the sound material. I obviously had
no preconceived notion about what the structure would be. It would come
out of what they were doing. The dance itself has a fixed physical vocabulary,
but the choreography varies according to choices the dancers can make about
when they go on and off the stage. We have ten dancers, but there are only
three belts for financial reasons. The dancers change belts from one to another
any way they want to, so there may be occasions when there may be no belts
at all on the stage. There are other occasions when all three of them are going.
In the pit I can control the sound by choosing to have the belt switched on
or off—that it's heard by the audience or not—and by mixing them together.
Essentially it's a collaboration between myself and the dancers.

BC: But these essentially ephemeral, immediate things cannot be done again?

GM: Right. The performance is done many times, but the details are not the same.
The character is much the same—the tweedledum sound that these belts make
is part of the character of the piece.

BC: I can't say I'm going to do *Telepos* without the Merce Cunningham Dance
Company.

GM: That's not necessarily true. Though the original idea came from working with
this dance group, it could be another dance group doing something else. Or it
could be something else that moves.

BC: I'm thinking back to many of the early '60s pieces for specific players. You've
moved out of that?

GM: Not really. These are for players, except that they are players that move. Essentially I'm using them as my source of sound. Another piece I've done just
this past May, called *Ambivex*, uses an extension of this principle. It's for any
number of instrumentalists—it happens to be one at the present time because
that's the only amount of equipment I've got. I play it on trumpet in which
the accelerometers are mounted on my fingers. There's notated material for
the trumpet player. The modifications of the trumpet sound occur according to accelerations and decelerations of the fingers, which are different for
each player. You can push down the first valve and get a certain sound on the
trumpet. But pushing down the first valve and what goes on muscularly varies from one person to another. Some people push down the first valve and

nothing happens to the other three fingers; other times, some combination of movement happens, so the neuromuscular responses of each player are going to be different. It doesn't necessarily have to be trumpet; it could be in the left-hand fingers of the cellist. I'm using something else for the formal structure: a notated score and specified instruments in which the peripheral modification of sounds comes from the unique myoelectric and muscular characteristics of each player. But the idea came from an even earlier piece using already exist-ing kinds of human activity to make modifications of sound effects where the material is somehow notated or given in advance.[7] Or, in *Telepos*, to generate the sound itself directly with dancers. I'm still concerned very much with live performance, and integrating the toys that I make with what people do, or with the circumstances that people are in.

The word "telepos" is very funny. I was interested in the idea of position at a distance. I messed around with words. The "tele" part, that was clear. What was I going to do about position? I called Christian Wolff (he's a Greek scholar), and he said the word would be "telephesis." I said, well, that's a little too academic for me. Maybe I can make use of the word "pos"—that's just a fragment of the composition. He said, "Well, that's very interesting, since you're working with dancers. The Greek word 'telepoús' means 'far afoot.'" I said right on—we'll use it. I said it sounded like a Greek god to me. He said in Greek mythology there are probably thousands of concepts given various names that pass as minor gods and goddesses anyway. So it turned out to be one of those little twists that justified itself poetically.

BC: Looking back, do you have more perspective now of the importance of ONCE?

GM: Personally, the importance is greater than I would ever have imagined. I don't know historically. Certainly it affected the lives of many people to have such a free-swinging festival in the early '60s in the cornfields of the Midwest. Looking back on what we did, who we had there, we had an incredible bat-ting average. We brought in Berio in 1960. OK, that was a good bet—it was pretty clear then that he was going to make it. But we brought in some pretty obscure kooks at that time, and I'll bet that three-quarters of them have gone on raising hell in various successful ways.

Looking back over those programs, it is really pretty astonishing who we got. More important, personally, was that it was such an amazing proving ground. We were doing things which really would be impossible now, not only because of the cost. But somehow our innocence about what we were getting into then gave us a great protection. We used to do concerts with nine pieces, the shortest of which was twenty-five or thirty minutes. It was unbelievable. The audiences sometimes complained that they were very long, and yet now and then I run into these marathon concerts. What should one's concept of the length of a concert be? I go to forty-five-minute concerts and to six-hour concerts, and it's all very much more an acceptable possibility. On occasion I listen to tapes and the quality of the performances for the most part could always have been better. But some of it was just remarkable. I still don't quite know how we did it, except we did it—a lot of us, six, eight, ten or twelve people, plus a peripheral ladies' auxiliary of remarkable people in Ann Arbor.

The most extravagant festival we did must have been six concerts in 1964. I don't think we spent more than three or four thousand dollars on that. We did things that would be just out of the question—more than a hundred players from all over: chamber chorus from Brandeis University, Illinois percussion ensemble. You couldn't do that now for less than forty or fifty thousand dollars.

I was a country boy, basically, when I finally came to New York in 1966. I came with a job, because I was working with Merce Cunningham, but I had no particular sense that I was conquering the big city. The conquering had been done. I felt very sure about what I had done and what I was doing. I never got intensely involved in the concert life of this city, outside of the Cunningham dance company, until the past year or so. A very strong group sense has developed here among various composers who are unrelated musically, but related very strongly in a sense of social need. That was an amazing time. It happened in San Francisco; it happened in various [cities]. At the time, I thought, "It's a damn shame that it doesn't make more of a dent in the American cultural fabric." Why doesn't the *New York Times* decentralize more effectively? Actually, it did in a funny way. Nobody in New York recognized it, but people elsewhere did. Now all kinds of stuff in the last ten years goes on everywhere, and it doesn't make any difference about New York. But it's a little hard for the paranoid in those positions, at that time, to feel like they're not pissing upstream.

BC: Are you still with the Sonic Arts Union?

GM: The Sonic Arts Union still goes on. We made a recording four years ago, but it just got out.[8] For the first time we got a grant from the State Arts Council of New York. We made some new works with it and did some concerts in New York City under fairly carefully controlled conditions. The Sonic Arts Union had the sense of collaboration only in a social way, really not so much musically. We used to call it the Sonic Arts Group, but Bob Ashley decided that "group" didn't represent what we were in the traditional sense. We support each other's logistics of putting on these concerts together.

We just finished a European tour in May. It was only a two-concert tour, but one was at that big festival in Bremen [Pro Musica Nova]. And because we're spread out across the country—Ashley in California and Lucier in Connecticut—David Behrman and I are really the only two people who collaborate in a creative sense. We've always collaborated technologically, and we're now working on a piece which uses chamber-sized multimedia aspects as well as music.

I'm not as comfortable with the Sonic Arts Union as I would like to be, partly because I'm getting spoiled. In the Cunningham Dance Company, there's somebody who takes care of the management. I don't have to think about it. Sonic Arts is still a quasi-guerilla operation. If I go on a four-week tour with the group, I can't tell anybody where I'm going to be, because I don't know. On the other hand, what we do artistically is still extreme enough in its risk that after some concerts I have trouble deciding what I liked and didn't like. It's still challenging my sensitivities and sensibilities, and I often feel indignant about things that happened artistically. That's good to have not gotten so comfortable about that.

BC: What do the Europeans think?

GM: The Europeans tend to be less enthusiastic than the Americans. But that's not unique to the Sonic Arts Union. It has to do with a lot of innovative art activities depending on where you are. Germany and France are now a lot more conservative than England or Sweden. We get some pretty funny reviews. Drumming up concerts there is becoming increasingly difficult because there are places that always want you back, but there are also places that had you once that wouldn't think of inviting you again. We performed in Bremen some weeks ago, and some guy sent out letters for the next tour. We got a letter from Hamburg from a person who said they had heard our performance in Bremen and there would be no room for the Sonic Arts Union in Hamburg. Which is nice: no room at the inn.

Each time we go, something is different. The repertory is different; the person who creates the scandal one time is not the same one who creates it the next time, so it always varies. The only thing that I'm distressed about, in Europe particularly, is discovering that you've been invited because you are to be that year's scandal. That's beginning to piss me off. The glamour is fun the first time, but it's usually those big festivals where they've gotta have one weird novelty number, some young American freak-o thing. The guys who run those festivals look around and know what's going to happen. I'm tired of not being able to hear my piece while I'm playing it for the ruckus in the audience. Those scandals have lost their kick since *Le Sacre*.[9] It doesn't mean anything any more. I'm sorry that we weren't able to collaborate on a basis which the ONCE group did. Times have changed.

BC: There was collaboration in Ann Arbor.

GM: Yeah. People got mad at each other, and we didn't really do collaborative pieces so much but we started into that area with the ONCE group, which was a theater ensemble. There we had some fundamental collaborative endeavors.

But logistically we were able to get some very complicated concerts organized, under circumstances which are now out of the question.

BC: Why do you suppose there are so many groups now? You read the groups that are to be at [the ICES festival] in England this summer.

GM: Certainly the problem of sharing equipment. We aren't just playing piano trios any more. Somebody's got to have the preamplifiers and the power amplifiers. There's no question that the rock phenomenon gave a strong impetus to the idea of what the electronic music group was. The fact that groups are so flexible—they come and go (personnel change); they expand or diminish—would not make it as sturdy an institutional idea as one would expect. But it's just the efficiency of being able to share equipment, of being able to collaborate with ideas when that becomes feasible. This has happened gradually over a period of ten or fifteen years. There's a lot of music which implies collaborative group activities. Cage's work, your work—a lot of things in which you could put together the elements of a social ensemble. Historically minded groups play a lot of that music. I expect to see some soloist-type activity involved with live electronics becoming more prevalent.

BC: That's [Salvatore] Martirano's bag now: a virtuoso performing.

GM: It's happening because it's time for it to happen. But it's also happening because it's getting cheaper to use equipment that way. The technology is getting relatively inexpensive. Most of my works in the past three or four years have been solo live-electronic works because I could take the full responsibility for them. I could afford complicated enough circuitry to keep me involved in the process of each piece while I can play it enough times to make it a repertory piece. That would have been out of the question six or seven years ago. I couldn't have afforded either the time or the money, nor could I have carried the stuff around. As usual, the technology has a good bit to do with it.

The group effort also makes it possible to promote recordings. I've tended to consider recording as secondary because of my concern for live performance activity. We do that on the side, but it's not our prime issue. But for people who are involved in recordings it's the issue of making a diverse program on the recording, getting it out, and being able to peddle it. When the Sonic Arts Union made their recording, we did all the engineering ourselves. We went to Brandeis, where Alvin Lucier was teaching. We got recording machines in, and we took turns doing that work. It was really very much a collaboration. Although we did individual pieces, we played in each other's pieces, but in the recording process, we exerted a lot of control. We did everything with that recording including, and right up through, the lathe work. We worked with a custom pressing service and we were at the cutting session; when decisions had to be made, we made them. We got a very good recording as a result. That's becoming more common, particularly as little rock studios are going up. People can work on that group basis very efficiently with recordings. The Sonic Arts Union is now concerned about recordings simply because we do a piece six, eight, or ten times, then it's time to go on to another piece. The configuration of equipment, the personnel that are involved, gets lost. There's nothing left unless we make a recording.

BC: The documentation.

GM: We're trying to do very high-quality documentation. I don't think any of us really had that concern until two or three years ago. We discovered that we could do it when we made the Sonic Arts Union recording in late 1967. It was a *lot* of work: eighteen-hour days, seven days per week. We ended up with something terrific, and we had tapes we could peddle to anybody. Like being a small businessman again. We had a product we believed in.

BC: You feel that continuing in this fashion is superior to academic . . .

GM: Well, I decided several years ago that I wanted to do my own work and see if I could survive at it. I've had the incredibly fortunate circumstance of being invited to join Merce Cunningham. That's a part-time project, as most modern dance companies are, but it's twenty weeks of the year or better, so it's a guaranteed situation for me. I've done the academic thing, but I do it on a limited basis, partly because most academic circumstances are concerned about moonlighting. When I've been invited to teach at schools—Illinois, Dartmouth, Brandeis, various places—they are very interested in me precisely because I have that performance experience. I don't have any academic credentials. They want me because I perform, but they don't want me to perform; they want me for what I do, but they don't want me to do it any more. I'm sympathetic with them and I understand their problems. The class shows up at nine o'clock in the morning and the teacher's got to be there. Only one of those teaching experiences was so attractive that I considered seriously staying on: Illinois. Illinois for many years has maintained a remarkably performance-oriented, experimentally minded environment, a remarkable group of people there. That's a *very* special situation; I just don't find that in too many places. I'm not putting it down, it's just not for me.

BC: You feel happier outside of it?

GM: Freedom is more important to me than the sense of security. I've been able to get by in the last four or five years without having to do that. There's been some heavy, brief moments, but Jesus, it's better than going to faculty meetings. Because of my heavy performing schedule, I don't always have a lot of time for musical creativity—for making new pieces, for designing circuitry. If I was in the academic world, I'd be fighting the teaching schedule for the same thing. But I dig performing, something I liked from my first recital.

BC: Whatever happened to the old ONCE scores?

GM: Some of them are published. Roger Reynolds's works have been published. Ashley's works are published. A few of mine are. Some of George Cacioppo's are published. [Don] Scavarda, one of the most interesting composers then, has not published any of his works. He has also withdrawn largely from musical activities. That's the work of the ONCE composers themselves, but I mentioned earlier how impressed I am looking back at some of the stuff we did by other people. I'll bet at least a third of that music is published or recorded. I'm not claiming clairvoyance, but we were in where things were happening—we knew everybody. The underground was big. We did it all, and a very good part of it is available.

BC: What ever happened to the concern for visuals?

GM: That still goes on. I'm working with film now on a very experimental basis, using it as something that goes with sound but on a chamber scale rather than on the extravagant space theater scale that we did with Milton Cohen [Space Theater]. We're working on the same basis with the Cunningham Dance Company. The lighting designer, Richard Nelson, has collaborated with the sound people and with special lighting. David Behrman is working with special slide projections with the Sonic Arts Union. Ashley's still messing around with George Manupelli with film. The Sonic Arts Union has tended not to get too elaborate, because our specialization has been more heavily with sound and there's presently too much to do. If the right combination of visual or video artists could come along and work well with us, we would very likely get involved. But for me, when you project something on the wall, it's just that much more equipment. That's feasible with the Cunningham Dance Company, but the Sonic Arts Union is still too guerilla-like to get with that.

I haven't personally held the visual direction as a primary aspect of my work. Not for lack of interest, but for lack of feasibility, and because I'm so busy with the other aspect of sound control. I've just recently finished writing a section of a book which is concerned with live electronic music.[10] I considered everything in which electronic control is used for live performance arts as part of live electronic music. It has a whole section on lasers, on videotape, on television, and on multimedia generally. I keep up with it technically, generally on a collaborative basis with somebody else because it's too damn much to do.

BC: People today talk about the concert situation being intolerable.

GM: I'm certainly uncomfortable with it. Partly because what we do, we do in a concert situation almost as a cop-out. We're taking so much control and responsibility for the technology and all the other kinds of innovations that we're involved with. Yet there's that inertia, a point at which we say the sponsor's got a concert hall, we'll do it there. Sometimes we tear up his concert hall—movie screens, players wandering around the audience. The nature of our work would imply a greater freedom for the audience, and most concert situations bolt the audience in the seats. You just can't change the space. That's made it very uncomfortable. We take every occasion that we perform in something other than a traditional concert presentation in a traditional concert situation. In the musical activities that we do with the Cunningham Dance Company, it's become almost an obsession trying to stay the hell out of proscenium stages. For this forthcoming European tour, I don't think there's one out of four performances that are proscenium situations. In the United States, we seek out gymnasiums and the like just to be able to live with ourselves a little better and not have to make those kinds of compromises. This is not against proscenium theaters as such; it's just that our work has become more diversified in many ways. Everyone's work has. Audiences have gotten to expect, and even now demand, a different freedom about the performance ritual. A great part of the audience still buys records, or stays at home and watches the TV, drinking a can of beer. Live performance arts have had a more formal aspect, but there's clearly no need for it. Everybody seems to feel much better when there's no pressure to stay in one place.

The only waste has to do with these art centers, which are built duplicating—badly—previous institutions. That whole business is just going to dwindle away. Even in New York, where the performance traditions are pretty heavy, a lot of experimentation is being done in the presentation of traditional music in the concert situation. And the audiences really much appreciate it. The biggest thing here is the Metropolitan Opera in Central Park. It's free, but that's not the whole story. It's where you're not captive as an audience, and not quite as captive as a performer. I don't even worry about it unless I'm up against the wall somewhere. If you make a commitment to a concert and get into a situation which is deadly, you have to make the best of it, and by that time it's too late. For the Sonic Arts Union, we don't have the money to send an advance man. But for the Cunningham Dance Company, very often someone, if not Merce Cunningham himself, will very often go ahead, see what the spaces are and really size it up—if not Merce, then the lighting designer, someone who has got all that stuff together, to determine what all the possibilities are.

BC: A really luxurious format.

GM: It's costly, but it isn't necessarily luxurious. You can decide, as the Cunningham Company has done, that that's important. Otherwise we're just doing the circuit like the old Ballet Russe de Monte Carlo. We're paid badly enough, so we might as well have a good time. To do that, we have to do something else.

BC: What if someone came up and asked you for a piano trio?

GM: I would like that. I don't make any music unless it's going to be played. Now I would love to do a piano trio, or a work for string orchestra, or something. There's hardly a medium, hardly a combination of resources that doesn't interest me in some way. I would try very hard to schedule the circumstance so that I would do a piano trio. I can't immediately imagine what I would do, but I have some little ideas—those things always go through the head. It's funny how many times I think about writing a big orchestra piece. There's something immoral about it now—not artistically, but socially immoral. Virtually 90 percent of the orchestras in the United States are leftover racist bastions. It's an extravagance which requires massive subsidy to support. I believe in subsidy, but I had rather put my energy in something that just wasn't going to cost so much for the kind of effort that goes into it. But leaving out the social and economic thing, which is a drag, it's terrific. If someone were to pay a lot of money so that I not only could afford it but might come out with money in the bank . . . that wouldn't be enough. I'd have to have assurance that it would get performed quite a bit or that its performance circumstances would be in some sense innovative, so that I could learn from the performance experience as well as from the compositional experience. I stood to make a little money at great effort in a project for Expo '70.[11] It didn't have a great deal of performing life because the expo situation was time limited, but the innovative aspects of the performance circumstances were *so* attractive that it was really worth doing it. As it turned out, the project never made it through its scheduled time. The most innovative work I ever did, the most reckless I ever became, was trying out kooky ideas which proved to be successful within that project. I have yet to do that well in circuit design innovation. The same attraction would exist if someone wanted me to do a piano trio. I'd try to raise a little hell.

BC: When I visited you in Ann Arbor, you were even then concerned about what the well-appointed studio should be. Are you still concerned with this?

GM: Even more. It's become more involved, because the idea of the studio has expanded in our minds. The studio then was a place to work on tape primarily, though we were already involved with live electronic music. Now that there are hundreds of studios, many of which are the same and which tend to fix the working procedures, my concern with the idea of the studio has increased. What should a practice room be? What should an organ department do? The innovation in social use in this direction is going on at places like Mills [College], where actually it's more like an organ depot than a studio. They get all the equipment in there and put it together in different ways. Also, the technology changes so rapidly—you can update anything three months later. Some of the technological change is getting spectacular, and you can do it cheaply. I am not concerned for the studio as much in my own work, for two basic reasons. First, I move around too much; second, it all got ripped off when I moved to New York. The idea of bolting anything down became ridiculous. There's no point in keeping a tape recorder at home, as within a few months it's going to get ripped off. That's new; I never had to put up with that ten years ago. Also, there's no economic liability in a studio—there never was—but now performing live is an economic liability. My concerns are technically very similar. Circuit innovation is the same now as it was then; the drive for it, to improve my access to the sound material by electronic means.

One thing that's very much the same is my concern for access, in not making these huge devices, studios, or configurations of equipment that are very hard to use, except for maybe a few people. That was my feeling about the pedagogical situation a few years ago. It's still my concern, but not so much because there's a big commerce in electronic music. You can go uptown to Manny's Music, which used to sell guitars and drum practice pads, and it looks like NASA: synthesizers and rhythm synthesizers all stacked up, and kids in there buying wireless microphones. The irony is that access is easier outside the academic institutions now than it used to be, and with very few exceptions it's not much easier in the academic institutions. You still have to be involved with irrelevant prerequisites and all that. So my gripe is that we're moving in the same direction.

An interesting situation with studios is that there's now commercial equipment for electronic music. It's really international, not just the United States. I don't just mean that we can buy things cheaper from Japan or England, but rather the artistic approaches as well as technological approaches are different in those places than they are here. It helps in diversifying what's happening here. The cheapest synthesizer one can buy is a British import. It has its problems, but it's eminently accessible and has a switching matrix on it. That's made a whole lot of changes coming in from the outside.

BC: They were playing a bunch of tapes at Dartmouth. The guy sitting next to me said, "Say, this sounds like it was made in Stockholm!," and indeed it was. It seems you can always tell that the guy's used Buchla apparatus, you can always tell Putney sounds.

GM: I agree. We're in a situation when you talk about commercial synthesizers you can recognize the Putney or the Buchla or the ARP or the Moog. But you can recognize the Steinway as opposed to the Baldwin. It's part of the issue of mass production. The tape from Stockholm is a special situation. That's a really bizarre situation, Stockholm—all that money to build a state-of-the-art studio ten years old? That problem is common all over the United States. It's just not done on that scale. The University of Michigan duplicated the Columbia-Princeton studio ten years before they did it. They decided, "We don't want to take any risks, so we'll do something that has been proven to work." And it's absolutely irrelevant. The output of that studio is practically . . . well, not zero, but there's been a half-dozen pieces in the past ten years that have come from it. The Stockholm situation is just an incredibly extravagant music box. Those things have to do with misguided philosophies. I'm not distressed by being able to recognize all those synthesizers.

BC: I'm not suggesting that. The distressing thing is that, just as you are playing on this piano or that piano, the synthesizers constrain the composers into a kind of shape that really they might not have wanted.

GM: But that situation is no different from playing the clarinet or the bassoon. If you choose a certain resource, you can stretch it and batter it around as much as you want, and you can sometimes do some pretty freaky things. But finally you have to add other resources or work in some situation. I'm not distressed by that. I am distressed at finding in university situations that a music department has decided to buy six of one kind of synthesizer. If they have that kind of money, they might as well diversify it, if they're going to make the commitment. That kind of thinking is the same problem as buying six Selmer clarinets.

BC: Or Baldwin Microsonic pianos.

GM: Diversity is of prime importance, and now we've got it and can use it. I'm in no worse position being asked to make a piece on a Buchla synthesizer than being asked to write a piano trio. It doesn't intimidate me at all.

BC: Another thing against your having your own studio—in addition to the reasons you've already given—is that with the Cunningham Dance Company, you've got all the goodies there anyway.

GM: Besides which, I'm out of the stream of things because I don't treat instruments the same way that most people treat instruments—electronic as well as conventional instruments. I essentially build the instrument for a particular piece. For the next piece, I need a different resource, so I build instruments for that. If I use a conventional instrument like a French horn or a piano, and modify it electronically, it's for a particular piece. In the Cunningham repertory, every piece has a different configuration of equipment. I try my best to keep the redundancy low, so that we have continued diversity. If we did a piece for the Cunningham Dance Company that uses Moog synthesizers, we wouldn't do another piece that used Moog synthesizers. That would tie up that piece right there. One has enough trouble with diversity in the repertory without playing the same instrument all the time.

BC: Are the dances ready-made by the time you get the piece, or is it all mutuality?

GM: That depends again on the circumstances. There are works in the repertory in which the music was made first, the dance was made second. Sometimes the dance is independent; sometimes there are dependencies, cues and the like. Half of what we do is to work simultaneously with independent moving. The dance tends to be made before the music, if John or David or I are making the music. And sometimes the lead timing is disastrously short, really terribly short. I had about four weeks' notice in the most recent work, the *TV Rerun* piece, *Telepos*. That's the way of working, and the kind of confidence that Merce places in me when he doesn't give me any more time than that. I'm putting that gently—I could have used ten weeks, or ten months. But I have to be realistic in that circumstance. There are circuit ideas I'd had in my head or breadboarded, things that I'd tried out. That's the way to go: take a step that is working in the right direction and make something for it. But that's what we do in any circumstances. We work independently, but we know a lot about how each other is thinking. I generally get a chance to see the dance material before the piece is done. Not because I make a special effort because I'm doing the piece, but because I like watching those dances. I like going to rehearsals a lot; it's more fun than going to the movies.

BC: What do you think about what the next generation is doing?

GM: There's almost several generations now. The composers in electronic music who interest me most are those who are getting very early into the technology of it and have gotten by all the historical requirements. They don't study vacuum tube technology. They're already into particular individual electronics. I learn a great deal technically from kids who are barely getting their stuff together musically but who are at some conference somewhere. It's not that I didn't know about digital technology, but they came into it from a different direction. It's like meeting Lou Harrison. The view that you have of western music, say, is very different from him because he came into it from two other places. And it's sad in a way that music education is not as diverse as technological education. I'm very interested in the people who are working with procedures that I wouldn't dream of because I was never in that world.

I'm also pleased that access to dissemination is easier now for the younger kids. Records, we always thought, should be as cheap and dispensable as paperback books, so that you can get that stuff out and let it die a natural death. That's making a whole different kind of young composer. The fact that these kids are running around organizing concerts! In Ohio, a group called the Hunted for Newer Music came out of the University of Ohio this past year. David Behrman was there teaching, only for a semester. The students around him caught the spirit of what the Sonic Arts Union is into, at a time when there seemed no possible way to put it to use. They're touring around giving concerts for twenty-five dollars at every little college in Ohio. They're pretty weird concerts, just as kooky a thing as anybody ever did. They get through with a year of that, and they've got all the bugs out of the procedure. They're making pieces, which are often very efficient in the way they're working with concerts, whether people dig them or not. These kids are in their late teens. There was no possibility for anybody my age to do anything like that at that time. I run into people who put me down for being too old—I don't know what to think about that yet. It happens occasionally in seminars and things in universities.

It delights me that I'm finding myself in the middle often. People know that I work with John Cage a great deal. I'll run into people who are putting him down for all kinds of reasons beyond musical: social, economic reasons. And there are still people in the class that find Cage's work much too far out. Then I discover after we've worn Cage out that really they want to pick on me because I'm there and John isn't. And the group is split the same way. It's very flattering to defend your activities from being too reactionary. Do you get that?

BC: Yeah, I do. It's about half on both sides. I'm a generation back yet, and that makes it even more strange.

GM: Are you really?

BC: Not musically, but age-wise. I identify musically with guys your age.

GM: I've been thinking about the dominance of New York. A newspaper and all the magazines which are read throughout the country all come from here. And there's probably only a half dozen, maybe eight, critics who write about new music. Of those there's probably only two or three that have any brains and those two or three (giving them the benefit of the doubt), do a lot of shabby work, due to the pressures of writing and working in New York City (one of them is not in New York, but all the rest are). They're exhausted by the nature of things here and things outside are not covered. The one outside of New York City, Alfred Frankenstein, is very good. He has chosen his own style of life and he writes good reviews. There's a fellow in New York writing for the *Voice*, named Tom Johnson.

BC: A composer?

GM: I think he's still a composer. He wrote a four-note opera lately which I missed. Several friends of mine said it was really quite charming work. Johnson is the best critic we have in New York now for new music. The reason I say he's the *best* is, first, he's truly interested in it. Well, Eric Salzman is interested, too, but Eric has other things going. But by and large Johnson tells the truth about what happens. He speaks his opinion consistently, so that if you read his writing over a period of say several months, you have some assurance about what might have happened or about your own reaction might have been had you been there. I read his writing each time because I want to keep up with what's going on. I've got to know him, in a sense, through his writing, in a way that's predictable.

I can't say that about Donal Henahan or Harold Schonberg. You never know how grouchy they were before the concert. It is really a sad situation in that the dominance of the press in New York has made a kind of corruption out of it, which everybody knows. And that there's so damn few critics. I've hoped that *Source* or one of those other magazines might encourage some people to do reportage that was accurate and really informative. There's a magazine coming out of Seattle now, called *Numus West*. I've seen only one issue of it, but I learned some things about what's going on in parts of the world I don't get to. It was primarily reportage instead of critical writing, but that's beside the point. That function is really still awfully bleak. The universities might do something about

. . . I don't want to say "training" music critics, but nourishing some interest and activity in that direction. The situation may never change until the publication situation changes, but I wish it would. But that problem has gotten to be so acute now that the sensation of our time is the disputes about whether Robert Craft told the truth about Stravinsky. Are you ever tempted to get into it?

BC: I've got some theoretical articles; I've done reviews of concerts, reviews of records, yes, but I have no wish to become a professional critic. The only time I was so tempted was in Tucson. There was an available opening for a summer guy for the *Arizona Daily Star*, but it turned out that you might go to one concert you really wanted to talk about, then you had accordion graduating class recitals and hometown things, and this rapidly disillusioned me. Hal Budd had a job reviewing in LA, but he wrote so virulently about things that were bad. Why should anybody waste time doing a review of the Vienna Boys Choir?

GM: Wow. There may be no direct solution. Most of us are discouraged from taking any responsibility in that direction save an article now and then, which we can control fairly carefully. Because it's precisely what you say: there's so much garbage. Well, the problem is also with the dance and other areas. I thought for a long time that the critic really had no useful function in society.

BC: With the dance company, what possible difference can it make when you do the same dance in Cleveland, Omaha, Milwaukee, Denver?

GM: That doesn't make a lot of difference when you get reviewed out there. It was the surprise of my life to do a concert with Robert Ashley in New York in the early '60s and to get one or two or maybe even three terrible put-down reviews. Really, they really laced us all over the place. From those reviews we got concerts, whereas good reviews from elsewhere didn't make a damn bit of difference. It was the power situation in New York. I'm not sure that the critic doesn't have a function. I didn't read reviews. I never bothered to get up early the next morning and get a paper. One has to collect them for publicity purposes if you're trying to survive. But there *would* be a function if the critic could illuminate what's going on in new music and newer performance arts: we could get some real information.

BC: He can't most of the time. But what other function?

GM: Well, then the only function I can see would be publicity. You get a good review or a bad review; you clip out what you need, you put the guy's byline on it if he's got a good enough byline. One of the first brochures I made for an organization was with a professional brochure maker. I supplied all the information. We had some very astute comments from obscure papers and various places. But we didn't want any of that shit. We just wanted the stuff that came out of the *New York Times* or *Newsweek* or *Neue Zeitschrift für Musik*.

There's concern about reviews in New York because this is a publicity town. We have the whole publicity madness here. I had a kind of absurd situation last week; we did a John Cage concert at the New School. Gregory Reeve, a composer and percussionist, organized it and it involved five musicians: Max Neuhaus, Phil Corner, James Fulkerson, Reeve, and myself. Because this is Cage's sixtieth birthday year, the place was swarming with photographers. In the performance of *Atlas Eclipticalis*—which was a very gentle, quiet thing for percussion instruments—the racket from the cameras was just ridiculous. I'm conducting, making the clock; I'm going very slowly and everybody is making these small sounds. You could have done it all with seven pictures. When the piece started off, the clicking started clanking. OK, I'm not going to stop the performance; after fifteen or twenty shots you'd think it would stop. It didn't. My left arm would get down and the right arm would start; now it was time for a new picture. The trombone player would turn a page and that was time for a new picture. Absolute lunacy! We had tried very hard to make a recording of the concert. We had placed our microphones very carefully. Somehow the photographers were standing under the microphones. Peter Moore, the photographer of the avant-garde, was backstage, having taken considerable precaution because he knows about those things. He wasn't audible to the audience, but he was standing right beside a very critical microphone. A number of people asked for their money back because of the racket of photographs, and then I got a letter from John Vinton, which he sent in duplicate to a number of people involved with the concert, complaining bitterly about this publicity mongering. I had to agree with him entirely.

It's part and parcel with the problem of looking for things like *Source* and *Numus West* and whatever the hell else can get going. We lost *Synthesis*, right? It came and went like a bubble. . . . It was actually worth it for the article of Thaddeus Cahill. I suspect it's going to have to get diversified outside of the New York area. The power block is going to have to change. Then the only other hope is publishers who will do books and anthologies. If you get enough trenchant treatises like Virgil Thomson's book, it might be all right, but it's got to be a lot of those to make it.[12] Yet there certainly seems to be more interest on the part of publishers in the last four or five years. There's a lot of stuff on the way, making better access for the general public who want to get more information.

Notes

1. For a deeper treatment of the topics of this interview, see Gordon Mumma, *Cybersonic Arts: Adventures in American New Music,* ed. by Michelle Fillion (Urbana: University of Illinois Press, 2015).

2. See Virginia Anderson's introduction to Christian Wolff's interview, chapter 22 in this volume.

3. Gordon Mumma, "What We Did Last Summer—A Commentary on ICES 1972," in Mumma, *Cybersonic Arts*, 73–78.

4. David Vaughan, *Merce Cunningham: Fifty Years*, ed. by Melissa Harris (New York: Aperture, 1997), 182–86.

5. Mumma, *Cybersonic Arts*, 266.

6. *Signals* (1970) and *Landrover* (1972).

7. Mumma is alluding here to his *Hornpipe* (1967). The finicky technology of *Ambivex* would discourage him from extending this technology to other instruments.

8. Sonic Arts Union, *Electric Sound*, Mainstream Records MS 5010, 1972, LP.

9. The premiere of Igor Stravinsky's *Le Sacre du Printemps* (*The Rite of Spring*) is infamous for inciting what is commonly referred to as a riot.

10. Mumma, "Live-Electronic Music," in *The Development and Practice of Electronic Music*, ed. Jon H. Appleton and Ronald C. Perera, 286–335 (Englewood Cliffs, NJ: Prentice-Hall, 1975); excerpted in Mumma, *Cybersonic Arts*, 79–90.

11. Mumma's Sound-Modifier Console was constructed for the Pepsi Pavilion at Expo '70 in Osaka, Japan; see Mumma, *Cybersonic Arts*, 65–71.

12. Thomson wrote several books, so it is impossible to know which Mumma was referring to, but it may have been the recently published *American Music since 1910* (New York: Holt, Rinehart and Winston, 1971).

17 Loren Rush (b. 1935)

STUART DEMPSTER

I met Loren Rush when we both were in different nearby high schools in the East Bay. Rush, a year ahead of me, began at San Francisco State in 1953. I arrived there in 1954, meeting Pauline Oliveros in early 1955. When I first visited Wendell Otey's Composers Workshop class, I stayed to listen to Oliveros's music in the company of Rush and Terry Riley. We became a troika of support for her, a story for another time. This convergence of activity was prescient in light of the upcoming decade.

New music in 1960s San Francisco actually began in 1957 with the *Vortex* events created by Jordan Belson (visuals) and Henry Jacobs (music), with a dozen loudspeakers installed overhead on the perimeter of San Francisco's Morrison Planetarium. Rush was one of many who were very excited about this, and by the time I returned from military service in 1960 and had attended one of the *Vortex* events, they had twenty loudspeakers. I was ecstatic over the surround sound and overhead visuals that were a precursor of countercultural multimedia "happenings" to come. Also, in 1957 Riley, Oliveros and Rush founded a trio that "started the West Coast improvisation kick."

In San Francisco during the 1960s there was, besides the popular genres that became so famous, extensive underground activity in early electronic music as well as in new music for voices and instruments in more or less "classical" settings. Organizations and individuals presenting new music included then fledgling Pacifica Foundation's KPFA radio station; Oakland Symphony under Gerhard Samuel; Mills College; KPFA's Performers Choice, led by Rush and pianist Dwight Peltzer; and many independent composers and performers presenting their work. Most prominent was composer Robert Erickson who taught and/or mentored Oliveros, Riley, and Rush. Universities with progressive new music included, at Mills College, Luciano Berio, Darius Milhaud, Sal Martirano, and Morton Subotnick; at UC Berkeley, William Denny, Andrew Imbrie, Roger Sessions, others; at San Francisco

State, Wendell Otey, and William Ward; and at the San Francisco Conservatory of Music, Erickson and Rush.

However, the best-known organization was the San Francisco Tape Music Center (SFTMC), elegantly documented in a book edited by David Bernstein.[1] Principal composers and performers associated with the SFTMC included Oliveros, Ramón Sender (Baryón), and Mort Subotnick. The SFTMC had only rather temporary and loose relationships with universities in its early days. Interestingly, Robin Laufer, the director of the San Francisco Conservatory, was enticed to allow the beginnings of SFTMC to take place in a small room at the end of the large building-long costume attic where I happened to be teaching trombone. There Ramón Sender and I had many wonderful conversations.

It wasn't long before the SFTMC was "invited" to move elsewhere—the elsewhere being a dilapidated Victorian on Jones Street where many early electronic music concerts were held. After a fire that happened under murky circumstances, SFTMC moved to 321 Divisadero Street, where it remained for several significant years before relocating to Mills College in 1968 with Oliveros as director. A year before that, Erickson and KPFA's Will Ogden had moved to La Jolla to create the University of California at San Diego Music Department.

So much had happened in those six or seven years at SFTMC before those departures: a four-day Cage-Tudor festival, the premiere of Terry Riley's *In C*, Tony Martin's stunning visuals at many events, and various visiting composers from Japan, Sweden, and elsewhere. My solo performances of commissioned pieces by Berio, Erickson, and Oliveros represent an example of other performances by Robert Moran, Riley, Rush, and others. Meanwhile, the conservatory premiered works by Imbrie, Moran, Rush, and others. Improvisation was a regular impromptu "happening" around the conservatory, and we were all involved. At San Francisco State, Lukas Foss's improvisation ensemble concert was particularly notable. A last-minute improvisation with Rush, Erickson, George Duke, and me (recorded by George Craig) in a conservatory classroom was another astonishing gathering.

Just outside San Francisco important activities included Larry Austin's work at the University of California Davis, where I met Karlheinz Stockhausen (who was resident there in 1966–67) when I performed a concert that included my commissions. Barney Childs taught at Deep Springs, a small private college well east of Lone Pine, California. Even with that amazing isolation he was in touch with the burgeoning new music scene, especially in the Bay Area. In September 1966 I premiered his *Music for Trombone and Piano* at Deep Springs, with Childs on piano, a piece that I commissioned that featured many new effects and sounds including a passage in sixth tones.

John Chowning earned a PhD at Stanford University and developed and taught computer music programs for Stanford's Artificial Intelligence Laboratory. At the time of this interview, Rush had joined Chowning at the Stanford Music Project, and in 1974, Chowning, along with Rush and others, founded Stanford's Center in Computer Research in Music and Acoustics (CCRMA). By this time, Rush was developing his own work as well as assisting others. When I would visit Rush, he would take me to CCRMA and, eventually, he had designed a simulated abbey with lengthy reverberation modeled after the Abbey of Clement VI in Avignon, where I had recorded.[2] He especially enjoyed my imitations of electronic sounds on trombone. I was interested in special tunings because trombone lends itself to that. Rush talks about our work in tuning in this interview. However, I never understood the math of those tunings, whereas he did. At least, I managed well in building chords in just intonation, as evidenced in my solo recordings.[3]

Rush is as conservative and deliberate as I am. In his composing, however, the marvelous quality of his compositions makes the wait worthwhile. In this interview, he describes his work on a piece for trombone and soprano with electronic processing, a piece with great promise; alas, that work was never completed.[4] Rush is unique in his quest for beautiful sounds—a nearly lost art in an age of heartless electronics and computers—and very much a West Coast composer.

Loren Rush: Interview

LOREN RUSH: The qualities that characterize the West Coast development began in the '60s and came directly from Robert Erickson. It also came through the conservative establishment at the time. All of the young composers were encouraged to do something that made sense to us as individuals.

BARNEY CHILDS: This is true in San Francisco. Some western composers never heard of Erickson and are still very clearly individual.

LR: It has to do with the temperament of an entire state or country. If we have to tie something specific, then it comes down to individuals. Phil Winsor is a West Coast–type composer, even though he was raised and educated in the Midwest. But he lived here for a while. Something very marvelous happened to Salvatore Martirano when he was here for two years. His music was never the same again. All of a sudden he started writing with a new kind of vibrancy, freedom, and individuality, which you couldn't have predicted from his earlier music. I expect it was an influence back and forth; he was here with the rest of us. But might it have happened if he had just moved to some small town on the West Pacific Coast someplace? It's a kind of openness.

In San Francisco (which is all I can speak of because I spent very little time in the rest of the state), music is so superfluous that it doesn't really matter what you do. There isn't any game to play. You can do things in New York, become successful and build a career. In San Francisco you can't even figure out what they might be, let alone even possibly think about building a career. At Tanglewood [in 1964], I realized I had nothing at stake, because I ran across all these composers who really had something at stake. I thought it's not going to make any difference to *me* what happens. When I go home I'm going to have the same job, do the same things, and not worry about it. So we just don't have those pressures to conform.

BC: Do you think this has anything to do with the fact that a lot of younger composers are also jazz players? You are, Phil is. Does this really count for anything?

LR: I don't think so.

BC: Hasn't left any kind of . . . ?

LR: Surely it left some impact. You know Mel Powell was a jazz player?

BC: He's older. Maybe that's not the point, because if it works it should work for him, too.

LR: I just wonder because he was certainly a better jazz player than I was. Many other composers are jazz players. Martirano is a jazz player. It's hard to know what that might mean. One can say the freedom that he has comes from the jazz background. The other thing is that none of us who were jazz players were exclusively jazz players.

BC: Subotnick was a jazz player.

LR: Pauline [Oliveros] wasn't really a jazz player. Terry [Riley] only started playing ragtime jazz. He was a very fine Mozart pianist and didn't have any interest in jazz at all.

BC: I guess it doesn't work. What did you get from being in Italy for two years? Did it leave any mark on you compositionally or in the way you've thought about music?

LR: I don't think so. I used the two years to catch up on my instrumental music. I worked on existing projects. That was wonderful. Rome is just as decadent musically as it is architecturally; that's a vacation. I used to feel that if I didn't go to a concert I might miss something. Now, ever since having been in Rome, I've lost that compulsion, because I learned that I wouldn't ever miss anything.

BC: So it could have been two years of Ulan Bator. Did you get to know the scene there? Is there one?

LR: I don't think so. It's hard to be sure because you hear only the music of those composers being played. There might be a lot of wonderful things if I were to be introduced from person to person, but I didn't make that much personal contact. I was really busy just trying to get my own work done. It's a difficult situation. The European composer has the opportunity in terms of performance, recording, printing, all the publishers, but he can't make a living. So they are all at work doing something else. At least teaching music is related somewhat. When one teaches music, it is expected that one will also continue composing, whereas they don't have music in the universities. This can be very destructive, especially in the twentieth century, for composers to function. It's difficult for European composers, in that sense. So it's sad to go to new music concerts in Rome or Paris to hear things which have already been worked to death in this country in concerts! They've discovered improvisation in the last four or five years. They have an improvisational ensemble in Rome which is so naive. They'll give concerts totally out of control and uninteresting—just the worst improvisation that anyone could hear. In Paris, Marius Constant had a group which was much more sophisticated and did much nicer things, but after working four years they came to the level of improvisation that we had done here about ten years previously. They also came to the rational conclusion that this isn't a very worthwhile way to continue, and stopped doing it. Which is much more creditable: to have done a fairly good job and then stopped, rather than doing an atrocious job and continuing.

BC: Pauline said that they've discovered live electronics in Europe, and it's time we started doing something else. It seems that except in university music departments, the fascination for having everybody plugged in and contact mikes, amplifiers, and controls is no longer with us. People explored it, found out what it had, and shipped it out. Have you been tempted to fiddle around with it?

LR: Yeah, I do it.

BC: *Hard Music* [1970] is a live electronics piece. But the live electronics isn't the part that the music is all about. It's an aid rather than an end.

LR: My live electronics always have to do with straight amplification. That's a fantastic filtering system all by itself without doing anything else. I don't put any other filters of any type on the sound. Most pieces that I've done for the last five years have been for amplified situations, including the *Cloud Messenger*, which is really for amplified orchestra. It will have to have quite a few performances before anybody will get up the nerve to amplify that entire orchestra. *Dans le Sable* [1968] is for amplified chamber orchestra, and I've never had a performance when I've been able to amplify the whole thing. We still just end up amplifying parts of it, because one of the most difficult things in live electronics to do is to amplify a large ensemble. Although it's not new: they were doing it in the big bands for years. Woody Herman, Stan Kenton, and all of those guys were amplifying the whole band. But when you want to balance it as well as you would when you balance a recording, and have the same kind of quality control (which of course the jazz bands didn't have), then it's very difficult. The last performance we did with the ensemble, we used about six microphones and then we ran out of channels. I could have used about three more.

BC: Are you dissatisfied with the unamplified piece?

LR: Certain parts have to be. The speaker speaks in a low voice; he has to be amplified. The soprano has to be amplified because I don't want her projecting and because she's humming part of the time. This very sensual kind of hum comes only by putting the ear or the microphone up close. I amplify the other singers because I want the quality of singing softly, but I want the big sound.

The idea is to have very soft music which is bigger than life. It's what we get when we go to the movies, with the wide screen and the sound. A whisper fills the whole auditorium. People can watch movies and forget that that's happening. It's fantastic.

BC: It's accepted.

LR: Robert Erickson has this concept: in early *concrète*, with all the people making music, there was probably only one piece possible to make.[5] He didn't identify which piece that was. He did identify that with pure electronica that Stockhausen, with *Gesang der Jünglinge* [1955–56], borrowing some concrète technique, made the piece for that period, for that medium.

BC: Who wants to rewrite [Stravinsky's] *The Rake's Progress*?

LR: Yeah. I suspect that Pauline Oliveros has done that with live electronics: the piece. It's not that it was so limited as that it was good enough for the whole medium. You make one piece. When you get the best piece, that's the piece, and all the other stuff works up to that. She's probably doing other pieces, as she can't keep doing that piece. Some composers would, but she won't. Erickson also projected that computer music may have only one piece in it. Now his view is much more limited than mine—but I worry. There might only be one piece—maybe I won't do it. It wouldn't be so bad if I did it.

BC: Do you find computer music is developmentally at a point now where, like with languages, you can feel at ease with what you're doing? Do you feel occasionally vague frustrations that somebody hasn't done more to make your job easier?

LR: No, the Stanford Music Project [from 1974, the Center for Computer Research in Music and Acoustics] is so highly developed and so flexible that the only frustration I feel is with myself: either the limits of my own ear or imagination, or my own abilities for handling the material. It's so different from working instrumentally. This is the big stumbling block. I've been working with the project for six months, and the main problem has been that I had to change my whole concept of what it is to write a piece. I had an idea of what it was to write a piece: I would think of a piece, sit down, and do it. It was clear what I had to do without frustration, without confusion, without getting stuck. Working with a computer, I find out that you can't pre-form everything that you are going to do successfully in your head. With an orchestral piece, it's possible (I use "orchestral" because that's a standard reference for instrumental music). We know all the timbres that are ground into our heads from childhood, and we know intuitively how to mix them. Some people mix better than others, but we still know what they sound like. Most composers are extremely adept; orchestration is never considered a problem. You don't think about what you're doing; you just do it naturally. You forget how much information we have when we do this. Okay, I'm going to use middle C, and I have a tuba

and a flute, and I'm going to put them together, and I'm going to have the
tuba just a little louder than the flute. I can say that to you and we know two
things: the individual thing and one being a little louder. It's clear what happens when they go together.

These things do not exist with a computer. You have one sound, you have
your idea, you visualize what it's going to be. "Flutelike": it takes a long time
to make an adequate flutelike sound. We don't know how they construct the
sound from the group up. Some people with computer music have spent fantastically large grants with a lot of people working to synthesize a flute, and
not successfully. With this project we came very close in a very short amount
of time. John Chowning has virtuosity with almost any given sound. Given
one evening, he can come damn close, closer than any research project has
ever come in the past. Given a week's work on it, he'll make a very elegant and
close approximation. He's done it with bowed string sounds, which is fantastic,
because the complexity of that is almost overwhelming.

Once you get to that point, then you develop the other sound that you are
going to mix. When you put them together, they don't mix the same way. It's
funny. We have these given components and mixtures that we can put together
in traditional instrumental music, which we don't have with this kind of pure
electronic computer music. You can't predict how two things are going to go
together—at least I can't predict very well. I have a tendency to preconceive
entirely the sound in the finest detail the way I will with instrumental music.
Then I'm stuck with the problem of trying to make that sound, and then make
it thinking in terms from the instrumental to the computer. You can't lower
your standards the other way around. You can't say, "I'll start with a sine wave
and build it up; when I get something interesting I'll stop." If you do, you
don't know how they mix. You get mixing through experience, which people
in synthesizers get fairly quickly. They can mix them and see what happens.
They learn rather quickly, and they predict quite well what's going to happen
if you put things together. The synthesizer is a musical instrument which you
can learn and predict.

BC: Are you conceiving this computer piece as a tape piece to be performed to the
    audience through two speakers? Are you writing for the home player?

LR: No.

BC: You're not getting away from the concert situation? Many have vilified the
    concert situation extensively as a meaningless ritual.

LR: I'm not so fond of all those seats in rows facing the same direction. I'm wor-
    ried about the social implications of the architecture of concert situations.
    But it's perfectly nice to have a lot of people get together and listen to music.
    The two pieces where I'm using computers are both concert pieces. One, for
    the pianist Dwight Peltzer, uses amplified piano and four-channel tape. Four

loudspeakers for the tape playback and another four loudspeakers that amplify the piano surround the audience. With this computer we can actually do music which people can have nothing to look at. Loudspeaker music can be effective. John Chowning's done two pieces, neither of which have instruments. There is so much liveliness to the sound, and the presence of the loudspeakers isn't so obvious, because the sound moves through space so well. But we don't have points that this is coming from a box over here on the right, and this is coming from a box on the left. When the music is this genuinely spatial, you don't expect to have performers. There's no problem with the audience coming into that without previous experience; they can handle that well. It's not the same problem previously with electronic music, where it's coming out of two boxes.

Electronic music has tried to confront this problem (I don't think ever successfully), because they can't really move the apparent source of sound. We can do that with Chowning's program; we can plot the exact location in the room of where the sound is coming from. So it doesn't have to come from the loudspeakers any longer. It's a trick: you fool the ear. You make the ear think it's coming from there, or it's coming right through the room, or flying out. We also can change the acoustics of the room itself by changing the type of reverberation used, so it may sound as if the room is condensed into a long tunnel or it may be opened up into a wide reverberant space. This eliminates that problem of putting lots of people in a theater. Except it is more obvious why you don't have to have all the seats sitting in a row facing the same direction.

BC: On the other hand, here's Peltzer, and he's got to be somewhere.

LR: Naturally, his place is on the stage and he plays his piano. I'm doing something with the audience, which is special to this kind of piece and audience: to go to a concert and listen to a guy sit on stage and play the piano. But the piano sound doesn't appear to come from the piano, although it's recognizably a piano sound.

BC: And he is recognizably playing it.

LR: You also don't know the location of the tape. So you just have the pianist, and then you have this other business going on which he joins in. Part of the theater of this piece is the audience realizing first the distance between themselves and this pianist, and then this distance grows greater and greater as the piece goes on. It seems as if he's having less effect and that it's getting out of hand. There's something happening that doesn't have to do with the concert situation of sitting down and watching a performer play. In a sense, that goes against the concert tradition, except that I'm *using* that tradition. Listening to a recording of that piece couldn't be effective. The piece has to do with space and perception of space, and has to do with the fact that space is expanding. It's not expanding in your mind; it's expanding by the fact that the pianist is going further away. If you notice the way which we think about objects in space, sometimes they do have a way of moving. We're never too clear exactly what our relationship is to them. Is that thing really just there, or is it out twice as far as we first thought? This expands the concert hall: the sounds come from beyond the walls, and the piano.

BC: Will an engineer control his sound, or will he be controlling his own?

LR: Levels are set and he's amplified.

BC: And the other piece you're doing?

LR: For Stu Dempster, with soprano and computer tape.

BC: Again you are working with real sounds, so-called computer sound.

LR: For the Dempster piece I'm using also prerecorded sounds. I'm recording his trombone.

BC: Are they all trombone?

LR: Not all. It's like concrète music: just going out, recording your sources, and then manipulating them. I'm using the computer also. So, much to his amazement while he's playing, I can make his trombone turn into six or eight. He will try to perform in a duet with the soprano, and then pretty soon her voice just starts circling all around the room and then gradually changes into a set of bells. Then he's left with the problem of trying to relate to this occurrence.

BC: So the performance is the acting out of the dramatism in the music in a very real way. As you describe it, each time it's not just playing notes—a dynamic is happening. The trombone is in relationship constantly to these sounds and must respond in certain ways; it's conditioned to respond to the score.

LR: This demands a lot of the performer because he has to be extremely sensitive and also be able to match pitches with an uncanny skill, which Dempster can do. I wouldn't ask this of a standard orchestral player. It also demands the ability to make source tapes in tune to start with, so that I don't have to keep retuning his stuff. He can do it. One time when he recorded Erickson's *Ricercar à 5* [1966], he did each track on separate days, not listening to the previous track, because he was busy. They had some sort of sync method for recording them. Bob was listening to something and conducting Stu. Plus they didn't have the playback facility; they could just make one channel at a time. After four days, they put the four channels together, and they were all in tune. When it comes to listening, by God, there it is. You wouldn't ask that of very many players. He's done other pieces which work similarly, so I can ask Stu to record this. I'm also using various tunings with the computer, and I will want him to match those tunings. All I have to do is to give him a drone tape for the recording. If I say this is the sort of fourth I want and just play it for him, well, then he'll make it. And he will always be able to come back and match it later because the entire piece is done with Pythagorean tuning.

BC: When you get to do computer pieces, what will be next? Will it be a piece for a specific virtuoso?

LR: I haven't any idea.

BC: If somebody came up and said, "Write me a piece for bassoon and piano," would you do it?

LR: I can't handle commissions very well. Even the idea is an infringement. I've been trying to write the piece for Stu Dempster for about eight or ten years. At first he asked for a trombone piece, and I couldn't imagine what anyone would do with a trombone. I heard a lot of pieces, and I got the idea that I could write a trombone piece. I had enough interest in that because the performer stuck with it. But having someone ask me to do a piece for bassoon and piano for next year: it might take me five years to figure out what I wanted to do. I don't want to write a piece that I can just turn out.

BC: On the other hand, if suddenly an idea came to you in terms of bassoon and piano, then you'd write it. Like, who writes pieces for two pianos? But you did one.

LR: I'm not against it, but if I were asked to do another piece for two pianos, I couldn't do it because I don't have another idea. I don't get many ideas. I'm willing to wait for them because I have enough ideas to keep me busy. Usually I get about one idea a year; it takes me a long time to work out the one.

BC: What have you done with your student pieces?

LR: I don't know what to do with them. They are in a pile. I've used the backside of a lot of them for scratch paper. But then I wrote an awful lot of pieces, and I don't need that much scratch paper.

BC: You're not interested in having your early works played? How far back do you still consider legitimate?

LR: I have a piece that I wrote in '59 for soprano and small ensemble, and that's still performed. My string quartet was finished in '61. When I look at that, it still seems OK. That was my last student piece. I was still studying with Robert Erickson and also with William Denny. Anything before that is really not any good. I've written an incredible amount of bad pieces.

BC: When you got the Guggenheim, did you have a specific project that you were going to do?

LR: Yes, it was to come to the Stanford Computer Music Project. I didn't have any more instrumental pieces I was planning to do. I was thinking only of the pieces that I was going to do with the computer. Well, I still had another orchestra piece in my head.

BC: You said that the earlier orchestra piece had a sense of drama that you wanted to get away from in the later piece. Do you think in a sense of dramatism now or did you in the orchestra piece?

LR: I have for a very long time, but it's been hard to do it. That's the sole thought, as opposed to making pieces which fit together beautifully, or that you can say is a good piece. I don't think it's all that hard to make good pieces.

BC: Why is everyone making bad ones then? Well, not everyone. Are people setting aside a kind of immediacy, a dramatism?

LR: I should make a differentiation. Either you're trying to do a piece which has impact upon the listener, or you're trying to do something else. If you're trying to do something else, I'm not interested. So all the something-else pieces could be very good, but I would say that this isn't very good music. A piece which has dramatic impact is a lot more difficult than it seems on the surface. It's taken a long time to come even somewhere close to defining what I mean by it. What I'm saying right now will be very likely not the pieces I'm writing, because that's where I clarify myself. *The Cloud Messenger* was a statement which was clarified, finished, and it said something which I had worked toward. But by the time it was completed, I realized that I really wanted to do something else.

BC: Ben Johnston says that the rehearsal and performance of a piece of his is in *itself* this dynamism or tension. The drama is in the performance, the realizing, the reenactment.

LR: That's certainly the composer's experience.

BC: When you hear the piece done, do you think of it doing it again for you? That it's like a play, some isolated section of a closed dramatic form which is being reenacted?

LR: I would say there is a separation. One thing is what the composer and performers go through in preparation, which is very exciting about being in music. But the area I'm most interested in is entirely separate from that, which is what happens to a person who comes into a concert hall or listens to a recording.

BC: So you're thinking of a concert situation involving an audience? It's not a kind of pure discharge of an exercise where a work is performed?

LR: No, it matters very much to me. I judge a performance on the basis of how the audience feels. I'm able to listen to it technically and say whether it's a nice performance or not, but if it's successful, it depends on what happens.

BC: That puts considerably more of a responsibility on the players, doesn't it? About your piece where the guys just weren't able to do it; this hamstrings the piece because they are not able to communicate as well as to put out the notes.

LR: There are different circumstances. For example, for the average high-quality symphony orchestra, I write so that if they play their parts well it will work. And if it doesn't work, it's not their fault. I don't demand that they put in that extra rehearsal. Hopefully the conductor can do something. That's a different circumstance than in a piece for a small ensemble.

BC: Like the string quartet, for example, the virtuosity coefficient is very high. It seems to me in *The Cloud Messenger*, a non-virtuoso orchestra can play this piece well technically.

LR: I think in terms of orchestras that way. I write for large ensembles at the level of a good high school orchestra. The difference is that a good high school orchestra couldn't play it. The reason is that they can't play their instruments that well. I mean the virtuosity in which a clarinet player can play his instrument well, can play the notes, and, given luck, can play in tune. If I get that much to work with, it's fantastic. I don't demand anything else in terms of virtuosity or in terms of ensemble rehearsal or complex rhythmic situations and so on. I feel it's not necessary with an orchestra, and it's not the medium of an orchestra.

BC: For a small group you can ask this and expect to get it?

LR: A small group lives on this extra kind of virtuosity. It's why so few orchestral players are good chamber players.

BC: Do you feel that nowadays with guys like Dempster there is a greater store of intelligent virtuosity to draw upon, which has opened things up for the composer?

LR: Sure. If you are doing a piece for Stu Dempster, you don't write a piece for trombone. You write a piece for Stu Dempster. Then you assume that there may be sometime someone who may want to try that also and may be able to come close to what Stu Dempster could do. But you wouldn't set out to write a piece for Stu Dempster without a Stu Dempster.

BC: Some hypothetical virtuoso that hasn't been invented would be ridiculous.

LR: The virtuosity in the string quartet has double payoff. One, it's guaranteed that if they can't play it well, it will fall apart. If there's no chance that they'll get through a performance, I don't have to worry about bad performances. There's no way to fake it. The other is the biggest mistake I've ever made in a piece, in that I didn't have the quartet in mind. It's for a virtuoso string quartet with a second violinist that doubles on viola. The viola also has the problem of having the C string tuned down to an A, so he has to relearn his viola a little. I had some fantastic virtuoso string quartet idealized in my mind and which is given every possibility of the virtuoso string player on that instrument. What if you put them all together and play it? And this is the only piece, including all my student pieces, which never had a performance.

BC: What has interested me very much about your work is despite your presence in the very important San Francisco scene in the early '60s, you resisted going into indeterminacy in a way that very few people have. I don't know of a piece of yours that moves totally in that direction. Why do you think that happened?

LR: The West Coast improvisation kick really started in San Francisco with a trio that was organized with Terry Riley, Pauline Oliveros, and myself. This was before Lukas Foss and the other group in Los Angeles. You will find none of those three of our group ever wrote much music which requires improvisation because we realized improvisation was a different art. It was different when we were working together, giving concerts, doing recordings for film and things. We had a response to each other which we thought we could engender to other players and other pieces. I think we found out very early that we couldn't. It means that those who knew the most about it decided not to put it in pieces.

BC: That makes a lot of sense. The early '60s in San Francisco: it must have been really exciting. Whatever happened to the idea of an unself-conscious group? Nowadays there are so many groups all over the world. Yet there's not that spontaneous feeling of being together that the *ONCE* people and you people had that really changed the whole face of music. Are such groups kaput?

LR: I can't explain it because it's been here before I was here. There's been always an appreciation for variety among composers. It covers the entire West Coast, but specifically the San Francisco area. In the earliest times when composers were organizing concerts, the most conservative and the most radical would be working together without cliquishness. In a sense we just grew into this period. It's very clear: there wasn't a prejudice among many of our really solid old-time conservative composers in this area. There was no prejudice toward the new young composers, and there was never this feeling among the so-called avant-garde. And there never was any setting up and choosing sides. I find this every other place that I've been. In 1965 when I went to Tanglewood to have a commissioned piece played, I was welcomed as a representative of the West Coast avant-garde. This was a really big surprise to me because in the West Coast I have always been considered a very conservative composer. Therefore to deal with questions on panel discussions and have to represent and justify the avant-garde was a very annoying problem. That was my first realization that people think in terms of categories and pigeonholes. I hadn't really even thought of myself as being a conservative as such, except that I knew that Pauline and Terry and Bob Erickson were doing much more radical things than I was. But I just assumed that they want to do those kinds of pieces and I want to do this kind of piece. We didn't think of ourselves as being polarized in any sense.

BC: What did they think of you over there in Italy? Were you a certified genuine American avant-gardist when you got there?

LR: No, they didn't pay any attention. That was very nice. They had their own established performance group practice. They were playing a very uninteresting kind of new music; they were trying to pick up the most interesting things from around the world that pleased them, using the local composers and then visiting composers who have some kind of reputation. I had very little contact with the typical Roman new music audience. But when I had performances, I can't say they expected me to be any one thing. For one thing, they had never heard of me. Then when the orchestra played my music, on two occasions, they were dumbfounded by the surface conservatism and other confusing aspects which they couldn't quite identify. I think they just figured I was crazy.

BC: One of those things they couldn't quite identify with, which I've always found in your things, is your interest in making good sound happen. I think maybe this is a western thing—a distaste for bad sounds. The process, or anything else, has to go if bad sounds are the result.

LR: It's more general than that. I don't think that the many composers who are using the synthesizers say to themselves, "I'm going to do a piece which has bad sounds." There are two problems. First, if you are talking just about sound itself, you begin to think about what makes interesting sounds. Once you start doing that, then you are not likely to do pieces which have bad sounds. Second is the medium; for example, the synthesizing medium prohibits it. I suspect that you cannot get good sounds with synthesizers. The problem is that if a composer is determined to use that instrument, he has to accept getting dull, uninteresting, lifeless sounds, or he has to be naive enough to assume that these are good sounds. You don't have to accept that limitation with a computer, which is a bigger problem, because at least you have an easy cop-out with standard synthesizer music—that's what they sound like. With a computer it's extremely difficult to *make* good sounds. You have to face something that we've never really had to deal with, defining precisely what it is with the sound that you want to do. With a computer, if you define it, then you can get it. It takes a lot of work and a lot of time, and then you can get any kind of sound you desire. It also turns out that maybe there aren't any new sounds. In a sense there weren't any new sounds with synthesizers, because we had all kinds of buzzy, whangy, lifeless, and dull sounds. This was the new class of linear sound—new in a sense, but they're useless. The problem is, are there new sounds which are not useless? I suspect so, but I don't think there's going to be any fantastic new sound that we've never heard before or that doesn't sound very much like some other sound which we identify as being a very precious and personal sound.

BC: Even with a computer?

LR: Yes. Our environment is so noisy that we're bound to hear one way or another some damned good sounds. With a computer, you can make those sounds—if you can identify them, if you can construct them. But you don't have a new sound. You have a sound somebody heard before. This is the class of sounds which are useful. They're new in the sense that they're not instrumental sounds, but they're sounds which we're used to. I've never heard a sound which is so new that it does not belong in the class of some sound. This is very much like the ocean or maybe a little more like a waterfall. Maybe this is an interesting complex, nonlinear sound. Sounds like some gong I've never heard before, but it's clearly a gong sound. I just haven't heard that particular gong, but one might assume that gong might exist someplace.

Where the new sounds can be is in-between. We have one known sound—for example, soprano, human sounds—and we have mechanical sounds, like some high tinkly bells. I work toward creating sounds that are on the continuum between those two. I'll just change the timbre gradually until it's half a bell and half a soprano. That, in a sense, is a new sound, except we also start some classifications: even the new sound that was never in existence before has references. Our references are so strong and so varied that every sound that we have should fit somewhere on some continuum between two known sounds. I'm not really interested in new sound.

BC: What are you interested in with the computer?

LR: Let me give you an example. When I worked with traditional instruments, I very rarely asked them to do unusual timbres. I prefer to make "new" timbres of combinations of existing timbres. The timbral quality of the instrumental pieces comes from mixtures of timbre rather than asking the players to do something new or unusual. That has to do with virtuosity. You can ask that kind of virtuosity of a Stu Dempster. But you can't ask it from the fourth trombone player of the San Francisco Symphony. When they try, you wish you hadn't asked. It turns out better to give them something that they can do well, leave them alone, and then mix it, even unbeknownst to them.

BC: Which is what you are doing in the orchestra piece. It seems to work very well.

LR: I'm most interested in this marvelous area of known and loved sounds. For example, the sound of a harp, which is so simple that it usually only sounds good in very complex ensembles. But there is a concept of a super-harp: what could a harp sound like if it could be as resonant as if you had your ear right up next to the soundboard, or even more resonant? It still has all the characteristics of the harp. What could a harp sound like which is thirty feet tall rather than the standard height? That's not a new sound, but a very special category, and that's something we can do very well with a computer. John Chowning did one of the earliest studies with a computer. He did a synthesis of tabla drumming, but the tabla set ranged all the way from about one inch to thirty feet. When we identify the range of the tabla, this is its range and it sounds very much like that instrument. It definitely belongs in the class of the plonk, plonk, tabla instrument. Once it gets expanded, then in a sense it is an entirely new experience and a new instrument. Of course, we have this limitation of playing through loudspeakers, but also an advantage. It can be louder than any tabla you ever heard before in your life. He's continued taking known sounds, because, of course, if you try to synthesize a known sound, artistically it's stupid. Why do you need it?

BC: Just bring in a clarinetist and have him do it.

LR: However, if you're trying to find out how you're going to do it you'd better have some clear goal. Once you make a trumpet, then you may never do that again, but you have defined a class of sounds. Then you can make variances from the entire range. And this has been pretty much the direction that Chowning has developed and explored. The others of us who use this system have inherited it. It seems clear: in order to gain experience, to develop your own ear to timbre, you start off with a known object and move it out from that.

BC: Why do you say that 1915 is the year that it all goes downhill or uphill?

LR: That has to do with music history.

BC: Is music history a valid option to those of us now who are writing? I think it is. Are we really concerned with what guys were doing in 1915 as far as sounds are concerned?

LR: I think so.

BC: But then it is a live music history.

LR: I think it's especially live, because in a sense music history deserted us in 1915. It all goes back to poor Arnold Schoenberg trying to figure out what to do with himself and coming up with this absurdity, the twelve-tone row. He had apparently some compulsion to do something that didn't make any sense, and he succeeded. So we were deserted by music history because we had a whole period between 1915 and the time that composers in my generation started working, where people were writing music that didn't make any sense. This never happened to any of our predecessors before that. In any other time you grew up in an ongoing musical culture which made sense when you could use the terminology, the tools . . .

BC: . . . the common practice.

LR: The common practice, which you had at the time. It comes back to synthesizing sounds with the computer. You have clearly defined points in time, concept, and so on from which to develop. What happens is that in our generation all the common practice music is not making sense. It's a very difficult spot to be in and also very challenging; first you have to master the current craft in order to really decide for yourself that it's silly.

BC: Is this what an academic education is for? So that you can learn what's foolish? The whole academic learning thing: they say all it does is set you back.

LR: I don't think so. It varies so much from place to place and location to location.

BC: How did it work in your own terms? Did you learn what not to do?

LR: I was fortunate because my first composition teacher was Robert Erickson, and I studied with him constantly for a period of at least six years. When I was first in college I was taking privately with Erickson. I was also studying at Berkeley. Berkeley was at this time a very marvelous school of profoundly conservative composers. In order of conservatism from least to most was William Denny, Andrew Imbrie, Seymour Shifrin, and Charles Cushing. No one was pushing twelve-tone technique. These people were trying to find something in music which was valid and based on not just traditional values, but proven values and communicable ideas. I resisted them very much, being at the age when you resist that thing. What I got from them only showed up much later: I learned a lot about craft. And they were carrying on the tradition. It was almost a last stand; it had been criticized. Indeed, I criticized them at the time. Simultaneously I was studying with Bob Erickson. His teaching had nothing to do with style. I never found out until much later that he was writing tonal music at that time; I thought he was a raving avant-garde composer. As well as I thought I knew him, I would only find out after several years what his music was like. He was intent on helping his students develop their own individuality, to an unusual extent when you consider that Terry Riley and Pauline Oliveros were studying with him at that time. And we have almost nothing in common in any obvious sense.

I think that the only time that the academic became too academic is when they started buying the avant-garde after everybody else decided it was finished. They weren't buying it with conviction. They were teaching stuff which they really couldn't believe, but they felt they could trick themselves. Historically, this is in correlation with the time when Aaron Copland and Arthur Berger start writing twelve-tone music. All of these guys had been so critical of it. They didn't believe in it any more after they started doing it than before. Then all of the universities had their own twelve-tone composer come in. At that point, you might say that that kind of academic education is not even useless, but maybe a waste of time. It's possibly harmful. I question whether you can do any harm to a talented student and if a teacher has than much influence, but a teacher can certainly waste a student's time.

BC: It's curious that your summer at Tanglewood there were so many other people there who have since gone on to make shapes for themselves. It must have been a very marvelous time.

LR: Of course I don't have any follow-up experience. I was there just one time. That was the first time they were doing a commissioning series. It was all pretty safe; most composers were doing exactly what you would expect for the period.

BC: Was Tanglewood a good thing?

LR: Not particularly. Sure, it was good in a sense that when you live in the San Francisco area, you're extremely isolated. You're isolated not in the sense of music tradition and good performance practice (this is all extremely well-developed in this area as any other) but you're isolated in the sense that you're not too sure. Take San Francisco and New York. In San Francisco we know no more what was going on in New York than New York knows what was going on in San Francisco. However, since New York assumes that the only thing of importance is going on in New York, therefore if you're going to San Francisco, you might as well be going to New Zealand. Maybe there's something going on in New Zealand! So it was a very good experience to be confronted with this. In fact, I was really disappointed that I didn't come well-prepared with Stetson hat and cowboy boots and six-guns, because that's what they expected. It was an education for me just to see what their reaction was to this strange creature who came from San Francisco. At that time I was the only composer west of Chicago in that series for that year, and, I suspect, probably for the entire history of it up until that time. There certainly weren't very many, and many of those have been tempered by living in New York for a while. Another enlightening experience from that was seeing the power that the musical establishment has over the young composer. Also, I wasn't accustomed to panel discussions; it never occurred to anyone here to ask a composer when he thought about what the future of the orchestra should be, would be, or could be. People who had a good feeling for me would warn me to be more careful, that I shouldn't be just going around saying the kind of things I was saying, because it would do me no good. There was probably a period in which it did me no good.

Notes

1. David W. Bernstein, ed., *The San Francisco Tape Music Center: 1960s Counterculture and the Avant-Garde* (Berkeley: University of California Press, 2008).

2. Stuart Dempster, "Standing Waves 78/87," for trombone and effects, prod. by Loren Rush (1978), on *In the Great Abbey of Clement VI* (New Albion Records NA013, 1987). This track uses the CCRMA simulated Abbey.

3. Dempster, "Standing Waves 78/87."

4. A two-minute version appears in Loren Rush, "Study for *Reverie*," Stuart Dempster, trombone, Renée Grant Williams, soprano, on *The Digital Domain: A Demonstration*, Elektra 9 60303–2, 1983.

5. *Musique concrète* is a style of electronic music that uses recordings of sounds as source materials that are then modified by the composer.

18 Michael Sahl (1934–2018)

DAVID NEAL LEWIS

On March 29, 2018, composer Michael Sahl died in New York City; when I checked a year and a half later, Google thought he was still alive. Such is the lot of the outsider American composer who does not attach himself to, or is not embraced by, the halls of academe, which sometimes rewards composers and musical educators with plaudits in the wake of their passing. By the time of the Childs interview, Sahl preferred the lack of contact, mounting his theatrical productions in modest circumstances, accepting purely commercial work when it came, and cultivating specific performers.

It wasn't always this way for Michael Sahl. In the 1950s he studied with Roger Sessions at Tanglewood and Princeton (where "they *gleich-geschalt*ed me"); he was then a Fulbright scholar to Italy.[1] He then spent several years in Europe, experiencing firsthand the heady atmosphere of the avant-garde scene associated with the Darmstadt Festival and its figureheads: Pierre Boulez and Karlheinz Stockhausen.[2] Childs included Sahl's work in an annotated repertoire list for the Tucson New Art Wind Ensemble, Childs's first new music ensemble at the University of Arizona, published in the *Music Educators Journal* in 1964. The annotations consist of comments on the playability of pieces in the repertoire. The group describes Sahl's *Wind Piece* (ca. 1962–63), written for the ensemble, as "Some notational problems at first, but much easier than it looks. Performer choice to some extent."[3]

In Sahl's work list on his tribute page, one will look in vain for *Wind Piece* or any other music close to it, as his String Quartet (1969) is the earliest work listed (though *Mitzvah for the Dead* [1966, for violin and tape] gained much critical note only a couple years earlier).[4] Written five years after he returned to the United States, it followed Sahl's work as musical director for folk singer Judy Collins. This—actually his second quartet (the first, as he notes to Childs, was in 1957)—was created as a reaction to rock arrangements for strings, especially "Eleanor Rigby." From 1969,

Sahl left the international avant-garde and pursued a varying concoction embodying jazz chords, romantic melodic lines, electric instruments, ideas from rock and pop, the tango, show tunes, and the blues. This shift in attitude shares some confluence with the later Uptown versus Downtown conflict in new-music circles in New York City. In fact, Kyle Gann has named Sahl as a prophet of this phenomenon, coining the term "Sahlesque" to signify certain polystylistic preferences found in Sahl's music.[5]

There is a professional dimension, however, to Sahl's decision to turn away from serialism and chance composition that resonates in the context of circa 1970: "It has cost me dearly, in the lack of a 'career' and in the scorn of my colleagues."[6] Sahl continued to write concert music for his friends, including *Memorial* (1978, for clarinet and piano), a commission from Childs for his duo with Phillip Rehfeldt, clarinet, and friend. Sahl cofounded, with accordionist William Schimmel, The Tango Project, which recorded two albums of classic Argentinean tangos for Nonesuch.[7] One track, "Por una Cabeza" by Carlos Gardel, appears at key moments in the films *Scent of a Woman* and *True Lies*.[8] Sahl himself wrote a tango, "Exiles' Café," for Yvar Mikhashoff, which has seen subsequent popularity both in concert and recordings.[9] He worked as a music editor and arranger for several documentary and other films, and as composer in others, including the execrable 1976 horror shocker, *Bloodsucking Freaks*.[10] Sahl collaborated with Eric Salzman on several projects, including cocomposing and cowriting the libretto for the satirical musical theater comedy *Civilization and Its Discontents* (1977) which gained critical notice and was recorded for Nonesuch.[11] Salzman and Sahl also cowrote *Making Changes: A Practical Guide to Vernacular Harmony*, a primer devoted to the arrangement and harmonization of popular music.[12]

Michael Sahl did not regret his decision to wave farewell to the Darmstadt School and follow his own muse; he wrote, "It ended by making me really happy in a way I couldn't have imagined. Eventually I found some people who like what I do."[13] Perhaps Gann's description of Sahl's style as Sahlesque is as close as we can come to the wide-ranging output of this composer. As long as Sahl's proponents refrain from devising adjectives to describe his music, then perhaps more work by Michael Sahl will find a place in the repertoire yet.

Michael Sahl: Interview

BARNEY CHILDS: Your present style: why is it the way it is?

MICHAEL SAHL: My God! Once upon a time . . . I learned music from my father, who was (and occasionally still is) a singer who sang two entirely different things: real lowbrow music and real highbrow music. He sang popular songs of the '20s and '30s; he also sang operas, lieder, and church stuff for the Handel-Haydn Society in Boston. He also sang in another genre that I've just recently rediscovered: the semi-serious English and American songwriters of the 1990s and 1910s, like [Charles Marshall,] "I Hear You Calling" and [Ivor Gurney,] "By a Bierside"; Arthur Foote, Oscar Fox, "The Hills of Home"; Cadman. You can't place whether Charles Wakefield Cadman wrote really serious chamber music. My father told me that he learned those songs from his singing teachers, but for himself he either picked things from opera on one side or from popular music on the other. That was my early musical environment. There were two early musical events in my life which were roughly contemporaneous with each other, both when I was about three years old. One was that I was taken to the Shell Concerts on the Esplanade, which were like the Young People's concerts by the Boston Pops under [Arthur] Fiedler. The other was that I was taken to hear the Benny Goodman Sextet in Boston Common on the bandshell. Those events made the same impression on me: fantastic! And when I was in junior high school, around 1946–48, I got very interested in folk music. I dropped classical music entirely for a couple of years and did nothing but play the piano. I got totally wrapped up in that.

I went to college and got more involved with Stravinsky, and I went to Tanglewood and got more involved with modern music. I was very involved in modern music in graduate school. I went to Princeton, and there they really *gleich geschalt*-ed me. The people who shaped me up did it, as far as they could see, for my own good, because these cultured people had no grasp of vulgar music as being something important. There was culture and there was dreck, and very little continuity between them. Milton Babbitt was interested in some show music, but it wasn't possible to take it seriously or flow between them. Then I went to Europe where there was nothing but culture music, and actually was very unhappy about it.

All those immortal tunes were being done. I was very much swept up in them, and everyone was excited about them, at least from the city. I shifted. I would do tape music, then rock music, and then avant-garde music. I really wanted to get things together. Now I realize that I have been trying to do that my whole life, because that was my natural taste. In the last couple of pieces I actually achieved that. I've written something like semiclassical music, but I certainly had a terrible time arriving at it. It isn't an individual story. Things have happened in musical society and in the audience's taste to make it easier to do this. I was never the strong and individualistic enough person to take the [Charles] Ives approach—go up on the mountaintop and write my own music—because at least I needed the imaginary picture that the audience was there. I wouldn't have made a good modern artist, the kind who nobly starves to death with his music unheard. It was tremendously frustrating when I lived in Europe and had my music unheard, and it was a tremendous satisfaction to me to come back to America and be able to make useful music even if it was really second-rate music. That's more or less the story: the events encouraged me in doing this, and the things that I did for a living encouraged me.

BC: You haven't been tempted to go into the academy?

MS: No, I don't like academic work because there is a class bias. Maybe from the outside it seems ridiculous, but I have a very definitely lower-middle class or working-class background. In commercial work it doesn't make any difference. People originate in all walks of life, some of the lowest. The humor that one hears with one's colleagues in commercial business is not too tasty, or even too interesting, but there is no pretense. When you get into academic work, you get into the class situation, where taste stands for something like, "A gentleman knows without knowing that he knows" (I forget whose mot that was). That's always held me back. Also it's just very slow going in the academic world. There are great advantages, but you have to stand in line for a long while. I have a kind of personality that offends some people and not others, and I offend more people in academic life than I do in commercial life. It's quite possible to offend people in commercial life; some of my highbrow friends do it without knowing they are doing it. When they come back to America and have to earn a living, they find out they don't know how to get along with ordinary people. With me it's easier to do that than it is to get along with academic people.

Time soothes it out, though. I was up in Buffalo just this spring. I got along very well with the academic people, so I think people don't mind me anymore. I was more obnoxious as a young man, if you can believe that, than I am now. I was snobbier, or I didn't keep it to myself as well. I suppose I'm not allowed to ask you things?

BC: You can ask me anything you want.

MS: When you heard these pieces I just played, what was your impression? I don't mean did you like the pieces, but did you say to yourself, "What's happened to poor old Sahl?"

BC: No. I said, what a good thing, because now he's back to the things that he did best when I first knew him. It was a full circle that I hoped you would achieve; the things you did best when we first met at Tanglewood.

MS: It really is a full circle? I haven't learned anything since I was eighteen?

BC: It's really a spiral. You're some years later and have learned more. The things that you did best then you are now doing exclusively. And all the hokey "mo-drun" things that you were doing for a while which didn't suit you.

MS: You don't believe those things are necessarily hokey in themselves. You just think they were hokey when I did them.

BC: No, I think they were hokey, period.

MS: Look, you do a lot of "modrun" things in *your* music and you don't think they're hokey, and you hear other music in which they exist. Here's what I'm trying to get at: there is music that I wouldn't write myself in a million years, for example, pieces of Stockhausen, but I would program and listen to it. There's music that I really like that isn't anything like the music I'm going to write, that has manners and sounds in it that I wouldn't touch with a ten-foot pole. But it is possible for some people to produce that music and mean it. Listen to the Webern opus 30; he did those things and really *meant* them.

BC: I'm trying to say that the things that you were doing didn't feel at ease, they felt like contrivance.

MS: That's true.

BC: I thought during those years that it would be nice if he comes back to doing those things he does best, which seemed natural, easy, and which one can be "creative" with. This has happened and pleases me very much.

MS: I had a very clear distinct idea fifteen years ago that I could never do anything with that kind of music, because that wasn't serious music. You couldn't make Beethoven quartets. But a study of the classics helped me. When I was in Italy, I would get the Mozart A Major Concerto. I would play it over and over for hours every day, and I would immerse myself in the sound world. When you are listening to it, you forget that this is great classical music of the past; you realize that here is a very childish idea, here is a buffoon-like idea, and here is a very sensual idea. You get a sense that when the people were actually writing and playing the music, whatever it sounded like, it didn't sound like classical music. When you hear classical music on WNCN at night, it's several feet off the ground. Every once in a while with Beethoven you get a glimpse of something and say, "That would sound awfully vulgar if it weren't Beethoven." Then you realize that if it *does* sound vulgar, it did sound vulgar! That's the way it was supposed to be. There's no special second level of listening. People have a second level of listening, but you're not supposed to listen to music that way. You are supposed to listen to the music like just as it is. That's one of the nice things about the WBAI Free Store. You always play music for people that are not a cultured audience. Even if they are cultured people, they don't come there as a concert audience. And people are exposed to music in a different way. They hear rock and roll one night, Renaissance music another night, and string quartets another night. To them it's all music; they are not trained to give it that special gloss.

I realized that the people who were writing two hundred years ago, the people that I admired and wanted to emulate, were writing what they heard. In the rash of modern string quartets, they tried to be the way the guest classical string quartets sounded if you weren't really listening to them. They had a kind of *paralyzing* quality. The Schoenberg Third String Quartet, which I think is a really good piece, nevertheless just reeks of misheard classical music all the time.

BC: People have said that the whole distinction of "classical" is a fake, a cultural thing that we have had to boggle with for a long time.

MS: No, because there's a difference between America and Europe. In America classical music is something that comes from somewhere else. Very few people in America have the opportunity to get with classical music and really dig it. If, however, you go to the opera in Vienna, and it's *Fidelio*, which is fairly obscure, not what you would call a tuneful opera, they're singing along. Everybody's going *hmmm*, and it's like *Fiddler on the Roof*. Obviously the music is real to the audience. That's more true of opera than of the symphony, because opera was always more popular. In Europe there's obviously more of a real link with that stuff. Going to the opera in Europe is nothing like going to the Met or a university opera workshop.

Something else people don't take seriously: this nostalgia thing, which is easy to laugh at, is actually the effort of people who have always been ashamed of being interested in history. It's their first miserable strivings toward a consciousness of their own history, their own culture, and a belief in themselves. The nostalgia business shouldn't be pooh-poohed. Madison Avenue nostalgia is, of course, a manipulation of that. But people go and dig around in Victorian houses simply to try to find something about the past, and find something worthwhile in the past of somebody else.

BC: The European past is already made. You have eight hundred years of tradition.

MS: Yes. It also doesn't belong to the people in this country. What belongs to them is Cedar Rapids. Everybody used to laugh at it in the '20s, but now they are not laughing at it anymore!

BC: What can we replace the European thing with?

MS: That's a good question, but it's not a question of replacing the European thing. It's simply a question of finding out who you are.

BC: That involves replacing.

MS: Yeah, because in the recent past, the Europeans are not in a very enviable state culturally. It's wicked to envy them; they have their own troubles. You had a generation of young people grow up after the war in Germany who can't listen to classical music at all because to them it means Hitler, because all kinds of other signal reflexes come into it. It's wrong to envy Europe and say, "How come we don't have a situation like the Europeans?" Martin Buber said, "When I die, God will not ask me why you haven't been so-and-so, God will ask me why haven't you been Martin Buber?" This is true of culture. It's odd: at the same time when people actually are more ashamed of their country than they have been in the past, they are more attached to it. Maybe the two are connected. I lived in Europe for four years as an American; before that I lived in graduate schools for two years in a European-orientated American environment, and I suffered from the most terrible, unspeakable inferiority because I was an American. What is an American, after all? "American" is a Texas oil millionaire.

I never told you the "Someone to Watch Over Me" story? Richard Ronshem and I both lived in Florence. Ronsheim was born in Cadiz, Ohio, and he was a much less successful pseudo-European than I was when I was there. His accent in foreign languages was worse and his mannerisms, his walk, and his suits were more American. I got away with it much better than he did; Frederick Rzewski got away with it better than anybody. Despite the fact that he was a very unsuitable pseudo-European, Ronshem was preoccupied with this mystery that enabled Europeans to make real art and Americans not. He was struck by Boulez. Boulez was never a favorite composer of mine; I preferred Stockhausen. We used to have agonizing discussions in which we mutually, collectively, and individually tore our skin off ourselves—our self-hatred and abnegation about why we are Americans. Sometime in about 1961, in the middle of one of these discussions, I had one of these visions and walked over to the piano and I played the beginning of "Someone to Watch Over Me," which has that descending scale pattern. I didn't remember what it was (I thought it was Jerome Kern, but of course it was Gershwin), and I said I would have rather written that than X's string quartet.

From that moment I made my mind up to get home. I was still a couple of years after that getting home because of difficulties. But I realized that one thing that an American was, besides a Texas oil millionaire, was a Jewish songwriter. I realized that those Jewish songwriters were real musicians and I had something in common with them: an eastern, urban, Russian Jewish environment with a similar bias. Of course I was a stage removed from that because I'd had a much better education. It's my own version of down-home, nitty-gritty soul music. Someone, like [Arnold] Franchetti, who taught at the Hartt School, would say, "What are you talking about? Is that Jewish music?" That's not what I'm talking about; it won't stand up to that kind of test. Simply, there was somebody who made some real music in my background, so there was a reason why I could write music. It's still perfectly irrational, but that's what people mean when they talk about finding roots. That meant a great deal to me.

BC: You had to be in Europe to do it?

MS: No, because when I was at Princeton I was already in Europe. "Why this is Europe, nor am I out of it."[14] If I'd gone to graduate school at Princeton, then to teach at some eastern college, in that environment, in that whole twelve-tone thing, I still would have been in Europe. I would have been in a backwater of Europe—Luxembourg—but I still would have been there.

By the way, one thing which happened to all of us and really changed something about American feelings was the tremendous Cage boom. Cage enabled

Americans to just absolutely stop worrying about whether they were artists at all. The abstract expressionists first, then Cage. It had an effect on me, who really wasn't terribly interested in Cage's music. The fact that this guy did something, he had the nerve, there was a whole movement, and it was taking the world by storm. It's tremendously important.

When you and I used to talk fifty million years ago in Tanglewood, the ideal that we set ourselves in terms of an "artist" (and I think that wasn't just us, it was consistent for that time) was the ideal of a lonely, powerful, completely independent individual who first of all shapes out of chaotic and unwilling nature, an order by an exertion of will. He's independent of the performance, he's independent of the audience, he's not a social being in any way. It had to do with the political climate of the times and other things. I tried to live that way; what it meant for me and for a lot of people of my generation was simply actually being involved in a clique. It didn't turn out to be real individualism at all. True, there were those guys of the real older generation, such as [Carl] Ruggles, Ives, John Alden Carpenter. I don't know what their lives were *really* like. It turns out that Ives moved for quite a while in the 1890s in musical circles in New York. Even though he didn't agree with anybody, he had some kind of contact, some cultural richness. But they created a false impression that they tried to live with. You have been tremendously involved in the reality of performance situations. It also had something to do with the part of the country you came from. Being from the West, you had to be a pioneer. Now there is a tremendous musical development in Los Angeles, where people from the West no longer have that feeling about themselves. A guy from the West in his twenties doesn't have that feeling and wouldn't know what you were talking about, because the world has changed.

There's something else: the purpose of life. I honestly believe that the purpose of life is not to make art—the purpose of life is to live, and art is something that comes off that living. My work dramatically improved when I started earning a living. Before that my work was my whole justification for my existence. Every time I made a piece, it had to justify the fact that I was in the situation that I was in, that I was living where I was living, and that I existed. It's a wonder that I wrote anything at all with that kind of tension. I've always had diarrhea of the pen, so I always managed to write something, but often it was meaningless and contentless, because it had too much awareness and consciousness. When I was earning a living, I didn't worry about who I was. I made peace with myself—if I never was anybody and if I never did anything important at all, that was really all right. For another thing, I got to be thirty. You know, *le malaise de Tom Thumb*.[15] I became thirty and I hadn't made it, whatever "making it" was. So I gave up. As soon as I gave up, I started to do Ensemble '65 and *Fantasy Music* [for organ, 1967], and

Mitzvah for the Dead. I began to make real music because nothing was riding on it any more.

BC: Which is an American thing: if we are careerists, we aren't going to work.

MS: Highbrow culture in Europe still has some relationship to reality. Highbrow culture in America never had much relationship to reality. Like the ladies with their diamonds going to the opera—it didn't have anything to do with listening to the opera. The opera was an artifact. As long as that's true, it's very difficult for any American artist to get spontaneous recognition from that highbrow establishment because the highbrow establishment only recognizes fakes. They'll recognize real things only after the most tremendous battle. They haven't recognized Ralph Shapey yet! How old is Ralph Shapey, fifty? Of his age group he's astounding, the nonpareil, the greatest composer within twenty years of him. But he's more obscure than ever! The cultural establishment—things in Grace Rainey Rogers Auditorium, Ford Grammer Hall, and all—don't take Ralph Shapey seriously. It happens over and over again because he doesn't seem like a cultural paragon, but he *is* a cultural paragon. It's like Baudelaire recognizing Poe; it's like the oldest story in the world. The same with Cage: Europeans recognized Cage and then he was all right for the American elite.

Our elite just doesn't work. That doesn't mean that no elites work, it just means that ours doesn't work. So you must find it somewhere else. This is why I involve myself as much as I can in experiments with a nonelite audience. Now it's very frustrating, and it's very difficult to make these experiments. Outside of the Free Store it's very hard.[16] But you always fool around with this. After I stopped working for Judy [Collins], I tried to get Paul Zukofsky to open for her in some big concert. You remember Loren Hollander? He played classical selections on an electrified concert piano as part of an evening of rock music in the Fillmore. Well, I just thought that was the greatest thing in the world. I can't wait until the elite make up their fucking minds that somebody is doing something that I think is valuable and worthwhile. Bill [Bolcom] is in exactly the same position. Bill quit Queens [College CUNY]; when he was teaching there he had a good gig. That's criminal, that's treason! If he quit Queens, there is something wrong enough with him; he also won't get that recognition that he needs. I got some recognition recently after Buffalo, and God willing, I'll get more. I never would have got it unless I turned my back on that and done something else than worried about what was real.

BC: How do you feel about writing a quartet?

MS: A string quartet?

BC: I mean, after the great string quartet slavery that so many of us have been through!

MS: I wrote a string quartet in 1957, and I didn't write another one, or it didn't occur to me to write another one, until 1969. I don't know whether it was that

I heard "Eleanor Rigby." After that, rock arrangers began using string quartets in their work. I would listen to them and say, "*That's* no way to write a string quartet!" It just gradually got to me. Zukofsky had this quartet that was in residence at Swarthmore, but he hadn't asked me for a piece. I said, Jesus Christ, I'm really going to try at writing a string quartet! A string quartet is really a nice combination and, used as it is, it's not worn out.

I don't believe a sound gets worn out; I don't believe that a sound gets old. Ten, fifteen years ago we all believed that tonality had somehow got to the point when it just doesn't work any more. People at Princeton were trying to sell you the twelve-tone system as a substitute for tonality because tonality doesn't work. It didn't not work! People were just afraid to do those things. Now people aren't afraid, and you find that tonality works just the same. The little old lady only drove it on Sunday and it works just as good as ever! Things come back. You can see this by the history of the appreciation of the music of the past. People liked Baroque music when it was new, then they lost their taste for it in the style following, then they got it back in the 1950s. Now it's so beat to pieces that people are going to lose their taste for it again. But that doesn't mean it's finished. That just means that it goes in the freezer. Do you agree with any of these things?

BC: I find Baroque music very dull. I don't find tonality dull at all.

MS: I can't live very well without tonality. Tonality doesn't have to do with tonal sounds. It's when you have harmony that you are dealing with tonal sounds. The difference is if you want chords. I tried to live without chords. I went through such a drubbing about this because in graduate school, everybody said [Jean-Philippe] Rameau was wrong. I suppose Rameau was a very simple-minded man, and in some ways he really was wrong. But that doesn't mean that harmony isn't harmony: you cannot get away from it. Church tunes and Mendelssohnian tunes based on harmony are not primitive music or stupid music—that's harmonic music. Sir Arthur Sullivan is just harmonic music. If you start throwing it out, as the Princetonians did, you can go crazy. It turned out to be a real necessity for me. If I have a good tune, harmony, and a bass, I'm really quite happy. Witness the two last pieces: they're just reeking with that. Fortunately, my old composition teacher is not around to tell me that you can't do it, that it's no good and it's primitive.

BC: The *harmony* you are using in these new pieces is stretched-out harmony, with more to it than just verticalities. These ornate winding lines are ostinatos of a sort, which, if you squeeze all the ostinatos together, you don't get a simple harmony.

MS: Sometimes you get real simple harmony where you need it. It's funny; I heard the Piston Quintet on WNCN the other night. It is a very pretty piece, but you felt that he was chickening out of all the cadences, for very "taste-y" reasons. I remember that in 1954 we talked about Copland, who was just about as brash as anybody could be about the cadences. Even *he* chickened out the chords; every finger in the music was pointing to *doh*. They couldn't do it. Now, out of perversity, a lot of us started to do it again: to put the chords, to call a spade a spade, to call a major chord a major chord, and then even worse, to call a dominant seventh a dominant seventh. There is a great kind of relief when you do that. Of course you find that what you thought were simple harmonies aren't simple harmonies, so you start building up from the beginning. You find out about non-chord tones again, just like you did when you studied harmony, except that there is a reason for it now. You don't turn to a page in a book and it says the 6/4/3 always resolves down the lower two notes except in the case of such-and-such, when it doesn't. If you bother to go through all the suffering—and I'm not really advocating it—you really find out finally what it means that the 6/4/3 resolves down.

BC: How much did being on the road with Judy Collins change what you are doing?

MS: I hate being on the road with a passion. When you are on the road you have to play the same material. You don't have time to do anything but to do sound, to get balances. You don't really rehearse, you meet at twelve or nine or ten o'clock Friday morning, get on the plane and fly somewhere, get off the plane, go to the Holiday Inn, watch television for a while, then go and do sound. You hang around the dressing room for about an hour, then do the concert. Afterwards you go out to McDonald's if you're unlucky, or some better place if you are lucky, and eat. You stay up drinking and talking because you can't unwind, then you go to bed about two o'clock. Then you get up at six because it's always an early plane; you get on the plane the next day, go to the airport, drive, go to the Holiday Inn, turn on the television. You fall asleep during the football, then the manager comes. When you get back to New York on Monday, you don't want to *hear* the fucking material. Nobody wants to see anybody, because you have been jammed together for four days, so you don't do any rehearsals and you don't prepare any new pieces during the season. You only do that about once a year. As a result, the material degenerates gradually. The lead singer can always get off, but the band doesn't get off. The time gradually sags on a piece, and it gets slower and slower. Then you eliminate it from the program and next month, when you put it on again, it's faster. The constant performance doesn't agree with me, because I get very tense when I perform. You have to perform in all kinds of situations, so you have to get tough like a paratrooper. I don't like it.

BC: These pieces are for electronic piano, electric harpsichord . . . ?

MS: I got interested in using electronic instruments because I wanted to use in-line recordings. Instead of recording with a microphone, if you have an electric instrument you can plug right into the mike or your reverb—right into the tape recorder—and you can make a direct clean recording. I bought that electric bass. I was aware of all those instruments and curious about them before I ever worked in rock and roll. But once I worked for Judy, of course I had many more contacts and many more ways to borrow things, so I made more use of it. Lots of people are using those electronic instruments now. The tape situation forces it on me. Take your Walt Whitman piece.[17] The kind of sound that you are using there is not available in the city. If you are teaching somewhere out in the country, then forces of that size are available to you; instruments are available to you. In the city, you have other problems and you have certain compensations. But the idea getting hold of a big band like that—I just wouldn't even know where to begin. The way to begin is to get a job at Northwestern if I were lucky, or go up to Buffalo where I have contacts and try and get in contact with that band. But it's all through colleges and universities, so you have to do whatever you can.

BC: This is why your symphony appears only in chamber size.

MS: Seven instruments. I didn't even make a score for the full version. If I go around with that tape and that score, I may lie to the conductor and say I have an orchestral version but it's in pencil at home. If somebody hears it and says yes, then I'll make a score. But the day is gone when I'll make a score in ink for some nonexistent performance in order to carry the score around under my arm to Darmstadt to show a lot of other people who are carrying scores around under their arms. I use to make quite nice-looking scores, but now I make pig scores. I don't take care with my calligraphy the way I used to. You've probably got a copy of a piece of mine, *Four* (1960), which is a kind of post-Webern piece for orchestra. It is unquestionably the most beautiful score that I ever made; it's as close as I could come to making the kind of score that [Richard] Maxfield made. That was at a time when there was absolutely no possibility of ever hearing the piece played. The score was the performance. You should see *Mitzvah for the Dead*. It's such a hairy-looking score that it is almost illegible, and that's my big success.

I'd like to go back and write more songs. I want to write something simple, like the things I'm writing now. And although some rock lyrics aren't bad, I don't want to do rock lyrics. It's a kind of pretense about it. I have to write something that has something to do with the way that *I* talk. I like some of my old songs, like the David Hemingway songs and the Hopkins songs from Florence. The Hopkins songs have never been performed. They fall into a funny genre, and it's very hard to get somebody to perform them. At [SUNY] Buffalo [they] performed "In My Craft or Sullen Art" [Dylan Thomas], once badly, which of course was taped, and once beautifully, which of course was not taped.

BC: You really don't have that much freedom in the academy. You get to know band guys who know other band guys. In the academy you don't carry your score around and show it to people. Clarinetists will tell other clarinetists, and trumpet players will tell other trumpet players. In New York apparently it never gets out. I've seen several pieces written for a percussionist around here. But none of these pieces will get out to guys like Ron George or G. Allen O'Connor, who are teaching.

MS: As a matter of fact, there *is* no communication. There is no community, and you can't legislate a community, you can't administrate communication. There has to be some natural way for it to grow, like trying to get ivy to climb. You can put something for it to climb on but it's got to climb there. It's a combination of helping and the thing doing it itself. People have made efforts; *Source* certainly made an effort to get music around, but it all fell dead. I'm sure that people in provincial places buy every goddamn periodical they can; they look at every score and take it out and try it on the piano, but there's still no communication. In New York, there's been a lid on the things that I thought were interesting in the last five or six years. I'll bet that has also been happening in the grassroots, way outside of New York. They must: people aren't that different.

BC: Not so. There is communication back and forth between players, instrumental-ists. Pieces written for specific virtuosos or specific groups got around, because they would tell their friends, send tapes.

MS: I thought of something else to ask you. To the serial school, the player is the servant. He's not really a human being, he's a second-class citizen. Therefore you can't expect anything out of a player. If he's competent, he does his job; but when he's through, like a studio man, he packs up his ax and forgets it and goes home. Now this isn't the situation *you* are talking about. You rely on the players. You write a piece the players are going to have fun playing, and the players tell other players, and you owe the performances to the players. Enlightened self-interest! Now, in most situations, players do not determine what is played. In "important" situations, the players do not determine that at all. The men in the Philharmonic want to play pinochle, but suppose they wanted to play a piece? It wouldn't make any fucking difference. I mean it's determined, like Nixon says, by "responsible people."

BC: But in unimportant situations, players do choose. Faculty recitals; they have a good student to give a piece to; they have a small ensemble . . . they'll play the work.

MS: I've been thinking a lot about something. It struck me that the symphony orchestra is basically a nineteenth-century industrial product. There's *one* man who knows what's going on. Other people have die stampers or grid things to do. Of course it takes greater skill. But if you're playing the second bassoon, you're supposed to watch the conductor and play what it says. You sit there in this big booming, buzzing confusion, and you can't hear anything properly, but it's not supposed to make any difference to you. If you have *faith*, and you play what you are given, then everything will come out right because there's a man up there who's watching. People will say that that is the only way it can be for an orchestra, but there's something basically dehumanizing about it. In a society where people aren't so willing to take orders and aren't willing to *trust* the field marshal, then people don't want to play in an orchestra.

BC: The interesting thing in some orchestras is the number of first chairs, notably wind players, who want to play new music. A good group may be largely dependent on four, five, maybe six, symphony players who aren't content with watching the "Man" do the "Thing."

MS: How do you square this perception with the desire to hear orchestra music? Because I've recently got this craving to hear and make orchestra music. Is there some kind of legitimate basis? Maybe there's a situation in the orchestra where you have really good conductors; where people really feel what they are doing, like they do in a big band. I just don't know.

Notes

1. John Hammond, "Michael Sahl, '55: In Memory," https://www.amherst.edu/amherst-story/magazine/in_memory/1955/michaelsahl (accessed August 15, 2019).

2. Unpublished letters from Michael Sahl to Barney Childs, 1955–61, document his moves from Amherst College to Princeton, Los Angeles, Rome, Darmstadt, and Spain.

3. Barney Childs, "Young Performers and New Music," *Music Educators Journal* 51/1 (September–October 1964): 42. In addition to Sahl, the annotated repertoire contains pieces by Robert Ashley, Gordon Mumma, Donald Martino, and Fluxus artists Jackson Mac Low and Joseph Byrd.

4. Barry Drogin, "Michael Sahl (1934–2018): Mixed Ensembles with Rhythm Section," Not Nice Music, http://www.notnicemusic.com/Sahl.html (last updated 2018).

5. Kyle Gann, liner notes to *Michael Sahl: In Fashion at Last*, Joseph Kubera, Mary Rowell, Eric Liljestrand, William Sloat, Kevin Norton, Philip Bush, Albany Troy 825, CD, 2006.

6. Michael Sahl, "Modernism and Romanticism and Me," accessed at Drogin, "Michael Sahl."

7. *The Tango Project*, Nonesuch D-79030, 1982; *Two to Tango (The Tango Project II)*, Nonesuch 79057, 1983.

8. Martin Brest, dir., *Scent of a Woman* (Universal Pictures, 1992); James Cameron, dir., *True Lies* (Twentieth Century Fox, 1994).

9. Michael Sahl, "Exiles' Café," on Yvar Mikhashoff, *Incitation to Desire*, New Albion NA 073CD, 1995.

10. Joel M. Reed, dir., *Bloodsucking Freaks* (Joel M. Reed Productions, 1976).

11. Michael Sahl and Eric Salzman, *Civilization and Its Discontents*, Nonesuch N-78009, LP, 1981.

12. Eric Salzman and Michael Sahl, *Making Changes: A Practical Guide to Vernacular Harmony* (New York: McGraw-Hill, 1977).

13. Sahl, "Modernism and Romanticism and Me."

14. Sahl is alluding to "Why this is hell, nor am I out of it," in Christopher Marlowe's *Doctor Faustus*, scene 3, l. 74.

15. The folklore character Tom Thumb is no bigger than his father's thumb. Sahl is perhaps indicating here that he suffers from a desire for a larger stature as a composer.

16. The San Francisco street theater and countercultural activists the Diggers had "free stores," gave away food, and threw free parties featuring live music. Perhaps this is a reference to that Haight-Ashbury scene.

17. Barney Childs, *When Lilacs Last in the Dooryard Bloom'd*, for chorus, wind band, stage band (New York: American Composers Alliance, 1971).

19 Peter Westergaard (1931–2019)

JEFFREY PERRY

In 1972 Peter Talbot Westergaard was forty-one years old and had been a member of the composition faculty at Princeton University for four years. Two ongoing projects loom large in the interview: Westergaard's music theory textbook, *An Introduction to Tonal Theory*, finished just before the interview and published in 1975, and his opera on Shakespeare's *The Tempest*, already underway for two years but not to be completed until 1992. Westergaard had already completed the chamber operas *Charivari* (1953) and *Mr. and Mrs. Discobbolos* (1966). *The Tempest* was followed by several other stage projects: the children's opera *Chicken Little* (1997); the "imaginary opera" *Moby Dick* (2005); the ensemble opera *Alice in Wonderland* (2007), written for seven singers and a conductor, with no orchestra; and *Twelfth Night* (2015).

The continuous contrapuntal skein that weaves through each scene of his operas suggests an origin in pre-Monteverdian as well as in post-tonal repertoires. Echoes of Schoenberg's *Moses und Aron* and of Stravinsky's *Rake's Progress* abound. With Childs he discusses his quest for comprehensibility without necessarily writing "easy music." As Westergaard suggests to Childs, "a vocal line is not just a verbal utterance and a musical utterance at the same time. It's the way the two interrelate." Exploring that specific interrelation continued to occupy him until his death in June 2019.

Westergaard's instrumental works, which are freed from the responsibilities of collaboration with a sung text, distill key elements of his process. The kernel of each work's success is its rhythmic life—each event tends to have a unique point of incipience, and each phrase tends to have its own unique temporal trajectory. A counterpoint of registers and colors creates a lively polyphonic surface and constant interplay between melodic threads. Each instrument seems to unfold at its own informational pace, creating a dancing multiplicity of perceived tempi that are juxtaposed or superimposed, each one individuated through the dimensions of pitch class, register, and timbre. Such linear clarity facilitates the individualized musical portrayal of characters like Prospero and Caliban.

A question from Childs about Westergaard's 1965 article on twelve-tone polyphony leads directly into a discussion of how he explores these ideas compositionally in his *Variations for Six Players* (1963) in which he highlights the role of informational redundancy in promoting clarity. A covert influence from Shannonian information theory appears here—how much signal can one have before it collapses into noise? How must one structure a signal to prevent it from seeming like noise?

A remarkable thing about rhythm in Westergaard is the way that each phrase has not just its own rhythmic, harmonic, and timbral profile, but often a quite immediately grasped individual affect as well. Being able to write music as abstract as Westergaard's that can also convey sadness, frenzy, anguish, giddiness, flirtation, or joy is not a common gift; it is, however, one that is useful for an opera composer.

Westergaard's textbook *An Introduction to Tonal Theory* (1975) helps clarify many of the concerns articulated in the interview, in particular *Fasslichkeit* (comprehensibility). He once said to me, "the failure to account for time with the same precision we account for pitch is what's wrong with most tonal theories." This might serve as the mission statement for the entire text. The conceptual dependence of certain musical events (e.g., dissonances, embellishing tones) on other events (structural pitches) forms a backdrop for Westergaard's presentation of a generative theory of melody and tonal counterpoint that predates that of Fred Lerdahl and Ray Jackendoff (1977, 1979).

Westergaard also beats Leonard Bernstein to the punch by a year—Bernstein's 1973 Norton Lectures at Harvard make a spirited attempt to use linguistics to explicate musical structure and the evolution of art music from antiquity to Schoenberg, Stravinsky, and Bernstein himself. In the Childs interview, it is clear that Westergaard has been pondering such matters for quite some time; indeed, in the same year, Westergaard gave a paper in Copenhagen titled "Linear Operations Necessary to Generate a Palestrina Foreground" that provides the basis for the first part of the *Introduction to Tonal Theory*. By using operations that have clear analogues in Chomskyan transformational grammar to generate, and thus conceptualize, what Schenkerians term the fundamental line and its elaborations, it suggests a unification of tonal theory and compositional practice. Milton Babbitt and Edward T. Cone influence Westergaard, but he goes beyond them in his grasp of recent work in linguistics and human perception and cognition. Unlike Bernstein's facile insight, Westergaard approached questions of musical syntax from deep study of Renaissance polyphony, sung language, and tonal and post-tonal form. His 1977 article "What Theorists Do" places him in the vanguard of the field of music perception and cognition studies, a burgeoning twenty-first-century subfield.[1]

In speaking to Childs, Westergaard pushes back against the notion that he and a few Princeton colleagues formed what Tom Wolfe would later term an art compound—an exclusive club, a closed circle of aesthetically circled wagons. The implication of Childs's articulation of the "Princeton Syndrome" is that the actions of these composers were perceived as excluding and devaluing the work of those outside the compound. In the context of the interview, such accusations were fresh and nerves were raw; this conversation between Childs, a West Coast experimentalist and Westergaard, an East Coast serialist, is thus interesting as a respectful parlay between two composers seeking common ground and a common language of craft and aesthetic in an increasingly fractured, Vietnam War–era, Nixonian America.

Peter Westergaard: Interview

BARNEY CHILDS: I'd like to ask about your development of classical twelve-tone procedures and how you use them in your composing. Particularly, if you could go into the article for those people who may read this book and may not have read your article.[2]

PETER WESTERGAARD: What I've done since writing the twelve-tone-polyphony article has been to extend those operations a little further. Those operations were simply ways of making two-dimensional structures along traditional twelve-tone lines. Since then I've tried to extend that ideal to make structures that are easier to play and easier to hear.

BC: Why do you say "easier to play"?

PW: For example, in the *Variations*, there are passages that have a twelve-tone set exposed in three ways at once.[3] First, by the totality of all the notes that come: there may be, say, a succession of six different sets stated. Second, by the individual instruments: there are six instruments, and each one presents its own twelve-tone set. Third, by individual registers: the twelve highest notes in the whole passage present their own set, as do the next highest twelve, and so forth. Now, in order to intensify those registral lines *as lines*, I made sure that, whatever instrument projected a given note in a registral line, its player would alter the timbre of his or her instrument so as to make it easier to associate that note on his instrument with the preceding note, or the succeeding note in that registral line that's produced by some other instrument. For example, in each of the two halves of the middle section of the middle movement of the *Variations* [Ex. 1], each player plays six notes, contributing two apiece to three different registral lines. Or, put the other way, each of the six registral lines is created by pairs of notes contributed by three different players. Each player's part says not only how to play a given note, but also what other players' notes it should sound like: for a couple of Bartók *pizz.* notes in the cello, the instruction reads: "match Timp., and deadened notes in Pf." The instructions in the piano and percussion parts reciprocate.

So each note a player plays is an item in three different messages. First, it's a note in the succession of all notes, and therefore must begin at exactly the right point in time, so that both the duration from the attack of the preceding

EXAMPLE 1: Variations for Six Players, 2nd movement, beginning of middle section. All sets are transformations of one another. Each is a derived set, that is, one consisting of a trichord followed by its three symmetrical cousins, I, R, and RI. Each set is either a symmetrical transformation (I, R, or RI) of any other set, or a set in which the items within the hexachord have been rotated (thereby creating a set derived from a different trichord), or a combination of both. For example, the first all-notes hexachord is 2 3 6, 5 4 1; the first flute hexachord is 2 1 4, 5 6 3, which is R of 2 3 6, 5 4 1's first rotation. (2 3 6, 5 4 1 rotated becomes 3 6 5, 4 1 2, which, backward, is 2 1 4, 5 6 3.) If this seems complicated, it results in something that is actually pretty easy to hear, since it means that all three kinds of line are limited to just two interval classes between consecutive notes: ±1 or ±3.

note in the succession and its attack and the duration between its attack and the attack of the next note can help make the pattern of durations between attacks audible to the listener. (It also has to have just the right dynamic level relative to those of the notes before and after, but, fortunately, the pattern of dynamic levels is closely aligned to the one made by durations—the shorter the duration until the next attack, the louder the note—so the two help each other out.) In the second place, it's a note in the succession of all notes coming from that instrument. That's the easy one. You sit there and play it. No matter how odd it sounds, it's yours. And finally, it's a note in a registral line, and therefore has to be coaxed into a kind of sound that will connect it for the listener to the adjacent notes in that registral line.

That's not easy. Indeed, the convergence of all those demands makes for some moments that are extremely difficult for the performers. Wherever I had a choice, I chose whichever way would be easier for the performer, but it is still a ticklish business to play that stretch of *Variations*. So in my music since then I've tried to avoid those situations: they seemed unnecessarily difficult—doable, but risky. Even though the performer may get it perfect once, it's difficult to guarantee. I've been fortunate—in some performances of the *Variations* I've gotten very good results. But because each note that's played is the sole bearer of many messages, it has to be just right. Unless it is, the whole edifice may easily come tumbling down. That's pretty scary for the performers, and it also makes for a difficulty for the listener. If everything is just right, fine. If one or two things are off, the listener may easily be sidetracked and lose the thread.

You might say that what I was trying to do in that piece might better have been done by electronic means. This may be true. But I was intrigued with the traditional notion of each performer playing his or her part so it would make sense in and of itself, but also fit in with the other performers' parts to make another, larger sense. You do that when you play chamber music, and this was the kind of chamber music I was trying to create.

Since then, the direction I've moved in, as far as my counterpoint or my version of twelve-tone polyphony is concerned, has been to make my registral lines easier to hear by introducing redundancies in their projection. Instead of having just *one* succession of twelve pitch classes that partition out into, say, four different registral lines, I might have *two* such successions which would partition out into the same four registral lines, so you would hear each pitch in a given registral line twice before going on to its next pitch. In such a case, I would not have the two instruments try to make the same pitch have a similar timbre or envelope. The pitch-identity connection there would be quite strong enough; the redundancy is easier for both the performer and the listener. That's more or less the direction I've been going recently. To an extent this is already true in the opera *Mr. and Mrs. Discobbolos*.[4] In a twelve-tone more than a hexachordal sense, it becomes the modus vivendi in the flute piece, the *Diver-timento on Discobblic Fragments*.[5] In the next two pieces, *Noises, Sounds and Sweet Airs*, which is related to the opera—my new opera, it hasn't been written yet—and a piece for band called *Tuckets and Sennets*, in which, because I had a full-sized symphonic band to play around with, there are a large number of registral lines being projected, including some really low ones.[6]

BC: Redundancy is very high.

PW: The redundancy is very high, as I suppose it should be in pieces for band. It's still pretty hard to play, at least for a band, but on the other hand, one can hear what's going on.

BC: Yes, quite clearly with the high redundancy.

PW: If it's played in tune, moderately cleanly, it should all come through. Does that answer the basic question on my version of twelve-tone polyphony?

BC: Yes it does. I don't think it illuminates the thesis of the *article* sufficiently for those people who haven't read the article.

PW: I talked about the twelve-tone set as it was used by Schoenberg, basically as a one-dimensional object: the set can be a source for relationships either between simultaneously sounding notes or between consecutively sounding notes but *not both at the same time*. However, in music of the past—specifically in tonal music, but also in earlier music—we had methods for controlling at least a two-dimensional array of pitches. I was trying to find a way of using sets so that the same relationships that are found, say, in the total succession of pitches might also be found in various lines going though those pitches. Mine is far from the only way at getting at the problem. Godfrey Winham's "Composition with Arrays" attempts to solve a similar problem.[7] He doesn't put the problem the same way I do, and he doesn't come up with the same results, but both our approaches recognize the same difficulty with the original Schoenbergian syntax.

BC: We might go on to the "style and idea" idea, and your views on what style is thought to be, and what it oughtn't to be.

PW: Yes, "style" is an ill-defined term that really ought to be eliminated from musical discourse until that time when someone comes up with a reasonably secure way of using it. It's a word that I have marked prejudices against. It is used by anyone from your Aunt Tillie, who asks you "What style do you write in, dear?" to music critics . . .

BC: Who ask essentially the same senseless question with fancier words.

PW: They *think* there is such a thing; and if you ask them what they really mean, they say, "You know, *of course*, what I mean. Now stop asking me those questions!" It may be a perfectly useful notion, but now the word belongs to that dim gray area of terms that depend on an assumption of mutual understanding but are never defined. Most arguments that try to use style are just almost useless.

BC: Style, you would suggest, is as misunderstood as simply a gathering together of surface phenomena . . .

PW: What most people mean by "style" are those features that two or more pieces may have in common. That almost runs against the notion of a piece to me. A piece is something that *doesn't* have things in common with other pieces; that's what makes it a piece. This may be a funny twentieth-century notion about what a piece is—we can come back to that when we talk about syntax—because obviously pieces do have common modes of understanding. But the Schoenbergian notion that style is something really rather trivial, whereas idea is something worth striving for, is a well-established prejudice in my mind. It's not meant to condemn all surface phenomena—because idea in Schoenberg's notion is clearly a surface phenomenon—but it's that particular surface phenomenon which leads you into a greater understanding of the piece as a whole. And it seems impossible that such an item would also be common property to a larger number of pieces.

BC: This takes you directly into syntax as an idea.

PW: Yes, most people who talk about style have an insufficiently formed notion of what syntax is. In the first place, once you talk about what "style" a piece is in, you're assuming multiple possibilities. If you say that so-and-so has written a piece in such-and-such a style, there is presumably another style he could have written that same piece in—think about that one for a while! Certainly most syntaxes or most verbal languages have the possibility of saying the same thing in more than one way. That means that the syntactic constraints are such that you can construct two sentences that mean the same thing or have the same structure, but have a different style, by choosing a different set of ways of expressing that particular notion. There's no question but that tonal syntax, for example, is so constructed that there are multiple possibilities for various structural functions, for more than one way of doing the same thing. The composer's specific choice of *which* way to do that may well constitute style. He may have a personal style in that he tends to solve similar problems in a similar way.

BC: I've always liked to think of that as rhetoric rather than style.

PW: Certainly the classical sense of rhetoric; the ancients had a much clearer sense of this word than we do: the whole notion of having particular formulas or particular ways of channeling ideas, that there are certain means of persuasion. They're not necessarily a limited set, but there's a finite set of things that you might possibly do that's well-known. There might be other ways too, but these are assumed to be known to both the orator and his audience. That's of course quite a different problem. I'm sure that in the eighteenth century there were ways of doing things which the composer knew the audience would recognize as identifiable French style or something else. Those things are relatively limited; they'd have to be, and any investigation of them now has to limit itself to rather obvious kinds of relationships.

BC: I'm merely introducing this as "what happens on the next level up." After the syntax has been clarified, the next level up enables one to operate, if one wishes, within certain set rhetorical modes.

PW: I think that one would want to describe one syntax for all of tonal music. But within that there might be traditional things that would prove further limiting features. Most people who talk about style are so naive about syntax that they therefore cannot define what they mean by "musical style." Also, there's considerable confusion as to which of these two things one is talking about. [Knud] Jeppesen's book on style is absolutely terrific; but some of the time it's about style, and some of the time it's about syntax.[8] Much of what he did makes it possible to form a good, clear-cut syntax—one that would not need to be so detailed. Jeppesen observes large amounts of music and describes what happens. Although he says this is part of a history of dissonance, he's not concerned with the connection between dissonance and step. That would be a syntactical concern. He's just reporting what he finds in this particular body of music. So I suppose he's doing what one *could* do to talk about style without understanding syntax. But the study itself is much more efficient once one has a reasonably tight syntax.

BC: You have investigated transformational grammar and Chomskyan approaches to this, which have always interested me. Dealing solely with tonal syntax did you find that this helped?

PW: Yes. But although Chomskyan linguistics obviously bear strong resemblances to tonal structure, nevertheless, after you investigate that similarity up to a certain point, then suddenly there really isn't any more similarity because the purposes (what is being communicated) of the two languages are so completely different. It's interesting to observe that there is this correspondence—and we as musicians can be proud that, for once, we got there first with transformational grammar—but I don't *really* think that that's terribly significant. What I *have* found of interest in a much more general way came about mostly in my work on text setting—in that curious realm where, at one and the same time, the same materials and the same relationships among sounds were being used for two syntaxes simultaneously. When you sing a vocal line you are simultaneously, in some sense, making an utterance in a verbal language and making an utterance in a musical language.

BC: Isn't it possible to say that an art song is simply a text with phonemic values changed?

PW: No, it's much more than that. A vocal line is not just a verbal utterance and a musical utterance at the same time. It's the way the two interrelate. One of the things that interested me most was that, in what we consider as good prosody, there's a minimum of conflict between the actual sound relationships required by the two items—we say the text fits the music like a hand to a glove. However, there are exceptions—and these exceptions are certainly equally interesting. They led me to do some more reading in linguistics, not the new-fangled Chomskyan kind, but simply the old-fashioned descriptive kind, where they talk about the role of what musicians would call pitch, dynamics, and rhythm in projecting a particular syntax in a verbal language. I was concerned to show how these two things had to fit together, but I was also concerned to show that there might be cases where you would use specific musical structures for which we have no parallels in verbal structure. To project a particular word in the spoken language, you would have to project that emphasis by saying it louder or pausing just before the word. With music, you could direct the listener's attention to that word by purely music-syntactic means without making it louder or having a rest before it—simply by, say, making it the "expected" pitch.[9]

In studying the structure of languages, I was struck by the fact that the whole notion of a syntax—at least, say, for a language like English—seems to be that it allows unambiguous communication. Extremely complicated structures can be transferred from one person to another without loss of what that structure is. For example, in English we may use the same word for both a verb and a noun, we use the same ending to show whether it's plural or singular, or reverse in the case of nouns and verbs—so that one can say a single word in English and not know whether it's a noun or a verb. Once you put it in a phrase, the chances of it being ambiguous are greatly reduced but still there. But once it's part of a whole sentence, that is a complete structure, it's *almost* impossible to create an ambiguity. (That is, in the *spoken language*. In the written language, it's much easier to create syntactic ambiguities, although these are usually avoidable by the inclusion of punctuation, as in everybody's favorite, "We've got time to kill Mother" vs. "We've got time to kill, Mother." The punctuation tells you how to *perform* the sentence. That's why those Roman orators invented commas and periods.)

I don't like to argue from analogy of verbal structure to musical structure, because the more you study each, the more you became convinced that they really are basically different. It does give some notion, though, that first of all, it would be *possible* to construct a nonambiguous syntax, and second, my work in text setting—and particularly the whole notion of the use of things like duration, pause, dynamics, timbre, and pitch to indicate syntactic structure—makes me think that possibly *true* structural ambiguity in tonal music is very difficult to come by. Although you might have complete statements that could mean two different things—once you play them, you're going to commit yourself to one way or the other way of hearing that. I suspect that people would never have liked tonal music so much if it had been ambiguous. They would have sought something nonambiguous, something that they could grasp immediately. Composers like Haydn, Mozart, and Beethoven are in effect writing structures which are (well, their complete structures are *whole* movements) their "sentences." And they are sentences of *enormous* complexity. Nevertheless, I'm beginning to think that there isn't such a thing as an ambiguous movement; while I disagree with various analysts who use essentially similar analytic techniques as to what the structure is, our disagreements are the result of our imperfectly formed syntaxes, rather than the imperfectly formed sentences of Mozart, Haydn, and Beethoven. As we sharpen our understanding of the way tonal syntax works, we will find that there really *aren't* that many ambiguities—unless pieces have been deliberately constructed to do just that. Maybe one can do that with English, but there are other languages where I understand it's much easier to do. And maybe one could do it deliberately with music. But I suspect that that's probably a special case.

BC: You said before that you regarded the Schenkerian model as an incomplete one, although a precisely directed one.

PW: Certainly that's the productive direction. The problem is in defining the operations more closely. My own work has been in the direction of defining the rhythmic aspect more closely. In doing that, I have narrowed the possible interpretations of a given passage considerably. I'm also concerned with the way you play it, and how that has to do with the way you understand it; and I think that, given a single phrase, there are phrases that could be interpreted in two different ways. You could analyze them two different ways. However, once you play them, you commit yourself to either one way or the other. I suspect, furthermore, that one of these ways will usually be the "right" way, or the other the "wrong" way, once you get to the relationship of that phrase to either the next phrase, or maybe the whole movement.

BC: How about the opera?[10] This will involve you in text setting, as well as in musical work. You said that you hadn't been writing very much in the past few years, as you'd been working on a book.

PW: Yes, the book has been handed in to the publisher.[11] I had thought the book would take me a year to write, and so I told myself, "Don't write any music until it *is* written; that's only way to get this thing done." Unfortunately, it took *three* years and therefore made me very unhappy because I had told myself that I wouldn't do any writing of music until I finished the book. Now I have returned to an opera on *The Tempest*, which I find much more interesting than writing books on theory!

BC: What problems in text setting are you up against in the opera?

PW: The biggest problem for me is the danger of blank verse. Blank verse has certain terrific advantages for spoken drama. It allows the actor a great deal of freedom as to how he uses the verse form—indeed, so much freedom that most actors don't use it at all. In fashioning the libretto from Shakespeare, first of all, I use only about a quarter of his text. This hurts now and then; on the other hand, it isn't as though I were consigning the lines I didn't use to the dustbin forever. You can still read the play. Certainly most of the marvelous lines I have omitted, particularly those lines that talk about the kinds of sounds one hears on this island—the noises, sounds, and sweet airs—I omitted presumably because I've got the music there to do that. But once I've cut down the amount of language—way, way down—the next problem is the particular *kind* of language, the length of sentences. There are a number of characters in the play who use very complicated sentence structures. Prospero is certainly one of them; he's always qualifying himself, turning back on his sentences, doing it again another way and then, at the end of an extremely long sentence, giving it a final twist. This is a very hard sentence structure to do in music. The danger is that you'll come out with very boring vocal lines. In contrast to my last opera, which had very tight rhyme scheme, elegant diction, very quick turns of phrase—this one, you're going to have to take a big, long breath. I don't want to say that it will be Wagnerian in its syntactical approach, but something like that. That is going to be a problem.

Another problem in this opera, as opposed, let's say, to the last one, is the large number of characters. In *Mr. and Mrs. Discobbolos* I had two characters, and the idea of the piece is that they are very similar. They talk in different ways, and there are discrete numbers in which they react in different ways, but they form a balanced pair and stay that way throughout a very short opera. In *The Tempest* I have eleven characters, and each one of them is very different; yet there are all kinds of cross-resonances among the characters. Various people resemble Prospero (the central character), but in various ways: Gonzalo in his convoluted speech, Antonio in his manipulating of people, and Caliban in his propensity for invocation, magical power and all. Yet these people are all clearly very different from and *differentiated from* Prospero. My initial problem is to separate out my characters by the kinds of vocal lines they have. Some of these are relatively easy choices and go directly to old operatic traditions, such as Ariel as coloratura soprano, Miranda and Sebastian as lyric soprano and lyric tenor, and Antonio as villain baritone.

BC: Is it going to be full opera or, like the other, seven instruments? Six?

PW: Six instruments in *Mr. & Mrs.* I haven't decided that yet. I have to find out more about the kind of vocal lines I want. Once I get those people moving in my mind and singing their lines and contrasting with one another, once I have some sense of contrasting scene structures, I'll be able to tell better how many instruments I'll need—clearly more than six; anywhere, therefore, from twelve instruments on up to a full orchestra. Related to this would be just simply economic facts—by the time I've got this thing put together, *who* is likely to play it, and what have they got? That would also, of course, affect the difficulty. I think judging from current performance practice, a composer is well advised, for the opera house, to keep the difficulty of his music pretty far down, for the singers, at least.

BC: How traditionally operatic are you going to be? Are you going to have all the Italianate set pieces?

PW: The structure is very much defined by Shakespearian structure, with certain strong exceptions. For example, I am leaving out the opening scene of Shakespeare, on the boat, entirely. I am just going to have a good blast of storm music, which will cut out to *subito pianissimo*—storm in the distance, Prospero, and Miranda. That seems to be the obvious solution. By and large, my structure will simply follow Shakespeare's quite closely. Shakespeare's is rather interesting. For example, the middle of his play is completely symmetrical, around the central scene between Miranda and Ferdinand, which is observed by Prospero. The characters present in each of the scenes moves outward in a symmetry that's quite complete and very nicely placed. This kind of shaping has something to do with Prospero's magic. Although Prospero's a magician, he is, of course, the kind of magician who has to take his chance when it comes. That chance is, of course, that Alonso's ship has sailed so near his island. But there is a larger sense that the critical moment has arrived—as he says in his opening scene with Miranda: "The time has now come when I must inform thee farther." He now knows that she must know what has actually happened in the past. He also knows that this is the time when he must act; he cannot just plot his revenge—which is what he's been doing for twelve years. What one has is a situation in which events that are loaded with significance, both from the past and the future, are crammed into one very small time, which he is trying to control. I think that that has something to do with its symmetrical arch. That, in a certain sense, is something that I don't have to do too much about; it just sits there in the middle. I've got three short acts, the middle one of which is completely symmetrical. No, I don't think there are "numbers." There are scenes, though; and those scenes will be heard as movements, in some sense.

BC: One of the problems in Shakespeare's later work is increasingly analogical with cinema. Instead of in the earlier plays where there's a fairly wooden sequence of events, one after the other, in the later plays—*Hamlet*'s a very good example—there's almost a sense of the announcer saying, at the end of a scene, "Meanwhile, somewhere else . . ." After you've seen the "meanwhile," you know that the action you've just seen has been going on, so there is a sense of several lines of development simultaneously. This is not just true in *The Tempest*; in this play Shakespeare is even going further. Not only do you have the sense of many things happening in different parts of the island at the same time, but you have Prospero as a pervasive presence in all these things.

PW: Yes, Prospero as represented by Ariel.

BC: Prospero through his "agents."

PW: It's significant that he's not going to send Ariel to observe his daughter and Ferdinand. That's *his* life, that's *his* own intimate concern. For handling monsters or kings or anything like that he can trust Ariel. Ariel makes it clear that his relation is simply that of spy and messenger. I certainly agree—there is the sense of simultaneous threads and we just see a certain segment of each thread. Do we know whether these scenes are all going on simultaneously? No, we don't. But on the other hand, that's one reason for putting them in this A-B-C-B-A pattern; they have to have some form.

BC: It's a kind of meta-order that Shakespeare uses.

PW: I don't think there's any reason why what happens with Caliban, and Trinculo and Stefano, has to precede or succeed the central scene. But it's essential that the scene between Ferdinand and Miranda is central in a different sense; it's central in the metaphorical sense rather than central in an operative order-in-time way. The whole notion of "time," in the sense of the choosing of a moment in time to do something, is critical. One of the reasons *The Tempest* appeals to me as an operatic subject—aside quite from the obvious operatic subjects of having monsters and spirits and all that—is that these are two rather important things that are very closely connected: time and identity. Identity would be the "true" identity of people, and there is a time to reveal the true identity of people. I'm not sure how operatic that is. Certainly the unmasking of people, the revelation of people on the stage, is stage worthy; but I'm not too sure how to do that musically.

BC: We're obscuring your musical ideas for the work in discussing the dramatic and the metaphorical.

PW: These things have somehow got to be taken into account in planning the music. As I say, the *successful* revelation of identity is one of the ends of the play. Surely, then I must arrange for musical identities which can be revealed and perceived by the audience with sufficient clarity so that they grasp them. I haven't got that one figured out yet. Other more traditional operatic things are easier to figure out. I have already worked out various of Ferdinand's vocal lines, and I'm sure he will resemble many other tenors in operatic literature. There certainly is a strong enough tradition for between vocal line and type of character represented to take care of him. There isn't for Caliban. He does not have any prototypes; and I will have to invent my own way of handling Caliban. One notion I have played with—I don't know how successfully it will work out—is that the relationship between Caliban and Prospero is a very important one: Prospero taught him how to speak. His profit is that he can curse; and when he curses, his language becomes closest to Prospero's. So I would imagine an extremely slow-moving but extremely ornate kind of writing for Caliban. Have we talked about cross-reference between characters? Well, we mentioned the fact of differentiating from Prospero. And yet there must be some way in which there is some connection. How to do that for many characters is a very large problem.

BC: Are you going to include the masque?

PW: Yes, but not the words. I'd make it a fourth-act ballet; you have to in order to nail down the whole notion of Prospero's ability to control the world so that it seems like a play controlled by an author. He thinks he can do it. Then of course, right in the middle he remembers that he *hasn't* gotten everything nailed down *quite* yet. I would also like to include the anti-masque and make something of that—the chase, the hunting down, directed by spirits in diverse shape. You can't have that without having had the masque before it. Neither has to be very long. But together they present the problem to Prospero in a nutshell: if he is to take revenge on these people, then he is himself a blot on his own view of an ordered universe. The ordered universe appears in the way he's arranged the spirits to work together harmoniously. He realizes that, in his desire for revenge and control, he himself is far from that ideal. But finally he can control that. I would consider that that's the turning point in my opera: his realization that were he to pursue revenge, he'd be no better than the people on whom he pursued revenge. When Ariel says that he would feel sorry for these people if he were human, Prospero realizes this. That seems to me an operatic turning point of the kind that then leads on to the whole last section of the piece. The moment he realizes that Ariel, who has no feelings, who is not a human being, can do this, he knows that he, as a human being, must.[12]

BC: This is counter-structure, in a sense, to the *Bogenform* [arch form] that we discussed earlier.

PW: Yes. At that moment the *Bogenform* disappears, because the middle—my second act—is completely symmetrical. Then the opening of the third act would correspond to the end of the first act which would include the characters of Prospero, the two kids, and Ariel. But then he sends them off—now this would correspond back, in retrospect, to the first scene in which Caliban makes his entrance. He suddenly realizes the presence of Caliban—it's still part of that; but, from then on, we're not just simply going backwards.

BC: How are you going to end?

PW: The end is the part in my libretto that is really left unresolved. The question that bothers me most, for purely traditional reasons, is that in comedy one generally has everybody sing at the end, and I would like to have everybody sing—but what do they sing? Do they simply join in with Prospero? That's no good. So there's a possibility of Prospero giving the epilogue simply as a tab. I really don't know. I think it's only after I begin to get a little further into the way that people sing on the other occasions that I'll be able to solve it. Maybe I'll never be able to solve it. It's perhaps unwise for me to plunge in without a good solution to that.[13]

BC: Do you have views on the state of music as it is being written today? What's happening among your students or your younger colleagues that you find worthy of remark? Is music changing—the ideas about what it ought to do, how it's done?

PW: It may be true that we're in a field where it's very difficult to write . . .

BC: I should interrupt by saying that I'm kind of asking for a specific purpose— because in many places the word "Princeton" has kind of an "Antichristly" connotation to many people.

PW: Let me answer your first question without reference to your comment. I think that in almost any period there are relatively few people who can write really *good* music. But at certain points, certain times, there were many people that could write *decent* music. I don't think that this is one of those times. You have to work like hell to write *decent* music nowadays. And the problem really is the syntactical limit we were referring to earlier. Of course, there's a marvelous syntax at everybody's disposal—that of tonal music. I just don't know of any regular composers who are really that much interested in writing tonal music. I don't know why that is. That's a very difficult question. To even pose it right now the right way seems to me hard.

BC: Perhaps it's the fear of not being thought "hip."

PW: Well, of course you could be "un-hip" that way. But if I were to come up with a completely tonal piece, why, they'd think it was a put-on.

BC: This has happened among people I've talked to.

PW: Right, but suppose, on the other hand, you really want to write a good piece, so you write a tonal one. That's another problem entirely. It might well be that you could not do that without being . . .

BC: Have you been tempted to?

PW: No, I don't think I'd be particularly good at it; I'm out of practice. After all, tonal music is something I *teach*, but not whole pieces, or not whole, long pieces. I think the difficulty really is the lack of available syntaxes. But I do find that the composers who think more and write less generally write more interesting pieces—not necessarily better pieces.

During the course of these three years when I was writing this book, I didn't go into every concert in New York. However, I hear a good deal of music and I see scores. I hear a good deal of music that's written by students here—there seems to be a good deal of hope there. It really has come to the point where each composer, in order to write a piece, has to first come up with a completely formed syntax, that is, a completely formed set of relationships that are going to be used in this piece. That's a pretty tall order. And I suspect that this may be one of the reasons why so much of the music I hear sounds so hopelessly confused. It is too tall an order. You hear pieces that have some very striking things in them; and you hear other pieces that totally baffle you. But the pieces that you hear in which there is some sense of ordered relationships being behind the whole piece—they come few and far between.

BC: How about Princeton?

PW: Yes. There are certain things that are curious about what has come to be known as the Princeton Syndrome. The Princeton Syndrome is presumably not something that is held by people who are *at* Princeton but is presumably something that is held by people who *aren't* at Princeton. That would include people from all over the U.S., even in such un-provincial centers as New York, I assure you. It has to do with an image of what we are supposedly doing here and how we act and what we think music is—an image which I've found to be totally false. I think because we write about music and we talk about music and we use symbols—mathematical or logical symbols—to describe musical structures, that somehow or other, that we, let's say, never *hear* what it is we're talking about, aren't quite concerned with how a listener might understand what it is we're writing. It's the old *Augenmusik* notion—the old "music as mathematics" fear. It's just silly. I can understand some of the reasons why this might have come about, but what strikes me as far more significant is that Princeton has, in fact, become an intensely traditional center of music study, particularly in its concern for understanding tonal music.

I was struck with it most when I went from Princeton as a graduate student, to Europe as a Fulbright student: the enormous difference between our American attitude towards the German/Austrian classics and my German and Austrian colleagues' attitudes towards them. We were and are still intensely interested in Mozart. At that time the Europeans were embarrassed by tonal music. And this is true that the people who teach here tend to take very seriously the notion of teaching and continuing to teach the structure of tonal music, take very seriously the notion that a composer's training should include an understanding of those works. Whereas, as I look across the country and talk to colleagues in various other places, I discover over and over again either that the colleague himself or some of his colleagues have been fighting in their own departments to clear out all this old music crap and just work on new music, and leave the study of tonal music to musicologists.

I think that the real conflict that will emerge in the long run between the Princeton department and many other departments would be that the Princeton department has a different set of concerns in its choice of subject matter.

We're not much concerned about the latest thing. We may be concerned about the latest way of looking at the same old thing. But we're not concerned with what around here is called "showbiz"; it may not quite resemble what showbiz people call showbiz, but showbiz for us is what Mr. Harold C. Schonberg writes about in the paper and what goes on at Carnegie Hall and so-and-so's latest success in his musical career. That really doesn't interest me very much. I have observed that there is a good deal of suspicion for people who don't play the game the way other people play it. So many Princeton composers have plainly opted out of the career-as-competition business, or make disparaging remarks about showbiz, that there is something suspicious about that—"Why would he do that?"; "Why isn't he like other people?"; "Why doesn't he want to have his piece played by Lenny and the Philharmonic?" Well—I don't think I'll give you my reasons for not wanting Lenny and the Philharmonic to play mine. Now, does that answer your question somewhat?

BC: I think that makes it very clear.

PW: I think that's a hard subject.

BC: I think it's fading out, frankly. The whole careerist thing is something we inherited, and it's still very alive in Europe.

PW: Sure. But there you can make a living by being a composer. In this country you can't unless you choose to turn out a product that has some sale value. You can make a living here by being a composer and convincing other people to support you because you *are* a composer. That, in a sense, is the way many people take their university jobs. They take them not because they want to teach or because they want to talk to other people about how they're thinking, but because they figure that society owes it to them, that they're composers, and therefore society ought to support them. And the only institution within society that seems willing to do this is the university, so we'll just have to put up with this pretense of doing what a university does. I don't care for that. I would say, though, that the differences between local notions of what a composer is doing in a university aren't necessarily that different from those held in other places. There seems to be a good deal of misinformation. The curious thing is that although the usual popular beliefs seem to put all the blame on Milton Babbitt, the same kind of nonsense seems to have existed before, when [Roger] Sessions was the dominant figure here, before Milton became the household word. I guess if you feel resentment, you've got to find some channel for it—and this is a possibility.

BC: The audience is, then, of concern to you?

PW: "The audience" is perhaps the wrong phrase. "A listener" might be ideal. I certainly don't mean the audience that's going to come here and hear my piece when it's done at such and such a hall. I do mean somebody who's going to hear it in the best possible way. That's not necessarily an easy job, even for listeners game to give it a try. So I try to make it easier for them, in the sense of some redundancy or structure . . .

BC: You *wish* to make it easier for them?

PW: Sure. Are you going to use specific examples in this book? It's just that a lot of these things would be much easier if I could just write a few lines down that show exactly what I'm about with this redundancy.

BC: OK. Good. At this point in the transcript the composer will insert such musical lines as he feels necessary to.[14]

PW: The idea of making it easier . . . Maybe it would be good to introduce one of Schoenberg's favorite words, which was *Fasslichkeit* (literally, "graspability"). He obviously wasn't the kind of person who wrote "easy music," and in his remarks he talks about different kinds of ease of grasping. (He even talked about the Offenbach and the Strauss family.) He is very much concerned that what you do be graspable, be intelligible. And his students are always concerned about clarity of the ideas, that they be strongly and sharply put. To a large extent, most of the compositional systems out there—the source of the kinds of relationships we might want to project in a piece—make it very difficult to do that. I have recently been working on things that are going to be easier to grasp, not so dependent on a single detail as dependent on a general redundant interrelationship between a number of details.

BC: What is your concern with immediate surface detail? For example, in the '50s you get a kind of European music which is micro-phenomenal, and it appears to be surface almost completely. Yet in this country this didn't happen except by imitators, generally in post-serial development.

PW: You could say that what I was trying to do in the *Variations*—these were micro-events, yet they were all supposed to connect.

BC: But one had the feeling that they all "belonged."

PW: Well, if it's not in European '50s music, that's just a failure of technique. Because what they were *trying* to do *was* to present something that was logically consistent.

BC: Yes, but in a Stockhausen *Klavierstück* can you hear anything but a micro-phenomenal kind of structure?

PW: No, and it's very difficult *to hear that*, because it doesn't fit very well. [Pierre] Boulez's *Structures* is maybe a better example, in that Boulez is putting together some pretty fancy relations among various serial entities, but then he doesn't choose those ways of projecting said relationships that would be easiest to grasp. For example, he doesn't use register; yet register would be far more *graspable* than all those twelve different attack forms, which may be graphemically distinguishable, but in terms of sound, I don't know how you're supposed to be able to distinguish one from its neighbor, either as a listener or as performer.

Such a procedure does provide a constantly varied surface; therefore, I think the combination of that and the combination of choice of how many lines to have going at once—that music is not very far from aleatoric music, in that you set up a formula; you plug it in; you get something. Well, you can compose aleatoric music that way: you get the right formula; you plug it in; you get something. The formula tells you what to write, never mind what you might wish to write. And I don't think that the leap—people talked then about the enormous shift from serially determined music to chance determined music—was that big at all. There was a change in ideology; but not much change in the music.

BC: Not much change in the *sound.*

PW: Certainly, not, no, or the *results*, let's say. A shift to a *theatrical* attitude, a theatrical presentation, was marked—and still is. You still get reports of festivals here and there, and that's basically all they seem to be interested in—some kind of fun and games. There may be exceptions—I don't know.

Notes

1. Peter Westergaard, "What Theorists Do," *College Music Symposium* 17/1 (1977): 143–49.

2. Peter Westergaard, "Toward a 12-Tone Polyphony," *Perspectives of New Music* 4/2 (1966): 90–112. See also George Crumb, "Peter Westergaard: *Variations for Six Players,*" *Perspectives of New Music* 3/2 (1965): 152–59.

3. Peter Westergaard, *Variations for Six Players* (Hackensack, NJ: Jerona Music Corporation, 1967). Recording: Acoustic Research 0654 088, LP, 1970.

4. Peter Westergaard, *Mr. and Mrs. Discobbolos* (Hackensack, NJ: Jerona Music Corporation, 1967; originally Alexander Broude). Recording: CRI SD271, LP, 1971.

5. Peter Westergaard, *Divertimento on Discobbolic Fragments* (Hackensack, NJ: Jerona Music Corporation, 1967; originally Alexander Broude). Recording: *20th Century Flute Music*, Nonesuch HB-73028, LP, 1975.

6. Peter Westergaard, *Noises, Sounds and Sweet Airs,* (Hackensack, NJ: Jerona Music Corporation, 1968); Peter Westergaard, *Tuckets and Sennets* (Hackensack, NJ: Jerona Music Corporation, 1969).

7. Godfrey Winham, "Composition with Arrays," *Perspectives of New Music* 9/1 (1970): 43–67.

8. Knud Jeppesen, *The Style of Palestrina and the Dissonance* (1926). Peter Westergaard, "On the Notion of Style," in *Report of the Eleventh Congress of the International Musicological Society, Copenhagen, 1972*, ed. Henrik Glahn, Søren Sørensen, and Peter Ryom, 1:71–74 (Copenhagen: Edition Wilhelm Hansen, 1974).

9. See Peter Westergaard "Sung Language," *Proceedings of the Second Annual Conference, 1967* (New York: ASUC, 1969), 9–37.

10. *The Tempest* (premiered 1994), then in progress.

11. Peter Westergaard, *An Introduction to Tonal Theory* (New York: W. W. Norton, 1975).

12. Peter Westergaard, unpublished score to *The Tempest: Opera in Three Acts after Shakespeare,* ca. 1990.

Prospero: How fares the King and his followers?

Ariel: All three distracted. Your charm so strongly works them that, if you now beheld them, your affection would become tender.

Prospero: Dost think so, spirit?

Ariel: Mine would, sir, were I human.

Prospero: And mine shall. Hast thou, which art but air, a touch, a feeling of their afflictions, and shall not myself, one of their kind, be kindlier moved than thou art?

(Shakespeare, *The Tempest*, act 5, scene 1, ll. 8, 14, 19–28)

13. "In its final version (1992), *The Tempest* differed from the project I described here. Shakespeare's opening storm scene ends up as a full-fledged scene (even though it is called 'overture') with both singing and action. 40% (not 25%) of Shakespeare's text survives. There are plenty of clear-cut numbers throughout the opera. (Some of the ones for Ariel were collected and arranged for high soprano and ensemble in *Ariel Music*.) The masque is sung, words and all, albeit only the last stretch of it—'Honor, riches, marriage blessings. . . . ' And Prospero ends up singing the epilogue as is, with everybody else just joining in with a polyphonic echo of each of the final couplets of his two stanzas" (Peter Westergaard to author, e-mail October 6, 2018).

14. This occurs in the discussion of *Variations* and its example earlier in this interview.

20 Olly Wilson (1937–2018)

HORACE J. MAXILE JR.

With an eclecticism that espouses influences ranging from Black vernacular forms to Edgard Varèse, Olly Wilson's compositional voice is among the more distinctive and celebrated in contemporary/modern music circles in the United States. Included among his numerous honors and recognitions is winning the 1968 Dartmouth Prize, the first competition devoted to electronic music. In fact, the timing of this interview sits squarely between the prize-winning *Cetus* (1967–68) and the completion of one of his most enduring and major works, *Sometimes* for tenor and tape (1976). This interview occurred in 1972, during a period of significant advancement for Wilson, as a move from Oberlin Conservatory to the University of California, Berkeley, commissions, Guggenheim fellowships, and thoughtful examinations of his compositional philosophy and aesthetic constituted his professional life for the early 1970s. In regard to the composer's evolving aesthetic, his interests and explorations with electronic mediums expanded. In addition to *Eighteen Hands of Jerome Harris*, each of the three additional works mentioned in the interview involve electronics: *Akwan* (1972, for piano, electronic piano, and orchestra); *Black Martyrs* (1972, a commissioned sound installation for Pitzer College); and *SpiritSong* (1973, for soprano, double chorus, and orchestra). Whereas *Eighteen Hands* and *Black Martyrs* are more conventional representations of then contemporary electronic (tape) music, Wilson uses sound amplification techniques in *SpiritSong* and *Akwan*. Of these works, *SpiritSong* is the most pivotal because it displays the composer's increasing proclivities toward timbral manipulations (with and between acoustic instruments and voices), and also because it marks a decided shift in the composer's choice of materials and approach.

Fellow composer Thomas Jefferson (T. J.) Anderson noted that Wilson began to intentionally incorporate musical emblems from Black culture in the early 1970s after returning from his fellowship residencies in Africa, and *SpiritSong* is among the first works to show that characteristic. According to Anderson, the work is inspired by "the evolution and development of the black spiritual."[1] Various elements from Black musical culture surface in his compositions from the time of this interview onward, but an affinity for the spiritual is noted in subsequent interviews in tandem with his output for various performance forces: *A City Called Heaven* (1988, for chamber ensemble), *Of Visions and Truth* (1993, song cycle for voices and chamber ensemble), and *Sometimes* for tenor and tape. The deliberate move toward more compositional uses of Black vernacular musical emblems in the early 1970s does not signal a sudden awakening to cultural and social issues that faced Black people during those years and the previous decade. Indeed, Wilson articulated a keen awareness of the counterpoints and distinctions between culture, history, and experience in a vigorous discussion on Black music in 1969:

> I would prefer to believe that you are in fact a result of all your experiences, so that a Black man cannot exist outside of his Blackness. That's why I say when I write a piece, if I'm honest with myself, and I profoundly think I am, it obviously reveals my blackness, whether it is demonstrable of not, whether you hear it or not. . . .
>
> It's impossible for anybody to have the same experiences I've had, irrespective of his color. Nobody else can have the same set of experiences.[2]

It appears that, for Wilson, themes of homage and hybridity informed his philosophy and approach within or without emblematic references to Black musical culture, as his artistic means and experiences involved various mediums, techniques, and genres.

Ultimately, Wilson prioritized the experience and expression of the individual, favoring these over the restrictive dogmas linked to prescribed practices advocated by some of his contemporaries. His dissatisfaction with insular (Western) viewpoints on electronic music are noted in this interview, but such sentiments were equitable when addressing those within his own culture when his methods and choices of medium were scrutinized. In 1973, Wilson offered an account of his early experiments with electronic media where "associates accused [him] of cop[p]ing out, of using the white man's machine to express [his] black humanity." His eloquent response reminded his "brothers" that "the Belgian Adolf Sax invented the saxophone and Jimmie Smith's last name was not Hammond. The point here is that, as in African Bantu philosophy, a thing is given meaning by the will of the human being. The media is the vehicle of expression, not the substance of expression. Since the substance stems from the well springs of the individual, the media may be derived therefore from any source."[3] The references to Sax and Smith speak directly to the rightful pride that his associates had in the advancements of Black musicians in jazz and, even more ironically, to the probable lack of criticism of those jazz musicians' choice of medium. Whereas apropos to the immediate critique of his associates, the subtle, and sometimes complex, distinctions between substance (creator/culture) and source (medium) and the ways in which they interact are essential to reading the structural and expressive potency of Wilson's music from the late 1960s to the early decades of the twenty-first century. One particularly profound and illustrative work is *Of Visions and Truth*. Unlike *Sometimes* for tenor and tape, this piece features acoustic instruments and three vocalists. With regard to substance and experience, *Of Visions and Truth* "considers the optimistic vision of an egalitarian America . . . while simultaneously acknowledging the harsh, colossal hypocrisy of the historical truth that is a mockery of that ideal."[4] The politically charged work employs folk spiritual songs and texts by Black poets as well as various postmodern compositional techniques. Additionally, his handling of formal boundaries with the chamber ensemble is reminiscent of strategies used in his electronic works. The dexterous treatments of cultural and technical elements are notable in a number of Wilson's works from the time of this interview until the end of his career. Indeed, Childs's engagement with Wilson in this year yielded telling commentaries not only on musical subjects but also on topics related to history, social concerns, criticism, and culture.

Olly Wilson: Interview

OLLY WILSON: As a person you're involved in this all the time. What is your role in society? What is your role as an individual? One can spend all of his time trying to justify his existence so much that he does that instead of concentrating on what he wants to do, which is, of course, to make music. The role of the composer is to consciously transform his experience through the medium of sound and to hope that this experience gives meaning to other people by manipulating sound sources around. Of course his experience is extremely broad. It takes in his social situation, the daily intimate personal situation, everything. I'm a Black composer; I think of myself as a "Black composer" as opposed to a composer who is "Black." My experience involves attempting to transmit some of this "Blackness," which has to do with this existence in contemporary America. At the same time, and this becomes very complicated, it has to be a natural point of view. I can't start all of my pieces with some quotation which immediately identifies me as Black. But at the same time, I'm conscious of this. I hope that the music in some way will reflect my Blackness, which is an extremely important and central thing.

BARNEY CHILDS: It seems that a lot of Black painters are copping out by using a more obvious way to get in through a kind of symbology, which is denied anybody working in music, unless he goes into quotation.

OW: Right. At the same time, I don't object to that. In some of my recent pieces, I have used things—say, a certain approach to rhythm—which one might say that somebody who is at least cognizant with traditional Black music, who is conversant with that musical expression, had to write that particular piece. I don't exclude that; at the same time, I don't feel compelled to force this as a major thrust of each of my pieces. There is something else, which is a broader approach to expression, an approach to time, an approach to the musical situation which involves a dynamic percussive approach and a very high-tension emotion. While it is not excluded from other people, it is something which I tend to hear in most Black composers and Black music. That's why it becomes complicated. On the one hand, I don't consciously say, "Boom, Baccy, every tune has a blues!" and on the other hand I don't exclude blues. There is something about the approach to the musical experience, which grows out of my Black experience.

BC: So this becomes an extra level in dealing with the process of composition. How have your African trips influenced your composing, your thinking about what music is, what it ought to do?

OW: It's so recent. I just returned a month or so ago. I completed a piece for piano, electronic piano, and orchestra including an amplified orchestra while I was there. Look at the medium: electronic piano, piano, orchestra, and amplified orchestra—and Africa? It seems somewhat incompatible. Yet I think my approach to the media may have been influenced by my day-to-day experiences. Then again it's such a subtle, mysterious kind of thing that I can't pinpoint it. I certainly don't think there has been a dramatic change in my compositional style; I'm simply more informed by additional resources and musical practices.

BC: How has it affected the way you feel about music in general?

OW: Prior to going to Africa, in the last five or so years, I began to look more carefully at the whole musical experience. Perhaps in my younger days—after I was right out of undergraduate school and graduate school—I may have been more inclined to accept notions of rigid lines between that which was more so-called entertainment music and that which was so-called nonentertainment music; with an implicit value system the latter was more important. My own musical experience from a child included a very heavy Black musical experience: the church choir, say. The first tune I ever played on anything was "Do the Hucklebuck." I learned to play clarinet and jazz piano at the same time I studied in regular school. I had the church experience, the secular jazz experience, and the school experience, and I kept these things rigidly separated in my mind.

The big evolvement was in being able to cut these lines down, being able to see that these distinctions were not necessarily valid or rigid ones. That was one of my motivating reasons for wanting to go to Africa, because by this time I'd already been extremely interested in looking at Afro-American music in a more analytical way. Prior to around 1966, I hadn't really looked at it in an analytical way, using not the same kind of tools, not the same kind of principles, but trying to develop new principles that were applicable to that kind of music. I started it around 1966, and a logical extension of that, of course, was the interest in Africa. I found things tended to confirm my basic ideas, so in a way, it's very fulfilling. So that other facet of my experience, that Black facet, has now suddenly become a much broader one, both intellectually and emotionally. Earlier it was only emotional: I knew it, I felt that I would never deny it, I wanted to deal with it. But now it's intellectual as well as emotional, and I can relate to it. Frankly, it fulfills me at a time when I find what some people refer to as American contemporary music not quite as thriving, because I don't make those rigid distinctions. I'm as excited by some of the things that Miles Davis or Herbie Hancock has done recently as I am by some things that [Karlheinz] Stockhausen invented a few years ago. Because I now recognize that, both intellectually and emotionally, the whole picture has become different.

BC: Even if the whole African experience has not really settled into your music, perhaps in five years, who knows what might be transmuted and come out in subtle, maybe unrecognizable ways?

OW: I don't mean to say the African experience has not settled into my music. It has, but the surface level of the African experience has not, because that would be a transformation. I think of the Afro-American experience as being a facet of the African experience. And I've come from that; I start out from the Afro-American experience, I'm expanded by other things I hear, and I'm working from that perspective. So I think of myself as grounded in this tradition. But recently that tradition in which I have been grounded has been firmed up, simply by learning more about it, simply by trying to understand it more. Since I'm looking at it from a contemporary perspective, I don't know whether this will be immediately perceptible in future pieces; I would hope so. Then we get back to the question, how is it perceptible? That's where this goes.

BC: Are you still working with electronics? I remember the studio compositions—are you still composing with electronic assistances? You've got amplified orchestra.

OW: Very much so. As a matter of fact, I have two commissions that I have to get out soon. One of them is for Pitzer College, which is an all-amplified, all-electronic piece to be played in the campus situation. For once I have an opportunity to build in regular performances and part of the condition is that it will be played on the birthdays of Malcolm X and Martin Luther King. I just finished a piece entitled *The Eighteen Hands of Jerome Harris* a week ago. It originated as a poem a poet friend of mine wrote. Jerome Harris is the Black jazz drummer from St. Louis. On one of his readings I performed double bass behind him, and one of my former students performed cello behind him. Then I took this tape of the poem plus our performance into the studio, and I developed it. The piece is designed to be danced to, so in a sense it's a ballet. But it developed out of that poem, "The Eighteen Hands of Jerome Harris," and that's an all-electronic piece, so I'm very much involved in electronics.

What has changed in my approach to the electronic source is first, I've done it more so I'm more familiar with it, and second, the technology involved in electronic production is a lot easier. Third, it's proven pretty conclusively in the last ten years that those admonitions that used to come out of Cologne in the early days, "This is a whole new era and we demand a whole new aesthetic; you must do this, you must not do that" is BS. Some of the most exciting electronic music I hear is on television commercials—guys just plinking stuff out for a coin—and every now and then they come up with something that might be interesting. On the other hand, people still write all-electronic pieces that are not entirely interesting. I personally tend to be less interested in that, unless it's for a specific setting like the Pitzer commission.

BC: This sounds theatrical. Not in the sense of activities, but in the sense that it's working in an environmental sound space.

OW: Although it's somewhat different from the usual environmental sound in that the music is clearly the central medium. But I do have the environment to work in, I do have to realize that everybody is not going to be standing in reverence, listening to sounds of wisdom. In fact, most students will be going to class and they'll hear this stuff going on. I hope that there's something about the piece that enriches their lives and at the same time relates to my social existence and to the social existence of Martin Luther King and the significance which lies with the life of Malcolm X. Without being cheap, everybody could write a piece, have somebody say "Malcolm X" or "Martin Luther King," and everybody else will say, "Ah, that's it!" I hope it comes on a subtler but a more meaningful level.

BC: But the technical problems in this music for a campus . . . Suppose somebody wants to do it on a different campus, with an entirely different setup: the buildings, the areas, the sound sources. It's a pretty challenging idea.

OW: It is. Of course, like most composers you try to get as much mileage out of it. Let's face it, we're all egoists. If you can create something that more people will hear, within some limitations, then of course you shoot for that. Even though it's designed for Pitzer, it's not going to be designed that precisely that it wouldn't go elsewhere. But the technical problems that you mention do exist. Now there are two speakers at various parts of a long quadrangle, and I have to try to work within those kinds of limitations, and realize that it's an outdoor piece, that some of the subtleties will be lost.

BC: Last winter we had a seminar with the wind ensemble, music of Mozart and Beethoven. For the first time I heard it outdoors and I realized why they wrote it that way. The sound is so different. You get it out of the room and it's real. What is the other piece?

OW: The other piece is a commission from the Oakland Symphony. I've just started sketches for it, and I've got another year for it. I actually started the piece because I thought at one point it was due this year. But the piece is for soprano and for two kinds of choruses and orchestra. One of the choruses will be capable of handling difficult contemporary idioms. The other chorus will be—and these aren't necessarily mutually exclusive, some of the people might be involved in both things—a Black chorus, with experience in singing gospel music.

BC: Is it a gospel piece, as such?

OW: I hope we'll have a combination with enough people to be able to read enough to be a good deal. I'm really looking for a kind of vocal quality, and that particular piece I hope will sort of grow out of that media idea I have.

BC: You don't seem as pessimistic about the future of orchestra pieces as a lot of people.

OW: In a way I'm pessimistic; on the other hand I'm not, because the orchestra is like everything else in our society. What I see around me in Northern California is orchestra conductors jumping to try to get on some kind of bandwagon, which has to do with social relevance. I see this primarily in Oakland, and I see it less in San Francisco. This might be a reflection of the relative budgets of each of the orchestras and the people who are able to produce the budgets.

Oakland recently has been very interested in trying to relate to the community, and there are a great many public concerts, free concerts and on-the-street concerts. And then in Northern California—I don't know much about Southern California—I see musicians out in the streets playing for the people. People are tossing the coins in the hat, and they're playing every kind of music. In SF yesterday I heard a group playing sort of Afro-American reinterpretation of African music on one corner across the street from Macy's in Union Square. Then I walked up the street and I heard a flutist and a guitarist trying to play a Mozart concerto. You walk down the street and you see string quartets in public squares, and people are stopping, listening, and being fascinated. They're not concerned with the chairs, the plush carpet, and the acoustics in this type of situation: people are sitting and listening. Those establishment things are perhaps important, but we have probably reached a point where they have become the most important thing, where the most important person involved in opera was Rudolf Bing, where the most important person is the big impresario. Clichés about the music scene being simply the plaything of the elite are not necessarily about the performer or the audience.

Because of that, certain orchestras have to go over and meet that need. Since orchestras want to exist, musicians want to play, and they discover that there is a need over there, they will move over. I don't think that the orchestra will disappear. It does exist and they are commissioning composers—few and not nearly as much as they should. They aren't playing nearly as much contemporary music as they should. But since some of them are saying, "I'll commission you to do this piece," then I'll write the piece. I can't honestly say that the next piece I wrote would be a piece for orchestra, if an orchestra didn't come and say "Do it." I'm enough of an egotist, pragmatic enough to want the music I write to be played, that I'm not into writing music for somebody to discover fifty years later. I want people to hear it, I want people to relate to it, I want it to mean something.

BC: You're very much concerned with response.

OW: I don't buy the notion that I only care if five or three people hear my piece. I'd like for many people to hear it. Although I'd like to be, I recognize that I'm never going to be as popular as James Brown or Igor Stravinsky.

BC: Either or both!

OW: Sure, yes!

BC: Now that you've been out in the West for quite a while, do you feel that there is a kind of "western" stance, a feeling about new music that is a little different?

OW: Though legally my residency is going on its third year, I have only been here actually a year and a half. I think the difference in the West is simply a continuation of the difference in the social attitude that I see in the West. People in the West are freer, tend to be more responsive to change, tend to be readily amenable to new ideas. As the old cliché says, much of what purports to be or will probably be the future social situation in the country, and ultimately in most of the world, emanates from the West. You can find that reflection in attitudes toward the music, so that if a particular concert of "new music" is properly advertised, you can generate a fairly decent audience.

On the other hand, because there is tremendous search for the new, the novel, it is also easy to do very cheap things and get big crowds. You can go down to certain places in SF or in Berkeley and say, "Hey, everybody, come on, we're going to do this," and a lot of the young people will come, simply because it's an in thing to come: it's "follow the buffalo." But my attitude is, independent of how you get them there, the people are there, if you're doing something meaningful, they'll come back. I've seen this happen at a lot of concerts on the West Coast—people come because it's supposedly an in thing. It's got the word around that this is really cool, man. Then before the concert's half over, three-fourths of the audience is gone. That's sad, too, because on one hand you got 'em there because they can say, "Yeah, I went to this way-out concert, man, and they were doing some way-out stuff." But nobody is really listening: everybody's lighting up and copping out.

BC: About the fact that you wanted people to become involved: do you feel personally like a revolutionary? Does music have social and political power, and to what degree can it go? Second, how about your own stance?

OW: To answer the first question, obviously yes, music has social and political power. Secondly, I think certain kinds of revolution, using the word very loosely, are necessary in this society. Thirdly, as a composer, are you a revolutionary? Are you using music as a social and political force? Can you justify your existence any other way? The question usually comes to me hard and fast, "Man, are you with it? Are you a revolutionary or are you part of the problem?" That's a good objective way of putting it. However, subjectively I am bothered by other things: musical expression, to get back to what I said earlier, being a conscious transformation of your experience. Your experiences are so broad, and music involves so many dimensions of experience. At one point they're revolutionary, in the sense of "Boom! Here you are!" You hope everybody gets the message, and you hope you change and motivate people. On the other hand, there are other parts of your experience which are independent of that: very intimate things. In that sense the average person certainly wouldn't perceive those expressions as being revolutionary. As a composer, if you're honest with yourself, that has to come, too. Therefore some of my expression is revolutionary. There are other things which have nothing to do with revolution; though looking at it from a very broad perspective, in the sense that you hope to change and to enrich people's lives, to make them more human, then of course they are revolutionary.

Every piece that I do doesn't say, "get a gun and do it now!" On the other hand, I have written pieces when I have felt exactly that way and hoped that the music would convey that. The most important musical personalities coming out at least the last ten or fifteen years in Black music are John Coltrane, Cecil Taylor, Eric Dolphy, and of course Miles Davis, who changes and yet maintains his drive, like a Stravinsky or a Picasso. In all those people there is a revolutionary fervor, but there is an intensity, which encompasses that but also a million things the immediate listener wouldn't say "Ah, that's revolutionary!" Although you can put any label on any music that you want; you can listen to *any* music and say, "Ah, that's revolutionary!" If that's what people want to accept at that particular time, they can certainly do it. But again we get to the same old problems with the meaning of music. If our confusion is simply in attempting to apply a certain syntax which is not really applicable, we're talking about a different kind of response to a different kind of experience. It's natural to try to do the old nineteenth-century things—this is beautiful, Fate knocking on the door—and somebody saying, "No, it means this," and then somebody finally saying "It means *that*," it means that musical expression, that musical gesture can only be understood in the context of its musical environment. But since it is music and since we are social beings and since we put these interpretations on it, then one can say, "Ah, that's revolutionary!"

BC: What role can we play as educators in getting the young into music in a way that we feel is real?

OW: Again, the most important role that we can attempt to play is simply to get people to listen. The first year I was here I taught a course in contemporary music. I don't know how it had been taught before. When I was in under-graduate school, contemporary music was taught like here are the really great people. We start at the late nineteenth century and move up. Of course the class ends. Maybe we're up to very early Stravinsky because we started with Brahms, so that's it. So people go and hear the concerts that are going on, and they are totally unprepared.

My approach to it was to start with today, to give them a glimpse of the diverse things that were going on. You familiarize them with the syntax involved in that kind of musical expression, and to show them what a person is about and what his impact has been. Contemporary music for the last ten to fifteen years or longer has been eclectic; there have been borrowings and cross-cultural things going back and forth. People are influenced by Indian music and African music and at the same time conversant with electronic techniques—all kinds of things, in addition to the mass media, which communicates the effect that that has had, and the kinds of musical experience that a person will have. You say, "This music is not necessarily on a plateau, somewhere up here, and your musical experience of the Rolling Stones is on this level. Just listen to it and be honest, do you dig it? If it has that immediate kind of attractiveness to you, then let's see who can understand." Then you talk about why you dig it, or why you don't. Now admitting that there are some intangibles, who really knows what the distinction is between composer A and composer B? You know we think we know. But we all know that familiarity is certainly one of the most important things, because if you're not familiar with style obviously you aren't in any position to make any value judgments. So we say, "Listen, and try to develop an open attitude towards it." In answer to your question about what can we do as educators, we can simply try to teach people, or try to get people to teach themselves, to listen with a broad mind.

BC: At what point then should any kind of scholarly analysis come in? Does it ruin someone once he has learned Schenker analysis, for example?

OW: I don't think so. That logically comes in after a person is already committed, if a person says "Wow, this really turns me on." If he's intellectually curious, then you say, "Well, if this turns you on, why does it turn you on, and what are the various approaches to ascertain this? Let's get into the musical syntax; what is happening here? Is there something happening here that is perhaps not happening there?" If in practice you're already convinced, then you can get into the theory aspect. You can say this really excites me, let's get into it. But if you're fascinated by the intellectual rigors involved in the theory, and the practice is secondary, that will die very quickly. Once you have mastered at least one iota of that, then you go on to something else which is interesting. But if you really have a firm interest then, recognizing that although you'll never be able to find out totally, there are certain things you can ascertain.

BC: Is it possible to take analysis too far?

OW: There is, since we're talking about somebody's transformation of their experience, the pouring out of their souls, transforming it, and making it a beautiful and meaningful experience. The things we can learn through analysis deal with syntax, grammar, musical logic, but the limitations of analysis in that sense don't really get to the heart of the total meaning of that experience. It tells us something about the syntax, the grammar, but then the other aspects that you could never get to. I always try answer the student who says, "Yeah, so now I know that this musical event is logical and appears to make sense in this context because of that, fine. But now that doesn't tell me about my own psychophysical reaction." I say, "But I'm not a psychoanalyst, and I can't deal with it. All I can deal with is the syntax and the kinds of grammar in this particular musical situation which I think certainly adds to it." I don't think it is the definitive thing about that musical experience—I'm a mystic in that sense.

BC: That's what I want to get at. In your own musical speech, you're really not contradicting yourself, but at one level you might be. You're saying analytically we cannot get at a gut reaction, but as a composer you are concerned with reaching inside and making this happen.

OW: But as a composer, I never have to analyze it.

BC: Therefore you feel that the thing where you're asked up on stage and the MC says, "Now tell us, Mr. Wilson, something about the piece."

OW: I can talk in technical shop terms to composers and I can say, well, I do this, but ultimately when they say, "Define the essence of your piece," I say "BS—you know I don't think I can." There are perhaps some people who think they can. I've never heard anybody yet, or read anywhere yet, that satisfactorily defined the essence of any piece I've heard yet. I'm not denying the possibility, but on the basis of my experience I haven't heard it. Therefore the other explanation seems more logical, which is the mystical one. We can describe how it psychologically affects you—and that's what we're talking about—and we certainly know on the basis of recent studies how it's related to the social situation, social prejudices, and social learning. But in terms of really defining it, we'll miss. We can perhaps make analogies; some analogies might be apropos, and others might not be. You go up to the board and you say this piece means this, and everybody says "Wow, far out." It might capture for you what the piece means; whether it captures it for anyone who has ever heard the piece is something else. But that's not the piece, that's just an analogy.

BC: How can a composer reach this level with his listener? Well, that's a stupid question, because we're all doing it and we all know why, but we could never explain it. If we put down how we sincerely feel about it, hopefully they too will feel a sense of immediacy of response. You mentioned earlier, when you were talking about Cologne's strictures about how tape music should be—an emphasis on process. This applies to so many things: one of them is that it's fairly easy to teach a piece if you can show someone how it's written. Any Webern piece, if analyzed, is like any simple music. But what about the relationship of process to sound? Should the listener feel that there is some kind of intellectual rationale going on? When you're composing, are you concerned with structural, syntactical matters on the audience level or simply for your own self?

OW: I'm concerned about it for my own self and on the audience level too. I think of that as a means to an end. I think of music as being a process, music as listening in time, and therefore, at least in every piece I've done up to this point, I do think of as existing over some span of time. I am concerned with continuity. I just happen to think in those musical terms; something is going to happen here, and something is going to happen over there. In most instances, I am concerned that there should be either what appears to be some logical musical progression—I am concerned about something happening here—or I can certainly conceive of some things happening. I would be very pleased if the listener came back to me and said, "Hey, I understand musically what you're doing in that piece," and if you can sit down and diagram it. But I think I would be pleased more by his emotional response. In other words, the craft involved in it—that's the means to an end. What I'm really trying to predict is something which I don't think can be expressed in those didactic terms.

BC: The process is merely a means to an end.

OW: Process is a means to an end. At least in my own music, what I feel comparable with that is that the whole process thing is important, it's the only way I know how to do it. I am concerned that the listener is aware of that, but not to the exclusion of the other things. The process on the syntactical level, you see, is subservient to the other kind of process, which is more important. So if a guy says, "Emotionally the piece turned me on," I'd be infinitely more pleased than a guy saying "In the fourth page and the thirty-second minute I heard something which sounded like something that happened in the first minute and a half; however, it was slightly altered this way," or "that gesture was different from that gesture here." That kind of talk is more shoptalk.

BC: Yes, you're appealing to a certain ear with that. It's there, but it's merely a vehicle to carry what is really happening. People are coming back to this more nowadays. They're concerned with the process as a means rather than process as an end. The whole European 1950s show you what you get into when you start thinking of process as an end.

OW: Right. Then you end up doing the end, why write the piece?

BC: Like somebody who says, "I can read a good analysis; I don't have to hear the piece."

OW: That kind of thing. Then the analysis is the piece.

Notes

1. Thomas Jefferson Anderson, "Wilson, Olly Woodrow," in *International Dictionary of Black Composers*, ed. Samuel A. Floyd Jr. (Chicago: Fitzroy Dearborn, 1999), 2:1246–47.

2. Olly Wilson quoted in "Black Composers and the Avant Garde," *Black Music in Our Culture: Curricular Ideas on the Subjects, Materials, and Problems*, ed. Dominique-René de Lerma (Kent, OH: Kent State University Press, 1970), 72–73.

3. Olly Wilson, "The Black-American Composer," *Black Perspective in Music* 1/1 (1973): 35–36.

4. New Black Music Repertory Ensemble, *Recorded Music of the African Diaspora*, vol. 1, Albany Records, Troy 1200, 2010, CD, liner notes.

21 Phil Winsor (1938–2012)

PETER GENA

There ought to be a saying that if you remember a Chicago experimental music scene in the '60s, you weren't there. If you don't, then you were. The legacy generated by a cadre of individualists who worked in Chicago, from Ruth Crawford and Florence Price to John Becker and Alexander Tcherepnin, had long since faded. On the South Side, the University of Chicago began enjoying a strong academic avant-garde tradition led by the Contemporary Chamber Players, directed by composer Ralph Shapey. However, those rare creative geysers that erupted rather spontaneously, spouting a fertile experimental milieu in New York, Buffalo, and Ann Arbor, skipped over Chicago, and sprang up downstate in Urbana-Champaign.

When I moved to Chicago in 1976 to teach at Northwestern, the robustly creative environs that I took for granted in Buffalo were absent. I quickly began to invite like-minded guest composers for lectures and concerts. To my delight, I learned about an individual at a local conservative Catholic college that might well be a kindred spirit. Almost immediately I sought out Phil Winsor from DePaul University, and soon we became immediate and inseparable friends. Phil avoided a competitive posture before he settled in Chicago in 1968—he already had won nearly every prestigious award and grant in composition that there was to be had. He held many residencies, most notably Tanglewood, American Academy in Rome, Radio-Televisione Italiana (Milano), and Darmstadt, and was at the San Francisco Tape Music Center from its origin to 1965 with its directors, Pauline Oliveros, Morton Subotnick, and Ramón Sender.

While he learned a great deal abroad, Winsor recognized that European musical thought at the time was still based in nationalistic identities. He sensed that visiting American composers were seen primarily as a conduit for established Europeans to get to America. However, young European composers found themselves bored with their musical surroundings and started looking to America for inspiration. Phil eschewed the necessity to pad his musical thought with any trace of philosophical polemic or rhetoric involving politics, sociology, history, or the like. We later shared the same disdain for the "critspeak" craze brought to us by our visual arts brethren, that is, the "verbicized" nouns and abstruse verbosity—taking paragraphs to express what John Cage could have said in a couple of sentences.

At the time of this interview in 1972 or 1973, previous achievements had placed Phil in a position of autonomy at DePaul, so much so that he could openly harbor a cynical mien regarding the composer's place in academia. Although almost ten years his junior, I found myself, for better or worse, quickly sharing those sentiments. His rendering of aspects of academia, including teaching composition, performing, appreciating new music, and the perceived success of a faculty composer, had taken on a rather sardonic tone. His manner was not unlike that of a character out of a J. D. Salinger short story; there was often an acerbic component to his temperament, but palliated by negligible misanthropy and plenty of humor. By the time we met, Phil lacked any trace of widespread anger—quite the contrary: he was mild-mannered and laid back. Nonetheless, there was always the opportunity to do as he does here: engage in critic bashing, the futility of composition prizes, East Coast snobbery, and so on.

Soon we agreed that, in addition to some innovative programming at the Museum of Contemporary Art, there was a need for a vibrant "downtown" (as in lower Manhattan) musical life in Chicago. We formed the Chicago InterArts Ministry, a nonprofit presenting organization, and subsequently began offering programs in spaces alternative to universities. Our guest composers were literally a who's who of the experimental scene: Terry Riley, Pauline Oliveros, AMM, Salvatore Martirano, Diamanda Galás, Rova Sax Quartet, Linda Montano, and Laurie Spiegel, among others.

We attempted in part to encourage the general public as well as our students to take on a more holistic aesthetic in contrast to what appeared to prevail at the base of academic music departments. It seemed that the individualism spawned by the '60s required what Phil characterized as "constant revision," rather than fixed dogma. Accordingly, his discussion with Barney rehashes the tedium of whether one can teach composition, and if so how to be critical *and* constructive. Indeed, Phil evokes the Cagean dismissal of arbitrary value judgment and direct criticism of student work, taking on the role as catalyst and avoiding any hint of imposing any doctrine on young composers. I recall that even at this time, Cage's ideas were widely ridiculed in academia, and he was regularly a target of ad hominem attacks—one could find little relief until the 1980s, twenty-plus years after *Silence*, when academic journals began to publish cute little aphorisms à la Cage. Worse yet, conceptual music and minimalism were viewed as trivial by the ivory tower.

Phil's conceptual repertoire ran the gamut from instrumental to electronic music. He collaborated, as he discusses here, in many genres, including film and new media; in addition, he was a talented photographer. Surely, he embraced a myriad of experimental tenets, but he made them his own. He partook of current musical trends, but no composer pruned the excesses quite like Phil. In *Melted Ears* (1967), he embraced quotations and improvisation. This was soon after the practice of borrowing material, widely evinced throughout music history, resurfaced though works like *Baroque Variations* (1967), by Lukas Foss, or Berio's *Sinfonia* (1968). Still, it showed itself well before the postmodern condition of appropriation became de rigueur in the visual arts. Remember that Stravinsky once declared that a good composer borrows, but a great one steals. In *S.T.O.C. (Same Tired Old Changes*, 1982), premiered at New Music America 1982 in Chicago, Phil boldly took what could be seen as modern-day pitfalls—such as tonal licks, repetitive patterns, phasing, and metamusic—and created a familiar yet distinctive sound and texture.

Shortly after New Music America '82 in Chicago, around the time that I left Northwestern University, Phil accepted an offer for a position at North Texas State University. I remained in Chicago, teaching at the School of the Art Institute of Chicago from 1983 until 2017, where I continue as an emeritus. The InterArts Ministry persevered with new membership through the mid-1990s, though our concerts diminished in number as Chicago grew as a center for experiment in music. From 1983 until his untimely death, Phil's enviable ambition, industry, and recognition snowballed. Yet he was always the witty character that I knew, confident but never taking himself too seriously. Although we infrequently stayed connected since the '80s, our mutual respect endured, if only—regrettably—through remote observation.

Phil Winsor: Interview

BARNEY CHILDS: People nowadays seem to feel pressure to produce music, that they have to write. Do you think this is built-in?

PHIL WINSOR: There's pressure to be productive that runs counter to what the case should be for a particular composer. If it isn't the next piece that he should write, or needs to write, then why should he write it?

BC: Where do you think the pressure comes from?

PW: Probably in response to professional conditions—the desire to advance his own position. There's a certain amount of ego involved, and ambition. Everyone feels this to an extent; if someone says he doesn't, he's probably independently wealthy.

BC: Is there some sort of "fame" pressure?

PW: It's not fame as much as a desire to earn a living at what one wants to do— which is normal.

BC: Suppose a composer found that he could do this essentially by writing a new piece every two years.

PW: That would be fine.

BC: You think each of us should pace himself by his own demands on himself. You want to write a piece? Then, dammit, write a piece!

PW: Good music is not something that can be squeezed from a tube like toothpaste. A commission that specifies the instrumentation can be a boost if that ensemble happens to fire any ideas which may preoccupy me. But if I have a piece in mind for twelve unusual instruments and that's the only combination that will satisfy my requirements, then it can be disastrous to translate those ideas into the requested ensemble.

BC: So it's possible to write a piece for twelve freaky instruments even though you know it may never be played?

PW: Sure, if I want to write it. The beauty is that it *will* be played today.

BC: And this wouldn't have happened twenty years ago?

PW: It would have been impossible twenty years ago.

BC: The instrumental fluency is now such that we can write anything we want.

PW: There are so many new music performing groups in and around universities looking for pieces, it's possible to write whatever we want and get at least one good performance of it.

BC: Has this contributed to a decentralizing—you don't have to go to New York?

PW: It's better *not* to rely on New York. If traditionally oriented professionals play your music, they probably won't understand what you're doing.

BC: A lot of action nowadays is from West Coast composers: people that have been there, grown up there, or were born there. You weren't born or raised there, and yet you lived on the West Coast. Did it influence your thinking in any way?

PW: When I moved there in 1960, I had just graduated from college, had only been writing music for a year or so that was clearly in an academic twelve-tone idiom. The composers active at the San Francisco Tape Music Center and the conservatory had a tremendous impact on my thinking.

BC: So many strong young composers were at Tanglewood the summer of 1966. Do you think you inter-influenced each other?

PW: Some of us enjoyed each other's company.

BC: So many outstanding people were there at once.

PW: It was an accident. I doubt that the particular criteria used for selecting composers that summer have been used since.

BC: By popular demand?

PW: Right!

BC: Some years ago, Larry Austin talked about open style, which was his coinage. And he said this was a western thing.

PW: That might seem true, but only because his statement is an analytical generality so vague and nondescriptive that its meaninglessness can coax one to seriously consider it as a realistic statement of fact.

BC: He wrote an article for the *Times* about what he calls the new romanticism. Do you think there's anything to this? People are now turning away from live electronics, multimedia, and all the experimentalism of the '60s.

PW: The 1960s idea was of group interaction. Multimedia was a popular way of making music on a grand scale. I'd use the word "personal" to describe my own orientation, but because it implies developing a style and adhering to it, I prefer "idiosyncratic."

BC: You don't think that developing an official style is how it should be done?

PW: I don't think the word "should" ought to be involved. The only purpose for anyone intentionally developing a personal style is to be able to favorably impress grant and prize juries and commission committees, for whom stylistic consistency and predictability is comforting. Juries don't think well of a composer whose music doesn't exhibit development in a particular direction, because to them it means he's not formed yet as a "serious" composer; he's just groping around, experimenting with a variety of compositional means as a preliminary to formation of a style.

BC: When you were in Rome, did you associate much with what was going on musically?

PW: Not at all.

BC: Was this from choice or necessity?

PW: A bit of both. First, I'd lived in Milan for a year when I was on a Fulbright to study with Nono, two years before I went to Rome. That year I participated in concerts, and with financial backing from USIA, I co-organized a concert of American music. During this period I also composed in the Italian Radio Electronic Music Studio and met a number of Italian composers. Through both Nono and Niccolo Castiglioni I learned a helluva lot about the significance of the philosophic orientations that seemed to direct many of the European maestri, and the general state of European composers in relation to their music, performers, and public—enviable, for the most part. It became clear, though, that national boundaries were even more important than musical considerations, and what the Italians had, they intended to keep Italian. An American was welcome in Europe as a visitor and medium of international communication; he was useful mainly as a passport to the United States.

I went to Darmstadt the summer before my year in Rome. The clique of European superstars was still ruling, and I heard nothing new coming either from them or their work. But the younger composers were walking out of master classes and beginning to boo at the concerts of their own national hero. One German student thought that this was the beginning of a new trend in Europe—that the younger composers were looking more toward America for inspiration and were thumbing their noses at the established European composers.

In Rome, I just wrote music. The American Academy did not provide funds for Fellows to live outside its walls, resulting in a very cloistered existence. One's contacts were primarily with other Americans, which wasn't conducive to active participation in Roman musical life. My sole contact that year with the Italian music scene was a performance by the Rome Radio Orchestra of my chamber orchestra piece, and by the time it was performed and broadcast, I was back in the United States.

BC: Is the European scene a philosophic war?

PW: It seems to be part of one's role as a composer: to participate in polemics, and to have a very clear philosophic stance on a variety of subjects—sociology, economics, politics, history. I found these discussions repetitious and tedious.

BC: There was a tendency to cite other people's work—the collage pieces. What happened to this?

PW: Personally, I've never thought of the collage technique as citing other composers' work, but as using preformed material. In *Melted Ears* [1967], for example, I was concerned with including a wide variety of content—-quotation as well as controlled improvisation and newly composed material.

I've used quotations because of extramusical associations people have with them. Most audiences are accustomed to hearing particular passages within their original contexts, and their associations include the conditions under which they heard the piece, how often, and whether they liked it or not. But when these passages are placed within new contexts, they're accessible as a fresh experience. The quotations perform totally different structural functions and acquire new connotations.

BC: So, when you hear two bars of Mozart in another context, it sounds different. How does this relate to certain graphic artists of the late '50s and early '60s who would take ordinary objects and put them in new settings?

PW: It's closely related, but the inspiration for this idea is contemporary life itself. Our entire experience has shifted, thanks to the electronic revolution, from one of static permanence to perpetual transience. In the nineteenth century, one had relatively little control over his daily environmental experience; today, our lives are truly McLuhanesque. The range and breadth of encounter that is available through the communications and transportations media is staggering. Our values and preconceptions are in an unending process of revision. This state can be disconcerting, but it's as if we are ascending to a higher level of awareness as human beings. Now that myriad connotations of events and experiences are the order of the day, we should accept and make use of this condition.

BC: Doesn't this lead to a compositional dilemma in terms of structure?

PW: No. For several years composers have commonly employed variability—a more appropriate term than "randomness"—on several different structural levels. The important breakthroughs achieved by Cage and others in this area have given composers a set of new tools which can be applied in very personal ways to one's own work. A popular method is to precisely notate individual parts, then allow the performers to determine when they will be played, how many times they are to be played, etc. The technique can be very workable, but right now I'm preoccupied with variability on a sub-formal level. I prescribe the sequence of events over the duration of a work; however, the compositional details may vary within limits according to the performer's discretion, allowing what could be called a new focus with each performance.

BC: Are we entering a new era in relation to the use of synthesizers?

PW: I feel that the synthesizer is emerging from the electronic music studio and becoming part of a more generalized compositional process. In the past, one was labeled as an "electronic composer" simply because he may have had occasion to use electronic sounds in a particular piece. With the advent of portable polyphonic synthesizers many composers are exploring the real-time possibilities; in effect, we now have a new, live performing instrument which can be integrated into the concert ensemble. I believe that within a few years the title "Director of the Electronic Music Studio" will evaporate simply because it'll no longer be necessary to depend on that rather insular situation. It's possible that advances in computer technology will cause a merger of facilities, and a new laboratory experience will evolve, but it will be a radically different concept. Until now, we have been forced by necessity into the lab because of the primitive state of equipment development; in the future, the lab will probably emerge as a true experimental and research facility.

BC: What about the tendency to put synthesizers in every Middlesex village and farm? Music educators seem to be acquiring small synthesizers and starting kids off at the junior high school level.

PW: I can't see anything wrong with it. It's simply another instrument which may be more appealing to a student than the relative inactivity of playing trumpet in the school orchestra. The disadvantage is that if he avoids ensemble situations by using the synthesizer, then his music reading and performance skills won't develop. It *can* provide direct access to composition, an avenue formerly available only through the piano or other keyboard instrument. It can also introduce them to a sound world that has quite a flexible vocabulary, and expose them to sonic events from which they might have recoiled otherwise.

BC: The New York Public Library has a notational survey project which will last three years. Is there going to be a common practice notationally?

PW: There already is.

BC: But it's so varied.

PW: That's the way it should be. Performers will have a wide vocabulary of notational means at their command. They'll be forced to learn unfamiliar systems and symbols in order to play new music. The performers who are members of today's contemporary music groups at our universities will teach them. They understand that individual composers devise unorthodox notational systems in an effort to precisely realize their musical intentions. We've become increasingly aware of the influence the visual appearance of the score has on the results we get from the performer. The more accurately the notation represents our aural imagery, the more likely the result will conform to our expectations. This requires a diverse set of notational systems. Of course, it is usually possible to *transcribe* a piece from unorthodox notation into conventional form, but this is a distortion: a more familiar script masks the clues to the concept of the piece.

BC: Are performers generally producing what you want?

PW: I've been fortunate; mostly the results I get are very close to what I had in mind. Occasionally a performer will be unfamiliar with an instrumental effect or a notational symbol, but they seem to grasp the notation used without undue effort.

BC: You used to play jazz. Is this reflected in your composition at all?

PW: It was a direct, immediate way for me to make music and it was an outlet for my own inventive urge. In jazz, especially small combos, one has the opportunity to improvise, and so it was fascinating for a time. Eventually I lost interest, not in jazz, but in playing jazz. It faded when I realized that I would have to devote my entire energy to it in order to make a living. Composition gradually assumed priority, and I stopped playing jazz entirely.

BC: You don't feel that it shows up in your composing—certain phrases?

PW: No, because I've stopped thinking in phrases.

BC: No phrases?

PW: The idea of "phrase" is so closely related to language that I avoid using the term. It appears in the general category of articulation, grouping of ideas, and occupies a relatively small corner in that category.

BC: Do you think of a piece of music in dramatistic terms then?

PW: I relate more closely to graphic art in terms of articulation of ideas on a broad plane. It's possible to conceive an entire piece which doesn't contain a single "phrase," yet may be built entirely of phrase quotes. I mean that the structural phrase function is missing.

BC: By "dramatistic" I mean the work as a whole in a dramatic sense.

PW: I do think in those terms, since I prefer at present to specify a particular order of event sequence.

BC: How about works in which there are apparently no sections at all, as in so-called minimal pieces? For example, Loren Rush's *Hard Music* [1970].

PW: The articulation occurs on a submerged level. It's partly timbral composition, partly internal rhythmic activity. This type of music is a good example of nonlinguistic composition. What sense does it make to discuss the piece in terms of phrases? And yet there is articulation.

BC: So it's simply vocabulary?

PW: The problem is always discovering what the variables are, on what level the constants lie. If one looks for "phrase" he will miss the music of the piece. It requires a total flexibility with regard to listening habits. In *Hard Music* the variables may not be immediately apparent because one is predisposed to listen to the surface gestures of music; but they are there.

BC: What about a piece like [Cage's] *4'33"*? The listener provides his own variable while listening. Is this sort of music still important to students? Do your students get turned on by Cage?

PW: They relate more to his ideas than to the musical results. There appears to be a real polarity: students either totally hate him or adore him.

BC: Are people less interested in historical musical influence? Do they look back thirty years and say, "Here's an important composer that I feel akin to"?

PW: The students don't give a damn for history. And why should they? The past exists in the present, we are the result of the past, and therefore the clues are always around us. Any rock station is full of the past. The younger composers I know are also not interested in developing a kind of common language as existed for centuries in music. I'm more interested in music as an art object, which means that *any* organizational idea can be fair game if I feel it has merit.

BC: Their professors don't see things that way?

PW: They're wrong. Perhaps it simply reveals a lack of imagination. After all, how many fugues does one have to study to understand contrapuntal devices and procedures? Once a composer has a fund of information about devices that have been used throughout music history, why should he bury himself in the archives? It is more important for him to project unorthodox uses for the techniques he has learned than to reiterate the past. A canon is a canon . . . better the student apply the idea to grossly different material, discover unique ways to proceed with his composition. The easiest way to alienate students is to belabor the past.

BC: Emphasize music history and empty your classes! The students don't seem to be concerned with elite careerism any longer.

PW: No, and they're not at all impressed by a composer's professional stature. I think it's very healthy, because often the fact that one is impressed leads him into blind alleys. Emulation can lead to imitation.

BC: Should a young composer stay in the academy and work for the doctorate as opposed to plying his craft on the outside?

PW: Now that the [Vietnam War–era] draft is over, I can see no reason for staying in the university beyond the master's degree except for ready access to a variety of performing ensembles. I don't believe that a doctorate will make an individual a better composer; on the contrary, I know several cases in which the effect of prolonged institutionalization was debilitating. If a composer intends to teach at colleges, then the doctorate will bring a slightly higher salary in state universities. However, he can achieve a similar status by building a reputation as a composer—writing and getting his music widely performed, applying for grants and prizes. This will probably take ten years or more, longer than most doctorates, but he will have been working at his primary interest instead of running an arbitrary obstacle course in the academy.

BC: You implied that theory is going to have to develop alternative methods of description for much of the new music, that language-related description is no longer satisfactory. Are attempts being made now to formulate a theoretic under which this music can be subsumed?

PW: We are in the process, but at the present the theoretic is being developed piecemeal. Many computer-programming concepts are being applied to analysis, and I'm sure that a codification will evolve before too long. Right now we're still groping toward a generalized body of concepts for analytical use.

BC: How important is it to any listener to know how much of the process is happening? When people listen to your woodwind quintet, is it important that they know the process before they can grasp your intent?

PW: That's a difficult question. If the idiom is foreign to their experience, then even the most elaborate program notes will not accomplish much. It's important for someone who really wants to understand the piece to listen to it several times until the surface novelty is no longer obtrusive; then he'll be able to absorb the structural process on a subconscious level. This doesn't mean that he'll come to like the piece, but a comprehension of the compositional process might begin to emerge.

Sometimes a listener is so offended by the first hearing of a piece that he completely dismisses it as worthless. This is a mistake. My first experience listening to the so-called new diatonicism—1962—made me furious. I lumped the whole business in the "mindless drivel" category, until I became suspicious of feeling so vehemently about something I thought was so innocuous. After more listening, I heard the world that lay beneath the surface of this music.

BC: Wouldn't it have been simpler to read an analysis?

PW: I don't think so. I don't believe this kind of acceptance is achieved on a rational plane. Analysis can "explain" only in superficial terms; understanding is accomplished only by listening and is related more to the idea of direct comprehension, or intuition.

BC: Feldman said in an interview in the mid-'60s that there was a feeling of wanting to be the fastest gun among younger American composers.

PW: He may have been referring to eastern composers. From what I've seen they seem to be fiercely competitive. Most young composers I know are from the

Midwest and West, and I don't think his statement applies to them. I've often witnessed a light-hearted sparring between individuals, but never that deadly seriousness or duplicity that seems to haunt the "New York school."

BC: Does not taking one's self too seriously show up in the music? It's much more relaxed. When you write a piece, you're not aiming for a masterpiece, a profound expression of the soul which will resonate through the ages.

PW: By the same token, we're not flippant in our approach either. It's a different perspective; while an earthshaking masterpiece isn't the objective, we want to write a piece that hits the mark.

BC: But it's a different mark.

PW: A more realistic one that rejects contrivance. The masterpiece syndrome requires that a composer wrap it up once and for all and throw it away, slaying every other composer with his insight and mastery of the "language."

BC: The great American symphony!

PW: It'll win the Pulitzer!

BC: Are you worried about audiences?

PW: Never.

BC: Neither am I. What about critics?

PW: "Crickets" burn me.[1]

BC: Bad reviews bug you?

PW: No, crickets bug me, no matter what they say. They're looking a gift horse in the mouth. If it weren't for us, they'd have nothing to write about, yet they act as if they'd just as soon be elsewhere doing something more fitting of their station. There are exceptions, of course. I feel that the job title "critic" should not exist; the most positive service a reviewer can provide is nothing more than a surface description of a piece for the potential audience. He ought to function, if at all, as a sportswriter and give a play-by-play account of what happened. Unfortunately, newspapers pay for more sensational copy than that would produce.

BC: Suppose a critic says your work is clearly a masterpiece, one of the greatest works of all time?

PW: I'd think he was full of shit.

BC: You wouldn't praise him for his good judgment?

PW: Hell no! But I would thank him for giving me a usable review.

BC: When I was at Oxford, a particular reviewer wrote such things as "The flute G sharp in bar 84 was a trifle unsteady."

PW: Critics could do a small service by confining themselves to providing a running commentary after the fact, instead of issuing "pronunciamentos." Invective or unwarranted praise give one absolutely no information about a composition.

BC: Do you find it difficult to get performances?

PW: I find it difficult to keep up with secretarial chores attendant to performances. Some opportunities for performance go by because I'm rather disorganized when it comes to mailing scores and answering letters.

BC: Suppose you get sent a tape of a performance and it's just appalling?

PW: It's happened several times; I recently received a tape of the two-piano piece, *Melted Ears*, which is thirteen minutes long. I listened to the first few seconds, then stopped. I didn't want to go sour on the piece. It was a terrible performance.

BC: So if you hear a bad performance, you may decide the piece is a loser?

PW: Especially if it happens on the first performance. But that isn't exactly what I meant by "going sour" on a piece. A completely distorted performance of a composition transforms it into a caricature of itself. Sometimes this is advantageous if the caricature is imaginative, suggests other ideas, or uses the material in ways that I had not considered. More often, however, the distortion reflects the performers' lack of imagination and technical facility. Incompetence on an executional plane can "smear" the structure of the piece and upset the balance of material that was specified in a particular order and proportion to represent my intentions. A listener might not react negatively to an incompetent performance if he is hearing the piece for the first time, because at that point he has no model against which to measure the fidelity of the rendition. He is not aware that the ensemble didn't give him the experience I intended him to have.

BC: Does it make any sense at all to talk about expressivity in music? Suppose a part of one of your pieces elicits an emotional response which you intended to create.

PW: The problem arises in the act of verbalization. We respond to sonic events, and our perception of unique musical structures induce a variety of psychological states. In attempting to categorize our reactions, we fail miserably by virtue of the utter uselessness of words to describe highly complex psychic states. We are reduced to rough-hewn, nebulous, nondescriptive terms: Joy, Despair, Love, Anger, Compassion. So, language, an extramusical channel of communication, is inadequate as a descriptive tool. When I compose, I relate directly to the material I'm using, I am aware of its relative degree of power to alter psychological states, but I don't try to attach verbal analogues. I use them only as instructions to the performer in the conventional sense—to play a particular segment joyfully, with spirit, delicately, or heroically. And, always, the instructions are ones we associate with human gestures in the broadest sense; I'm not fond of cryptic instructions that leave the performer more confused than enlightened.

BC: Don't you think there are musical moments that are "expressive" in the sense that they automatically trigger a given emotional response?

PW: Yes, but not in an absolute sense; it's conditioned response in the Pavlovian meaning. Hollywood composers probably have the most complete catalog of musical mood clichés which will produce the predictable audience salivation. One could turn this conditioned response characteristic to advantage in an entirely different manner. There is tremendous potential in material that has collected numerous extramusical connotations over the years.

BC: In other words, if a composer is asked to write a piece that will sound joyous, he could put together enough clichés.

PW: Yes, but this is not the romantic notion of expressivity.

BC: The idea that there are innate, built-in reactions in every human being. What about the use of experimental music along with experimental films, where the concern is likely to be the direct opposite from that of the Hollywood composer?

PW: I'm glad you asked that question, because filmmaker Tom Palazzolo and I have experimented quite a bit with segments of film footage and electronic tape which, individually, and apart from each other, seemed to create totally different response effects. We tried each film "scene" several times, each time with a different tape event; the fusion of the media produced a fresh response with each repetition of the film, but at all times the film and tape sounded as if they were made for each other.

BC: A great idea!

PW: The context and juxtaposition of film and tape material created a different flavor with each screening; they were "expressive" of a variety of experiential states, so to speak.

BC: That certainly shoots down the Doctrine of Affections, as far as I'm concerned.

PW: The problem was for Tom and I to decide exactly what the impact of each scene was to be. We both understood that almost any piece of tape would "work" with any film footage, and the solution lay on the macro-formal plane. All the scenes and tape segments taken collectively had to be shaped to produce the chosen result. The only absolute in the entire process is that the film alters the musical aura, and vice versa. The same thing happens when a purely musical composition is played in diverse concert/environmental situations. How many times have you heard a piece of yours that scared the hell out of you in one situation . . .

BC: . . . and was endless tedium in another. I suppose that multimedia has by now filtered down to the colleges. Most students seem to think if there's something for the eye and something for the ear, that's multimedia.

PW: There's much interchangeability of terminology—mixed media, multimedia, intermedia, etc.—but it all reduces to the common denominator of several information channels functioning at once regardless of the degree of integration or stratification. I don't care what you call it, or how many categorical distinctions are made, as long as the composite is successful. Newly coined terminology can give one a fresh feeling toward an old concept. For example, one of the composition students at DePaul who is enamored of "multimedia" recently began listening to opera. He recently remarked to me, "That Wagner cat got into some pretty heavy shit." If *I* had suggested that he study Wagner, he probably would have told me Wagner wasn't relevant. It's more important that he approached another composer's music of his own volition; what does it matter that it was accomplished via a redefinition of theater experience— multimedia as opposed to opera. The exciting thing is that he suddenly saw Wagner not as an historical relic but as another composer who had an élan he could identify with and learn from.

BC: Are live electronic pieces more trouble than they're worth? Say three guys put on a concert and set up all their equipment; they amplify the instruments, they've got loops and feedback systems?

PW: The experiential results always determine whether it was worth lugging all that equipment. It's simple enough to buy a dozen two-dollar contact microphones, attach them to live instruments, put them through a mixer and/or ring modulator, and do a show. But the limitations are very severe with this setup because contact mikes usually have incomplete frequency response and act as stationary filters. Therefore, the results will depend entirely on the composer's ability to create an interesting composition, not in spite of the limitations but *because* of them. The limitations will have to be central to his compositional frame of reference. For a composer with a fitting idea, any conceivable combination of live and/or electronic instruments can produce a worthwhile result. Even if only one piece out of twenty turns out to be a winner, then the effort is well spent.

BC: How much does it help a composer today to be his own engineer?

PW: A composer will find the skill useful if he can learn during the compositional process through practical experience. But spending several years working to become an engineer when one is actually a composer can prove both distracting and detrimental. They should go hand in hand. Actually, your question implies the quarrel I've had with traditional music education; I've always been able to absorb skills most quickly when I had *need* for them. Force-fed training invariably evaporates through disuse, making it necessary to reacquire that tool when a meaningful situation arose.

I don't suggest that an individual can always objectively discern what he needs to solve a particular problem. This is perhaps the only good argument for having "teachers" at all. For example, a composition student at DePaul whom I had treated fairly flexibly by allowing him to progress at his own pace in whatever style he chose, recently complained that I wasn't providing enough direction for him. I asked him what he meant by "direction" and he eventually arrived at the statement "I'd like to learn some different styles of composition." I pointed out that he had already been exposed to most twentieth-century composers' music at one time or another during his study; it finally dawned on me that he wanted me to require that he get hold of a contemporary music theory text and learn to write in the styles of Stravinsky, Hindemith, Berg, Bartók, etc. He knew that he needed to accomplish this project, but I had to say it for him.

BC: How much and what sort of "criticism" should a teacher provide about a student's creative work?

PW: I don't think it is ever necessary to directly criticize students' work. Arbitrary value judgments contribute little in an instructional sense, and are easily mis-construed. I've found it more productive to let the student do the talking, state his own view of how well a particular sequence of musical events conforms to his intentions, and then discuss other possible solutions and ways of handling material if he feels revision is necessary. So, in private teaching situations I confine my comments to concrete techniques for shaping and ordering sound, rather than impose my personal aesthetic on him. Teachers should interfere as little as possible with the educational process, serving as catalysts rather than alter egos.

Group composition courses are another matter entirely. The students con-stantly judge each other's work and don't hesitate to state their reactions. They don't seem to be offended by the harsh comments that are often made. If I were to state that a particular piece was ineptly composed, the student might interpret this to mean "you'll never be a composer," whereas the same comment from a peer would carry less weight, because it's only another student saying it. I try to counter that kind of attitude, but it's built-in. Students have been taught all their lives that the teacher is master.

BC: The whole musical-artistic-historical syndrome is behind them to that degree. Do you think, as I do, that students ought to listen to bad pieces?

PW: Yes. If the general consensus in a class is that they have just listened to a flop of a piece, all the teacher needs to ask is why, then step back and moderate the discussion. Good pieces rarely draw much comment; they are satisfying in themselves.

BC: How much should a player know besides technique?

PW: Almost as much as a composer. He has to have the ability to look beyond the musical surface and see what makes a piece tick.

BC: I have trouble with some of my works in which certain performer choices are admissible, but then they make choices which are not admissible. "We decided to choreograph this choral piece of yours and to play it for laughs." They simply add things which are not in the piece.

PW: Then you, the composer, are forced to write a damn book of rules and regula-tions for performing the piece. With more perceptive new music groups this would never happen. They look at the score as well as their parts and develop a sense of what *is* admissible within the framework of a particular composition, choices or no choices.

BC: Sometimes perfectly reputable outfits will take a piece, rehearse it, and when you show up for the performance, they've included things which have no business being in the piece.

PW: I'm sure that some groups secretly hate new music even though they may play it to be hip. They'll look for every loophole in the composer's instructions and not give a thought to the intent of the piece, instead of saying "This would be in bad taste," or "This would not be appropriate even though it's not specifically prohibited by the score." They seem to feel that if the score permits a few choices that the license is there to make a vaudeville act of it.

BC: Are you writing easier pieces than you were four or five years ago?

PW: They look superficially simpler, but from the performance tapes I'd say they are more difficult.

BC: In their demands?

PW: For some time the demands have been of a technical nature: more effects, extended registral usage, etc. The music I write now doesn't require that type of virtuosity, but it requires precise intonation and absolute control over timbre. In some respects, this is more demanding than asking a performer to play a pointillistic line full of irrational rhythms, wide pitch leaps, and constantly shifting dynamics.

BC: Performers today are more prepared to do such a thing, and are past the stage where they were striving for technical feats without listening to what they were playing.

PW: Yes, now that the struggle for expanded instrumental resources seems to have abated, the good performers are stressing flexibility and adaptability to a wide variety of musical idioms.

BC: What's going to happen now that younger composers are taking responsible academic positions, even heads of departments? Are the young fireballs becoming establishment?

PW: Maybe, but it will be a far healthier establishment. There is a growing trend in universities toward hiring active composers, whereas in the not-too-distant past one was expected to be a theory teacher first, a composer second. There is more recognition now that a good composer is not necessarily a good theory teacher, and vice versa.

BC: We disagreed upon this point when we talked about it two years ago. If you're teaching composition to people who are not going to be professionals, but are required to take a year of composition for their certificate, do you (1) as you have done, introduce them to new things, or do you (2) as I used to do, take what they're doing and try to get them to do it better, even though it's second-team Brahms?

PW: I haven't changed my position. If people are in a composition course simply because it is a requirement for graduation, then I see them as a potential audience for new music rather than a group of composers. They should be exposed to the broadest range of idioms that time will permit. Why help them to write better Brahms?

BC: Isn't writing just learning a process of self-discipline and self-expression?

PW: If they have no impulse toward creative work, then why waste the time?

BC: Because you're trying to teach them how to think, and they have come to you because you're the guy who teaches it and it's required.

PW: If they want to learn to think, they should study thinking; and if they want to learn to compose, the best way *is* to compose. But if they come to my class and want neither, then I'm going to indulge in a little "conditioning" of my own. I'm self-centered about this to the extent that the least I can do is try to build an audience for the rest of us guys who do want to compose. If they leave the course with an ounce more appreciation for contemporary music, then it's worth foregoing all that second-team Brahms. If they want discipline, they can learn knot tying or other crafts. Imagination is harder to come by and is the quality most often lacking in student pieces. All the educational emphasis on discipline puts the cart before the horse. An imaginative, inventive individual always finds the means to realize his ideas, but the vision comes first, the discipline incidental.

BC: And what do you do with a graduate student who already has a thorough, concrete means of composing, an idiom which you can't jar them out of with dynamite?

PW: I don't try to jar them out of it; I let them continue in whatever style they are working. And if they seem to be blocked up, I make definite assignments for composition projects and ask them to listen to music since 1960. It's a way of exposing them to new idioms. You can't force anyone to write good music. If they are in a rut, they are stuck for a variety of reasons, and I'm no psychoanalyst. Mostly they eventually work free by expanding their horizons. This happened recently with a graduate student who had been writing essentially the same piece over and over. One day he asked, "Would it be all right with you if I tried something else?" As if I were making him stay with the old style.

BC: I've found that the real composers are always doing something experimental or exploratory—it's going to be their next piece.

PW: Quite a pleasant change from the run-of-the-mill student who seldom brings anything to class.

BC: Do you get good results from students who are not composers but take electronic music so they can plug around with the sounds?

PW: Occasionally, but after they discover that compositions do not automatically issue from the machinery, they often lose interest. When this happens, I encourage them to audit the course, so grading is avoided.

BC: At many places now, if they fail, the course is as though it never existed. It's a kind of convenient ignoring. A composer has to learn how to deal with failure to be serious.

PW: That may have been true twenty years ago.

BC: You don't think it's possible to fail today if you are serious?

PW: No. In the past a composer was a failure before he began. Performances were rare and hard to come by, there was no chance of a living at anything but teaching, he was totally unnecessary to our society. Many composers fell by the wayside out of sheer inability to survive a system which saw them only in their role as teachers. How many university composers listed their occupation as "Composer" on IRS forms? No, they saw themselves as teachers first, which is back-asswards. Teaching today is beginning to assume its proper place as [a] spin-off of creative work; it is possible to declare oneself a composer, even though the bulk of income is from teaching. Makes a tremendous psychological difference. So I don't see any way of failing if one can get performances and feels personally satisfied and fulfilled by his efforts. What type of failure do you mean? Why should I learn to accept failure?

BC: When one has personal views of what he can do, and he realizes that he cannot ever do them; for example, to be on the cover of *Time* magazine someday, or to be Stravinsky.

PW: Oh, that's so like the romantic's eternal striving, the unrequited love theme. Young composers today have a much more pragmatic attitude toward their careers: they write music, pursue performances, and attend to promotional matters in a businesslike way. Once, one may have ignored everything except writing music because it was going to languish in a drawer, unperformed. Failure in the sense of not being on the cover of *Time* doesn't exist in the same world; it's simply a silly dream that has no bearing on the "success" or "failure" of one's music.

BC: I hadn't thought of it in those terms. I think you are right.

Note

1. Winsor tended to use cynical monikers when referring to detractors. Perhaps "crickets" cleverly evokes the idea that criticism is senseless chirping.

22 Christian Wolff (b. 1934)

VIRGINIA ANDERSON

Barney Childs recalled that this interview occurred on an idyllic day in 1972 or 1973 at Christian Wolff's farm, sitting outside and talking until the sun set. This was a crucial point in Wolff's life, just after his first year at Dartmouth College, teaching music rather than classics for the first time. It came just after the English premiere of *Burdocks* (1971), a suite of ten pieces for orchestra or orchestras written in text, graphic, and common-practice notation.[1] In this format, *Burdocks* parallels Cornelius Cardew's seven-part *The Great Learning* (1968–71). Wolff was about to begin his "next step" toward music concerned with social and political topics, again paralleling Cardew, who was just making his big switch from Cagean experimentalism to Maoist socialist realism. If anything, Cardew (1936–81) was the absent guest at the interview, and the Scratch Orchestra, which Cardew cofounded and which premiered *Burdocks* in London, is inextricably woven into its context.

From the youngest member of the Cage group in the 1950s, Wolff's indeterminacy elicited social and psychological reactions to group playing, which, as Childs and Wolff discuss, can lead into impossible situations for continuing the performance. In his first published article on experimental notation, Cardew claimed that in these situations, "Christian would frown faintly, then smile a solution."[2] Cardew met Wolff in Darmstadt in the late 1950s, with John Cage and David Tudor. After their meeting, Cardew left his former mentor Karlheinz Stockhausen to write graphic pieces with a heavy philosophical and spiritual content. Rather than pursue music, Wolff studied, and then taught, classics at Harvard University until his move to Dartmouth in 1970. Childs had only begun teaching music composition at Milwaukee College Conservatory in 1969 after years of teaching poetry and English literature. The enthusiasm of both composers for music education in this interview is obvious.

At Dartmouth Wolff established a course in experimental music, where students learned Paragraph 2 of *The Great Learning* and *Burdocks*. They performed with the Merce Cunningham Dance Company—an incredible experience for young students. In 1971, Wolff recorded *Burdocks* at Dartmouth with a small group, including David Tudor, bandoneon and organ; Wolff, bass guitar and flute; Gordon Mumma, horn and harmonica; Frederic Rzewski, piano and percussion; David Behrman, viola, melodeon, and whistle; and John Nash (the British artist and Wolff's brother-in-law), violin.[3]

The background to *Burdocks* involves an amazing synchronicity in unusual instrumentation. While resident in London in 1967–68, Wolff took "Stones," part of his first text music collection, *Prose Pieces* (1968), to Cardew's house. As Wolff remembered, Cardew "smiled, walked over to his desk and handed me a page of Paragraph 1 with the stones passage on it."[4] For the premiere of Paragraph 2 in 1969, Cardew recruited what would become the nucleus of the Scratch Orchestra, a group of reading and nonreading professional and amateur musicians and nonmusicians who were mandated to improvise, perform, and compose music. The definition of music, according to their draft constitution, "depends entirely on the members of the Scratch Orchestra."[5] The prevailing ethos of the membership was anarchic, steadied by a disciplined core of experimental musicians. *Burdocks* premiered at Cecil Sharp House on March 28, 1972. Performers were members of several London new music groups, including the improvisation group AMM, Gentle Fire, the Promenade Theatre Orchestra, and the Portsmouth Sinfonia. The Scratch Orchestra and its satellite groups also played. The Scratch rock band CUM contributed what Wolff calls the "messy" performance of the melody-and-accompaniment section, *Burdocks* VI.

That August, after the Childs interview, the Scratch Orchestra performed *Burdocks* at a festival associated with the Munich Olympics. This event produced one of the oddest protests in new music, when Carole Finer chose to interpret one element of *Burdocks* V, the number "7," by playing seven folksongs on her banjo. Morton Feldman, Cage, and David Tudor were in the audience. Feldman made a loud vocal protest during the performance. Richard Ascough, leader of a Scratch Orchestra delegation to mediate with the Americans, gave this report: "Feldman and Cage . . . were upset at the inclusion of the folksongs. I explained that this was in one of the last spokes in which there was a number 7. Cage decided that should be seven sounds. . . . Cage, Feldman and Tudor went through the score trying to find the interpretation for this number 7. He couldn't find it; Tudor reckoned there was another page of the score, which explained all these symbols, but I said this is the score we've got."[6] Wolff, in America, did not hear this concert until 2015, but said before then, "given the nature of that particular group, that it would have been very beautiful."[7]

Both Scratch Orchestra performances of *Burdocks* occurred after a group crisis that resulted in a turn to a Maoist aesthetic. As Wolff mentions in the interview, Cardew arranged "Va pensario" (the Chorus of the Hebrew Slaves) from Verdi's *Nabucco*, and political discussion occurred in the interval. Cardew introduced the

Munich concert by attacking Cage and Feldman's "ivory-tower approach," and the orchestra performed a group-penned "revolutionary opera."[8] Cardew had already written articles condemning Stockhausen and Cage for bourgeois music and would soon denounce his own previous work.[9] After noting that these attacks were "crude," Wolff states that Mao offers a challenge, so that "I want to try to see what's right and wrong with it."

Although Cardew would later denounce Wolff for not going far enough, Wolff's commitment to social reform has informed his music to this day.[10] Cardew worked as a Communist activist and party member until his death by a hit-and-run driver in 1981. Wolff and Childs met for the last time in 1994, at the Scratch Orchestra Twenty-Fifth Anniversary concert at the Institute of Contemporary Arts in London. Fittingly, the featured work on the program was *Burdocks*.

Christian Wolff: Interview

BARNEY CHILDS: Your approach to notation has opened up some ways of thinking about music—both in performance and in analytic approach—which I find very challenging.

CHRISTIAN WOLFF: You must mean notations that involve rhythms that are created by coordination, interaction. The first idea came about not so much from the notation of note-to-note procedure, as structural-unit-to-structural-unit procedure. I had that in mind in a piece for two pianos, which had much the same layout as the Stockhausen *Klavierstück XI* (1956). That piece struck me as wrong in that you let your eye wander. There's nothing in particular to guide your eye except your intention. I once heard a two-minute version of that piece by David Tudor at Darmstadt, under very official circumstances. Everybody sat back for a good twenty minutes of Stockhausen, and suddenly the thing was over. I suspected hanky-panky at work.

That situation interested me, but how to get it into a livelier, structurally more functional framework? I stumbled on the idea of making your procedure depend on what you had last heard as you got through a structural unit. The rhythm within that structure still depended on various prescribed time lengths, within which sounds could be freely disposed by the player. Something very short would be quite precise. If you've got a fifth of a second to do something, there isn't much leeway, but if you've got twenty seconds and only two sounds to make, then you have plenty of time to make a choice. In such a situation, you have time not only to think about what you might do next, but you can also listen to what the other fellow's doing. Even if you don't intend to make a response, often you can't avoid it, so the idea of moving from sound to sound must have come from that. I got that idea of having players proceed some of the time by coordination from note to note from Cornelius Cardew's

Octet [1959], where the coordinations are marked by vertical and angled lines between the players' notes. The notations were more precise. Cardew did that for [the] convenience of ensemble playing, whereas I was interested in having certain flexibilities in the same situation. I adopted that notation but made some of the note values indefinite. That changed the character of the coordination, and hence the rhythm, considerably. If you didn't know when you could stop, or if you didn't know when you'd start, that would affect your playing considerably. The simple coordination, when you're supposed to play with the next sound you hear and then stop with it, is given a different character, because you couldn't start playing until you'd heard something. In practice I've found one tends to look; you can almost get it right when you can see someone getting ready.

BC: That's fudging?

CW: In a way, but it depends on what you want. Once I found that out, I was very pleased, because it produced a rhythm that I wanted but I hadn't heard. It seemed the most economical—sometimes the only—way to notate it. The notation itself had a functional logic. It wasn't standing for something else, nor something could easily just as well have stood in its place.

BC: You use an analogy on the back of a record jacket about people walking along . . .

CW: The landscape. I first thought of making a piece out of sections, which then could be freely repeated. In other words, the sections became locations in the landscape. As in any analogy, you can go just so far. When the piece is performed, you move among them as you would in a landscape and as you hear it. First time round you just hear a succession of events, and you don't necessarily see any connection. There may be a certain amount of structural cohesion or continuity by virtue of the pitch choices available, but on the whole, you don't get too clear an idea. As sections get repeated, you begin to see the shape of each of them. It's a funny situation in which the landscape begins to be defined by the movements of the people in it. I tried to express that in the piece *Edges* [1968]. Because you avoided the notations, my notion (not that it's ever been realized in my experience of the piece) was that if that piece went on long enough, you would begin to hear what was notated by virtue of its not being present, by virtue of its being constantly avoided.

BC: Student performers always express instant terror when they see the music; and yet, after a week of fuddling around, they discover that it is very straightforward.

CW: I've had that experience. At first I was dismayed because I'd thought I'd got something very nice and simple and found people troubled by it. The first time we tried the two-piano piece [*Duo for Pianists II*, 1958] it was just a disaster. Frederic Rzewski and myself had a pretty good idea of what we were after, but it just wasn't going. Suddenly, after working a couple of hours, it clicked.

BC: Something else that always amazes me is the fact that, with several players, nobody is left over. There isn't somebody who's waiting at the end for some-body to do something. Everybody comes out right, even though they may be enormously different each time through. Sometimes people are stuck on long notes, desperately trying to keep the thing going.

CW: There's two things: the idea that the thing can break down, that you can get into situations when you have to make a radical decision. You're at an im-passe—the situations in which I didn't go out of my way to avoid—where you would be hung up on a note. The other players might be waiting for a sound, so they couldn't go on until you produced one, and you couldn't produce one. Of course—and this is what it's partly about—it produces a theatrical situa-tion, because that does get communicated to the audience. At first it's tense and almost unpleasant, but after a while you get to enjoy it. Whatever efforts you have to make to keep the sound going also have a special character. When there's an impasse, you have to make your decision, because there's several you could make. You could pretend that the necessary coordination has in fact been given you, or you could stop and start again. Different pieces include directions that way. But I've been struck by the end of pieces. You find that remarkable when you improvise: it doesn't take much attunement between people; you don't have to be playing together a long time. At times you're tempted to think it's a natural sense of completion. It's not absolute. I have been in improvising groups where we could have come to an end, and somebody decided, "Well, no, I can see this thing pick up again." But you can hear that that's happening. But the sense of the end of the phrase, certainly the end of a larger movement—it's very easily communicated.

BC: When we did the *Septet*, there was a quasi-theatricality of this sort; people know who they want to look at for the next cue, but it's never the same per-son twice. You have a good deal of a chamber music interaction, especially in sections where the conductor isn't doing things, and each player in turn has to cue in chords or attacks. As such, there's a sense of participating in a piece that is not present in other situations.

CW: Those pieces are much stricter than they look. When people pick up a piece, like *For One, Two or Three People* [1964], they think . . .

BC: . . . it's a piece of cake.

CW: That's always led to problems. Logical coordination problems are not so great; but then you run into another situation: namely, how you rehearse. Certain things are absolutely out of bounds within a piece, but there are not very many, so it's very hard to tell when people make mistakes. All you can do is to develop an honor system. Everybody has to monitor themselves; you get into what amounts to an ethical domain.

BC: Is the situation where you're working now convenient to performance?

cw: Yes. I'm partly connected with a music department for the first time in my life. It's fantastic. It's all right to use the piano if I want. I've never had that before! I do about one course a year—next year it'll be two. But I did a course called A Practical Introduction to Music.

bc: Was this for beginners?

cw: Theoretically it's for beginners. In the last few years I've got very interested in getting people to make music who don't have any professional training, who may never have played an instrument at all. You've got more of it in the fine arts—people who have never drawn before are required to take a drawing course. They may never become artists, but they'll at least get an idea of what it's all about. That was the idea, to introduce people to basic musical situations by making them try them out. You can always teach people to sing and drum in some form, so the barriers are not so great. Some students were interested in this; others heard that this was going to have something to do with experimental music, so we had a very curious mixture. How do you accommodate that combination? There were fifteen altogether, so it's not too big a group. But it ran the whole gamut from total ignorance to the very competent. That was our orchestra for the spring; we *were* an orchestra.

bc: Did you plan what they did?

cw: Since I'd never taught a formal course of that kind, I did it partly as we went along. One nice thing happened when we were over halfway through the course. I was to do music for Merce Cunningham. He tries to find the most interesting space he can find—usually a gymnasium or some vast place. He programs a combination of dances which runs continuously. He makes it up more or less on the spot, and they run about an hour and a half. All the Cage-Cunningham musicians were in Europe. It was not so far away from us, so I got hired to do it. I decided to use this class to prepare them. The term divided roughly into drumming and singing; we spent quite a bit of time in the first part just learning rhythms, then also making up pieces to develop different ideas about rhythm. We also had two compositions we worked on steadily. One is this piece of mine called *Burdocks* [1970–71]. The other one is Cardew's *The Great Learning*, Paragraph 2 [1969].

bc: Is that the one with the chanters and the stones?

cw: No, it's the one with the drumming and the singing. It's quite hard because you need lots more voices than we had. But the drumming isn't so hard that you can't do it. I found this group much less inclined to sing than they were to drum. I encouraged them to make pieces (that was the next thing), but I did not insist on it because it's up to a person if he wants to do that. But quite a few got interested in doing that, and some of them were OK. The last thing we did was a concert almost entirely of student compositions.

bc: How did the Cunningham end up?

CW: I was really pleased and surprised. He was in residence, so they wanted two shows. The first one was more or less a straight concert, and that was really hard. The other one was just music for them dancing. That's not so bad, because they just dance and don't worry too much about what's going on. What we did for the dancing was partly because of the space. It was a field house; the space was three basketball courts side by side. It also had a large balcony, where they did gymnastics, and a big PA system which came down from above. We scattered our forces throughout that space: a group up in the balcony and four groups down below. The dancing took place in the middle court, the far court was the audience, and the backcourt behind the dancers along with the balcony was our space. Using the PA system from above, we could saturate the place completely with sound. Yet there weren't so many of us that we were overdoing it. We must have had fifteen pieces. We moved from one to the other, constantly flowing. It had interesting problems of coordination. We'd been working all this time in a room only about twenty yards long, and to coordinate with somebody way in the balcony got to be very interesting.

We also used material from *Burdocks*. That comes in ten parts. Each part is rather strongly differentiated from the others; it's a suite, really. We did some other pieces of mine, which again were originally written for people who were not necessarily professionally trained. That came about when I was in England about four years ago. I decided I should give some talks about music, but I found that I got tired of just talking to people. I found it much more interesting to have them involved with the music. I would find people who'd like to play music they could learn in a short time. Mostly art students—at the time it was much easier to find jobs in art schools than it was in music situations! I had people who might strum a guitar or could do nothing, but were interested. Being artists, they knew what it was about, but they didn't know how to go about it. So I made a set of pieces that were just prose instructions. You wouldn't have to read music.

BC: There's a considerable movement over there to write this.

CW: Yes. Brian Dennis edited a collection of pieces of music for schools, and I did one for him, for that first collection.[11] I heard a concert which schoolchildren did of works by David Bedford. The English idea of amateur music is very strong. Do you know the Scratch Orchestra? That's sort of a quasi-organized version of that situation. They've produced quite a body of this kind of music. That was later—they organized just after I left. Perhaps it's not just accidental that that came up while I was there. Another thing that I did was an idea introduced by the Scratch [Orchestra]: taking very familiar music and trying to make amateurs play it the best they can. So, on our program, we did a song called "The Great Wall of China."

BC: These were performed on whatever instrument was handed the student?

cw: Whatever was available. I think the only restriction was to make sure that somebody was representing every line of the music where possible. And those who couldn't do melody instruments at all would do the rhythm, so everybody was busy. Have you ever done that or heard it?

bc: I heard the Musical Club and Union second orchestra at Oxford when I was over there, where you played any instruments.

cw: It's an amazing sound. In one way it's very comical; it's enjoyable from that point of view. But musically it's not uninteresting. It's not only a distorting mirror, it also gives the music a kind of transparency. It's a very nice experience, a mixture of comic and clarifying. The pieces might be awful, everyone is so tired of them; suddenly they take on a whole new light. Then we did *Burdocks*. I'd never written any orchestra music, primarily out of pragmatism. I could just never see an orchestra playing my music! I've also always been interested in writing music that was clear, where you didn't lose the details. The idea of writing supporting parts, or filling out harmony, or any of that business, I just couldn't see that at all. So I just put the problem off, encouraged by the fact that I couldn't see anybody playing it. I've almost always tried to write pieces with some performance in mind.

bc: Is *Burdocks* playable by large numbers?

cw: Very large. That was the idea.

bc: Are there restrictions on instrumentation?

cw: No. Instruments aren't specified and actually the numbers can vary a lot. The piece is subtitled "for one or more orchestras."

bc: There is no specification of what the orchestra is composed?

cw: There are some structural suggestions. It's in ten parts. For nine of them it's specified what the minimum number of players must be. One doesn't specify and could be done by solo player.

bc: A sort of concertino?

cw: I think the largest minimum is fifteen. The instructions suggest that if you do have large forces, you do both multiple versions of the same part and you combine different parts. "For several orchestras": like a number of bands going, which has a practical side. You can rehearse large numbers of people independently, bring them together at the last minute and still have it go the way it should. But aside from making something that would make sense for orchestra, the idea of the piece was this problem of quantity. I could deal with large numbers only by having quite different things going on.

bc: Has an orchestra done this piece?

cw: The largest number has been forty-five.

bc: Amateurs?

cw: It was a combination. The nucleus was the Scratch Orchestra. I had them in the back of my mind when I wrote the piece. Some parts are difficult, but others are not technically demanding at all, so amateur groups could easily do it. But they got together with a number of the smaller new music groups in London. There are quite a few now, four or five—in total, forty-five people. That was interesting because the larger the numbers, one tends to make the arrangements more simple. The idea of clarity seems to have gotten through, though I never say anything about it in the instructions. The versions tend to be increasingly pliant. Each part tends to run just one page, so that everybody has what amounts to both the score and his part. This one is quite simply a melody, a two-part tune which can be repeated indefinitely. They could play one part and then the other part, in any combination of repetitions, as well as three rhythmic sections which constitute the accompaniment. There are practically no restrictions. Either the accompaniment or the melody has to be represented at least at one point during the performance. But you could do it all accompaniment and have the melody come in only once.

BC: This requires a considerable amount of preplanning by the conductor?

CW: It's not specified. You can do it freely; no conducting at all. We've done performances with just six, seven, or eight people. Everybody tends to pretty much do what they want to; they improvise freely on the structure, from the material itself. The other extreme is one version that the Scratch people did. Because it had a melody and was very popular, it got about five different versions. People got very tired of that melody by the time it was finished. The strictest one was almost all accompaniment. They played a B minor chord on just two of the accompanying rhythmic figures—only melody or harmony instruments. The melody is more or less modal; it's a little queer, but if it suggests any key, it suggests B minor or B major. So they made these very beautiful B minor chords in the given rhythms for quite a while, then a bass clarinet played the melody. All of this was in one tempo. That's another thing: the tempos are free, so each person can do the melody or accompaniment at any speed he wants.

BC: It must make for some astonishing textural things coming through.

CW: It's not a bad tune—well, it takes a while to get on your nerves! But it's really a tune. One person came up and said, "Where did you get that tune?" He assumed that I just lifted it out of some folk music. I don't doubt that you could find something like it somewhere, but I did make it up. They also did a rock version, where they accentuated it very heavily, and amplified it loudly—a standard rock setting. It was a little less satisfactory—not because it was rock, but mostly because it was very ramshackle and hadn't been very well-prepared. Which is the ethos of the Scratch people: it was fun, but it wasn't too clean. I don't know what value judgment to put on it. Mostly it was just too messy. I enjoy occasional messiness, but this was like a cardboard box that had gotten very soggy and very wet; you lost the sense of the box completely.

Other parts are very simple. One is the instruction to play 511 sounds, all of them different in some way. They did two versions of that. The first one was free: everybody did their own notion of how to solve the problem of getting through 511 sounds and making each one different. One man had a glass and he struck it once, and then he had water and an eyedropper, and he put one drop of water in and hit it again, until he'd done 511. It was very ingenious. And then—this hadn't come up in rehearsal, so when it happened at the performance it was just electrifying—one man decided he would pop 511 paper bags of different sizes. He fortunately got some assistance—otherwise he would have been there all night. There was this tremendous clatter going on somewhere in the back, and then this very delicate business with the glass. Other people were playing scales, doing fairly ordinary things, but that state of messiness was very enjoyable, very cheerful. After a while, the structure of it began to emerge. You began to see that people were really going through to the end. The second version that they did was to play scales, generally speaking moving up—occasionally you could come down again—and the difference would be the notion that any two sounds are different. By proceeding scale-wise, you could make different sounds, but you could repeat a scale, because you'd probably do it in a slightly different way. The 511 was beat by a conductor at a fairly rapid pace, and the whole thing was over in about two and a half minutes. But that's how they ended the concert. So you can see what the range of possibilities would be.

BC: It sounds like an enormously satisfactory piece.

CW: I'm very pleased with it. You can do shorter versions of it, and they're quite fine. But they took up the better part of an evening for this. They broke it in half; they went through it twice. It's mostly the changes, and you recognize them; you really do see the structure. Whether things follow one after the other or when they overlap, you see different things going on. There are simplified versions of my coordination ideas, described without the notes. For example, you play with the person nearest you, and then with the next nearest, and then after that until you've reached the outermost space of the performance area, and everybody's doing it.

Some parts are more elaborate. One consists of a hundred fragments, some melodic, some rhythmic, some a mixture. The only instruction is that they should all be played; you just distribute them among the players, depending on how many you have. If you have an orchestra that has just a hundred players, each has his part. You do it, and it's a short movement! If you have two people, well, it gets a bit long.

BC: Has it yet been done by . . . ?

CW: An "official" orchestra? Richard Dufallo was going to Europe—Amsterdam— and he was to get an orchestra together and conduct a concert of American music. He was going to do that piece. I was a little wary, because you have to know what you're about, especially if you're going to instruct a conventional orchestra in what to do. It's very difficult if they haven't been used to the Scratch Orchestra. I don't know if he did it, or what happened when he did do it.

BC: Will you continue teaching this music course?

CW: Practical Introduction to Music. Yes, slightly differently next year. Jon Appleton suggested that we do an introductory course together. He's technologically minded, so he wanted to use the computers they have, these machines with which you can do exercises. They're like language-lab machines, where you do something and it tells you if you've done it wrong. It doesn't slap you but suggests how you might improve it and get it right. They have simple ones for doing harmony exercises. He wanted to make them somewhat more interesting—have programs where students learn by trying out what it's like to make a piece, not by surveying the literature. The electronics were convenient, because you had the immediate material; you didn't have to go to the trouble of getting performers. I am going to do a "live" version where the students would devise pieces they could play together themselves. It's going to be a little tricky to organize, because we'll probably have quite a few students. The other course will happen again, under the title of Experimental Music. There I'll aim to do a concert. I think a course should organize itself around a concert, so that you're not just fiddling around in a classroom by yourselves, you're moving towards some kind of social event.

BC: If someone said, "Here's some money—write us a wind quartet," would you still be interested?

CW: I like to do as many things as possible. I just did a string quartet on commission. Even in that situation, I'm making material that's available. The string quartet can be done by any number of string players, but obviously and immediately it's directed towards a classic string quartet.

BC: It's seemed that your music isn't played much compared to the amount of mileage that Cage and Feldman get, and other people; that nobody knows your pieces. I'm not sure why. Has this just been my own experience?

CW: I suppose I'm in a transition. When I first began, I was amazed that anything ever got played. After ten years I thought things were getting better. BMI lost my address for ten years, so I got nothing. Suddenly I got communication from them covering that time. There were only two pieces that were recorded on it. One of them was *Summer*, a string quartet, but that had gotten played about three hundred times. I couldn't figure it out! It's recorded. People would hear it, then they would be interested in trying it. So things have improved. New music gets played and there are more groups, especially in colleges. There must be a lot out west. I'm not familiar with that situation, but I get the impression. But it hasn't taken the musical world by storm; it's a situation we all face.

I think John Cage is, for various reasons, a very special figure. He's terrific, he's very powerful, but part of the reason that his music is played must be by virtue of his writing. He went over the top with that first book, *Silence*, because that appealed to people who'd never dream of learning much about the music. If you're planning a new music concert, it's a good idea to put a Cage piece on, because you're assured initially of an audience. Feldman has done very well, partly by virtue of being closer to the New York situation for a long time, and he's worked very hard at it.

I haven't; all this time I've had other jobs. I've not been able to push my own stuff a great deal. The breakthrough came when I went to England and had a free year. My music probably gets played more in England than anywhere else; it really does well there. That's where that performance of *Burdocks* was put on, and a lot of people came.

BC: I have never heard a group do a work of yours. I take it back: I've heard the trumpet, cello, and flute trio.

CW: I'd say that's partly on account of the music. Even the string quartet does not immediately appeal to the professional group. There's the Concord [String] Quartet, kids who want to make a reputation on contemporary music. I don't think anybody told them about it; they just found it. But it's in the music itself. I hadn't noticed until fairly recently that I wasn't writing music for the established musical scene. Which isn't to say they can't do it, but it's not the first thing that they would pick up. Hence there aren't that many performances.

BC: The pieces *are* accessible. We did *In Between Pieces* [1963] at Milwaukee, with three electric guitar players. They learned that piece as well as anybody ever learns a Schubert song. Their performance after about a year was something else. They discovered through that and a couple of other works that you could make more exciting quiet sounds on the electric guitar than they thought possible. And this was a very, very quiet piece. They also did Cardew's *Treatise* [1963–67], which was essentially and practically inaudible. One of these three players who is continuing in music now has the piece on his own.

CW: That's very encouraging.

BC: There isn't anything inherent in the works that should keep them away. People get put off by the notation; once they discover that the notation makes complete sense and is a pretty sensible operation, then they relax. A professional group is another matter.

CW: There's getting to be a dichotomy between the groups that have sprung up— Weisberg's group, one in Chicago, and so on—and I think, why shouldn't they do a piece like *Septet* [1964]? Perhaps it's unfair to say, but I get the impression they are attracted by a page that's really black with notes, where something clearly challenges the virtuosity of the players. That's the only thing. It's *not*, in that sense, virtuoso music.

BC: With virtuoso players it can be very exciting.

CW: It takes a lot of dedication; that's the disadvantage. There's an interesting case. Right before I got to London for *Burdocks*, the closest English equivalent to one of these American groups, the Fires of London, Peter Maxwell Davies's group, did an all-Feldman concert. Friends said it was awful. The music on the surface, technically, seems too simple, anti-virtuoso. They just play it off, but it's dead as a doornail because it's very difficult. The problem in all of Feldman is playing as quietly as possible and yet still making a sound. Somehow they didn't even notice that that was the problem.

BC: This is a European thing. What's in the Feldman piece, and in a lot of your pieces too, is an American thing. It requires a way of hearing that the conservatory-trained virtuoso is just not going to have.

CW: I'm not sorry about that. This story about the guitar players is very encouraging. That's really what I would like the music to do: to permeate or infiltrate in as many odd corners as possible. Of course it's not very visible. It won't get reviewed in the journals or the papers because it won't get done at official concerts, but if it gets played that way, that's fine with me. I suspect to a certain extent that's happening—if you hang around long enough, things get done.

BC: Your much harder pieces are the earliest ones.

CW: Those are clearly virtuoso. They're mostly piano pieces, and they're written for David Tudor. That was the time of the Stockhausen piano pieces, [Pierre] Boulez's second sonata. There was a wave of virtuoso pieces, and we all wrote them.

BC: I think that *Burdocks* and whatever follows it would be enormously acceptable. Can there be a wrong reason for playing something? Music educators who are interested in [Carl] Orff and [Zoltán] Kodály, and band people who refer to new music as "novelty numbers," might well find the piece useful to its purposes.

CW: That would be nice. Because I flatter myself to think it would be a process of infiltration. There might be a hope of . . .

BC: . . . subverting their ears, regardless of the means by which the piece is presented to them.

CW: I still fear that the format is a bit off-putting. It doesn't look like music at first. Some of it does—you can see notes here and there—but even the part with the melody, what do you do? Whoever's conducting this has to do quite a bit more than he is accustomed to because it's a lot different than what he's accustomed to. Have you had some experience with that kind of situation? Writing for or working with a larger school group?

BC: I was commissioned to do a choral piece for an Iowa high school choir [*A Glasse of Truth*, 1968]. I also was commissioned to write for high school band [*Six Events for 58 Players*, 1965], which is an almost inaudible piece that can last for five hours if they want.

cw: And what was their reaction?

bc: The high school chorus piece was for chorus, lights, tape, and projections, all made to furnished instructions. With younger people there is this initial moment of disbelief in, and even of repugnance to, the music. But if the conductor works a little, then you break through into a time when the group as a group is doing its own special thing, and they become quite captivated with it. That's why pieces such as you are describing can't help but succeed if people are willing.

cw: That's what happened when that class began. When I first showed them *Burdocks*, they couldn't believe it; they were astounded. But they realized that there were many things you could do. You have to stir them a bit; in this case it was slightly different, because you get them to think. The course is not only designed for playing but also for examining what music was—thinking about this phenomenon of shapes on paper, verbal remarks, and so on. Even something like "511 sounds, all different." . . . We had long discussions on what makes one sound different from another. Then you realize, why 511? Many questions like that. Another thing I like very much and I try to do (which goes back to where we began with notation) is economy. It pleases me to get two sentences on one page which will produce an hour's worth of interesting music.

bc: This gets into aesthetics: we're stuck with a "masterpiece" complex with a lot of contemporary composers who, if they were asked to write for amateurs or high school players, would either write down to them or not write at all. What does a work have to *have*? When they hear a not-very-good student new music group perform a work to the best of their ability, but the performance is clearly not the Fine Arts Quartet, people say, "This is *bad*, you shouldn't do this, it's a lousy performance, the work isn't there."

cw: That's already in the music itself. Mistakes have been an idea with me a long time. It's not that you set out to do a shabby performance. Obviously you try to do it as well as you can, but the music is arranged so that certain things will present insurmountable obstacles. I have written things which I had not expected someone to play, where I wanted precisely the sound of the effort, or even of the failure. Sometimes I've been disappointed because somebody could do it! This goes back to the Cagean notion that we're not making more masterpieces in the sense of being absolutely perfect, complete objects; where everything's in place and in marble, so to speak, forever and ever. Clearly that idea is losing ground among some of us. So if it's already in the aesthetic, in the music itself, then you can address people who wouldn't be technically capable of representing those sounds.

bc: There's a line in Cardew's "Notation: Interpretation, etc.," saying that it's rankly unfair to tell a performer "Do anything you want" and then growl at him because you think it's a bad performance.

CW: Pieces get played and mistakes get made, yet somehow the feeling is so strong and they have so much authority that it doesn't matter. It's a very dangerous area, obviously, because it's what you encourage in the performers. It's so easy to try to throw a performance together as fast as possible.

BC: Many of us face this problem with a work in which there is some option. A lot of players think that simply because they have two feet of rope they've got twenty-five yards. All manner of liberties are taken.

CW: It's quite astonishing, that total misreading, total misrepresentation, with pretty clear instructions. The opposite idea may be useful. The more you restrict the players—not in the sense of making them be reproducers the way they are mostly in nineteenth-, early twentieth-century music—the clearer the freedom becomes, and in that sense the more enjoyable.

BC: We work with certain kinds of players. But other kinds of players won't work at all. I can't see, for example, players who get together to read chamber music doing one of these pieces because they *like* to. I can see playing this music for pleasure after you've put away the Haydn and you're ready to go on to other things.

CW: It's an educational problem. Slowly but surely people will just have to be converted. I've avoided it because I've addressed myself ideally to musical dropouts: people who *have* got an instrument under their belts, but somehow are not interested in the standard line of the music school.

BC: A lot more people play now because of the spread of so-called popular music. These people are really interested in new music; people who don't want to play the official list one more time. And these are the people in my student new music groups who stay with the group semester after semester, who are seriously interested. They complain because their teacher wants them to play a concertino on their recital, and they'd much rather do a Cardew piece or a piece of yours. Some of them are damn good at it too—their feeling, their sense. They're as suited to the idiom of music since 1955 as your standard conservatory violinist is going to be to the official concerto literature.

CW: I've been out of touch, and I'm just beginning to get into it. Dartmouth doesn't have much of a tradition of music.

BC: It would be nice if you could do the general introduction course at a school with three hundred instrumental majors.

CW: There's a band and a glee club. Of course I've just got there, so perhaps I'll make inroads in that direction too.

BC: A large state university would have, for example, a giant stage band. I've had a lot of success with people who are essentially jazz musicians who take to this, yea, even as the duck to water. The three Milwaukee players were rock guitarists when they came in. This is where the real gold mine is.

CW: How do you find the audience situation when these new pieces get done?

BC: Oh, it varies incredibly. Ralph Shapey said that often in Chicago he had tremendous audiences—four hundred, five hundred—which is unthinkable elsewhere at a new music concert. The general sense of the audience? Everything from violent enthusiasm to what Dick Maxfield once referred to as "hysterical apathy." We put on a concert in Milwaukee for an audience of two. Essentially what we did was come down off the stage and put them right in among the players and let them participate. There *is* an increasing audience outside the university, but it's not increasing very fast. It seems very difficult to try to sell European 1950s Darmstadt music; people don't want to hear it. They find it dull. But for later, more relaxed music, yes, there is an increasing audience.

CW: I've had the same. I find small audiences tend to work better, especially if you can get them involved: break up that dividing line between stage and seats; have no seats or scatter the seats around. Once we simply invited them to come up. It was a large stage; they didn't get in the way. That's another aspect of the music. Aside from the fact that it can tolerate mistakes, or lack of virtuoso polish and so on, it's no longer interruption, it becomes participation. Someone looks over your shoulder in a long silence and starts talking to you. They think you're not doing much right now: "Tell me about it." I guess we really want to turn the audience into musicians.

BC: In some places this isn't going to happen. In large sophisticated cities, you'll still get people who think the function of the audience is to sit in the red plush upholstered seats and wait until the end so they can applaud. If they go to a string quartet concert, they're watching themselves listening to string quartets, which everybody knows are the greatest means of musical expression of the human soul. Look at Beethoven! So there they sit.

CW: I've decided to if possible discourage it. Yet there are various strategies, aside from fixing the hall. You may become self-conscious, but you become self-conscious in a different way. Make it difficult for people to realize when a concert has begun or ended, for people to realize that they're allowed to applaud now. Begin before the announced time: something is happening when they go in there, so they can't sit down and say all right, show me. They have to start working before they even start. Then, "Is it over? Isn't it over yet?" Run one piece into the next so they have no idea where you are in the program. Things like that are all very useful.

BC: I've always wanted to put on a concert at which the names of the composers are not given at all, so that you don't have the automatic canned response. But I can't find many composers who would lend their weight to this.

Working in classic literature, you deal with one of the most polished and sophisticated ethical and aesthetic apparatuses that man has ever set up. Does this overlap into your musical thinking?

cw: Less and less. My early music did have that notion behind it, in that I wanted to make something that was very pure. I didn't think so much about permanence, but that's part of it, because there'd be very little that would drop off or waste away, resulting in these pieces with a restricted number of notes. I suppose that's where classics had its effect. The other idea that comes through is clarity of statement. It's not rational clarity, so much—that's one view of the Greeks, which is too simple—but it's surface clarity. There comes a point where it gets mysterious, where the principle is just out of reach—it's there, but you don't quite know what it is. That idea always appealed to me; that affected the music in various ways, especially the earlier music. It doesn't come out too directly—only in the '50s, when people wrote very complicated music—but the notion of making something that was both clear and mysterious is there. The idea of economy, too, is probably a classical notion. But the connection of those two activities, music and Greek literature, has become simply a peda-gogical one. The Greek material is clearly valuable, so in that way, it's good for teaching. Also you'll never completely comprehend it, so that you won't kill that—it'll always escape you.

bc: The mystery is there.

cw: But then you get larger pedagogical situations: how ideas are communicated, or how you get people to start making their own ideas, aesthetically, ethically, or both. At the moment I don't know enough really to say anything yet. I think there are three stages. First is a formal aesthetic one, and the next one, "ethical," is the best word I can think of. We were talking about that earlier, the development of a sense of "honor" among the players. It's not that you avoid professionalism and that you're amateurish, but you realign the sense of what a performer feels he ought to do. It's not to be able to play a scale at a fantastically rapid pace and get all the notes in place. It's responsibility to a certain situation, a relationship to other sounds, other players, or even the whole concert situation. The third stage would be social and political, and that's the one I'm floundering around in now. That's the next step one has to take. The ethical one seems easy for it to fall into the given social structures that we have that clearly need overhauling. A simple one: the concert situa-tion. We've already been doing it without noticing, but one probably has to get more systematic about it.

bc: I think the political step is a very dangerous one: for example, the Cardew letters about Cage and Stockhausen.

cw: I like Cardew very much. I admire everything he's done; he's a good friend, so everything he does I take very seriously. And this last stage, I'm battling; not in the sense of battling him, but of just wrestling with the whole problem. The Cage article . . . I suppose it's relevant to think about his own private relationship to what he's written. It's obviously very crude, yet if it hadn't been crude it wouldn't have had nearly the impact that it clearly does. It gets one's mind up, if not one's feelings, and then you have to try to answer it. There's nothing more dangerous than politics. But it seems very important to come to grips with that.

BC: I don't like to think of music as the servant, willing or unwilling, of any kind of topical cause.

CW: That's the danger. But we have also been very self-indulgent, and that's partly as a reaction to that. Very beautiful in the *Burdocks* concert. Cardew arranged that, partly because he wanted to do the music, but also as an experiment in seeing how the Scratch Orchestra would work with these other groups ... well, "politically" seems very fancy; it's only music, after all! He also arranged a discussion with the audience in the middle of the concert, not afterwards, to see what they were getting out of this. There were mixed results: reactions both on the right and the left. Those on the so-called right thought that the aesthetics of the piece had been violated, and the ones on the left thought it hadn't been politicized sufficiently. Still, it was a very lively situation; both players and audience enjoyed themselves. At the beginning they did an arrangement by Cardew of the chorus of the Hebrew slaves from Verdi's *Nabucco*. Apparently, when this piece was done in Milan, it picked up a resonance in the working-class movement at the time. Cardew explained in the program note that he put the chorus on this program because he felt that it was an allegory of the situation of the composer now who had been relegated by society to a kind of ivory tower and thereby rendered homeless.

The language is curious. What perhaps bothers us most in his articles is that so many terms are borrowed. We've all got used to trying to make up our own language where we could. Cardew has been a very prominent figure, and now suddenly he's talking Mao. It comes as a shock. At the same time, it has obviously certain advantages: Mao's thought is very consistent, it's remarkably clear. So it's a point of reference. You then have to attack the point of reference—and that's quite an undertaking. I'm involved in that now, because I want to try to see what's right and wrong with it. So far I've found it a very interesting exercise. I don't know how it will eventually take me back to music or connect with it, but it's worth doing simply as a reaction to what's been happening, which is that we have—in a sense—been disconnected. You can say it's not our fault, that the musical situation is barren in many ways. What do you do? Surely you want to influence it; as soon as you're interested in that, then you're into a political situation. It's a question now of how you want to influence it, where you want to influence it. If you want to influence it, you might as well do it effectively. And so it goes.

Notes

1. Text notation uses written language; graphic notation uses pictorial elements.

2. Cornelius Cardew, "Notation, Interpretation, etc.," *Tempo* 58 (Spring 1961): 25.

3. *Christian Wolff: For Piano I/For Pianist/Burdocks,* Wergo LP, Wer 60 063, 1972.

4. Christian Wolff to the author, e-mail July 24, 2008.

5. Cornelius Cardew, "A Scratch Orchestra: draft constitution," *Musical Times* 110/1516 (June 1969): 617.

6. Richard Ascough, unpublished report of Scratch Orchestra concert, Munich, August 1972.

7. Christian Wolff, *Cues/Hinwein* (Cologne: MusikTexte, 1998), 256.

8. Ascough, report.

9. Cornelius Cardew, *Stockhausen Serves Imperialism, and Other Articles: With Commentary and Notes* (London: Latimer New Directions, 1974), particularly "Cage: Ghost or Monster?" 34–40, "Stockhausen Serves Imperialism," 46–55, and "Self-Criticism: Repudiation of Earlier Works," 78–103.

10. Cornelius Cardew, "Introductory Talk for Discussion at a Wolff/Rzewski Concert," in *Stockhausen Serves Imperialism,* 66–68.

11. Brian Dennis, *Experimental Music in Schools: Towards a New World of Sound* (London: Oxford University Press, 1970). Wolff's piece, *Toss* (1968), appeared in *Materials,* a supplemental envelope of twenty pieces.

23   Charles Wuorinen (1938–2020)

BRUCE QUAGLIA

      In 1972, when he sat down with Barney Childs for this interview, Charles Wuorinen could be described as a "young lion" who was already well into a successful career; one that would be marked by periodic controversies reflecting the strong positions that he has always held on the role of the composer, and more generally of the place of new music and art in society. In 1970 he had become the youngest composer to ever win the Pulitzer Prize in music for *Time's Encomium* (1968–69), an electronic work (his only work that is entirely electro-acoustic) realized on the RCA synthesizer at the Columbia-Princeton Electronic Music Center.

      This work closed a decade during which he burst forth onto the New York music scene, receiving numerous accolades, including awards and citations from BMI (1959, 1961–63), the American Academy of Arts and Letters (1967), and the Guggenheim Foundation (1968). Most notably, he founded the Group for Contemporary Music (GCM) in 1962 with Harvey Sollberger. The GCM set new standards for the performance of difficult contemporary music and championed composers who would come to define the Uptown New York style. Appointed to the music faculty at Columbia University in 1964, where he had only recently graduated, Wuorinen's strong political and musical stances would lead to his becoming a contentious figure within a highly conservative department at a university that was suddenly at the center of many of the turbulent political crises and protests of the late 1960s. Despite his many musical accomplishments, Wuorinen would be denied tenure at Columbia in 1970–71, resulting in a rare case of academic acrimony that would reverberate across the pages of the *New York Times*.[1] When the interview with Childs took place, Wuorinen had very recently left Columbia and joined the faculty of the Manhattan School of Music. However, it would be misleading to characterize Wuorinen as ever having been an "academic composer," given his persistent focus on practical aspects of composing and music making, and his general antipathy toward academic musical disciplines and their discourses.

Childs begins this conversation with some questions about Wuorinen's recently composed String Quartet No. 1 (1971), noting some palpable new directions for the composer in terms of both style and execution. Although Childs mentions only the Chamber Concerto for Flute and 10 Players (1964) as a counterexample, the entire series of chamber concerti from the mid-1960s is exemplary of the strict style of dense, intensely focused dodecaphonic techniques that Wuorinen had begun to move away from. This move began first with the *Duo* (for violin and piano) (1967) and *Politics of Harmony (A Masque)* (1967) but was then realized more completely in the *String Trio* (1968). The *Trio* is marked by newer processes that compose the largest structure of the work down into smaller time spans to the level of formal units and phrasing, and sometimes even into the surface details. These processes also often result in substantially sustained tonal centers, expressed as drones and other points of repeated pitch-class emphasis.[2] Though published several years later, many of the techniques Wuorinen described in his book, *Simple Composition*, come from this period.[3] While *Simple Composition* mainly describes the techniques of strict twelve-tone composition from his earlier music of the mid-1960s, it also lays out the principals of "nested form" that first appeared in the works leading up to the first string quartet. Wuorinen's use of self-similar structures that reappear at different time spans and structural levels of a musical work would reach a zenith in the late 1970s and 1980s in a series of pieces that engage directly with the fractal geometry of Benoit Mandelbrot.

Throughout this interview, Wuorinen declines to make substantive predictions about the future of contemporary art music or the outlook for contemporary composers. Yet if we compare this interview to some of his later ones, we do find some degree of optimism still present.[4] In 1972, Wuorinen still imagined a future for composers with some degree of artistic independence from and/or within institutions, likening this potential situation to that of "the wandering scholars of ancient China," a point of comparison that may require some context. Wuorinen had recently been studying the culture and thought of ancient China, perhaps in a search for universal constants. His student and friend Jeffrey Kresky has described this as Charles's period of "Chinoiserie."[5] We may regard the 1967 work, *The Politics of Harmony (A Masque)*, set in ancient China, as using that same cultural context to get at broader social and artistic truths. Here "forbidden tunes," once performed, bring about a calamity amid a narrative concerning the progression of moral, social and political order into disorder over time.[6] A little later in the interview, Wuorinen compares the situation of the composer in 1972 to that of the art of ancient China, where "the entire past is available." More than these references to China, synthesis of the music of the past with that of the present remains one of Wuorinen's most persistent technical and aesthetic concerns to the present day. Wuorinen's thoughts on this, and the techniques to achieve such a synthesis, are already fully mature in 1972 when he sat down to talk to Childs.

Charles Wuorinen: Interview

BARNEY CHILDS: I was interested in your thinking about pitch organization. The string quartet, especially in the last movement, seems to be different from your earlier works.

CHARLES WUORINEN: The whole issue is rather complicated, since I never think of pitch organization independently of other aspects of organization. That quartet is one of a series of my works in the last several years that all share a common reorientation from earlier works: a tendency to make the compositional continuity from the large into the small. The works are all conceived, at first, in very general terms over the entire span that they're occupying; and the progressive processes refine them rather than involving an accretion of small-scale continuity of the generally larger continuity is rather the subdivision of very generalized continuity specifically. This approach, even if it is not defined any further than that, tends to return one's interest to a goal-directed pitch-relation situation by its very nature. Beyond that, the specifics in the application of these principles support it as well. So if there's a change, it may result from that.

BC: Maybe I'm not familiar with the interim pieces. There is an earlier sequence of works which are also related, like the flute concerto. But this is a different relationship that these works attain?

CW: Yes, these works were all around '68.

BC: The violin piece—the duo?

CW: That's in between.

BC: Your talk about that piece had ideas about pitches. So was this transitional?

CW: Yes. Over the last two years my interests have shifted more and more away from the establishment of comprehensive predefined arrays of twelve-tone-derived pitch relations. Although still twelve-tone, it's become much simpler in its underpinnings, because the surface of my music has become more complicated in its execution—not necessarily in actual sound, but because it's being much more freely elaborated than before.

BC: In the quartet, the rhythmic underpinnings seem to be more relaxed somehow and the rhythmic surfaces are more ornate and tangible.

CW: It is. What goes on in that specific work is something that I do occasionally, a variation within my present practice. [*Tape malfunction.*]

CW: I was saying that even a half dozen years ago it was possible for a composer or a whole group of composers to present scores for performers, which were somewhat separated, notationally speaking, from what is normally recognizable and understandable by most performers. I'm not speaking of graphic or aleatoric music, but music which is conventional in its ambiance but is notated illiterately, and to excuse such practices on the grounds that they simply didn't perform—that they didn't have the experience. There are relatively few composers today who would dare to make that kind of statement, who would acknowledge rather than be proud of their separation from more immediate acts of music making. Also, the reunification of "musical functions" has a very important effect on all kinds of basic conceptual attitudes about music. For example, there is a school of thought which suggests that the process of perception (or the process of analysis, which I presume is closely related to that) and the process of composition are largely the same, although perhaps the reversal to each other or something like that. My own conviction is, of course, quite other.

BC: This is music making on every level? The players are also compelled to take this stance? It's no longer sufficient to show up at seven o'clock with the pieces in the folder, noodle through them, and go home?

CW: Not as possible as it once was. It still happens. But it is no longer assumed that the humble composer is to be grateful for any attention at all that is given to him. Now it's assumed that a slightly higher standard of artistic morality must be observed.

BC: There are now players who commission pieces for their instruments, which a composer would have never thought of writing without these commissions. And these works make the composer come to grips with musical problems that he might not have come to.

CW: That's undoubtedly true, of course, but this phenomenon is nested inside of a more general one, namely a reorientation of instrumental or performing resources. Every age has interests in characteristic combinations, instruments, and what have you. Our own appears quite a bit richer than past ages, in that we have not dispensed with the combinations of instruments of the past, to any marked degree—we still write our string quartets—but there are certain new areas of previous neglect (percussion is the most obvious) as well as areas of addition (electronically) which are receiving a great deal of attention. Those players—of tubas, of percussion instruments and others who are not cursed with an enormous historical repertoire—seem to be recognizing more that they are in an age in which the classic literature for their instruments is being created. This is certainly true of percussionists. As a result, dealing with such players is much more rewarding than dealing with players with more mainstream instruments.

BC: Often percussionists will be more musically aware, than, let's say, string players.

CW: Certainly, because they have no opportunity to develop the kind of self-satisfaction and complacency that string players do. It's interesting that the proof of all this lies in the fact that there are violinists and other string players—a couple of cellists—who really *are* concerned with contemporary music. The struggle that they have, in order to deal with or to keep at arms length the repertory they have inherited, is equally revealing.

BC: Is it possible for a composer to lead a completely independent life now?

cw: Independent in what sense? Financially?

bc: Well, financially is the main part—but is it possible to become, as one becomes a writer, say?

cw: I don't see how it could be. I don't think that anyone leads an independent existence. Much of that is illusory, certainly for a person involved in an art which depends on the presence and cooperation of other people. It's a question of trying to achieve the maximum freedom and flexibility within such a life, and to modulate between the desirability of stability and security and the necessity for freedom of action. There is much more possibility for composers to exist as independent professionals now than there used to be. Not so much free of institutional involvement, which is probably what you're really talking about, as more like the wandering scholars of ancient China, going around peddling their knowledge in practical ways. In those days they were military technologists—as well as the best moralists. I can foresee a role somewhat like that for composers and other artists via the institutions. Not a full-time exclusive and lifetime involvement with one or another, but a rather peripheral series of visiting composerships on leave.

bc: Back to the peripatetic philosophers.

cw: Something like that is much more in the wind, especially as nonacademic, noninstitutional means of support become more available. And they will, inevitably, because when one sees, for example, in New York State the first burgeonings of state-supported program of commission grants to individual artists. I'm sure this is going on elsewhere in the country. It's a very small program, now in its second year. We will see this increasingly as the government moves more and more into these areas. No doubt it will be hideously abused, as all government subsidies are, but nevertheless, it will exist. That and the resulting response which is inevitable in the private sector will have a good deal to offer. Even if the sums of money involved are not that great, the fact that a person can receive some kind of support outside of present existing channels for his work is a very powerful psychological factor.

Another point: many people are very interested in bringing educational radio and television—public radio and television—to heel somewhat, to stop their exploitive free-of-charge use of music. If that battle is ever successful, and I think it will be ultimately, the whole economic picture for contemporary music obviously will change. There are what our last president used to call nervous Nellies who are afraid that if force is applied to these institutions, they'll stop performing contemporary music. That is absurd. Just as the popular song writers of the '20s were told by the then-burgeoning broadcasting industry that they should be glad to have their stuff played for nothing because they were being exposed, we are told that by the very same educational television which finds $85,000 to pay a well-known commentator to do a once-a-week show for a year. I think that the funds, minimal as they may be, could be dug up for us. The point is that in this atmosphere of increasing fiduciary respect, I think a professional can develop a degree of independence—although not a complete one. That was not possible before.

Another point, while we are on this subject, is that it now seems evident that whenever there is an adequate distribution system for recordings of contemporary music, they go very well indeed. The failure of the products of certain companies to sell very widely is purely the result of inadequate distribution. Nonesuch, on the other hand, is an excellent example of what happens when there is an efficient distribution system. This demonstrates that there is a tremendous untapped audience, an enormous financial base for us, if certain intermediary problems can be removed. One can hardly estimate whether this will solve all economic problems. Undoubtedly, they won't. There is certainly a change for the better.

BC: But what about the system in Holland, where just about everything anybody writes gets government publication and performance? Peter Schat had a recent piece for a cast of thousands, and it had all been laid on, all the ornate electronics and everything else.

CW: Do you mean is this in the cards?

BC: Europe is doing all these things for its broadcasting companies, too.

CW: It's very hard to say. I wouldn't want to predict. If it is, it's a long way off. And one of the reasons that there is a very high degree of disinterest in this sort of thing persisting in established cultural institutions. For example, I remember a proposal last year to put on some short stage works at the [New York?] City Center making use of federal funds. But the project never materialized. There was no American work among them. There were three short works of Hans Werner Henze, there was a piece of Ligeti. Not the slightest sense from people who were putting it on, or the government agency that was prospective underwriter, that government funds should be used to support the citizens of the country. This point has been made very strongly a number of times by very distinguished composers—two on the National Council on the Arts. And there is only so far the most casual response to all of this. What is going to be necessary is a long period of education, until the government finally gets the profound, the complicated, the sophisticated idea that tax money should be spent first on the product of artists who are citizens of the country. When that realization is reached, then maybe we will be able to see some of this. It's all very well for a small East European socialist country to publish every work of every composer who has any claim to professional status. Whereas this country is the musical center of the world, in which there is an incredible amount of activity and an incredible range of diverse views represented. It would be very difficult to imagine a government body's being able to deal with the volume of material that's produced. So I rather doubt that that day is coming very soon.

I'm not entirely sure that it's a good thing, either. Certainly our condition is far from what it ought to be. But our condition should not be made so automatically easy that we have happen to us the terrible disaster that's happened to Europe. Whatever Europe may have been worth from the compositional point of view after the Second World War, now has become a complete waste. A large part of that has arisen from the fact that too much support was available, and that composers and other musicians interested in contemporary music were automatically assumed to be right in every excess they committed. There was no balance. Again, we return to the necessity of having a balanced and mature point of view. A certain amount of adversity is worth something.

BC: We help this by extending a golden hand to these men to come over.

CW: You have one of the sorest points, in my view. In this late date, with the twentieth century almost over, we (not we as musicians—but so many people who make economic cultural decisions for us now and then) still must live with a three-quarter-century out-of-date American cultural inferiority complex. There may never have been any real justification for it, but there has been none whatever for the last twenty-five or thirty years, and particularly none justifiable with respect to a European scene which is utterly barren and destitute.

BC: Yet you have in universities the visiting official European, dragging down as much salary as the football coach and not there for the rest of his three months. And American musicians are getting beans.

CW: One of my favorite examples of that was a young French composer who was, without an hour of teaching experience in his life and without a word of English to his credit, hired at a large California university at a very substantial salary at an age and at a rank which no American in the country could have possibly come into. Also, it is still considered necessary to import orchestral conductors from abroad. In the case of the [New York] Philharmonic, a man like [Pierre] Boulez, who has his merits and deserves respect in certain terms. Nevertheless, it should be felt by everyone here that his appearance on the scene would make a support of contemporary music that was not possible otherwise. It is absurd, insulting, and infuriating, and of course has been proved to be quite opposite from the truth. Witness the announced programs of the Philharmonic next year, which include two contemporary American works.

BC: It's a tacit assumption, something that's automatic.

CW: Yes. There's something else that's interesting in the case of the Philharmonic. You know of their [Prospective] Encounter series. They intend to justify their failure to perform orchestral music on the grounds that they are discharging their responsibilities to contemporary music in that domain. They muscle in on the one area which is already well served, and attempt by that to get out of the institutional responsibility to play orchestra music. This is a very unpleasant situation. One almost wishes that they would withdraw back into their museum. When they pretend to relevance in an area where they have no competence, it's very distressing. Those were the highly skilled professionals who were brought in to take care of the humble composer. If the orchestras wish to exist as kindergartens, that's all right with me. What I cannot endure and will not accept is the derogation of standards that they take.

BC: There are still universities in which this happens. We spoke earlier about the presence of very talented young players who are not just competent to handle music but play it with considerable know-how. This ersatz professionalism works against it. If there's one thing that bugs me about some universities, it's this sense that there is still an attempt to hold to this old line despite the presence of very talented and interested young players and instructors. There is still the feeling that the orchestra is the important unit, where you go and sit through the official fifty repertoire pieces. It's very scary.

CW: This simply demonstrates, as does the American cultural inferiority complex, that these attitudes last far longer than we want them to. When one cannot believe that anyone can still retain a given conviction, one finds there are in fact millions who do. That is ever our role: to be disappointed in our expectations.

BC: It's a half-life, retained after you've seen its visible power go out.

CW: The main mistake artists make about such matters is in assuming that other people care about an artistic issue as much as they do. The people you are talking about may be administrators or musicologists, music educators—other people only peripherally involved with music and for whom it is far simpler to persist in a given attitude than to bother adopting a new one. One always is distressed by this indifference, assuming that it represents actual opposition to one's point of view. In fact it doesn't. It simply represents an indifference to any point of view and the resulting unwillingness to change.

BC: You mentioned that you wrote a group of works related about a set of ideas, then made a transition to another group of works that generally explored certain areas. Is this going to turn out to be a pattern, that a single work is insufficient for you to realize the compositional implications of your intellectual approaches and constructs?

CW: I wouldn't presume to predict the future, but I can answer that to some extent. I am unconcerned to the point of almost active hostility with the notion of the uniqueness of the individual work. It is artistically unhealthy. I am also unconcerned with the notion of individual artistic identity; that is, the primarily nineteenth-century notion (although it had roots much earlier) of the unique artistic personality producing the unique artistic work. It's an attractive and seductive notion, but if it's to be achieved, it's to be achieved only by being ignored. For that reason, I can never regard an individual piece as carrying an obligation to sum something up entirely. Sometimes that appears and sometimes it doesn't. As I move from work to work, I certainly don't feel like I'm writing the same piece again, but because I frequently work on more than one thing at a time there's a far greater degree of connectedness among my adjacent works than there is for some others. Yet I also find certain composers who don't produce a piece for two or three years doing exactly the same thing with the piece after the long hiatus. And this is a very important lesson, because nothing is served by preoccupation with the new, with the individual, or with the unique in one's self.

My point of view is subsumed in a broader attitude and a broader conviction, which I feel very strongly, that the Western music at the present moment ought to reconcile itself with its own past. People have many different ways of going about it, some of which I am sympathetic to and some of which I'm not. The notion of a nineteenth-century evolutionary progressivism or historical determinism, in which some line is pursued and ultimately wipes out all the rest because it's better is not really the point at all. We are now, and I've said this for many years, in the same situation that Chinese art used to be; the entire past is available, in a simultaneous way, for use in whatever way the artist feels is appropriate. I don't think the immediate future holds the historical reappearance of old ways of composing pieces. But I do think that the kinds of oppositions and antitheses that used to be asserted as absolutely basic between, say (because it concerns me more than other kinds), twelve-tone music and tonal music really are not as pronounced as one might think. And there's no reason why those cannot be united on a higher plane.

BC: This is a redefinition of style, perhaps?

CW: "Style" is a word I don't understand and never use, because the word is a kind of generalization to cover up a lack of clarity of detail. That is if one hears every note in a work and that's the work. There really is no part of it that can be extracted and called style, although in many cases one can speak about the surface of a piece as opposed to something deeper down in it. That's a verbal prejudice I have. The word has been misused so many times and it has sometimes been used to mean methodology—sometimes process, or whatever. But I'm not comfortable with it.

BC: I'm thinking in terms of citation of past works in one's work: appearance of work by a Baroque composer, a few bars, which has been done. People say this is mixing up the styles.

CW: First of all, I don't know whether that's a good or bad thing to do. It's so contextual in its aspect, there's no point in generalizing about it. When people say mixing of styles, I think what they mean is that mutually antithetical musical systems are being revised. If the process of unification can be carried out to a point where the mutually antithetical are no longer so, then there isn't an issue. As for abruptions and discontinuities on the surface in pieces, I don't see any reason why they shouldn't be there.

This may be of some bearing: quite naturally, as a result of the extension of the compositional idea that I was talking about before, certain quotations have appeared. In my last completed work, for example, I have a couple of peripheral references to two Mozart symphonies and the Beethoven Ninth. These were not part of the plan of the piece; the piece has nothing to do with quotation or allusion. It simply was of great interest that as an act of purely local caprice in the final elaboration of the surface of the piece, I was able to insert those things because the pitch-class configurations that surrounded the areas where I put them made it appropriate. And although they are quotes and allusions at the same time, they are not grafted on to anything.

BC: They are organic?

CW: I regard them as so. I found it very interesting that a piece which was composed out of the twelve-tone past with modifications and expansions now can include that thing as a mere incident. I could have elaborated the surface in another way, so there was no dialectical point behind it all. If it is possible, and if there is anything that could summarize my present aims, it would be the broadening and expansion of that kind of flexibility of language.

BC: Could this expand to alter the structure at the next level down? You're talking about surface . . .

CW: I think it's entirely possible.

BC: What major modifications do you think the twelve-pitch-class system has benefited from?

CW: The first is that the notion of a musical system—particularly the twelve-tone system, since it's been more precisely defined than any other in certain respects—always carries with it the notion of boundaries. There has been a tendency in recent musical thought to try to fix boundaries very firmly. That's useful for purposes of reference. But that obscures the fact that between the tonal and twelve-tone systems there is not absolute disjunction and raises the question: at what point does something stop being twelve-tone? If one takes a classic view of the twelve-tone system with its arrays of set forms, set forms primarily treated, or with set forms being treated as abstractions of line, whether verticalized or not, etc., then I wouldn't regard my own music as twelve-tone at all. But one can raise the same kind of question about tonal music. I find myself unable to believe the tonal system exists outside of a very small period and number of people. Perhaps eighteenth-century Viennese are the only really tonal composers; maybe one can broaden that a bit. The point is whether or not a system can be said to be developing or not depends on where its boundaries are said to be fixed.

If you say that all that I have been vaguely alluding to in my own practice are no longer twelve-tone because they don't do thus and so, then the twelve-tone system is, in fact, a fixed and inflexible thing. If you say, as [Milton] Babbitt has wanted to for years, that the twelve-tone system and tonal system are fundamentally opposed, then the process of reunification that I'm referring to is also manifestly impossible or ill-advised. So it seems terribly difficult to form any precise notions until we all can agree on these boundaries. I see nothing wrong with defining late eighteenth-century Viennese music as tonal music or one work exemplifying the system and everything else as a variant of it. Or taking certain classical twelve-tone works and saying *they* represent that, and anything else is a departure. But there would have to be some conventional agreement before we could go that far along. Most of the arguments that we have artistically, of course, are simple confusion of terms.

BC: In a compositional approach such as yours, in which the small things are an essential result of starting outside and working in, it seems that your view of the details, when you get to them, is going to be quite different than it would have been if you'd done it the other way. They are going to surface in quite a different way and become dominant to a degree that they could never have done if you had begun with them.

CW: Absolutely, because if one tries to build up large continuity out of small detail, then the detail is not a detail any more, it's a generator. Every detail, therefore, comes to carry with it an enormous burden of responsibility and an enormous set of either exciting and/or threatening potentialities. As a result, one has very little flexibility locally within a work. It is, in fact, precisely that problem which led me to this other attitude. The way I work now, when I arrive at the surface whatever I choose to reflect of the underneath structure of course is mine to do. I no longer feel, as I once did, any inhibition about elaboration of the surface. Now I feel I can solve contextual problems contextually. My attitude derives from a conviction that I've developed out of—to behave in the same way on every level of organization. And while it may be a kind of superficially attractive ideal, that overlooks the fact that one's perception of musical time does not operate the same way in the large as it does in the small. The larger the dimensions get, the more the quantitative begins to be received and experienced as qualitative. For that reason, I don't see how a surface can be made to do in a couple of seconds what the whole piece is doing over twenty minutes.

BC: That's what strikes me about the quartet. There is leisure and relaxation; it's as though you have all the time in the world to handle the surface details. You do, in a sense, because the process has given you this. As a result, it's a totally different kind of gesture that is very attractive.

CW: I have to add one other thing to this, which is that once the surface exists, it is the way through which the entire work is perceived. I am sure that the choices one makes contextually and locally, and sometimes casually, reach down and affect the basic structure very profoundly in some instances. So be it. My point is that that fact is the cleanest demonstration that composition and perception are different. Because the way I work my pieces—a work is always in an equal state of completion in every one of its parts—my dealing as composer in the process of composition with the surface simultaneously over the entire work is one thing, because I feel that I'm putting a final coat of paint on a building which has a secure foundation. However, when the work is heard and experienced in that way, what is going on in the mind of the hearer is a generalization from the moment-to-moment detail. He cannot regard the detail in the same way that I have when I composed it, no matter how well he knows the work.

BC: It seems that there are two end points on the surface activity concept. One is kind of post-Darmstadt, where every surface detail is of equal importance in its impact because there isn't anything else. You've got a whole plenum of tiny individual actions. The other is where surface details are so fully independent of any other kind of macrostructure that they become qualifying in themselves. They are not generated to do so; they just sit there and organize things in a very curious way. What you're doing, in a sense, is resolving a dichotomy and getting away with the best parts of each one.

CW: That's the intent. But the attempt is made by denying the existence of a dichotomy to begin with, and simply trying to reflect on what the various levels of organization of the piece contribute to the overall coherence of it. So what happens in the small can be only metaphorically reflected in what happens in the large, not literally so. We have suffered in recent years from an overdose of literalism trying to transfer from one domain to another, things that don't transfer literally so easily. When we have managed to define systematically, with consistency, the operations of transfer, we will have solved all the problems.

BC: One of the features about music of the last twenty years has been an emphasis on a kind of organic growth, a feeling that you come into the piece at one end and you're no longer going through a set of shapes and balances; you're developing, growing—maybe not always predictable. Perhaps the Elliott Carter piano concerto, which is essentially an organic piece?

CW: Well, it has been very important and continues to be, because it is one of the few respects in which large-scale form in Western music has changed. Now, it would be unwise to try to assert that as a replacement for the past. What I look forward to with some interest is a possibility of again reconciling that kind of continuity. Carter's work is the most familiar example of it, and secondarily perhaps composers like Wolpe, but equally in the works of composers like Babbitt one finds, although with a different intent, that sense of continuity unfolding and developing. What is unfolding is somewhat different, but it's the same general idea. There is the same tendency to avoid the metaphorical periodicity as it existed in music of the past. Now, however, we should have both resources available.

BC: This parallels your earlier view that we're simply saying OK, the limitations are not what we thought they were. If you take the idea of organic growth, this brings back an expressivity, a means of dramatism which had not previously been there. This dramatism is opposed to the dramatism of [Jean] Racine, [Pierre] Corneille, which is a dramatism of balances; and this is a dramatism of dynamism. It makes the pieces work in a peculiarly immediate way. Larry Austin wrote an article for the *Times* in which he talked about the "New Romanticism."[7] I'm not sure what it means, but there the phrase was.

CW: I don't know what the phrase means, either, so it would be hard for me to comment on it. I suppose what is in his mind—I haven't read the article either—has to do with the throwing over of shackles, kicking over of traces.

BC: Perhaps getting back to a lyrical and personally expressive idiom.

CW: I don't know what that means, either. Unless it means simply aping a certain set of rather unpleasant mannerisms, which in the past were defined as expressive of personal position. I reject all that. I don't know what's intended beyond this very specific meaning. Such statements, of course, refer to feeling that music has been unduly constrained. Certainly Larry Austin's music has never been unduly constrained, so I don't know why this should preoccupy him. It's awfully hard. When everyone deals with journalistic phrases like that, if one tries to invest them with real meaning, then one is in real trouble. If one plays along with them and says "I guess I know what it means," then one falls into a worse trap.

BC: It seems that younger composers are standing closer to the piece than they were twenty years ago.

CW: Well, the ideological lines that seem quite sharp have been blurred. Therefore, the individual work has become more important than what it represents.

BC: What is happening with your students?

CW: The best of them are like the performers I spoke about before, without any observed self-effacement. They seem free of the competitiveness that used to characterize many composers; they seem without question devoted to serious artistic ideals in ways that some earlier generations, including my own, were not necessarily so involved in. Where it will lead, I cannot say. Maybe they come to me because they know I will be sympathetic to it, but I find a lack of interest in my students in the avant-garde for its own sake, a lack of concern with that progressive reactionary dichotomy and that whole general range of opposition. It doesn't seem to enter anybody's mind as particularly important.

BC: The recent works that you mention are all instrumental pieces. Are you going to continue with synthesized work?

CW: I imagine so. I'm not engaged in that at the moment. I'm beginning an opera.

BC: What's the libretto going to be?

CW: It is a pornographic restoration type.

BC: That's almost redundant.

CW: But it's newly written by a brilliant friend of mine.

BC: Think of a restoration comedy that doesn't get pornographic?

CW: Well, this is nothing else but. It's called the *W. of Babylon.*[8] It's rather small scale. It was planned as a chamber opera that has nine characters. It will be followed by a much larger work, which is not supposed to be funny. This one is.

BC: The works which you have written over the last several years have been largely commissioned by particular virtuoso players. Does it bother you that some of these works don't get out, that you don't get a program from Hog Jowl State saying that there has been a performance of your piece?

CW: None of my music is played in places where people can't play. Most of it is very difficult. It is certainly not played the way the works of [Alan] Hovhaness or [Henry] Cowell are. And that simply seems to be a fact of life. I don't make things to be withheld deliberately. My mind just seems to work in those ways.

BC: There's an awful moment when you get a tape which some well-meaning guy has done when you weren't there, and it's just abominable.

CW: Yes.

BC: I know a lot of tuba players who would be very happy to try the concerto. But there's something about New York, all clichés aside, that those of us outside of it don't have a hotline to find out what is happening. The programs for the Group [for Contemporary Music] come out, this is true.[9] But people don't find these things out. I know tuba players that don't know you have a tuba piece. They ought to know it.

CW: We've always suffered nationally, because of the size of the country and the diversity of artistic activity, from lack of information about what's going on. There are few people around now who are trying to figure out ways of doing that. But even if there was some kind of clearinghouse, it wouldn't really make that much difference, because an active artist can't really bother to keep a diary of his activities.

BC: But that doesn't bother you?

CW: It would be nice if communication were better, obviously. I welcome every effort to improve it, but I see basic problems, because everyone is primarily self-involved.

BC: What about your early works?

CW: I like to leave those things alone. Pieces that are really student pieces are more or less withdrawn. But it's not as if I have to resist countless heavy pressures to have them performed or otherwise disseminated. One or two works accidentally receive a kind of dissemination in currency that they shouldn't have. But what's done is done; I certainly make no effort to falsify the past. I've always been impatient with artists who try to present themselves as fully formed from the brain of Zeus. An artist's responsibility lies, in part, in leaving all of his traces. That is very important, because if one has any real achievements to his credit, they can only be measured against his failures.

I certainly have my own preferences amongst my works. But if someone comes along and wants to do an early piece of mine that I don't think very much of any more, I would never prevent it. I would be denying my own past.

BC: I have some failures that are just *too* bad: anomalies that should have been drowned.

CW: An artist wishing to disguise his failures is again part of that hero business, the superficial notion from the past, and I think it's very unheroic, rather cowardly. It's far more worthwhile to have the stuff around, primarily because, although I have infinite contempt for the judgment of a public at a given moment, I have a good deal of faith in the overall reliability of the historical weeding-out processes. It's true there are a number of worthwhile works by worthwhile composers that aren't known as they should be. But I don't think there are any major figures in the past or any really major works that we don't know about.

Notes

1. See Charles Wuorinen, "Are the Arts Doomed on Campus?" *New York Times*, August 8, 1971, 1; Donal Henahan, "Columbia Music Unit Faces Extinction," *New York Times*, May 20, 1971, 47.

2. See Anton Vishio: "On Wuorinen's *String Trio*: Two Analytic Sketches," and JoAnn Kuchera-Morin: "Structure in Charles Wuorinen's *String Trio*," both in *Perspectives of New Music* 56, no. 2 (Summer 2018): 317–47 and 113–48.

3. Charles Wuorinen, *Simple Composition* (New York: Longman, 1979).

4. See Joan Peyser, "Wuorinen's Bleak View of the Future," *New York Times*, June 25, 1988; and William Robin, "Why Is Charles Wuorinen So Cranky?" *New York Times*, May 25, 2018. Also see James Romig, "A Conversation with Charles Wuorinen," *Perspectives of New Music* 56/2 (Summer 2018): 11–21.

5. Jeffrey Kresky, unpublished interview with the author and Sumanth Gopinath, April 23, 2018.

6. See William Hibbard, "Charles Wuorinen: The Politics of Harmony," *Perspectives of New Music* 7/2 (Spring–Summer 1969): 155–66. Hibbard also places this work in the context of the Columbia protests during Wuorinen's time on the music faculty there.

7. Larry Austin, "Can Electronic Music Be Romantic?" *New York Times*, September 19, 1971, sect. D, 15.

8. *W. of Babylon* (1976), "a baroque burlesque," libretto by Renaud Charles Bruce.

9. Wuorinen and Harvey Sollberger founded the Group for Contemporary Music in 1962.

Contributors

VIRGINIA ANDERSON researched graphic and text notation, time, indeterminacy, British systems minimalism, and the London Scratch Orchestra; she recorded as a clarinetist, percussionist, and free improviser. She was treasurer of the Experimental Music Catalogue and editor of the *Journal of Experimental Music Studies*.

JAY M. ARMS is a Visiting Lecturer of Ethnomusicology at the University of Pittsburgh. He researches American experimental music and the internationalization of Indonesian gamelan. His current project traces evolving discourses about gamelan tunings, situating them at the intersection of divergent theories of tuning, ethnomusicology, and creative practices.

THOMAS S. CLARK was a colleague of Larry Austin at the University of North Texas. They founded the Center for Experimental Music and Intermedia, hosted ICMC (International Computer Music Conference), and coauthored their landmark book, *Learning to Compose: Modes, Materials, and Models of Musical Invention* (1989). Clark wrote *Larry Austin: Life and Works of an Experimental Composer* (2012).

STUART DEMPSTER is a trombonist, composer, didjeriduist; professor emeritus, University of Washington; and founding member, Deep Listening Band. His recordings have been produced by Columbia (Sony), Nonesuch, and New Albion. Grants include Fulbright Scholar, Australia (1973), and a Guggenheim Fellowship (1981). He has received three Golden Ear Awards to date: Deep Listening 2006, Earshot Jazz 2009, and the International Trombone Association Lifetime Achievement Award 2010.

MICHELLE FILLION is Professor Emerita at the University of Victoria British Columbia, and taught at Mills College and McGill University. She specializes in the music of Haydn and Beethoven. She is the author of *Difficult Rhythm: Music and the Word in E. M. Forster* (University of Illinois Press, 2010) and edited Gordon Mumma's *Cybersonic Arts: Adventures in American New Music* (University of Illinois Press, 2015).

ROBERT FINK is Professor of Musicology at UCLA. He has published widely on contemporary music (both art and popular), most notably *Repeating Ourselves: American Minimal Music as Cultural Practice* (2005), and, as lead editor, *The Relentless Pursuit of Tone: Timbre in Popular Music* (2018).

PETER GENA, composer, studied with Morton Feldman and Lejaren Hiller. His works—instrumental, electronic/computer, and VR—have been presented in the Americas, Europe, Asia, and Australia. He writes primarily on new music and composers, and is Professor Emeritus at the School of the Art Institute of Chicago.

SARA HAEFELI is an Associate Professor at Ithaca College. She is author of the monograph *John Cage: A Research and Information Guide* (2018) coauthor of *Writing in Music: A Brief Guide* (2021), and editor-in-chief of the *Journal of Music History Pedagogy.*

ROB HASKINS, Professor and Chair of Music at the University of New Hampshire, writes on Cage and others. His *Classical Listening* (2016) collects writings from his first twenty years writing for the *American Record Guide.* He is also a performing and recording artist.

DAVE HEADLAM is Professor of Music Theory at the Eastman School of Music. He has published widely on music post-1900, popular music, rhythm in music, and music and technology. His *Music of Alban Berg* (1996), received an ASCAP Deems Taylor award.

KEVIN HOLM-HUDSON is Professor of Music Theory at the University of Kentucky. He holds a doctor of musical arts in composition from the University of Illinois, where his instructors included Salvatore Martirano, William Brooks, and Morgan Powell. His doctoral thesis was a multi-parametric analysis of Robert Ashley's *Perfect Lives.*

RONALD KUIVILA is Professor of Music at Wesleyan University and a former student and colleague of Alvin Lucier. He is a composer and sound artist whose music and installations center on physical and technologically mediated relationships to sound. Kuivila has performed and exhibited in the Americas, Europe, and Asia.

DAVID NEAL LEWIS is a composer, writer, scholar, and radio host. A pioneer in Cincinnati's underground music scene, Lewis has worked as a buyer for Tower Records, an editor at the All Music Guide, and for the Library of Congress. Currently, Lewis manages a record store in Luray, Virginia.

GAYLE SHERWOOD MAGEE has published extensively on the compositions of Charles Ives, the film soundtracks of Robert Altman, and transnational music in World War I. She is currently completing a book on William Bolcom for the American Composers series at the University of Illinois Press.

HORACE J. MAXILE JR. is Associate Professor of Music at Baylor University. His primary research interests involve concert music by African American composers and musical signification. His publications include articles in *Perspectives of New Music*, *Journal of the Society for American Music*, and *Annual Review of Jazz Studies*.

JEFFREY PERRY has taught at Louisiana State University since 1994. A composer and theorist, he holds degrees from Williams College, the California Institute of the Arts, and Princeton University. He has published on the music of Schubert, Cage, Mel Powell, and others. Music-text relationships are a major interest.

JAMES PRITCHETT is the author of *The Music of John Cage* (1993). From 1986 to 1992, he wrote software for composers at the computer music centers at Brooklyn College and Princeton University.

BRUCE QUAGLIA is a composer and scholar of twentieth-century music. He has served on the music faculty of the University of Minnesota, Utah Valley University, and the University of Utah. He was recently guest coeditor of the "Wuorinen at Eighty" *Festschrift* in *Perspectives of New Music*.

JOHN SCHNEIDER is the Grammy Award–winning guitarist, author, and broadcaster who has released over twenty CDs and is the founding artistic director of MicroFest festival, MicroFest Records, and the groups Just Strings and the PARTCH Ensemble. He can be heard weekly on Pacifica Radio's *The Global Village* (www.KPFK.org).

FRANCES WHITE is a composer of instrumental, vocal, and electronic music. She is particularly known for her works combining live performers and computer-generated electronic sound spaces. She studied composition with Charles Dodge at the Brooklyn College Center for Computer Music in the 1980s.

Index

BARNEY CHILDS (1926–2000) was an experimental music composer, poet, and educator. His compositions included chamber music and music for keyboards.

VIRGINIA ANDERSON maintained the Experimental Music Catalogue and was the editor of the *Journal of Experimental Music Studies*. She died in 2021.

Music in American Life

Pressing On: The Roni Stoneman Story *Roni Stoneman, as told to Ellen Wright*
Together Let Us Sweetly Live *Jonathan C. David, with photographs by Richard Holloway*
Live Fast, Love Hard: The Faron Young Story *Diane Diekman*
Air Castle of the South: WSM Radio and the Making of Music City
  Craig P. Havighurst
Traveling Home: Sacred Harp Singing and American Pluralism *Kiri Miller*
Where Did Our Love Go? The Rise and Fall of the Motown Sound *Nelson George*
Lonesome Cowgirls and Honky-Tonk Angels: The Women of Barn Dance Radio
  Kristine M. McCusker
California Polyphony: Ethnic Voices, Musical Crossroads *Mina Yang*
The Never-Ending Revival: Rounder Records and the Folk Alliance *Michael F. Scully*
Sing It Pretty: A Memoir *Bess Lomax Hawes*
Working Girl Blues: The Life and Music of Hazel Dickens *Hazel Dickens and*
  Bill C. Malone
Charles Ives Reconsidered *Gayle Sherwood Magee*
The Hayloft Gang: The Story of the National Barn Dance *Edited by Chad Berry*
Country Music Humorists and Comedians *Loyal Jones*
Record Makers and Breakers: Voices of the Independent Rock 'n' Roll Pioneers
  John Broven
Music of the First Nations: Tradition and Innovation in Native North America
  Edited by Tara Browner
Cafe Society: The Wrong Place for the Right People *Barney Josephson,*
  with Terry Trilling-Josephson
George Gershwin: An Intimate Portrait *Walter Rimler*
Life Flows On in Endless Song: Folk Songs and American History *Robert V. Wells*
I Feel a Song Coming On: The Life of Jimmy McHugh *Alyn Shipton*
King of the Queen City: The Story of King Records *Jon Hartley Fox*
Long Lost Blues: Popular Blues in America, 1850–1920 *Peter C. Muir*
Hard Luck Blues: Roots Music Photographs from the Great Depression *Rich Remsberg*
Restless Giant: The Life and Times of Jean Aberbach and Hill and Range Songs
  Bar Biszick-Lockwood
Champagne Charlie and Pretty Jemima: Variety Theater in the Nineteenth Century
  Gillian M. Rodger
Sacred Steel: Inside an African American Steel Guitar Tradition *Robert L. Stone*
Gone to the Country: The New Lost City Ramblers and the Folk Music Revival
  Ray Allen
The Makers of the Sacred Harp *David Warren Steel with Richard H. Hulan*
Woody Guthrie, American Radical *Will Kaufman*
George Szell: A Life of Music *Michael Charry*
Bean Blossom: The Brown County Jamboree and Bill Monroe's Bluegrass Festivals
  Thomas A. Adler
Crowe on the Banjo: The Music Life of J. D. Crowe *Marty Godbey*
Twentieth Century Drifter: The Life of Marty Robbins *Diane Diekman*
Henry Mancini: Reinventing Film Music *John Caps*

The University of Illinois Press
is a founding member of the
Association of University Presses.

———————————————

University of Illinois Press
1325 South Oak Street
Champaign, IL 61820-6903
www.press.uillinois.edu